MODERN INTERNATIONAL ECONOMICS

Third Edition

WILFRED J. ETHIER

UNIVERSITY OF PENNSYLVANIA

MODERN INTERNATIONAL ECONOMICS

Third Edition

W • W • NORTON & COMPANY

NEW YORK   LONDON

PHOTOGRAPH CREDITS

Stock Montage (p. 6)
Archive Photos (p. 48)
Peter Lofts (p. 70)
Warder Collection (pp. 92, 438)
Swedish Information Service (p. 124)
Wassily Leontief (p. 154)
Harvard University Archives (p. 402)
New York Public Library (p. 438)
Wide World Photos (p. 496)
Yale University Archives, Manuscripts and Archives, Yale University Library (p. 524)
Christ's College Archives (p. 546)

The text of this book is composed in Times Roman, with the display set in
Eras. Composition by TSI Graphics. Manufacturing by Quebecor/Martinsburg.

Library of Congress Cataloging-in-Publication Data

Ethier, Wilfred J.
    Modern international economics / Wilfred J. Ethier. — 3rd ed.
        p.   cm.
    Includes index.
    ISBN 0-393-96311-X
    1. International economic relations.   I. Title.
HF1411.E824   1995
337—dc20   94-27931

W. W. Norton & Company, Inc., 500 Fifth Avenue, New York, NY 10110
W. W. Norton & Company, Ltd., 10 Coptic Street, London WC1A 1PU

1 2 3 4 5 6 7 8 9 0

In Memory of My Father

Contents

PART FOUR

Monetary Mechanics   **339**

CHAPTER 12.   The Balance of Payments   **341**

CHAPTER 13.   International Financial Markets   **355**

Part Five

International Monetary Economics 399

Preface

Beware of a thick book.

—RICHARD WAGNER

The world is changing. The Eastern bloc is no more, its former members presently struggling to restructure their societies and to join the modern world economy. Less dramatically but just as significantly, economic reform is sweeping through much of the developing world. Meanwhile, Western Europe deepens and broadens its economic integration, and economic integration has also come to North America.

This textbook is changing, too. Like its predecessors, this third edition of *Modern International Economics* offers an up-to-date view of the issues and, more importantly, a systematic way to analyze them. But those who used the first or second edition will notice changes. For one thing, there are more chapters. The division of chapters into small, distinct sections has always made this book more flexible than others; now this flexibility is further enhanced by the new and more detailed organization of chapters.

For example, the new chapter organization increases emphasis on scale economies and imperfect competition as distinct causes of trade. The first edition of this book pioneered the inclusion of these topics in an undergraduate text, and this third edition continues to provide the most thorough treatment available of the newer theories of international trade.

Conveying to undergraduates a sense of how economists think about issues involving international payments becomes more challenging as the material required in an undergraduate text bears less and less relation to how the subject is approached in most graduate schools. This book deals with the problem by introducing intertemporal issues in an elementary way. The second edition pioneered the intertemporal treatment of international capital movements and the current account; this new edition moves the material center stage.

While a textbook cannot compete with the daily newspaper as a source of issues, it can begin to link up the analysis with current events. I have once again tried to use the theory to illustrate the most pressing issues of the day. The "Case Studies" that earlier users liked so much are still here, joined by many new ones.

The presentation continues to be almost entirely verbal and geometric. More advanced or specialized material is provided by asterisked sections labeled *Exploring Further.* These sections contain no algebra or advanced mathematics, but they do on occasion make intensive use of geometry. They can all be skipped without loss of continuity. The mathematically trained student is directed to Appendix I, which provides a technical treatment of international trade theory keyed to Parts One, Two, and Three of the text. A typical one-semester course would cover the unasterisked sections of the core chapters (1–6, 13–15, 17–19) plus whatever the instructor wishes from other chapters. A one-year course might cover the entire text and supplement it with readings. Appendix I is suitable for graduate students and more sophisticated undergraduates.

The majority of sections are followed by a selection of problems. The problems are arranged more or less in order of increasing difficulty, and especially challenging problems are distinguished by asterisks. Students should at least attempt the unasterisked problems before going on to the next section. A *Study Guide* is available, which contains the answers to nearly all of these problems as well as additional problems, self-tests, detailed review of basic ideas, and review questions for every chapter in this text. I have also prepared an *Instructor's Manual,* which is available from the publisher.

Acknowledgments

The following economists read various parts of the manuscript and provided many useful suggestions:

Laurel Adams
Northwestern University

Christopher Bell
*University of North Carolina at
Asheville*

Arthur I. Bloomfield
University of Pennsylvania

Jorge A. Braga DeMacedo
New University of Lisbon

Barbara J. Craig
Oberlin College

Amy H. Dalton
*Virginia Commonwealth
University*

Alan V. Deardorff
University of Michigan

Slobodan Djajic
*Graduate Institute of
International Studies, Geneva*

Jonathan Eaton
Boston University

Charles Engel
University of Washington

James D. Gaisford
University of Calgary

Javier Gardeazabal
*Universidad del Pais Vasco,
Bilbao*

Elizabeth Goldstein
Lehman Brothers

Thomas Grennes
North Carolina State University

Gunvald Grønvik
Norges Bank, Oslo

Donald Keenan
University of Georgia

Peter Kenen
Princeton University

Kyung-Soo Kim
Sung Kyun Kwan University, Seoul

James A. Levinsohn
University of Michigan

Richard Marston
University of Pennsylvania

Steven Matusz
Michigan State University

Daniel E. Nolle
Middlebury College

Farhad Rassekh
University of Hartford

Assaf Razin
Tel Aviv University

Raymond Reizman
University of Iowa

Michael Schmid
Universität der Bundeswehr, Hamburg

John Sheahan
Williams College

Edward Tower
Duke University

Michael A. Webb
University of Kentucky

David Wharton
Wells College

Elliot Zupnick
Columbia University

Carol Flechner, Donald S. Lamm, and W. Drake McFeely, of W. W. Norton & Company, provided valuable editorial help. I thank them all.

Introduction

International trade meaning in plain English trade between nations, it is not surprising that the term should mean something else in Political Economy.
                                                              —F. Y. EDGEWORTH

Everyone knows what international economics is all about. It is about international trade and whether we should restrict imports of Japanese automobiles or Korean refrigerators. It is about nagging balance-of-payments problems and spectacular foreign-exchange crises. It is about the gnomes Zurich, the sheikhs of Araby, and the millions of poor migrants who are trying to find better jobs by leaving southern Europe for northern Europe or the Far East for the Middle East or by paying someone to smuggle them into the United States. It is about multinational corporations larger than countries, fuel bills that seem huge to those who must pay them, and automobiles that look smaller than ever before. It is about European complaints that interest rates are too high in America and American complaints that Europe is not charging us enough for her steel.

This book is about all these things and many others as well. We discuss them by developing the basic ideas of international economic theory and then putting those ideas to work. What makes international economic theory distinct from general economics? Is it perhaps really the same—except for a more cosmopolitan terminology and distinctive practical applications? To a large extent the answer is yes. The fundamental tools, ideas, and modes of thought of general economics are basic to this book. But there are two key aspects of the subject that make international economic theory distinct.

1. *In the world economy some markets are national while others are international.* The most important example of this feature is the assumption that the factors of production—land, labor, and capital—are perfectly mobile within nations but completely immobile between nations (national factor markets), whereas commodities can be traded both nationally and internationally (international commodity markets). This assumption has characterized international trade theory since its development by the classical economists, and the assumption will be basic to the first six chapters of this book. But, of course, the assumption is not true. Anyone can think of exceptions. Capital flows into projects around the globe—but perhaps not into certain

blocks in your town. No North American student can be blind to international human migration, yet families often refuse to leave depressed areas for more favorable regions of the same country. Our assumption, then, is not a literal description of reality, but an abstraction of an underlying tendency. As such, the assumption is useful for thought, but we must not make a religion out of it. Consequently, international factor mobility is examined in detail in Chapter 10 and is mentioned elsewhere in the book, as are still other departures from the assumption.

2. *National sovereignty influences the character of economic activity.* This point first arises in Chapters 7, 8, and 9, where we examine commercial policies that tax or otherwise impede commodity exchanges between countries but not within countries. Almost every nation has its coin of the realm, so that transactions between nationals involve a common currency whereas transactions between residents of different nations require one type of money to be exchanged for another. A large part of this book is concerned with issues related to the existence of distinct monetary systems.

The two features are not independent. International factor movements are certainly inhibited by national policies and by the reluctance of factor owners to expose themselves or their wealth to foreign jurisdictions.

This book first examines—in Parts One, Two, and Three—those issues that do not involve money, and then—in Parts Four, Five, and Six—those that do. In each case we first present the basic theory as a few fundamental ideas, which are developed gradually in the light of basic characteristics of the modern international economy and are linked together. Then we further exploit and apply the theory. In conclusion, Part Seven serves as an overview, incorporating both monetary and nonmonetary analysis in discussions of some of the most pressing issues of our times.

Part One

Why Nations Trade

Why do nations exchange goods and services? Who exports what to whom at what prices? Which countries produce which goods? Is international trade a good thing for the world, and, if so, how are the gains distributed among nations? Do all benefit, or are some countries made better off at the expense of others?

The pure theory of international trade deals with issues like these. Part One approaches them by asking the most fundamental question of all: Why should nations trade?

As we study this theory, keep in perspective actual international trade. The figure below shows the network of world trade in 1993. Each number gives exports plus imports as a percentage of world exports plus imports. Thus Japanese exports to Western Europe plus Western Europe's exports to Japan equaled 2 percent of all goods exported by all nations plus all goods imported by all nations. Trade among the countries of Western Europe likewise accounted for 35 percent of world trade. Altogether, 69 percent of world trade is accounted for in the figure (the remaining 3 percent is accounted for by the twenty-five trade flows that round off to 0 percent, plus the countries, such as Australia, that are excluded).

If you study the figure for a few minutes, you will concoct hypotheses about geographic, political, and historical influences on trade flows. Note in

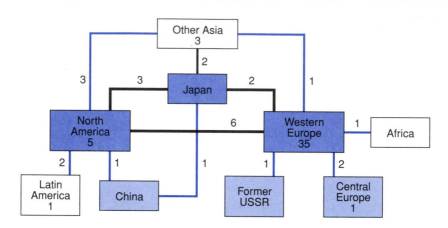

Who Trades with Whom: Network of World Trade, Third Quarter of 1993

particular the very large part of world trade accounted for by exchanges among industrialized market economies (North America, Western Europe, and Japan), known as the *North,* the small part of world trade accounted for by the *East* (the former USSR, Central Europe, and China), and the peripheral role played by the *South* (Latin America, Africa, and Other Asia), whose modest trade tends to be concentrated with particular parts of the more developed world.

Our perspective on world trade can be broadened by looking at the characteristics of specific countries. The table below lists eight countries ranked according to exports. Examination of the first column of figures shows little relation between national size—as measured by population—and trade: India, the most populous country, trades the least. When size is instead measured by the gross national product, it correlates more closely with trade, but there are exceptions. Large continental countries (the United States and Brazil) tend to trade proportionally less than smaller countries, with the European industrial nations the heaviest traders. Thus, 21 percent of the United Kingdom's national income is spent on imports, compared with 9 percent for the United States, and the average German spends nearly three times as much on imported goods than does the average American.

The table contains two apparent anomalies. Canada is geographically large, like the United States or Brazil, but trades more than they do relative to GNP. The reason is twofold: because most of Canada's economy is close to the American border, it trades heavily with the United States; and since the Canadian economy is only about one-tenth the size of the American, this trade is relatively much more significant for Canada. The strangest entry in the table is Singapore, which exports more than it produces and imports goods worth almost twice its own GNP! How does Singapore do it?

Characteristics of Selected Countries, 1992

Country	Population (millions)	GNP ($ billions)	Imports ($ billions)	Exports ($ billions)	Imports per capita ($)	Imports/GNP (%)	Imports/world (%)
United States	253*	5,962	536	439	2,225	9	14
Germany	64*	1,776	402	422	6,281	23	11
Japan	124	3,704	233	340	1,879	6	6
United Kingdom	58*	1,056	222	191	3,828	21	6
Canada	27	548	129	134	4,778	24	3
Singapore	3*	47	72	63	24,000	153	2
Brazil	156	395*	23*	32*	147	6	1
India	850*	265*	20*	18*	24	8	1

*1991 data.

SOURCE: International Monetary Fund, *International Financial Statistics.*

Singapore is an entrepôt: large quantities of goods are imported and then, per-haps after some processing, reexported to final buyers. Singapore serves as a middleman.

Well, then, why *do* nations trade? There are just three fundamental rea-sons, each the subject of its own chapter.

The classical explanation is comparative advantage, treated in Chapter 1. Until fairly recently, the classical theory and its extensions formed the basis for how most economists looked at the world, and theoretical research con-sisted mainly of polishing and applying this established body of thought. But now many economists suspect that this is not adequate, a suspicion generated both by empirical investigations of international trade and by the way that ac-tual trade has been changing over time. The result has been to give new life to competing explanations. The chapters in this part try to convey the excite-ment of this competition among theories induced by observation of the world in which we live and to explain why it all matters.

CHAPTER 1

Comparative Advantage

> No real Englishman in his secret soul was ever sorry for the death of
> a political economist.
> —W. BAGEHOT

The principle of comparative advantage is one of the great feats of economics: simple and elegant, applicable under very general circumstances, and central to an understanding of a host of phenomena. The basic idea was developed in the early nineteenth century by the English classical economists and is attributed primarily to David Ricardo.

We first illustrate comparative advantage in a very elementary framework called the simple Ricardian model and then discuss it under more general circumstances. We then look again at world trade to see how the theory stacks up against reality.

As we develop the theory of comparative advantage, you might want to consider how it relates to two interesting phenomena.

1. *International Wage Differences*. Wage rates vary dramatically over the globe. For example, in 1990 average hourly wages in manufacturing in three countries were

United States	$10.83
South Korea	3.94
Malawi	.57

What accounts for these differences? How can countries like these compete with each other and profitably trade? Can they?

2. *The Great Tomato War*. During the winter, tomatoes and other fresh vegetables reach American tables from producers in Florida and Mexico. Field hands in Mexico are paid a wage about one-third of that received by their Florida counterparts. Mexican growers have gradually expanded their share of the market at the expense of Florida growers and have captured about one-half of the total market for winter vegetables. Farmers in Florida have reacted to this with demands—unmet—for protection from unfair Mexican competition. What should U.S. policy be?

DAVID RICARDO (1772–1823)

David Ricardo was the son of a Jewish financier who had migrated to London from Holland. The family was of Portuguese origin. At the age of twelve David went to work for his father, but he was disowned when he converted from Judaism to marry a Quaker. Ricardo made a fortune on the London stock exchange and retired young. He purchased an estate and a seat in Parliament, from which he would on painful occasion expound his views. Ricardo's estate—Gatcombe—is now the residence of Princess Anne. Despite his fabulous practical success as a businessman, as an economist Ricardo emphasized abstract theory. He analyzed growth and income distribution and was a major architect of the classical system of thought, from which both Marxism and modern capitalist economics have developed.

1. THE SIMPLE RICARDIAN MODEL

Suppose that two countries—say, France and Germany—can produce but two goods: butane (a chemical used as fuel) and apples. Each apple produced in France requires exactly 2 units (say, man-hours) of labor for its manufacture. Table 1.1 shows the amounts of labor necessary to produce 1 unit of each good in each country. Note that both goods require more labor for their manufacture in France than in Germany.

Suppose that initially each country is producing some of both goods, and consider the following experiment. France cuts back production of butane and uses the labor released from the butane industry to produce more apples, which are sent to Germany. The Germans can then cut back apple production and use the labor released from the apple industry to produce more butane, which can in turn be sent to France. What would result? If the French produce 1 less unit of butane, 6 units of labor will be released, which will be able to produce 3 additional apples. If these apples are sent to Germany, enabling the Germans to reduce their apple production by 3 apples, 3 units of German labor will be released. Now only 1 unit of German labor is required to produce

TABLE 1.1 **A Simple Ricardian Model: Labor Required in Each Country to Produce One Unit of Each Good**

	Butane	Apples
France	6	2
Germany	1	1

TABLE 1.2 A Simple Ricardian Model: Possible Results of the Experiment

	Additional butane	*Additional apples*
In France	−1	+3
In Germany	+2	−2
In world	+1	+1

the unit of butane necessary to replace the original French cutback. Therefore, France and Germany are now able to produce together just as many apples and as much butane as before, and in addition there are now 2 units of German labor left over with which to produce 2 more units of butane, or 2 more apples, or some combination of apples and butane. Table 1.2 shows the final result if these two German laborers are divided equally between the apple and butane industries. This additional output can be divided between the two countries, making both of them better off.

Be sure that you understand fully the above reasoning. It is the heart of the principle of comparative advantage and will be made use of again and again in this book under many different guises and for many different purposes. To test yourself, show that if France instead shifts labor from the apple industry to the butane industry, exporting butane to Germany for apples, France and Germany will together become *worse* off.

Clearly, this experiment can be repeated, and the two countries together can be made even better off. That is, additional French labor can be shifted from the butane industry to the apple industry, and the trade of French apples for German butane extended. This process can continue until either the entire French labor force is producing apples, the German labor force is specialized in butane, or both countries are specialized. Thus only these three final possibilities are compatible with an efficient pattern of world production.

Note that this result depends not at all on the *absolute* levels of the four labor requirements in Table 1.1, but only on the *ratios* of the requirements within each country. For example, if French labor became much less efficient so that both numbers in the first row were multiplied by 100, we would still get the same result. Similarly, both German labor requirements could be multiplied by any positive number at all, and none of the conclusions would be changed. Everything depended only on the fact that 6/2 is greater than 1/1.

KEY CONCEPT

An *efficient pattern of production* is one for which it is impossible to increase the production of any good without reducing the output of some other good.

More generally, letting a_A^F denote the labor necessary to produce one apple in France and so on, everything depended on the fact that

$$\frac{a_B^F}{a_A^F} > \frac{a_B^G}{a_A^G}.$$ (1.1)

You should verify that if this inequality were reversed, efficient world production would call for France to produce butane and Germany to produce apples.

These ratios also shed further light on our result. They are expressed in the following units:

$$\frac{a_B^F}{a_A^F} = \frac{\text{labor/butane}}{\text{labor/apples}} = \text{apples/butane}.$$

Thus each ratio tells us the cost, in terms of apples, of producing one more unit of butane in each country. The inequality says, then, that the world must sacrifice more apples to make butane in France than to make it in Germany. Hence, we may conclude that as much of the world's butane as possible should be produced in Germany.

The inequality in Equation (1.1) can equivalently be written

$$\frac{a_A^G}{a_B^G} > \frac{a_A^F}{a_B^F}.$$ (1.2)

In this form the inequality says that the cost in terms of butane of producing 1 apple is greater in Germany than in France. Hence, as many of the world's apples as possible should be produced in France. When we speak in this way of the cost in terms of apples of producing butane, we are referring to *opportunity costs*. That is, butane is obviously not produced by using up apples, but, rather, the true cost of butane to the economy is the apples that *could* be produced by the labor actually used to make the butane *if* that labor were instead used by the apple industry.

When the labor requirements are in the relation shown in Equation (1.2), we say that "France has a comparative advantage over Germany in apples relative to butane." Just as the inequality could be written in two equivalent forms, this statement is equivalent to the statement "Germany has a comparative advantage over France in butane relative to apples." These two sentences are interchangeable; each implies the other. The important point about each is its double-barreled relativity; we speak of nothing in absolute terms but of apples *relative to* butane, of France *over* Germany.

What conclusions can be drawn in this simple Ricardian world directly from a knowledge of the pattern of comparative advantage? Notice that we cannot tell *exactly* what the pattern of production would be. If, to take an extreme example, everyone in the world wants only apples and has no use for butane, then both countries will produce only apples and international trade will be pointless, regardless of the pattern of comparative advantage. Or, to

---

KEY CONCEPT

The *opportunity cost* of a good to an individual or to a society is the amount of some other good that must be forgone in order to obtain one unit of it. Suppose you have ten dollars and want to buy a ten-dollar pizza and ten dollars' worth of gas. You obviously cannot afford both and so must choose. The *opportunity* cost of the pizza is the gasoline, and the *opportunity* cost of the gasoline is the pizza. The *money* cost of each is ten dollars.

---

take a more realistic case, if the world wants more apples than France can produce, Germany must produce some apples also. But comparative advantage narrows things down by distinguishing between efficient and inefficient patterns of production. In our example, France should never produce any butane if Germany is producing some apples, and Germany should never produce any apples if France is making some butane. For these are precisely the situations to which we can apply the reasoning used at the beginning of this section to show that by exploiting the pattern of comparative advantage the world can have more of both butane and apples.

Thus comparative advantage tells us something about the pattern of production. Its implication for the pattern of international trade is even simpler: a country should export that good in which it has a comparative advantage and import that good in which it has a comparative disadvantage. In the example given in Table 1.1, France should export apples and import butane.

Problems

1.1 Suppose that in England 5 man-hours of labor are required to produce each cask of wine and 5 man-hours are required to produce each bolt of cloth, whereas in Portugal 1 man-hour of labor is required for a cask of wine and 4 man-hours for a bolt of cloth. (Except for the choice of numbers, this is the example used by Ricardo to discuss comparative advantage.)

    a Who has a comparative advantage in what and why? Make two equivalent statements.

    b Prove that your answer to Problem **1.1a** is correct by showing in detail that when both countries are producing both goods, the world can be made better off by allowing England and Portugal to reallocate labor and trade in accordance with the pattern of comparative advantage. Derive the analog of Table 1.2.

    c Now suppose that it becomes possible to move labor between the two countries. What should be done?

1.2 In the content of Problem **1.1,** suppose that there is also a third country, France, where 1 man-hour of labor can produce either 1 bolt of cloth or $1/2$ cask of wine. What statements can you make about comparative advantage? Which patterns of production and international trade are efficient?

1.3 An executive in a firm happens to be an excellent typist but is, nonetheless, given a secretary, who in fact types more slowly than the executive.

   a Formalize this situation in terms of our discussion of comparative advantage and show explicitly how this assignment of people to jobs could be efficient from the firm's point of view. (Hypothesize that each individual can either type so many pages or make so many decisions in one hour—make up your own numbers.)

   b Suppose instead that this job assignment reflects only sexist discrimination. Use the idea of comparative advantage to show that the firm is paying a cost for this discrimination.

2. EFFICIENCY IN THE SIMPLE RICARDIAN WORLD

The previous section showed that if the pattern of trade and production conflicts with comparative advantage, it is possible to increase world output of all goods through increased trade and international specialization. Now we shall reexamine this conclusion from a slightly different point of view, both to drive home further the basic point and to introduce some concepts and techniques of use later on.

Look first at the various possible total outputs of both goods that can be produced by each country. To do this, we need to know not only the productivities of labor, but also how much labor is available. Assume that France has a total labor supply of 600 units and Germany a total labor supply of 500 units. Then if France devotes its entire labor force to the butane industry, it can produce $600/a_B^F$ or, in view of Table 1.1, 100 units of butane; if it specializes in apples, it can produce $600/a_A^F$ or 300 apples; if it divides its labor equally between the apple and butane industries, it can produce 50 units of butane and 150 apples; and so forth. The possibilities are depicted by the line in Figure 1.1(a). This line, known as the French *production possibility frontier,* can be thought of as the collection of all alternative feasible French outputs of the two goods having the property that the output of one good can be increased only by lowering the output of the other. That is, it depicts all possible French outputs that are efficient. Point C involves more of both apples and butane than does A, but C lies outside the production possibility frontier and thus requires more labor resources than France possesses. Point B, on the other hand, is inefficient; it lies inside the production possibility frontier and involves less of both apples and butane than does A. If the French economy is producing the outputs denoted by B, then some French labor must be either idle or employed in a wasteful manner. Point D, like A, is efficient; it involves less apple output than does A but more butane. In similar fashion we can derive Germany's production possibility frontier, which is depicted in Figure 1.1(b).

The slope of the French production possibility frontier is

$$-\left(\frac{600}{a_A^F} \, / \, \frac{600}{a_B^F}\right)=-a_B^F/a_A^F.$$

KEY CONCEPT

The *production possibility frontier* of a country or other entity shows the alternative combinations of various goods that the entity can produce, given its technology and its stock of productive factors such as labor.

Thus the slope of the production possibility frontier is determined *only* by the labor input requirements, whereas its distance from the origin depends upon the size of the French labor force. (Verify that if France's labor supply triples, say, the French production possibility frontier will be shifted outward by a factor of 3 but will retain the same slope.) Thus the inequality (1.2), which determined the pattern of comparative advantage, translates geometrically into a French production possibility frontier steeper than the German. We usually term a_B^F / a_A^F, the negative of the slope, the "*marginal rate of transformation* of apples for butane," denoted MRT_{AB}. It tells us the quantity of apples that must be forgone to produce more butane—that is, the opportunity cost of butane in terms of apples. Similarly, it tells us the amount of additional apples that France could produce if it reduced its butane output by 1 unit.

We thus have a second method of determining comparative advantage: *if the MRT_{AB} in France is greater than that in Germany, France has a comparative advantage over Germany in apples relative to butane.* This method is

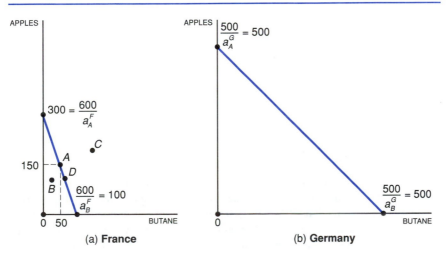

FIGURE 1.1   Production Possibility Frontiers   A country's production possibility frontier displays the menu of alternative output combinations that that country can produce. It depends on the size of the country's resources and on its technology for producing goods from resources.

> **KEY CONCEPT**
>
> The *marginal rate of transformation* of one good for another is the amount by which production of the first must be reduced in order to free enough productive factors, such as labor, to produce one additional unit of the second.

conceptually distinct from the earlier method of using ratios of labor productivities. But in the simple Ricardian world, the two must be equivalent.

The production possibility frontier is intimately connected with the question of efficiency in a country *by itself,* but we are also interested in the efficiency of the world as a whole. Clearly, the world will not be operating efficiently unless each country is operating efficiently—that is, unless each country is operating on its production possibility frontier. But is this all that is necessary for world output to be efficient? No. For we saw in section 1 that unless comparative advantage is followed, world output is not as high as it could be. Let us, therefore, examine efficient world output patterns—that is, the *world* production possibility frontier.

Suppose that France is specialized in apple production. Then world output will equal whatever Germany produces plus the 300 French apples. These possibilities are given by the line *AB* in Figure 1.2(a). For example, at point *A* France produces 300 apples and Germany 500; at *B* France produces 300 apples, and Germany 500 units of butane. When Germany is specialized in butane, world output will equal whatever France is producing plus the 500 units of German butane. This gives the line *BC* in Figure 1.2(a). The world production possibility frontier is then *ABC*.

But we could have proceeded differently. If Germany is specialized in apples, world output equals France's output plus the 500 German apples; this gives *AD* in Figure 1.2(b). Similarly *DC* is obtained by supposing that France specializes in butane. Clearly *ADC* lies inside *ABC*. That is, except for *A* and *C,* where both countries specialize entirely in the same good, any pattern of world output on *ADC* is inefficient because more of both goods can be obtained at some point on *ABC*.

What is the difference between these two attempts to find the world production possibility frontier? The first case looked at what world output would be for all patterns of production *compatible* with comparative advantage. But the second case looked at situations that *violated* comparative advantage. At *D,* for example, Germany specializes in apples and France in butane. The world production possibility frontier illustrates in geometric terms the meaning of comparative advantage.

Points *A, B,* and *C* on the world production possibility frontier correspond to complete specialization in both countries. At *A* both specialize in apples; at *B* France produces only apples, and Germany only butane; at *C* both

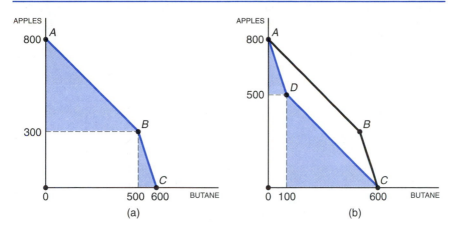

FIGURE 1.2 **The World Production Possibility Frontier** The world production possibility frontier is obtained by adding together the frontiers of individual countries.

specialize in butane. Between *A* and *B* France is specialized in apples, while Germany produces both goods. Here the world marginal rate of transformation of apples for butane equals that in Germany. This reflects the fact that if world output is to change, it must come about through changes in Germany; France remains specialized in apples. Between *B* and *C,* however, the situation is reversed. France produces both goods, while Germany is specialized in butane, and the world marginal rate of transformation equals that in France.

Where on the world production possibility frontier should the world produce? We cannot say. That depends upon world tastes for the two goods, about which we as yet have said nothing. This reflects the conclusion in the previous section that comparative advantage does not tell what world production should be: it specifies the efficient alternatives.

Problems

1.4 As in Problem **1.1,** 5 man-hours of labor are required to produce each unit of wine and each unit of cloth in England, while in Portugal 1 man-hour of labor produces 1 unit of wine and 4 man-hours of labor produce 1 unit of cloth. Suppose also that each country has 100 man-hours of labor available.

    a Draw the production possibility frontiers for England, Portugal, and the world. How do they change if England's labor force increases to 1,000?

    b If everyone in the world always consumes 1 cask of wine for each bolt of cloth, what should each country produce and what should the direction of trade be?

    c Draw the world production possibility frontier if the labor is *internationally* mobile.

1.5 In the above problem, suppose that in France 1 man-hour of labor can produce 1 unit of cloth while 2 man-hours of labor are required for 1 unit of wine, and, in addition, that France has 200 man-hours of labor. Draw the world production possibility frontier. Who is producing what at various points along it? Depict the inefficient patterns of specialization.

---

3. THE ECONOMICS OF THE SIMPLE RICARDIAN WORLD

In the previous two sections, we discussed what international trade and specialization *should* be but said nothing about what they actually *would* be. This distinction is important; for example, one might conjecture on the basis of Table 1.1 that both French industries would be driven out of business by more efficient German competition, and this would not be efficient for the world as a whole. Also, our discussion has so far dealt entirely with production; we have said nothing about the economics of international trade. It is time to turn to these questions.

Suppose initially that we can observe the French economy in *autarky*—that is, free of any economic relations with the rest of the world. Then the French must supply their own apples and butane. Suppose that the (autarkic) wage rate in France is w^F, expressed in some unit of account (say, dollars or francs or apples). Then if the labor market is competitive, all French firms must pay w^F for each unit of labor they use, and since labor is the only input required in either industry, the cost of producing apples in France must be $a_A^F w^F$ and the cost of butane must be $a_B^F w^F$. These must, in fact, be the actual prices, P_A^F and P_B^F, *if* the apples and butane are competitive and *if* both apples and butane are produced. If $P_A^F > a_A^F w^F$, for example, then French apple producers are earning a profit that will ultimately be bid away by competition. If $P_A^F < a_A^F w^F$, then apple producers are receiving less for their product than it costs them to produce it and so will eventually close down if the inequality persists.

Since France cannot trade, the French economy will be in equilibrium only when demand equals supply in all three markets (labor, apples, and butane). Suppose this occurs at point A in Figure 1.1(a). If w^F is equal to 1, for example, we have $P_A^F = a_A^F = 2$ and $P_B^F = a_B^F = 6$. The 150 apples produced at A are thus worth 300, and the 50 units of butane are worth 300, so that the value of national output is 600. Similarly, the total wage bill (that is, national income) is 600. There are three markets and three prices here, but note that only relative prices really matter in the sense that if all prices change in the same proportion, no one will act differently, so that the economy will remain at A. Suppose, for example, that $w^F = 2$. Then $P_A^F = 4$ and $P_B^F = 12$. The prices faced by each individual have doubled, but so has his income. He will behave no differently.

Let us, then, look at the relative price of butane in terms of apples: $P_B^F / P_A^F = a_B^F w^F / a_A^F w^F = a_B^F / a_A^F = 3$, the marginal rate of transformation of apples for butane. That is, P_B^F / P_A^F can be unequal to the marginal rate of transformation of apples for butane only if France specializes completely in one of the goods. But in autarky the French must produce both goods to consume both.

If we examine Germany, we arrive at similar conclusions. The German autarkic relative price of butane in terms of apples, P_B^G / P_A^G, must equal the German marginal rate of transformation of apples for butane, a_B^G / a_A^G (again, unless all the Germans do completely without one of the goods). We thus have a third method for determining the pattern of comparative advantage: *if the autarkic relative price of butane in terms of apples is greater in France than in Germany, France will have a comparative advantage over Germany in apples relative to butane*. This third method is conceptually distinct from the other two. They both depended upon technological parameters, whereas this method depends upon economic data: autarkic market prices. But in this simple Ricardian world, all three methods must give the same result.

KEY CONCEPT

France has a comparative advantage over Germany in apples relative to butane if, in autarky, the relative price of apples in terms of butane would be less in France than in Germany.

What will happen if France and Germany begin to trade with each other? Suppose that, initially, both French prices are higher than both German prices—for example, w^F and w^G both equal 1, so that the numbers in Table 1.1 are the initial prices. Then German firms will be deluged with customers and will try to hire more workers, thereby bidding up wages and thus costs—and German inflation will take place. French firms, on the other hand, being undercut in world markets, will begin laying off workers, thereby causing French wages and costs to fall, relative to German wages and costs. This state of affairs will persist at least until German costs rise sufficiently relative to French costs so that some French good becomes competitive in world markets. Suppose for simplicity that French prices do not fall at all, so the relative change in costs consists entirely of German inflation. Then German wages must rise by at least 100 percent (in which case, German costs will be as indicated in the third row in Table 1.3); otherwise, no French firm can compete on world markets, and the inflation must continue. With 100 percent inflation, the table shows that French apples can compete, but French butane cannot. France must specialize in apple production, while both goods may be produced in Germany: world output must be somewhere along the line AB in Figure 1.2. Use $p = P_B/P_A$ to denote the international relative price of butane in terms of apples that is established when the countries trade. With 100 percent German inflation, $p = 2/2 = 1$, the German relative autarkic price.

TABLE 1.3   **Wages and Costs of Production When Trade Takes Place**

	Butane	Apples	Wages
France	6	2	1
Germany (initially)	1	1	1
Germany (after 100% inflation)	2	2	2
Germany (after 200% inflation)	3	3	3
Germany (after 500% inflation)	6	6	6

The German wage can rise by no more than 500 percent (in which case, German costs are given by the bottom row of Table 1.3); otherwise, all German firms would cease to be competitive, and the process would be repeated in reverse. With 500 percent German inflation, only German butane will be competitive, while France may produce both goods: world output must be somewhere on the line BC in Figure 1.2, and $p = 3$, the French autarkic relative price.

If German wages rise by more than 100 percent but less than 500 percent, Germany must specialize in butane and France in apples: world output will be given by point B in Figure 1.2, and p will lie somewhere between 1 and 3, the autarkic relative prices. The third line of Table 1.3 illustrates such a case.

All this sheds light on international wage differences, pointed out on page 3. First, wage differences reflect general differences in labor productivities between countries. In Table 1.3, German labor is two to six times as productive as French labor, and, as we have seen, the German wage will be two to six times as large as the French wage. Thus international differences in wages actually make it possible for countries to compete with each other. Second, and more subtly, the actual degree of wage difference depends upon world demand. In our example, if world demand for butane is high, the wage in Germany will be three times as high as the French wage, forcing the Germans to specialize in butane, where their productivity advantage is greatest. A high world demand for apples, on the other hand, results in a German wage only twice as high as the French wage, forcing the French to specialize in apples, where their productivity disadvantage is least.

When the economics of the simple Ricardian world are spelled out, all the conclusions in section 1 about what trade and production patterns should be are, in fact, guaranteed by the international economic mechanism. Comparative advantage is not merely a prescription for how international trade should be organized, it is also an explanation of how such trade is determined. In addition, it tells us something about the international price p: it must lie somewhere between the two autarkic relative prices inclusive. We have thus been able to answer substantially the first of the three basic questions presented at the beginning of Part One as the purpose of a pure theory of trade. But we cannot tell exactly what p will be or what the pattern of production will be until we know something about world demand—that is, how the world values the two goods.

Problems

1.6 We have seen that the pattern of comparative advantage can be determined by comparing relative prices in the two countries when free trade is restricted. When the restriction is removed, trade proceeds according to comparative advantage and prices in the two countries are driven toward common international prices. But if prices are the same everywhere, why would anyone bother to trade?

1.7 Suppose, in the context of Table 1.1, that $w^F = 1$ and $w^G = 1$. Then both French prices are higher than both German prices, and, as we saw in section 3, international competition will cause the French wage to fall if the two countries trade. Does this not indicate that free trade will hurt the French worker?

1.8 In Problem **1.4b,** what will be traded, and what will all prices be? Do both countries gain as a result of trade? By how much? If the world suddenly decides it will consume 1 cask of wine for every 2 bolts of cloth, how will your answers change?

1.9 The discussion in the text supposed that wages and prices in France and Germany adjusted themselves to each other entirely through inflation in Germany. Suppose instead that it happens entirely through French deflation, with German prices constant. Restate the argument of the text, and write down the analog to Table 1.3.

1.10* *The Exchange Rate.* French prices are expressed in francs (Fr) and German prices in marks (DM). If the French wage equals Fr 1 and the German wage is DM 1, what are the costs of production of both goods in both countries with the technology of Table 1.1? The exchange rate is the price of one currency in terms of another: it allows us to compare prices in the two countries. With an exchange rate of 1 franc per mark, compare the costs of the two goods in the two countries. Suppose that, unlike the discussion of this section, there is no inflation or deflation in either country so that the wage rates do not change but the exchange rate can adjust. What must the exchange rate equal for both countries to be able to compete? Derive an analog to Table 1.3 for different values of the exchange rate. Can you think of any economic mechanism that would tend to alter the exchange rate to make it appropriate?

4. THE GAINS FROM TRADE

We can now answer the basic question: Are there gains or losses from international trade, and, if so, how are they distributed? Section 1 demonstrated that free trade is beneficial to the world as a whole. But how are the benefits distributed between the two countries? Can France be harmed while Germany greatly benefits?

To answer this question, look again at each country's production possibility frontier, reproduced in Figure 1.3. The production possibility frontier depicts the alternative combinations of the two goods that a country can consume in autarky, when anything that is consumed must be produced at home. If free trade takes place, the relative price p of butane will be between the two autarkic relative prices or equal to one of them. Suppose that $p = 2$. Then

France will specialize in apples, producing 300. The French can consume all or some of the apples, receiving 1 unit of butane for every 2 apples they export. The darker line in Figure 1.3(a) depicts all such consumption possibilities. It is now easy to see that France must benefit from free trade. The darker line lies outside the production possibility frontier so that every possible autarkic consumption pattern, such as *A,* is dominated by some free-trade consumption pattern, such as *B,* featuring more of both apples and butane. Only if the French do without butane and always consume 300 apples will this not be true. But in that case, France will never enter the international market at all. Two things should be noted about these gains from trade, unambiguous though they are. First, France will not *necessarily* consume more of both goods under free trade than under autarky. Consumption could take place at *C,* for example, which involves more butane but fewer apples than *A.* But in this case the French have simply chosen to spend their incomes on *C* in preference to *B,* which costs the same. Second, we are arguing that France as a whole gains from trade, not that every individual Frenchman does. The Ricardian model is too simple to discuss adequately the internal distribution of income, which we will come to later in this book. But for now, we can say that gainers gain more than any losers lose, and France as a whole gains: it is possible to give each French citizen more of both goods than in autarky.

What is the reason for these gains? They occur because the world relative price *p* differs from the autarkic relative price. In France, the autarkic relative price is higher than *p,* so France specializes in apples. Then exporting one apple gives France more butane as imports than it could obtain by producing one less apple and using the labor to produce butane itself. The darker line in Figure 1.3(a) is flatter than France's production possibility frontier. From Germany's point of view, the opposite is the case. The autarkic relative price is lower than *p,* so Germany specializes in butane, and Germany can obtain more apples for a single unit of butane by exporting butane than by not producing it and using the labor to make its own apples. The darker line in Figure 1.3(b) is steeper than the German production possibility frontier. Germany must gain from trade in the same sense as France does.

The distribution of the gains from trade should now be clear. If a country's autarkic relative price is the same as the international price, it will not benefit from trade and all the gains will go to its partner. The more the inter-

---

KEY CONCEPT

The *terms of trade* measure the number of units of imports a country can obtain for each unit of exports. Thus $1/p$ is France's terms of trade, and p is Germany's. The terms of trade can be taken as an index of the gains from trade. The more favorable (that is, the higher) the terms of trade, the more a country gains.

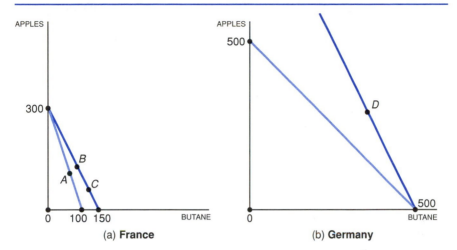

FIGURE 1.3 Consumption Possibilities in Autarky and with Free International Trade   A country's production possibility frontier and international prices together determine the menu of alternative consumption possibilities that the country can afford.

national price differs from the autarkic price, the more it gains from trade (and the less the partner gains). But trade will never actually harm either country. In Figure 1.2(a), along *AB* all the gains accrue to France, and Germany is no better off; along *BC* Germany obtains all the gains; at *B* the gains are divided among the two countries in a way that depends upon what *p* is.

Problems

1.11 As in Problem **1.4,** suppose that England has 100 man-hours of labor and requires 5 to produce each unit of wine and of cloth, whereas Portugal has 100 man-hours of labor with 1 required to produce each unit of wine and 4 to produce each unit of cloth. If the world relative price of wine in terms of cloth is 1, what will be the pattern of trade and production, what will be the prices in each country, and who will gain from trade?

1.12 Discuss the gains from trade in relation to Problem **1.3.**

1.13 Use the framework of the simple Ricardian model to discuss the Great Tomato War. Should the United States restrict imports of Mexican vegetables? Does the model help explain why Florida growers in fact want these imports restricted?

1.14 How would you explain the gains from trade to an unemployed New England textile worker?

1.15 Suppose that when trade opens, France is forced to continue producing at point *A* in Figure 1.3(a), instead of specializing in apples. How is the argument in the text altered? Compare this situation with both autarky and the case where France specializes.

1.16* From 1792 to 1900, the United States was legally on a *bimetallic standard:* the dollar was defined in terms of both gold and silver. As a result of the Coinage Act of 1792, the U.S. Mint stood ready to convert gold or silver into coins at the prices in the first line of the table below, for anyone presenting either metal. Alexander Hamilton, Thomas Jefferson, and Robert Morris were chiefly responsible for this act. (While its essential features were readily adopted by Congress, there was intense debate over whose likeness should appear on the coins.) France was also on a bimetallic standard from 1803 until 1874, and the bottom line contains French prices illustrative of the early part of this period.

From the first line of the table, we see that the official U.S. relative price of an ounce of gold in terms of silver was $11.60/ $0.77 = 15 ounces. Similarly, the French price of gold in terms of silver was Fr 60/ Fr 3.87 = 15½ ounces.

a Use the logical structure of the simple Ricardian model to deduce what happened after passage of the 1792 act. France was economically much larger than the United States in those years.

b The U.S. Mint ratio was changed in 1834 and 1837 to about 16 silver ounces per gold ounce. The world price ratio by and large remained near 15½ to 1. What do you think happened from 1834 to 1862 (the U.S. government abandoned metallic standards during the Civil War)?

Mint Prices of One Ounce of Gold and Silver, Representative of 1803–1834

	Gold	*Silver*
United States	$11.60	$0.77
France	Fr 60.00	Fr 3.87

1.17* In the discussion of the simple Ricardian model, we were concerned with trade in commodities. But in a sense, the two countries were actually exchanging their labor services because a unit of each good is actually an embodiment of the labor that produced it. Define *factoral terms of trade* as the number of units of foreign labor a country can obtain by the sacrifice of 1 unit of domestic labor in this sense. What is the relation between the factoral terms of trade and the commodity terms of trade? What values can the factoral terms of trade assume? What condition must the factoral terms of trade satisfy for a country to gain by trade? Suppose that France becomes more efficient in its export industries (say a_A^F falls from 6 to 3) and thus exports more, causing the world relative price p to rise. What will happen to the factoral terms of trade? Which terms of trade do you think is a better index of gains? Why?

5. EMPIRICAL TESTING OF THE SIMPLE RICARDIAN MODEL

The Ricardian model is useful for explaining and manipulating basic ideas of international trade and for understanding related complex phenomena. But can it also explain actual trade flows in terms of relative labor productivities? This question was addressed in a famous study by English economist G. D. A. MacDougall. He examined 1937 data for twenty-five U.S. and U.K. industries and compared for each industry the ratio of American and British output per worker with the ratio of British and American exports to third countries. (He used exports to third countries—that is, to all countries except the United States and United Kingdom—rather than exports to each other because in 1937 the two countries exported relatively little to each other and because they imposed different tariff barriers to imports, whereas British and American firms competed in third markets on terms of relatively more uniform equality.)

MacDougall found that, in twenty of the twenty-five industries, the United States had a larger share of the export market than did the United Kingdom whenever American labor was more than twice as productive as British labor, and a smaller share otherwise. American wages were about twice as high as British so that American labor had to be twice as productive to give equal labor costs. These findings were taken as support for the view that comparative advantage can be explained by labor productivities.

A further striking fact emerged from MacDougall's data: there seemed to be a significant, functional relationship between relative labor productivity and relative exports. When MacDougall's twenty-five observations were plotted on a graph, as in Figure 1.4(a), they seemed to cluster around a curve, which was a straight line when the axes were measured in a logarithmic scale. Such a relationship is not implied by the Ricardian model. Theory suggests that whenever American productivity is less than twice that of Britain, British firms would produce at lower cost and capture the entire market. The United States would have the entire market whenever its labor productivity was more than twice Britain's, and the two countries would perhaps share the market of a single good produced at equal cost in both countries. One can think of many complications, ignored in the simple model, that could muddy the waters and

(a) **MacDougall's results**   (b) **Example of export price results**

FIGURE 1.4 **Empirical Tests of the Simple Ricardian Model** The dots indicate MacDougall's observations for distinct industries.

account for the departure from theory. For example, each of the twenty-five industries is, in fact, an aggregate of related products; thus even if Britain has a productivity advantage in footware, on the average, the United States might still be able to produce some kinds of shoes more cheaply. Or there could be quality differences: if British cars are perceived by consumers as different from American, some people will continue to buy British cars even if they cost more. Or transportation costs and other trade barriers could be significant: even if woolen clothing costs more to produce in the United States than in the United Kingdom, American firms might be able to undersell British firms in those markets "closer" to the United States. These reasons and others like them would lead us not to expect the simple all-or-nothing result that comes from the theory in its elementary form. But neither would they necessarily cause us to expect to find a systematic functional relation between relative productivity and relative exports across different industries.

A number of subsequent investigations using different data and covering different periods have obtained results similar to MacDougall's. Thus the empirical evidence seems to be at least consistent with the view that trade patterns are largely determined by relative labor productivities. Of course, some other theory might perform even better. In principle we would like to consider all the factors that could possibly influence trade patterns and to test for their relative importance. The procedure of looking instead to see whether a specific simple theory is consistent with the data is a more practicable but second-best alternative.

In section 3, we saw how comparative advantage could be expressed in terms of relative autarkic prices. MacDougall and other economists have also inquired as to whether trade patterns could be explained in terms of relative prices. But in order to do this, two problems need to be faced. First, data on actual, internationally comparable transaction prices are hard to come by. Economists have had to make do with quoted values of aggregates of commodities (ignoring, for example, quality differences). The second, more fundamental problem is that comparative advantage depends on relative *autarkic* prices, and trade establishes a single international price in each market. Since we observe countries trading with each other, it is impossible, even in principle, to measure what autarkic prices would be. Economists have attempted to deal with this problem by comparing British and American export prices (that is, prices at the point of export rather than in the market where actually consumed). Transport costs and other barriers prevent these prices from being completely equalized by trade.

MacDougall found that in twenty-one of twenty-three industries, the country with the lower export price had the larger share of the third-country export market. Similar results have been obtained by other researchers. However, economists have not found a significant functional relationship between relative export prices and relative exports. (MacDougall did find such a relationship, but it failed to turn up in subsequent investigations.) This is illustrated in Figure 1.4(b). Such a relation is not predicted by the basic theory, but we do not know why it turns up with relative labor productivities but not with relative prices.

MacDougall in effect tested the *joint hypothesis* that comparative advantage is determined by labor productivities *and* that comparative advantage determines trade. Economist H. Glejser of the University of Brussels focused on the latter by itself. In 1957 six European countries agreed to form the Common Market and gradually eliminate tariffs and other restrictions on mutual trade. Glejser compared relative prices in 1958, before the agreement took effect, with trade flows in 1966, when considerable tariff reduction had been implemented. He found that low relative prices tended to be correlated with large market shares. This supports the view that comparative advantage determines trade, independently of whether the simple Ricardian model adequately describes reality.

6. COMPARATIVE ADVANTAGE IN MORE GENERAL CIRCUMSTANCES

The first four sections examined comparative advantage in the simple Ricardian model. The remainder of this chapter tries to make clear that the concept is an extremely general one, independent of the specific technology.

The Ricardian world is simplified in many ways. Some of these simplifications seem palatable. The two goods and two countries, for example, can be taken as proxies for "aggregate imports" and "aggregate exports," and for the "home country" and the "rest of the world." In any case many of the specific problems caused by a multiplicity of goods and of countries can be dealt with as they arise. Still other simplifications, such as ignoring transportation costs or such as the clear-cut distinction between domestic markets, where labor is perfectly mobile, and international trade, where labor is completely immobile, allow us to focus on the essentials while avoiding unnecessary details. But other assumptions ought not to be accepted so readily. Since the special technology of the Ricardian model appeared to be the crux of comparative advantage, it is the technological assumptions that must be examined.

We supposed that the production of a unit of each good entailed simply the use of a certain amount of homogeneous labor. But in reality many factors beyond "raw labor," such as various types of capital equipment, labor skills, natural resources, and entrepreneurial ability, play varying roles. Thus a simple description of the technology, such as that in Table 1.1, is not possible. But at least one of the technological concepts of the preceding sections can still be used. The various factors of production are available only in limited amounts, so that there is a basic scarcity of resources, and the economy must still decide among alternative patterns of production. We can still talk about the production possibility frontier, although it will not in general possess the simple properties discussed in section 2.

More general production possibility frontiers for France and Germany are depicted in Figure 1.5. These frontiers are downward sloping since, if an economy is producing efficiently, the only way to increase production of one good is by decreasing production of the other. But these curves are also

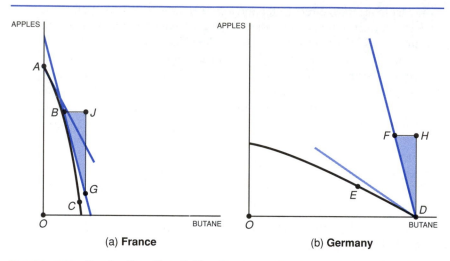

(a) **France**   (b) **Germany**

FIGURE 1.5 **Production Possibility Frontiers Displaying Increasing Opportunity Costs** Increasing opportunity cost causes a production possibility frontier to bend outward. But here, *each* point on France's frontier is steeper than *every* point on Germany's.

bowed outward rather than inward or some combination of the two. Why? Suppose France is producing at a point such as *B,* which calls for most of its resources to be devoted to apple production. Then, if it wishes to reduce apple output in order to produce more butane, it can do so by shifting from the apple industry to the butane industry those factors, such as skilled industrial workers, that are not suited to apple growing but productive when producing butane. If, on the other hand, France is producing mostly butane, such as at point *C,* then the only way to decrease apple output and increase butane output still more is by transferring from apples to butane factors of production, such as apple pickers or peasants with big hands, that are much better suited for the apple industry. The production possibility frontier will therefore be flatter at *B* than at *C*. In other words, the MRT_{AB} increases as we move along the production possibility frontier from the apple axis to the butane axis; there is increasing opportunity cost to shifting the pattern of production.

   Although the labor requirements that we originally used to determine the pattern of comparative advantage are no longer available, the marginal rate of transformation still is, but its value will depend upon the actual pattern of production. The marginal rate of transformation of apples for butane is still equal to minus the slope of the production possibility frontier at the point in question. If France is producing some of both goods, then the relative price of butane in terms of apples is equal to MRT_{AB}. Why? Suppose, for example, that $P_B^F / P_A^F > MRT_{AB}$. Then $P_B^F > P_A^F MRT_{AB}$. This means that the value of one additional unit of butane is greater than the value of the reduction in apple output necessary to produce it. Thus entrepreneurs will increase butane output and reduce apple output, and, as a result, MRT_{AB} will increase. This process will be repeated until either France specializes entirely in butane or the marginal rate of transformation becomes equal to relative prices. Thus if France is producing at point B, say, then the straight line through B depicts all those combinations of apples and butane that cost the same as the output at B, and the negative of the slope of this line must be the relative price of butane in terms of apples.

The problem now is to speak of comparative advantage without the simple labor requirements originally used for this purpose and even though the marginal rate of transformation and the autarkic price ratio are no longer simple parameters but can assume many possible values. Suppose that the French and German production possibility frontiers bear the simple relationship to each other depicted in Figure 1.5: *each* point on France's production possibility frontier is steeper than *every* point on Germany's—that is, the slope at point A in Figure 1.5(a) is steeper than the slope at point D in Figure 1.5(b). Then the marginal rate of transformation of apples for butane must always be greater in France than in Germany. Regardless of what the autarkic patterns of production are (say, C in France and E in Germany), it must be the case that $P_B^F / P_A^F > P_B^G / P_A^G$. The experiment in section 1 can now be repeated for this case with exactly the same result. (If there is any doubt in your mind, work through the reasoning again in the context of this section.) Indeed, we will obtain all the conclusions of sections 1 through 4 about the gains from trade, about the efficiency of world output, and about how the international economy will bring about patterns of trade and production compatible with comparative advantage. If, for example, the international relative price is equal to minus the slope of the line BG in Figure 1.5(a), then France will produce at B, and Germany at D, specializing in butane. French consumption will be given by some point on the colored line, say G. Then German consumption will be given by F (the line FD has the same slope and length as BG). France exports JG ($= HD$) apples to Germany for BJ ($= FH$) butane. Both countries gain from trade, and the amount of the gain depends, as before, on how favorable the terms of trade are—that is, on how much the international relative price differs from what the autarkic relative price would be. A country must gain if these two relative prices differ, regardless of whether the country actually specializes or not.

Thus all our earlier conclusions about comparative advantage remain valid in this case of increasing opportunity costs. But suppose that the two production possibility frontiers do not have the simple relationship assumed above but are instead as in Figure 1.6. We can no longer say that one is unambiguously steeper than the other. For example, the marginal rate of transformation at point A on France's production possibility frontier is the same as at point B on Germany's. Even in this case we can talk about comparative advantage if we define it, as before, in terms of actual autarkic relative prices. If, for example, autarkic French production and consumption of the two goods

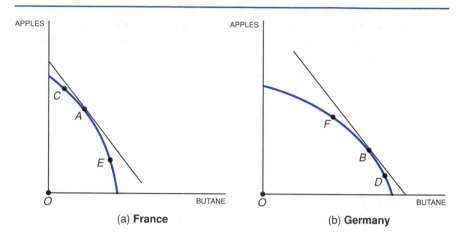

(a) **France**   (b) **Germany**

FIGURE 1.6 **Increasing Opportunity Costs and Incomplete Specialization with Free Trade**   With increasing opportunity costs, both countries may continue to produce some of each good even with free trade. Here, some points on France's frontier are steeper than some points on Germany's but flatter than some other points.

are given by point *E,* and German by point *F,* then the autarkic relative price of butane in terms of apples is higher in France than in Germany and so France has a comparative advantage over Germany in apples relative to butane. But if, on the other hand, France is at point *C* in autarky and Germany at point *D,* then it is Germany whose comparative advantage lies in apples.

The experiment of section 1 can now be repeated here as well. That is, if the autarkic positions are given by *E* and *F* respectively, world output can be made more efficient if France shifts resources from butane to apples and Germany does the reverse (verify that if the countries are originally at *C* and *D* they should shift resources in the opposite direction). We can once again arrive at the same results concerning both world efficiency and free international trade. If you are at all troubled, you should work this out in detail. There are, however, two differences between this case and our previous examples. First and most fundamentally, comparative advantage cannot be deduced on the basis of technology alone. In the earlier cases we could tell which country had a comparative advantage in which good simply by looking at the two production possibility frontiers. But now we must also know exactly *where* on those frontiers each country would produce in the absence of free trade—that is, we must know something about domestic demands. In addition, one of our earlier conclusions must be slightly altered: it is no longer certain that at least one country will be driven to complete specialization under free trade. If, for example, France at point *E* in Figure 1.6(a) shifts resources from butane to apples and Germany at point *F* does the reverse, the French marginal rate of transformation will fall and the German will rise. It is now possible that they will become equal before either country specializes completely. This is illustrated in Figure 1.6, where France produces at *A* and Germany at *B* under a common international price. Thus, in general, it is true only that a country will increase the production of that good in which it has a comparative advantage and decrease the production of the other good once trade begins. With the exception of this minor alteration, all of the conclusions concerning comparative advantage in the simple Ricardian world remain true in general situations.

Problems

1.18 Recall that in section 1 we considered the experiment of shifting labor from butane to apples in France and the reverse in Germany, recording the result in Table 1.2. Do the same now, in the context of increasing opportunity costs, and derive a table analogous to Table 1.2.

1.19* Suppose that France exports apples to Germany in exchange for butane under increasing opportunity costs. Neither country is specialized. Now suppose that the cost of transporting butane from Germany to France equals 50 percent of the (German) cost of producing the butane. The cost of transporting apples, however, is so low that it can be ignored. What must the free trade relationship be between the prices of each good in the two countries? Suppose that a "transportation revolution" is expected to reduce by one-half the cost of shipping butane within the next four years. Can you predict anything about the likely effects of this upon international trade and upon the pattern of production in both countries?

7. TASTES AS A DETERMINANT OF COMPARATIVE ADVANTAGE

In the previous section we emphasized that comparative advantage is general and does not depend on a special technology. We shall now drive home this point even more by showing that we can talk about comparative advantage even when there is no production structure. Suppose that France and Germany each possesses 100 apples and 100 units of butane. This is depicted in Figure 1.7, where *A* and *B* denote these endowments of the two goods. Since these endowments cannot be altered, we can no longer speak of the marginal rate of transformation. But we can still use autarkic relative prices to define the pattern of comparative advantage. If each country were in autarky, prices would be determined at which the domestic demands for the two goods equal the (fixed) domestic supplies. The lines *FF* and *GG* in Figure 1.7 are drawn with slopes equal to minus these relative autarkic prices. Clearly, $P_B^F / P_A^F > P_B^G / P_A^G$. Then we say that France has a comparative advantage in apples relative to butane with respect to Germany. But what does that mean in this case?

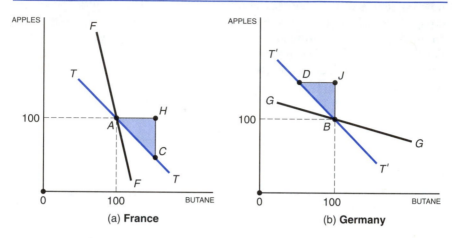

(a) **France**   (b) **Germany**

FIGURE 1.7 **Comparative Advantage in the Absence of Production** Differences in tastes can generate trade: the French are willing to sacrifice more apples for one more unit of butane than the Germans require as compensation for giving up the butane.

KEY CONCEPT

An individual's *marginal rate of substitution* of one good for another is the largest amount of the first good that the individual would willingly sacrifice to obtain one more unit of the second.

To answer this question, first look at the situation from the point of view of an individual (French) consumer—say, Marie. By the "marginal rate of substitution of apples for butane," denoted MRS_{AB}, we mean the amount of apples that must be given to Marie to compensate her exactly for the loss of 1 unit of butane. Or, equivalently, the amount of apples that must be taken away from her to leave her just as satisfied as she was originally if she is given 1 more unit of butane. Each individual's MRS_{AB} depends upon her own tastes. But it also depends upon her pattern of consumption (just as the marginal rate of transformation depends upon the pattern of production). Suppose, for example, that a consumer has a very large quantity of apples but very little butane. She will then find additional butane a good deal more useful and the loss of 1 apple considerably less irksome than she would if she had, instead, a large quantity of butane and only a few apples. In other words, a consumer's MRS_{AB} normally diminishes as she substitutes butane for apples. Now, any consumer facing given market prices for two goods will always spend her income in such a way as to make her MRS_{AB} equal the relative price of butane in terms of apples, P_B^F / P_A^F. Why? Suppose, for example, that she instead spent her income so that $P_B^F / P_A^F > MRS_{AB}$, or $P_B^F > P_A^F MRS_{AB}$. This means that the money she would save by purchasing one less unit of butane is greater than the cost of the apple necessary to compensate her for the loss of the butane. She could spend this excess on both goods, making herself better off. Similarly if $P_B^F / P_A^F < MRS_{AB}$, the consumer could make herself happier by spending less on apples and more on butane. We are not imagining the consumer to be a calculating machine, always computing her *MRS:* if she spends her income in the way she most prefers, she must be causing her *MRS* to equal the relative price she faces, whether she is aware of the concept or not. Since all French consumers face the same relative prices, P_B^F / P_A^F equals the MRS_{AB} of *every* French consumer. This does not mean that they all spend their incomes in the same way. Different individuals have different incomes and different tastes and will purchase different assortments of goods. But if they face the same prices, they must have the same MRS_{AB}. Similarly, each German consumer will spend his income so that his MRS_{AB} equals the autarkic relative German price. These conclusions are valid regardless of the structure of production in both countries.

Since $P_B^F / P_A^F > P_B^G / P_A^G$, it must be that in autarky the MRS_{AB} of each French consumer would exceed that of each German consumer—that is, $MRS_{AB}^F > MRS_{AB}^G$. Suppose now that 1 unit of butane is taken from some German consumer—say, Fritz—and given to Marie. Marie will be just as well off as she was originally if MRS_{AB}^F apples are also taken from her. But only MRS_{AB}^G apples need to be given to Fritz to compensate him exactly for the original loss of 1 unit of butane. Thus there are apples left over that can make both of them better off. Notice the precise formal similarity between this reasoning and that of section 1. We have come to the same conclusion, that trade according to the pattern of comparative advantage can benefit all. Only now we are doing this not by making world output more efficient, but by making the world distribution of goods more efficient.

What will happen if these countries trade? Initially, $P_B^F / P_A^F > P_B^G / P_A^G$. Then in Germany butane costs (P_B^G / P_A^G) apples. This many apples can be obtained in France for $P_A^F(P_B^G / P_A^G)$, which is less than P_B^F, the amount the butane can be sold for in France. Thus there is profit to be made by exporting French apples for German butane. The relative price of butane in terms of apples will fall in France and rise in Germany until a common international relative price p is determined. This is depicted by the lines *TT* and *T'T'* in Figure 1.7; France consumes at *C,* and Germany at *D.* Thus France exports *HC* (= *BJ*) apples to Germany for *AH* (= *DJ*) butane.

The principle of comparative advantage leads to the same conclusion as before about the pattern of trade, and, again, both countries gain from trade. And, again, the gains from trade accruing to a country depend upon how favorable its terms of trade are—that is, upon how much the international relative price differs from what the autarkic relative price would be.

> ## KEY CONCEPT
>
> An *efficient pattern of consumption* is a distribution of goods among individuals for which it is impossible to redistribute the goods to make someone happier without making someone else less happy.

This example also makes clear that the gains from trade do not result solely from altering the world pattern of production. There is, to be sure, a *production gain* from trade: as the previous sections demonstrated, free trade causes world output to be on the world production possibility frontier. But we have now seen that there is in addition a *consumption gain:* free trade ensures that the actual assortment of goods produced will be distributed efficiently among the world's consumers.

8.* *EXPLORING FURTHER:* INDIFFERENCE CURVES

An Individual's Indifference Curves

An individual's tastes can be described by a collection of indifference curves. This is done in Figure 1.8 for Marie, our typical French consumer. Point A indicates a consumption bundle consisting of 5 apples and 2 units of butane. The curve through A, labeled *I,* shows all combinations of apples and butane that Marie regards as neither better nor worse than A. Thus if the bundle A were replaced by *E,* Marie would not care. The actual shape of such an indifference curve is subjective, reflecting Marie's individual tastes. But some general conclusions can be drawn. For example, an indifference curve must have a *downward* slope, because more apples compensate for less butane. Indifference curves further from the origin depict better alternatives. In Figure 1.8, bundle *C* must be better for Marie than *A,* because *C* has more of everything; likewise *B* is worse than *A.* Thus the indifference curve through *C* (labeled II) lies outside that through *A,* and the curve through B would lie inside if that curve were drawn. Bundle *D* lies on a higher curve than does A, so Marie prefers *D* to *A.* If we did not know the shape of these curves (that is, Marie's tastes), we would not be able to compare *A* and *D* because one bundle has more apples but the other has more butane.

The MRS_{AB} at any point equals the slope of the indifference curve at that point (more precisely, *minus* the slope since the latter is a negative number). Thus if Marie consumes the bundle *C,* her MRS_{AB} will equal OF/OG. The "bowed in" shape of the indifference curves reflects diminishing marginal rate of substitution: MRS_{AB} falls as more and more butane is substituted for apples— that is, as we move downward and to the right along an indifference curve.

Suppose that the relative price of butane in terms of apples equals OF/OG and that Marie's income enables her to buy OG units of butane or OF

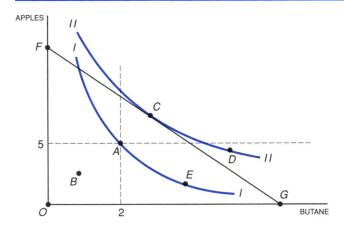

FIGURE 1.8 **Marie's Indifference Curves** Marie is indifferent between bundles *A* and *E* and between bundles *C* and *D*. She prefers either *C* or *D* to either *A* or *E*.

apples. Thus she can purchase any bundle in the triangle OFG. She will buy the bundle that puts her on the highest indifference curve. This will be at a point, such as C in Figure 1.8, where an indifference curve is just tangent to the edge of the triangle. Thus Marie will choose a bundle that makes her MRS_{AB} equal to the relative price of butane in terms of apples, the conclusion we reached in section 7.

Community Indifference Curves

We have used indifference curves to describe the subjective tastes of an individual Frenchwoman. Presumably distinct collections of indifference curves describe the tastes of all other French (and German) residents. Many parts of trade theory can be conveniently treated with community indifference curves: a set of curves describing the collective tastes of a nation as a whole. It is not generally possible to derive such curves from individuals' indifference curves in a wholly satisfactory way, and one would not want to use them when considering problems involving the internal distribution of income or other issues where differences between individuals matter. But in other cases community indifference curves can be heuristically convenient.

In that spirit, suppose that the tastes of the French nation as a whole are summarized by one set of community indifference curves and German tastes by another. Each country is characterized by two types of information: objective supply conditions, described by the production possibility frontier, and subjective tastes, described by the community indifference curves. Figure 1.9 shows this information for both countries. If a country cannot trade, it will produce and consume at that point on its production possibility frontier lying

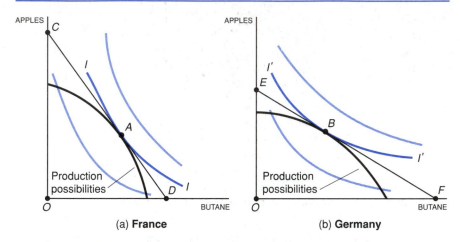

FIGURE 1.9 Autarky If France and Germany do not allow trade with each other, France will produce and consume at *A* and Germany will produce and consume at *B*.

on the highest community indifference curve: point *A* in France and point *B* in Germany. At such a point, the two curves are tangent, with the common slope reflecting the autarkic price ratio. Thus in France the relative autarkic price of butane in terms of apples (P_B^F / P_A^F) equals OC/OD $(= MRT_{AB}^F = MRS_{AB}^F)$, while in Germany $OE/OF = P_B^G / P_A^G = MRT_{AB}^G = MRS_{AB}^G$.

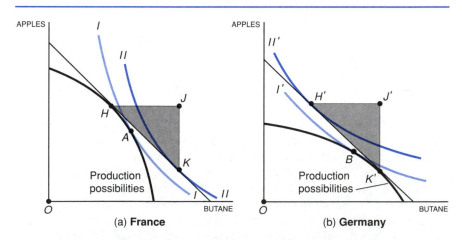

FIGURE 1.10 Free Trade With free trade, France produces at *H* and consumes at *K*, while Germany produces at *K'* and consumes at *H'*. The French "trade triangle" (*HJK*) is identical to the German (*H'J'K'*).

Figure 1.10 shows a free-trade equilibrium. France produces at H and exports $JK (= J'K')$ apples to Germany for $HJ (= H'J')$ butane. Thus France consumes at point K on the indifference curve II. Under autarky, France produced and consumed at A on the lower indifference curve I; so France has gained from trade. Likewise, Germany, now producing at K' and consuming at H', has gained from trade by moving from the indifference curve I' to the higher II'.

Problems

1.20 Prove that, for a single individual, two distinct indifference curves cannot intersect.

1.21 Draw community indifference curves in Figure 1.7 to show that international differences in tastes can serve as a basis for mutually beneficial trade.

1.22 Go through the discussion in section 3 of the gains from trade, using indifference curves.

1.23 Draw the community indifference curves that depict the tastes described in Problem **1.4b:** everyone always wants to consume equal numbers of bolts of cloth and casks of wine.

9. NORTH-SOUTH TRADE

How does comparative advantage measure up in terms of actual trade? We now take a detailed look at world trade.

One natural way to idealize the world, in terms of the two-country examples considered in the previous sections, is to view it as divided into two blocks: the developed countries (also called the "North" or the "Center") and the less developed countries (the "South" or the "Periphery"). And commodities can be classified into two groups: manufactured goods and primary products. One would expect the developed countries as a group to have a comparative advantage over the less developed countries in manufactured goods relative to primary products.

This accounting convention is used in Table 1.4, which shows the pattern of world exports in various years (the trade of former communist countries is excluded). The first number in each entry gives the value of the appropriate exports in billions of U.S. dollars, and the number in parentheses shows what percentage that value is of total exports for that year. *DC* stands for the developed countries as a group and *LDC* for the less developed countries.

Three striking characteristics of world trade are immediately apparent from these figures. First,

The largest part of world trade is that among the developed countries themselves, rather than between these countries and the less developed ones.

TABLE 1.4   **Trade of Developed and Less Developed Noncommunist Countries in Selected Years** *(billions of dollars)*

(a) 1953

Exports to	Exports from				Total	
	DCs		LDCs			
DCs	$29	(42%)	$18	(26%)	$47	(68%)
LDCs	16	(23)	6	(9)	22	(32)
Total	45	(65)	24	(35)	69	(100)

(b) 1973

Exports to	Exports from				Total	
	DCs		LDCs			
DCs	$294	(63%)	$80	(17%)	$374	(80%)
LDCs	69	(15)	23	(5)	92	(20)
Total	363	(78)	103	(22)	466	(100)

(c) 1992

Exports to	Exports from				Total	
	DCs		LDCs			
DCs	$1,923	(56%)	$610	(18%)	$2,533	(74%)
LDCs	623	(18)	267	(8)	890	(26)
Total	2,546	(76)	877	(24)	3,423	(100)

SOURCE: General Agreement on Tariffs and Trade, *International Trade.*

We would expect differences in comparative costs and tastes to be much more marked between the two groups of countries than between individual developed countries. The fraction of world trade accounted for by trade between the less developed countries themselves is minor.

A second salient fact is the very rapid growth in world trade in the period 1953 to 1992. Indeed, this growth has been rapid relative to world output.

> *International trade has grown more rapidly than world production in nearly every year since the Second World War.*

That this rapid growth has, however, not been balanced is the third feature revealed by Table 1.4.

Trade among the DCs has increased much faster than trade in general and thus accounts for an increasing proportion of total trade.

What about the commodity composition of trade, the exchange of manufactured goods for primary products? Table 1.5(a) reveals that the DCs do, on balance, export manufactured goods to the LDCs in exchange for primary products, as expected. (The number in parentheses in each entry shows what percentage of total trade between the two groups of countries consisted of trade in manufactures.) Trade among the DCs themselves also involves, to an increasing degree, manufactured goods. Since Table 1.5 revealed that trade between these countries was increasing more rapidly, we would expect trade in manufactures to be accounting for an increasing fraction of total trade. That this is indeed the case can be seen in Table 1.5(c).

The DCs, on balance, export manufactures to the LDCs in exchange for primary products. The DCs also exchange manufactures among themselves.

Thus the most significant part of world trade is the exchange of similar goods (manufactures) between similar economies (DCs).

Bela Balassa, Herbert Grubel, Peter Lloyd, and others have demonstrated that the rapid expansion of trade among the DCs has not taken the form of increased specialization, as comparative advantage would lead one to expect, but rather of a simultaneous increase by all countries of their exports of most industries.

Trade among the DCs features a large and growing volume of intra-industry trade, both absolutely and relative to interindustry trade.

Thus France exports steel and automobiles to Germany while also importing both goods (intraindustry trade) instead of just exporting one and importing the other (interindustry). It might seem senseless to both import and export automobiles, but there are several good reasons for doing so. *Product differentiation* is one: French and German automobiles are not the same, so trade gives consumers more choice. *Division of labor* is another reason: parts of the car might be built in France and other parts in Germany so that trade in automobile parts is necessary to assemble complete cars. Intraindustry trade need not, therefore, be different in principle from interindustry trade. What makes it interesting is that, since roughly similar goods are exchanged, comparative cost differences are unlikely to be large between countries.

Aggregate statistics mask some significant developments. We have already mentioned the rise in the price of oil. Another important trend is the rapid rate at which LDCs have increased their exports of manufactures since the 1960s. World trade in manufactures grew at an average annual rate of 8.9 percent from 1960 to 1975, with the DCs expanding their exports at 8.8 percent while LDC exports of manufactures grew at 12.3 percent—the most dy-

TABLE 1.5   **International Trade in Manufactures**

(a) The Pattern of Trade in Manufactures, 1985 (billions of dollars)

Exports to	Exports from	
	DCs	LDCs
DCs	$696 (73%)	$97 (33%)
LDCs	197 (78)	43 (37)

(b) The Pattern of Trade in Manufactures, 1992 (billions of dollars)

Exports to	Exports from	
	DCs	LDCs
DCs	$1,519 (79%)	$330 (54%)
LDCs	474 (76)	213 (79)

(c) Relative to Total Trade

Year	Value ($billion)	% of total trade
1928	12	39
1953	32	45
1973	350	61
1992	2,653	73

SOURCES: United Nations, *Monthly Bulletin of Statistics,* and General Agreement on Tariffs and Trade, *International Trade.*

namic part of world trade. (The fact that the global growth rate was so much closer to the DCs' rate reflects the latter's large absolute share.) Table 1.5(a) shows that LDC exports of manufactures in 1985 totaled $140 billion, or 12 percent of world manufactured exports. This is a modest share, to be sure, but in 1960 it had been only 4 percent. Comparison of Tables 1.5(a) and 1.5(b) shows further dramatic growth.

> *LDC exports of manufactures are the fastest-growing part of world trade, although their absolute share is still modest.*

Much of this growth is accounted for by a small group of newly industrializing countries (NICs) such as South Korea, Taiwan, Hong Kong, Singapore (sometimes called the "Gang of Four"), and Brazil. These countries have experienced rapid growths in incomes while expanding their exports of manufactures such as shoes, textiles, steel, and, more recently, automobiles and computers.

Problem

1.24 Since the Second World War, the DCs have substantially lowered trade barriers, but the LDCs have not. Explain how Table 1.5 seems to be consistent with comparative advantage. What would you expect to be true of the relative *gains* from the various trade flows as distinct from their sizes?

10. *CASE STUDY:* THE INTERNATIONAL TRADE OF THE UNITED STATES

A second way to split the globe is between the United States and the rest of the world. This trade is summarized in Table 1.6. The three most important trading partners of the United States are Canada, Japan, and the European Union (EU) as a whole. Trade with Eastern Europe has increased substantially but remains a small fraction of the total. The United States trades more with other DCs than with the LDCs. International trade accounts for a relatively low proportion of the U.S. GNP but, due to the size of the American economy, is nonetheless a substantial fraction of total world trade.

The large imbalance shown in these figures will be discussed later in this book. Now we are concerned with the *structure* of this trade. The United

TABLE 1.6 **International Trade of the United States, 1993** *(billions of dollars)*

(a) Direction				(b) Composition	
Partner	Exports	Imports		Commodity group	Exports-imports
DCs	271	348			
Canada	101	113		Food	12.8
EU	95	102		Petroleum	−44.0
Japan	47	107		Other raw materials	3.5
LDCs	180	237		Capital goods	29.9
Mexico	41	40		Automotive goods	−50.0
OPEC	19	33		Other consumer goods	−79.0
Others	120	164			
Eastern Europe	6	4			
TOTAL	457	589			
% of U.S. GNP	7.2	9.2			
% of world trade	12.5	15.4			

SOURCE: U.S. Department of Commerce, *Survey of Current Business.*

States appears to have a comparative advantage in temperate-zone agricultural products (notably wheat, corn, and soybeans, all of which contribute positively to the food item in Table 1.6(b)) and in high-technology manufactured goods (such as capital goods). On the other hand, America is a heavy net importer of low-technology manufactured products (such as consumer goods) and of mineral fuels (notably oil). All this seems consistent enough with what one would guess relative autarkic prices to be, considering the nature of the American economy.

Problem

1.25 What reasons can you think of for the patterns of comparative advantage apparently indicated by Table 1.6(b)?

11. *CASE STUDY:* THE INTERNATIONAL TRADE OF CANADA

Canada is the largest single trading partner of the United States, accounting for about 20 percent of the total U.S. trade. But since the Canadian economy is only about one-tenth the size of the U.S. economy, this trade is even more important for Canada. As is clear from Table 1.7, about 70 percent of all Canadian trade is with the United States. On balance, Canada exports raw materials and imports manufactures. The large two-way trade in automotive products reflects the fact that Canada and the United States basically share a common automobile industry. A 1965 agreement between the two countries eliminated all tariffs on shipments of auto parts by General Motors, Ford, Chrysler, and American Motors.

TABLE 1.7 **Canada's International Trade, 1992** *(billions of U.S. dollars)*

	Exports to		Imports from	
Commodity group	*United States*	*Others*	*United States*	*Others*
Agriculture	12.1	11.6	6.1	3.5
Fuels	12.2	1.6	1.3	4.0
Other primary	4.9	4.7	2.3	1.2
Capital goods	15.4	4.3	23.2	12.6
Automotive goods	29.8	0.9	19.8	6.3
Other manufactures	23.0	5.4	24.4	13.2
TOTAL	103.9	30.3	79.9	42.6

SOURCE: General Agreement on Tariffs and Trade, *International Trade.*

Problem

1.26 What reasons can you think of for the pattern of comparative advantage apparently indicated by Table 1.7?

12. *CASE STUDY:* U.S.-JAPANESE TRADE

Japan is the second-largest trading partner of the United States. Since Japan is economically much larger than Canada, we do not have the same dramatic disparity in relative importance. But there is another dramatic disparity: in recent years Japanese-American trade has been unbalanced, with the United States importing much more from Japan than exporting to it. This is clear from Table 1.8, which shows a U.S. balance-of-trade deficit with Japan of $43.8 billion in 1992.

This trade imbalance attracts a great deal of public attention. It also illustrates several points. One is the danger of focusing on *bilateral* trade balances in a *multilateral* world. Suppose that Japan on balance imported $30 billion worth of raw materials from the rest of the world (other than the United States), that Japan then exported $30 billion worth of manufactured goods to the United States, and that the United States on balance sold $30 billion of various goods to the rest of the world. The net trade flows would be as represented in Figure 1.11.

Here each country has balanced trade overall, but all the *bilateral* trade flows are extremely unbalanced! The United States, for example, has a deficit of $30 billion with Japan; but this is unimportant because the deficit is matched by an equal surplus with the rest of the world.

How important is such *triangular* trade in reality? A glance at Table 1.8 reveals that it accounts for a lot. Japan's trade with the rest of the world is more

TABLE 1.8 Japan's International Trade, 1992 *(billions of dollars)*

Commodity group	Exports to		Imports from	
	United States	Others	United States	Others
Food	0.3	1.6	13.3	26.5
Other primary	2.6	9.1	10.0	80.5
Automotive goods	30.8	47.4	1.2	5.2
Other consumer goods	8.4	26.5	5.8	28.3
Other manufactures	54.3	158.6	22.5	39.9
TOTAL	96.5	243.2	52.7	180.3

SOURCE: General Agreement on Tariffs and Trade, *International Trade.*

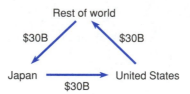

FIGURE 1.11 **A Hypothetical Trade Pattern** Despite huge *bilateral* imbalances, each country's *total* trade is in balance.

nearly in balance than its trade with the United States. Table 1.6 shows that United States trade with the rest of the world is also much more nearly balanced than its trade with Japan. But the U.S.-Japanese imbalance is not entirely due to a triangular trade pattern, for the United States is running a large deficit with the world as a whole, and Japan has a large surplus with the world as a whole.

Two other points deserve mention, although we will not pursue them until later. First, we have been looking at merchandise trade, but other types of international transactions are also important. Countries *borrow and lend* to each other, and they also trade *services:* insurance, transportation, the interest on loans and investments, and so on. Imbalances of commodity trade should be viewed in the broader context of all international exchanges. Second, our theory has looked at free-trade situations, but in practice countries restrict trade in many ways. The nature and extent of such restrictions is dramatically controversial for U.S.-Japanese trade.

Now let us look at the structure of this trade. Japan is clearly a net importer of primary products and an exporter of manufactures. The country has few natural resources and so must import large quantities of raw and semi-processed materials that are paid for with the manufactures that these materials help to produce. Note that the United States is a net exporter of both food and other primary products to Japan. But the United States is proportionally a more important source for the former than for the latter: over one-third of Japan's food imports comes from the United States whereas less than 15 percent of its imports of other primary products are American. This partly reflects the fact that primary products include oil; the Japanese import virtually all their oil, and most of this comes from the Middle East.

The greatest imbalance in U.S.-Japanese trade is with consumer goods, especially automobiles. The Japanese surplus here is a large part of the total bilateral imbalance; the Japanese export almost six times as many consumer goods to the United States as they import. There is also a large imbalance in the trade of other manufactures (which includes capital goods and technologically advanced goods), but the trade flows here are more nearly proportional to the overall flows between the two countries. Again, there is an asymmetry with respect to the rest of the world. The Japanese export more consumer goods to the United States than to the rest of the world, whereas a dispropor- tionately small share of their exports of other manufactures is sent to the United States. Similarly, Japan imports almost two thirds as many other manu- factures from America as from the rest of the world, and a disproportionately small share of imports of consumer goods comes from the United States.

It appears from this that the United States has a comparative advantage over Japan in primary products and that Japan has a comparative advantage over the United States in consumer goods. Other manufactures seem to be in the middle so that the direction of trade here is sensitive to the overall bal- ance. Also, the United States seems able to compete well, relative to the rest of the world, in the Japanese market for food and other manufactures but rel- atively poorly in the market for consumer goods.

Problem

1.27 What reasons can you think of for the pattern of comparative advantage apparently indicated by Table 1.8?

13. *CASE STUDY:* THE NICs AND THE NECs

The Japanese economy has grown rapidly since the Second World War. Much of the stimulus for this growth has come from the dynamic expansion of the country's exports of manufactured goods. Japan first developed strong export markets in textiles and other simple manufactures. Then it gradually expanded exports of more complex goods, displacing traditional exporters, until it developed the trade pattern described in the previous section.

In contrast to this, LDCs have typically followed closed policies, dis- couraging international trade. (These policies will be discussed in Chapter 4.) However, since the 1960s a small group of LDCs (the *newly industrializing countries*—or NICs—mentioned in section 9 of this chapter) have been rapidly expanding their own exports of simple manufactures in apparent emu- lation of the Japanese pattern. First in textiles and clothing, then in other sec- tors, including, more recently, automobiles and electronics, these countries have now achieved significant market penetration with most simple manufac- tures. Often this has been at the expense of Japanese firms, just as the Japanese had earlier displaced Western firms in many world markets.

The export success of the NICs is clear in Table 1.9. The ten countries here classified as NICs experienced average annual rates of growth of exports much above the world average throughout the period 1964–1984. In that time their share of world exports more than doubled, from 5 percent to 11.5 percent.

TABLE 1.9   **Export Performance of the NECs* and the NICs†**

	Exports as a % of world exports (in value)			Average annual rate of growth of exports	
	1964	1984	1990	1964–80	1980–90
NECs	1.7	2.3	3.0	17.2	25.4
NICs	5.0	11.5	11.0	20.5	18.2
World	100.0	100.0	100.0	17.0	11.1

*NECs: Colombia, Malaysia, Philippines, Thailand, Turkey, Uruguay.
†NICs: Brazil, Greece, Hong Kong, Korea, Mexico, Portugal, Singapore, Spain, Taiwan, Yugoslavia.
SOURCE: International Monetary Fund, *Direction of Trade.*

More recently, a second tier of LDCs have been experiencing accelerating export growth. These are sometimes referred to as *newly exporting countries* (NECs). The collection of NECs whose performance is reported in Table 1.9 increased their exports at an average annual rate only slightly better than that of the world as a whole during 1964–1980. But from 1984 to 1990 their growth rate was significantly higher. Some people expect that the NECs will overtake the NICs in regard to export penetration, just as the NICs are beginning to overtake the Japanese. Indeed, some of the NECs are now increasing their exports more rapidly than are the NICs.

Japan's export success has caused competing industries in other DCs to clamor for relief, and strains have been put on Japan's relations with these other countries, notably the United States. Japanese trade has also been restricted in various ways, such as with the export restraints on automobiles (these will be discussed in Chapter 7). The NICs' export penetration in many light industrial sectors is now producing a similar result. Thus far there are few signs that the expansion of these countries' trade has been affected in the aggregate, but there is increasing external criticism of some of them, especially Korea and Taiwan. Some DC politicians and industry spokesmen claim that the NICs try hard to increase exports while continuing to restrict imports. There is some basis for these charges. Although the NICs are export-oriented and have few trade restrictions relative to other LDCs, they remain protectionist by the standards of the DCs. If the NECs continue to expand their export shares, they will likely also figure in similar controversies. Perhaps this is what we can expect in the rest of the 1990s.

14. HOW DOES COMPARATIVE ADVANTAGE STACK UP?

Quite well, thank you. Each of our case studies displayed trade patterns readily understood by combining the ideas of comparative advantage with basic knowledge of the countries and regions involved. And the basic theory has a useful broader application. This is just what theory should do.

But, still, in recent decades doubts have grown dramatically about how relevant comparative advantage really is to contemporary trade. Why? Mainly because the largest and most dynamic portion of world trade is the exchange of similar products between similar economies—in particular, the intraindustry trade of manufactures among the DCs.

An essential point of comparative advantage is that countries trade in order to exploit their *differences*, whether these are differences in the relative ability to supply goods or in the relative desire to consume them. But this actual trade seems to be based on *similarities*. So maybe something other than comparative advantage is at work here.

But this is not necessarily so: extensive trade in similar goods between similar economies is *not* logically inconsistent with comparative advantage. The DCs have much larger market economies than do the LDCs (this is, after all, what development means) and would, therefore, be expected to trade more. Also the DCs as a group are much less inclined than the LDCs to limit their trade with taxes, controls, and other protectionist devices. Indeed, the basic logic of comparative advantage can potentially be turned on its head actually to offer an *explanation* of this trade: if the exchange of similar commodities yields only modest gains, then similar economies, which must exchange similar goods, need to trade a lot to realize gains!

The prominence of intraindustry trade between similar economies is important not because it cannot be explained by comparative advantage (which is *not* true), but because it can also easily be explained by other theories. Deciding the relative importance of each is ultimately a problem for empirical research. But this can't be done until we understand how the other theories work. This will be addressed in the next two chapters.

Problem

1.28 Write down as many reasons as you can think of why two countries should trade with each other. For each reason, indicate either that (a) it has nothing to do with comparative advantage or (b) it helps to determine what the pattern of comparative advantage is. Justify your answers.

15. SUMMARY

1. The basic reasoning underlying the principle of comparative advantage was presented in section 1. It is essential that the logic of the example in section 1 be thoroughly understood. The balance of this first chapter has been devoted to exploring the actual economic implications of comparative advantage and to emphasizing the general nature of the idea.

2. If, in the absence of free international trade, the relative price of butane in terms of apples is higher in France than in Germany, we say that France has a comparative advantage over Germany in apples relative to butane or that, equivalently, Germany has a comparative advantage over France in butane relative to apples.

3. If trade is allowed, then (a) each country will tend to increase the output of that good in which it has a comparative advantage and will tend to decrease the output of that good in which it has a comparative disadvantage; (b) each country will export the good in which it has a comparative advantage and import the other; (c) world output will tend to become more efficient; (d) each country will gain from free trade relative to autarky; and (e) the gains enjoyed by a country will be greater the more favorable its terms of trade—that is, the greater the difference between relative prices before and after trade is liberalized.

4. The actual world relative price and the actual pattern of production in each country cannot be deduced from comparative advantage alone. Detailed knowledge of world demand for the two goods is also necessary.

5. The DCs on balance export manufactures to the LDCs in exchange for primary products, but the largest part of world trade is the intraindustry exchange of manufactures among the DCs themselves.

SUGGESTED READING

Balassa, B. *Trade Liberalization among Industrial Countries.* New York: McGraw-Hill, 1967.

Bhagwati, J. "The Pure Theory of International Trade: A Survey." In *Surveys of Economic Theory.* New York: St. Martin's, 1967. Pages 159–72 contain a discussion of the Ricardian theory and a critique of statistical tests of it.

Cooper, R. *The Economics of Interdependence: Economic Policy in the Atlantic Community.* New York: Columbia University Press, 1980. A discussion of the development of the postwar international economy.

Glejser, H. "Empirical Evidence on Comparative Cost Theory from the European Common Market Experience." *European Economic Review* (1972).

Grubel, H. G., and P. J. Lloyd. *Intra-Industry Trade.* New York: Wiley, 1975.

Haberler, G. *The Theory of International Trade.* New York: Macmillan, 1937. See Chapter 10 for a good discussion of comparative costs.

Jones, R. W. "Comparative Advantage and the Theory of Tariffs: A Multi-Country, Multi-Commodity Model." *Review of Economic Studies* (1961). The basic statement of comparative advantage in the general case of many goods and countries.

Leontief, W. "The Use of Indifference Curves in the Analysis of Foreign Trade." In *Readings in the Theory of International Trade.* Edited by H. S. Ellis and L. A. Metzler. Homewood: Irwin, 1950.

MacDougall, G. D. A. "British and American Exports: A Study Suggested by the Theory of Comparative Costs." In *Readings in International Economics.* Edited by R. E. Caves and H. G. Johnson. Homewood: Irwin, 1968.

Ricardo, D. *The Principles of Political Economy and Taxation.* Baltimore: Penguin, 1971. Ricardo's treatment of comparative advantage is found in Chapter 7.

Samuelson, P. "The Gains from International Trade." In *Readings in the Theory of International Trade.* Edited by H. S. Ellis and L. A. Metzler. Homewood: Irwin, 1950.
———. "Social Indifference Curves." *Quarterly Journal of Economics* (1956). When community indifference curves exist.

CHAPTER 2

Economies of Scale

> As it is the power of exchanging that gives occasion to the division
> of labor, so the extent of this division must always be limited by the
> extent of that power, or in other words, by the extent of the market.
> —ADAM SMITH

Chapter 1 revealed trade patterns consistent with comparative advantage, leaving open the question of whether that theory explains the large volume of intraindustry trade in manufactures between the DCs. Comparative advantage could also explain trade between the DCs, but such trade might also reflect something else entirely. What difference does it make? Comparative advantage implies that gains are likely to be greatest for trade between economies that are least similar. Thus one might conclude that expansion of DC-LDC trade is relatively important for global welfare, whereas changes in the already extensive trade among DCs are relatively unimportant. This policy conclusion becomes questionable if trade is significantly due to some other cause. Accordingly, this chapter and the next successively examine the two principal alternatives to comparative advantage as an explanation of trade: scale economies and imperfect competition. Both explanations have been around for a long time, but only recently have most economists begun to pay them a lot of attention.

1. INCREASING RETURNS TO SCALE

Comparative advantage is very general: most reasons to trade are special cases of comparative advantage. One of the few possibilities not included is increasing returns to scale—the idea that production is most efficient when

FRANK D. GRAHAM (1890–1949)

Frank Graham was born in Nova Scotia, did his graduate work at Harvard, and spent most of his professional life as a professor of economics at Princeton, where he instigated a succession of professional controversies. The best known was a strong attack on the classical theory of international trade, even though Graham accepted the basic features of the Ricardian model discussed in Chapter 1, emphasizing instead the possibilities that arise with more than two goods and two countries. Graham also advanced a controversial argument that increasing returns to scale—the topic of this chapter—could justify tariff protection. Although he was himself a free-trader who thought his argument of little contemporary practical importance, the discussion was an early and prominent demonstration that the implications of comparative advantage can fail if trade is in fact due to something other than comparative advantage.

conducted on a large scale. The simple Ricardian model, by contrast, assumes *constant returns to scale:* varying all inputs in proportion causes output to vary in the same proportion. In Table 1.1, for example, *each* ounce of butane produced in Germany required 1 unit of labor, so that 2 units of labor produced 2 ounces of butane, 3 units produced 3 ounces of butane, and so on.

Suppose instead that the technology for producing butane from labor is as described in Table 2.1 in each country. Thus the first ounce of butane produced requires 4 units of labor, and each additional ounce of butane requires 1 additional unit. This means that the average (labor) cost *declines* as output expands: with 1 butane unit produced, the average cost is 4; with 2 produced, it is 2.5; with 3, it is 2; and so on. Equivalently, the average productivity of labor *increases* as more labor is employed in butane production.

KEY CONCEPT

A technology has *increasing returns to scale* if an equiproportional increase in all inputs increases output in greater proportion, *constant returns to scale* if it increases output in the same proportion, and *decreasing returns to scale* if it increases output in a smaller proportion.

TABLE 2.1 Technology for Butane Production in Each Country (*increasing returns to scale*)

To produce this much butane . . .	. . . Requires this much labor . . .	. . . So the average labor cost is . . .	. . . And average labor productivity is
1	4	4/1 = 4.00	1/4 = .25
2	5	2.50	.40
3	6	2.00	.50
4	7	1.75	.57
5	8	1.60	.63
6	9	1.50	.67
7	10	1.43	.70

External versus Internal Economies of Scale

An important consideration is whether the scale economies are *internal* to an individual butane firm or *external* to it. In the former case, the individual firm knows it can enjoy low average costs if it produces at a high scale. This would be so if the scale economies reflect the efficiency of a large plant—an automobile assembly plant is a good example. But with external economies the individual firm cannot itself influence its average costs; instead they depend on the size of the entire industry. For example, a large manufacturing sector in a country might generate a labor force with skills and habits useful for industrial life, support an extensive infrastructure, allow many specialized crafts to develop, and so on. All this would lower average cost for all firms in the sector as the sector expands. But an expansion of any individual firm, unmatched by an expansion of the sector, would not lower that firm's costs. The Swiss watch industry, with its many specialized crafts, was often pointed to as an example.

KEY CONCEPT

Scale economies are *internal to the firm* if the firm's average costs depend upon the firm's size. They are *external to the firm* (and *internal to the industry*) if the firm's average costs depend upon the size of the industry, but an expansion of the firm with the industry unchanged in size will have no effect on the firm's average costs.

Why does it matter whether economies of scale are internal or external to the firm? Internal economies are not consistent with the perfect competition we have been considering so far. Suppose that a butane firm believes it has no control over the market price of butane and that the entry of competing butane firms has driven profits to zero. If the firm has internal increasing returns to scale, it can lower its average costs (and thus generate a profit since the price of butane is given) by increasing output. Thus competitive firms will always want to increase production and will never be in equilibrium. Equilibrium requires *either* that the firm not be competitive, so that it expects an increase in output to push down the price of butane, *or* that the scale economies be external, so that it expects the increase in output to have no effect on average cost.

KEY CONCEPT

In a *perfectly competitive market,* individual firms cannot influence the price they can charge for their products. This will be so if there are many sellers of identical goods. In an *imperfectly competitive market,* each firm is aware that its actions will have some effect on the price it receives.

National versus International Economies of Scale

Scale economies can work in other ways. One of the most important reasons for scale economies at the industry level is that a larger market permits a greater division of labor. Take Adam Smith's example of the pin factory: if each worker produces entire pins from scratch, productivity is much less than if pins are produced in assembly-line fashion, with each worker specialized to an individual step in the process. The key requirement is that the market for pins be large enough so that enough workers can be employed to allow them to specialize in different crafts: the division of labor is limited by the extent of the market. This sort of scale economy is obviously central to modern industry. A final good such as an automobile is built from thousands of special parts, each of which is in turn produced by many workers with specialized crafts and equipment.

Scale economies resulting from the division of labor differ in one crucial way from the scale economies we considered earlier. These other examples had required *geographical concentration* of production: to exploit the advantages of large plant size, production must take place *at* the plant; to imbue a population with industrial skills, industry must be sizable *where* the population is. But this is not true of Smith's pin example. If each worker concentrates on a distinct part of pin making, there must be enough work concentrated where each worker is to keep him fully employed; but the workers themselves need not be concentrated in the same factory, city, or nation, provided that it is not too difficult to ship pin parts from worker to worker. Likewise, all the parts that go into an automobile need not be produced in Detroit in order to profit from the division of labor. These scale economies are *international:* they depend upon the size of the world market rather than upon the amount of geographical concentration of production.

KEY CONCEPT

Increasing returns to scale are *national* if average cost depends on the size of the national industry. They are *international* if average cost depends on the worldwide size of the industry.

Scale economies that are respectively internal or external to the firm may be either national or international in scope. For example, economies that come from concentrating production in a single, large, efficient plant are national and internal to the firm; those that come from a division of labor within a global manufacturing sector are external to the firm and international in scope. As another example, consider an automobile firm spending millions of dollars to design a new model. This will generate scale economies because more production allows the firm to spread the design cost over more vehicles, reducing the design cost per vehicle. Such scale economies are internal to the firm. But many automobile producers are *multinational firms,* operating plants in several countries. Such a firm might use the new design in some of its plants in different countries; in this case the economies of scale are international in scope as well as internal to the firm.

The nature of economies of scale is often sensitive to circumstances. For example, the extent of the division of labor is determined by the size of the world market if tariffs, transport costs, and other trade barriers are insignificant: various stages of production can be located anywhere if it is easy to ship parts from place to place. But sufficiently high trade barriers will make these economies national since they will require all stages of production to be located in the same country.

Another example. Suppose that the scale economies are due to a large industry allowing specialized craftsmen or -women, each of whom learns a particular job especially well. For years the Swiss watch industry has been cited as an example. Such economies are likely to be external to the firm. But whether they will be national or international in scope is sensitive to exactly

TABLE 2.2   Types of Scale Economies

	Internal to the firm	*External to the firm*
National	Concentration of production in a large, efficient plant	A large industry supporting an industrial labor force and extensive infrastructure
International	Research and development by a multinational firm	Extensive division of labor in an industry with low barriers to trade and communication

how the workers learn their crafts. If they bear the cost themselves (through schooling or a long apprenticeship at low wages), they will be most likely to do so if most of the world's firms that could employ them are located near where they themselves live: that way they could be most sure of having a job at a competitive wage once the training is completed. Thus the scale economies will likely be national. But if the firm is to pay the cost (by paying for the worker's education or by paying a full wage during the training period), it will be most likely to do so if there are no competitors nearby, thus making the defection of a newly trained worker to a competitor unlikely. In this case the scale economies will not require geographical concentration and so will be international.

Table 2.2 shows the various types of scale economies with typical examples of each.

Problems

2.1 If France has 5 labor units and if Table 2.1 describes the technology of both the apple and butane industries, draw France's production possibility frontier.

2.2 Suppose Germany is identical to the France of Problem **2.1**. Draw the world production possibility frontier if the scale economies are *national*.

2.3 How does your answer to Problem **2.2** change if the scale economies are *international*?

2. SCALE ECONOMIES AS A BASIS FOR TRADE

To see how scale economies themselves may cause trade independently of comparative advantage, consider a simple example in which France and Germany are identical: same size, same technology, same tastes. This rules out comparative advantage as a cause of trade. We use the example of Table 2.1, whose first two columns are mostly contained in Table 2.3.

Suppose, for simplicity's sake, that apple production still has constant returns to scale, with 1 unit of labor required to produce each apple in each country, and that France and Germany each possesses 10 units of labor. Suppose that, if France and Germany do not trade, each country divides its labor force equally between the two industries. Thus, in France, 5 units of labor produce (from Table 2.3) 2 units of butane, and the other 5 units of labor produce 5 apples.

National Economies of Scale

Suppose first that the scale economies depicted in Table 2.3 are *national*. Since the countries are identical, they must have equal relative autarkic prices so neither country has a comparative advantage in anything. But there is still

TABLE 2.3 **Production in Autarky and with Trade**

To produce this much butane . . .	. . . Requires this much labor . . .	. . . Allowing this many apples	
0	0	10	France with trade
1	4	6	
2	5	5	Each in autarky
3	6	4	
4	7	3	
5	8	2	
6	9	1	
7	10	0	Germany with trade

good reason to trade. Suppose France specializes in apples and Germany in butane. Then, from Table 2.3, the 10 units of German labor produce 7 units of butane, and France produces 10 apples. If the French trade 5 apples to Germany for 3.5 units of butane, each country can consume just as many apples as in autarky but more butane. Note two features of this trade.

Increasing returns to scale furnish a basis for trade independent of comparative advantage.

This simple example abstracts entirely from comparative advantage.

The pattern of trade tends to be indeterminate if the cause of trade is increasing returns to scale.

Suppose instead that France had specialized in butane and Germany in apples. We would have obtained the same consumption pattern with the opposite pattern of trade! Since the two countries are identical in this example, their roles are interchangeable, and no theory can prescribe or predict the pattern of trade.

International Economies of Scale

Now suppose that the scale economies illustrated in Table 2.3 are international. This means that, with free trade, the economies of scale in butane production come from an increased division of labor worldwide, so that the first two columns of the table refer to the *global* butane industry, regardless of how it is divided between France and Germany.

Suppose that autarky is the same as before, with each country producing 2 units of butane and 5 apples. If trade commences, one possibility is the same outcome as before, with France specialized in apples and Germany in butane. With the entire butane industry located in one country, it will not matter whether the scale economies are national or international. Thus our two conclusions still hold, and trade consists again of the *interindustry* exchange of apples for butane.

But international scale economies do not require the butane industry to be concentrated in one country. In this example, with the two countries identical, it makes no difference which country produces what! The gains from trade come from increasing the division of labor within the global butane industry. For example, the two countries could even maintain their autarky allocations of resources, with each country employing 5 units of labor in each industry. Trade allows the two countries to establish a single large butane industry of 10 labor units with a global output of 7. This is attained by an increased division of labor, with the 5 French workers doing part of the production process and the 5 German workers the other part. This requires the *intraindustry* exchange of unfinished and finished butane between the two countries. Indeed, in this particular case there would be only intraindustry trade and no exchange of apples for butane: the two countries produce identical quantities of apples, and, with identical tastes, they consume identical quantities as well. This example thus illustrates another potential feature of this trade.

> *When increasing returns to scale are international, trade between countries with similar patterns of resource allocation will tend to be* intraindustry, *and trade between countries with different patterns of resource allocation will tend to be* interindustry.

Note the analogy to the fact, pointed out in Chapter 1, that intraindustry exchange is more prominent relative to interindustry exchange in trade among the DCs than in that between the DCs and the LDCs

We have seen, then, that economies of scale furnish a motive for trade that is logically distinct from comparative advantage. The tendency for the pattern of this trade to be indeterminate actually reflects the basic difference between comparative-advantage trade and scale-economies trade. Under comparative advantage, countries trade to *exploit their differences* (whether of abilities or of needs); this tends to assign specific roles to specific countries in the world economy. But with scale economies, countries trade to *specialize in narrow tasks* and thereby do them better; what they actually specialize in is secondary.

Problem

2.4 Industries are sometimes described as having *decreasing* returns to scale: increasing all inputs in proportion increases output in a smaller proportion. Try to deduce the consequences of such scale diseconomies for international trade when they are national and when they are international.

3. NATIONAL EXTERNAL ECONOMIES OF SCALE

The previous section established that scale economies can motivate trade. To discuss this trade in more detail, we need to be more specific about the nature of the scale economies. In this section we look at increasing returns to scale that are external to the firm but national. For example, they might reflect the development of an industry-oriented population or of opportunities for investment in infrastructure as a country's industrial sector expands.

There are two reasons to focus on this case, which is, after all, only one of the four possibilities present in Table 2.2. First, such economies have often been central to debates about alternative trade-and-development strategies for LDCs, a topic this book will address later. Second, we have seen that external economies are consistent with perfect competition, whereas internal economies are not. Since we will address imperfect competition in the next chapter, we would rather not muddy the water by slipping it in now.

Since the scale economies are national, Table 2.3 applies to each country individually. Suppose as before that the two countries are identical and that each country allocates 5 workers to each industry in autarky. Now allow free trade. What happens depends upon world demands for the two goods. One possibility is that, just as above, one country—say, France—specializes in apples, and one—Germany—specializes in butane. Then our earlier discussion continues to apply, and world production becomes more efficient. How the gains are distributed between the two countries depends upon the terms of trade, as was true in Chapter 1 with trade based on comparative advantage.

But there are other possibilities as well, and these are illustrated in Table 2.4, which, for convenience, reproduces our example once again. One possibility is that the world might desire more butane (and fewer apples) than would be produced if both countries specialize. Then France must produce some butane as well. This can be illustrated in Table 2.4 if we suppose that France produces 1 unit of butane and 6 apples while Germany specializes in butane, producing 7. Since the French butane industry is competitive, it must earn zero profits. Therefore, a unit of butane, which requires 4 units of labor to produce, must sell for the same as 4 apples, which also require 4 units of labor. If the French buy a second unit of butane, it will therefore cost them 4 apples, leaving them with only 2: they can no longer afford to buy their autarky consumption of 2 units of butane and 5 apples. The French are necessarily harmed by this trade since they are producing less butane even though it costs more. We have a form of exploitation here; Germany reaps all the gains from trade and then some, so that France would be better off not trading at all!

With increasing returns to scale, free trade might possibly be worse for an individual country than autarky.

This can never happen if trade is due to comparative advantage.

TABLE 2.4 Production with Alternative Trade Patterns

To produce this much butane . . .	. . . Requires this much labor . . .	. . . Allowing this many apples	
0	0	10	France: trade harmony
1	4	6	France: trade jealousy
2	5	5	Each in autarky
3	6	4	
4	7	3	
5	8	2	
6	9	1	Germany: trade harmony
7	10	0	Germany: trade jealousy

Why has trading made France worse off? Since Germany becomes the primary producer of butane in this example, France is reduced to operating a smaller butane industry than in autarky. This means that French labor will be very inefficient in producing butane, because of the economies of scale. But German labor will be efficient in the large German industry. Since competition requires French butane to sell for no more than German butane, the French wage needs to be very low to compensate for the low French labor productivity.

Note that, just as in the preceding section, the roles of the two countries can be reversed in this example: the pattern of trade is indeterminate. But now it makes a great difference to each country which role it plays: the butane exporter necessarily gains and the butane importer, whose wage must fall enough to preserve a small, inefficient butane industry, necessarily loses. This is a recipe for international conflict. If the countries have governments conducting trade policy, each will try to ensure that it becomes the country specialized in butane production. The loser will be tempted to refuse to trade at all. For this reason Table 2.4 refers to this case as "trade jealousy." This contrasts sharply with comparative-advantage trade, where the two countries share gains and neither has an incentive to refuse to trade.

Another possibility is that the world might desire less butane (and more apples) than would be produced if both countries specialize. Then Germany must produce some apples as well. This can be illustrated in Table 2.4 if we suppose that France specializes in producing 10 apples while Germany diversifies, producing, say, 6 units of butane and 1 apple. Since the German butane industry is competitive, it must earn zero profits. Therefore, a unit of butane, which requires on average $9/6 = 1\frac{1}{2}$ units of labor to produce, must sell for the same as $1\frac{1}{2}$ apples, which also require $1\frac{1}{2}$ units of labor. If the Germans buy 3 apples, these will, therefore, cost them 2 units of butane, leaving them with 4: they have more of both goods than their autarky consumption of 2 units of butane and 5 apples. Likewise, if the French sell 3 apples for 2 units of butane, they will have as much butane as in autarky but more apples. Both countries clearly must gain from trade in this case.

Not only does trade benefit both countries, it also makes them equally well off. Since they both compete in the world apple market, and since 1 worker is required to produce an apple in each country, the wage must be the same in each. In contrast with the preceding example, neither country has an incentive to force its partner to exchange roles. So Table 2.4 refers to this case as "trade harmony."

Suppose next that, as in section 7 of Chapter 1, we allow more factors of production than just labor. The production possibility frontier of a country could look like Figure 2.1. The "bowed in" shape, or *decreasing opportunity costs,* illustrates the increasing returns that can be captured by specialization in either commodity—that is, by producing close to either axis. Suppose, again, that the two countries are identical so that Figure 2.1 applies to each. Then in autarky each country must produce and consume at a point such as C. If the two countries trade, one can produce at A and the other at B, and each can consume at a point like D. Again, trade and specialization pay. Recall that in section 7 of Chapter 1 incomplete specialization became more likely when labor was no longer the sole factor. But now complete specialization is still called for.

Trade is likely to be characterized by complete specialization if it is due to increasing returns to scale.

Such scale economies can give a different perspective to DC-LDC trade than does comparative advantage. For if the former explains this trade, LDC exports of primary products are basically a result of historical accident: the DCs simply specialized in manufacturing first. Such a view of the role of LDCs in the world economy has sometimes been used to justify policies of protecting the LDCs' manufacturing industries in the hope of realizing scale economies as the industries grow. We will return to this in Chapters 4 and 5.

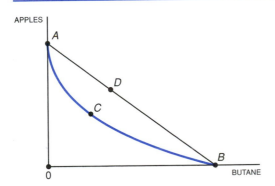

FIGURE 2.1 Decreasing Opportunity Costs Decreasing opportunity costs cause a production possibility frontier to bend in. They can be caused by sufficiently strong increasing returns to scale in one or both sectors.

But the anomalous aspect of world trade is the large volume of intra-industry trade among the DCs. This does not seem to fit in well with our discussion of scale economies. At the industry level, such economies imply (as we have seen) extensive industrial specialization and interindustry trade, just the opposite of the nonspecialization and intraindustry trade we actually observe. At the plant level, the larger DCs seem sizable enough generally to support efficient-sized plants irrespective of changes in trade policy. International economies of scale seem more relevant to DC-DC trade.

Problems

2.5 Suppose that France has 10 labor units and that Table 2.3 describes its technology. Each French resident always spends one-fifth of her income on apples and four-fifths on butane. Describe autarky equilibrium: How much of each good is produced and consumed and what is the price of butane in terms of apples?

2.6 Suppose England has 6 workers and the following technology for producing cloth and wine:

To produce this much cloth . . .	. . . Requires this much labor . . .	. . . Allowing this much wine
0	0	6
1	3	3
2	4	2
3	5	1
4	6	0

Describe autarky equilibrium if all the English always consume equal quantities of wine and cloth.

2.7 Suppose that Portugal has eight workers and the following technology for producing cloth and wine:

To produce this much cloth . . .	. . . Requires this much labor . . .	. . . Allowing this much wine
0	0	8
1	3	5
2	4	4
3	5	3
4	6	2
5	7	1
6	8	0

Describe autarky equilibrium if all the Portuguese always consume equal quantities of wine and cloth.

2.8 Suppose that the England of Problem **2.6** and the Portugal of Problem **2.7**

engage in free trade. Describe an equilibrium in which England completely specializes in the production of cloth. What is the free-trade relative price, and how does it compare with autarky prices in the two countries? Who gains and/or loses relative to autarky?

2.9* Find another possible free-trade equilibrium in Problem **2.8**, and describe it as completely as you can. Compare the various free-trade and autarky equilibria from the perspective of world welfare.

4. INTERNATIONAL EXTERNAL ECONOMIES OF SCALE

Suppose America and Britain trade pins and automobiles, with both goods produced under internationally increasing returns to scale due to the division of labor. Trade is possible in both finished pins and automobiles and also in unfinished pins and automobile parts. Either or both industries might be geographically concentrated in one country or dispersed between the two countries, with some stages of production taking place in one country and other stages in the other country.

Where should the industries be located? Scale economies are not now a relevant consideration: since they are international, these economies depend only on the global sizes of the two industries and not on where they are located. So location should instead be determined by comparative-advantage considerations. If America and Britain have different comparative costs, each industry is likely to be geographically concentrated in one country so that finished pins will be exchanged for finished automobiles: trade will be *interindustry*. But if the two countries have similar costs, incomplete specialization is likely; part of each industry will be located in each country, and *intraindustry* trade will be necessary to produce finished pins and finished automobiles.

Evidently there is a big contrast between the effects of national scale economies and those of international scale economies. But the prominence of the latter also depends upon the former in a subtle way. The reason is as follows.

The basic idea behind international scale economies is that industrial production becomes more efficient if it splits into separate stages, with different individuals or firms specializing in the different stages. If the products of the various stages can be easily traded, they need not be located in the same country. Thus if producing automobiles from raw materials can be divided into 10,000 distinct stages with 10,000 labor units each specializing in a distinct operation, many more automobiles will be produced than if each of the 10,000 labor units attempted the mad task of producing automobiles from start to finish. If each unit can easily ship the part it processes to the unit that needs to use it, the 10,000 units can be dispersed around the globe. But if it pays to split the production of automobiles by 10,000 labor units into 10,000 stages performed by 1 unit each, shouldn't it be better to split it into 100,000 stages performed by each unit devoting one-tenth of its effort to a single stage? Of course not. The efficiency gains come from having each unit specialize in a single stage and so do it very well; 100,000 stages would be practical only if the demand for automobiles was great enough to employ 100,000 labor units. This is the meaning of Adam Smith's dictum that "the division of labor is limited by the extent of the market." But another way of expressing the same thought is to say that each unit operates under increasing returns to scale: it will be less productive when it devotes one-tenth of its time to a single operation than when it devotes all of its time. Since a unit is located in a single place, these economies are national.

This is illustrated in Figure 2.2, which refers to a single sector, such as pins or automobiles, subject to international economies of scale. The horizontal axis measures the total number of stages into which production is divided and so indicates the division of labor. The vertical axis measures the total productive effort of all stages added together; given the division of labor, this indicates the size of the industry.

The line labeled *NE* shows the influence of national economies of scale in each of the individual stages. The position of this line is determined by the total amount of labor (and other resources) employed in the industry; increase this employment, and *NE* shifts out. If all these resources are used in a single stage, its productivity is measured by q. Suppose these resources were split into two stages, each with one-half the resources used in the original single stage. If each stage operated under constant returns to scale, each of the two

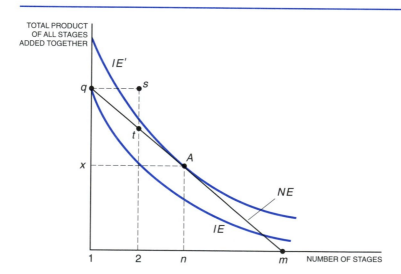

FIGURE 2.2 National and International Economies of Scale National scale economies in the production of each stage imply that a given amount of resources produces fewer total parts the larger the number of different types of parts, or stages (*NE*). International scale economies in the production of finished output mean that productivity increases with more stages (*IE*). Efficiency requires that these countervailing influences be balanced.

new stages would have one-half the productivity of the original so that their total productivity would not change: we would be at *s* in Figure 2.2. But with increasing returns to scale, each stage will be less efficient than the original, larger stage, so we will be below *s:* at *t* in the figure. The slope of *NE,* therefore, reflects the strength of the national scale economies within each stage. If these are absent, so that we have constant returns to scale, *NE* will be horizontal. The stronger the national scale economies, the steeper the *NE* line.

The lines labeled *IE* and *IE'* show combinations of total productivity and division of labor that result in the same final output for the whole sector. Curves farther from the origin correspond to more output. Thus final output can be increased either by increasing production at a given division of labor (moving vertically up) or by increasing the division of labor for given production (moving horizontally to the right). The greater the international increasing returns to scale—that is, the larger the payoff to a greater division of labor—the steeper the *IE* and *IE'* curves.

If the sector is originally operating at *q,* in a single stage, it can utilize its resources to greater effect by undertaking a division of labor: moving along *NE* to *t* and beyond. As it does so, the increased division of labor allows for more and more final output. But the division of the sector's resources into more and more stages of a smaller and smaller size becomes more and more costly because of the national economies of scale at the level of the individual stages. At *A,* where the division of labor is *n,* the sector is doing the best it can: the benefit of a greater division of labor from creating another stage is just offset by the cost resulting from operating each stage at a smaller scale.

If the national scale economies at the stage level are sufficiently strong relative to the international economies at the sector level, *NE* will be steeper at *q* than *IE.* In this case the best the sector can do is to stay at *q:* it doesn't pay to undertake any division of labor. At the other extreme, the national economies could be very weak relative to the international economies so that *NE* is flat relative to *IE'.* In this case *n* will be very large: the division of labor should be carried a long way.

Now let us look at Figure 2.3. Suppose that the sector expands—perhaps because trade has begun and the sector has become integrated into the world industry. The expansion of the sector shifts *NE* up to *NE':* for any given number of stages, more of each stage can be produced. (*NE* shifts up in greater proportion than the expansion in the sector's resources because of the scale economies in producing each stage.)

If the number of stages does not change, the sector shifts from *A* to *B,* and final output expands, as indicated by the shift from *IE* to the higher *IE'.* But the sector can do even better by increasing the division of labor and moving from *B* to *C,* thereby shifting to the even higher *IE*.*

The division of labor is limited by the extent of the market because of economies of scale at each stage of the division of labor. These economies are likely to be national, as discussed above. They also might be internal to the firm. If so, imperfect competition must be considered. This is discussed in the next chapter.

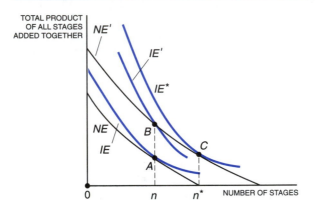

FIGURE 2.3   A Larger Market Permits a Greater Division of Labor   An expansion of the sector shifts *NE* up, resulting in an increase in the division of labor from *n* to *n**.

Problem

2.10   Suppose that scale economies are due to the division of labor and that there are two countries. Discuss the relation between the production possibility frontiers of the two countries and of the world.

5. PRODUCT DIFFERENTIATION

Product differentiation can also become important with regard to economies of scale. Consider now economies that are national and internal to the firm. As we saw earlier, this will not allow a competitive equilibrium.

Suppose that the technology for producing apples in France and that for producing butane in France is each as described in Table 2.1, and that this technology applies to each individual firm. France has 20 units of labor. Suppose that in autarky, 10 of these labor units are allocated to apples. Then they can produce 7 apples, from Table 2.1. But perhaps the French would prefer to consume two kinds of apples—eating and cooking, say—rather than just one, or perhaps some French consumers prefer cooking apples while others prefer eating apples. Then instead of allocating all 10 apple workers to a single apple-making operation, the French might establish two operations, with 5 workers each, to make two varieties. From Table 2.1, they could thereby produce 2 cooking apples and 2 eating apples. Suppose that the French would, in fact, rather have this combination instead of 7 of a single apple type and do, therefore, conduct two operations. Suppose, once again, that Germany is identical to France and that, therefore, Germany also produces and consumes 2 eating apples and 2 cooking apples in autarky.

Now suppose that France and Germany trade. We could then have all eating apples produced in France (7 units, by Table 2.1) and all cooking apples produced in Germany. If France exports 3.5 eating apples and Germany 3.5 cooking apples, each country can now consume 3.5 of each type. Alternatively, the two countries could now differentiate apples even more. For example, France could continue to produce 2 eating and 2 cooking apples, as in autarky, while Germany produces 2 tart and 2 sweet apples. In this case the two countries together produce the same amount of apples as without trade (8 units), but each consumer can choose from four varieties rather than two.

Regardless of whether trade causes an increase in output or an increase in variety, the result has been intraindustry trade: apples are exchanged for apples. If, instead of assuming that France and Germany were identical, we had allowed one country to be relatively more efficient than the other, then all apple types would have been produced in that country, and we would have had interindustry trade: all apple varieties exchanged for butane. Thus product differentiation, like the division of labor, enables returns to scale to shed light on the apparent anomaly observed in Chapter 1.

> *With product differentiation, countries with substantial comparative cost differences tend to each produce all varieties of different goods so that trade is interindustry. Countries without substantial cost differences will be nonspecialized at the industry level and trade will be intraindustry.*

Product differentiation benefits an economy by producing a variety of different goods within a sector rather than a single homogeneous product. If more variety is better than less, why not carry this to extremes and make each unit a distinct variety? In fact this is sometimes done: firms offering certain services, such as law or hairdressing, or producing some sophisticated capital goods, tailor their products to individual customers. But more often, the degree of variety is limited by increasing returns to scale. As the number of varieties increases and the output of each individual variety falls, the average cost per unit rises. Suppose, for example, that Table 2.1 describes the technology for producing each variety of apples, and that France has 20 workers in the apple sector. If variety is maximized, France can produce 5 apples—each distinct—with 4 workers required for each. But if the French are willing to settle for only 4 varieties they can have 8 apples in all, with each pair requiring 5 workers. Similarly, 14 apples can be obtained if there are only 2 different types. Thus there is a basic trade-off between quantity and variety. If increasing returns to scale characterize the production of individual varieties, it is unlikely that the scale economies will be external to the firm. Thus we would expect to find at last some degree of imperfect competition. The next chapter will take this up.

6. *CASE STUDY:* THE WORLD AUTOMOBILE INDUSTRY

The global motor-vehicle industry is a mature manufacturing sector located largely within the industrialized part of the world economy. Approximately 50 million vehicles are produced each year, of which about 90 percent are built and sold in North America, Western Europe, and Japan. Each major country in this part of the world has its own automobile industry, but the countries also undertake extensive automotive trade among themselves.

The industry thus well illustrates the common pattern of *large-scale intraindustry exchange of manufactures among similar industrialized economies*. It also well illustrates the roles of the various types of economies of scale.

Mass Production

Ever since Henry Ford introduced the assembly line, efficient automobile production has called for long production runs of single models in large plants. These are examples of *national* increasing returns to scale that are *internal* to the firm. This method of making cars ("mass production") revolutionized life in the industrialized world.

The minimal efficient plant size is small relative to the global automobile market, so many plants can be accommodated by an efficient world industry, but it is large relative to many small economies. Several South American countries, for example, long maintained automobile industries of inefficiently small scale. Very low wages would have been required for these industries to be internationally competitive. Instead, these countries used high trade barriers to shield their industries from foreign competition so that automobiles were very expensive to purchase there. Now some of these countries have automotive industries integrated into an efficient world operation. For example, Volkswagen produces cars in Mexico, using parts manufactured in Germany and elsewhere, for export to the United States.

Efficient plant size is one important source of economies of scale in automobile production. Another is product development: this takes three to five years and a huge investment. Larger production allows the development cost to be spread over more units and so reduces the development cost per unit. Suppose, for example, that a company spends $1 billion to design, develop, and test a new model. If the company then produces and sells 500,000 of these vehicles, product development has added $2,000 to the cost of each vehicle. But if instead 5 million of these cars are sold, the development cost per vehicle is only $200. Thus product development is a source of economies of scale just as surely as is efficient plant size. The difference is that an efficient plant must be located in a single country, but a newly developed product can be manufactured and sold in any number of locations. Thus these scale economies are *international* and *internal* to the firm.

Henry Ford also pioneered the use of interchangeable parts in automobile production. This is an aspect of the division of labor (indeed, the assembly line can be thought of as a device for facilitating the division of labor within a plant). Vehicles are assembled from thousands of distinct parts supplied by producers around the globe. Some of these producers are subsidiaries of the major automobile firms, but many are independent; some deal exclusively with a single automobile firm, but many sell to several. The resulting economies of scale are potentially *international,* and they are sometimes *external* to the firm, sometimes *internal.*

More generally, the motor vehicle production process involves steel, rubber, and many other industries that supply inputs to the automotive industry or to its suppliers. This larger division of labor generates international external economies of scale that are obviously massive (relative to the lifetime or more required for an individual to construct a single car from scratch with raw materials).

Product differentiation is important in this market and becoming increasingly so. Typically, a country's industry builds the types of vehicles most preferred by residents of that country and also exports its products to the minorities in other countries with similar tastes. Thus international trade offers consumers in all countries a wider menu of choices.

Lean Production

Japanese firms became successful in the world automobile market as they developed a new method of making cars called "lean production." This technique emphasizes the organization of the workforce into teams, just-in-time delivery of parts, continuous improvement by the workers themselves in production methods, and an unremitting attention paid to quality. Once a firm learns the method, it can employ it in its factories wherever they might be located. Thus effort devoted to learning lean production and to the continuous improvements it calls for involves economies of scale that are *international* and *internal* to the firm. But lean production also implies some international economies of scale *external* to the firm. Improvements made by one firm can be copied, to a degree, by other firms; with the improvements generated by the workers themselves, the larger the world workforce, the larger the number of improvements. Japanese firms have successfully employed lean production in their North American and European plants, and American and European firms have copied their techniques with varying success.

Transplants

American automobile firms established European subsidiaries during the 1920s, and for years General Motors and Ford have been among the largest European producers. (Chrysler also once had European subsidiaries but sold them when times were bad.) These corporations now operate in many countries. More recently, Japanese and European producers have set up foreign operations. For example, Japanese firms have eight plants in the United States, three in Canada, and five in Europe; Korea also has a U.S. plant, and the German firm BMW is establishing one.

Scale economies are usually not the primary motives for establishing these subsidiaries. Often the goal is to penetrate markets where exports are limited or prevented by trade policy. For example, Japanese firms began to establish U.S. subsidiaries when their exports from Japan were limited by quotas and when they feared future U.S. trade restrictions. Many of the foreign subsidiaries of U.S. firms were also established to leap over trade barriers. Foreign operations are also often intended to take advantage of lower production costs abroad. For example, BMW is establishing its U.S. operation in part because of its belief that it is cheaper to supply the American market from a plant in America than from one in Germany. These motives are easily understood in terms of comparative-advantage trade. But economies of scale are also important for foreign investment within the automobile industry. The national internal scale economies of plant size ensure that foreign investments will not be modest: it is either a large, efficient plant or nothing at all. And international scale economies have been crucial to the success of the Japanese transplants, which draw on the global organizations for production methods, product designs, and numerous components.

International economies of scale and foreign subsidiaries have facilitated the development of the *world car:* a single model that can be assembled and sold in numerous locations and that can use standardized components produced around the world. Volkswagen has followed this strategy, and Ford has tried it, with limited success, with its Escort and, with more determination, its Mondeo. But it is the Japanese who have made the most extensive and successful use of the world-car approach.

The U.S.-Canada Automobile Agreement

U.S. firms established subsidiaries in Canada in order to avoid Canadian barriers to automobile imports. Prior to 1965 these subsidiaries constituted a smaller version of the U.S. industry (the Canadian economy is only about a tenth the size of the U.S. economy), with fewer models available and labor productivity only about two-thirds of that in the United States because of the smaller scale of operations. Since 1965 an agreement between the U.S. and Canadian governments has allowed the automobile firms to move automotive parts and finished automobiles freely between the two countries. This agreement allowed the two countries to establish a single integrated industry. As a result, the volume of two-way intraindustry trade in automotive products greatly increased, and labor productivity in Canada approached that in the United States. Fewer models were actually produced in Canada, but trade allowed Canadian consumers a greater choice.

The automobile agreement was limited to producers and did not include consumers. But in 1989 Canada and the United States negotiated a Free Trade

Agreement to eliminate trade barriers generally, including those on automobiles, and this framework was to be extended to include Mexico in a North American Free Trade Agreement, negotiated in 1992.

Flexible Production

As the world market becomes more integrated and as producers learn from each other and increasingly use components from the same or similar sources, differences in price and quality shrink. Product differentiation then becomes an important way for firms to compete. If this is so, those firms will be especially concerned about being able to produce a wide variety of models in moderate volume (rather than a small number in great volume) and about being able to introduce new models quickly. With this as the outlook, automobile firms are now developing yet another new way of making cars: flexible production.

Flexible production involves a technology that allows rapid product development, the ability to produce a number of distinct models simultaneously in a single plant, a short "down time" while switching a plant from one model to another, and ease in configuring individual vehicles in response to customers' needs. The new production techniques are still being developed, but they have begun to have an impact. For example, Mazda's plant near Hiroshima in Japan can simultaneously produce four distinct models; conventional plants can produce one or, at most, two. Flexible production implies an interesting sort of economies of scale. Since a large, expensive plant is still important, for the *firm* we still have significant economies of scale that are both national and internal. But scale economies are much less significant for *individual differentiated products:* the whole point is to be able to produce a number of distinct models in moderate volume with little cost penalty.

The world automobile industry illustrates economies of scale at work. It also illustrates that the various types of scale economies need not display themselves one at a time in isolation: a specific production structure often exhibits several different types of economies of scale interacting and working together.

7. SUMMARY

1. A technology possesses increasing returns to scale if increasing *all* inputs in proportion increases output in greater proportion.

2. Economies of scale are internal or external to the firm, depending on whether average costs rely on the output of the firm or upon that of the industry. Scale economies are national or international, depending upon whether that output must be located in one country or not.

3. External economies of scale furnish a basis for trade that is independent of comparative advantage. Specialization is likely, and the role of individual countries might be ambiguous. A country might be worse off with free international trade than in autarky.

4. Economies of scale that are due to the division of labor or that are accompanied by product differentiation imply that trade between economies with modest comparative cost differences will be largely intraindustry and that trade between economies with substantial comparative cost differences will be largely interindustry.

SUGGESTED READING

Ethier, W. "Internationally Decreasing Costs and World Trade." *Journal of International Economics* 2 (1979). Scale economies and the division of labor.

Graham, F. "Some Aspects of Protection Further Considered." *Quarterly Journal of Economics* 37 (1923). An early and forceful argument that economies of scale might cause trade to harm a country.

Helpman, E., and P. R. Krugman. *Market Structure and Foreign Trade.* Cambridge: MIT Press, 1985. An extensive treatment of the theory of international trade with scale economies and imperfect competition.

Lancaster, K. "Intra-industry Trade under Perfect Monopolistic Competition." *Journal of International Economics* 2 (1980). Scale economies and product differentiation.

Matthews, R. C. O. "Reciprocal Demand and Increasing Returns." *Review of Economic Studies* (1949/50). Geographically concentrated scale economies.

CHAPTER 3

Imperfect Competition

They want market share. Business is like warfare to them. Gaining ground. Wiping out the competition. Getting control of a market.
—MICHAEL CRICHTON

The economies-of-scale explanations of trade in Chapter 2 naturally lead to one based on imperfect competition because economies of scale internal to the firm are inconsistent with a perfectly competitive equilibrium. Therefore, imperfect competition and scale economies often go together. But each can motivate trade independently of the other. This chapter considers imperfect competition, the last of the three fundamental reasons for why nations trade.

1. IMPERFECT COMPETITION

In a perfectly competitive market all participants are *price takers:* buyers and sellers act as though they have no influence on market prices and so do the best they can, given those prices. In an imperfectly competitive mar-

---

KEY CONCEPT

In a *perfectly competitive* market, individual firms cannot influence the price they can charge for their products or the prices that they must pay for what they buy. This will be so if there are many sellers and buyers of identical goods. With *imperfect competition,* some firm is aware that its actions will have some effect on some price that it receives or that it pays.

JOAN ROBINSON (1903–1983)

One of the preeminent economists of this century, Joan Robinson was a member of the faculty at Cambridge, England, where she was awarded a professorship almost a quarter century after the appearance of her 1933 classic *The Economics of Imperfect Competition.* This work, together with a contemporary contribution by E. Chamberlin of Harvard, established a central position in economic theory for imperfect competition—the subject of this chapter. Joan Robinson also made seminal contributions to Keynesian economics, capital theory, and many other subjects. She was iconoclastic in her economic methodology and arguments as well as in her lifestyle. Since much of her work has proved to be outside the mainstream of modern economics, it is perhaps not surprising that she was overlooked for a Nobel prize.

ket someone behaves as though she has some influence on some price, either a price at which she sells or a price at which she buys. A majority of markets presumably have some imperfection. You probably see yourself as a price taker in most markets in which you deal, but chances are that in most of them you can point to someone you think has a significant influence on price.

Imperfect competition can take many forms. We often think that market participants will be price takers if there are a lot of them, so imperfect competition may arise if there are not too many on at least one side of a market. Thus one way of classifying imperfect competition is according to how many participants there are.

For example, a market in which there is a single seller is called a *monopoly.* A monopolist can charge any price she wants without fear of being undercut by a rival and need only concern herself with whether her potential customers will be tempted to buy or not. Such a firm clearly has a lot of control over its price. A market that instead has one buyer is called a *monopsony.*

A market with several sellers is called an *oligopoly,* and it may be referred to as a *duopoly* if there are just two sellers. This adds another dimension. Like a monopolist, an oligopolist will not be a price taker because he knows that altering his supply will influence the price it fetches. But he also knows that altering his supply will influence his oligopolistic rivals and that what they do will likewise influence his own profit. Thus *strategic interaction* between the oligopolists becomes important: each will decide his own actions, taking into account how that decision might influence his rival's actions. This gives an additional way of classifying oligopolistic markets: choice of strategy variable.

For example, an oligopolist might employ a strategy of setting a price for her product. Her actual sales would then depend on demand conditions plus the actions of her rivals. Alternatively, she might choose a certain amount of her product to sell. The price that it would fetch would then be determined by demand conditions plus the actions of her rivals.

Were this firm perfectly competitive, her only available strategy would be the amount to sell: she would have neither the need to settle for less than the price prevailing in the market nor the ability to sell for more. If the firm were instead a monopoly, the two strategies would just be two ways of describing the same strategy since demand conditions link price and quantity sold. Only with an oligopoly are the two available and distinct.

KEY CONCEPT

A *monopoly* consists of a single firm, and an *oligopoly* consists of several. A *monopolistically competitive* industry has many firms, but each sells a distinct differentiated product.

There may be other possible strategy variables as well. Choice of capacity is one. A competitive firm or a monopolist would want to install whatever capacity can most efficiently supply the output the firm wishes to sell. But a decision by an oligopolist to install a modern, efficient plant will also send a message, or perhaps a threat, to rivals and potential rivals. Her choice of capacity might, therefore, be influenced by the message she wants to send as well as by the output she thinks she will provide.

Further scope for strategy arises with *differentiated products.* A product is differentiated if it possesses characteristics that can vary from seller to seller. Thus automobiles are differentiated: a Ford Taurus and a Honda Accord, though fundamentally similar, are perceived as distinct by consumers. The word-processing software offered by Microsoft and by WordPerfect do the same job, but they may differ in specific features, in "look and feel," or in the customer support offered by the two firms. Two retail shops may offer the same products and provide the same services and yet be differentiated by location. In all of these cases, an important strategy for a firm is to choose the characteristics with which to endow its products.

A market characterized by differentiated products may sometimes have an extreme form of oligopoly known as *monopolistic competition.* Such a market has many sellers of differentiated products and possesses one key feature: the strategic interaction of oligopoly vanishes because each firm, being one of many, believes its own choice of strategy will have little impact on the other firms. Thus the firm can act as a minimonopolist in providing its differentiated product, maximizing its own profit without regard for any impact of its own actions on other sellers of similar but differentiated goods.

KEY CONCEPT

An oligopoly is characterized by *strategic interaction:* each firm chooses its strategy knowing that its choice will influence the behavior of its rivals and that it will itself be influenced by those rivals' behavior. Strategic interaction is absent from a monopoly because there is only one firm, and it is absent from monopolistic competition because there are enough firms so that the strategy of a single firm is unimportant to all the others.

Problems

3.1 Give examples of actual markets that are characterized by the following: perfect competition, monopoly, oligopoly, and monopolistic competition.

3.2 In your answer to the preceding problem, can you point to any characteristics of the examples that explain why the markets have the structures that they do?

3.3* A *market demand curve* shows the amount of a good that consumers will purchase at each hypothetical price. Suppose that the demand for widgets is *downward-sloping:* at higher prices consumers buy fewer widgets. A *firm's demand curve* shows how much a particular firm could sell at each price. How is the demand curve of an individual widget firm related to the market demand curve for widgets if the widget market is (a) a monopoly, (b) perfectly competitive, (c) a duopoly.

---

2. MONOPOLY

Now we review the behavior of a single monopolistic market in a closed economy. This will refresh your memory of some concepts important for imperfect competition and also set the stage for the discussion of international trade to come.

The monopolist wishes to maximize his profit: the excess of revenue over cost. His profit accordingly depends on market conditions—which help determine revenue—and on cost conditions. Let us look at the latter first.

Suppose that the monopolist's costs consist of a *fixed cost,* which must be incurred just to keep operating, and a *variable cost,* which depends on how much is produced. In Figure 3.1, the variable cost is strictly proportional to output. The height c measures how much each unit of output contributes to this cost, and the distance f to c measures the firm's fixed cost.

Increasing production by 1 unit always adds c to the firm's costs. The *marginal cost curve,* depicted by MC in the figure, shows for each level of output how much it would cost to increase production by 1 unit. Since in our example this is always c, the MC curve must be a horizontal line at the height c.

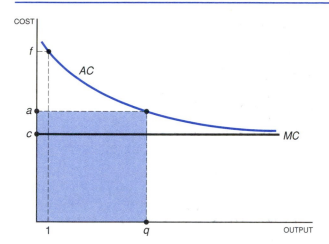

FIGURE 3.1 **Cost Curves** The height of the *MC* curve measures the cost of increasing output by 1 unit; *AC* measures the average cost per unit. The total cost is measured by the area of the rectangle under the *AC* curve.

The curve labeled *AC* shows average cost per unit at each level of output. This curve falls because as output rises, the fixed cost is averaged over more and more units, while variable cost always averages just *c* per unit. If the firm's output were *q* in the figure, marginal cost would be indicated by the height *c* and average cost by the height *a;* the shaded area measures the total cost for the firm.

Suppose, for example, that a firm has fixed costs of 5 and variable costs of 1 per unit. Then an output of 4 would generate total cost of 9 (4 × 1 plus the fixed cost of 5) for an average cost of 9 ÷ 4 = 2.25. Marginal cost is 1; if production increases to 5, total cost goes up by 1 to 10 and average cost falls to 2 (= 10 ÷ 5).

Now turn to the market conditions facing this monopolist. These conditions are summarized by the market demand curve showing how much will be bought at each price. Such a curve is depicted by *D* in Figure 3.2. By setting an appropriate price or offering an equivalent quantity for sale, the monopolist can operate at any point he wants on the demand curve: his problem is to choose the point that maximizes his profit.

If the firm were to sell the quantity *q* in the figure, it could be sold for the price *p*, yielding revenue *pq*, measured by the shaded area in the figure. The line *MR* measures *marginal revenue*, the effect on this revenue of selling one more unit. If the firm's actions had no effect on price (which would be the case if it were competitive), the additional unit could be sold at the going price *p* which would, therefore, measure marginal revenue. But this is not the case. Since the firm faces a downward-sloping demand curve, selling one

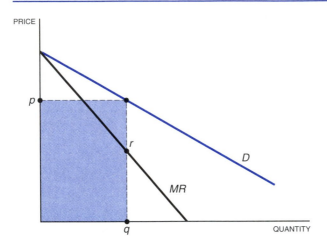

FIGURE 3.2   Demand   The height of the *D* curve measures the price for which a quantity of output can be sold; *MR* measures the effect on revenue of selling one more unit. Total revenue is measured by the area of the shaded rectangle under the *D* curve.

more unit will depress the price at which all its output is sold. Thus marginal revenue must be less than *p,* which is why the *MR* curve lies below the *D* curve in the figure.

What, then, should the monopolist do? He wants to maximize his profit, or the excess of total revenue above total cost. He will be doing this if he sells the quantity of output that makes marginal revenue just equal to marginal cost. This is shown in Figure 3.3.

Selling the amount *q* in the figure causes *MR* to equal *MC.* Why is this good for the monopolist? If he sold less than *q, MC* would be less than *MR.* This means that selling one more unit would raise his revenue by more than his costs: he should sell the unit. Similarly, if he were selling more than *q,* reducing his output by 1 unit would lower his costs by more than his revenues and, therefore, raise his profit. Only if *MR* equals *MC* is he doing the best he can.

A monopoly has two potential features that may characterize imperfect competition in general and that will matter for what follows. First, as shown in Figure 3.3, the monopolist may be able to maintain a *profit.* In a competitive market such a profit would be dissipated by the entrance of the new rivals that it attracts, but this mechanism is absent in a monopoly. Second, a monopoly is *socially inefficient* because it produces too little. This is reflected by the fact that price (which indicates what one more unit is worth to society) exceeds *MC* (which measures what one more unit would cost society). Intuitively, the two are related: a monopoly generates a profit by restricting supply and so forcing price up.

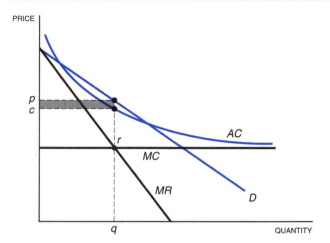

FIGURE 3.3 **Maximizing Profit** The monopolist will maximize his profit by selling the quantity *q* for which *MR* equals *MC*. In this case his profit is measured by the area of the rectangle determined by the vertical distance between the *AC* and *D* curves.

Problems

3.4 Show how Figure 3.1 and Figure 3.3 would change if the firm's fixed cost were 0.

3.5 The text distinguished between variable costs, which depend on how much is produced, and fixed costs, which arise simply from operating at all. But a firm might also have *sunk costs,* which have already been made or committed to and which, therefore, cannot be avoided even if the firm does not operate at all. How do sunk costs change Figure 3.1 and Figure 3.2?

3.6 Suppose that the production of fried clams entails a fixed cost of $6 per pint and a marginal cost of $2 per pint. Draw the *MC* and *AC* curves of a fried-clam firm.

3.7 In the isolated hamlet of Marbletoe, residents would consume 10 pints of fried clams if the clams were free, and each dollar's price would reduce demand below 10 by 1 pint—that is, if a pint costs *p*, residents of Marbletoe would demand 10 − *p* pints of fried clams. Draw this hamlet's demand curve for fried clams and its associated *MR* curve.

3.8 The supply of fried clams in Marbletoe is controlled by a lucky monopolist, Rufus. What should Rufus do to maximize his profit, and what would that profit be? How many pints of fried clams would Marbletoe enjoy, and what price would Marbletoe pay for them?

3.9 How does your answer to the previous problem change if the fixed cost of producing fried clams falls from $6 to $3? Who gains from this? What happens if instead the marginal cost falls from $2 to $1?

3. IMPERFECT COMPETITION AS A BASIS FOR TRADE: INTERNATIONAL OLIGOPOLY

Now we can show that imperfect competition can be an independent cause of trade. Suppose, as in an earlier example, that each apple and each unit of butane requires 1 hour of labor to produce in either France or Germany. Suppose further that the two countries are identical and that there is only one possible variety of each product. Under these circumstances, since neither comparative advantage nor scale economies could motivate trade, if it takes place, it must be because of something else.

To introduce imperfect competition as simply as possible, suppose that in each country there is a single producer of butane but many competitive producers of apples. Thus the butane producer is a monopolist and behaves as discussed in the previous section. Trade will now matter: each butane producer may be a monopolist in her own country in autarky, but the two of them will compete with each other if the countries are open to trade.

Let us look at this in detail. Imagine France to be in autarky initially. Since 1 hour of labor can produce either 1 apple or 1 unit of butane, $MRT_{AB} = 1$. Since apple producers are competitive, profits are driven to 0 and the price of an apple accordingly equals the wage. But the butane producer has no competition, so she maximizes her profit and charges a monopoly price—that is, she sets MR equal to MC, as explained in the previous section. Now in this case, MC is simply the wage, so the monopolist's price, which exceeds her MR, is higher than the wage. Thus the price of butane in terms of apples, p, exceeds unity.

Consumers, as always, choose a consumption pattern that equates their marginal rate of substitution to p, so $MRS_{AB} = p > 1 = MRT_{AB}$. Since MRS_{AB} exceeds MRT_{AB}, consumers would be willing to give more apples to obtain additional butane than the economy would have to sacrifice to obtain the butane. That is, the French are producing (and consuming) too many apples and not enough butane. This is the social cost of the butane monopoly, referred to in the previous section. Since Germany is identical, the same thing happens there.

In Figure 3.4 the line *CHM,* called the French *best-response curve,* shows how much butane the French producer will sell in France for each level of imports from Germany. If there are no imports, the French firm is a monopolist and so sells the monopoly amount, *OM.* Suppose instead that the German firm ships *Oe* to the French market. The French producer knows that if she continues to sell the monopoly amount, the price of butane will be driven down and her profit will fall. On the other hand, if she accommodates the imports by reducing her own sales by the same amount, *Oe,* the monopoly price will be maintained, but her profits will still fall because she will have a reduced share of the market. The most profitable response will likely be an intermediate one: she will reduce her sales, but by less than *Oe,* and the price will fall some. In the figure, the French firm can minimize its loss of profit by reducing its sales from *OM* to *OE'.* As we move up the French best-response

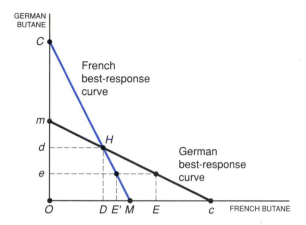

FIGURE 3.4 **International Oligopoly** Each firm's best-response curve shows the amount of sales that would maximize its own profit, given the sales of its rival. Equilibrium is at the intersection because only there is each firm doing as well as it can, given the behavior of its rival.

curve, we observe the response to larger and larger volumes of imports from Germany. French sales fall, but by less than the increase in imports; the price of butane falls, as do the profits of the French producer.

The volume of butane sales that will just wipe out all monopoly profit is *OC* (and this is what would be sold if the butane market were competitive). If this much butane is imported, the French producer will not sell anything because she knows that any sales would drive the price still lower and so result in losses.

KEY CONCEPT

The *best-response curve* of a firm in a duopoly shows what the best strategy for that firm is for each conceivable strategy of its rival.

Thus Figure 3.4 shows what happens when trade is allowed. The line *mHc* is the German best-response curve. It shows how much butane the German firm would like to sell in France, given the sales of the French firm. Since the two firms are identical, the German best-response curve must resemble the French best-response curve, the line *CHM,* with the roles of the two axes reversed. Since the two countries are identical, a similar diagram describes the German butane market.

Now compare autarky and free trade. In autarky each butane firm is a monopolist in its own market. The French firm sells the quantity *OM* in France and the German firm sells *Om* in Germany. If trade is allowed, the butane firms become a *duopoly*. Point *H* shows sales in France; the local producer sells *OD*, and her German rival exports *Od* to France. Why is this so? Suppose that the French firm sold something else—say, *OE*. Then the German firm would maximize its profit by selling *Oe*, as revealed by its best-response curve. But if *Oe* is imported into France, the French firm would in fact want to sell *OE′*, not *OE*. Thus *H* is the only equilibrium in the sense that each firm sells what it wants, given the behavior of its rival.

With trade allowed, total butane sales (*OD* plus *Od*) exceed what they would be in autarky (*OM*), and the price is lower. The French are better off, with the gap between MRT_{AB} and the MRS_{AB} shrinking. A similar description applies to Germany. This simple example makes seven useful points.

1. The trade that takes place is intraindustry (apples are not traded in the example).

Indeed, the trade is not even in *differentiated* products, but in *identical* products, and so might seem pointless if we did not understand it.

2. This trade is gainful because it reduces the degree of imperfect competition, not because of what is actually exchanged.

In fact in this example actual trade is not really necessary; each producer could continue to supply only her own market, instead of shipping half her output abroad since there is really only one world butane market. The important point is that each firm must react to the presence of a rival by behaving more competitively.

3. If economies of scale are present, average costs will fall since the level of production increases.

In this example we have assumed away scale economies to focus on oligopoly, but they could be important in practice. If our butane firms had fixed costs, and so the cost curves shown in Figure 3.1, an increase in production would move a firm down its declining *AC* curve.

4. Each country tends to export those goods whose industries are most competitive, relative to the other country.

Suppose, for example, that France has two identical butane firms and Germany only one. Look at autarky in each country. In Germany the single producer sells the monopoly amount, *Om,* and charges the monopoly price. Autarky equilibrium in France can be represented by Figure 3.4 if we reinterpret the axes to refer to the two French firms. One firm sells the amount OD, and the other firm sells the (equal) amount Od. Their total is greater than the amount Om sold in Germany, and the price of butane is lower. Thus the country with the more competitive industry in autarky has the lower autarky price. If the two countries trade and the three firms are all identical, the French firms will produce more butane than the single German firm; thus France will be a net exporter.

    5. We now have an example where trade alters the domestic distribution of income, harming some even if it makes the country as a whole better off.

Free trade benefits France as a whole by resulting in more butane at a lower price, but the butane producer suffers because her monopoly profit is reduced.
    Imperfect competition introduces the possibility of profits, and international trade causes the firms of each country to vie with each other to wrest as many of those profits for themselves as possible. The success of a country's firms in this contest helps determine the effect of trade on that country's welfare.

    6. Profit switching—the effect of international trade on the distribution between countries of profit in an oligopolistic market—helps determine how trade affects individual countries.

    Table 3.1 summarizes the normal effect of international trade due to imperfect competition on the welfare of specific groups. There are three basic effects. First, trade causes a *consumption increase* of the good produced in the imperfectly competitive industry. Since imperfect competition inefficiently limits supply, this is a good thing: it benefits consumers in each country without hurting firms, and so benefits each country individually and, therefore, the world as a whole.
    The increased competition induced by international trade lowers the total profits earned by the French and German butane firms together. This *profit*

TABLE 3.1   **Effects of Trade on Various Groups**

	Home consumer	Foreign consumer	Home firms	Foreign firms	Home	Foreign	World
Consumption increase	+	+	0	0	+	+	+
Profit reduction	+	+	−	−	0	0	0
Profit switching	0	0	+	−	+	−	0
			−	+	−	+	

reduction effect redistributes income from firms to consumers within each country, but it does not affect aggregate welfare in either country or, therefore, in the world as a whole.

Finally, *profit switching* may transfer profits from the firms of one country to those of its trading partner. This redistributes welfare *internationally,* with one country gaining and the other losing, but it does not affect aggregate worldwide welfare.

Profit switching introduces the possibility that trade generated by imperfect competition just might be harmful for an individual country. If a country's firms fare badly in the contest for oligopoly profit and if the profits lost exceed the gains to consumers from more consumption at a lower price, the country will lose on balance.

> 7. *Profit switching introduces the possibility that trade might harm an individual country, even as it makes the world as a whole better off.*

Thus trade due to imperfect competition, like trade due to economies of scale, might harm an individual country. This can happen only under special circumstances and so seems unlikely, but with comparative advantage trade it can never happen at all.

Problems

3.10 Suppose, as in Problems **3.6** and **3.7,** that the production of fried clams by the supplier Rufus entails a fixed cost of $6 per pint and a marginal cost of $2 per pint, and that, if a pint costs p, residents of Marbletoe would demand $10 - p$ pints of fried clams. Suppose, now, that there is a second supplier of fried clams, Violet, who has the same costs as Rufus. Violet is selling 2 pints. Given this strategy by Violet, what is the best that Rufus can do? Does your answer tell you anything about Rufus's best-response curve? Does it tell you anything about Violet's?

3.11 Given that Rufus sells the quantity of fried clams you found in your answer to Problem **3.10,** should Violet continue to sell 2 pints? If so, why? If not, what should she sell? Does your answer tell you anything about Rufus's best-response curve? Does it tell you anything about Violet's best-response curve?

3.12* Draw Rufus's best-response curve and Violet's best-response curve. Describe the duopoly equilibrium, and compare this with the monopoly equilibrium you described in Problem **3.8.**

4.* EXPLORING FURTHER: PRICE-SETTING INTERNATIONAL OLIGOPOLY

The previous section reached important conclusions. But a distinctive feature of oligopoly is that behavior can change a lot from case to case. Rival firms can compete with each other in different ways, and different notions of equilibrium might seem reasonable. For example, we have supposed that the firms compete in *quantities*—that is, each firm, keeping a nervous eye on its rival, decides how much to sell, and price then adjusts to clear the market. But firms might instead compete in *prices*—each firm would set its price, again, keeping a nervous eye on its rival, and then supply whatever the market demanded.

Suppose that the French and German firms produce differentiated products and compete with each other in prices. Figure 3.5 shows the French butane market in this case.

The French best-response curve now shows what *price* the French firm should charge to maximize its profit, given the price the German firm is charging for butane in France. If the German firm were to raise its price, the French firm would also be able to charge a higher price, but it might not increase it as much in order to attract customers from the German rival. Thus the best-response curve might slope up, as shown in the figure, and the French firm's profits rise as we move up the curve. *OM* measures the highest price the French firm would ever charge—that is, the price that would maximize French profits if the German firm did not sell in France (or, equivalently, if the German firm charged a price so high that no one would buy from it). Thus *OM* must be the French autarky price of butane.

The German best-response curve has an analogous interpretation. Equilibrium is at *H,* the intersection of the two curves. Thus trade causes the price of butane in France to fall from *OM* to *OP.* Also, to the extent that German butane differs from French, product variety has also increased.

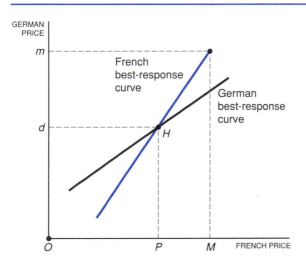

FIGURE 3.5 An Oligopolistic Market with Price Competition   Each firm's best-response curve shows the price that would maximize its own profit, given the price charged by its rival. Equilibrium is at the intersection because only there is each firm doing as well as it can, given the behavior of its rival.

All this is different from quantity competition. But since, by and large, the basic conclusions of the previous section still apply, the difference may not seem that important. This is not always true, however, as we will discover later in this book.

Problems

3.13 The previous section made seven basic points about trade and oligopoly when firms compete in quantities. Discuss in detail how valid each of these points remains if instead the firms compete in prices.

3.14* Suppose, as in Problems **3.10** and **3.11,** that the production of fried clams by the supplier Rufus entails a fixed cost of $6 and a marginal cost of $2 per pint. And suppose that Violet, who has the same costs as Rufus, sells steamed clams. If Violet charges q for a pint of steamed clams and Rufus charges p for a pint of fried clams, residents of Marbletoe would demand $10 - p + \frac{1}{2}q$ pints of fried clams. Violet is charging $q = \$4$. Given this strategy by Violet, what is the best price that Rufus can set? Does your answer tell you anything about Rufus's best-response curve? Does it tell you anything about Violet's?

3.15* Suppose that, if Rufus charges p and Violet charges q, residents of Marbletoe would also demand $10 - q + \frac{1}{2}p$ pints of steamed clams. Draw Rufus's best-response curve and Violet's best-response curve. Describe the duopoly equilibrium, and compare this with the monopoly equilibrium you described in Problem **3.8** and the duopoly equilibrium you described in Problem **3.12*.**

3.16* This section supposed that the duopolists sold differentiated products. Try to discuss what might happen if instead they sold identical products.

5. MONOPOLISTIC COMPETITION

Monopolistic competition is an extreme form of oligopoly in which firms sell differentiated products and are sufficiently numerous so that each ignores the possibility of strategic interaction between its own deeds and those of any particular rival. It is clear that product differentiation is important in practice because we see it all the time. It is not clear that imperfect competition without strategic interaction is also important. But we have looked at oligopolies with small numbers of firms and at strategic interaction, and now we want to see what can happen if the number of firms can grow large. This is much easier if we do not worry about strategic interaction at the same time. For this reason monopolistic competition is useful to study.

The Division of Labor, or Differentiated Consumer Goods

The theory of monopolistic competition can be used to study markets for differentiated consumer goods. The world motor vehicle market is a good example: there are many producers, each offering vehicles that are substitutes for those of other producers but that still possess characteristics special to the individual firm. As we saw in Chapter 2, this establishes a basis for *intraindustry* trade between similar economies: such economies are both likely to produce automobiles, but they can gain by producing different varieties and exchanging them. This way, consumers in both countries have more varieties to choose from if trade takes place than if it does not. But if variety is such a good thing, why not go all the way and provide each consumer with the unique automobile she most prefers? Because of economies of scale in the production of individual varieties: it doesn't pay to introduce another variety unless it can be produced in enough volume to bring average costs down to a reasonable level. A larger market allows more varieties to be produced in such volume; this is why trade is such a good thing. But if the economies of scale apply to an individual variety, they will be *internal* to the firm producing that variety, and Chapter 2 showed that internal economies of scale are not consistent with a perfectly competitive equilibrium. Thus we need to look at imperfect competition. Furthermore, monopolistic competition is of special interest because we are concerned here with a large number of sellers of distinct varieties and how that number is affected by trade.

The same considerations apply to markets characterized by international economies of scale due to the division of labor. As we also saw in Chapter 2, this establishes a basis for *intraindustry* trade between similar economies: such economies are both likely to have an automobile sector, but they can gain by concentrating on different stages of the production process and exchanging the intermediate goods required for finished automobiles. The division of labor is limited by the extent of the market because of internal economies of scale in the operation of individual stages: it doesn't pay to add another stage unless it can be operated in sufficient volume to get average costs down to a reasonable level. Thus again we need imperfect competition, and monopolistic competition is an interesting way to look at the intraindustry exchange of producer goods also.

Monopolistic Competition Equilibrium

So let us turn to monopolistic competition. Trade in producer goods is in fact much larger than trade in consumer goods, but both are important and the latter is more visible in our daily lives. Since the basic properties of intraindustry trade in consumer goods because of product differentiation are, by and large, shared by intraindustry trade in producer goods because of the division of labor, it doesn't pay to analyze first one and then the other. Therefore, let us examine just trade in differentiated consumer goods, remembering that the basic points will also apply to trade in producer goods associated with international economies of scale.

Consider the producer of a single variety of a differentiated product— say, automobiles. This producer faces a market demand curve for his particular

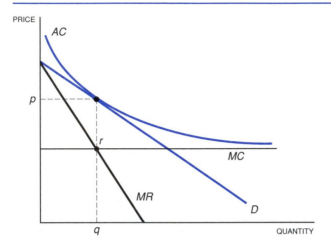

FIGURE 3.6 Monopolistic Competition Equilibrium The monopolistically competitive firm maximizes its profit by selling the quantity *q* for which *MR* equals *MC*. Entry and exit into and out of the industry shift the *D* and *MR* curves faced by the individual firm until the representative firm is making a zero profit (*p* = *AC*) when it is maximizing its profit (*MR* = *MC*).

variety. Since he is only one automobile producer among many, he does not worry about the possibility of the other producers responding to his actions—that is, there is no strategic interaction. So this producer simply picks the point along his demand curve that maximizes his profit, just like any monopolist. That is, he sells the quantity that causes his *MC* to equal his *MR*.

But this is not all. Although he is the only supplier of his particular variety, our producer is but one among many. If he is making a profit and if he is typical of the industry, this will induce new firms to enter the industry. Conversely, if the typical producer is operating at a loss, even while doing the best he can, varieties will be withdrawn from the market. If a new firm enters, our firm will lose some of its customers—that is, its demand curve shifts down (and so its marginal revenue curve shifts down, too). Also, existing customers now have more choice and so are likely to be more price conscious—that is, the demand curve becomes flatter and thus more responsive to price changes. All of this is unfortunate for our firm, but there is nothing it could have done to prevent it: the new entrant came into the market because existing firms were on average making a profit, not because of anything any one of them was doing.

Entry and exit will continue until the representative firm is just breaking even so that no one else has an incentive to come in or to leave. Thus the demand curve facing the representative firm adjusts so that that firm is earning 0 profit (that is, price equals average cost) when it is doing the best it can and maximizing its profit (that is, marginal revenue equals marginal cost). This is shown in Figure 3.6.

International Trade

Now suppose international trade begins with two countries, each with a monopolistically competitive sector such as that just described. Suppose that initially there are n automobile firms at home and n^* abroad. With international trade there will now be $n + n^*$ automobile firms in a single world market, before any entry or exit takes place as a result of trade. Since each consumer can now choose from $n + n^*$ varieties rather than just from n (or from n^*), many consumers will now be able to find a variety preferable to what they would be able to find with autarky. Thus trade confers a clear benefit: consumers have more choice. Since entry and exit will keep the profits of a representative firm equal to 0 with either free trade or autarky, the profit reduction and profit switching caused by trade and oligopoly do not occur now.

But there may be other effects. Since each firm now has $n + n^* - 1$ competitors rather than just n (or just n^*), it probably faces a flatter demand curve than in autarky—an increase in price will likely drive away more consumers than before because they now have more alternatives from which to choose. As always, firms will enter or exit until this new demand curve shifts so that the representative firm is left with 0 profit when doing the best that it can. The new international equilibrium is shown in Figure 3.7.

In this new international equilibrium the representative firm produces more than in autarky. This increased output moves the firm down its average cost curve, so each automobile costs society less than in autarky. With price equal to average cost because profits are 0, consumers face a lower price than

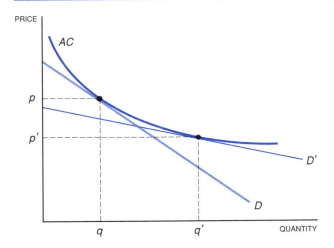

FIGURE 3.7 Monopolistic Competition: Autarky to Free Trade The representative monopolistically competitive firm has more competitors with free trade than with autarky and accordingly faces a flatter demand curve. As a consequence, the firm sells more at a lower price in free trade than in autarky.

they would in autarky. International trade has intensified competition among firms, each of which faces more rivals than in autarky, and this forces prices down. It will also tend to force some firms out of the market so that the number of varieties could be reduced below $n + n^*$ in the international equilibrium, although it would still exceed both n and n^* individually so that consumer choice will have widened. But the lower price will stimulate demand, and this could reduce or even eliminate the need for firms to exit.

International trade has generated gains in two primary ways. First, consumers have more choice; thus many are enabled to obtain automobiles that meet their needs better than would be possible in autarky. Second, each automobile is cheaper than it would be in autarky.

This section has looked at monopolistic competition in markets for differentiated consumer goods generated by a desire for product variety. Similar considerations apply to producer-goods markets generated by the division of labor.

6. SUMMARY

1. A market is imperfectly competitive if it contains some participants who are not price takers.

2. Imperfectly competitive markets can be classified on the basis of how many sellers (or buyers) there are and according to the type of strategic interaction between them.

3. The major types are monopoly (a single seller); oligopoly (several sellers with strategic interaction of some sort), and monopolistic competition (a number of sellers without strategic interaction).

4. International trade can increase the degree of competition in an imperfectly competitive market. This can be expected to improve social efficiency and is another reason for countries to trade.

5. If imperfect competition allows nonzero profits, these will be affected by international trade. This allows trade to redistribute income both within countries (profit reduction) and between countries (profit switching).

6. International trade in monopolistically competitive industries allows consumers to have more choice and industry to employ a greater division of labor. It can also lower the cost of individual varieties by allowing a greater exploitation of internal economies of scale.

SUGGESTED READING

Chamberlin, E. H. *The Theory of Monopolistic Competition.* Cambridge: Harvard University Press, 1933. The classic statement.

Ethier, W. J. "National and International Returns to Scale in the Modern Theory of International Trade." *American Economic Review* (1982). Monopolistic competition and the division of labor.

Feenstra, R. E., ed. *Empirical Methods in International Trade*. Cambridge: MIT Press, 1988. Contains several interesting empirical studies of international trade with imperfect competition and economies of scale.

Grossman, G., ed. *Imperfect Competition and International Trade*. Cambridge: MIT Press, 1992. A collection of basic journal articles.

Helpman, E., and P. R. Krugman. *Market Structure and Foreign Trade*. Cambridge: MIT Press, 1985. An extensive treatment of the theory of international trade with scale economies and imperfect competition.

Kierzkowski, H., ed. *Monopolistic Competition in International Trade*. Oxford: Clarendon Press, 1984. A collection of papers dealing with trade and imperfect competition.

Part Two

How Nations Trade

H ow do nations trade? At a superficial level this is straightforward: merchants and manufacturers in one country negotiate contracts with customers in another country. But we are interested in deeper issues such as how international prices are determined. In Chapter 4 we discuss this. We consider other issues as well—for example, the links between how a country trades and its domestic economic characteristics such as the distribution of income. The theory developed in Chapter 5 will allow us to investigate these links. Finally, in Chapter 6 we will confront the theory with the facts of world trade. This is critical: tension between theoretical prediction and empirical fact has been just as important for the development of the topics discussed in Part Two as it was for those discussed in Part One. The evolution of trade theory during the last forty years or so has been driven largely by two sources of tension between existing theory and apparent fact. One source is the large volume of trade in similar goods between similar industrial economies; as we saw in Part One, this stimulated interest in reasons to trade other than comparative advantage. The other source is the Leontief Paradox, which will be discussed in Chapter 6.

CHAPTER 4

International Equilibrium

> The produce of a country exchanges for the produce of other countries, at such values as are required in order that the whole of her exports may exactly pay for the whole of her imports.
>
> —JOHN STUART MILL

Comparative advantage explains the pattern of trade. It also furnishes a strong argument for trade gains and tells much about production and the terms of trade. But to explain the actual pattern of production or the exact terms at which one country's products exchange for those of another, we also need detailed knowledge of demand. In this chapter we explore these problems and answer completely the first two of the questions posed at the outset of Part One: What explains the pattern of international trade and production? What are the welfare implications of international trade?

You may recall from elementary economics how demand and supply curves describe how price is determined. We want to do the same now for international trade. But the situation is complicated: we have at least two goods, imports and exports, and two market participants, the home country and the rest of the world, which are both simultaneously buyers and sellers. This is a problem of general equilibrium. As we develop the theory, you might consider how it relates to the oil crises of the 1970s and 1980s, which changed everyone's life. The prime features then were dramatic changes in the world price of oil. Why did these changes happen? Why did they happen then?

1. THERE IS NO SUCH THING AS A FREE LUNCH

Imagine a single economy in isolation—say, the French economy with but two commodities, apples and butane. Anyone who wishes to buy butane must offer for sale an equal-valued number of apples, and the only reason apples are ever offered for sale is to purchase butane. This elementary observa-

JOHN STUART MILL (1806–1873)

John Stuart Mill survived an unusual educational regime imposed by his father, the economist James Mill, to become a great philosopher and economist, and one of the major intellectual figures of his day. In his writing and (briefly) in his speeches in Parliament, he was also a major exponent of the liberal viewpoint on such issues as reform and women's rights. He was apparently much influenced by Harriet Taylor, with whom he had a relationship for about twenty years before the death of her husband allowed Mill to marry her. (Mill was also the friend at whose home the only copy of the manuscript of the first part of Carlyle's *The French Revolution* was inadvertently destroyed.) Mill's *Principles of Political Economy* was published in the revolutionary year 1848—also the year of the publication of *The Communist Manifesto*—and became the supreme statement of classical economics and, for nearly half a century, the standard textbook.

tion is universally true: if I agree to purchase a $10,000 car, then I am simultaneously offering to sell $10,000—that is, to sell my right to $10,000 worth of goods. The demand for the car and the offer of $10,000 worth of goods are one and the same. In the French economy as a whole, then, the value of the total demand for apples plus the total demand for butane must always equal the value of the total supply of apples plus the total supply of butane. That is, it is *always* true that $P_A^F D_A^F + P_B^F D_B^F \equiv P_A^F S_A^F + P_B^F S_B^F$, or

$$P_A^F (D_A^F - S_A^F) + P_B^F (D_B^F - S_B^F) \equiv 0, \tag{4.1}$$

where D_A^F denotes the total French demand for apples and so forth. The values of the economy's excess demands (the excesses of demands over supplies) of the two goods always sum to 0. This property is known as Walras's Law, after the French economist Léon Walras (1834–1910).

KEY CONCEPT

Walras's Law: For any individual, group, country, or the entire world, the sum total of the values of the excess demands for all goods, services, and assets is always equal to 0. This is because a demand is by its very nature a supply of something else of equal value.

Walras's Law is a general one: if there were 10,000 goods in this economy instead of 2, the same reasoning would imply that the values of the excess demands in the 10,000 markets would always sum to 0. Two other aspects of Walras's Law deserve emphasis. First, it is an identity that always holds, apart from whether the economy is in equilibrium or not; this is the meaning of the three-barred equality sign in Equation (4.1). If the French economy is in autarkic equilibrium so that demand equals supply in each market, then Equation (4.1) must hold since each term in parentheses is itself equal to 0. But Walras's Law will hold even outside of equilibrium. We deduced Equation (4.1) directly from the fundamental meaning of *demand* and *supply,* and never said anything about equilibrium. Second, Walras's Law is a statement about the relationship *between* the two markets and tells us nothing about the markets individually. For example, it does not say whether the apple market is in excess supply ($S_A^F > D_A^F$), has excess demand ($D_A^F > S_A^F$), or is in autarkic equilibrium. But it does imply that *if* the apple market is in equilibrium, then the butane market *must* also be in equilibrium; if there is an excess demand for apples, then there must be an excess supply of butane, and so on.

Problems

4.1 Suppose that in addition to apples and butane there are 9,998 other markets in the French economy. Then what does an excess demand for apples imply? If the other 9,999 markets are in equilibrium, what must be true of the apple market? If the answers to these questions do not come to you at once, go back to the beginning of this section and rededuce Walras's Law directly for an economy with 10,000 markets.

4.2 Fill in the blanks in the following table:

Price of apples in terms of butane	Excess demand for apples	Excess demand for butane
1/10	1,000	
1/5		−80
1/2		−20
2/3	0	
1	−10	
3/2		30
2		50
5		100
10	−15	

4.3 A man sold a bond for $10,000, bought a $7,000 automobile, and put the remaining $3,000 in the bank. Since the value of the bond supplied exceeded the value of the car demanded, did he not (heaven forbid!) violate Walras's Law? What if you give a beggar 50 cents for a cup of coffee?

2. IMPORT DEMAND CURVES

Suppose that there are no economies of scale or imperfect competition, so that all trade will be due to comparative advantage. The French can trade at the international prices of apples and butane. If there is an excess French demand for butane, this excess is the net French demand for butane imports. By Walras's Law there must simultaneously be an excess supply of apples— that is, a net supply of exports of apples of equal value at the international prices. So define $M^F = D_B^F - S_B^F$ and $X^F = S_A^F - D_A^F$, and rewrite Equation (4.1) as $-P_A X^F + P_B M^F \equiv 0$, or

$$pM^F \equiv X^F, \tag{4.2}$$

where $p = P_B/P_A$. Note that (4.2) is nothing more than (4.1) rewritten in such a way as to emphasize the role of international trade. It simply says that the French demand for imports is always equal in value to the French supply of exports; this is always true whether or not world markets are in equilibrium— that is, whether or not the rest of the world is willing to satisfy the French demand for imports and to purchase the French supply of exports.

An *import demand curve* summarizes the possible roles a country can play in the world economy. In Figure 4.1 the horizontal axis is measured in units of butane and will be used to depict the excess demand for butane, while their price in terms of apples will be marked off on the vertical axis. Point A, for example, indicates a demand for imports of OB at a price of OC; point E represents a supply of EJ of butane *exports* (that is, negative imports).

From Walras's Law, seen in (4.2), $pM = X$. Thus at any point in Figure 4.1 the demand for imports and their price are given by the coordinates, while the supply of exports of apples equals the product of imports and their price. At point A, for example, $X = OBAC$. The French autarkic equilibrium price, P_B^F / P_A^F, is given by OD; at this price domestic demand equals domestic supply in both markets, and the import demand curve passes through the price axis. If the world relative butane price p is less than p^F—say, that indicated by OC—then comparative advantage indicates that France will import butane and export apples, as discussed in Chapter 1. This is illustrated by point A. On the other hand, if p is above the autarkic price, the French will export butane and import apples, as at E.

Three important features of the import demand curve should be apparent. First, it is a general equilibrium concept; if the international price changes, the import demand curve indicates the effect as the entire economy adjusts: both consumers and suppliers, both import markets and export markets. Second, the import demand curve is itself relevant only to the French

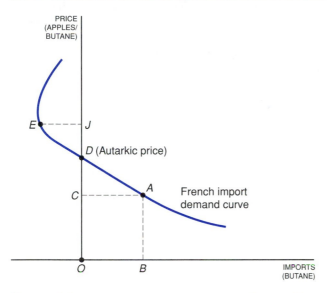

FIGURE 4.1 **The French Import Demand Curve** This curve shows how much butane France will want to import at alternative international prices. *OD* is the autarkic price; at lower prices France will want to import positive quantities, and at higher prices it will want to import negative quantities—that is, to export butane.

economy. We had to know nothing about Germany to derive it, and it itself tells us nothing about Germany. Finally, we need not know what the international price actually is because the import demand curve indicates how an economy would behave under all hypothetical values of this price.

Problems

4.4 Graph the observations in the completed table from Problem **4.2,** and "connect the dots" to draw an import demand curve.

4.5 Use the completed table from Problem **4.2** to graph an "export supply curve" showing the supply of exports of butane corresponding to each price of *butane in terms of apples*.

4.6 Suppose France has 100 apples and no butane. French tastes are such that the country would wish to behave as follows:

If P_B / P_A is . . .	The French wish to . . .
greater than 3 *A/B*	consume only apples
3 *A/B*	export 60 apples
not more than 3 *A/B*	consume 20 apples

Use Walras's Law to deduce M^F and X^F for each case. Draw the French import demand curve by graphing the observations and connecting them. Also draw the French export supply curve.

4.7 Suppose you have the following data for Germany:

P_B/P_A	B demand	B supply	A demand	A supply
4		120	140	20
4/3	80	110		30
1	100	100	50	
	140	80	45	85

Fill in the blanks. Draw Germany's import demand curve for apples by graphing the observations and connecting the dots. Also draw Germany's export supply curve.

4.8* Suppose that in England 5 units of labor are required to produce either 1 bolt of cloth or 1 cask of wine, that England has 100 units of labor, and that each Englishman always consumes 1 cask of wine for each bolt of cloth that he consumes. What can you say about his marginal rate of substitution? Derive England's import demand curve exactly. (Hint: draw England's production possibility frontier. What is the autarkic price? For each value of the relative price ask yourself: What will England produce; what will it consume? Record the differences to draw the import demand curve.)

4.9* Suppose that in Portugal 4 units of labor can produce 1 bolt of cloth, 1 labor unit can produce 1 cask of wine, 100 labor units are available, and each Portuguese always spends one-half of her income on each good. Derive Portugal's import demand curve exactly.

3.* *EXPLORING FURTHER:* INCOME AND SUBSTITUTION EFFECTS

The import curve in Figure 4.1 is drawn so that a fall in the price of imports causes a rise in M. But it is not clear whether X rises or falls. This is worth investigating. A change in relative prices can be thought of as exerting its influence upon M and X in three logically distinct ways. First, there is what can be termed a *consumption substitution effect:* a fall in the relative price of butane, say, will induce consumers to substitute butane for apples. Second, if the economy is not already specialized in apple production, there will be a movement along the production possibility frontier so that apple output is substituted for butane output: a *production substitution effect.* The net result of both substitution effects is an increased excess demand for butane and an increased excess supply of apples—that is, M and X both tend to rise.

Finally, there will also be an *income effect:* the fall in the relative price of butane means that the income of apple exporters has in fact risen—that is, the apples that they are exporting will now buy more butane. (By the same token the income of butane sellers has fallen.) For example, if in Figure 4.2 the rel-

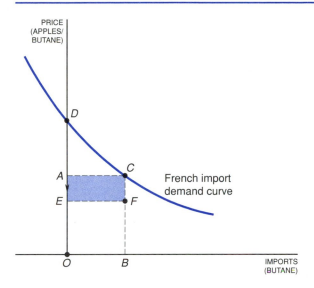

FIGURE 4.2 An Improvement in the French Terms of Trade   If the international price of butane falls from *OA* to *OE,* the quantity of apples that France must pay for *OB* units of butane is reduced by *ACFE.*

ative price of butane falls from *OA* to *OE,* the French need export only *OBFE* apples rather than *OBCA* to buy *OB* units of butane. This increase in income will normally cause the French to consume more of both goods (although there are some goods, such as gruel and secondhand clothes, that we consume less of as our income rises). The income effect, then, usually causes *M* to rise and *X* to fall since the only way to consume more of the export good is by exporting less of it. In this case, the improvement in the terms of trade will necessarily increase *M* but may cause *X* to rise or fall, depending upon whether the substitution or income effect is dominant. At point *D* the substitution effects necessarily dominate since the income effect is 0—the fact that our exports are worth more cannot help if we are not exporting. But as we move away from *D* along the import demand curve, the income effect becomes more important.

An illustration may prove of use at this point. Suppose you are a pea picker working as long as you want at a certain wage. Then you are essentially "exporting" your labor in order to "import" the goods you purchase with your wages. If your wage increases, your income will rise and you will perhaps respond by working more. But if your wage increases again and again, you decide there is more to life than picking peas and you will begin to cut back on your labor so as to have more leisure in which to enjoy your new-found affluence. That is, the income effect will eventually dominate. There is nothing farfetched about this example: labor unions frequently take part of their wage increases in the form of a reduced workweek, and the average workweek has tended to fall over the years as incomes have risen.

Problems

4.10* Discuss the roles of income and substitution effects in Problems **4.8*** and **4.9***.

4.11* Suppose, as in Problem **2.6,** that England has 6 workers and the following technology for producing cloth and wine:

To produce this much cloth . . .	. . . Requires this much labor . . .	. . . Allowing this much wine
0	0	6
1	3	3
2	4	2
3	5	1
4	6	0

The English always consume equal quantities of wine and cloth. What can you say about the consumption substitution effect, the production substitution effect, and the income effect in this case?

4. THE VOLUME AND TERMS OF TRADE

The French import demand curve summarizes how the French economy will behave under all possible relative prices. To analyze world markets we need similar information for Germany.

For France we arbitrarily referred to butane as imports and apples as exports. This did not reflect a prediction about what the actual trade pattern would be: the imports and exports might turn out either positive or negative. But regardless of what the actual pattern is, certainly Germany exports whatever France imports and vice versa. Therefore, define M^G to be the German excess demand for apples and X^G to be the excess supply of butane. Then draw the German export supply curve of butane. This is combined with the French import curve in Figure 4.3.

We are now equipped to understand the basic idea contributed by Mill. The intersection of the two curves reveals the world relative price and the pattern of trade. In Figure 4.3 France will import *OD* units of butane from Germany at the price *OE*. Germany will import *ODAE* apples from France. Only at *A,* the intersection of the two curves, can both world markets be in equilibrium. If, for example, the international relative price were *OH,* then the German supply of exports of butane would be given by *B* while the French demand for imports of butane would be indicated by *C*. There would thus be an excess world demand for butane and an excess world supply of apples. Only at *A* do the desired exports and imports of the two countries match.

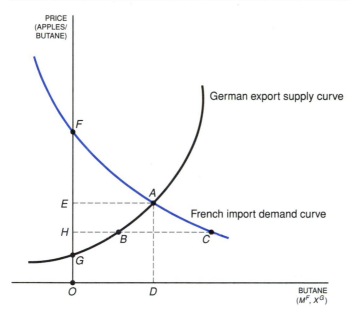

FIGURE 4.3 **The Terms of Trade** The international price of butane is determined by the intersection of the French import demand curve with the German export supply curve.

Note that the German autarkic price of butane in terms of apples, OG, is lower than the French, OF—that is, France has a comparative advantage over Germany in apples relative to butane. If the French curve instead intersected the price axis below the German curve, they would intersect in the left-hand quadrant, indicating that France exports butane and Germany apples. Thus the curves illustrate the principle of comparative advantage.

Problems

4.12 Redraw Figure 4.3 as if France had the comparative advantage in butane.

4.13 Suppose that France and Germany, as described in Problems **4.6** and **4.7**, enter into free trade. By drawing the French import demand and German export supply curves, find the terms of trade and the volume of goods exchanged. Do the same with French export supply and German import demand curves.

4.14* England has 100 labor units, 5 of which are required to produce either 1 cask of wine or 1 bolt of cloth. Each English resident always consumes the two goods in equal quantities. Portugal also has 100 labor units with 1 required to produce 1 cask of wine and 4 to produce 1 bolt of cloth; each Portuguese always consumes quantities of wine and cloth equal *in value* to each other. What will the terms of trade between these countries be? Who exports how much of what? What are the wages and prices in the two countries? Suppose that England's labor force increases to 1,000 units and nothing else changes. Which curves shift? What are the new terms of trade and pattern of trade? What size must England's labor force be if that country is to export wine?

5. ELASTICITY

Because it summarizes how the economy would react to any international price, the import demand curve is one of the main tools of international trade theory. And its shape is a basic characteristic of the economy. One measure of this shape is the elasticity of import demand, given by the formula

$$e = \frac{\text{percentage rise in } M}{\text{percentage fall in } p}. \tag{4.3}$$

A great virtue of the elasticity concept is that it gives you a pure number reflecting a fundamental property of the economy: the value of e does not depend upon whether M or p is measured in pounds, ounces, gallons, or quarts.

KEY CONCEPT

The *elasticity of import demand* is the percentage increase in the demand for imports resulting from a 1 percent improvement in the terms of trade—that is, a 1 percent fall in p.

Since an increase in p implies a decrease in M, e will always be positive. Import demand is elastic or inelastic if $e > 1$ or $e < 1$, respectively. If $e > 1$, a 1 percent fall in the price of imports increases the volume of imports more than 1 percent. Thus the total amount spent on imports increases. An improvement in the terms of trade will, therefore, cause the economy to increase its expenditure on imports if import demand is elastic and to decrease such expenditure if import demand is inelastic.

You may have met with the notion of demand elasticity before, and perhaps even learned a method of reading it off a demand curve. To find the value of e at, say, point A on the import demand curve of Figure 4.4, draw a straight line through A tangent to the curve at A and extend it until it intersects both axes. Then the value of e at A will be given by AB/AC.

Verifying that this procedure does indeed yield the true value of e is a largely manipulative affair. Notice that the value given by this procedure depends upon the exact point at which the elasticity is measured; e does not

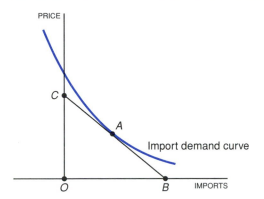

FIGURE 4.4   Finding the Elasticity of Import Demand   The elasticity of the import demand curve at *A* is *AB/AC*.

have the same value at all points of the curve. Elasticity is intended to tell us how the economy will respond to a change in a given situation. It is only natural that this response should depend upon the situation.

If the import demand curve is elastic and *p* falls by 1 percent, then *M* increases by more than 1 percent, so that the total amount spent on imports (price × quantity) rises. But exports are what is spent on imports. Thus if *e* exceeds 1, a fall in *p* raises *X*.

The Elasticity of Export Supply

We have investigated the elasticity of import demand. But it is just as natural to look at the elasticity of export supply, *f*, which is the percentage increase in the supply of exports resulting from a 1 percent improvement in the terms of trade:

$$f = \frac{\text{percentage rise in } X}{\text{percentage fall in } p}. \qquad (4.4)$$

Of course, *e* and *f* must be two ways of looking at the same thing; given the value of one, we should be able to calculate the other. The relation is simple. If *p* falls by 1 percent, *M* rises by *e* percent and *X* by *f* percent. Now a 1 percent fall in *p* reduces the cost of imports by 1 percent so that the total spent on imports (that is, exports) rises by *e* − 1 percent. Thus

$$e - 1 = f. \qquad (4.5)$$

The Elasticity of Exports with Respect to Imports

The final possibility is the elasticity, *g*, of *X* with respect to *M*:

$$g = \frac{\text{percentage rise in } X}{\text{percentage fall in } M}. \tag{4.6}$$

From formulas (4.3), (4.4), and (4.6),

$$g = \frac{f}{e}. \tag{4.7}$$

Problems

4.15 Suppose you have the following observations:

p	M	X
100		100,000
99	1,030	

Fill in the blanks. Calculate $e, f,$ and g for the change from the first observation to the second.

4.16 In Problem **4.2** calculate $e, f,$ and g for each pair of successive observations, using the definition of each elasticity. Also calculate f and g from your values of e, using the relationships derived above. Try to explain any discrepancies.

4.17* What can you say about the elasticities of the curves you derived in Problems **4.8*** and **4.9.***?

4.18* Prove that the geometric technique for finding the value of e is correct. Prove the relations among $e, f,$ and g.

6. *CASE STUDY:* SOME INTERNATIONAL ECONOMIC PROBLEMS OF THE LESS DEVELOPED COUNTRIES

As we saw in the first chapter, less developed countries (LDCs) as a group export primary products to developed countries (DCs) for manufactures. Many assert that the demand of the DCs for primary product imports is inelastic, reasoning that because these goods are often necessities, demand for them cannot vary much in response to price changes. Also the supply of primary products by the LDCs is often asserted to be inelastic, at least in the short run, since this supply depends upon past planting, mining, exploration, and so forth, and can be varied only after a substantial time lag. Such a situation is depicted in Figure 4.5.

The Issues

Three distinct areas of concern to the less developed countries follow from this description.

1. *Fluctuations of Export Earnings.* Natural events such as crop failures, the business cycle, inventions, taste changes, and so forth cause these curves to shift around year by year. With low elasticities, minor shifts can cause substantial variations in the terms of trade and, therefore, substantial year-by-year fluctuations in the export earnings of individual countries. For example, in Figure 4.5, if the LDC export supply curve shifts slightly to become curve *L'*, the terms of trade change substantially. Low elasticities mean that substantial price changes cause small quantity changes; therefore, a moderate quantity change requires a large price change to be effected.

2. *Terms of Trade.* If the DCs' import demand curve is inelastic, the LDCs face less favorable terms of trade than need be. Suppose the LDCs as a group were permanently to trade less with the DCs. Thus they permanently shift their export supply curve to the left—say, to *L'* in Figure 4.5. This permanently improves their terms of trade. The LDCs would be using their position as a monopolist in the primary product market (and monopsonist—or sole buyer—in the market for manufactures) to restrict supply (demand) and thereby force price up (down). This process cannot be pushed too far because, as we saw in Chapter 1, autarky is worse than free trade: it matters not how

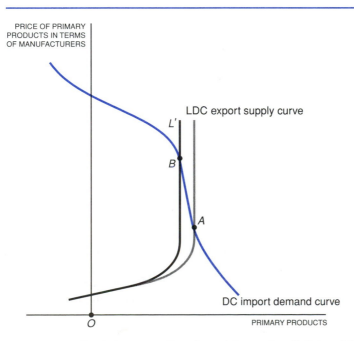

FIGURE 4.5 **Trade between Developed Countries (DCs) and Less Developed Countries (LDCs)** Because both curves have low elasticities, even small shifts of either one can cause large price swings.

favorable the terms of trade are if a country does not trade much. But if the DCs' demand is inelastic, the LDCs would be better off by trading less. In Figure 4.5, for example, the LDCs are clearly better off at *B* than at *A* because they are importing more manufactures while sacrificing fewer primary product exports. By the same token the DCs are worse off. Low elasticities, then, furnish the LDCs with a potentially powerful motive to abandon free trade even though such a move would be inefficient for the world as a whole.

3. *A Secular Decline in the Terms of Trade.* Spokesmen for the LDCs often argue that their terms of trade are steadily worsening. This is asserted to be due to many causes. The two that concern us are low elasticities and a tendency for the LDCs' export supply curve to shift outward, relative to the DCs' import demand curve, as the world economy grows. The argument is that as income grows, a smaller fraction of it is spent on necessities such as food and a larger fraction on manufactured goods. Also development itself requires large imports of manufactured goods. Finally, the DCs are constantly developing new products, such as plastics, that substitute for primary products. Figure 4.5 illustrates the implication. Suppose in some time period the LDCs' export supply curve shifts outward from *L'* , while the DCs' import demand curve expands hardly at all. Then equilibrium shifts from *B* to *A,* and the LDCs experience a decline in their terms of trade. This is asserted to be the long-term trend.

The Evidence

Before examining attempts and proposals, let us look at the evidence.

Indications of low elasticities abound, and many primary product prices have in fact fluctuated markedly relative to prices of manufactures. Table 4.1 illustrates quarter-by-quarter changes in the indices of selected commodity prices and compares them with the behavior of the U.S. wholesale price index. Since many LDCs concentrate their exports in only a few products, they must have experienced significant fluctuations in their terms of trade. But beyond this the evidence is unclear.

Consider the first issue: export earnings. Calculations of export earnings of groups of LDCs frequently show only moderate fluctuations. The reason is simple. Suppose a bad crop shifts the LDC export supply curve to *L'* in Figure 4.5. The decrease in quantity and consequent rise in price cancel each other at least in part; export earnings fluctuate less than the terms of trade. But the situation of individual LDCs is more complicated, and the reason is a good lesson. A frost in Brazil that decimates the coffee crop may have only a moderate effect on the earnings of coffee exporters in the aggregate. But Colombia, unaffected by the frost, will experience only the sharp rise in price, whereas Brazil will have to bear the full decline in quantity. Even if individual LDCs do experience large swings in earnings, this need not hamper development. Such fluctuations will be expected, recognized as transitory, and perhaps adjusted for. The few studies that exist of the effect of such fluctuations on LDC development largely fail to reveal any significant impact.

TABLE 4.1 Indices of Selected Commodity Prices and of U.S. Wholesale Prices (*1975 average = 100*)

	Quarter	Coffee	Copper	Groundnut oil	Sugar	Superphosphate	Tin	U.S. wholesale price
1973	II	82	132	58	46	41	96	76
	III	88	164	67	45	56	75	80
	IV	89	178	76	52	56	83	82
1974	I	90	191	123	94	105	107	85
	II	95	226	128	112	146	135	88
	III	85	140	123	148	169	125	95
	IV	85	110	129	230	173	103	98
1976	I	139	101	83	69	49	98	103
	II	175	124	78	68	41	111	104
	III	185	126	90	51	45	120	105
	IV	225	104	95	38	44	120	106
1980	I	248	212	87	99	96	254	148
	II	255	166	84	136	85	252	151
	III	253	171	105	153	82	252	156
	IV	255	161	125	176	84	231	159
1991	I	111	189	104	21	64	83	231
	II	109	182	97	21	61	85	229
	III	104	176	92	21	57	85	229
	IV	97	180	73	21	61	83	230

SOURCE: *International Financial Statistics.*

The evidence for a secular decline in the LDCs' terms of trade is even sketchier and has received abundant criticism. Relevant price indices are hard to find and do not adequately account for changes in the quality and variety of manufactures. Also a decline in the terms of trade would not in itself imply a deterioration in the LDC's position since it could be due to an increased ability to export. The position of LDC spokesmen on this issue is the opposite of that of the classical economists, who believed that the pressure of a growing world economy on a limited stock of arable land and mineral resources would inevitably drive up primary product prices, a view that has found modern expression in the concerns of conservationists and neo-Malthusians over the "limits to growth."

The Attempted Remedies

Despite the ambiguous evidence, the LDCs have pushed for policy measures. The most natural would be for the LDCs to control their export supply curves with export or production quotas or purchases and sales of primary products. Such measures could apply to all three issues.

Individual LDCs have in fact followed such policies. Brazil has restricted coffee exports to hold up prices, and Cuba has even burned part of its sugar crop. But single countries can at best achieve only transitory success in this way. If some LDC restricts exports, a competitor will step in to fill the gap so that the restriction will result in a loss of market share rather than a higher price. Thus Brazil's restriction of coffee exports allowed other Latin American countries to increase their markets and helped stimulate the development of coffee cultivation in East Africa. Geometrically, although the producers (and potential producers) of a primary product may *in the aggregate* face an inelastic foreign import demand curve, any individual producer faces a much more elastic curve because, from its point of view, the rest of the world includes competitors as well as customers.

International Commodity Agreements. There is thus good reason for LDCs to join together, in what is called a "producer cartel," for multilateral action. There have in fact been many such attempts. Most of these have had little success. One basic problem is the temptation to cheat. If export restrictions are binding and price is being held up, individual countries will be tempted to violate their quotas (and this can be done with little fear of detection). The temptation would be enhanced by a suspicion that other countries are cheating or by dissatisfaction with the quota allotment. Similarly, new producers have little incentive to join the agreement, rather than taking a "free ride." Thus such agreements have proved unstable. LDCs have sometimes tried to deal with this by involving the DCs in the agreement, essentially as enforcers. The International Coffee Agreement involves both producer and consumer nations, with the United States, as a large consumer, in a key position. This brings up a second problem. While both the LDCs and the DCs may desire stable prices, and so be in basic agreement over the issue of price stabilization, the interests of the two groups clearly conflict with respect to the issue of improving LDC terms of trade. Even if the agreement is limited to price stabilization, the participants must agree where the price should be stabilized. The International Coffee Agreement has broken down in the past because of such producer-consumer variance. Further DC reluctance is due to a belief that commodity agreements, whatever their aims, tend in practice to respond more to the needs of producers than to those of consumers. The United States has long opposed such agreements, although the opposition has gradually eroded in recent decades.

Many economists are skeptical of stabilization agreements because of the ambiguous evidence for their need and the proven difficulty of implementation.

There is a third reason as well. Private speculators can play a stabilizing role. If the price of tin were to fall below its "normal" level, speculators would purchase tin to sell later at a profit and thereby limit the price decline. A commodity agreement could be justified if there were reason to believe that its managers would be more effective than professional speculators would be. Otherwise, the efforts of the agreement would simply displace those of speculators, and the agreement could succeed in limiting price fluctuations only if its activities were more extensive than those the speculators were willing to undertake. This means that an effective stabilization program could require larger resources and substantial costs. Many economists question the wisdom of using scarce LDC resources in this way.

Import Substitution. Many LDCs have tried to limit dependence on the world economy by shifting resources from traditional export sectors to the production of goods they have imported; thus they have attempted to shift their import demand curves to the left. Such "import substitution" policies have been forcefully implemented in the past by many Latin American countries and others.

Import substitution policies cannot effectively deal with the three issues for the same reason that attempts by individual countries to control prices are ineffective. But import substitution does insulate an LDC from external fluctuations by reducing the role of world markets. Such a reduction has also often been desired for noneconomic reasons. The cost should be obvious after Chapter 1: such a country is forsaking the benefits of comparative advantage. Significant import substitution requires that some goods be produced domestically at higher opportunity cost than that at which they could be purchased abroad. These programs have lost much of their appeal in recent years as awareness of their inefficiency has spread. This awareness is due both to the success of some LDCs, such as Taiwan and South Korea, that have relied on foreign trade and to many recent studies documenting the cost of import substitution. (Of course single-country studies will miss any terms-of-trade improvement due to many LDCs simultaneously pursuing import substitution.)

Generalized Systems of Preferences (GSPs). In UNCTAD the LDCs have pressed for *tariff preferences* on manufactures—that is, lower DC tariffs on imports from the LDCs than on similar goods imported from other DCs. Note that this contrasts sharply with import substitution in emphasizing trade rather than limiting it. The hope is to foster the development of light manufacturing industry in the LDCs (and so deal with the three issues indirectly). The European Economic Community instituted a preferential tariff system in 1971, Canada in 1974, and the United States, after initial opposition, began such a program in 1976. Other DCs also have GSPs. These schemes have significant limitations. Benefits have thus far been limited, although in recent years the LDCs have expanded manufactured exports to the DCs faster than world trade has grown, as we saw in Chapter 1.

Problems

4.19 The alleged secular decline in the LDCs' terms of trade was explained by low elasticities and the relative shifts of import demand and export supply curves. How would the argument be affected by elastic curves? What is the role of elasticity?

4.20 Unilateral action is unlikely to be effective because an individual LDC faces a much more elastic import demand curve than do LDCs in the aggregate. But if so, how could the three issues ever arise for individual countries?

4.21 The International Monetary Fund (about which more will be said when we come to international monetary economics) has a facility to lend to LDCs with temporary shortfalls of export earnings. What are the pros and cons of such a measure? Compare it to commodity agreements.

4.22 The LDCs are sometimes urged to follow *export diversification.* If they exported many primary products rather than just a few, fluctuations in individual prices would tend to cancel so that the overall terms of trade should be more stable. Discuss this proposal and compare it to import substitution.

4.23 Suppose that the LDCs succeed in improving their terms of trade by interfering with free trade in world markets. This makes the DCs worse off. Suppose the latter are considering using foreign aid as a bribe to induce the LDCs to return to free trade. Is it possible for the DCs to offer a tempting bribe—that is, one large enough so that the LDCs are at least as well off as they are now but not so large that the DCs are worse off? Why?

7. "ELASTICITY OPTIMISM" AND "ELASTICITY PESSIMISM": EMPIRICAL ESTIMATES

In our discussion of the LDCs, high elasticities were generally good and low elasticities bad. This is true of other applications as well. The classical theory is basically a story of adjustment through relative price changes. If elasticities are high, substantial quantity adjustments can be effected by moderate price movements and the process can be expected to work well; low elasticities spell trouble. Thus those who believe that elasticities are in fact high are called "elasticity optimists," and those who doubt this are called "elasticity pessimists." The former tend to have considerably more faith in the price system.

Economists have made many attempts to measure trade elasticities. At first the estimates were low, and much pessimism was generated. But more careful methodology has subsequently led to higher estimates.

There are many reasons why good estimates are hard to come by. Satisfactory data are a big problem. Another can be illustrated by Figure 4.6. Suppose the economist wishes to estimate the shape of the DCs' import demand curve. She will have a set of observations of actual prices and quantities traded at various times; points *A* and *B* in each panel represent two such observations. The natural way to proceed is to fit a curve to the data—to connect

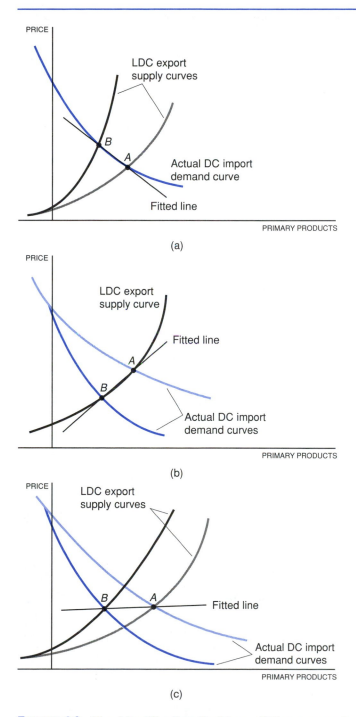

FIGURE 4.6   The Identification Problem   Fitting a curve to data can be misleading if we have an incorrect notion of how the data were generated.

TABLE 4.2 Estimates of Long-Run Price Elasticities of Aggregate Imports

Country	Number of estimates	Range of estimated values	"Best" estimate of home demand	"Best" estimate of rest-of-world's demand
United States	21	.41–3.00	1.66	1.41
Canada	7	.60–1.59	1.30	0.79
Japan	5	.77–1.47	0.78	1.25
France	6	.39–1.53	1.08	1.31
West Germany	8	.24–1.48	0.88	1.11

SOURCE: R. M. Stern, J. Francis, and B. Schumacher, *Price Elasticities in International Trade.*

A and *B* in this case. This will be appropriate if the movement from *A* to *B* (and to the other observations) was in fact due to a shift of the LDCs' export supply curve, as depicted in panel (a). But if the data were in fact generated by shifts of the DCs' import demand curve, as in (b), or, more likely, by shifts of both curves, as in (c), the procedure will not work. This is known as the *identification problem*. The way to deal with it is to use additional information about the determinants of the import demand and export supply curves to estimate both simultaneously. (You will perhaps think of yet another problem. We have assumed that the data are observations of equilibrium positions—intersections of the curves. If the observations are in fact of transition between equilibria they need not lie on either curve.)

Table 4.2 provides a summary of the estimates obtained by economists of import elasticities of some major countries. For each country, the "best" estimate of the home elasticity of import demand plus that of the rest of the world sum to more than unity. Table 4.3 shows some estimated price elasticities for the U.S. demand for imports of specific commodity groups. Note the low primary product elasticities.

TABLE 4.3 Price Elasticities for U.S. Imports of Selected Commodity Groups

Crude materials	0.18
Crude foodstuffs	0.21
Semi-manufactures	1.83
Finished manufactures	4.05

SOURCE: H. S. Houthakker and S. P. Magee, "Income and Price Elasticities in World Trade."

Figure 4.7 shows stylized trade patterns. A" small country" is one that has no influence over international prices. A more technical way of saying the same thing is that such a country faces an infinitely elastic export supply curve from the rest of the world. An example is shown in panel (a). Panel (b) depicts trade between a pair of large industrial areas (and ignores trade with other parts of the world). Neither country is small, but the elasticities are likely to be high. These countries trade much in manufactures—where elasticities tend to be high—and a large part of this trade involves the intraindustry exchange of similar goods. If European goods are close substitutes for American goods, small price changes will cause demand to shift between them: demand will be highly elastic. Panel (c) shows trade between the DCs as a group and the LDCs as a group. As we know, this trade consists to a large degree of the exchange of manufactures for primary products and so features relatively low elasticities.

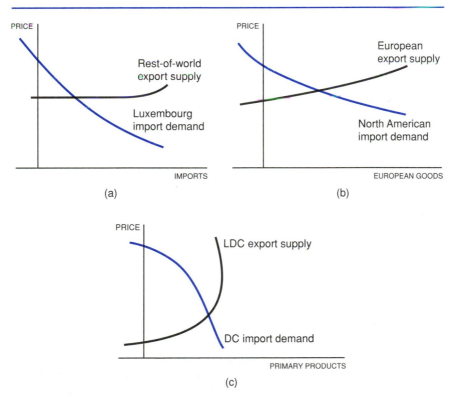

(a)

(b)

(c)

FIGURE 4.7 Stylized Views of Typical Trade Patterns Panel (a) represents the typical situation faced by a small country, panel (b) the case of two large industrial areas (DC-DC), and panel (c) the pattern between DCs and LDCs.

Problems

4.24 Suppose we represent a restrictive national trade policy by a shift in a country's import demand curve that causes it to demand fewer imports at each price, or by a shift of its export supply curve that causes it to supply fewer exports at each price. Discuss the effects of such a policy shift by each of the countries depicted in Figure 4.7.

4.25 When is a shift in a country's import demand curve that causes it to demand fewer imports at each price the same as a shift of its export supply curve that causes it to supply fewer exports at each price?

8. *CASE STUDY:* THE INTERNATIONAL ECONOMICS OF ENERGY

The most important economic event of the 1970s was the dramatic rise in the price of oil; its equally dramatic fall was big news in the 1980s. The oil market is the world's largest, and oil is the most prominent internationally traded good in both tonnage and value. The commodity is important to us all—directly, to fuel our automobiles and heat our homes; indirectly, for the energy essential to modern industry.

Development of the World Oil Market

The petroleum market began after the discovery of a well at Titusville, Pennsylvania, in 1859; international trade in the commodity began two years later, when it was exported to Europe from Philadelphia. The automobile created a large demand for oil, and the first three decades of this century witnessed the exploitation of major oil fields in the American Southwest and the Middle East as well as the development of what were to become the seven large international oil companies, or "majors" (Exxon, British Petroleum, Royal Dutch/Shell, Texaco, Mobil, Gulf, and Standard of California). Prior to the Second World War, the majors constituted a producer cartel with reserves of easily extractable oil that must have seemed almost limitless and certainly overshadowed demand. This combination of oil-company solidarity and large supply forced the countries that actually possessed oil into a passive position. This was dramatically illustrated in 1951, when radicals in Iran overthrew the shah and nationalized foreign oil interests. The majors simply refused to buy Iranian oil. They could do this because the plentiful world supplies allowed them to get the oil they needed elsewhere; the Iranians could not sell their oil to anyone else because the majors controlled the world market. Thus Iranian oil earnings disappeared, and in 1954 a CIA-assisted coup ousted the regime and returned the shah to power.

Figure 4.8 shows the situation faced by an individual oil exporter in those years. The large supply of oil available at a fixed price meant that such a country faced a straight-line demand curve such as *ADB*. Any attempt to seize control of production and shift its own export curve would fail to influence price and so only reduce the amount of imports it could buy, from *ABCO* to *ADEO* in the figure.

The long availability of plentiful oil had two major results: the industrial economies became dependent upon cheap energy, and oil became the most important source of that energy. The automobile conquered America; postwar reconstruction in Europe and Japan produced an industry dependent upon oil rather than coal. An insignificant source of energy at the start of this century, oil accounted for 45 percent of world energy supplies by the end of the 1960s. Natural gas contributed almost 20 percent more, and the share of once-dominant coal fell to less than 30 percent.

OPEC and the Oil Crises

The Organization of Petroleum Exporting Countries (OPEC) was founded in 1960 in response to a reduction in oil prices (and thus in producer-country revenues) brought about by a glut in the market. Throughout the 1960s producer countries became stronger relative to the majors, and membership in OPEC grew from the original five nations to thirteen. By 1977 OPEC accounted for about one-half of world oil production and two-thirds of

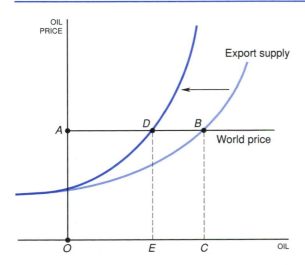

FIGURE 4.8 Restriction of Oil Sales by a Single Supplier A single supplier cannot influence the world price; therefore, cutting back sales simply means that customers are lost to competing suppliers.

TABLE 4.4   **Price of Crude Oil (Arabian Light)** *(dollars per barrel)*

				First shock			Second shock		Collapse	
Year	1960	1969	1971	1973 (Aug.)	1974	1977	1980	1985	1986	1989
Price	$1.91	1.51	2.49	3.03	11.65	13.66	28.00	30.00	15.00	14.40

world reserves. About 1970 oil prices began to rise (see Table 4.4). This reflected in part not only the emerging power of OPEC, but also a fundamental change in market conditions: world demand was overtaking supply. This is not to say that the world was suddenly confronted with the specter of an imminent depletion of oil. Rather, the rapid rise in demand made it clear that supplies were not inexhaustible and would become tighter in the decades ahead.

In late 1973 and early 1974 OPEC was able to restrict supply and effect a fourfold rise in oil's price. This is shown in Figure 4.9, where a (modest) shift in OPEC's export supply curve causes equilibrium to shift from *A* to *B* and dramatically increases the price of oil. There are two key ingredients: the ability of OPEC to control supplies, and the low elasticity of the rest of the world's import demand curve. In 1979 the market tightened up, partly in response to the revolution in Iran, which choked off oil supplies from that country and engendered fears of other future disruptions, and OPEC was again able to raise the price dramatically (the second "oil shock").

Response to the Shocks

By 1981 the oil market had loosened up, and prices fell a bit. People began to speculate that OPEC was losing its grip. Early in 1986 oil prices collapsed. They have never really recovered since, despite some attempts by OPEC to bring this about and despite various shocks—such as the Gulf War in the early 1990s—that produced price fluctuations. Two influences seem responsible.

The Effect of Higher Oil Prices in the Importing Countries. Individuals have responded to the high oil prices by conserving energy overall and by switching to nonoil sources of energy. Examples of the former are fuel-efficient automobiles and appliances, increased insulation, and so forth. Aggregate effects are reflected in Table 4.5. The three countries in the table are in different positions. Japan is the most vulnerable to increases in the oil price—99 percent of Japan's oil is imported. The United States imports less than half its oil, and Canada, the only country of the three to increase its energy intensity, has adequate supplies of its own (as well as a government policy of keeping energy prices low).

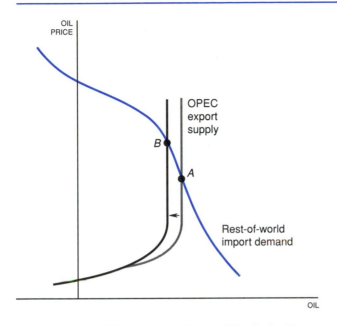

FIGURE 4.9 A Rise in the Price of Oil A simultaneous reduction in sales by many suppliers can force prices up.

The Difficulty of Maintaining a Cartel. As OPEC restricted output, other oil supplies developed and OPEC's share declined. The solidarity of the cartel deteriorated, with the uniform price policy abandoned for years at a time and with two charter members (Iran and Iraq) even going to war. In addition to the problems inherent to any cartel—discussed in previous sections—OPEC has a distinctive problem of its own. Some members (notably Saudi Arabia) have vast reserves and shallow populations. The Saudis will be selling oil for a long time and so do not want to spoil the market for the long term by stimulating the large-scale development of synthetics. But other OPEC members, such as Iran and Nigeria, are selling off their oil rapidly and have large present-day revenue needs. It is in the interest of these countries to exploit to the full the short-run inelasticity of the demand for oil, regardless of the long-term

TABLE 4.5 Energy Consumed per Million Dollars of GNP (at 1979 U.S. Prices), in Terms of Equivalent Barrels of Oil

Country	1960s average	1979
United States	6,500	5,800
Canada	6,700	7,000
Japan	3,600	3,200

consequences. From time to time countries with such different needs have been able to reach agreements to limit output, but they have not been able to sustain adhesion to such agreements.

9. *CASE STUDY:* COMPUTABLE GENERAL EQUILIBRIUM MODELS

This chapter has focused on international equilibrium, where prices adjust to balance demands and supplies of commodities worldwide. The effects of shocks and other policy actions can be analyzed by the method known as *comparative statics:* the shocks and actions shift demand and supply curves, and the new intersection is compared with the old to determine the effect of the actions. This is how we looked at the oil shocks in section 8, for example.

To make things simple we have usually considered only two goods and two countries. But practical policy analysis often demands more detail. The most straightforward way to obtain it is to estimate and test a disaggregated world model—that is, to determine demand and supply curves for all goods by all countries as well as other economic relations with which these curves interact. But this is impossible. The data are not available; and if they were, the computation would be forbidding, even in the age of the supercomputer. Thus second-best alternatives are used.

One alternative is a computable general equilibrium model of the world economy. As explained at the beginning of this chapter, general equilibrium examines the relations between a number of markets in simultaneous equilibrium. To construct a computable general equilibrium model, the economist first assembles available data on resources, production, trade flows, prices, and so on. Since the data come from many different sources, much detailed labor is required to make them mutually consistent. Next, the general structure of the model is specified. This is where the basic theoretical assumptions are made. The final step is to calibrate the model for a benchmark year. This involves specifying the values of model parameters, such as the various elasticities. The economist typically chooses these values from existing studies, such as those of trade elasticities mentioned in section 7 (but sometimes it is necessary to guess). The essential point is to calibrate the model consistently so that it can replicate the benchmark year. Suppose, for example, that 1984 is our benchmark year. Then the model will be calibrated so that when the exogenous variables (government policies, natural resources, and so on) are set equal to their 1984 values, the equilibrium solution of the model will yield endogenous variables (trade flows, production, prices, and so on) equal to what they really were in 1984. The model can then be used for comparative statics. To analyze a hypothetical change in government policy, for example, the alternative policy is plugged into the model, which is then solved for its new equilibrium. This is compared to the benchmark equilibrium to determine what the effects of the policy change would have been.

During the last fifteen years or so computable general equilibrium models have been employed with increasing frequency in international economics and other fields as well. Their big advantage is that they allow the economist to analyze the effects of policy actions and other exogenous events in the context of a consistent, interrelated global system. But their use is controversial; detractors claim that too many compromises have to be made to obtain the models ("garbage in, garbage out"). Two are especially important. First, the basic theoretical assumptions are often untested and sometimes untestable. Second, the parameter values that are stipulated during calibration are often of necessity highly questionable. Thus some economists regard the models as nothing more than intellectual toys. But users of the models say that they give insight into how the complex world economy actually functions, even if the numbers that the models yield should not be taken very seriously. Also other methods would face the same problems, and these models at least force one to make those problems explicit and visible.

Consider an actual example. John Whalley, of the University of Western Ontario, has constructed and used a number of computable general equilibrium models. One of them consists of six sectors and seven regions—the United States, the EEC, Japan, other DCs as a group (ODCs), OPEC, the newly industrialized countries (NICs), and the LDCs. The benchmark year was 1977.

Table 4.6 shows the effect in 1977 of the removal of all tariffs and other barriers to trade. These barriers were set equal to 0, and the model was solved for its new equilibrium. The table reports the differences, between the new equilibrium and the benchmark one, in the welfare and the terms of trade of each of the seven regions.

Several features stand out. First, some regions gain, and some lose: we have a case where free trade is not advantageous to all parties. Basically, the DCs are made better off and the LDCs worse off. The fact that some lose from free trade is consistent with comparative advantage; we are comparing free trade to restricted trade, not to autarky. Second, the terms of trade effects are substantial and may be important for the welfare effects, with which they are correlated. Finally, the worldwide gain of $33.1 billion, though nothing to sneeze at, is only a small fraction of 1 percent of world GNP. The distributional effects are more prominent: the four blocks that benefit gain more than

TABLE 4.6 Effects of the Removal of All Trade Barriers (1977)

	U.S.	EEC	Japan	ODCs	OPEC	NICs	LDCs	World
Welfare (billion $)	+9.3	+35.5	+20.8	−1.8	+8.3	−21.0	−18.7	33.1
Terms of trade (%)	+1.5	+12.7	+23.1	−4.7	+1.7	−23.0	−29.3	

SOURCE: J. Whalley, *Trade Liberalization among Major World Trading Areas* (Cambridge: MIT Press, 1985).

twice the global gain; the blocks that are harmed lose by more than the entire global gain. The general picture is that free trade would have a small aggregate welfare effect, would substantially alter terms of trade, and would benefit the DCs at the expense of the LDCs. These are very important conclusions, if true. So it is important to be as clear as possible about such limitations of a computable general equilibrium model as its basic assumptions and the values of its key parameters.

This model assumes away economies of scale and imperfect competition, which Chapters 2 and 3 showed could each be a basis for trade, and does not allow changes in the pattern of specialization, one of the ways in which comparative advantage works. The welfare gains come about through exploitation of the other aspects of comparative advantage (more efficient production and consumption). Perhaps this is why the welfare effects are so modest. In any case it is interesting that they are modest when the other bases for trade are absent. The large terms of trade effects reflect relatively low values of the trade elasticities. Our discussion in the previous section of the response to the oil shocks makes it clear that the time horizon is critical here. The general picture that emerges (of large terms of trade effects that basically determine the welfare consequences) is a pretty straightforward consequence of how the model was put together. But the actual pattern of changes (who gains and who loses, and how much) cannot be grasped without solving the model.

10.* *EXPLORING FURTHER:* HOW TO DERIVE IMPORT DEMAND AND EXPORT SUPPLY CURVES

An economy's import demand and export supply curves depend upon all conditions of production and consumption in that country. This section shows explicitly how the curves can be derived from the production possibility frontier and community indifference curves.

Panel (a) of Figure 4.10 shows the production possibility frontier and two community indifference curves (U_I, U_{II}) for the French economy. The French import demand curve for butane will be derived in panel (b), so the horizontal axis there measures butane and the vertical axis measures the relative price of butane in terms of apples. Panel (c) will be used for the export supply curve of apples, so apples are measured on the horizontal axis and the relative price of an apple in terms of butane on the vertical axis.

Autarky equilibrium is at point *C* in panel (a), where the production possibility frontier is tangent to an indifference curve. The common slope, *OD/OE*, is, therefore, the French autarky price of butane in terms of apples. Mark this height out on the vertical axis in panel (b); this is where the import curve will cut the vertical axis. Similarly, the reciprocal of this, *OE/OD*, is recorded in panel (c) as the autarky price of an apple in terms of butane.

The basic technique is as follows. The relative price is varied, with French production and consumption at each price deduced in panel (a). The

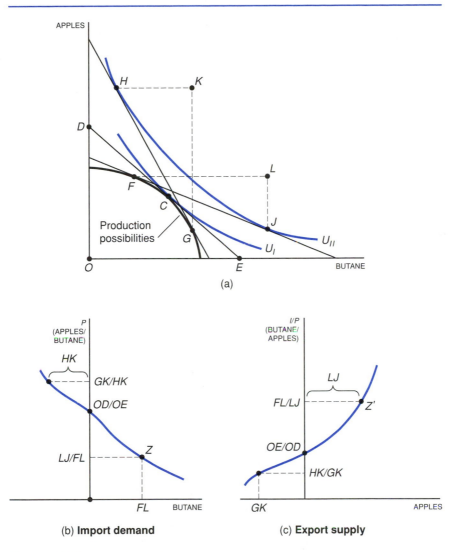

(a)

(b) **Import demand**

(c) **Export supply**

FIGURE 4.10 **The Derivation of Import and Export Curves** As the price line is shifted in panel (a), horizontal excesses of demand over supply are recorded on the horizontal axis in panel (b), and vertical excesses of supply over demand are recorded on the horizontal axis in panel (c).

differences between production and consumption are then recorded in panels (b) and (c) as imports and exports. The figure shows two other relative prices as illustrations.

When the relative price of butane in terms of apples is LJ/FL, the French produce at F in panel (a) and consume at J. Thus they import FL units of butane and export LJ apples. These quantities are recorded appropriately in panels

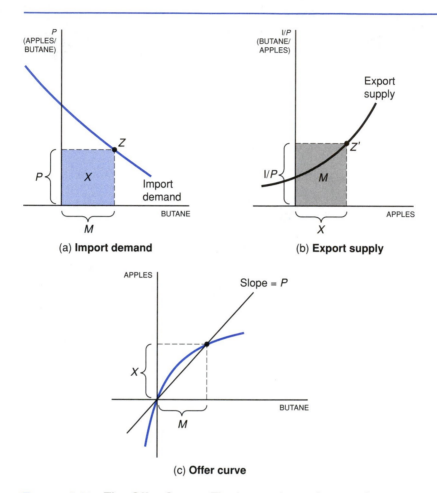

FIGURE 4.11   The Offer Curve   The import demand curve, the export supply curve, and the offer curve record the same information in three different ways.

(b) and (c) as points Z and Z', respectively. Note that this is a lower price of butane in terms of apples than in autarky and, therefore, a *higher* price of apples in terms of butane. The opposite pattern of trade appears with the price GK/HK.

The import and export curves are merely two different ways of recording the same information. The import curve records combinations of p and M, but Walras's Law tells us that $pM \equiv X$, so we can deduce X. Thus the value of X corresponding to point Z in panel (a) is the product of the coordinates or LJ, which is just the number of apples recorded at point Z' in panel (c). Similarly, the export curve records combinations of $1/p$ and X, while $M \equiv (1/p)X$ from Walras's Law. Thus the product of the coordinates at Z', which is FL, is the quantity of butane recorded at Z.

Sometimes economists use a third method to record the same information. An *offer curve* (sometimes called a "reciprocal demand curve") shows combinations of M and X, leaving p to be deduced from Walras's Law ($p \equiv X/M$). Figure 4.11 shows the relation between import, export, and offer curves.

Problems

4.26 In Figure 4.10, derive a French export supply curve of butane and import demand curve for apples.

4.27 What would the offer curve in Figure 4.11 look like if exports were measured on the butane axis and imports on the apple axis?

4.28 Suppose that in England 5 units of labor are required to produce either 1 bolt of cloth or 1 cask of wine, that England has 100 units of labor, and that each English resident always consumes 1 cask of wine for each bolt of cloth. Use the techniques of this section to derive England's import demand, export supply, and offer curves.

11. SUMMARY

1. A demand is, by its very nature, a supply of something else of equal value. This leads to Walras's Law: the total value of excess demand in all markets always equals 0.

2. An import demand curve shows the amount of imports a country is hypothetically willing to buy at each price.

3. International equilibrium can be pictured as the intersection of the home import demand and foreign export supply curves: the relative international price will be determined at that level at which the domestic demand for imports and (equal valued) supply of exports simultaneously equal the foreign supply of exports and demand for imports.

4. The elasticities of import demand and export supply curves measure the responsiveness of quantities to price changes. High elasticities usually imply a smoothly functioning price system, whereas low elasticities spell trouble.

5. The LDCs are generally thought to have, and to face, low elasticities because of the nature of their exchange with the DCs of primary products for manufactures. This is the source of many LDC policy issues.

SUGGESTED READING

Behrman, J. N. *International Economic Order and Commodity Agreements*. Reading: Addison-Wesley, 1978.

Bhagwati, J. N., ed. *The New International Economic Order: The North-South Debate*. Cambridge: MIT Press, 1977.

Bhagwati, J. N., and T. N. Srinivassan. "Trade Policy and Development." In *International Economic Policy*. Edited by R. Dornbusch and J. Frenkel. Baltimore: Johns Hopkins University Press, 1979. A useful survey.

Dixit, A. K., and V. Norman. *Theory of International Trade.* London: Cambridge University Press, 1980. See Chapters 2, 3, and 5 for an advanced treatment.

Houthakker, H. S., and S. P. Magee. "Income and Price Elasticities in World Trade." *Review of Economics and Statistics* 2 (1969).

Jones, R. W. "Stability Conditions in International Trade: A General Equilibrium Analysis." *International Economic Review* 2 (1961). Contains a detailed algebraic treatment of elasticity.

Krueger, A. *Foreign Trade Regimes and Economic Development: Liberalization Attempts and Consequences.* Cambridge: Ballinger, 1978. An assessment of LDC policies; part of a large project.

Leamer, E., and R. M. Stern. *Quantitative International Economics.* Boston: Allyn and Bacon, 1970. See Chapters 2, 3, 6, and 7 for a treatment of problems in empirical work.

Marshall, A. *Pure Theory of Foreign Trade.* London: London School of Economics and Political Science, 1930. The first (1879), and still one of the best, treatments of offer curves.

Mill, J. S. *Principles of Political Economy.* Edited by W. J. Ashley. London: Longman, 1909. Contains a statement of Mill's theory of international values.

Newbery, D., and J. Stiglitz. *The Theory of Commodity Price Stabilization.* Oxford: Oxford University Press, 1981. An insightful theoretical approach.

Stern, R. M., J. Francis, and B. Schumacher. *Price Elasticities in International Trade.* London: Macmillan, 1976. A comprehensive bibliography of estimates of price elasticities from 1960 to 1975.

Whalley, J. *Trade Liberalization among Major World Trading Areas.* Cambridge: MIT Press, 1985. Computable general equilibrium models.

CHAPTER 5

Factor Endowments

> Generally, abundant factors are relatively cheap, scanty factors are
> relatively dear, in each region. Commodities requiring for their pro-
> duction much of the former and little of the latter are exported in ex-
> change for goods that call for factors in the opposite proportions.
> Thus indirectly, factors in abundant supply are exported and factors
> in scanty supply are imported.   —B. OHLIN

This chapter seeks to uncover the effect of trade upon the domestic allocation
of resources and distribution of income. This demands a closer look at the internal workings of the economy. Up to now we have taken the production
possibility frontier as given. True, in the simple Ricardian model different
marginal rates of transformation were a consequence of different labor productivities. But this was mainly an illustration, and the different productivities were not themselves explained. We now probe below the surface to discover why production possibility frontiers have the slopes they do. More
generally, we wish to explain the pattern of comparative advantage.

   This is difficult because there are obviously many different reasons for
countries to trade. Anyone can see that climate gives tropical countries a
comparative advantage over temperate zones in tropical fruits relative to fir
products. Geographical proximity plays a role: New England and New York
are closer to much of Canada than to most of the United States, and trading
patterns have historically been sensitive to the location of waterways and to
changes in transportation technology. As we saw in section 7 of Chapter 1,
tastes can also help to determine comparative advantage. In this chapter we
first focus on yet another explanation: *factor endowments*. Factors are the
productive ingredients available to an economy: land, labor, capital, natural
resources, skills, and so on. The United States, for example, is highly endowed with physical capital—factories, equipment, and so forth—whereas
India relies much more on labor power. The importance of capital relative to

ELI F. HECKSCHER (1879–1952)

The Swedish economist Eli Heckscher is probably best known to English-speaking economists
for his book *Mercantilism,* a study of the economic
doctrine that preceded classical thought and
viewed the power of the nation-state as a policy
objective. Heckscher devoted much of his work to
a monumental study of Swedish economic history, but he also developed the essentials of the
factor-endowments theory of international trade in
a short article published in Swedish in 1919 and
translated into English thirty years later.

BERTIL OHLIN (1899–1979)

Heckscher's follower Bertil Ohlin developed and
elaborated the factor-endowments theory and
was responsible, through his writings, for the
wide exposure that the theory received, beginning in the 1930s. In addition to being a professor at Stockholm, Ohlin was a major Swedish
political figure. He served in the Riksdag
(Sweden's parliament), headed the Liberal party
for almost a quarter of a century, and was minister of trade during the Second World War. In
1979 Ohlin was awarded (jointly with James Meade of England) a Nobel prize
for his work in international economic theory.

labor in most other countries is somewhere in between, with Western Europe
closer to the U.S. end of the scale, and the less developed world closer to the
Indian. It is on these differences that we shall focus.

The theory we examine originated in the first half of this century and is
frequently referred to as the *Heckscher-Ohlin theory* after the Swedish economists Eli Heckscher and Bertil Ohlin, who developed it. The theory has been
refined and elaborated by many economists, a process that continues.

With all the conceivable explanations of comparative advantage, why
focus on this particular one? There are a number of reasons. First, different
factor endowments seem to be one of the more important (if not the most important) explanations, although the extent to which this is true is still a point
of lively debate among economists (and one to which we shall return).
Second, this particular approach will link international trade to the domestic
allocation of resources and distribution of income. Also, a country's factor
endowment is itself determined in part by economic phenomena: the present
capital stock is determined by past behavior, and the present state of the econ-

omy will determine the future capital stock. Thus it becomes possible to examine relationships between international trade and economic development and growth, and between trade and international capital movements. Finally, the factor-endowments approach can be made conceptually general enough to include many other possible explanations. That is, we can regard climate, technical secrets, patents, geographic location, and so forth as themselves factors of production. We can do this either by complicating our analysis with a large number of factors or by defining "capital" and "labor" in a general fashion. The more we do this, however, the more cumbersome or vague our conclusions become and the more difficult they are to apply to real situations. A theory that explains everything really explains nothing.

The factor-endowments approach is a powerful and useful one. But keep in mind two fundamental limits: (1) it addresses only trade due to comparative advantage (ignoring scale economies and imperfect competition); (2) it presumes a particular source of comparative advantage (international differences in relative factor endowments rather than differences in size, tastes, or technology).

1. THE HECKSCHER-OHLIN-SAMUELSON MODEL

The vehicle we shall use for presenting our theory is called the Heckscher-Ohlin-Samuelson model. (Paul Samuelson of MIT was instrumental in developing the structure of this model.) As before, assume two countries—called France and Germany, respectively—and two goods—apples and butane.

The Assumptions

The Heckscher-Ohlin-Samuelson model consists of four basic assumptions:

1. There are two countries, two goods, and two factors of production (call them capital and labor).

We need at least two factors in order to study the role of relative factor endowments; limiting the number to two makes the model as simple as possible.

2. The two factors are available in fixed amounts in each of the two countries, are fully mobile between industries within each country, but are immobile between countries; all markets have free and perfect competition.

This assumption establishes the difference between international and domestic trade, just as in the classical theory.

*3. The two countries are alike in every respect except for their endow-
ments of the two factors. In particular, the technologies for producing
apples and butane are available to both countries, and these countries
have identical tastes in the sense that if they face identical prices for apples and butane, they will consume them in identical proportions.*

The purpose of this assumption is to ensure that our conclusions reflect only
differences in factor endowments and not a mishmash of many causes.

*4. For each of the two goods there is a given technology (available to
both countries) indicating how capital and labor can be combined to
produce output. This technology possesses constant returns to scale
(varying both capital and labor in the same proportion will vary output
in that proportion).*

These assumptions are made for two distinct reasons. Assumptions 1, 2,
and 4 try to make the theory as simple as possible. If they do not correspond to reality, the arguments that follow from them may have to be made
more complex, but the factor-endowments basis of comparative advantage
will not be challenged. Assumption 3, however, ensures that our theory reflects only the basic idea that trade is due to different endowments. This assumption can be defended directly. Technology is really just knowledge,
which is not constrained by national boundaries; tastes for broad aggregates
should reflect basic human needs rather than national peculiarities. But
whether these arguments are relevant at an operational level is an empirical
question. We make assumption 3 simply to focus on the effects of different
factor endowments.

Some Definitions

According to assumption 3, the only difference between France and
Germany is in their endowments of capital and labor. A little jargon is appropriate to describe this difference. Denote the French endowments of capital
and labor by K^F and L^F and the German endowments by K^G and L^G. We shall
use the following definition:

KEY CONCEPT

France is said to be *capital abundant* relative to labor compared to
Germany if

$$K^F/L^F > K^G/L^G.$$

Notice that this definition has a double-barreled relativity, as does that of "comparative advantage" in Chapter 1 (since they involve a comparison of ratios, not of absolutes). It is interchangeable with the following:

Germany is labor abundant *relative to capital compared to France if*

$$L^G/K^G > L^F/K^F.$$

For concreteness we shall call the capital-abundant country France and the labor-abundant country Germany.

In each country apple and butane firms employ labor and capital to produce their products. The wages and rents the firms pay for these factors constitute the firms' production costs. All apple and butane firms in the same country must pay the same wages and rents since they compete with each other in factor markets. But since the two goods are different, they will not use capital and labor in equal proportions. Thus we need another definition.

KEY CONCEPT

The apple industry is said to be *capital intensive* relative to labor compared to the butane industry if, at identical wages and rents, the apple industry employs more capital per worker than the butane industry does.

This definition also has the by-now-familiar double-barreled relativity and so is equivalent to the following:

Butane is labor intensive *relative to capital compared to apples if, at identical wages and rents, the butane industry employs more workers per unit of capital than does the apple industry.*

We shall assume that apples are always the capital-intensive industry and that butane is the labor-intensive industry.

These are the two definitions suggested by the assumptions of the model. Factor *abundance* classifies the two countries since, by assumption 3, they differ in no other respect. Factor *intensity* classifies the two industries; it applies to both countries because they share the same technology.

Problems

5.1 Recall the discussion of U.S. trade patterns in section 10 of Chapter 1. Try to explain the apparent U.S. comparative advantage in terms of relative factor endowments (do not confine yourself to capital and labor; try to think of other relevant factors). Do the same for trade between the DCs and LDCs.

5.2 Suppose that England has 100 workers and 160 units of capital, whereas Portugal has 100 workers and 70 units of capital. Also suppose that 1 cask of wine requires 4 workers and 1 unit of capital to produce, whereas 1 bolt of cloth requires 5 units of capital and 2 workers to produce. Apply the definitions of factor abundance and factor intensity.

5.3 What do you think is true regarding the relative factor abundance of the following countries: the United States, France, Israel, Taiwan? What do you think is true regarding the relative factor intensity of the following industries in the United States: steel, wheat, research, street cleaning, teaching?

2. A BASIC RELATIONSHIP

In each country capital and labor are hired to produce outputs, and firms use no other inputs. Firms must pay a wage to hire labor and a rent to hire capital. Thus the wage and the rent in a country fully determine the costs of producing apples and butane in that country. Consider an increase in the wage with the rent remaining constant. This increases costs in both industries. But the two industries will not be affected the same way. Since the butane industry is labor-intensive, its costs will be increased proportionally more than costs in the apple industry, where labor is not as important. A rise in the wage relative to the rent increases the cost of the labor-intensive good (butane) relative to that of the capital-intensive good (apples). This relation is shown as the *relative cost* curve in Figure 5.1. (We can say more, but we will postpone until section 4 a detailed discussion of the relation between relative factor prices and relative commodity costs.)

Three features of the relative cost curve deserve emphasis. First, it is a *technological relationship;* its slope depends on relative factor intensities. Our assumption of constant returns to scale is important here; otherwise costs would depend upon scale, which could vary across countries, in addition to wages and rents.

Second, because the curve is a technological relationship and because the two countries have the same technology, the curve applies to *both* countries. Since factors are not internationally mobile and French labor does not compete with German labor, wages and rents in France need not equal those in Germany. Thus the two countries may be at different points on the relative cost curve—for example, France could be at F in Figure 5.1 and Germany at G. But both countries must be somewhere on the *same curve* as long as they have the same technology.

Finally, there is the relation between the costs of butane and apples and the prices of these goods. If a good is produced in a country, its price must equal its cost in long-run equilibrium—if cost exceeds price, no one will wish to produce it and the industry will close down; if price exceeds cost, the profit will induce competition, forcing the two into equality. Thus if the wage-rental ratio in Germany equals OA in Figure 5.1, and if apples and butane are both

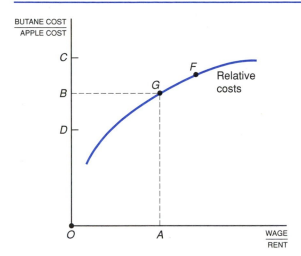

FIGURE 5.1 **Relative Factor Prices and Relative Costs** With constant returns to scale, the ratio of wages to rents determines the ratio of the cost of butane to that of apples.

produced in Germany, then OB must equal the relative price of butane in terms of apples. But if a good is not actually produced, cost could exceed price (the reason for not producing it). Thus if Germany is specialized in apples, the relative price of butane in terms of apples could equal OD, for example. Or if Germany is specialized in butane, the relative price could equal, say, OC.

Problems

5.4 Redraw Figure 5.1, reflecting the case in which butane production is capital-intensive. What would the curve look like if, by a fluke of nature, butane and apples used exactly the same technique of production?

5.5 Suppose that in England 1 cask of wine requires 4 workers and 1 unit of capital to produce and 1 bolt of cloth requires 2 workers and 5 units of capital. Derive a curve like that in Figure 5.1. What could you conclude about English production if the wage and the rent in England both equaled 1 and the price of cloth in terms of wine was 2?

5.6 Suppose that, as a result of some innovation, it is now possible to produce butane with fewer workers per unit of capital than before. No change occurs in apple technology. What is the effect on the curve in Figure 5.1?

5.7* What would the curve in Figure 5.1 look like if butane was relatively capital-intensive at low wage-rental ratios but relatively labor-intensive at high wage-rental ratios, with apples and butane using the same technique at some intermediate wage-rental ratio? What circumstances could cause two industries to have this relation?

3. THE HECKSCHER-OHLIN THEORY: COMPARATIVE ADVANTAGE AND FACTOR PRICES

The model described in section 1 is used to develop four basic propositions, all of which have frightening names. We will discuss two of them in this section and two in the next.

The Heckscher-Ohlin Theorem

The Heckscher-Ohlin theorem explains the pattern of comparative advantage in terms of factor endowments:

> *A country has a comparative advantage in the good that makes relatively intensive use of the country's relatively abundant factor.*

Thus in the present case France will have a comparative advantage in apples and Germany in butane. Note that the theorem is consistent with the definitions of the last section: it will not claim that both countries have a comparative advantage in the same good.

Once the Heckscher-Ohlin theorem tells us the pattern of comparative advantage, we can apply the results of the previous chapters: France will export apples to Germany in exchange for butane, and so forth.

The Heckscher-Ohlin theorem is easily proved using the relative cost curve discussed in the previous section and reproduced in Figure 5.2. Recall that the relative cost curve applies to both countries. Suppose that France and Germany are both in autarky. Since both countries have the same tastes, the relative labor abundance of Germany will be reflected in a lower autarkic wage-rental ratio (equivalently, the relative capital abundance of France will be reflected in a lower rental-wage ratio and a higher wage-rental ratio). This is shown in Figure 5.2, where *OG* denotes Germany's autarkic wage-rental ratio and *OF* denotes France's. In autarky each country must produce both goods for itself, so *OB* denotes the German autarkic price of butane in terms of apples, and *OA* the French autarkic price. The relative autarkic price of butane is higher in France than in Germany: Germany has a comparative advantage in butane and France in apples.

Figure 5.3 shows the same production possibility frontiers for France and Germany as did Figure 1.6. France is the relatively capital-abundant country and, therefore, is better equipped to produce the capital-intensive good, apples. This is reflected in the figure by the generally steeper slope of France's curve. (The next section will demonstrate why this is so.) Since the two countries are assumed to have identical tastes, autarkic equilibrium in France (at *A*) will feature a steeper slope than autarkic equilibrium in Germany (at *B*). Thus, without trade, apples are relatively cheaper in terms of butane in France than in Germany.

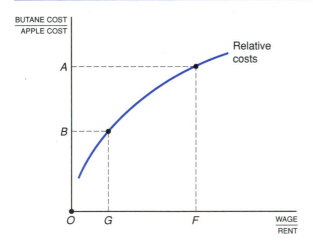

FIGURE 5.2 **The Heckscher-Ohlin Theorem** In autarky, the country with relatively more labor will have a relatively low wage and, therefore, a relatively low cost of production of the labor-intensive good.

The greater the dissimilarity in French and German relative factor endowments, the greater the dissimilarity in their production possibility frontiers. If the two countries had identical endowments of capital per worker, their frontiers would have identical shapes—the frontier of the larger country would be simply a blowup of that of the smaller country. If, on the other hand, France's relative capital abundance exceeded Germany's by enough, each point on France's frontier would have a steeper slope than every point on

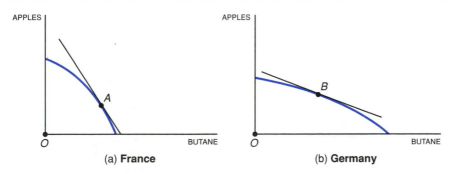

FIGURE 5.3 **Production Possibility Frontiers** Each country's production possibility frontier is skewed toward the good that makes relatively intensive use of the country's relatively abundant factor.

Germany's (as was true of Figure 1.5). In this case, you will recall, free trade must cause at least one country to specialize completely. This brings us to the second basic proposition.

The Factor-Price Equalization Theorem

Our second proposition, the factor-price equalization theorem, is as follows:

Free international trade between two countries will cause factor prices in the countries to become more equal. If both countries continue to produce both goods with free trade, their factor prices will actually be equal.

Thus if France and Germany each produce both apples and butane while freely trading, the French wage will equal the German and the French rental will also equal the German. This proposition can be proved with the aid of Figure 5.4. Suppose that German and French autarkic wage-rental ratios equal *OG* and *OF,* respectively, so that relative autarkic prices in Germany and France equal *OB* and *OA*. If these countries engage in free trade, world prices must be somewhere between the autarkic prices—say, equal to *OC*. If each country produces both goods, then *OC* also equals relative costs in both countries, and *OH* must, therefore, equal the wage-rental ratio in both France and Germany. Since relative factor prices are equal, absolute factor prices must be equal also. Otherwise one country would have uniformly higher factor prices than the other, and so costs—and thus prices—could not be the same.

If either country specializes, factor prices need not be completely equalized because costs need not equal international prices and, therefore, each other. Suppose, for example, that Germany specializes in butane while France produces both goods. Then French costs equal relative prices, *OC*, but German costs could be somewhat less—say, equal to *OD*. Then the German wage-rental ratio equals *OJ* while the French equals *OH*. Factor prices are not completely equalized by trade, but they are more nearly equal than they would be in autarky.

The factor-price equalization theorem reflects the basic presumption of the Heckscher-Ohlin approach: trade is due to different factor endowments because factors cannot be moved from country to country. Suppose that France and Germany freely trade and that both countries produce both goods so that their factor prices are equalized. If some revolutionary development were to enable labor and capital to move freely between countries, just as they can move within a country, nothing would happen. With equal factor prices, no factor has any incentive to move. Free trade has been a complete substitute for international factor mobility. If specialization prevents complete factor-price equalization, trade in goods is only a partial substitute for factor mobility.

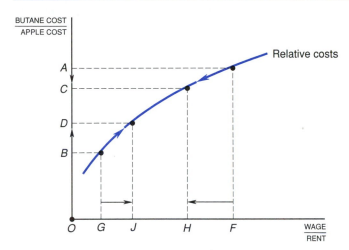

FIGURE 5.4 **Factor-Price Equalization** By forcing commodity prices together, international trade also tends to force factor prices together across countries.

Problems

5.8 Refine your answers to Problem **5.1** in light of the discussion of this section.

5.9 Agricultural trade between the United States and Europe is not free. The yield per acre on a French farm is typically much higher than on an American farm devoted to the same crop. Does this indicate relative American inefficiency or backwardness? Explain in terms of the theory. What would you expect to be true of relative French and American prices of relevant factors? What do you think would be the effect of a movement to free trade?

5.10 Suppose that when each cask of wine produced requires 4 labor units and 1 capital unit and each bolt of cloth requires 2 labor units and 5 capital units, the wage and the rent each equal 100. What is the cost of wine and cloth? Suppose the wage and the rent both increase to 110. By what percentage have they risen? What are the new costs of the two goods, and by what percentages have they changed? Answer the same questions if instead the wage increases from 100 to 120 and the rent from 100 to 105. Answer the questions if instead the wage falls from 100 to 90 while the rent rises from 100 to 120.

5.11* Discuss in detail the Heckscher-Ohlin and the factor-price equalization theorems in the context of Problem **5.7***.

5.12* Suppose that we retain all of the assumptions of the Heckscher-Ohlin-Samuelson model *except* that we assume that all French citizens have a much greater relative preference for apple consumption than all German citizens (who, therefore, have a much greater preference for butane consumption). How is the Heckscher-Ohlin theorem affected?

4. THE HECKSCHER-OHLIN THEORY: INCOME DISTRIBUTION AND GROWTH

We now discuss the remaining two of the four basic propositions of the Heckscher-Ohlin theory.

The Stolper-Samuelson Theorem

The Stolper-Samuelson theorem links international trade to the domestic distribution of income. The relative cost curve in Figures 5.1, 5.2, and 5.4 implies that if both goods are produced, an increase in the relative price of the labor-intensive good (butane) increases the wage relative to the rent so that labor's income rises relative to capital's. But in 1941 an even stronger result was obtained by Paul Samuelson and Wolfgang Stolper, now at the University of Michigan.

> *An increase in the relative price of the labor-intensive good will increase the wage rate relative to both commodity prices and reduce the rent relative to both commodity prices.*

If an increase in the relative price of butane raises the wage-rental ratio, laborers gain relative to capitalists. But this does not mean that they gain absolutely. If the wage were to rise less than the price of butane, a worker who spent his income mainly on butane would be worse off in spite of the wage increase. The theorem asserts that this will not happen. Wages will rise relative to *both* commodity prices, so workers will be better off no matter how they spend their incomes; rents will fall relative to both commodity prices, so capitalists will be unambiguously worse off.

By combining this result with the Heckscher-Ohlin theorem, we can see how trade affects domestic income distribution. A country has a comparative advantage in the good intensive in its relatively abundant factor. Free trade will increase the relative price of that good and so, by the Stolper-Samuelson theorem, increase the real income of the relatively abundant factor and reduce that of the relatively scarce factor. Since the country as a whole gains from trade, the abundant factor gains more than the scarce factor loses. The former could in principle compensate the latter for its losses and still gain. A sufficiently elaborate political system might undertake such compensation. Otherwise there will be a class in the economy permanently harmed by free trade, even though the country as a whole gains.

For example, the United States in its early history had an abundance of land and scarcity of capital relative to Europe. The farmers of the West and South (who owned land) favored free trade, whereas the businessmen of the Northeast (who owned capital) favored restrictions on trade.

Proving the Stolper-Samuelson Theorem

The theorem is easy to prove. Suppose, for example, that the price of butane rises by 10 percent and that of apples remains unchanged, both goods being produced. Then the cost of butane rises by 10 percent, and this cost consists of the cost of labor and capital. The wage and rent cannot both rise by exactly 10 percent because wages rise relative to rents. They cannot both rise by more than 10 percent because the cost of butane would have to rise by more than 10 percent; similarly, the wage and rent cannot both fail to rise by at least 10 percent. Thus one rises more than 10 percent and one does not. As wages rise relative to rents, it is the wage that rises more than 10 percent and thus increases relative to both commodity prices.

The price of apples, and so its cost, has not changed. But the wage has increased. Thus the rent must actually fall since otherwise the cost of apples would have to increase. Therefore, the rent falls relative to both commodity prices.

The Rybczynski Theorem

While he was still a student, T. M. Rybczynski, now chief economist at Lazard Bros. Co., Ltd., in London, proved a proposition relating trade and economic growth. The latter will be reflected in changes in a country's endowments of the factors. Like the Stolper-Samuelson theorem, this proposition applies when both goods are produced.

At constant prices, an increase in one factor endowment will increase by a greater proportion the output of the good intensive in that factor and will reduce the output of the other good.

Suppose, for example, that the French capital stock increases by 10 percent, the labor force remaining constant. Then the theorem asserts that French apple output will increase by more than 10 percent and French butane output will fall. This is illustrated in Figure 5.5. The increase in capital must shift the French production possibility frontier outward. In the figure it shifts from curve *ABC* to *DEF*. Suppose France is initially at *B*. Then the Rybczynski theorem asserts that point *E* on the new production possibility frontier, which has the same slope as *B* on the old (thus the same MRT_{AB} and corresponds to the same relative price), lies to the northwest of *B*, as illustrated.

By combining this result with the Heckscher-Ohlin theorem, we can see how economic growth affects a nation's trade. If a country's capital stock increases by, say, 10 percent, national income will rise by some smaller proportion because only part of national income comes from the earnings of capital.

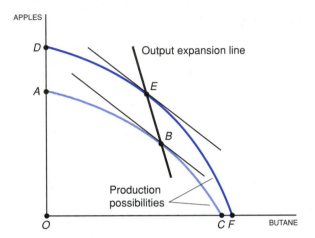

FIGURE 5.5 **The Rybczynski Theorem**   An increase in the capital stock shifts the production possibility frontier out in such a way that *E* is northwest of *B* if the slope of the new frontier at *E* is the same as that of the old frontier at *B* and if capital-intensive goods are measured on the vertical axis.

This increased income will normally be spent on both goods so that, at constant prices, national *demand* for both goods will rise by less than 10 percent. The Rybczynski theorem tells us that the *supply* of the capital-intensive good (apples) rises by more than 10 percent while the supply of butane falls. Thus apple supply rises relative to demand, and butane demand rises relative to supply. If the country is capital-abundant, the Heckscher-Ohlin theorem tells

---

Proving the Rybczynski Theorem

The Rybczynski theorem is proved with the same logic as the Stolper-Samuelson theorem. Suppose the capital stock increases by 10 percent and the labor force is unchanged. If both goods continue to be produced, factor prices will not change by the factor-price equalization theorem, and so the techniques of production will not change either. The output of both goods cannot rise by 10 percent since this would require 10 percent more labor and the labor force has not increased. Similarly, the output of both goods cannot rise by more than 10 percent. They cannot both fail to rise by 10 percent either, or else the increased capital stock could not all be utilized. Thus the output of one good rises by more than 10 percent, and that of the other does not. Since apples are capital-intensive, it must be apple output that rises by more than 10 percent. The labor force has not changed, but the apple industry has expanded and so increased its use of labor. Therefore, the output of butane must actually fall.

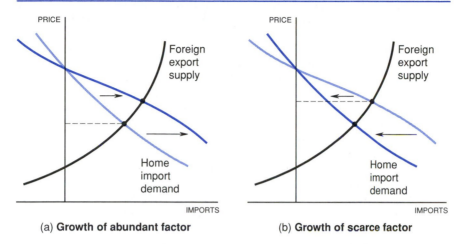

(a) **Growth of abundant factor**   (b) **Growth of scarce factor**

FIGURE 5.6   **The Effect of Economic Growth on International Trade**   The Rybczynski theorem is used to describe the effects on a country's trade of the growth of one of its factors.

us that it exports apples and imports butane so that the growth of capital causes the country to trade more at each price: its import demand curve shifts to the right. If the country is instead labor-abundant, its import demand curve shifts to the left. The general conclusion, illustrated in Figure 5.6, is that economic growth that accentuates a country's relative factor abundance (and so makes the country less like the rest of the world) shifts its import demand curve out; growth that moderates the country's relative factor abundance shifts the import demand curve in.

Problems

5.13 What do you think is the consequence of the historic rise in the American wage, relative to other factor prices, on the cost of a university education? On the cleanliness of city streets? Specifically relate your answers to the theory.

5.14 Show how your answers to Problem **5.10** illustrate the Stolper-Samuelson theorem.

5.15 The savings rate in Japan after the Second World War has been much higher than in most other countries. What is the likely effect on relative Japanese factor abundance? Use the theory of this section to predict the likely consequences.

5.16 Suppose that a country, where a cask of wine requires 4 and 1 units of labor and capital, respectively, and where a bolt of cloth requires 2 and 5 units of labor and capital, respectively, produces 200 casks of wine and 200 bolts of cloth. How much capital and labor is this economy using? Suppose wine output falls to 80 casks. What are the changes in percentage terms? How much capital and labor is now required? What are these changes in percentage terms? How does this illustrate the Rybczynski theorem?

5.17 Calculate the outputs of wine and cloth in Portugal and England if the countries have the technology described in Problem **5.16,** if England has 100 workers and 160 capital units, and if Portugal has 100 workers and 70 capital units. (Do this either by trial and error or by setting up and solving two simultaneous equations in two unknowns.) Show how a comparison of Portugal and England illustrates the Rybczynski theorem. Show how it also demonstrates the Heckscher-Ohlin theorem, if the two countries are freely trading.

5.18 Using the results of this section, describe the possible effects of economic growth upon the terms of trade. Upon internal income distribution.

5.19* The Stolper-Samuelson and Rybczynski theorems apply to situations in which both goods are actually produced. Suppose instead that France specializes completely in the production of apples. How would French wages and rents be affected by a rise in the price of apples? By a rise in the price of butane? How are *real* wages affected? How would French outputs respond to a change in factor endowments with the prices of apples and butane unchanged?

5.20* The Stolper-Samuelson theorem assumes that both factors are freely mobile between industries within a country. But in fact this is not true, at least for substantial time periods. Suppose, for example, that labor is freely mobile between apple and butane production but that capital is immobile so that each industry's capital stock is fixed. Discuss the Stolper-Samuelson theorem in this case.

5.* *EXPLORING FURTHER:* ANALYSIS OF THE HECKSCHER-OHLIN-SAMUELSON MODEL—THE FIRM

Consider the behavior of a single firm—say, a French producer of apples. The firm has two decisions to make: how much capital and labor to hire, and how many apples to produce. That is, it must determine its technique of production and its scale of operations. Its problem is illustrated in Figure 5.7.

The curved line through points A and B gives the combinations of capital and labor that can be used to produce 1 bushel of apples. This curve, called an *isoquant,* must slope downward since the only way to continue producing the same output with less capital is by adding more labor. A distinct isoquant corresponds to each level of output, and larger outputs correspond to isoquants farther from the origin. The negative of the slope of an isoquant is called the marginal rate of technical substitution of capital for labor and is denoted $MRTS_{KL}^{A}$.

The isoquants in Figure 5.7 are "bowed inward"—that is, $MRTS_{KL}^{A}$ increases as successive units of labor are replaced by capital. Why? At a point such as A the bushel of apples is produced by a very low capital-labor ratio— that is, many workers are employed per unit of capital. If 1 worker is laid off,

---

KEY CONCEPT

The *marginal rate of technical substitution* of capital for labor is the amount of additional capital that must be employed to keep output unchanged if 1 fewer worker is employed.

---

she will hardly be missed and there will be little loss of output; only a small amount of capital need be added to maintain output at 1 bushel. But at point B there are fewer workers per unit of capital; 1 fewer worker implies a substantial loss of output, and 1 more unit of capital a relatively slight gain. Thus $MRTS_{KL}^A$ must rise as we go from A to B—that is, the isoquant is bowed inward.

Suppose that the firm has somehow decided to produce exactly 1 bushel of apples. The firm knows its scale of operations and presumably knows what it must pay for capital and labor. The question is which technique to employ. What point on the isoquant costs the least?

Suppose first that the firm were to spend exactly Fr 100. If the full Fr 100 were spent on capital, Fr 100/r units would be employed where r denotes the rent; if only labor were hired, Fr 100/w units would be employed where w denotes labor's wage. By dividing the Fr 100 between capital and labor, any combination on the line FC in Figure 5.8 can be employed. Thus FC denotes all combinations of capital and labor that cost exactly Fr 100 at the given

---

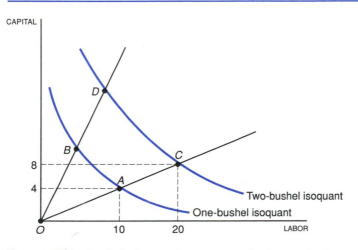

FIGURE 5.7 **Apple-Industry Isoquants** An isoquant shows the alternative techniques available for producing a specified amount of output.

rental and wage rates. The slope of FC is given by

$$-\frac{OF}{OC} = -\frac{\text{Fr } 100/r}{\text{Fr } 100/w} = -\frac{w}{r}.$$

Therefore, the slope of this "budget line" reflects the ratio of wages to rents and nothing else. The total amount spent determines how far the budget line is from the origin. If the budget were reduced from Fr 100 to Fr 50, for example, the line FC would shift to DE, which has the same slope but is only half as far from the origin as FC. (How would FC be affected if instead the wage rate were to double?)

The firm's problem of finding the least-cost technique to produce 1 bushel of apples is the geometric problem of pushing the budget line FC as close to the origin as possible while still touching the one-bushel isoquant. This must occur at a point of tangency such as A in Figure 5.8. The firm will always produce at least cost if it uses capital and labor in such proportions as to cause the $MRTS_{KL}^{A}$ to equal w/r, the wage-rental ratio.

Thus the wage-rental ratio determines the technique of production once the firm knows which isoquant to produce on. But what determines the scale of operations? This problem is simplified by the assumption of constant returns to scale, which means that an equiproportional change in *both* capital and labor will always change output by that same proportion. Doubling the amount of capital and labor used by an apple firm, for example, will double its output of apples. Constant returns to scale are more relevant the more long run our point of view because in the short run it is impossible to vary all inputs. Since we are interested in long-run questions such as the allocation of resources, this is no problem.

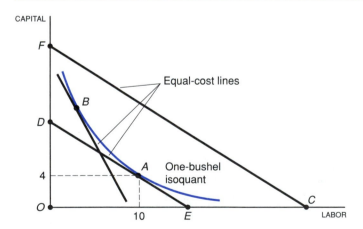

FIGURE 5.8 Finding the Technique of Production At the least-cost technique, an isoquant is tangent to a budget line (as at point A).

The one-bushel isoquant now tells us everything we need to know about the technology of producing apples. If, for example, the wage-rental ratio is equal to the $MRTS_{KL}^A$ at point A on the one-bushel isoquant in Figure 5.8 so that the cheapest way to produce 1 bushel of apples is by using 10 units of labor and 4 of capital, then the cheapest way of producing 2 bushels of apples is to use the same technique at twice the scale—that is, to employ 20 units of labor and 8 units of capital. In other words, point A is the technique that should be used for *each* unit of apples regardless of how many apples are produced. Constant returns to scale ensure that the problem of choosing the technique of production is entirely independent of the problem of choosing the scale of operations.

Suppose that the wage-rental ratio increases, say, to the value indicated by the slope of the straight line through B in Figure 5.8. The least-cost technique for producing apples is now given by point B, where the $MRTS_{KL}^A$ equals the new wage-rental ratio. Firms will substitute capital for labor so that each unit of apples will now be produced by technique B regardless of how many total apples continue to be produced. In this way we can use the one-bushel isoquant to determine the technique of production—that is, the ratio of capital to labor employed in the apple industry for each value of the wage-rental ratio.

Problems

5.21 Suppose that the production of each bushel of apples requires 4 (or more) units of capital together with 2 (or more) units of labor. Draw the one-bushel isoquant. What can you say about the $MRTS_{KL}^A$ in this case? What technique of production would an apple producer choose if $w/r = 5$? If $w/r = 1$? For other values of w/r?

5.22 Suppose that each bolt of cloth requires 1 unit (or more) of capital plus 4 units (or more) of labor to produce. Answer the same questions as in Problem **5.21.**

5.23 Suppose that any quantity of cloth can be produced either as described in Problem **5.22** *or* by using 7 (or more) units of capital plus 1 (or more) units of labor. Answer the same questions as in Problem **5.21.**

5.24* Suppose that K units of capital plus L units of labor can always produce $(K/L)^{1/2}$ units of wine. Answer the same questions as in the above problem.

6.* *EXPLORING FURTHER:* ANALYSIS OF THE HECKSCHER-OHLIN-SAMUELSON MODEL—THE GENERAL EQUILIBRIUM OF PRODUCTION

Suppose that the prices of apples and butane, P_A and P_B, are given. These might be free-trade prices determined by reciprocal demand, or they might be autarkic equilibrium prices. It matters not; we take them as starting points.

The apple technology, as we have seen, can be completely described by any single isoquant, and so can the butane technology. Figure 5.9 shows the isoquant that produces one franc's worth of apples and that which produces one franc's worth of butane. For example, if a bushel of apples costs half a franc, the isoquant that has been drawn is that which shows how to produce two bushels of apples.

Each firm, regardless of how much it produces, will use the point on its isoquant where the $MRTS_{KL}$ equals the wage-rental ratio. The line $CQRD$ in Figure 5.9 has been drawn tangent to both curves. If the wage-rental ratio is equal to minus the slope of this line *(OC/OD)*, the cheapest way to produce one franc's worth of apples is to employ technique Q, and the cheapest way to produce one franc's worth of butane is to use technique R. The figure shows apples to be relatively capital-intensive.

If both goods are produced, each franc's worth of apples will be produced by Q, and so the total amounts of capital and labor employed by the apple industry will lie somewhere on the ray through O and Q. Similarly, the total capital and labor devoted to butane must lie somewhere on the ray through O and R. Suppose that G denotes the amounts of the two factors available to the economy as a whole. Then this total must be divided between apple production and butane production in just such a way as both to give each industry the factor proportions indicated by its respective ray and to add up exactly to G. To see this geometrically, complete the parallelogram formed by the two rays and by points G and O in Figure 5.9; draw a line *(EG)* through G parallel to *OR*, and draw another line *(FG)* through G parallel to *OQ*. The completed parallelogram is *OEGFO*. Point E indicates the total capital and labor used in the apple industry, and F shows the factors allocated to butane production. *EG* is parallel to, and the same length as, *OF*. Thus adding *OE* and *OF* together is the same as adding *EG* to *OE* or adding *FG* to *OF;* we end up at G.

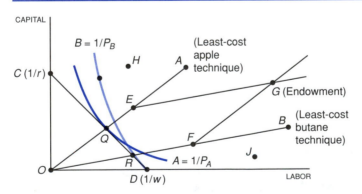

FIGURE 5.9 **The General Equilibrium of Production** For factor markets to clear, the least-cost techniques must operate at scales that together require the economy's total endowment, G.

Since Q shows the capital and labor required to produce one franc's worth of apples, E will produce OE/OQ francs' worth of apples. For example, if E is twice as far from the origin as Q, then two francs' worth of apples is being produced (or four bushels at a price of half a franc per bushel). Likewise, OF/OR francs' worth of butane is being produced.

Figure 5.9 also reveals what factor prices must be in equilibrium. The line $CQRD$ is the common tangent to both one-franc isoquants and, therefore, shows the combinations of capital and labor that cost exactly one franc. Thus C shows the amount of capital that can be hired for one franc: $1/r$ units. The rent is, therefore, $r = 1/OC$. Similarly, D shows the labor that can be hired for one franc, $1/w$, so that $w = 1/OD$.

Problems

5.25 Suppose each wine cask requires 4 units of capital and 2 units of labor while each bolt of cloth requires 1 unit of capital and 4 units of labor. What will be produced if the economy has 10 units of labor and 6 units of capital? What will factor prices be if the price of wine is Fr 2 and that of cloth is Fr 1?

5.26 What will happen to the outputs of the two goods if, in Problem **5.25,** the capital stock increases to 8 units? What happens to factor prices if the price of cloth increases to Fr 2?

5.27 The discussion in this section assumed that the economy-wide capital-labor ratio was between the least-cost capital-labor ratios in the two sectors—that is, G in Figure 5.9 was between the rays OQ and OR. What would happen if instead the economy's endowment were as indicated in Figure 5.9 by point H? By point J?

5.28* How do your answers to Problem **5.25** change if a bolt of cloth can be produced *either* by the technique described in that problem *or* by 7 units of capital plus 1 unit of labor.

5.29* Use isoquants to illustrate, in a diagram like Figure 5.9, the situation described in Problem **5.7*.**

5.30* Suppose that an economy is producing both goods, as in Figure 5.9. Now introduce a third good, cloth, with its own distinctive isoquants. If the prices of apples and butane do not change, under what circumstances will cloth be produced instead of one of the other goods? When will all three goods be produced? Complete the parallelogram in this latter case.

7.* *EXPLORING FURTHER:* ANALYSIS OF THE HECKSCHER-OHLIN-SAMUELSON MODEL—BASIC PROPOSITIONS

The Rybczynski Theorem

In Figure 5.10 the ray OA indicates, as in Figure 5.9, the least-cost technique for producing apples, and the ray OB indicates the least-cost technique

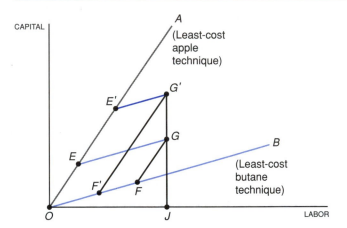

FIGURE 5.10 Proving the Rybczynski Theorem An increase *GG'* in the capital stock expands the apple sector from *E* to *E'* and contracts the butane sector from *F* to *F'*.

in the butane industry. The economy's endowment is indicated by *G* so that *OJ* units of labor and *JG* units of capital are available. *E* and *F* indicate the allocations to the apple and butane industries, respectively, so that apple output is proportional to the distance *OE* and butane output is proportional to *OF*.

Now suppose that the capital stock increases in the amount *GG'*, the labor force and all prices remaining unchanged. Then the endowment point moves from *G* to *G'*. Completing the new parallelogram, we see that the allocations to the apple and butane industries are now *E'* and *F'*, respectively. It is clear from the geometry that the output of the labor-intensive good, butane, must fall (in an amount proportional to *FF'*) and the output of the capital-intensive apples must increase. Furthermore, the proportional rise in apple production, *EE'/OE*, exceeds the proportional increase in the capital stock, *GG'/JG*.

The Stolper-Samuelson Theorem

In Figure 5.11, point *Q* again shows the capital and labor required to produce each franc's worth of apples, and *R* the requirements for one franc's worth of butane. The wage is $1/OD$ and the rent $1/OC$. Now suppose that the price of butane increases, that of apples remaining unchanged. Since butane is worth more, less butane corresponds to a franc's worth: if the price of butane rises from one-third of a franc to one-half, for example, the number of units of butane worth a franc drops from three to two. Thus the one-franc isoquant for butane shifts inward; in Figure 5.11 the isoquant through *R* shifts to that through *H*, the quantity *HR/OR* reflecting the proportionate rise in the

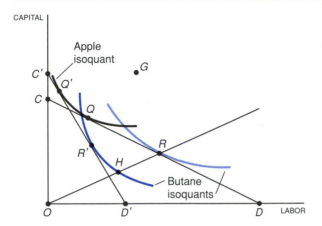

FIGURE 5.11 **The Stolper-Samuelson Theorem** A rise in the price of butane shifts its unit-value isoquant inward, altering factor rewards.

price of butane. Since the price of apples is unchanged, the one-franc isoquant for apples stays put.

The new common tangent to both isoquants is the line $C'Q'R'D'$. Since $1/OC'$ is less than $1/OC$, the rental has fallen, and the wage has risen because $1/OD'$ exceeds $1/OD$. Furthermore, $D'D/OD$ exceeds HR/OR: the proportionate rise in the wage exceeds that in the price of the labor-intensive good (butane). Thus we have the Stolper-Samuelson theorem: an increase in any commodity price produces a proportionally greater increase in the price of the factor intensive to that good and a fall in the price of the other factor.

Note that the change in factor prices induces both industries to alter their techniques of production. The butane industry replaces the technique H by R', and the apple industry replaces Q by Q'. Both industries respond to the rise in the relative cost of labor by switching to more capital-intensive techniques. How is it possible for *every* firm in the economy to become more capital intensive if the overall amounts of available capital and labor do not change? The labor-intensive industry (butane) must expand, and the capital-intensive industry (apples) must contract. The *intraindustry* substitution of capital for labor must be accompanied by an *interindustry* substitution of butane for apples so that the total employment of capital and labor does not change.

The Factor-Price Equalization and Heckscher-Ohlin Theorems

In proving the Stolper-Samuelson theorem we have shown that the wage-rental ratio is positively related to the cost of the labor-intensive good. This justifies Figure 5.1, which was used to establish the Heckscher-Ohlin and factor-price equalization theorems. But we can add to our understanding of these propositions by looking at them again from a slightly different point of view.

Consider first the Heckscher-Ohlin theorem. In Figure 5.10 point G' can represent the endowment of the capital-abundant country and G that of the labor-abundant country. Clearly, the former must have a greater output of capital-intensive goods, relative to labor-intensive goods, than the latter. By assumption, the two countries consume the two goods in the same proportions. Since imports and exports equal the differences between production and consumption, the capital-abundant country must be exporting the capital-intensive good, and the labor-abundant country must be exporting the labor-intensive good. If point G' is moved up (or G is moved down) enough to cross the ray from the origin and thus cause specialization to the good intensive in the relatively abundant factor, this argument will not be changed.

We turn next to factor-price equalization. For given international commodity prices we can proceed, as in Figure 5.9, to find the budget line corresponding to production of both goods and, thereby, the factor prices that must hold and the techniques of production that must be used if both goods are produced. Suppose these techniques are as indicated by the rays OA and OB in Figure 5.10. Then any pair of countries with endowments (such as G and G' in the figure) between these rays will in fact produce both goods and have identical factor prices, and use identical techniques, provided that the countries engage in free trade at the given international commodity prices. If, on the other hand, a country has an endowment that is not between the two rays, free trade will cause that country to specialize completely in the production of one of the goods and to have factor prices different from those in the other country.

Problems

5.31 Using the technology described in Problems **5.21** and **5.22,** illustrate the four propositions with specific numerical examples.

5.32 In Figure 5.11 complete the parallelograms from point G to find the allocations of capital and labor to the two industries both before and after the price change. Compare the two situations.

5.33* Illustrate the Rybczynski theorem, if possible, in the case described in Problem **5.30*,** when all three goods are produced.

8. *CASE STUDY:* THE INTERNATIONAL WHEAT MARKET

This and the following two sections illustrate the factor-endowments theory.

One would expect, in accord with that theory, that countries relatively well endowed with the lands and climate so important for wheat cultivation would have a comparative advantage in the crop. This is indeed the case since the major wheat exporters are the United States, Canada, Argentina, and Australia. Historically, Eastern Europe, with its plains, has had a comparative advantage over Western Europe in wheat. The difficulty of transporting the crop formerly limited trade but did not eliminate it: ancient Greece imported wheat from southern Russia, and for centuries Western Europe has imported the crop from the East. In the latter part of the nineteenth century, Australia and the Western Hemisphere were opened up to wheat cultivation, and transportation costs dropped dramatically. The crop now enters international trade on a large scale, and patterns of trade and production are as suggested by our theory. But it is also true that much of the industrial world heavily protects its agriculture. Trade in wheat is far from free; Western Europe, formerly a minor exporter, continues to be a large producer of wheat and now exports a significant amount.

Table 5.1 shows data about wheat production and trade for selected countries. Several features emerge from the table. First, there are substantial differences in yields, even among those countries with broadly similar economic structures and between whom trade is otherwise free: compare yields in the United States and Canada with those in the three Western European countries. Our theory predicts that, if trade is free and if countries do not specialize completely, they will have equal factor prices and, therefore, will employ the same techniques of production. But the absence of free trade in wheat prevents this from being as true as it otherwise would be. A second notable feature of the table is the fact that the countries with a comparative advantage in wheat (the United States and Canada) have *lower* yields than those with a comparative disadvantage. This seems strange since comparative advantage is associated with relative efficiency. But our theory explains such a state of affairs. The United States and Canada, because they are relatively land-abundant, employ more land-intensive methods—that is, each farmer works a larger quantity of land than does a farmer in France, Germany, or the United Kingdom, where the high yields reflect a large input of labor per acre. The United States is also a capital-abundant country and employs capital-intensive methods of farming; otherwise the U.S. entry in Table 5.1 would be even lower.

TABLE 5.1 **Wheat Production and Trade of Selected Countries, 1990**

	Yield (metric ton/hectare)	Production (million metric tons)	Net exports (million metric tons)
United Kingdom	7.0	14.0	3.6
France	6.5	33.3	17.0
West Germany	6.6	11.1	−1.6
United States	2.7	74.5	27.0
Canada	2.3	31.7	18.0
USSR (1985)	1.7	83.0	−19.0

SOURCE: Food and Agriculture Organization, *Monthly Bulletin of Statistics.*

Two countries look a bit strange in Table 5.1. We have said that France is not a relatively efficient producer of wheat, but the third column reveals that country as the third-largest wheat exporter in the table. The reason is that French agriculture is protected by the Common Agricultural Policy (CAP) of the European Union (EU), so France, which is an efficient wheat producer relative to the rest of the EU, can sell the crop in a market shielded from the rest of the world. In addition, the CAP subsidizes agricultural exports from the EU. Thus the large French exports do not reflect free international trade but, rather, the reverse. We shall examine the CAP further when we study the EU in Chapter 20.

The former USSR has both the lowest yield and the highest production in the table, yet it is a hefty importer. With a large endowment of suitable lands, the region employs land-intensive methods, as indicated by the low yield. Russia has historically been a major exporter of wheat and has a comparative advantage over much of the world in the crop, although her wheat-growing areas are less desirable and have a more unpredictable climate than those of the United States and Canada. Also the former USSR is a large wheat *consumer* and has often been a large net importer even though it is the world's largest producer and still an exporter of the crop to Eastern Europe.

Problems

5.34 On the basis of Table 5.1, what can you conjecture about the relative sizes of the prices of wheat cropland in the various countries, relative to other factor prices?

5.35 Suppose that all the countries in Table 5.1 were to adopt completely free international trade, including wheat. How do you think the various entries in the table would be affected?

9. *CASE STUDY:* RELATIVE WAGE MOVEMENTS

An examination of relative wage movements since the Second World War furnishes another application of the factor-endowments theory. As pointed out in Chapter 1, trade in manufactured goods between developed countries has expanded rapidly since the Second World War. This expansion has been accompanied by (and partially caused by) a significant lessening of trade barriers: tariffs and transportation costs have fallen, business executives have become more internationally minded, communications have become more efficient, firms have gone multinational, and so forth. If the expansion is interpreted as a movement toward free trade, the theory implies that factor prices and production techniques should become more similar across countries. Such developments have taken place, as any international traveler can attest. Table 5.2 provides an illustration. The table clearly shows that between

TABLE 5.2 **Hourly Wages in Manufacturing in Selected Countries As a Percentage of the U.S. Wage**

	1959	*1979*
Canada	82	95
Japan	11	82
Sweden	39	109
France	27	60
Italy	23	72
West Germany	29	107
United Kingdom	29	76
United States	100	100

SOURCES: *International Financial Statistics;* United Nations, *Monthly Bulletin of Statistics.*

1959 and 1979 wages in the various countries converged in dramatic fashion. (The mean of the eight entries rose from 43 to 88, while their standard deviation fell from 29 to 17.) A similar convergence of factor rewards apparently also took place between countries maintaining liberal trade during 1870 and 1914, when significant reductions in transportation costs had the effect of lowering trade barriers.

All this is illustrative but should not be interpreted as "proof" of the theory. Other influences have also been at work: for example, capital and labor have become increasingly mobile internationally, and agriculture has remained protected. A more formal investigation was undertaken by the economists Manouchehr Mokhtari and Farhad Rassekh, who examined the performance of sixteen industrial countries during 1961 through 1984. They also found a strong convergence of real wages between these countries and, furthermore, that increasing trade openness was the single most important determinant of that convergence.

10. *CASE STUDY:* SOUTH KOREAN EXPERIENCE WITH EXPORT-LED GROWTH

As noted in Chapter 4, South Korea has differed from many LDCs by relying on foreign trade to help stimulate economic development, a policy known as *export-led growth*. In recent years, Korea has accumulated capital at a rapid rate, both absolutely and relative to the rest of the world. The Korean experience has been examined in detail in various studies, and Table 5.3 contains a few calculations from one of these studies. The first column shows the increase in the capital-labor *(K/L)* ratio for the Korean economy—about 115 percent between 1966 and 1975. Note that the overall capital-labor ratio is between the capital-labor ratios in the two sectors, manufacturing and agriculture.

TABLE 5.3   **South Korean Experience** *(K/L ratios in thousands of dollars per laborer)*

Year	(1) Overall K/L	(2) Wage index	(3) K/L in manufactures	(4) K/L in agriculture	(5) K/L in exports	(6) K/L in noncompeting imports	(7) Total exports ($ million)
1966	0.7	100	1.8	0.3	1.0	6.5	250
1975	1.5	183	3.0	0.7	3.1	16.7 (1972)	5,081

SOURCE: Wontack Hong, *Trade, Distortions and Employment Growth in Korea* (Seoul: Korea Development Institute, 1979).

The second column shows that the wage has increased substantially; in fact, wages have risen relative to rents (not shown in the table). As a result, capital has been substituted for labor in both sectors, as revealed in the third and fourth columns. But the increases in the capital-labor ratios in the two sectors are not large enough to accommodate the overall increase in the capital stock per worker, indicated in the first column. Thus there must have been the sort of reallocation of resources from the labor-intensive sector to the capital-intensive sector that is predicted by the Rybczynski theorem. This is revealed in the last column, where exports are shown to have increased dramatically—Korea exports both primary products and manufactures, but the latter accounted for most of the export increase. The fact that the fifth column resembles the third much more closely than the fourth is indicative of the relative importance of manufactures in exports. Indeed, Korean exports changed from consisting mainly of ores and other raw materials to manufactures such as textiles, shoes, steel, and electronics. A comparison of columns 5 and 6 furnishes support for a factor-endowments explanation of trade: exports are much less capital-intensive than noncompeting imports—goods that are imported and not produced at all at home.

The illustrations in this and the preceding two sections demonstrate the use of the Heckscher-Ohlin theory and lend that theory support. But they are far from formal tests of verification.

11. SUMMARY

1. This chapter has investigated the factor-endowments theory of comparative advantage: countries have a comparative advantage in those goods whose production makes relatively intensive use of those factors with which the country is relatively abundantly endowed.

2. The factor-endowments theory is given explicit form in the Heckscher-Ohlin-Samuelson model, which hypothesizes a world of two goods, two factors, and two countries that are identical in all respects except factor endowments.

3. The Heckscher-Ohlin-Samuelson model yields four basic propositions that explain the pattern of comparative advantage and establish links between international trade and domestic factor markets, income distribution, and growth.

4. The four basic propositions give powerful results, but at the cost of demanding assumptions: trade is assumed due to comparative advantage, comparative advantage is assumed due to relative endowment differences, and the special assumptions of the Heckscher-Ohlin-Samuelson model are imposed. This puts a large burden on empirical verification of the relevance of the basic propositions.

5. The Heckscher-Ohlin theory studied in this chapter is basically an extension of the classical theory, which it both builds upon and complements. Thus it is sometimes referred to as the *neoclassical* or modern theory of international trade.

SUGGESTED READING

Heckscher, E. "The Effect of Foreign Trade on the Distribution of Income." In *Readings in the Theory of International Trade*. Edited by H. S. Ellis and L. A. Metzler. Homewood: Irwin, 1949. The original article in English translation.

Johnson, H. G. *International Trade and Economic Growth*. Cambridge: Harvard University Press, 1965. Chapter 1 contains an alternative geometric treatment of the factor-endowments theory.

Jones, R. W. "Factor Proportions and the Heckscher-Ohlin Theorem." *Review of Economic Studies* (Oct. 1956). A basic treatment of the Heckscher-Ohlin theorem.

————. "The Structure of Simple General Equilibrium Models." *Journal of Political Economy* 6 (1965). An algebraic treatment.

Mokhtari, M., and F. Rassekh. "The Tendency towards Factor Price Equalization among OECD Countries." *The Review of Economics and Statistics* 71 (1989). Factor-price equalization and trade among the industrial countries.

Ohlin, B. *Interregional and International Trade*. Cambridge: Harvard University Press, 1933. The classic statement.

Rybczynski, T. M. "Factor Endowment and Relative Commodity Prices." *Economica* 88 (1955). The Rybczynski theorem.

Samuelson, P. A. "International Factor-Price Equalization Once Again." *Economic Journal* 234 (1949). The factor-price equalization theorem.

Stolper, W. F., and P. A. Samuelson. "Protection and Real Wages." *Review of Economic Studies* 1 (1941). The Stolper-Samuelson theorem.

Travis, W. P. *The Theory of Trade and Protection*. Cambridge: Harvard University Press, 1964. The effects of tariffs.

CHAPTER 6

Explaining Trade

> When you can measure what you are speaking about, and express it in numbers, you know something about it; but when you cannot measure it, when you cannot express it in numbers, your knowledge is of a meager and unsatisfactory kind: it may be the beginning of knowledge, but you have scarcely, in your thoughts, advanced to the stage of science.
>   —LORD KELVIN

The Heckscher-Ohlin-Samuelson model leads to powerful and interesting results, like the four propositions discussed in Chapter 5. But the price is high: the model makes an imposing list of assumptions. Is the price too high? Are the model's implications relevant to the world in which we live? Empirical investigation is called for.

This could concern three questions: the most general one of how important comparative advantage is as a cause of trade, the still general question of whether factor endowments are important determinants of comparative advantage, and the specific one of whether the Heckscher-Ohlin-Samuelson model is an adequate description of reality. It is natural to start with the latter question since a positive answer implies positive answers to the former as well.

1. THE LEONTIEF PARADOX

In 1953 Wassily Leontief published the results of one of the most famous empirical investigations in economics: an attempt to test the consistency of the Heckscher-Ohlin-Samuelson model with U.S. trade patterns. Leontief wished to measure the capital-labor ratio actually used in the production of U.S. exports and imports. One complication is the existence of interindustry flows. The automobile industry, for example, uses as inputs not only factors such as capital and labor, but also steel and other *intermediate goods* (that is, goods that are used to produce goods). The steel industry also uses intermediate goods, including motor vehicles! Leontief (who received a Nobel prize for the development of input-output analysis) used a 1947 input-output table for

153

WASSILY LEONTIEF (b. 1906)

Leontief was born in St. Petersburg, Russia, and undertook graduate study there (when the city was known as Leningrad). In the 1920s he went to Germany for further study and moved to the United States in 1931, taking a position at Harvard, where he was to remain for most of his professional life. Leontief is best known for the development of input-output analysis, a methodology for the study of the production structure of an economic system. Leontief's application of input-output analysis to international trade—which will be discussed in this chapter—may well have been the single most influential empirical finding in economics. He was awarded the Nobel prize in 1973.

the United States to cut through these circular flows and calculate the total use (both directly and indirectly—in the form of intermediate goods) of capital and labor in various industries.

Leontief then calculated, on the basis of the U.S. pattern of trade in 1947 (and, in a subsequent recalculation, in 1951), the capital-labor ratio embodied in a representative collection of U.S. exports, as well as the capital-labor ratio embodied in a representative collection of U.S. goods that compete with imports, rather than those of actual imports, because he had only U.S. data. Thus he ignored imports that were not also actually produced in the United States—notably, coffee, tea, and jute. Also ignored were those sectors, mainly services, that did not enter into international trade at all.

Leontief found that U.S. exports used a capital-labor ratio of $13,991 per man-year, whereas import substitutes used a ratio of $18,184 per man-year. Given the presumption that the United States is relatively capital-abundant, this is just the reverse of what the Heckscher-Ohlin theorem predicts. Thus it is called the Leontief Paradox.

This type of test differs from MacDougall's study discussed in Chapter 1 and the elasticity estimates discussed in Chapter 4 in that it does not examine a large number of observations in the hope of discovering regularities. Instead, it is basically a description of a single observation—U.S. trade in 1947. Thus it raises the question of whether that observation is nonrepresentative; for example, 1947 was right after the Second World War, when the United States was the only major industrial economy free of devastation. Leontief's calculation has, therefore, been repeated, by Leontief and others, using different data. The paradox was found to be an enduring feature of U.S. trade, at least until well into the 1970s. The same type of calculation has also been made for other countries and regions, and similar paradoxes have sometimes (but not always) been found.

The Leontief Paradox has stimulated a huge amount of both empirical and theoretical research and still does: anything this glaring calls for an explanation. This chapter can be regarded as a partial response to the paradox.

Problems

6.1 Discuss in detail the compatibility of Leontief's procedure with each of the assumptions made in the Heckscher-Ohlin-Samuelson model.

6.2 Review the discussion in Chapter 1 of the commodity composition of U.S. trade and your answer to Problem **5.1**. How reasonable do you think it is to try to fit the United States into the Heckscher-Ohlin-Samuelson model on the basis of capital and labor as the two factors?

2. POSSIBLE EXPLANATIONS OF THE LEONTIEF PARADOX

In this and the following sections we discuss several competing explanations of the Leontief Paradox. In this section we consider two possibilities suggested by the Heckscher-Ohlin-Samuelson model; in section 3 we deal with extensions of the factor-endowments approach; in section 4 we look at alternative determinants of comparative advantage rather than factor endowments; and in section 5 we look at alternatives to comparative advantage itself.

Factor Intensity Reversal

Chapter 5 noted that the two industries would not normally use capital and labor in identical proportions and so defined the capital-intensive industry to be the one using more capital per worker. But under some circumstances apples might be relatively capital-intensive, while under other circumstances butane might be.

Suppose, for example, that the butane industry is inflexible: 1 unit of capital plus 1 unit of labor can produce 1 unit of butane, and there is no other method. But suppose that capital and labor easily substitute for each other in the apple industry: there are many methods of producing a bushel of apples. If the wage-rental ratio is very high, apple producers will choose a capital-intensive method to economize on the expensive labor, and apple production will be capital-intensive relative to butane production. If the wage-rental ratio were to fall, apple producers would substitute labor for capital, but butane producers, hampered by their inflexible technology, would have to continue using 1 unit of capital with each unit of labor. Thus the capital intensity of the apple industry would decline relative to that of the butane industry. If wages fall enough relative to rents, the capital-labor ratio in the apple industry could fall all the way to that in the butane industry and below. Thus at low enough

wage-rental ratios, the apple industry would be labor-intensive relative to butane. Such a switch in the pattern of relative capital intensities is called a *factor
intensity reversal.*

How can such a reversal affect the Heckscher-Ohlin theorem? Suppose
that France is capital-abundant relative to Germany and that the two economies are in autarky. France thus has a higher wage-rental ratio than does
Germany, and each French industry employs more capital per worker than
does its German counterpart. Now suppose that because of a factor intensity
reversal, apples are relatively capital-intensive in France but relatively labor-
intensive in Germany. Then the Heckscher-Ohlin theorem would predict that,
if free trade were to commence, the capital-abundant country (France) would
export its capital-intensive good (apples), and the labor-abundant country
(Germany) would export its labor-intensive good (apples). This is nonsense:
the theorem predicts that both countries export the same good. Thus the presence of a factor intensity reversal nullifies the Heckscher-Ohlin theorem,
which must be violated by one of the countries.

The Leontief Paradox can, therefore, be due in principle to a factor intensity reversal between the United States and the rest of the world. Unfortunately, testing for a reversal on the basis of existing technological data is
extremely difficult. Economists have come to varying conclusions about the
likely practical importance of such reversals. We cannot say that there is in
fact very strong empirical evidence indicating that the Leontief Paradox is
due to factor intensity reversals.

Demand Reversal

The assumption of identical tastes in the two countries ensures that the
labor-abundant country has the lower autarkic wage-rental ratio. Suppose we
drop this assumption and that each country has a strong preference for the
good intensive in that country's relatively abundant factor. Thus the Germans
have a stronger preference than the French for butane and a weaker preference for apples. Then it is possible that Germany, despite her larger endowment of laborers per unit of capital, could have a higher wage-rental ratio than
France, if the demand for labor to satisfy the greater desire for labor-intensive
goods is sufficiently pronounced. Such a situation is called a *demand reversal.* In this case Germany would have a comparative advantage in the capital-
intensive good (apples), and France in the labor-intensive good (butane).

A demand reversal could potentially explain the Leontief Paradox. If the
United States has a sufficiently great desire for capital-intensive goods, it
could be led to import them from the rest of the world, despite the possession
of more capital per worker.

Is this the case? One can find examples where a country has a marked
preference for a good that it is relatively well endowed to produce. But international comparisons of consumption patterns have failed to reveal substantial systematic differences in tastes. Thus there is no empirical support for the

suggestion that the Leontief Paradox is due to demand reversals. This is really what we would expect: the same casual empiricism that makes us sure that the United States has more capital per worker than the rest of the world also makes us just about as sure that the United States would have a higher autarkic wage-rental ratio.

We have examined two possibilities, suggested by the Heckscher-Ohlin-Samuelson model, to account for the paradox. Although these cases increase our understanding of the theory, they do not have strong empirical support. We must look elsewhere for an explanation of the paradox.

Problems

6.3 Draw a diagram showing the relation between the wage-rental ratio and the ratio of butane cost to apple cost if a factor intensity reversal is present. If the relative factor intensities of the two industries reverse themselves twice.

6.4 If the Leontief Paradox were indeed due to a factor intensity reversal, what would Leontief have found if, instead of calculating the capital and labor used to produce a bundle of U.S. import substitutes, he had calculated the capital and labor actually used in the rest of the world to produce a bundle of U.S. imports? What would he have found if he had performed his actual calculation for the rest of the world rather than for the United States?

6.5* What can you say about factor-price equalization if a demand reversal is present?

6.6* Discuss the factor-price equalization, Rybczynski, and Stolper-Samuelson theorems in the presence of a factor intensity reversal.

3. EXTENSIONS OF THE HECKSCHER-OHLIN-SAMUELSON MODEL

Now we consider suggestions that depart substantially from the Heckscher-Ohlin-Samuelson model but that still view trade as explained by relative factor endowments.

Natural Resources

Some economists have argued that it is inadequate to consider only capital and labor, and that natural resources should also be included, thus restoring the traditional triad of capital, labor, and "land." Those, such as Jaroslav Vanek of Cornell University, who think that this point helps explain the Leontief Paradox employ a two-part argument. It is alleged, first, that many natural resources have become relatively scarce in the United States and that the United States imports natural-resource-intensive goods. Second, natural resources and capital could be "complementary"—that is, goods whose production requires large quantities of natural resources could also require large quantities of capital. This combination of circumstances could potentially explain the paradox. According to this story, the United States does indeed import capital-intensive goods, not because capital is scarce, but because capital-intensive goods are also natural-resource-intensive and natural resources are scarce. For example, the United States imports crude oil, which requires a large capital investment for extraction and transportation, so that the services of this capital are also imported. But the trade is due to an American shortage of oil, not of capital.

Empirical investigations have found that natural resources have become increasingly relatively scarce in the United States over the last century, and these investigations have presented evidence that this is a significant determinant of trade patterns. Thus this consideration seems to have some power.

Human Capital

Nations and individuals invest in their future not only by accumulating physical capital such as plant, equipment, and inventories, but also by spending on education, training, and other investments embodied in human form—that is, human capital. A portion of total wages is a return to human capital rather than a payment for simple labor services. This is why, at least in part, college graduates earn more than those who never went to college. A neglect of human capital could potentially account for the Leontief Paradox if export industries used more human capital than did import-competing industries. It is known, from the work of Irving Kravis at the University of Pennsylvania, that export industries do in fact tend to pay higher wages.

Measuring human capital is difficult because there is no explicit market for it. Methods of calculation have varied. For example, some studies have assumed that all wages, above the wage paid for unskilled labor, are a return to human capital; others have tried to construct measures directly by means of data on the costs of education, training, and so forth. The various studies have together established that human capital is significant and that U.S. exports are human-capital-intensive so that the phenomenon is an important determinant of trade. Indeed, one study (by Peter Kenen, now at Princeton) even calculated that the paradox could be reversed by adding human capital to physical capital.

Once they have been calculated, measures of human capital can be employed in two ways. Human capital can be added to physical capital to obtain a measure of total capital. If this is done, the basic Heckscher-Ohlin-Samuelson model remains intact, and the issue is solely one of measurement. Alternatively, human capital can be treated as a distinct factor, like labor and physical capital. In this case the model is substantially altered because the number of factors increases from two to three. Empirical studies have employed both methods, and, although some economists have concluded that it is better to treat human capital as a separate factor, the evidence is not conclusive on this point.

Labor Skills

A nation's labor force consists of many skill groups. Some economists, such as Donald Keesing of the World Bank, have sought the explanation of trade patterns in endowments of skills. Various studies have established a connection between the skill mixes of national endowments and the mixes embodied in imports and exports, and some studies have also established an influence of skill mix on the trade status of specific commodities.

Since this approach essentially treats different types of skilled labor as distinct factors, it departs from the basic Heckscher-Ohlin-Samuelson model by increasing the number of goods.

Taking account of labor skills is obviously closely related to taking account of human capital, and so the question arises whether this approach actually contributes anything additional. Some studies have accordingly employed both human-capital measures and indices of skills. The conclusion appears to be that the latter do in fact have explanatory power beyond that contributed by human capital.

Problems

6.7 Sometimes human capital is added to physical capital to obtain a measure of total capital, and sometimes the two types of capital are treated as separate factors. Now physical capital itself can take many forms (different types of buildings, different equipment, inventories of different goods), and the form it takes depends upon the sector in which it is employed. If the purpose of the theory is to explain trade in a long-run perspective where capital is completely flexible, how should the two types of capital be treated (added together, or separate)? What difference does it make? Can you think of any reasons to distinguish between human and physical capital but not between forms of the latter?

6.8 Suppose you were to discover that in nearly all countries wages are generally higher in export industries than in import-competing industries (there is some factual support for this). What would this imply about the empirical relevance of the human-capital explanation? Would this cause you to prefer one method of measuring human capital over another?

6.9 Specific skills are due in part to innate ability and in part to training (or human capital). If innate abilities are distributed in about equal proportions in the populations of different countries, should the skill groups and human-capital explanations be distinct?

6.10* Some commodities, because of high transportation costs, do not enter into international trade at all. Personal services are often of this sort. Suppose we alter the basic model by adding a third, nontraded good. Does this change the model in any way beyond increasing the number of goods from two to three? If nontraded goods consist mainly of service industries, what effect would they have on calculations such as Leontief's? Try to deduce the implications of the presence of a nontraded good on the four basic propositions of the Heckscher-Ohlin theory.

4. ALTERNATIVES TO FACTOR ENDOWMENTS

The previous section considered possibilities that depart from the Heckscher-Ohlin-Samuelson model but still preserve a factor-endowments viewpoint. Other theories focus on entirely different considerations. Some of these theories are inconsistent with a factor-endowments basis of comparative advantage, whereas others are consistent with and complementary to factor endowments. This section discusses several of these alternative approaches.

Technological Change

We saw in Chapter 1 that the United States exports technologically advanced manufactured goods. This fact has stimulated many studies, the common element of which is that the United States has a comparative advantage in research and development (R&D) itself. Thus goods that are relatively costly to produce at home might, nevertheless, be exported because of the R&D that they embody, and the actual export mix would have to change constantly in order for R&D, in the form of "advanced" products, to continue to be exported.

This approach would reduce to a form of the factor-endowments theory if one were to hypothesize that factor endowments explain the comparative advantage in R&D. The main modifications to the simple model would once again be increases in the numbers of factors and goods (and perhaps also an explicit dynamic element). But empirical investigations have not followed this path. Rather, they have attempted the more rudimentary task of relating exports to various industry characteristics thought to reflect the importance of research activities: the proportions of scientists and engineers in employment, the first trade date (to indicate the newness of a good), expenditure on R&D, the degree of product differentiation, and the like. Results have been mixed. Some studies have confirmed the importance of R&D for U.S. trade flows (as one would expect), but no clear framework of cause and effect has emerged.

This influence of technological advance upon trade is sometimes described in terms of a *product cycle*. According to this scenario, a new product is developed in the United States because of that country's comparative advantage in R&D. The product is initially produced at home for the domestic market because direct communication between producer and customer is essential to the development of the good. As that development proceeds and the good is perfected, production expands and an export market develops. Eventually, the good becomes standardized or familiar, and constant communication between buyer and seller declines in importance relative to lower production costs. Production, therefore, begins abroad. At first, foreign production is small as learning takes place abroad, and the foreign output is sold only on the local market, displacing some U.S. exports. Foreign production then gradually increases, and U.S. exports gradually fall, until the good is finally imported into the United States and foreign output supplies the entire world market. In the meantime, the U.S. firms have developed still newer products that are being introduced and will subsequently experience the same cycle. This sort of story obviously lends itself more readily to case studies of individual industries than to aggregate empirical testing of a country's entire trade. A number of such case studies have been made, notably in motion pictures and electronics, and they have revealed a product-cycle pattern.

Explanations of American imports and exports as trade in technology raise further questions. First, what is the source of the hypothesized U.S. comparative advantage in R&D? As noted above, the factor-endowments and alternative explanations presumably could enter here. Second, if the United States does in fact have a comparative advantage in R&D, what determines whether this causes exports of new goods rather than the direct export of research services for foreign customers or for U.S. firms with productive capacity abroad? This question will arise again in this book when we examine international investment and the multinational firm.

Tariffs and Other Distortions

All nations use tariffs and other measures to interfere with their international trade, and all experience at least some distortions in domestic markets as well. We saw in Chapter 4 that many LDCs have adopted policies that extensively influence trade flows away from those dictated by comparative advantage. In many of these countries the domestic markets likewise have been influenced to depart substantively from what would have come about in a purely competitive environment. Such measures are much less pronounced in the developed countries, but these nations do nonetheless impose tariffs. In some sectors, especially agriculture, the degree of protection from international competition can still be large. Some economists, notably the late William Travis, have suggested that the Leontief Paradox might be due largely to tariffs and other forms of protection. There is evidence that, in the United States and some other DCs, industries, such as textiles and footwear, that are relatively intensive in unskilled labor are relatively heavily protected. Investigations have shown that tariffs might contribute to the Leontief Paradox but that protection is not a major factor, at least as far as the DCs are concerned.

Linder's Hypothesis

Yet another theory has been proposed by the Swedish economist Staffan B. Linder, who assigns a central role to demand. Linder's theory is intended to apply only to manufactures, with trade in primary products presumably explained by endowments of crucial natural resources. The theory has two components.

1. *Potential exports are those goods for which a domestic market exists.* This assumption is defended by the same sort of alleged information requirement central to the early part of the product cycle: the knowledge of how to

develop, produce, and market a product cannot be acquired without a local market with which to interact. The assumption is asserted as a general tendency, and the existence of counterexamples, such as the Korean export of Christmas decorations to the United States, is acknowledged. Since a country would never import a good without a local market, this assumption implies that a country's potential trade is limited to those goods having a domestic market and that the potential trade between any two countries is limited to those goods for which markets exist in *both* countries.

2. *The range of goods for which domestic markets exist is determined by per capita income.* This amounts to assuming that income is the dominant determinant of tastes. (Recall that the Heckscher-Ohlin-Samuelson model assumed, by contrast, that relative demands are independent of income.)

The two assumptions together imply that the amount of potential trade between countries is greater the more nearly equal are their per capita incomes. According to the second assumption, countries with greatly different incomes will have domestic markets for different types of goods so that only comparatively few goods will have markets in both countries. But the first implies that only those goods with markets in both countries are tradable; thus there will be little trade between countries with greatly dissimilar incomes.

Linder's theory leads to conclusions different from those of the factor-endowments approach. Countries with high per capita incomes also have much capital per resident. Linder's theory accordingly predicts that the volume of trade will be the greatest between countries with similar capital-labor ratios and, therefore, similar per capita incomes. The Heckscher-Ohlin theory may seem to imply the opposite conclusion: countries with similar capital-labor ratios will have similar comparative costs and thus little basis for mutual trade. Nevertheless, there is some scope for complementarity between the theories. Linder's theory predicts which goods are potentially tradable but says nothing about the patterns of trade in those goods—that is, which will be imported and which exported by any particular country. Presumably this can be explained by other theories, such as that of Heckscher and Ohlin.

Linder's theory is in rough accord with the facts: the lion's share of world trade is among the DCs, with broadly similar per capita incomes, rather than between the DCs and LDCs. However, detailed empirical support for the theory has not been found, and tests of propositions thought to reflect Linder's theory have given it only mixed support.

5. INCREASING RETURNS TO SCALE AND IMPERFECT COMPETITION

As a final possibility, this section looks at the relation between factor endowments and those possible explanations of trade that have nothing to do with comparative advantage.

Increasing Returns to Scale: External Economies

The basic Heckscher-Ohlin-Samuelson model assumes constant returns to scale. We saw in Chapter 2 that scale economies could provide a basis for trade entirely independent of comparative advantage and, therefore, also independent of factor endowments working through comparative advantage. For example, suppose that France and Germany have identical factor endowments (so that the Heckscher-Ohlin theorem would predict no trade) and, therefore, identical production possibility frontiers, but that geographically concentrated scale economies cause that common frontier to be "bowed inward" as in Figure 2.1. Then, as we saw, there is a basis for trade and specialization not predicted by comparative advantage or, therefore, by factor endowments. Furthermore, the pattern of that trade is indeterminate.

Increasing Returns to Scale: Product Differentiation and the Division of Labor

All this applies to *national* scale economies, which require the geographical concentration of production. What if the scale economies are *international*—a result of the division of labor—or if product differentiation is significant? Then, as we saw in Chapter 2, *interindustry* trade will still be based upon comparative advantage, and countries that are relatively similar and so have minor comparative-cost differences will engage mainly in *intraindustry* trade. Now the factor-endowments theory hypothesizes that countries with large differences in factor endowments have large differences in comparative costs, whereas those countries with similar endowments have similar comparative costs. If this is so, two conclusions follow.

1. Trade between countries with similar endowments is largely intra-industry, whereas trade between countries with dissimilar endowments is largely interindustry.
2. International scale economies and product differentiation do not vitiate the factor-endowments theory.

Factor endowments are, of course, much more similar among the DCs than they are between the DCs as a group and the LDCs. Thus these conclusions are consistent with the trade patterns discussed in Chapter 1.

The fundamental message of the Heckscher-Ohlin theory is that trade and factor mobility are *substitutes* for each other. The presence of international scale economies does not alter this conclusion as far as interindustry trade is concerned. But they cause intraindustry trade and factor mobility to be *complements*. If factors were to become more mobile between countries, this movement would reduce comparative cost differences, thereby reducing interindustry trade but increasing intraindustry trade.

Oligopoly

Imperfect competition is our other alternative to comparative advantage as an explanation of trade. Recall from Chapter 3 that imperfect competition can induce both intraindustry and interindustry trade. If some sector has an imperfectly competitive market structure in each of two countries, intraindustry trade within the sector (or the potential for such trade) will increase competition in each country. If the relative degree of oligopoly across sectors differs between two countries, interindustry trade could result, with each country exporting the good produced by that country's relatively more competitive sector, compared to the other country. How does all this relate to factor endowments?

The volume of intraindustry trade may be indeterminate, as we saw in Chapter 3, since it is the competition between the two countries that matters, not the actual volume of trade. But relative endowment similarities, by making the sectors in the two countries similar in relative size, would seem to increase the scope for such trade. In any case, oligopoly does not weaken the implication of scale economies that intraindustry trade is stimulated by endowment similarities.

The relation between imperfect competition and factor endowments is more uncertain regarding interindustry trade. If a country's relatively competitive sector also makes relatively intensive use of the country's abundant factor, the two influences work in the same direction: that commodity will be exported. But if the competitive sector makes intensive use of the scarce factor, the two motives for trade are in conflict.

Scale Economies, Oligopoly, and the Leontief Paradox

Can scale economies or oligopoly account for the Leontief Paradox? Consider first interindustry trade. We have seen that product differentiation and international scale economies do not vitiate the factor-endowments theory, so they cannot themselves account for the paradox. External economies have an indeterminate effect on the pattern of trade, so they could be consistent with almost anything. But oligopoly has an opposite influence than factor endowments on interindustry trade if a country's relatively competitive sector makes relatively intensive use of its relatively scarce factor. This would produce the paradox if the effect of oligopoly dominated. However, there is no empirical evidence on whether this possibility is of any practical importance.

Endowment similarities promote intraindustry trade. This might seem at first to be a likely candidate for explaining the paradox since it is just the reverse of the Heckscher-Ohlin explanation of interindustry trade. But this is not so. The Leontief Paradox is in terms of the *factor content* of trade, the amounts of capital and labor indirectly traded in the form of the goods produced from them. But intraindustry trade involves similar goods: imports will typically embody about the same factor services as exports. Thus intraindustry trade will account for little of the indirect exchange of capital for labor, and it will not cause the paradox.

6. TESTING THE FACTOR-ENDOWMENTS THEORY

The best way to test various theories of international trade would be to estimate empirically a comprehensive model in which each potential explanation had a role to play. It would then be clear which are important and which are not. But existing data and resources make this impossible. Instead economists have attempted to test the factor-endowments theory by itself.

But how can we judge whether the theory has passed its test? One way would be to put it head to head against a rival theory (such as Linder's hypothesis, scale economies, or imperfect competition) and see which better explains the facts. But this is not done: the alternatives are further from empirical implementation than the factor-endowments theory. Instead the latter is examined alone, and a subjective judgment is then made of whether it is useful to ignore everything except relative factor endowments.

The Heckscher-Ohlin theorem asserts a relationship between three sets of parameters: factor endowments, technology, and trade flows. Empirical tests typically employ data about two of these and infer the third. For example, Leontief used data on technology and trade flows and inferred relative factor abundance. The inference was at odds with prior belief; hence the "paradox." But note that this procedure cannot judge whether it is the hypothesis that the world is adequately represented by the Heckscher-Ohlin-Samuelson model that is at fault, the prior belief, or both.

Empirical work subsequent to Leontief has sometimes replicated his calculation for other years and countries, but much of the work has gone beyond his study in at least one of three ways: (1) *Inference.* Some studies have used data on factor abundance and trade flows and have inferred the technology. (2) *Dimensionality.* Sometimes the data are not as aggregated, with account taken of more than two goods, factors, and/or countries. As we saw above, this is true of studies concerned with natural resources, human capital, or multiple skill groups. (3) *Regressions.* While Leontief in effect examined a single observation, some other studies have looked at many observations in order to uncover regularities. For example, data from many countries might be examined to see if trade flows are systematically related to factor endowments.

Relative Factor Abundance

So far in this chapter we have depended upon prior beliefs about relative factor endowments. Table 6.1 contains some estimates of 6 countries' relative endowments of 10 factors. The estimates are based on data collected by Harry Bowen of New York University and used by Edward Leamer of the

TABLE 6.1 **Relative Factor Endowments, 1975**

Factor*	Brazil	Canada	India	Japan	United Kingdom	United States
GNP	2.66	3.46	1.99	11.14	5.10	32.94
CAPITAL	1.85	3.65	1.18	14.92	4.87	29.36
PRO LABOR	3.56	2.37	13.47	8.03	6.00	24.53
LIT LABOR	4.28	1.74	14.29	11.05	4.77	17.11
ILLIT LAB	4.92	0.02	65.24	0.20	0.06	0.15
TROP LAND	52.19	0.00	9.09	0.00	0.00	0.14
DRY LAND	0.76	2.38	5.68	0.00	0.00	32.44
TEMP LAND	1.75	38.03	3.77	1.91	1.25	18.47
COAL	0.21	1.96	8.49	1.67	11.13	50.87
MINERALS	5.55	19.06	3.43	1.89	0.98	27.58
OIL	0.71	9.76	0.73	0.16	1.63	58.04

*PRO LABOR: professional and technical workers; LIT LABOR: literate, nonprofessional workers; ILLIT LAB: illiterate workers; TROP LAND: tropical rain land; TEMP LAND: humid, temperate land.

Each entry in the table represents the percentage of the "world's" total endowment of the respective factor that is possessed by the respective country. Thus 14.92 percent of the "world's" capital stock was in Japan. The "world" is defined as the 47 countries for which data were available.

SOURCE: E. E. Leamer, *Sources of International Comparative Advantage* (Cambridge: MIT Press, 1984).

University of California at Los Angeles in an empirical study of international trade. The 6 countries were chosen from the 47 represented in the data set. These 47 included most of the major trading nations.

Each number in the table shows what percentage of the total (for the 47 countries) endowment of each factor was accounted for by the respective country. For example, 1.85 percent of the total capital stock of the 47 countries was located in Brazil. Therefore, for each country higher numbers indicate relatively more abundant factors. Thus Brazil is relatively most abundant in tropical land and relatively most scarcely endowed with coal. The first row shows what fraction of total GNP each country contributed and so measures relative sizes. We can regard a country as abundantly endowed (relative to the other 46 countries) with each factor for which its endowment share exceeds its GNP share and scarcely endowed with each factor whose endowment share falls short of the GNP share. Thus Brazil is relatively abundant in each type of labor, in tropical land, and in minerals, and it is relatively scarce in capital, dry land and temperate-zone land, coal, and oil. There are other factors not included in the 10 reported here, and there are more than 47 countries in the world. The United States appears so abundant in coal and, especially, in oil because the 47 countries do not include some nations with large stocks (for example, the Middle East and the countries of the former Soviet Union are mostly excluded). But most of the important factors and trading nations are taken account of, so the table probably gives a good overall picture. Note that, after the questionable coal and oil, the United States is most abundantly endowed with dry land, capital, minerals, and professional labor, and is very scarcely endowed with illiterate labor and tropical land. Canada's relative endowment pattern is not all that different except that the relative abundance of temperate land and minerals is considerably more pronounced. Japan is relatively abundantly endowed only with capital, though the scarcity of literate nonprofessional workers is basically absent and that of professional workers modest. All other factors are scarce. The United Kingdom is relatively most abundant in coal and professional labor. India, as one would expect, is extremely well endowed with illiterate labor. But the more skilled types of labor are also abundant, in relative terms, as are coal, minerals, and all types of land, whereas capital and oil are scarce.

As an example of the type of work that has been done, look at some of Leamer's results, reproduced in Table 6.2. Leamer used the data set that Table 6.1 was drawn from. He treated each of the 47 countries as an observation and statistically analyzed the relation between endowments and trade flows. Each entry in Table 6.2 shows by how many thousands of dollars a unit increase in the endowment of the indicated factor would raise net exports of the indicated commodity. Thus a 1 unit rise in the stock of illiterate labor will increase a country's exports (net of imports) of petroleum products by $18,900, of raw materials by $2,500, of forest products by $11,500, of animal products by $17,900, of labor-intensive manufactures by $4,800, and of other manu-

TABLE 6.2 **Estimates of the Effect of Factor Endowments on Trade, 1975**

Factor	Commodity group*								
	PETR	RMAT	FORS	TROP	ANML	CERL	LABR	CHEM	OTHM
CAPITAL	−20.4	−8.8	−1.3	−2.7	0.04	−4.3	1.0	3.8	45.6
PRO LABOR	−507.6	303.1	−81.2	−301.3	−279.4	946.3	−699.7	481.7	−3,125.3
LIT LABOR	8.9	−59.4	−17.1	22.6	−17.3	−97.4	78.9	−53.4	204.4
ILLIT LABOR	18.9	2.5	11.5	7.9	17.9	−18.8	4.8	−4.4	47.4
TROP LAND	−0.4	−0.1	−0.2	2.9	−0.3	2.3	−0.5	−0.8	−1.5
DRY LAND	−0.2	−0.3	−0.2	0.6	0.7	1.0	−0.3	−0.2	−0.6
TEMP LAND	−1.4	−0.9	−0.4	2.3	3.7	10.3	−1.9	−4.3	−15.5
COAL	−0.1	0.4	0.0	−0.1	−0.1	0.0	−0.1	0.0	−0.1
MINERALS	0.0	1.1	0.0	0.0	0.0	0.0	−0.1	−0.1	−0.2
OIL	0.4	0.0	0.1	0.1	0.0	0.2	0.0	0.0	−0.3

*PETR: crude oil and petroleum products; RMAT: raw materials; FORS: forest products; TROP: tropical agricultural products; ANML: animal products; CERL: cereals, etc.; LABR: labor-intensive manufactures; CHEM: chemicals; OTHM: other manufactures. The unit of measurement for each commodity group is $1,000. The unit for each type of labor is 1,000 workers and for each type of land 1,000 hectares; for coal, minerals, and oil it is $1,000, and for capital it is $1 million.

Each entry in the table represents the increase in net exports of the respective commodity group that will result from a unit increase in the endowment of the respective factor. Thus an increase in a country's capital stock of +1 million will result in a +3,800 rise in that country's net exports of chemicals.

SOURCE: E. E. Leamer, *Sources of International Comparative Advantage* (Cambridge: MIT Press, 1984).

factures by $47,400. But net exports of cereals will fall by $18,800, and that of chemicals will fall by $4,400.

The Heckscher-Ohlin-Vanek Theorem

All this shows, like the case studies in Chapter 5, that factor endowments help us to understand the world. But this is not the same thing as testing a specific factor-endowments theory. For this, we first need a theory to test. The Heckscher-Ohlin theorem itself will not do because just two goods and two factors are not adequate. Economists have tried instead to test a version of this theorem that allows for more goods, factors, and countries.

Suppose that free trade takes place with factor-price equalization. Jaroslav Vanek has shown that, in these circumstances, much of the Heckscher-Ohlin theorem continues to hold. Because all countries have identical factor prices, they use identical techniques so that the quantities of the various factors used to produce a unit of any good are the same regardless of where that good is produced. Therefore, the assumption that all countries consume goods in identical proportions implies that all countries "consume factors" in identical proportions. For example, if some country's national income were 10 percent of world income, the goods that it consumed would together require for their production exactly 10 percent of the world endowment of each factor. Thus the country's exports would together require more of any factor for their production than would the country's imports when the country possessed more than 10 percent of the world endowment of that factor, and any factor for which the country's endowment accounted for less than 10 percent of the world endowment would be imported in the same sense. More generally, we can say that a country is relatively abundant in any factor for which the country possesses a greater fraction of world supply than the fraction of world income that the country accounts for, and that the country is relatively scarce in the factors for which it possesses a smaller fraction. Then each country's exports will, in the aggregate, use a greater quantity of each of its abundant factors and a smaller quantity of each of its scarce factors than will its imports in the aggregate. This result is known as the *Heckscher-Ohlin-Vanek theorem* (HOV). Note that it does not say whether any particular good will be imported or exported (unless there are only two goods), but it does justify aggregate calculations of the Leontief type.

Versions of this theorem have been tested, first by Keith Maskus of the University of Colorado and then more extensively by Harry Bowen, Edward Leamer, and Leo Sveikauskas. The HOV theorem did not fare well. Table 6.3 summarizes some calculations made by Bowen, Leamer, and Sveikauskas. They compiled data on trade flows and on factor abundances of 12 factors for the 27 countries in the table and, using data on U.S. technology, computed the factor content of each country's trade in 1967. Each number records the proportion of the 12 factors for which the factor content of the respective coun-

TABLE 6.3   **Test of Factor Content of Trade**

Country	"Correct" factor content
Argentina	.33
Australia	.33
Austria	.67
Belgium-Luxembourg	.50
Brazil	.17
Canada	.75
Denmark	.42
Finland	.67
France	.25
Germany	.67
Greece	.92
Hong Kong	1.00
Ireland	.92
Italy	.58
Japan	.67
Korea	.75
Mexico	.92
Netherlands	.58
Norway	.25
Philippines	.50
Portugal	.67
Spain	.67
Sweden	.42
Switzerland	.67
United Kingdom	.92
United States	.58
Yugoslavia	.03
Overall	*.61*

SOURCE: H. P. Bowen, E. E. Leamer, and L. Sveikauskas, "Multicountry, Multifactor Tests of the Factor Abundance Theory," *American Economic Review* 77 (1987).

try's trade was in accordance with the predictions of our theorem—that is, the proportion for which the country's exports embodied more (less) of a factor than did its imports, if the country's share of the world endowment of that factor was more (less) than its share of world income.

The table thus summarizes calculations analogous to those Leontief did many years ago. But note two important differences. First, this study involves calculations for 12 factors for each of 27 countries, a total of 324 calculations; Leontief's study involved 2 factors for 1 country. Second, this table reports the results of comparisons of the calculated factor content of trade with data on factor abundances rather than with prior beliefs about what those abundances are. That is, the study utilized data on trade, technology, and endowments, and not just on the first two.

The HOV theorem predicts that each number should be 1.00; if endowments have nothing to do with trade, we might expect the numbers to average to about .50 overall. As you can see, the results are disappointing, and other tests did not supply more encouragement. Apparently, this is due, in some combination, to the low quality of available data and to a theorem that is too simple to accommodate reality. Other investigations have consistently found that the predictions of the HOV theorem are not borne out by the data.

But this is not surprising. The HOV theorem assumes that trade is free and that it equalizes factor prices internationally, and both assumptions are dramatically at odds with reality. The important question, therefore, is whether the HOV predictions fail because of the absence of free trade and factor-price equalization or whether they fail because relative factor-endowment differences are not in fact the major cause of trade.

Daniel Trefler of the University of Toronto also used data on technology, trade flows, and endowments but proceeded differently from the work described above. From the data on trade flows and on U.S. technology, Trefler calculated what countries' endowments would have to be for the predictions of the HOV theorem to hold, and he then compared these with the countries' actual endowments. He found that international differences in divergences between actual endowments and the calculated HOV endowments were negatively correlated with international divergences between factor prices. That is, a country with an endowment of labor 20 percent greater than what the HOV theorem indicated was necessary for that country's trade also tended to have a wage about 20 percent lower than a country whose labor force just matched its HOV requirement.

This result might be due to international differences in factor productivity. For example, a country might need 20 percent more labor than what the HOV theorem predicts because its labor is 20 percent less efficient than that of the United States, whose technology data were used. Then free trade would require wages to be 20 percent lower in this country so that it could compete internationally. If this is the reason for Trefler's result, we have evidence that trade is caused by international differences in factor endowments *plus* international differences in factor productivities. But the result could reflect something else. For example, if trade barriers are significant, a labor-abundant country would export less than it would with free trade, so its labor force would exceed that country's HOV prediction. And, being labor-abundant, the country would also have a lower wage. In this case trade could be due solely to international differences in endowments. But, regardless of the reason for Trefler's result, it is intriguing.

Economists have been trying for about forty years to implement empirically the factor-endowments theory. This work can be summarized as follows.

1. The two-factor, two-commodity version of the theory is too simple to accommodate reality in a useful way.
2. The factor-endowments approach helps us to understand the world economy, which can be usefully and instructively approached with only a moderate number of goods and factors.
3. A version of the Heckscher-Ohlin theorem simple enough to be useful has not yet been found to be supported by the data.

Problems

6.11 Based on Tables 6.1 and 6.2, what would you expect the pattern of trade of the United States to look like? The trade of Canada? Of Japan? Compare your guesses with the descriptions in Chapter 1.

6.12 Table 6.1 shows illiterate labor to be abundant in India and scarce in the United States. What does Table 6.2 imply about the consequences for each country's trade of a migration of 1 unit of illiterate labor from India to the United States? Suppose that at the same time 2 units of capital move from the United States to India. What happens to each country's trade in this case?

7. *CASE STUDY:* THE FACTOR CONTENT OF AMERICAN TRADE

Table 6.4 shows the 1975 commodity composition of the net trade of the United States and of its two largest trading partners, Canada and Japan. The commodity groups are classified as in Table 6.2, above. The United States had large imports of petroleum products, labor-intensive manufactures, and tropical agricultural products, and there were large net exports of cereals, chemicals, and other manufactures. Except for petroleum (which we have discussed), this accords well with Table 6.1. Canada imported all types of manufactures and exported an assortment of primary products (remember, more than two-thirds of this trade was with the United States). Japan did basically the opposite, exporting all types of manufactures and importing primary products. On the whole these trade patterns seem sensible in terms of relative factor endowments.

TABLE 6.4   **Net Exports of the United States, Canada, and Japan, 1975 *(billions of dollars)***

	Commodity group								
Country	PETR	RMAT	FORS	TROP	ANML	CERL	LABR	CHEM	OTHM
UNITED STATES	−24.0	0.5	0.0	−5.0	−1.6	18.0	−6.2	5.0	22.3
CANADA	0.0	4.7	4.2	−1.3	0.0	2.5	−2.2	−0.7	−9.0
JAPAN	−20.1	−10.2	−3.1	−2.7	−1.9	−6.3	1.7	1.8	39.5

SOURCE: E. E. Leamer, *Sources of International Comparative Advantage.*

TABLE 6.5   **Characteristics of U.S. Trade, 1962**

Variable*	Ratio of M variable to X variable
PK/L	1.27
PK/L (−NR)	1.04
(PK + HK)/L	1.14
(PK + HK)/L (−NR)	0.97
S & E	0.74
S & E (−NR)	0.62

*PK/L: ratio of physical capital to labor; (PK + HK): physical capital plus human capital calculated as the cost of education of labor; (−NR): indicates that industries intensive in the uses of natural resources are excluded; S & E: proportion of employees who are scientists and engineers.

SOURCE: R. E. Baldwin, "Determinants of the Commodity Structure of U.S. Trade," *American Economic Review* 1 (1971).

A 1971 study by Robert Baldwin of the University of Wisconsin examined the international trade of the United States. Table 6.5 shows some of his results pertaining to the 1962 patterns of trade.

The first entry in the table indicates that the (physical) capital-labor ratio employed in the production of a typical $1 million of U.S. import substitutes was 1.27 times as large as the capital-labor ratio used in the production of a typical $1 million of U.S. exports. This is the Leontief Paradox once again, and not much different from the ratio Leontief had obtained earlier (1.30). The second entry in the table shows that when natural-resource-intensive industries are ignored, the ratio falls to 1.04. Thus the natural-resource explanation seems to be important in practice though not important enough to account entirely for the paradox by itself. That the same is true of human capital is revealed by the third entry, showing that the ratio drops from 1.27 to 1.14 when human capital is added to physical capital. Taking into account both the natural-resource and human-capital explanations does eliminate the paradox in the fourth entry. These conclusions are reinforced by the last two numbers, which show that scientists and engineers are proportionally less visible in import-competing employment than in export employment and that the disparity widens when natural-resource-intensive industries are dropped.

Problems

6.13 Compare the discussion of the factor content of U.S. trade (this section) with the discussion of its commodity composition (Chapter 1). Discuss whether the two seem intuitively consistent.

6.14 What do you think would be the consequences of a U.S. abandonment of liberal trade on the domestic distribution of income between factors?

6.15 If farmers and farm laborers are simply workers who happen to work on farms, does the relative intensity of such workers in imports and exports tell us anything about whether relative factor endowments *cause* the pattern of trade, as the Heckscher-Ohlin theorem asserts? Answer the question with regard to other skill groups.

6.16 Chapter 1 discussed the possibility of a triangular pattern of trade between the United States, Japan, and the rest of the world. Can you see any indications of this in Table 6.4?

8. *CASE STUDY:* THE FACTOR CONTENT OF CANADIAN TRADE

Canada's net trade in 1975 was summarized in Table 6.4. This pattern was understandable in a factor-endowments sense, using the relative abundances presented in Table 6.1 and the inferred technological parameters of Table 6.2.

Table 6.6 shows results of a study by Harry Postner. Canadian exports are most strongly intensive in natural resources, which accords well with prior expectations, and are also intensive in physical capital and labor with at most an elementary-school education. Human capital would appear to be scarce. These results dovetail nicely with our discussion of U.S. trade. This can also be seen in Table 6.7, which focuses on the trade between the United States and Canada alone. The basic picture that emerges is like that of Table 6.6, except that now even elementary labor is relatively more intensive in imports, and exhaustible natural resources are now the most export-intensive.

TABLE 6.6   **Factor Content of Canadian Trade, 1970**

Factor*	M/X	M−X
RNR	0.46	−83.0
ENR	0.61	−86.0
PK	0.82	−531.0
Elementary L	0.91	−3.1
Secondary L	1.07	3.8
University L	1.14	1.3
Total L	1.02	1.9

*RNR: renewable natural resources (such as forest products); ENR: exhaustible natural resources (such as minerals); PK: physical capital; Elementary L: labor with an elementary-school education only; *M:* factor content of a typical $1 million of import substitutes. Labor is measured in man-years, and capital and resources in thousands of dollars.

SOURCE: H. H. Postner, *Factor Content of Canadian International Trade, 1975* (Ottawa: Economic Council of Canada, 1975).

TABLE 6.7   **Factor Content of Bilateral U.S.-Canadian Trade, 1967**

Factor*	M/X	M−X
RNR	0.70	−35.0
ENR	0.55	−105.0
PK	0.81	−579.0
Elementary L	1.06	2.3
Secondary L	1.17	9.0
University L	1.14	1.2
Total L	1.12	12.5

* See note to Table 6.6. *M* refers to *Canada's* imports.

SOURCE: H. Postner, *Factor Content of Canadian International Trade, 1975* (Ottowa: Economic Council of Canada, 1975).

Problems

6.17 Compare the discussion of the factor content of Canadian trade (this section) with the discussion of its commodity composition (Chapter 1). Discuss whether the two seem intuitively consistent.

6.18 What do you think would be the consequences of a Canadian abandonment of liberal trade on the domestic distribution of income between factors?

6.19 What do you think would be the consequences for U.S.-Canadian trade of a large-scale disinvestment of capital in the United States and investment in Canada? Use Table 6.2.

9.* *EXPLORING FURTHER:* MANY GOODS AND FACTORS

The previous sections lead to three conclusions. First, the simple Heckscher-Ohlin-Samuelson model is inadequate for explaining world trade satisfactorily. Second, the factor-endowments approach in general is useful for such an explanation; nearly all the suggestions that had explanatory power could be thought of as simply the addition of more goods and factors to the Heckscher-Ohlin-Samuelson model. Third, no simple version of the factor-endowments theory has been supported by the data. Our four basic propositions, on the other hand, were developed on the assumption of just two goods and factors. Do these propositions retain any validity if we increase the number of goods and factors but do not compensate by simplifying the model in some other way? This question is discussed in section A.5 of Appendix I. Here we sketch out how the propositions fare if the numbers of factors and goods are equal but greater than 2, adhering in other respects to the description of the Heckscher-Ohlin-Samuelson model given in Chapter 5.

Factor-Price Equalization

The firms in each of the (possibly many) industries face market prices for each of the factors, and they choose the least-cost technique: that collection of quantities of the various factors that can produce 1 unit of output at minimum cost. Because of constant returns to scale, this technique can be operated at any level, so each industry will employ the various factors in the same proportions in which they are required by the least-cost technique. These requirements and the factor prices determine the cost of production of each good, and, if the commodity is actually produced, this cost must equal its price. When world prices equal these costs, any country whose endowment consists of factors in proportions between the proportions required by the various industries' least-cost techniques will produce all goods and will have the corresponding factor prices. Thus all such countries must have equal factor prices when freely trading with each other.

The Stolper-Samuelson and Rybczynski Theorems

The reasoning employed in Chapter 5 to prove the Stolper-Samuelson and Rybczynski theorems can still be used when there are many goods and factors, and substantial parts of those two propositions remain true. Consider the Stolper-Samuelson theorem. Suppose that the price of machines rises—say, by 10 percent—that the prices of all other goods are unchanged, and that machines and at least one other good continue to be produced. All factor prices cannot rise by more than 10 percent, or the costs of all goods would rise by more than 10 percent and nothing could be produced; all factor prices cannot rise by exactly 10 percent, or all costs would rise by 10 percent and no goods with unchanged prices could still be produced; finally, all factor prices cannot fail to rise by at least 10 percent, or the cost of machines could not rise by the 10 percent increase in price. Thus at least one factor price rises by more than 10 percent, and at least one factor price does not rise as much as 10 percent. If all factors were to rise in price or remain unchanged, the costs of all goods would increase; so at least one factor price must fall for a good with unchanged price to experience no change in costs.

We conclude, then, that an increase in any commodity price, with the prices of other commodities held constant, will cause a greater-than-proportional rise in *some* factor price and an absolute fall in *some* factor price. Thus the real income of the first factor unambiguously increases, and that accruing to the latter factor unambiguously falls.

The Rybczynski theorem can be similarly extended. An increase in the endowment of one factor, with all other factor endowments and all prices constant, would cause the output of some good to increase in greater proportion and would cause the output of some other good to fall.

Problems

6.20 What does the Heckscher-Ohlin-Vanek theorem imply about the validity of the natural-resources explanation of the Leontief Paradox if factor-price equalization takes place?

6.21 Go through the reasoning of section 7* of Chapter 5, as best as you can, if there are three goods and two factors. If there are two goods and three factors.

10. THE SPECIFIC-FACTORS MODEL

The Leontief Paradox—casting doubt on the Heckscher-Ohlin theorem—has been the primary source of suspicion about the practical relevance of the factor-endowments theory. But it has not been the only source. The Stolper-Samuelson theorem implies that a person should form his attitude toward trade policy on the basis of the factor that supplies his income and not on the basis of the sector in which his ownership of that factor is employed. But often this does not seem to be so. For example, Stephen Magee of the University of Texas once examined the lobbying positions over trade policy of trade associations (representing capital) and of unions (representing labor) in a number of industries. The Stolper-Samuelson theorem suggests that all the trade associations should take one position and all the unions should adopt the other. But Magee found that, in a strong majority of cases, trade associations in export industries supported free trade while associations in import-competing industries supported protection, and similarly for unions. If industry location does matter, our theory's assumption that capital and labor can freely move from sector to sector becomes suspect.

The Heckscher-Ohlin-Samuelson model treats factors of production as completely mobile between *industries,* though not mobile at all between *countries.* Mobility between countries will be examined later in this book. Consider now mobility between industries. A country's capital stock is embodied in physical form: factories, equipment, and inventories; the education and training of the workforce; highways, railroads; a judiciary; and so forth. This inhibits mobility: there is no magic wand to transform a cotton gin into a grape press, should production shift from cotton cloth to wine. *Specific factors are those that cannot be transferred from one industry to another—they are suitable for a specific use.* The notion is very sensitive to the time perspective one has in mind. Most factors are highly specific over a short time span but can be quite mobile when given sufficient opportunity. The cotton gin must gradually wear out or become obsolete; its depreciation allowances will eventually be able to finance a grape press. In this sense capital is very mobile between industries, but time is required. The same is true, in varying degrees, of other factors. Most laborers possess specific skills; but even un-

skilled laborers are often reluctant to switch jobs, especially if the switch involves a change in lifestyle or abode. The "little old winemaker" may stead-
fastly refuse to do anything else; but the old curmudgeon will eventually die
and be replaced by a member of a younger generation.

The degree of mobility also varies across factors: except for the extreme
short run or extreme long run, some factors will be quite mobile between sectors, and others will not. This is emphasized in the *specific-factors model:* an
analytical structure identical to the Heckscher-Ohlin-Samuelson model except that one of the factors—call it capital—is immobile between industries.

Thus suppose two goods—apples and butane—are each produced by
labor and capital. The supply of labor is fixed to the country as a whole and
perfectly mobile between the apple and butane industries, but each sector employs a fixed amount of specific capital. Since apple capital and butane capital
cannot substitute for each other, no mechanism ensures that they are paid
equal rents. But the wage will be the same in both industries.

The specific-factors model formalizes much literature antedating the development of the Heckscher-Ohlin-Samuelson model. Interest in the former
has revived recently in part because of the importance of specific factors in
determining the effects of tariff changes.

Equilibrium

Figure 6.1 shows the equilibrium of a single country as represented by a
specific-factors model. The distance HG measures the total labor supply of
the country, with labor in the apple sector measured off to the right from H
and labor in the butane sector measured off to the left from G. Thus point C
represents an allocation of HC labor to apple production and of CG labor to
butane production. Since the amounts of capital in the two sectors cannot be
altered, they are not shown in the figure. The AA curve measures, for each
level of labor employment in the apple industry, the value of the marginal
product of that labor: $P_A MPL_A$. (P_A denotes the price of apples and MPL_A the
marginal product of labor in the apple industry—that is, the increase in apple
production that would result from the employment of one more laborer.) As
more and more labor works with the fixed stock of apple capital, MPL_A falls;
thus the AA line slopes down. The BB curve analogously shows the value of
the marginal product of labor in the butane industry: $P_B MPL_B$.

Note that the AA curve—and, by analogy, the BB curve—depends upon
three things. First is the technology for producing apples from capital and
labor. If we follow the HOS model, this will be the same across countries. The
second feature is the price of apples: increases or decreases in P_A shift AA up
or down in proportion. Of course, P_A will be the same in countries trading
freely with each other. The third feature is the stock of apple-specific capital.
An additional laborer in the apple industry will raise production more if there
is more capital to work with. Thus increases or decreases in the amount of

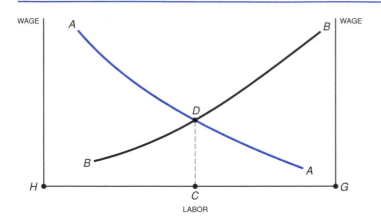

FIGURE 6.1 Equilibrium in the Specific-Factors Model Horizontal movements to the right represent shifting labor from the *B* industry to the *A* industry. This causes the marginal product of labor to rise in the *B* industry and to fall in the *A* industry.

apple-specific capital shift *AA* up or down. There is no reason to expect different countries to have equal amounts of each specific factor, so this feature will cause *AA* and *BB* to differ from country to country.

The value of the marginal product of labor in the apple industry, $P_A MPL_A$, is the amount by which any apple producer can increase his revenue by hiring an additional laborer. As long as that amount exceeds the cost of hiring that worker—the wage *w*—the firm will do so. Thus the apple industry will continue to hire more labor until $w = P_A MPL_A$. For similar reasons the butane industry will hire labor until $w = P_B MPL_B$. Since the two industries pay the same wage in equilibrium, it must be that $P_A MPL_A = P_B MPL_B$. That is, equilibrium is shown by the intersection point *D* in Figure 6.1 so that *HC* is the quantity of labor employed in the apple sector, and *CG* the amount in the butane sector. The wage rate equals *DC*.

Factor Endowments

Now consider changes in the endowments of a country with an equilibrium like that just described. Suppose that the prices of apples and butane do not change. The effects depend upon whether it is the mobile factor or one of the specific factors whose supply alters. Figure 6.2(a) shows the result of an increase in the supply of labor, the mobile factor, in the amount *GG′* (= *DE* = *CF*). Point *G* and the *BB* curve shift to the right by this amount, so the new equilibrium is given by point *D′*. The apple industry has increased its employment of labor by *CC′* and the butane industry its employment by *C′F*. Since each industry has an unchanged quantity of capital, output of both apples and butane

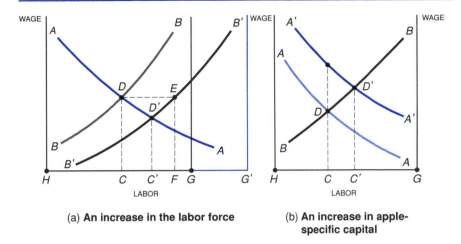

(a) **An increase in the labor force**

(b) **An increase in apple-specific capital**

FIGURE 6.2 **Endowment Changes** An increase in labor "stretches" the horizontal axis, while an increase in the stock of capital specific to one sector increases the marginal product of labor in that sector.

has risen. The wage falls from CD to $C'D'$. (The additional labor must be split between the two sectors so as to keep $P_A MPL_A$ equal to $P_B MPL_B$, and each MPL falls because each worker has less capital to work with.) The rents of both types of capital rise because each type is worked by a larger quantity of labor and, therefore, has a greater marginal physical product. Note how an increase in the supply of the mobile factor has consequences in this specific-factors model that are in sharp contrast to the effects, described by the Rybczynski theorem, of an increase in either factor—necessarily mobile—in the HOS model.

Panel (b) of Figure 6.2 shows the effects of an increase in the endowment of one of the specific factors, apple capital. Any given quantity of labor in the apple industry now has more capital to work with and thus a larger MPL_A: the effect of the endowment change is to shift AA upward. Labor must move from the butane industry to the apple industry to restore equality between the values of its marginal product in the two sectors. In the figure, CC' labor moves from butane production to apple production. Since the apple industry also has more capital than before whereas the quantity of butane capital has not changed, apple production must rise and butane production fall. Thus changes in supplies of specific factors produce results closer to those predicted by the Rybczynski theorem in the HOS model than do changes in the supply of the mobile factor. The wage rate rises from CD to $C'D'$, reflecting the fact that labor in each sector now has more capital to work with. The rentals of both types of capital must, therefore, fall to keep costs in line with the unchanged commodity prices.

Suppose that two countries engage in free trade, and also suppose, as in the HOS model, that the countries consume apples and butane in identical proportions and share an identical technology. Differences in labor supplies are unlikely to be related in any clear way to the pattern of trade between these countries because, as we have seen, a change in the supply of the mobile factor causes both outputs to change in the same direction. But a change in the supply of a specific factor alters outputs of the two goods in opposite directions, so it is likely that each country will export the good using that country's relatively abundant specific factor. Compare this with the Heckscher-Ohlin theorem.

Price Changes

Now that we have examined the structure of the specific-factors model, we are ready to consider the effects of price changes. A rise in P_A raises $P_A MPL_A$ in proportion and so shifts the AA curve up. Figure 6.3 shows the effects of an increase in P_A in the proportion ED/DC. Equilibrium moves from D to D'. Thus CC' labor shifts from butane production to apple production. The wage rises, but not by as much as P_A, since D' is lower than E: w rises relative to (the unchanged) P_B but falls relative to P_A. Thus the effect of the price rise on *real* wages is ambiguous and depends on spending patterns; workers who consume mainly butane will be better off, and those who consume mainly apples will be worse off. (Technology also counts. A little experimentation will convince you that w might rise nearly as much as P_A or hardly at all, depending upon the degrees of steepness of the AA and BB curves.) Contrast this result with the prediction of the Stolper-Samuelson theorem for the HOS model.

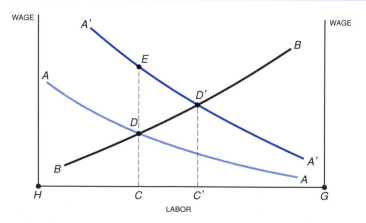

FIGURE 6.3   An Increase in the Price of Apples   An increase in the price of an apple increases the *value* of the marginal product of labor in apple production.

The real rewards of the specific factors, however, do change unambiguously. With more labor to work with, apple capital has a higher marginal product and, accordingly, receives a higher rental in terms of apples and, therefore, in terms of butane as well. Butane capital has less labor to work with, so its rent falls in terms of butane and so in terms of apples also.

Problem

6.22 Show how the effects of an increase in the supply of labor can be described geometrically by a shift, in Figure 6.3, of point *H* and the *AA* curve to the left. Compare the results with Figure 6.2(a).

11. SUMMARY

1. Leontief's finding that U.S. exports tend to use less capital per worker than do U.S. import substitutes and similar calculations by others have undermined faith in the two-good, two-factor Heckscher-Ohlin-Samuelson model as an adequate vehicle for the analysis of trade.

2. Theoretical and empirical investigations have studied alternative approaches. The approaches that have been most successful have typically exploited a factor-endowments explanation requiring more than two factors and goods. Those suggestions, such as demand reversals, tariffs, national increasing returns, and Linder's theory, which abandon the factor-endowments approach, have received less empirical support.

3. Empirical testing has failed to support any tractable version of the Heckscher-Ohlin theorem or any alternative.

4. Empirical work implies that it is important to know whether the four basic propositions derived from the Heckscher-Ohlin-Samuelson model are crucially dependent upon the assumption of just two goods and two factors. A central core of the four propositions does remain valid in the presence of many goods and factors.

5. The specific-factors model modifies the Heckscher-Ohlin-Samuelson model by assuming that one factor is unable to move between sectors.

SUGGESTED READING

Baldwin, R. E. "Determinants of the Commodity Structure of U.S. Trade." *American Economic Review* 1 (1971). An empirical test.

Bowen, H. P., E. E. Leamer, and L. Sveikauskas. "Multicountry, Multifactor Tests of the Factor Abundance Theory." *American Economic Review* 77 (1987). The poor performance of testable theories.

Deardorff, A. V. "Testing Trade Theories and Predicting Trade Flows." In *Handbook of International Economics*. Vol. I. Edited by R. W. Jones and P. B. Kenen. Amsterdam: North-Holland, 1984. Surveys the empirical contributions.

Dixit, A. K., and V. Norman. *Theory of International Trade*. London: Cambridge University Press, 1980. Chapters 1 and 4 discuss the factor-endowments theory with many goods and factors.

Ethier, W. "Some of the Theorems of International Trade with Many Goods and Factors." *Journal of International Economics* 2 (1974). The fate of the basic propositions with more than two goods and factors.

————. "National and International Returns to Scale and the Modern Theory of International Trade." *American Economic Review* 72 (1982). Scale economies, intraindustry trade, and the factor-endowments theory.

Feenstra, R. C., ed. *Empirical Methods for International Trade.* Cambridge: MIT Press, 1988. Contains several articles relevant to this chapter.

Hufbauer, G. C. "The Impact of National Characteristics and Technology on the Commodity Composition of Trade in Manufactured Goods." In *The Technology Factor in International Trade.* Edited by R. Vernon. New York: National Bureau of Economic Research, 1970. An empirical study.

Keesing, D. B. "Labor Skills and Comparative Advantage." *American Economic Review* 2 (1966). The empirical relation between trade patterns and skill groups.

Kenen, P. B. "Nature, Capital and Trade." *Journal of Political Economy* 5 (1965).

Leamer, E. E. *Sources of International Comparative Advantage.* Cambridge: MIT Press, 1984. Indispensable empirical study of the factor-endowments approach.

Leontief, W. "Domestic Production and Foreign Trade: The American Capital Position Re-examined." In *Readings in International Economics.* Edited by R. E. Caves and H. G. Johnson. Homewood: Irwin, 1968. The Leontief Paradox.

Linder, S. B. *An Essay on Trade and Transformation.* New York: Wiley, 1961. Linder's theory.

Magee, S. P. "Three Simple Tests of the Stolper-Samuelson Theorem." In *Current Issues in World Trade and Payments.* Edited by P. Oppenheimer. London: Routledge and Kegan Paul, 1980. Reasons to care about specific factors.

Maskus, K. V. "A Test of the Heckscher-Ohlin-Vanek Theorem: The Leontief Commonplace." *Journal of International Economics* 9 (1985). The first test: the theorem fails.

Mayer, W. "Short-Run and Long-Run Equilibrium for a Small Open Economy." *Journal of Political Economy* (Sept. 1974). Specific factors.

Mussa, M. "Tariffs and the Distribution of Income: The Importance of Factor Specificity, Substitutability, and Intensity in the Short and Long Run." *Journal of Political Economy* (Nov. 1974). Specific factors.

Postner, H. H. *Factor Content of Canadian International Trade, 1975.* Ottawa: Economic Council of Canada, 1975.

Travis, W. P. *The Theory of Trade and Protection.* Cambridge: Harvard University Press, 1964. The effects of tariffs.

Trefler, D. "International Factor Price Differences: Leontief Was Right!" *Journal of Political Economy* 101 (Dec. 1993). International differences in factor productivity and in factor endowments are together consistent with actual trade patterns.

Vanek, J. "The Natural Resource Content of Foreign Trade, 1870–1955, and the Relative Abundance of Natural Resources in the United States." *Review of Economics and Statistics* 2 (1959).

————. "The Factor-Proportions Theory: The N-Factor Case." *Kyklos* 4 (1968). The Heckscher-Ohlin theorem with many goods and factors.

Vernon, R. "International Investment and International Trade in the Product Cycle." *Quarterly Journal of Economics* 2 (1966).

Williams, J. R. "The Resource Content in International Trade." *Canadian Journal of Economics* 2 (1970).

Part Three

Using Trade Theory

The pure theory of international trade studied in Parts One and Two is built squarely on the assumption that commodities can be freely traded among countries but factors are completely immobile internationally. Thus commodity markets are international, whereas factor markets are national. This assumption was the ultimate cause of trade.

Part Three looks at international economic issues that arise when we depart from this basic assumption. Recall from the Introduction that international economics is distinguished from general economics not only by its treatment of markets of differing extent, as studied in Part One, but also by the limits of national sovereignty. This second distinguishing feature arises in Chapters 7, 8, and 9, where we discuss the role of national governments in controlling and limiting international trade. Thus we also depart from the assumption that commodities can be freely traded among countries. Chapter 10 then drops the other half of the assumption—that factors are immobile internationally—to examine issues involving the movement of productive factors from one country to another. The multinational firm is addressed in Chapter 11. In all five chapters we freely apply the basic ideas with which Part One has equipped us.

CHAPTER 7

Tariffs and Trade Theory

> We up in Massachusetts do not want that duty upon molasses, we
> trade our fish for molasses, and if you shut out molasses you shut
> in fish. —U.S. CONGRESSIONAL DEBATES (1790)

The theory of international trade makes on balance a strong case for free
trade. Yet governments have always attempted to control trade to at least
some extent, and deliberate free-trade policies have been very rare historically. We now examine commercial policy: the attempts of national governments to influence or control international trade.

Many instruments can be used to exercise commercial policy. Perhaps
the most familiar is a tax on imports, commonly called a *tariff*. Exports might
also be taxed, and both imports and exports are sometimes subsidized (a negative tax). In addition many *nontariff barriers* do not involve taxes or subsidies at all. Quantitative restrictions, for example, limit the quantities of specific goods that can be imported (or, sometimes, exported). In principle there
might be either maximum or minimum quotas on either exports or imports,
but a quota on the maximum quantity of a good that can be imported in a specific time interval is perhaps the most familiar form. Sometimes tariffs and
quotas are combined. A *tariff-quota* (or customs quota) does not prohibit imports above the quota amount but instead subjects them to a higher tariff than
that imposed on imports within the quota.

In addition to taxes and quantitative restrictions, many nontariff barriers
occupy a gray area: laws, regulations, and procedures that are not explicitly
aimed at international trade but that nonetheless influence it. Overzealous
health inspectors, safety regulations biased toward domestic production
methods, and regional development grants and tax privileges to export industries are examples of a host of measures that influence international trade despite ostensibly different purposes.

In what follows we shall at first be largely concerned with tariffs. This is
because tariffs historically have been the most important form of commercial

policy and because the conclusions we reach with respect to tariffs will easily be adapted to the other forms of protection as well.

1. THE TARIFF

A tariff is a tax on imports: the price a domestic purchaser pays for an imported good exceeds the amount the foreign exporter receives by the tariff payment. All the economic effects of a tariff follow from this simple fact. But a tariff can take many forms.

Specific Tariffs

Perhaps the simplest is a specific tariff: a tax of a specified amount on each unit of a specified good that is imported. If P denotes the foreign price of some good and t_S the specific tariff levied upon it, then the domestic price Q is

$$Q = P + t_S. \tag{7.1}$$

Ad Valorem Tariffs

Alternatively, tariffs are frequently ad valorem: a specified percentage of the price paid to the foreign exporter. If P denotes the foreign price of a good subject to an ad valorem tariff rate t_{AV}, then the domestic price Q is

$$Q = P (1 + t_{AV}). \tag{7.2}$$

The domestic price consists of the payment to the foreigner, P, plus the import tax Pt_{AV}.

Other Forms

Most tariffs are either specific or ad valorem, but other forms are also encountered. For example, the two types are sometimes *combined,* with the total tariff equal to a specific tariff plus a percentage of the price. Yet another type of tariff is a *variable levy:* the tariff is adjusted to keep the domestic price of imports equal to some target level. Thus if Q denotes the target, the variable levy will be equal to $Q - P$ so that a fall in the foreign price results in an increase in the levy. Such tariffs have most often been found on agricultural goods in connection with domestic price-support measures. The English Corn Laws of the early nineteenth century, which taxed grain imports, were of this type, and such levies are important today because the European Union employs them in connection with its Common Agricultural Policy.

Significance of the Forms

The economic effects of a tariff follow from the fact that it causes the domestic price of a good to exceed the price paid to foreigners. Only this difference really matters—not the form of the tariff that brings it about. It is simple arithmetic to calculate the ad valorem rate equivalent to a specific tariff in a given situation and vice versa.

Nevertheless, it sometimes makes a great difference in practice how tariff legislation is written. A general inflationary rise in all prices will cause tariff charges to rise in the same proportion with ad valorem rates, but a specific tariff will not change at all and so will become relatively less important. In the United States and elsewhere many actual tariffs are specific, and the substantial inflation since the Second World War has greatly reduced their importance.

A second practical difference between the forms arises from the fact that tariff laws necessarily apply to categories of goods, with some products in any category more expensive than others. For example, the U.S. specific tariff of \$1.17 per gallon on sparkling wine is proportionally much more significant for an Asti Spumante sold for \$4 per gallon by an Italian exporter than for a French champagne costing \$30 per gallon.

We are interested in the economic consequences of tariff protection, regardless of the form it takes. It is simplest to focus on an ad valorem tariff, even if the protection is actually due to some other form. Also, we shall be mainly concerned with the *overall* effects of protection rather than with the consequences of different tariff rates on different goods (we will turn to this later). Suppose that imports face a uniform ad valorem tariff of t. If P_M equals the price paid to foreigners and Q_M the domestic price, then

$$Q_M = P_M (1 + t). \tag{7.3}$$

Suppose that exports are not taxed, so that the price P_X that foreigners pay for our exports equals the price Q_X received by exporters. Let $q = Q_M/Q_X$, the domestic relative price of imports in terms of exports, and $p = P_M/P_X$ the foreign relative price. Then, since $Q_X = P_X$,

$$\frac{Q_M}{Q_X} = \frac{P_M}{P_X} (1 + t)$$

or

$$q = p (1 + t). \tag{7.4}$$

Thus the overall economic impact of a tariff is to cause the home relative price of imports in terms of exports to exceed the foreign relative price. This can also be emphasized by rewriting (7.4) as

$$t = \frac{q - p}{p}. \tag{7.5}$$

The tariff rate equals the percentage by which q exceeds p.

Problems

7.1 In the example of the specific tariff on sparkling wine, calculate the equivalent ad valorem rates on both Asti Spumante and champagne, and compare the two. Suppose instead that sparkling wine is subject to a 10 percent ad valorem rate. Calculate the equivalent specific tariffs on both products. Suppose that both export prices rise by 50 percent. Calculate the changes in tariff payments in all cases.

7.2 Explicitly derive expression (7.5) from expression (7.4).

7.3 The text discussed some ways in which it would matter in practice whether a tariff is specific or ad valorem. Try to think of some ways in which a variable levy could in practice differ from the other two.

7.4 The United States has always had many specific tariffs and many ad valorem tariffs. By contrast, European tariffs became largely specific during the 1920s and have become largely ad valorem since the Second World War. Can you think of any reasons for this change?

2. COMPARATIVE ADVANTAGE AND TARIFFS

Suppose that a country taxes all imports at the rate t, producing that gap between q and p indicated in (7.5). What are the economic consequences? To answer this we apply the basic ideas of the pure theory of international trade, starting with comparative advantage.

The fact that q exceeds p implies that a tariff is inefficient for the world as a whole. Recall from Chapter 1 that if an economy produces both goods, their relative price equals the marginal rate of transformation (*MRT*) between them: the amount of one good that must be forgone in order to produce one more unit of the other. Then if both importables and exportables are produced both at home and abroad, the fact that q exceeds p means that MRT_{XM} is greater at home—that is, more exports must be sacrificed to produce one more importable at home than abroad. This means that the world can produce more of either or both goods if the home economy switches resources from importables toward exports, if the rest of the world does the opposite, and if the two countries trade more. This is a straightforward application of the reasoning in Chapter 1, which you should review now if the above argument is not clear.

In similar fashion, q equals the MRS_{XM} of each domestic consumer and p the MRS_{XM} of each foreign consumer. Thus the former exceeds the latter: each domestic consumer is willing to sacrifice more exports to obtain one more import than each foreign consumer would require to supply it. So consumers in both countries can be made better off by trading more. This is just a straightforward application of the reasoning in section 7 of Chapter 1.

Thus a literal application of comparative advantage gives the first conclusion about tariffs: *tariffs are inefficient for the world as a whole.*

Comparative advantage also shows that a country that levies a tariff itself suffers in two ways: it pays a *production cost* and a *consumption cost*.

The production cost refers to the fact that a country that levies a tariff produces a mix of goods worth less at international prices than the country is capable of producing. International relative prices equal p, and domestic prices q equal the MRT_{XM}. Since q exceeds p, MRT_{XM} likewise exceeds p. Thus the exports that could be produced by producing one less unit of importables (MRT_{XM}) exceeds the number of exports that are worth the same as one importable (p). The value of national income could be increased by producing fewer importables and more exports.

This is illustrated in Figure 7.1. The international price p is equal to OA/OC, which is the same as OB/OD: the lines AC and BD are drawn parallel. The domestic relative price q equals OH/OG; this exceeds the world price by the amount of the tariff. The domestic production possibility frontier is TT'. Domestic firms will produce where the MRT_{XM} equals q, the relative price they face. This is at E, where the slope of the production possibility frontier (the MRT_{XM}) equals the domestic relative price OH/OG. The line AC shows all combinations of the two goods that are equal in value to combination E at *international* prices. Thus OC shows the international value of domestic output expressed in terms of importables, and OA shows it expressed in terms of exportables.

If the domestic economy were instead to produce at F, where MRT_{XM} equals the international price p, the international value of domestic output would be OD in terms of importables and OB in terms of exportables. Thus, because of the tariff, the value of domestic output at international prices is

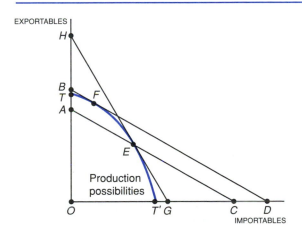

FIGURE 7.1 The Production Cost of a Tariff A tariff causes a country to produce too many importables and not enough exportables, reducing the value of national production by *AB* in terms of exportables and by *CD* in terms of importables.

less than it need be by the amount *CD* in terms of importables or *AB* in terms of exportables. This loss is the production cost of the tariff. It results from the fact that the tariff causes domestic firms to respond to a distorted price *(q)* rather than to the true international price *(p)*.

The *consumption cost* of a tariff similarly is due to the fact that consumers respond to a distorted price. Since *q* exceeds *p,* consumers purchase fewer imports than they would wish to do if they were free to buy at the international price: the fact that consumers collectively tax themselves by the amount of the tariff causes them to distort their consumption patterns. The loss of welfare resulting from the fact that each consumer purchases a combination of goods less desirable than what he can afford at the international price is called the consumption cost.

This cost can be viewed more formally. The domestic price *q* is equal to the MRS_{XM} of each consumer: the most exports the consumer would willingly sacrifice to obtain one more unit of imports. Since the MRS_{XM} $(= q)$ exceeds *p* by the tariff, the consumer is willing to sacrifice more exports to obtain an additional import than he has to pay on the international market (that is, *p*) to do so.

Despite the fact that a country burdens itself with both a production cost and a consumption cost by levying a tariff, we cannot conclude that the country is necessarily worse off. This is because a tariff could have additional effects. For example, the tariff could cause the international price to change. If the price declines so that the terms of trade improve, that constitutes a benefit to be weighed against the production and consumption costs. The former could conceivably outweigh the latter. But if a country does benefit from a tariff, it is at the expense of the rest of the world. This is because our first conclusion in this section was that a tariff necessarily harms the world as a whole.

Problems

7.5 Suppose you have the following data for Germany:

P_B/P_A	B demand	B supply	A demand	A supply
4/3	80	110		30
1	100	100	50	

Suppose the international price of butane is 1 bushel of apples and that Germany imports butane with a tariff of 1/3. What is the production cost to Germany in terms of apples? In terms of butane?

7.6 Industries often request tariff protection from foreign competition. But if a tariff *protects* industry, how can it cause a production *cost*?

7.7 The argument in the text concluded that a home tariff harmed the world because the MRT_{XM} and MRS_{XM} at home were larger than abroad. Go through the argument again under the assumption that the home and foreign countries *both* tax their imports.

7.8* As in Problem **2.8,** 5 labor units are required to produce 1 unit of either cloth or wine in England, 100 labor units are available, and the English always consume the two goods in equal quantities. Suppose the world price of wine is 1/3 bolts of cloth and that England imports wine with a 100 percent tariff. What are the production and consumption costs to England?

3.* *EXPLORING FURTHER:* THE GEOMETRY OF TARIFF COSTS

This section adds further geometric detail to the previous section. Figure 7.2 illustrates the consumption cost of a tariff. E represents production in the presence of a tariff. (To reduce clutter, the rest of the production possibility frontier is not drawn.) AC shows the consumption possibilities attainable by trade (OC/OA equals the terms of trade). The best obtainable consumption is at M, where AC is tangent to a community indifference curve. But the country will not in fact consume here. This is because at M, the MRS_{XM} (indicated by the slope of the community indifference curve U_0) equals p (reflected in the slope of AC), whereas the tariff causes consumers to equate the MRS_{XM} to the domestic price q, which exceeds p. Thus the economy will consume at that point on the budget line AC where the intersecting community indifference curve has a slope of q. This is N, where q, equal to NQ/QR, equals the MRS_{XM} (indicated by the slope of the indifference curve U_1).

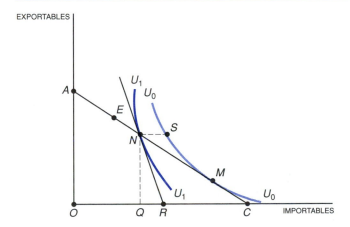

FIGURE 7.2 **The Consumption Cost of a Tariff** A tariff causes a country to consume too many exportables and not enough importables, reducing welfare.

The consumption cost of the tariff is reflected in the fact that N is on a lower indifference curve than M—the tariff causes the community to spend its actual income in a suboptimal fashion. This cost can be measured in terms of importables by the horizontal distance NS between the two curves.

Figure 7.3 shows the total effect of the tariff on the domestic economy. The relative price of imports again equals $OB/OD (= OA/OC)$. The highest indifference curve the country can attain at these prices is U_F, reached by producing at F (where $MRT_{XM} = p$) and trading to consume at F' (where MRS_{XM}). But the tariff distorts the decisions of domestic firms that produce at E instead, where the production cost of CD is incurred, so that the highest attainable indifference curve is now U_0. But even this is not reached because the tariff also distorts the decisions of domestic consumers, who consume at N rather than M. The steep gray lines through E and N are parallel, with the common slope reflecting domestic relative prices.

If the tariff has caused the terms of trade to differ from their free-trade value, Figure 7.3 does not capture the full effect. Figure 7.4 shows a case in which the tariff has caused the terms of trade to improve so much that the country is better off than without the tariff, despite the production and consumption costs. Without the tariff, the terms of trade would equal OC'/OA' and U_F is the highest attainable indifference curve, reached by producing at F and consuming at F'. The tariff has caused the terms of trade to improve to OC/OA, allowing the community to consume at N, which is on a higher indifference curve than is F'. Thus the country is better off with the tariff, despite the production and consumption costs.

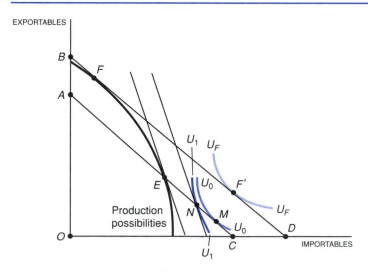

FIGURE 7.3   General Equilibrium of a Tariff   With a tariff, the country produces at E and consumes at N. If it could freely trade at the same international price, it would produce at F and consume at F'.

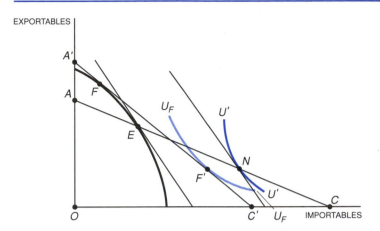

FIGURE 7.4 An Increase in National Welfare The tariff shifts consumption from F' to N and raises national welfare because, in this example, it causes an improvement in the terms of trade large enough to outweigh the production and consumption costs.

Problems

7.9 In Figures 7.3 and 7.4, the gray line through E is inside the parallel gray line through N: the combinations of goods equal in value at domestic prices to actual production are smaller than the combinations equal in value to actual consumption. Why is this the case? How can you interpret the distance between the two gray lines?

7.10 Prove that point N in Figures 7.2 and 7.3 must lie northwest of M—that is, the consumption distortion of a tariff reduces trade instead of increasing it. On what does your proof depend?

4. TARIFFS AND PRICES

A country suffers a consumption cost and a production cost from its own tariff, but we are unable to tell whether the country is worse off if we do not know what happens to the terms of trade. International equilibrium describes how relative prices are determined. We, therefore, use it to discover the effects of a tariff on both international prices (p) and domestic prices (q).

Recall from Chapter 4 that an import demand curve shows how much a country is willing to import at each price. The line through points 0, A, and B in Figure 7.5(a) and (b) shows a country's *free-trade import demand curve:* the import demand curve if no tariff exists. Suppose now that the country levies a tariff on imports at the rate t. What happens to the import demand curve?

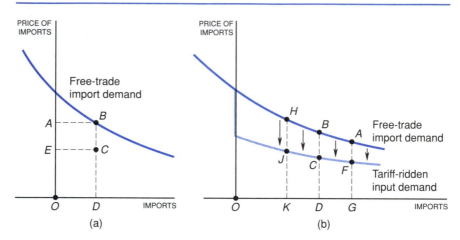

FIGURE 7.5   The Effect of a Tariff on the Import Demand Curve   Imposing a tariff shifts the import demand curve down by a proportion equal to the tariff rate. Thus $t = BC/CD = HJ/JK = AF/FG$.

Consider any point, such as B in Figure 7.5(a). Since B is on the free-trade import demand curve, it indicates that at a price OA, citizens of this country would buy OD imports, paying $OABD$ exports for them. Review section 2 of Chapter 4 if this is not clear. Under free trade, the whole quantity $OABD$ is what the country is willing to export to the rest of the world in exchange for OD. But if there is a tariff, part of the total payment $OABD$ must be paid to the government for the tariff, and only a portion will be left for the rest of the world. Point C in Figure 7.5(a) is drawn so that BC/CD equals the tariff rate t. Then in order to obtain the quantity OD of imports, the citizens of this country are willing to pay the price BD of which BC is the tariff, so that the country is willing to pay the price CD to the rest of the world in exchange for OD. In the proportion t, B has shifted downward to C as a result of the tariff. (This assumes that the government does not use any of the tariff revenue it collects to buy imports.)

The same is true of every point on the free-trade import demand curve: it shifts downward in the proportion t as a result of the tariff. In Figure 7.5(b), the curve through J, C, and F is the tariff-ridden import demand curve (so that $HJ/JK = BC/CD = AF/FG = t$).

The Tariff and the Terms of Trade

Now that we know what a tariff does to the import demand curve, we can see what it does to relative prices. First, the terms of trade. In Figure 7.6(a), (b), and (c), M represents the free-trade home import demand curve, and X the free-trade foreign export supply curve. Thus *OA* represents the quantity imported without a tariff, and the price is *AE*. Now suppose the home country levies a tariff. This produces no effect on the foreign curve because nothing has changed in the foreign country. But the home curve shifts downward in the proportion of the tariff. The new tariff-ridden home curve is illustrated by *M'*, and *OA'* represents imports. The new international price is *A'E'*.

The general conclusion is that *a tariff improves the terms of trade of any country sizable enough to influence international prices.* In Figure 7.6(a) the import price after the tariff, *A'E'*, is much lower than before, *AE*. Similarly, in Figure 7.6(b) the tariff improves the terms of trade, though not as dramati-

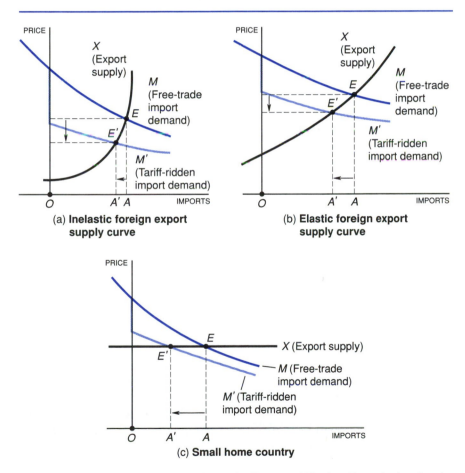

(a) **Inelastic foreign export supply curve**

(b) **Elastic foreign export supply curve**

(c) **Small home country**

FIGURE 7.6 **The Effect of a Tariff on the Terms of Trade** By reducing the demand for imports, a tariff forces down their price. The more elastic the foreign export supply curve, the smaller this improvement in the home terms of trade.

cally as in Figure 7.6(a). In general, by imposing a tariff a country shifts its import demand curve down and causes international equilibrium to move along the foreign export supply curve toward the origin. This improves the terms of trade of the tariff-levying country. As Figures 7.6(a) and (b) illustrate, the improvement is greater the more *inelastic* the foreign curve.

By levying a tariff, a country induces its citizens to demand fewer imports from abroad, thereby driving down their price. The more inelastic the foreign curve, the more the price of imports must fall in order to reduce foreign supply to the lower demand.

If the home country is too small to influence world prices, there can be no improvement in the terms of trade. The tariff simply causes the country to trade less at the same price as before. This is illustrated in Figure 7.6(c), where $A'E = AE$.

A tariff produces a terms-of-trade gain, which must be weighed against the consumption cost and the production cost to determine whether the tariff has on balance benefited the home country. A small country necessarily loses: there is no improvement in the terms of trade.

The Tariff and the Domestic Relative Price of Imports

How does a tariff influence domestic relative prices? In free trade, the domestic relative price of imports in terms of exports, q_F, equals the international relative price p_F:

$$q_F = p_F. \tag{7.6}$$

With a tariff, the domestic relative price exceeds the international price by the amount of the tariff:

$$q_T = p_T (1 + t). \tag{7.7}$$

Thus the tariff, by definition, causes q to increase, *compared to p*. But we have just seen that a tariff also improves the terms of trade—that is, reduces p. Thus it is not clear whether on balance the domestic price rises or falls: whether q_T is greater than or less than q_F. If the international price falls by a smaller percentage than the tariff, the domestic price must rise. For example, if a 10 percent tariff reduces p by 5 percent, then q rises by 5 percent. But if the 10 percent tariff reduces p by 20 percent, q falls 10 percent.

The slope of the foreign export supply curve influences the behavior of the domestic relative price. This is illustrated in Figure 7.7. Free-trade equilibrium is at E, and the tariff-ridden equilibrium is at E'. Thus the *free-trade* relative domestic price equals AE. To find the *tariff-ridden* domestic price, consider point G on the free-trade home curve directly above E'. In order to buy OA' of imports, domestic citizens pay the price GA', including the tariff payment. The domestic price has increased as a result of the tariff: GA' is greater than AE. In this case the foreign curve slopes up. But if the foreign curve instead bends back, as in Figure 7.7(b), the domestic relative price will fall as a result of a tariff. This strange outcome is called the *Metzler Paradox* after the late economist Lloyd Metzler of the University of Chicago, who showed when it could happen.

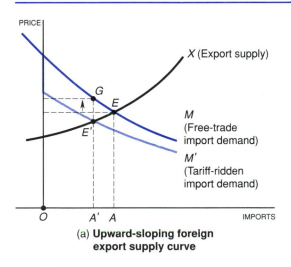

(a) **Upward-sloping foreign export supply curve**

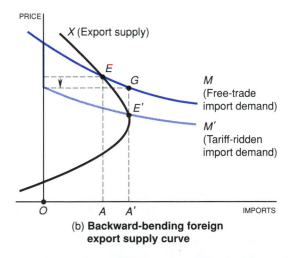

(b) **Backward-bending foreign export supply curve**

FIGURE 7.7 **The Effect of a Tariff on Domestic Relative Prices** The domestic relative price of imports is higher with a tariff than without if the foreign export supply curve slopes up, but it is lower if the foreign export supply curve bends back.

Problems

7.11 If you did Problem **4.7** correctly, you obtained the import demand curve below. How is it affected by a 50 percent German tariff on apple imports?

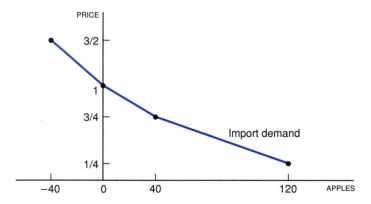

7.12 If you did Problem **4.6** correctly, you obtained the export supply curve below. Suppose that France levies no tariff and engages in trade with the Germany of Problem **7.11,** above. Show the effect of the German tariff on the trade between the two countries. What is the effect on the terms of trade and on domestic relative prices in both countries?

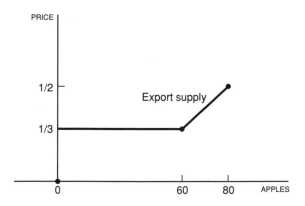

7.13* Show how a tariff on imports shifts a country's export supply curve. Use the export supply curve to show the effect of a tariff on international and domestic relative prices. How does a 10 percent French tariff on butane affect the curve in Problem **7.12?**

7.14* The discussion in the text implicitly assumed that the government spends all tariff revenues on exportables. In Figure 7.5(a), for example, domestic citizens pay *OECD* to the rest of the world for the import *OD*, and they pay *ABCE* to their government as tariff revenue. If some of this revenue, however, is spent on imports, total imports will equal not *OD*, but *OD* plus the imports that are bought with the tariff revenue. Suppose, contrary to the discussion in the text, that the government always spends *all* tariff revenues on additional *imports*. Show how a tariff affects the home import demand curve in this case. Under these circumstances, will a tariff still improve the terms of trade? When will it increase the relative domestic price of imports?

5. TARIFFS AND THE FACTOR-ENDOWMENTS THEORY

The previous section showed that a tariff raises the domestic price of importables relative to exportables (if the foreign export supply curve does not bend back). Recall from Chapter 5 the *Heckscher-Ohlin theorem:* a country has a comparative advantage in the commodity whose production is relatively intensive in the country's relatively abundant factor.

It follows, then, that a tariff raises the domestic price of the good that uses intensively the country's relatively scarce factor: if France is capital abundant and exports capital-intensive apples, then a French tariff raises the French price of labor-intensive butane relative to apples. The tariff tends to displace resources from apple production to butane production.

A tariff protects that industry which makes intensive use of the country's relatively scarce factor.

The factor-endowments theory also sheds light on how protection influences the domestic distribution of income. Recall the *Stolper-Samuelson theorem:* a rise in the price of any commodity causes the price of the factor used intensively in the production of that commodity to rise in even greater proportion, and the reward of the other factor falls. Since a tariff can be expected to raise the domestic relative price of the good intensive in the country's scarce factor, it follows that the reward of the scarce factor rises relative to both commodities and the reward of the abundant factor falls relative to both commodities. The French tariff on butane raises labor's real income and lowers capital's.

A tariff increases the real income of the country's relatively scarce factor and reduces the real income of the country's relatively abundant factor.

Thus the tariff redistributes income *within* the tariff-levying country so that some class will favor protection and some class will oppose it. As we have seen, the country as a whole will lose as long as the terms-of-trade effect of the tariff does not outweigh the consumption and production costs. This means that the abundant factor loses more from a tariff than the scarce factor gains: the former could in principle "bribe" the latter to forgo protection and still be better off than with a tariff. But in the absence of any sort of compensation or redistribution, those people whose incomes come from the earnings of the scarce factor have a definite interest in protection, even if it is harmful to their country overall.

All this presupposes that both factors are freely mobile between the two industries, as in the Heckscher-Ohlin-Samuelson model. But with a more short-run horizon the specific factors model, discussed in Chapter 6, might be more relevant. Suppose, then, that capital is specific to the industry in which it is located but that labor is still free to move between sectors.

Recall from Chapter 6 that a rise in the relative price of a good causes an even greater proportional rise in the reward of the factor specific to that sector and a fall in the reward of the factor specific to the other sector. Since a tariff can be expected to raise the relative domestic price of imports in terms of exports, a French tariff on butane raises the real income of butane capital and lowers that of apple capital.

A tariff increases the real reward of the factor specific to the import-competing sector and reduces the real reward of the factor specific to the export sector.

The mobile factor has no clear stake in either protection or free trade. Perhaps, being in the middle, labor will fare about the same as the country as a whole, suffering from protection unless a significant improvement results in the terms of trade. But the direction of change in the welfare of any individual laborer will be sensitive to her pattern of spending.

Problems

7.15 On the basis of the discussion in this section, which factors of production in the American economy would you expect to favor protection?

7.16 Discuss how commercial policy could help explain the differences in agricultural yields shown in Table 5.1. How could changes in such policy help explain the relative wage movements shown in Table 5.2?

7.17 What is the effect of a tariff upon the domestic distribution of income if the foreign export supply curve bends back?

7.18* Deduce how the factor-price equalization theorem would be affected by the presence of a tariff in one or both countries.

6. NONTARIFF BARRIERS

The previous three sections developed the theory of tariffs by exploiting each of the three fundamental ideas of international trade theory. The conclusions also apply in large part to nontariff forms of protection. For example, import subsidies operate like tariffs but in the opposite direction—they are in effect negative tariffs. Thus the earlier conclusions need only be reversed to apply to subsidies. In this section we consider several additional forms of protection. Instead of working out a complete theory for each form, we show how tariff theory can be adapted to include these alternatives.

Export Tax

Sometimes exports rather than imports are taxed. To isolate the effects, suppose that a country levies a tax at the ad valorem rate t on all exports but leaves imports free of tax. The domestic price of importables, Q_M, therefore, equals the price paid to foreigners, P_M:

$$Q_M = P_M. \tag{7.8}$$

Since exports are taxed, the price at which they are sold to foreigners, P_X, equals the domestic price, Q_X, plus the tax, tQ_X.

$$Q_X (1 + t) = P_X. \tag{7.9}$$

To examine relative prices, divide (7.9) into (7.8):

$$\frac{Q_M}{Q_X} \frac{1}{(1 + t)} = \frac{P_M}{P_X}$$

or, recalling that q equals the domestic relative price of imports in terms of exports, Q_M/Q_X, and that p equals the international relative price P_M/P_X,

$$q = p (1 + t). \tag{7.10}$$

Compare (7.10) with (7.4). They are identical. *A tax on exports is equivalent to an equal tax on imports.* This result is known as Lerner's symmetry theorem, after the economist, Abba Lerner, who elucidated it.

Tariffs and export taxes exert economic effects by influencing relative prices. An export tax differs from a tariff in two ways: (1) it applies to exports rather than imports, and (2) it causes the foreign price of the taxed good to exceed the domestic price (rather than vice versa). These two differences just cancel out so that, on balance, there is no difference. All the conclusions of the previous three sections concerning tariffs apply equally well to export taxes.

It is important, however, to realize the limitations of the symmetry theorem. It assumes that the only relative price that matters is that of imports in general with respect to exports in general. Thus it says that a uniform tariff on all imports is equivalent to an equal uniform tax on all exports. A tariff of 10 percent on oil is not equivalent to a tax of 10 percent on the export of wheat. The relative price of oil in terms of wheat is not the only relative price; there are many other goods to consider as well.

How important are export taxes in practice? They are certainly far less common than tariffs in the industrial countries. There are, in fact, *no* American export taxes; they are expressly forbidden by the U.S. Constitution. (This prohibition was inserted in part to mollify the South, the major export region of the country at the time, which feared that the new government might finance itself by taxing southern exports of cotton and tobacco.) Nevertheless, they are important. OPEC's primary instrument of commercial policy is an oil export tax (although it is not often called that). More generally, many LDCs tax the export of primary products, as Brazil does with coffee.

Import Quotas

Quantitative restrictions, or quotas, have become increasingly important in recent years. A quota is a blunter instrument than a tariff: instead of taxing imports, it directly limits the quantity that can be brought into the country. Figure 7.8 shows how an import quota works.

Figure 7.8(a) depicts the free-trade home import and foreign export curves. Equilibrium is at *E,* so the home country imports *OA* at price *EA*. Now suppose that the home economy imposes an import quota of *OQ*. This has no effect on the portion of the home curve from *B* to *F* because in this region the economy imports less than the quota. But the portion of the import demand curve beyond *F* is now ruled out; in effect, the home import demand curve becomes *BFE'Q*.

The home economy now imports *OQ*. In order to supply us with this quantity, the rest of the world must be paid the price *QE'*. But domestic citizens are willing to pay *QF* to obtain the imports. What happens to the difference, *FE'*? This measures the value of a quota allotment. Since a quota limits the right to import, those individuals who are allotted such rights have something of value. Since an import can be purchased for *E'Q* and sold for *FQ*, resulting in a profit *FE'*, this profit is the value of having the right to import 1 unit.

The disposition of this value depends upon government policy. The government could reserve for itself the right to conduct the country's trade and

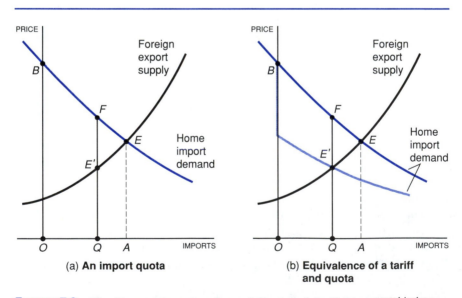

(a) **An import quota**

(b) **Equivalence of a tariff and quota**

FIGURE 7.8   **The Economics of an Import Quota**   A tariff rate of *FE'/E'Q* has the same effects as an import quota of *OQ*, with the quota rights auctioned by the government.

earn the profit *FE'*, which would thereby enter the coffers of the state. Alternatively, the government could auction off import rights to the highest bidder. In this case the government would be able to sell the rights at the price *FE'*, which would again be revenue of the government. In either case, *E'* represents the actual trade between the two countries. The home country imports *OQ*, for which domestic citizens pay the price *FQ*. Of this, *E'Q* is paid to the rest of the world, and FE' is paid to the domestic government. Thus the international relative price is *E'Q*, and the domestic relative price is *FQ*.

This is the same result that would have been obtained by an appropriate tariff, as shown in Figure 7.8(b). If the home country had instead levied a tariff at rate *FE'/E'Q*, the home import curve would have shifted down as is depicted in Figure 7.8(b). In this case, *OQ* would be the quantity imported, and *FE'* would have been the government's revenue per unit—the same result as achieved by an import quota *OQ*. Thus there is a basic equivalence between tariffs and quotas:

> *The results of any quota can be duplicated by an appropriate tariff policy, and the results of any tariff can be duplicated by an appropriate quota policy.*

Because of this equivalence, all our conclusions about the economic effects of tariffs apply equally well to quotas. But just as with the Lerner symmetry theorem, care must be observed in relying upon this result. Jagdish Bhagwati of Columbia University and other economists have emphasized that various circumstances might vitiate the equivalence between tariffs and quotas. For example, governments often do not appropriate the value of quotas. Quota allotments might be distributed in proportion to previous imports, or, especially in the case of intermediate products, they might be distributed in proportion to importers' abilities to process the imports. This method was used with the U.S. quota on petroleum imports that was in effect from 1958 to 1973. In these cases the value *FE'* goes not to the government, but, rather, to those firms or individuals who receive allotments. Alternatively, government officials might pass out the allotments in return for bribes. In this case *FE'* lines the pockets of corrupt bureaucrats. Under all the circumstances, a quota results in a different distribution of domestic income than does a tariff and could confront individuals with different incentives. It could also lead to a different international distribution. The government might not allocate import rights at all, but instead have foreign governments allocate rights to export to us. In this case, *FE'* is not captured by the domestic economy, but instead accrues to the foreign country. The domestic economy then pays the price *FQ* for *OQ*. This has been the case with some U.S. attempts to limit textile imports. Instead of imposing import quotas on textiles, the U.S. government has persuaded various foreign governments to adopt "voluntary" quotas on exports to the United States. This has ensured that the values of the allotments are captured by foreigners. This point will also arise when we discuss

Japanese automobile exports to the United States in section 10 below. The equivalence between tariffs and quotas also breaks down in the face of other circumstances, such as imperfect competition and uncertainty about the future, that alter the role of the import demand curve.

Problems

7.19 Show how your answers to Problems **7.11** and **7.12** could be duplicated by an appropriate quota.

7.20 Suppose that a certain country exercises commercial policy solely through an *export* quota. Discuss the economic effects, and draw the analog to Figure 7.8. To what extent are import quotas and export quotas related to each other in the way that the Lerner symmetry theorem relates import taxes and export taxes?

7.21 The Indian government has established import quotas on many goods used as productive inputs by that country's industry. In some cases these quotas have been allocated among importing firms in proportion to the output capacities of the firms. What is the effect of such an allocation system on economic incentives? Discuss the long-run implications, and compare them to those of a tariff.

7.22 Suppose that a certain economy uses three goods: imports, exports, and nontraded goods. There are thus two relative commodity prices: the price of imports in terms of exports and the price of nontraded goods in terms of exports. Show how a tariff on imports affects both relative prices (as Equations (7.4) and (7.10) do in the text), and do the same for a tax on exports. What do you conclude about the Lerner symmetry theorem?

7.23 Consider a quota and its equivalent tariff, as in Figure 7.8. Show how each form of protection causes equilibrium to respond to

a an outward shift of the foreign export supply curve.

b an outward shift of the home free-trade import demand curve.

7. TARIFFS WITH SCALE ECONOMIES

Chapter 2 showed that economies of scale can furnish a basis for trade independently of comparative advantage. In this section, we consider the effects of tariffs in this case.

The Scale Cost of a Tariff

Tariffs inhibit specialization. Often a country will produce some goods or varieties of goods that would be entirely imported in the absence of protection. If the production of these goods entails national increasing returns to scale, there is an additional cost to the protection, for both the tariff-levying country and the world. For suppose the former were to cease producing these goods and instead import them from the rest of the world, which, therefore, would increase its production. The foreign scale of operations would now be larger than the scale in each country with the tariff. Thus the goods imported and consumed at home would now be produced at lower average cost than before, and the goods consumed abroad would also be produced at lower cost.

The *scale cost* of a tariff is the increased cost of production that arises when the tariff causes some goods to be produced in more locations than necessary and thereby sacrifices available scale economies. Although it has to do with production, this should not be confused with the production cost mentioned earlier. The production cost arises when some goods are produced in the *wrong* location (one with a higher opportunity cost than somewhere else), whereas the scale cost arises when goods are produced in *too many* locations.

External Economies of Scale

Scale economies provide another addition to our catalog of possible tariff costs. But they can also cause tariffs to have other, dramatic effects. To see this, we need to be more specific about the scale economies. Suppose that, in both France and Germany, butane can be produced in the same way with increasing returns to scale that are external to the firm. That is, as a country's butane industry expands, average cost falls for all firms in the industry, but individual firms cannot reduce their own costs by expanding. Labor is the only factor, and apple production involves constant returns to scale.

Suppose that with free trade France produces both goods, exporting apples to Germany for butane. Germany produces only butane. If the two countries are about the same size, the German butane industry will be larger than the French, and so German costs will be lower. Since the two countries compete on equal terms in the French butane market, wages must be higher in Germany than in France.

Now suppose that the French introduce a tariff on butane. The French produce fewer apples and more butane, which reduces costs as scale economies are realized. Wages rise in France and fall in Germany. If the tariff is large enough, Germany could begin producing and exporting apples, with the French specializing in butane production. The positions of the two countries will have reversed. In this case the tariff will have become redundant—France is no longer importing butane—and can be removed. Tariff protection has been temporary and, in effect, amounted to export promotion.

Whether world welfare rises or falls depends upon the sizes of the two countries and on their relative efficiency in producing apples. If France and Germany are identical, world welfare will not change. The tariff is basically a weapon for one country to better itself at the expense of another.

International Economies of Scale and Product Differentiation

Additional consequences of protection emerge in the presence of international scale economies due to the division of labor. Suppose that such economies are important in automobiles, produced under free trade by a single, globally integrated industry with some stages of automobile production taking place at home, some stages abroad, and international trade in intermediate products. Tariff protection, by making this trade more costly, limits the division of labor, increasing the global cost of automobile production. We saw in Chapter 2 how protection had this effect on the North American automobile industry before the U.S.-Canada automobile agreement established free trade within the industry.

Tariffs can also influence how stages of the global industry locate at home and abroad. If one country levies tariffs on some intermediate goods and if these goods can be produced in either country at about the same cost, production will tend to locate in the country with the tariff and to export from there to the rest of the world, thereby avoiding the tariff. The threat of U.S. protection, for example, induced Japanese firms to shift part of the automobile production process to the United States.

Tariffs on differentiated consumer goods can produce analogous results. By raising the cost of foreign-produced varieties, they reduce consumer choice; if they cause some varieties to be produced in more than one location, they also generate scale costs as discussed above.

Problem

7.24 The text discussed the effects of a tariff if, with free trade, France and Germany both produced butane, which has increasing returns to scale, but only France produced apples, which are subject to constant returns. How does the argument change if initially only Germany produces butane but both countries produce apples? What do you conclude from this?

---

8. TARIFFS WITH IMPERFECT COMPETITION

Chapter 3 showed that imperfect competition can furnish an independent basis for trade. Now we investigate the consequences of protection in such a context.

Oligopoly

Suppose that the butane market is an oligopolistic one. There is one French producer and one German producer. Figure 7.9 shows their competition in the French market, with imports of butane from Germany measured on the vertical axis and domestic sales by the French firm on the horizontal axis.

Recall the discussion of Figure 3.4. Each firm's best-response curve in Figure 7.9 shows how much butane that firm would sell for each level of sales by its rival. Thus the French best-response curve shows, for each level of imports from Germany, the amount of French sales that would maximize the

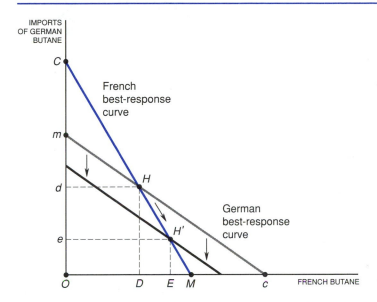

FIGURE 7.9   A Tariff in an Oligopolistic Market   A French tariff on German butane shifts down the German best-response curve, reducing imports of German butane and raising the sales of the French firm a smaller amount.

profit of the French firm. Moving up along this curve, from M to H' and H and toward C, the French reduce their sales in response to increased imports but by a smaller amount so that total sales rise and the price of butane falls. The German best-response curve has an analogous interpretation. Point H in the figure shows equilibrium: if the German firm exports Od to France and the French firm sells OD locally, each will be maximizing its own profit, given the behavior of the other.

Now suppose the French government imposes a tariff on imports of butane from Germany. For any level of French production, the German firm will now find export sales less profitable than before and so will export less. The German best-response curve shifts down, as shown in Figure 7.9. Equilibrium moves from H to H'. Thus German sales fall by de, while French sales increase the (smaller) amount DE. Less butane is sold in France than before, at a higher domestic price. The profit of the French firm has risen.

The tariff has evidently had two countervailing influences on French welfare. First, it has shifted oligopolistic profit from the foreign firm to the domestic one. This *profit-shifting effect* is beneficial to France but maybe not to Germany. Second, by reducing imports it has made the French butane market less competitive. This *anticompetitive effect* harms the French.

Now consider the effects of trade policy in an oligopolistic export market. (We saw in Chapter 3 that oligopoly could induce two-way trade in identical products.) Figure 7.10 shows French and German best-response curves

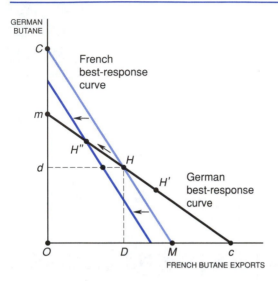

FIGURE 7.10 **Export Tax or Subsidy in an Oligopolistic Market** A French export tax shifts the French best-response curve to the left, reducing French exports of butane and raising the sales of the German firm a smaller amount.

in the German butane market. Again, equilibrium is at *H,* with the French firm exporting *OD* to Germany, and the German firm selling *Od* locally. France may either tax or subsidize its exports to Germany. An export tax will shift the French best-response curve to the left so that equilibrium will move to a point like *H″* in the figure. French exports fall, and domestic sales by the German firm rise, but not as much, so total sales fall and price rises. An export subsidy will instead shift the French best-response curve to the right, so equilibrium moves to a point like *H′* in the figure. French exports rise, and domestic sales by the German firm fall, but again not as much, so total sales rise and price falls.

Thus a French export tax makes the German market less competitive and increases the profit of the German firm, while an export subsidy does the opposite. But what is the effect on France? This depends on the profit of the French firm in the German market, but it is not clear what happens here. A tax reduces sales but raises price, while a subsidy lowers price but increases sales. It is not clear whether the French firm increases profit by moving to the left along the German best-response curve or to the right. Consider this more closely.

At point *m* in Figure 7.10 French profit is 0 because they sell nothing. Also at point *c* the German firm will not want to sell anything, so French profits must be 0 there as well (if French average costs are constant and equal to German). Evidently, as we move along the German best-response curve from *m* to *c*, French profits first rise above 0 and then fall. If they are still rising at *H*, a subsidy will increase profit and a tax will lower it; if profits have begun to fall at *H*, an export tax will instead benefit the French firm.

We can figure out what must happen once we recall that *H* is also on the French best-response curve. This means that, with German sales equal to *Od*, the French firm at *H* has increased its own sales to just the point where further small changes yield no additional profit. But a reduction in German sales will certainly aid the French firm. Thus profit must still be rising at *H*. A small rise in French sales and reduction in German sales (that is, a movement toward *c*) will on balance increase French profit.

An export subsidy thus raises national welfare by raising the profit of the imperfectly competitive export firm, while an export tax lowers welfare. This is interesting; it apparently pays to *stimulate* trade rather than to restrict it. But this should be regarded as an example of what might happen rather than as a general conclusion because we have looked at just one set of circumstances.

Suppose, for example, that there is more than just one French exporter. To keep things simple, suppose that there is no German butane firm so that each axis in Figure 7.10 refers to one of the French exporters. A French export subsidy will now affect both firms, and both best-response curves will shift out. Equilibrium moves to the northeast, and both firms increase their sales of butane in Germany. Since their joint exports were initially above what a single monopolist would have supplied, their joint profits must fall. In this case it would clearly be better, from a narrow French perspective, to restrict trade rather than stimulate it.

There is a simple reason for this difference in conclusions. When a single home firm competes with a foreign rival in a foreign market, we want the home firm to become *more competitive* and win some of that rival's profit. But when two or more home firms compete with each other in a foreign market we want them to become *less competitive* and collude to exploit that market; it is their joint profit that matters for home welfare, not its distribution between the two firms. So if home exporters compete mainly with each other, export restrictions are likely to be called for. If they compete mainly with foreign firms, export promotion is likely to be the optimal national policy.

Oligopolistic Price Competition

Suppose there are again only one French firm and one German firm competing in the German market, but that they sell differentiated products and compete by setting prices rather than quantities. Figure 7.11, based on Figure 3.5, shows the two best-response curves. Initial equilibrium is at *H*. If the French tax exports or otherwise restrict the amount of butane exported to Germany, the French firm will charge a higher price for any given price of its rival: the French best-response curve shifts to the right. Equilibrium moves to *H'* so both prices rise, but that of the French firm rises more. Moving from *H* to *H'* must increase

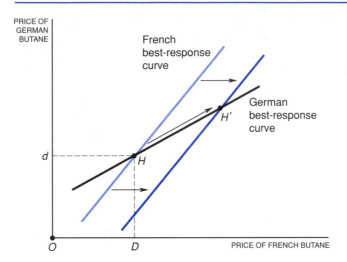

FIGURE 7.11   **Export Tax in an Oligopolistic Market with Price Competition**
The French export restriction shifts the French best-response curve to the right,
raising both firms' prices. French welfare rises, and German welfare drops, although the German firm increases its profits.

the profits of the French firm. This is because at H it had raised its price just
enough, given the German price of Od, so that a further small increase would
have no effect on profit. But an increase in the German price would raise French
profit so that the net effect of a movement from H to H', raising both prices,
must be to increase profit. An export subsidy would have the opposite effect, so
it is again in the French interest to restrict trade, not promote it.

 If the French restrict exports with an export tax, the French firm may not
be better off in the end. The tax payments must be subtracted from the rise in
pre-tax profit, and it is not clear which is larger. But France as a whole gains
since the tax is collected by the French government. Also the German firm
would welcome the French action since its own profit is higher at H' than at
H. The German price has increased absolutely while falling relative to that of
its French competitor. But Germany as a whole is worse off, because the anticompetitive effect of the trade restriction hurts German consumers, who now
pay higher prices for both types of butane.

9. *CASE STUDY:* THE EFFECTS OF ELIMINATING CANADA'S TRADE BARRIERS

 During the 1960s and 1970s a number of studies of Canada's tariff structure investigated the likely effects for that country of global free trade and
also of free trade with the United States alone (the two policies are not that

different since, you will recall from Chapter 1, about 70 percent of Canada's trade is with the United States). These often showed significant gains, with economies of scale playing a central role.

These implications also emerge in a study by David Cox of the University of Western Ontario and Richard Harris of Queen's University. They employed a computable general equilibrium model of the sort discussed in Chapter 4. The model contained 29 industries, with scale economies and imperfect competition present in 20. The benchmark year was 1976. The model was solved for what its solutions would have been in two alternative cases: if Canada unilaterally abolished all tariffs, and if tariffs were abolished by all countries together. The solution in each case was compared to the benchmark solution. Results are summarized in Table 7.1.

Multilateral free trade is calculated to increase the volume of Canada's trade by a large 88.6 percent. The relative importance of intraindustry trade declines a negligible 1.7 percent, so we basically have an equiproportional rise in both interindustry trade and intraindustry trade. The large increase in the length of production runs shows that the effect is to increase scale, giving scale economies the chance to work. The welfare gain to Canada is a substantial 8.6 percent of national income.

Contrast these results with those of the computable general equilibrium model discussed in Chapter 4. In that case free trade had only a slight proportional effect on global welfare, and its main impact was to produce modest international transfers as a result of terms-of-trade swings. A big difference between the two models is that scale economies and imperfect competition were not included in the earlier one but are central to the present results.

We need to be cautious in drawing conclusions from this exercise. It is subject to the inherent limitations of computable general equilibrium models discussed in Chapter 4. Also it has special features of its own. For example, unexploited scale economies and limited competition are far more important for a relatively small industrial economy like Canada than for a larger one. Nevertheless, a contrast of this study with the earlier one does point to the possible significance of scale economies and imperfect competition.

TABLE 7.1 **Estimated Effects of Free Trade for Canada**

	Unilateral	Multilateral
Welfare gain as % of national income	4.1	8.6
Length of production runs (%)	41.4	66.8
Total factor productivity (%)	8.6	9.5
Trade volume (%)	53.1	88.6
Relative intraindustry trade (%)	−0.7	−1.7

SOURCE: D. Cox, and R. Harris, "Trade Liberalization and Industrial Organization: Some Estimates for Canada," *Journal of Political Economy* (February 1985).

10. *CASE STUDY:* RESTRICTIONS ON JAPANESE AUTOMOBILE EXPORTS TO THE UNITED STATES

During 1980 the United States automobile industry lobbied intensively for protection from Japanese imports. The domestic industry was subject to the twin evils of a sluggish U.S. car market—due to both subdued aggregate demand and lessened demand for cars in particular as a result of the second oil-price shock—plus a shift in consumer preferences to smaller, more fuel-efficient cars. The latter benefited the Japanese, who were able to increase their share of the U.S. market. The domestic industry demanded a "breathing spell" of protection while changing its product mix so that it might finance investment in new models and put unemployed automobile workers back on the job. After an investigation, the United States International Trade Commission (about which more will be said in the next chapter) concluded that imports were not the cause of the domestic industry's problems. But public pressure continued, protectionist bills were introduced in Congress, and the new Reagan administration was able to persuade the Japanese government to restrict "voluntarily" exports to the United States. The Japanese announced that they would limit exports to 1.68 million units in the year starting April 1, 1981. The quota was renewed at this level for two more years. In 1984–1985, a 1.85 million vehicle quota was in force, and this was replaced by a 2.3 million unit ceiling on April 1, 1985, which was further extended for 1986–1987.

Figure 7.12 shows possible effects of the quota. In panel (a), the Japanese export supply curve of automobiles is flat over part of its range, reflecting a Japanese ability to supply cars at a constant price while extra capacity exists. With free trade, equilibrium is at A, and the United States imports DA automobiles from Japan at a price of OD. The initial quota of 1.68 million vehicles was 140,000 less than Japan had exported to the United States the previous year, and their sales were expected to grow without the restraint. Thus, as shown in the figure, the quota was binding and prevented point A from being attained. With Japanese cars more difficult to obtain, American car manufacturers were able to raise their prices. The higher prices of American automobiles made Japanese vehicles more attractive at each price, shifting the import demand curve to the right, as shown in the figure. The new equilibrium is at B, with the 1.68 million automobiles sold at the price OC. The area $CBED$ measures the value of the quota allotment of 1.68 million. The U.S. government would have received this much if it had sold the quota rights or if it had limited imports by an appropriate tariff. But instead it was the Japanese who limited exports, with the 1.68 million unit allotment apportioned among the Japanese automobile firms by the Japanese authorities. Thus it was the Japanese firms who received the $CBED$ in the form of profits.

Panel (b) looks at the situation in another way, focusing on the oligopolistic nature of the American automobile market. The line labeled USR is the best-response curve of American producers if they all act alike and if firms compete with prices. It shows what price all American firms will charge for

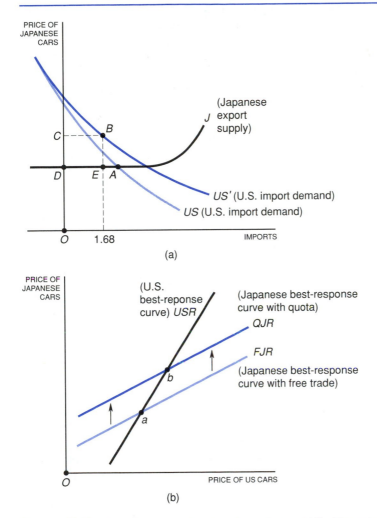

FIGURE 7.12 **The Japanese Restraint on Automobile Exports to the United States**   The Japanese restraint resulted in fewer U.S. imports of Japanese cars. The resulting higher prices of U.S. cars shifted demand for imports to the left. In terms of an oligopolistic market, the restraint shifted up the Japanese best-response curve.

each price charged by all Japanese firms. (For simplicity, ignore the fact that individual American firms—and individual Japanese firms—are different and take into account each other's actions as well as the actions of their foreign rivals.) *FJR* shows the Japanese best-response curve without a quota; it will be flat if the Japanese firms act competitively in the American market. Equilibrium is initially at *a*. The Japanese export quota shifts their best-response curve up to *QJR,* moving equilibrium to point *b.* The situation is just as discussed with respect to Figure 7.11 in the preceding section. The profits of the American firms increase, and because they get to keep the quota rents, the Japanese firms also have higher profits. The quota, in effect, promotes collusion in the American automobile market.

Several studies have attempted to measure the effects of the voluntary export restraint of Japanese automobiles on the U.S. economy. Let us look at some results of a study performed by David G. Tarr and Morris E. Morkre of the Federal Trade Commission. They examined the effect of the quota in the calendar year 1981. In that year actual U.S. imports of Japanese quotas totaled 1.911 million vehicles (this exceeds the initial quota of 1.68 million because the quota was not in force during the first three months of 1981; for the first full year of the quota, Japanese exports were right on target). Tarr and Morkre estimate that in the absence of the quota 1981 imports of Japanese cars (the distance *DA* in Figure 7.12(a)) would have been 2.696 million. Thus the effect was to reduce American purchases of Japanese cars by 785,000. But this does not mean an equal increase in sales of domestic vehicles. Some consumers purchased non-Japanese imports, and many others postponed or canceled new-car purchases altogether. Actual sales of domestic autos were 6.255 million, and the study estimates that without the restraint they would have been 6.134 million, so that 121,000 more American-made cars were sold because of the quota.

Employment. Tarr and Morkre used estimates that one job would be generated by an additional 26.3 cars produced. They, therefore, concluded that the sales of 121,000 vehicles were responsible for about 4,600 jobs. Other studies have claimed that each 5 vehicles would ultimately provide 1 job; this yields an estimate of 24,200 jobs. Each figure is small relative to the almost 300,000 automobile workers laid off before the agreement. To find the total effect on U.S. employment, we should add the increased employment in other U.S. industries to which demand has been switched from Japanese cars, subtract the decreased employment in U.S. export industries that have lost foreign sales as a result, subtract the employment provided by any jobs the rehired autoworkers held while unemployed, and account for any jobs created or lost by spending changes. The net effect of all these is a matter of speculation, but we might as well ignore them because the concern of the quota was employment in the auto industry.

Prices. Figure 7.12 shows the price of Japanese cars in the United States rising as a result of the quota. Retail prices of Japanese cars in the United States in fact rose dramatically after quotas were imposed, but there are two reasons why this rise probably exceeded the distance *CD* in the figure. First, Japanese firms shifted their export mix to higher-grade cars in an attempt to offset partly the reduction in unit sales by selling more car per unit. To this extent U.S. consumers received something in exchange for part of the higher prices even though they would not buy that something if given a free choice. Second, in order to preserve the solvency and good will of their dealer networks, the Japanese firms allowed their U.S. dealers to keep part of the price rise in higher profit margins. Tarr and Morkre calculated the average price received by the Japanese firms (*OC* in the figure) as $4,967 and the average price at which they would be willing to sell their cars *(OD)* as $4,573. The average price of a U.S.-built car was $8,940, and it was calculated that without the restraint it would have been $8,923. Thus the direct impact of the quota was estimated to be a 785,000-vehicle reduction in imports, a $394 rise in price for Japanese cars, a 121,000-vehicle increase in sales of American cars in the U.S. market, and a $17 rise in their price.

Effect on U.S. Welfare. Like any trade restriction, the voluntary export restraint on Japanese automobiles transferred income away from consumers of the product and caused a consumption cost and a production cost. Table 7.2 shows estimates of each. Consumers paid $17 more for each American-made car, a total of $104 million, and $394 more for each Japanese import, another $753 million. The first of these was certainly a cost to consumers but not to the United States as a whole since it was pocketed by the U.S. auto firms. The second would also not have been a national cost if imports had been restricted by a tariff (or by selling import licenses) since the $753 million would then have been collected by the government. But since this was not done, the money was instead collected by Japanese firms and so was a cost to the United States as a whole (though not to the world as a whole). Consumers would have bought 785,000 more Japanese cars if there had been no quota. They were willing to pay $4,967 for one more Japanese car, since that was the actual price, but without the restraint they would have to pay only $4,573, or $394 less. If they had bought the full 785,000 additional vehicles, the last one would have been worth just the $4,573 it cost. Thus, on average, each of the unbought autos would have been worth $197 (= $394 ÷ 2) more to consumers than what they would have to pay for it. This is the consumption cost of the restraint, the amount by which the goods actually consumed in the United States in 1981 fell short of the value of what the country could have bought with its income. The production cost was calculated in a similar way.

TABLE 7.2   Estimated Effect of the Restraint on U.S. National Welfare in Calendar Year 1981

	Dollars
Quota rents paid to Japanese firms ($394 × 1.91 million)	753 million
Consumption cost ($197 × 785,000)	155 million
[Higher price of U.S. cars ($17 × 6.134 million)	104 million]
Production cost ($8.50 × 60,500)	1 million
TOTAL COST TO U.S. ECONOMY	909 million
COST PER AUTO JOB CREATED ($909 million/4,598)	197,695/job

SOURCE: D. G. Tarr and M. E. Morkre, *Aggregate Costs to the United States of Tariffs and Quotas on Imports* (Washington, D.C.: Federal Trade Commission, 1984).

The consumption cost and production cost were pure waste, paid by consumers but not received by anyone else. They were thus costs to consumers and also to the United States and to the world as a whole. The quota rents were costs to consumers and to the United States but not to the world since they were received by the Japanese. The higher prices of American cars were costs to consumers but not to the world or to the United States since they were received by American firms. Thus the total cost to the U.S. economy was the sum of the unbracketed rows of Table 7.2, or $909 million. Note that the income transfers are much greater than the efficiency losses (production and consumption costs). The production cost in particular is small relative to the other three items. Note also how expensive it is to create auto-industry jobs in this way. The $197,695/job is excess cost, over and above the wages paid to the worker and the cost of the materials and equipment he used.

The above calculations apply only to 1981 (remember that the quota existed for only nine months of that year). Similar calculations can be made for the other years of the quota. Tarr and Morkre state that their estimates are on the low side because they have made conservative assumptions. Other studies of the effect of the Japanese automobile export quotas have made still different assumptions and reached different conclusions. But our figures clearly illustrate what is involved.

If we think of the United States as divided into the auto industry and consumers, the cost of the quotas to the latter group is larger than to the country as a whole. Table 7.3 uses our estimate of the national cost to estimate the cost to consumers. To the welfare cost of $909 million must be added the $104 million consumers paid to U.S. auto firms in the form of higher prices. The Japanese firms allowed their U.S. dealers to keep part of the rents generated by the quota. The list price of Japanese autos increased substantially, and newspapers reported that dealers were commonly charging $1,000 to $1,500 above list. Taking $200 as a guess of how much the quota increased what the dealers received per car gives a total of $382 million. Finally, the quota enabled competing producers of European cars also to raise their prices, and, since the Japanese cars were among the most fuel-efficient in 1981, their limited availability increased consumer gasoline spending above what it would have been for similar mileage. These effects are estimated at $20 million each. But because consumers are taxpayers, there were some savings also. It was estimated that each unemployed autoworker cost the government $14,700 per year in unemployment payments, welfare, and so on. These costs were saved for each worker put back on the job. Also the auto industry paid taxes on its higher earnings. These sum to $128 million in savings. Note that these are actual savings to consumers *only* if we assume that the higher employment and higher earnings of the auto industry did not come from lower employment and earnings elsewhere in the economy. Altogether this gives a total cost of $1,307 million to consumers to aid the automobile industry, which amounts to an extra cost of $284,254 for each job created.

TABLE 7.3 Estimated 1981 Effect of the Restraint on U.S. Consumers

	Dollars
U.S. welfare cost	909 million
Higher price of U.S. cars ($17 × 6.134 million)	104 million
Rents paid to U.S. dealers of Japanese cars	
($200 × 1.91 million)	382 million
Higher costs of European autos	20 million
Higher fuel costs	20 million
Total higher direct costs	1,435 million
Lower social expenses ($14,700 × 4,598)	68 million
Higher taxes for U.S. auto industry	60 million
Total indirect savings	128 million
TOTAL COST TO U.S. CONSUMERS	1,307 million
COST PER JOB TO U.S. CONSUMERS	284,254/job

SOURCE: Based on D. G. Tarr and M. E. Morkre, *Aggregate Costs to the United States of Tariffs and Quotas on Imports* (Washington, D.C.: Federal Trade Commission, 1984).

Aftermath. Within a few years the U.S. automobile industry was earning record profits. Although the industry's cost-cutting measures were much more responsible for this than the quotas, the latter certainly helped. But despite the profits, the quotas were not ended, as we have seen. Japanese firms also found the quotas very profitable, and soon a disproportionate share of their worldwide profits were coming from the protected American market. After the initial Japanese-U.S. agreement was reached, other countries demanded similar restraints. (Calculations such as the above were noticeably absent from the debates.) The Japanese agreed to restrict 1981 exports to Canada to 174,000 units (about 6 percent below the 1980 level) and to limit the rate of growth of exports to Germany to 10 percent per year. Britain, Italy, and France had already restricted imports from Japan.

Problems

7.25 Suppose that the United States had limited car imports from Japan by means of a $394 specific tariff. How would this affect the calculations of the costs borne by U.S. consumers, the domestic auto industry, and the nation as a whole?

7.26 Suppose that aggregate U.S. employment is determined by macroeconomic policy so that any job created in the auto industry by the restraint must be matched by a job lost in some other industry. How are our calculations affected?

7.27 Assuming that without the export restraint, Japan would have sold the United States an additional 785,000 units at an average price of $4,573, calculate the direct effect of the restraint on the U.S. trade balance on the basis of the figures in this section.

7.28 Recall that because of a 1965 agreement, the United States and Canada basically share a common auto industry. Discuss the effects on Canada of the restraint on Japanese auto exports to the United States. (Do not use specific numbers.)

11. SUMMARY

1. Tariffs and other forms of commercial policy exert real effects by causing the domestic relative price of imports in terms of exports to exceed the foreign price.

2. Tariffs are inefficient for the world as a whole; they cause the levying country to incur a consumption cost and a production cost, although the country could still conceivably be better off at the expense of the rest of the world.

3. Levying a tariff improves the terms of trade of a country if that country is sizable enough to influence international prices. Otherwise a country just trades less and loses.

4. A tariff protects the industry that makes intensive use of the scarce factor by causing factors to flow into that sector.

5. A tariff increases the real income of the country's relatively scarce factor and reduces the real income of the relatively abundant factor.

6. A tariff increases the real income of a factor specific to the import-competing sector and lowers the real income of a factor specific to the export sector.

7. A tax on exports and a quota each can be made equivalent to a tariff.

8. Protection can impose scale costs if it causes a country to operate industries at inefficient small scales.

9. With oligopolistic markets, trade policy can shift profits from foreign to domestic firms.

10. Protection of imperfectly competitive industries can make them even less competitive.

SUGGESTED READING

Brander, J. A., and B. J. Spencer. "Tariff Protection and Imperfect Competition." In *Monopolistic Competition in International Trade.* Edited by H. Kierzkowski. Oxford: Oxford University Press, 1984. Trade policy with oligopolistic industries.

Cox, D., and R. Harris. "Trade Liberalization and Industrial Organization: Some Estimates for Canada." *Journal of Political Economy* (Feb. 1985). Free trade for Canada.

Dixit, A. K., and V. Norman. *Theory of International Trade.* London: Cambridge University Press, 1980. See Chapters 5 and 6 for an advanced treatment of tariff theory.

Jones, R. W. "Tariffs and Trade in General Equilibrium: Comment." *American Economic Review* (June 1969). A neat mathematical statement of basic tariff theory.

Lerner, A. P. "The Symmetry between Import and Export Taxes." *Economica* (Aug. 1936). Lerner's symmetry theorem.

Metzler, L. A. "Tariffs, the Terms of Trade, and the Distribution of National Income." *Journal of Political Economy* (Feb. 1949). The Metzler Paradox.

Michaely, M. *Theory of Commercial Policy.* Chicago: University of Chicago Press, 1977. An extensive survey.

Tarr, D. G., and M. E. Morkre. *Aggregate Costs to the United States of Tariffs and Quotas on Imports.* Washington, D.C.: Federal Trade Commission, 1984. The costs of Japanese voluntary export restraints on automobiles and other U.S. protectionist measures.

CHAPTER 8

Why Nations Restrict Trade

> Around the splendid public buildings we are erecting in Philadel-
> phia, there stood till very recently a stiff and angular structure of
> wood. Like that scaffolding is the Tariff around the edifice of our
> national industries. It is not aesthetic. It adds nothing to the beauty
> of the edifice. But we cannot do without it.
>
> —ROBERT ELLIS THOMPSON

Chapter 7 exploited the pure theory of international trade to deduce the economic effects of tariff protection. These seem largely negative: the world is
made worse off by protection, and even the tariff-levying nation suffers a production cost and a consumption cost. Yet extensive protection has been en-
demic throughout history. In this chapter we examine the reasons for tariffs.

Reasons for tariffs can be classified into two groups. In the first are those
that address the economic relations of the tariff-levying nation with the rest of
the world. These *international* objectives are discussed in section 1. Other
reasons concern the tariff-levying country itself, and we discuss these *internal* objectives in sections 2 and 3. We shall examine eight reasons altogether.

We shall see that there is a basic difference between the validity of the
international objectives and the validity of the internal objectives. The international objectives result in arguments for protection that can be rational
from a *nationalistic* perspective: under the proper circumstances it makes
sense for a country to interfere with trade, at least if *global* welfare is not a
concern. But the internal objectives generally supply only *second-best* reasons for protection: although interfering with trade may sometimes help, it is
better to use other policy tools instead. Thus protection is generally not a
good thing.

1. MOTIVES FOR PROTECTION: INTERNATIONAL ECONOMIC OBJECTIVES

We saw in Part One that there are three independent reasons for countries to trade: comparative advantage, economies of scale, and imperfect competition. Each type of trade also generates a potential motivation to limit trade; this section discusses each in turn. A fourth international objective amounts simply to not wanting to trade for some reason.

(A) The Optimum-Tariff Argument

A tariff improves the terms of trade of the levying country if that country is large enough in world markets. It also reduces the volume of trade, generating production and consumption costs. But a moderate tariff could benefit a large country—that is, the favorable terms-of-trade effect could outweigh the unfavorable consumption and production costs.

This, then, is one possible motive for tariff protection: to increase national welfare by improving the terms of trade. It applies to comparative-advantage trade. The policy can be pushed just so far; an increase in the tariff increases the production and consumption costs as it improves the terms of trade. Eventually, the costs will predominate because, as Chapter 1 showed, free trade is better than no trade, and the result of a high-enough tariff will be no trade. The rate that squeezes out as much gain as possible is known as the *optimum tariff*.

The Optimum-Tariff Formula

We can derive a formula for the optimum tariff if we are willing to be a little more exact about the marginal savings curve MS. If imports are reduced by 1 unit, we save, first, their price p. Also, a 1-unit reduction in M is a percentage reduction of $1/M$, and each percentage reduction in M will reduce p by $1/f^*$ percent, where f^* is the elasticity of the foreign export supply curve. (Review Chapter 4 if necessary.) Thus the absolute fall in p is $p(1/f^*)(1/M)$. Multiply this by the volume of imports M to find the savings due to the price reduction: p/f^*. The total savings—what is measured by the MS curve—is thus $p + p/f^*$.

The value to the economy of one import is its domestic relative price, q. Imports should be restricted until MS is just equal to this, or until $p(1 + 1/f^*) = q$. Since $t = (q/p) - 1$, this gives the optimum-tariff formula

$$t = 1/f^*.$$

If the home country is too small to influence world prices, f^* is infinite. Thus t equals 0: the optimum policy for a small country is free trade. But if the home country is not small, the formula calls for a positive tariff. Free trade is not best.

When will all possible gains be squeezed out? The optimum tariff is illustrated in Figure 8.1. With free trade the home economy is at *E*, importing *OA* at the price *AE*. Suppose we were to import one less unit. How much would we save? Since we would no longer have to pay for that unit, we would save its price, *AE*. But the lessened demand for imports would also force down that price, so we would also save on what we still imported. Suppose that the distance *BE* in Figure 8.1 measures this additional savings. The marginal savings (MS) curve in the figure shows, for each level of imports, how much the economy could save by reducing imports by 1 unit. This marginal savings curve lies above the foreign export supply curve because we always save the price (which the export curve shows) and then some due to the price reduction.

At *E*, it pays the home country to restrict trade. By importing one less unit we save *AB* in exports needed to pay for it. But that unit is worth just *AE*, the price we are willing to pay for it. Thus importing less gives us a net saving of *BE*. The best we can do is to keep on restricting imports until we get to *C*, where the marginal savings curve crosses the free-trade import demand curve. Then we will be importing *OF*, and the marginal savings from a further reduction, *FC*, is just what 1 unit of imports is worth to us.

But point *C* is not on the foreign export supply curve. We will in fact import the quantity *OF* if we levy a tariff at the rate *CD/FD* so that *FD* would be the international price of imports and *FC* the domestic price.

Practical Relevance of the Optimum Tariff. The essence of the optimum tariff is the exploitation of monopoly power. If a country can influence world

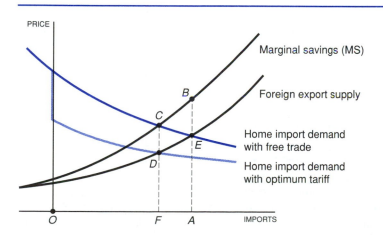

FIGURE 8.1 **The Optimum Tariff** A country has levied an optimum tariff when the domestic price of imports just equals the savings from reducing imports by 1 unit. This occurs when the free-trade import curve intersects the marginal savings (MS) curve.

prices, the citizens of that country collectively possess monopoly power; by withholding part of their export supply they can force the price up. Equivalently, they have monopsonistic power in the market for their imports, and by restricting demand they can hold price down. The tariff is the instrument by which the country's citizens collectively manipulate the market. It is important to realize that this argument is strictly a *nationalistic* one. From a global point of view the optimum tariff is 0. With a tariff, the home country imposes a loss on the rest of the world, a loss that exceeds the home country's gain: the country carves a larger slice for itself from a shrinking world pie.

How relevant is all this for actual tariff policy? It does not now seem very relevant for industrial countries. One examines the records of congressional tariff debates in vain for any mention of an optimum-tariff motive for protection. A major reason is that other motives are far more important. Another is the feasibility of an optimum-tariff strategy. This requires the home country to be able to influence world prices, and the degree of influence must be sizable enough for an optimum tariff to be worth bothering about. But even a large country needs to worry about the possibility of *retaliation.* Our discussion of the optimum tariff took the foreign export supply curve as fixed and, therefore, assumed a fixed tariff policy on the part of the rest of the world. But if we can use commercial policy to improve our terms of trade, other countries can presumably do the same to us. Our tariff could be countered by a foreign tariff and a resultant tariff war. The final outcome could easily leave both countries worse off than in free trade. In any case, the possibility of retaliation greatly reduces the appeal of an optimum-tariff policy.

Such a policy is, therefore, tempting only to a country that is both sizable and reasonably free of the fear of retaliation. The latter requires an asymmetric position vis-à-vis the rest of the world. For example, if a large country trades with many small countries, retaliation is unlikely. Each of the trading partners would be unable to exert significant monopoly power by itself, and, if there are many of them, they would be unlikely to collude. Asymmetry could also be due to the commodity composition of trade. For example, the home country might be the world's only exporter of a certain good that many other countries import, while importing an assortment of goods also imported by many other countries. Germany, as the predominant exporter of potash, and Chile, as virtually the only exporter of nitrates, were in this position at the turn of the century. Both countries were able to exploit their monopoly positions until the high prices of their exports induced the development of additional supply sources and of substitutes.

An asymmetry, either of size or of trade pattern, is not currently possessed by any of the industrial countries, with their roughly similar economic structures. The United States was perhaps in such a position at the close of the Second World War, when the other major industrial countries had been devastated. But American policy at the time was oriented toward reducing tariff barriers.

The optimum-tariff argument, then, seems to be largely irrelevant to tariff policy in the developed countries. But the argument is by no means irrelevant in the modern world economy, even for the industrial nations. Far from it. OPEC pursued such a policy. OPEC's policy instruments were not tariffs, but, in effect, export taxes and quotas. (This had also been the case with Germany and Chile early in this century.) However, these have basically the same economic effects as tariffs. OPEC possessed the necessary asymmetry. The manufactured goods and foodstuffs that OPEC imports are probably as vital to them as their oil is to their trading partners. But they can obtain these imports, or close substitutes, from a large and diverse number of countries. Accordingly, OPEC was not seriously threatened with retaliation. But now there are more sources of oil.

The success of OPEC spawned attempts by other primary-product exporters. But, as noted in Chapter 4, most of these had little success. A possible exception is bauxite, which rose sharply in price.

(B) Production Shifting

The optimum-tariff argument may apply to trade due to comparative advantage. Trade due to national external economies of scale introduces another possible motive: production shifting. Recall from Chapter 2 that a country operating an industry with such scale economies will benefit from supplying as much of the world market as possible: the more it can produce, the lower will be its average cost. If the economies are *national*, these costs depend on how much the home economy produces, not on how much the world produces. If the economies are also external to the firm, individual firms will be unable to realize these economies by themselves; so there is potentially a case for government intervention to, in effect, seize the economies collectively.

Tariff protection can help in such cases. Suppose that butane is characterized by national external economies of scale and that the home economy imports butane and also operates a small, import-competing butane sector. Then, as we saw in Chapter 2, wages at home will have to be low to allow the small, inefficient butane sector to compete. Indeed, such a country will be worse off than if it refused to trade at all—that is, a prohibitive tariff will raise welfare. If the country is aggressive, it might be tempted to go further and subsidize exports of butane in the hope that a large butane industry will be so efficient that wages and national welfare can rise.

The basic idea here is to make the home industry more efficient by grabbing market share from foreigners. If this is successful, the foreign economy could be left with a smaller butane industry and so be worse off. Thus this argument, like that for the optimum tariff, is basically nationalistic. But there is a subtle difference. The optimum-tariff argument implied inefficiency for the world as whole: the home country realized a gain by inflicting even more harm on the rest of the world. This is not necessarily true now: switching butane production from the foreign economy to the home one may or may not be inefficient from a cosmopolitan point of view—that is, the home country may or may not gain less than the foreign economy loses. Indeed, it is conceivable that, if the foreign economy ceases production of butane altogether, it might even share in the gains.

How important is all this in practice? Such arguments have been important in policy debates because they furnish the most significant justification for the *infant-industry* argument for protection, an argument with a long history and one that we will return to later in this chapter. But concrete examples are another matter. They are hard to come by, so production shifting should be regarded as a theoretical possibility of questionable relevance.

(C) Profit Shifting

Imperfect competition is the third possible reason for trade. When markets are not competitive, firms in those markets may earn positive profits. If there are both domestic and foreign firms in the market, trade policy can be used to divert profits from the latter to the former, making the home economy better off at the expense of the rest of the world. This was discussed in Chapter 7. Figure 8.2 is simply Figure 7.10 adapted to present purposes, so you might review the earlier discussion now if you do not remember it.

Suppose a home firm and a foreign firm compete with each other in some foreign market. Equilibrium is initially at *H*. Recall that moving away from *H* down and to the right along the foreign best-response curve will raise the profit of the home firm. But this will be true for just so long. If we go all the way to *c*, the home firm's profit will be 0. Thus there is some point between *H* and *c* on the foreign firm's best-response curve where home profit is maxi-

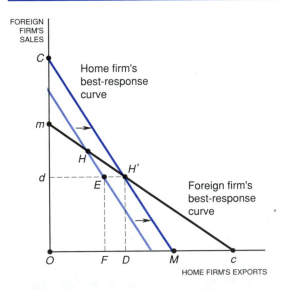

FIGURE 8.2 Optimal Export Subsidy in an Oligopolistic Market An export subsidy shifts the home firm's best-response curve to the right so that home exports of *OD* become a credible threat to the foreign firm.

mized. Suppose this is at point H' in the figure. A home export subsidy will shift the home firm's best-response curve to the right and move equilibrium from H to H', maximizing home profit.

The fact that a subsidy is called for here is not significant since we saw in Chapter 7 that under many circumstances a tax would in fact be appropriate. Rather, the point is that trade policy of some sort can make the home economy better off by obtaining for it a larger share of oligopoly profit. But what exactly is the role of the government? In our previous example the government was essentially the means by which the residents of the economy could combine and exercise their aggregate market power; individual residents had no such power by themselves. But this is not the case now. The home firm is part of a duopoly, not a competitive market. Why cannot the home firm simply announce that it will sell the quantity OD no matter what the foreign firm does? If the foreign firm believes this announcement, it will realize that the best it can do is sell Od, and so we will still end up at H'. Who needs the government? The problem with this is that such a home-firm announcement will not be *credible*. The foreign firm presumably understands the world as well as its home competitor and so knows that, if it sells the quantity Od, the home firm will in fact maximize its profit by selling OF, not OD. H is the equilibrium in the sense that only here is each firm's strategy credible. By establishing an export subsidy, the home government changes the incentives facing the home firm so that it becomes optimal for the latter to sell OD if its foreign rival sells Od. But this will work only if the government can credibly commit itself actually to pay the subsidy—for example, by passing a law. Otherwise there is no reason why the foreign firm should take the government's announcement of a subsidy any more seriously than it would take the home firm's announcement of an increase in exports. But if it does, the government has a role to play.

Like the optimum tariff, trade policy here benefits the home country at the expense of a foreign country. But whereas an optimum tariff is always bad from a global point of view, the same need not be true of trade policy in the face of an oligopoly. The reason is that an oligopolistic market is not efficient to begin with, so a change in behavior might either increase or decrease efficiency. The export subsidy illustrated in Figure 8.2, for example, might very well raise world welfare because it increases competition in a market where competition was restrained by duopoly.

(D) Trade Limitation for Noneconomic Reasons

Sometimes governments wish to limit imports for reasons that are not economic at all. For example, limiting oil imports to 8.2 million barrels per day was an objective of the U.S. government, enunciated by President Carter in 1979. In Figure 8.3, if national policy is to limit imports to OC, a tariff of AB/BC does the trick. The country must pay the production and consumption costs (unless the terms of trade improve enough), but these are the inevitable costs of the national objective.

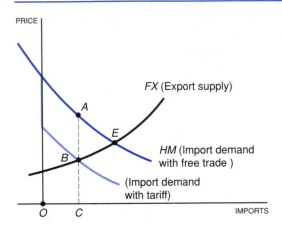

FIGURE 8.3   Import Limitation   If national policy is to limit imports to *OC*, a tariff of *AB/BC* will accomplish this.

Problems

8.1 Some people urged that the United States use the "wheat weapon" against OPEC—that is, force up the price that OPEC must pay for our agricultural exports just as they forced up the price of their oil exports. Discuss the feasibility of such a policy.

8.2 We shall see that tariffs are often *second-best* policy tools—that is, they are inferior in some ways to alternative methods of achieving whatever goals the tariffs are being used for. Examine each of the four motives discussed in this section to see if you can think of some other, superior policy.

8.3 The optimum-tariff policy $t = 1/f^*$ would seem to indicate that when on the backward-bending part of the foreign export supply curve ($f^* < 0$), a *subsidy* to imports ($t < 0$) is best. But we concluded that tariffs should be *increased* in such a case. Reconcile.

8.4 How would our discussion of an optimal export subsidy (or tax) change if the home and foreign oligopolists competed in the *home* market rather than in a foreign one?

2. MOTIVES FOR PROTECTION: INTERNAL ECONOMIC OBJECTIVES

Although the tariff is ostensibly a device for regulating a country's international economic activity, many motives for protection center upon its internal effects. We take up three motives involving internal objectives in this section and a fourth in the next one.

(A) Revenue

The tariff is a tax, and it can yield revenue. There is a limit: a higher tariff lowers imports, and a prohibitive tariff yields no revenue at all. But most governments can raise substantial revenues in this way. In order to do so the country must bear the production and consumption costs, so (unless a significant terms-of-trade improvement can be expected) the tariff is inferior to less distortionary taxes. That is, a tariff is a *second-best* tool.

If the tariff exists to raise revenue, the needs of the government become important in determining the degree of protection. Tariff policy becomes linked politically to how heavily a country wishes to tax itself and to how large a government it wants.

How important in practice is the revenue motive? Not very, as far as the modern industrial economies are concerned. Tariff revenues account for less than 2 percent of the total tax revenue of the U.S. government and are minor sources in other DCs. Public discussions of tariff questions seldom allude to revenue aspects. One must conclude that this is not important in such countries.

But it has not always been so. At one time most nations relied heavily on tariff revenues for government finance. Revenue was the reason Britain maintained some tariffs from the abolition of the Corn Laws in 1846 until the First World War. The American tariff was the principal source of federal revenue throughout the nineteenth century and was not displaced until the income tax was instituted. Even today, tariffs are important revenue sources for the governments of most LDCs. For example, in 1986 the government of Uganda derived over 75 percent of its revenue from taxes on trade, and Lesotho had similarly raised about 76 percent of its revenues in 1985. The DCs today rely mainly on broad-based taxes (income, sales, and value-added), which are much more effective for raising the enormous revenues required by the governments of modern industrial states. But the efficient administration of such taxes requires a large and reasonably effective government bureaucracy and a reasonably literate population, conditions that were not met in the past and are still not met in large parts of the world. A tariff, by contrast, requires only customs officials stationed (palms upward) in the trading centers and a police force to control smuggling. Seventeenth-century Britain banned tobacco growing because it was easier to tax tobacco imports than to tax a domestic crop.

(B) Domestic Distortions

Because a tariff affects a country's internal price structure and allocation of resources, it can deal with distortions in the domestic economy. These have various causes: monopolies, labor unions, external economies or diseconomies (social benefits or costs not reflected in private prices, such as pollution), government activities or regulations. The basic idea is to use a tariff to cancel partially the effect of such distortions. Suppose, for example, that a brewery, needing pure water for its product, reduces water pollution in its vicinity. The brewer is paid for his beer, but there is no one to reward him in materialistic fashion for purifying the water. Because of this the industry will not be as large as socially desirable. A tariff on beer could help deal with this problem by reallocating resources into the brewery industry.

The fly in the ointment (or in the ale) is the fact that a tariff introduces distortions of its own. These additional distortions must be weighed against those neutralized by the tariff. In the brewery example, a tariff on beer will lead to cleaner water but will also introduce a consumption cost. Although protection can be used to deal with domestic distortions, it is better to use more direct methods that do not have the undesirable side effects of tariffs. The best policy for the brewery is a subsidy for purifying water; this would ensure that brewers receive monetary rewards equal to the social benefits supplied without introducing the distortions of a tariff.

Protection, if carefully employed, can potentially reduce the damage caused by domestic distortions, but tariffs are not as good as measures that directly attack the distortions. Of course, direct measures might be ruled out by political or administrative considerations. There is a clear analogy to the use of tariffs to raise government revenue: other methods are more effective in principle, but they are not practical for some countries. Once again, they are *second-best*.

The Infant-Industry Argument. This is a good example of the domestic-distortion case for protection. Also, it is important enough in practice to deserve separate mention.

This argument does not dispute that, in the long run, countries are best off with free trade. But, so the argument goes, a country might not be able to realize its true comparative advantage under free trade if other countries are already established in the relevant sectors. For example, a certain LDC might possess all the natural advantages needed to become a successful exporter of steel. But it must compete with existing steel exporters, who possess enormous advantages simply by being in the market to begin with. Our potential entrant must be prepared to suffer huge losses while it establishes the necessary plants, trains the required labor force and managers, and gradually penetrates the international market.

The infant-industry argument is that such industries ought to be given tariff protection to help them get off the ground. Then they will gradually develop in the sheltered domestic market until they are ready to compete internationally. At that time tariffs will become unnecessary, and the country will export the products of the no-longer infant industry. The country will be trading according to its long-run comparative advantage; and if the infant industry has been wisely chosen, the gains from this trade will more than compensate for the losses the country had to suffer while the tariffs were effective.

Sometimes the argument is applied at a more general level. Industrialization requires much infrastructure and a sizable labor force with the requisite attitudes, habits, and skills. Thus we have what might be called an "infant country" argument. In any case, protection should cease when the long-run pattern of comparative advantage is attained.

The argument has been important in practice. One frequently hears it in reference to LDCs. Alexander Hamilton argued along these lines for the young American republic, as did Friedrich List for Germany. John Stuart Mill gave the argument his approval. In the eighteenth century the development of Britain's textile industry, a key element in the industrial revolution, was aided by protection from Asian competition. The growth of American industry in the nineteenth and early twentieth centuries took place behind high tariff walls.

The essential point is that the argument depends upon market distortions. An effective free market would not be hampered by the fact that a new industry must suffer losses before it can compete. Capital markets enable entrepreneurs to borrow to tide themselves over until their projects pay off. If a country has a long-run comparative advantage in steel production, potential steel producers should be able to borrow enough to develop to compete internationally. If they cannot, that fact is an indication that steel production is not really a good bet for the country. In order to justify protection there must be some distortion to be overcome.

For example, it might be unduly difficult to borrow funds for investment because of restrictive legislation, prejudice, or incomplete information on the part of private investors. This would constitute a distorted capital market. Or the infant industry might be one that generates external economies of scale: expansion of the industry reduces costs to all participants, not simply to the firms that expand. A single firm cannot capture the full social benefit from an expansion and is, therefore, not likely to expand as much as is socially desirable. This possibility was discussed in section 1. In any case, some distortion is necessary to justify protection.

This means that the infant-industry argument is subject to the same criticism as above: a tariff causes distortions of its own, which must be weighed against any benefits, so that direct measures are always better. Distortions in capital markets ought to be attacked head on; the best response to external economies of scale is a subsidy on output. This will expand activity and enable the external economies to be realized without the consumption cost of a tariff.

A political objection is also sometimes raised against the infant-industry argument. An essential aspect of this argument is that protection be temporary until the industry gets on its legs. Cynics argue that any industry politically powerful enough to obtain protection while it is an infant would have no trouble retaining special treatment once it had grown even more powerful.

(C) Noneconomic Objectives

Closely related to the domestic-distortion argument is the view that noneconomic objectives may justify protection. For example, a country might wish to produce its own military hardware, even if similar products are cheaper abroad, to ensure a domestic supply should the country suddenly find itself isolated from foreign sources. Such national-defense arguments are heard in Israel, for example. Similarly many countries, including the United States, protect their shipping industries. Some argued that the United States should develop domestic energy sources (or even strategic oil reserves) to free itself of the threat of "economic blackmail" by OPEC. The common denominator is a noneconomic reason to foster some industry.

Tariffs can be used to realize noneconomic objectives, just as they can attack domestic distortions. The United States can ensure a larger merchant marine by discriminating against foreign shipping; Israel can stimulate its defense industry by discriminating against foreign suppliers; America can stimulate domestic energy production with a tariff on imported oil.

The argument is illustrated in Figure 8.4. With free trade, the relative price of butane in terms of apples is *OB/OC*, so that the home country produces at *A*. Suppose consumption is at *D*, so *DE* apples are exported in exchange for *EA* butane. Suppose that this country does not wish to be so dependent on the rest of the world for butane and wants to produce at *F* even though this is more costly than free trade.

The country will produce at *F* if the domestic price of butane in terms of apples is *GF/GH* and the price can be raised to this level by an appropriate tariff.

The tariff imposes, as always, a production cost and a consumption cost. The production cost, measured by *LB* in Figure 8.4 (review Figure 7.1 if necessary), is unavoidable if the country produces at *F* rather than at *A*: this is the price that must be paid for the noneconomic objective. If it produces at *F*, the

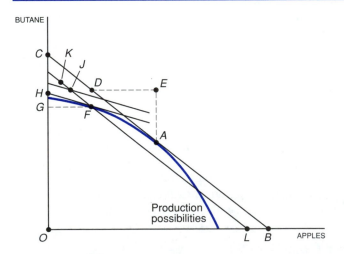

FIGURE 8.4   Noneconomic Objectives   If a country wishes to produce at *F* rather than at *A*, a production cost of *LB* is unavoidable. But a tariff also causes a consumption cost.

country must consume on the line through $K, J, F,$ and L. The consumption cost is due to the fact that the tariff prevents the country from consuming at the best spot on this line. For example, K might be the best combination of apples and butane to consume, but the tariff causes people to import less butane so that the country consumes at a point such as J instead.

Although a tariff can change the country's production from A to $F,$ other methods can do the same without the consumption cost. For example, the government might pay butane producers a certain sum for each unit of butane that they turn out. This will stimulate butane production and move the economy along its production possibility frontier from A toward $F.$ A sufficient subsidy will move the economy all the way to $F.$ But now consumers can buy at world prices; there is nothing to prevent them from consuming $K.$ The production subsidy is superior to the tariff because it aims directly at the noneconomic objective (to increase production), whereas a tariff is indirect and has undesirable side effects.

This conclusion is a general one. Although tariffs can attain noneconomic objectives, they are clumsy instruments. Other methods can attain the same objectives at less cost. Tariffs are, at best, *second-best.*

Problems

8.5 This section showed that a tariff was a second-best way of attaining a noneconomic objective because other methods can do the same without the consumption cost. Does this argument apply to the motive of trade limitation for noneconomic reasons discussed in the previous section? What is the essential difference between the two motives?

8.6 Is the tariff a second-best method of raising government revenue? If so, what methods are better?

---

3. MOTIVES FOR PROTECTION: PRESSURE GROUPS

We now come to the last of our eight motives. A tariff increases the real income of a country's relatively scarce factor while reducing that of its relatively abundant factor. A desire to redistribute income in just this fashion could, therefore, motivate protection. But this suffers from the same shortcoming as many other motives: a tariff involves undesirable side effects, which could be avoided by a more direct method. A tariff harms the abundant factor more than it benefits the scarce factor, so that the country as a whole loses (unless there is a large enough terms-of-trade improvement—a possibility we already examined with the optimum-tariff argument). This loss could be avoided by lump-sum redistributions of income: simply taxing the people who are to have lower incomes and giving the proceeds to those whose incomes are to increase.

The distributional consequences of protection are actually far more subtle than the above argument would suggest. One reason is that factors of production do not move easily between industries: in Chapter 6 we called them "specific factors."

Specific Factors and Income Distribution. The implications of specific factors can be best brought out by an example. Suppose that capital and labor produce apples and butane, with apples relatively capital-intensive. Apples are exported and butane imported. The production possibility frontier is illustrated in Figure 8.5. Point F shows production under free trade, with an international price of butane in terms of apples equal to AB/AF. Now suppose a tariff on butane raises its domestic price to AC/AF. New equilibrium production is at G (the line through G and H is parallel to that through F and C): if capital and labor are freely mobile, production moves from F to G. But factors are freely mobile only in the long run.

In the short run the economy remains at F. The tariff has raised the price of butane, so factors employed in the butane industry are better off: they receive more for the butane they produce. Factors employed in the apple industry are worse off. In the short run, then, the important consideration is *location;* both capital and labor in the butane industry are better off, and both capital and labor in the apple industry are worse off.

As time goes on, both factors begin to leave the apple industry for the higher rewards available in butane production. The departure might in some cases be involuntary if apple firms shut down; the factors that they had used could face an unemployed spell whose length depends on how specific they are. As resources move from apples to butane, production gradually shifts from F to G.

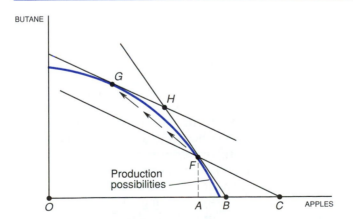

FIGURE 8.5   Short-Run and Long-Run Effects of Protection   In the long run, a tariff causes the economy to alter its output from *F* to *G*. But in the short run, factors are immobile, so output does not change.

Now relative factor intensities begin to matter. The shrinking apple industry is relatively capital-intensive. Thus the apple industry is releasing more capital but less labor than the expanding butane industry, which is labor-intensive, wishes to absorb. This causes wages in butane production to rise even more and rents in butane production to fall. At the same time, wages in the apple industry rise as those apple producers that wish to keep going begin to find that they have a harder time retaining workers than capital.

Eventually, the economy reaches point *G*. The two industries now pay equal wages and equal rents, so no factor has an incentive to move. The wage (in both industries) is higher in real terms than before the tariff, and the rent is lower. The important consideration now is the *identity of the factor* and not its location.

A factor's income is determined, in the short run, entirely by its location and, in the long run, entirely by its identity. During the transition both considerations matter. Another consideration that matters during the transition is the relative degree of mobility. Some factors move sooner than others. We can use the *specific-factors model* discussed in Chapter 6 to analyze this case. Suppose that workers can move before capital can, so think of the "middle run" as a period in which labor is mobile between sectors but capital is still immobile. The effect of the butane tariff is summarized in Table 8.1.

Some individuals are affected in the same direction in both the long run and the short run, whereas others are affected in opposite ways. Laborers in the butane industry, for example, are benefited both in the short run (they are located in butane production) and in the long run (they are relatively intensively used by the protected industry). But capital initially employed in butane production is in an ambiguous position, benefiting in the short run but suffering ultimately. We know from Chapter 6 that, in the medium run, the reward of butane capital will rise relative to both commodity prices and the reward of apple capital will fall relative to both. Thus the two types of capital fare the same in the medium run as in the short run but even more so. Labor, on the other hand, is in an uncertain position: the wage rises in terms of apples but falls in terms of butane. There is no such uncertainty in either the short run or the long. Note also that some rewards have a complex time pro-

TABLE 8.1 Income Effects of a Tariff on Butane *(labor intensive)*

	Higher real income	Lower real income	Uncertain
Short run	Butane labor Butane capital	Apple labor Apple capital	
Medium run	Butane capital	Apple capital	Butane labor Apple labor
Long run	Butane labor Apple labor	Butane capital Apple capital	

file. The rental of capital in the butane industry rises in the short run and rises further in the medium run, only to fall in the end; the wages of labor in the butane industry initially rise, then fall, and then reverse themselves again. Only capital originally in the apple industry fares consistently over time. Thus owners of other factors could either favor or oppose protection for their industry, depending upon their time horizon. This discrepancy helps explain why individuals sometimes adopt positions on tariff issues at odds with their own interests as predicted by the Stolper-Samuelson theorem. For example, the owners of capital invested in labor-intensive industries, such as textiles in the DCs, often plea for protection even though the Stolper-Samuelson theorem indicates it is contrary to their interests. Emphasis on short-run effects is also strengthened by the fact that factory owners are frequently organized politically on the basis of industrial location. Laborers in the capital-intensive apple industry might be organized in a Federation of Apple Pickers and Worm Squashers. Because it represents only apple workers, this federation could favor a tariff on apples even though it would harm laborers in general (and its own members in the long run): apple workers who leave the industry also leave the federation.

Importance of Distributional Considerations. The distributional motive for protection seems very powerful in reality, if we are to judge by how well individuals' positions on tariff issues accord with their self-interests. But it is hard to tell just how important the motive is. Unless requested by a group generally perceived to have an inequitable income share, an appeal for protection that is not couched in terms of national well-being is unlikely to be persuasive. Thus appeals will be based on noneconomic objectives and on the infant industry and other such arguments (or else on fallacious arguments). Despite this ambiguity, distribution is certainly an important consideration. Thus the tariff, ostensibly aimed at international economic relations, is also a domestic issue: part of the struggle over the distribution of the national income.

Problem

8.7 The optimum-tariff argument supplies a motive where the tariff is a first-best tool from a *nationalistic* perspective. But from a *cosmopolitan* perspective is it a first-best method for redistributing income among countries? Why? If it is not, what methods are better and why?

4.* *EXPLORING FURTHER:* THE SECOND-BEST NATURE OF THE TARIFF

Previous sections have shown that tariffs are *second-best* methods of dealing with domestic objectives. This section examines the issues more thoroughly. We consider a domestic distortion in the production of importables, but our analysis applies as well to the other motives discussed in sections 2 and 3.

In Figure 8.6 the terms of trade equal HA/GH so that with free trade and perfect competition the economy would produce at C. But the domestic distortion prevents this. The nature of that distortion is not relevant; suppose that all producers of importables are required to belong to a trade association, with a membership fee proportional to output. If that fee equals FG/HA in Figure 8.6, the economy will produce at A. The quantity HA of importables could be sold for GH exportables, but FG of that goes for the fee, leaving producers with FH. Thus producers behave as though the relative price were FH/HA rather than GH/HA. Consumers are not directly affected by the trade association, so the economy consumes at B.

If the trade association were broken down, production would shift from A to C and the economy would consume the free-trade collection of goods, D. This is a *first-best* solution. A subsidy of FG/HA per unit on the production of importables would produce the same result by neutralizing the association's fee.

But suppose a tariff is used instead. The idea would be to protect importables, thereby stimulating their production, thus countering the effect of the association in reducing production. Such a tariff cannot possibly be a first-best solution because it will impose a consumption cost. In fact, the tariff might not improve matters at all.

This is illustrated in Figure 8.7. Again, point B on the indifference curve U_F represents initial, free-trade consumption, and point D on the indifference curve U_1 represents consumption if the distortion is removed by a first-best method. With the tariff, production is at E, and consumption is at J on the in-

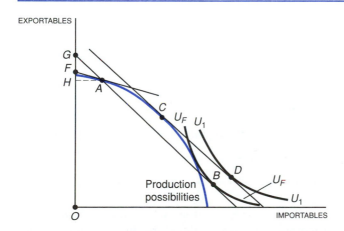

FIGURE 8.6   A Domestic Distortion   A production distortion causes production to be at *A* rather than *C* so that consumption is at *B* rather than *D*. A tariff can shift production back to *C*, but it would add a consumption distortion so that consumption would not be as good as at *D*.

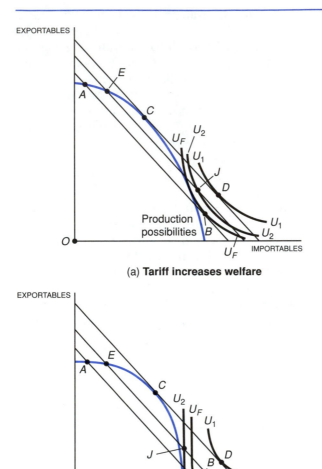

(a) **Tariff increases welfare**

(b) **Tariff reduces welfare**

FIGURE 8.7 A Tariff to Counter a Domestic Distortion A tariff that neutralizes a domestic distortion may either raise or lower national welfare since the tariff introduces distortions of its own.

difference curve U_2. By shifting production from A to E, the tariff has countered part of the distortion and increased national income. In panel (a) the country has been made better off since U_2 is above U_F. But the country cannot be as well off as with a first-best policy—that is, U_2 must be below U_1—for two reasons. First, the tariff has not been large enough to counter completely the distortion: production has moved only to E and not all the way to C. Second, the tariff has introduced a new distortion of its own in the consumption cost. U_2 is not tangent to the budget line between E and J; the slope of U_2 at J reflects the domestic (tariff-ridden) relative price. In panel (b) the country is actually worse off than before as a result of the tariff, U_2 is below U_F and would have been better off doing nothing at all. In this case the harm due to the consumption cost exceeds the benefit from countering the original distortion.

Two further conclusions are demonstrated in Figure 8.8. Panel (a) shows that a *small* tariff will always cause an improvement relative to free trade. With no tariff, the country produces at A and consumes at B, on U_F. A tariff distorts consumers' choices away from importables, causing consumption to move from B along the budget line in the direction of point A. This will put the economy on a lower indifference curve, thereby imposing the consumption cost. At the same time, the tariff will protect the importables industry so that

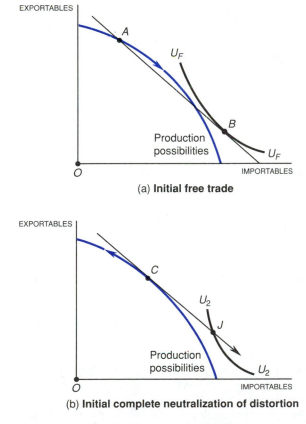

(a) **Initial free trade**

(b) **Initial complete neutralization of distortion**

FIGURE 8.8 The Effects of a Small Change in a Tariff A small tariff that partly neutralizes a domestic distortion is always better than doing nothing, and a tariff that completely neutralizes the distortion is always overkill.

production moves away from A, as shown by the arrow. This pushes the budget line outward, illustrating the increase in income from neutralizing the distortion. Suppose now that only a small tariff is imposed. The indifference curve U_F has the same slope at B as does the budget line. Thus a small movement along the latter will not be very different from moving along the former; the movement to a lower indifference curve will be negligible, and the consumption cost will be insignificant. But the production possibility frontier at A cuts the budget line from below, so any movement along the former must push out the latter to a commensurate degree. Thus for a *small* initial tariff, the increase in income due to neutralizing the distortion dominates the consumption cost. This argument applies only to a small tariff. As the tariff is raised, the production point moves to flatter parts of the production possibility frontier, whose slope, therefore, approaches that of the budget line, and the consumption point moves to steeper parts of the indifference curves.

Panel (b) of Figure 8.8 shows a case in which the tariff is just large enough to neutralize completely the domestic distortion. The production point C, therefore, coincides with what production would be with a first-best solution. But there is a consumption cost, illustrated by the fact that the indifference curve U_2 through the consumption point J cuts the budget line. The same logic as above now shows that a small tariff *reduction* must benefit this country. Such a reduction will move production in the direction of the arrow from C and consumption in the direction of the arrow from J. Since the production possibility frontier has the same slope at C as does the budget line, the reduction in income will be negligible for a small tariff. But U_2 is steeper at J than is the budget line so that the country must move to a higher indifference curve.

In sum, four conclusions apply to the use of a tariff to neutralize domestic distortions.

1. Because it introduces a distortion of its own, a tariff is necessarily second-best—that is, inferior to a more direct method.
2. A *small* tariff is always better than free trade.
3. A tariff that completely neutralizes the distortion is too large.
4. A moderate to large tariff may be either better or worse than no tariff at all.

Problems

8.8 This section suggested two possible first-best ways of dealing with the trade-association example of a distortion. Are those two ways equivalent? What would determine which should be used?

8.9 Prove each of the four conclusions of this section *without* using community indifference curves.

8.10 Formulate analogs of this section's four conclusions that apply to the use of a tariff to improve the terms of trade.

5. EFFECTIVE PROTECTION

Thus far we have ignored the fact that countries import many different goods subject to different tariff rates. Such differences become important in some cases, such as when dealing with intermediate goods.

Intermediate goods are used to produce other products, as steel is used to produce automobiles. The price of an automobile covers the cost of the steel embodied in the vehicle as well as the value added in the automobile industry itself. Now, a tariff on automobiles affects its total price, whereas an automobile producer is interested only in the part of the price represented by value added and not in the part that is simply passed on to producers of intermediate goods.

As an illustration, suppose that a firm produces an automobile that, with free trade, sells for $20,000. Suppose further that $10,000 of this pays for steel and that the remaining $10,000, the value added in the automobile industry, covers wages, rent, profit, and so forth. Suppose that a country imports both automobiles and steel. Consider the effect of a 20 percent tariff on automobiles with free trade in steel. The domestic price of a car is thus $24,000 (the $20,000 world price plus 20 percent), of which $10,000 is still required to pay for the (duty-free) steel. This leaves $14,000 ($24,000 less $10,000) for value added. Thus the 20 percent tariff on cars has enabled the domestic producer to increase value added from $10,000 to $14,000—a *40 percent* rise. It is this latter figure, rather than the 20 percent *nominal* tariff on automobiles, that is of immediate interest to individuals involved in automobile production.

Suppose, next, that trade in automobiles is free but that steel has a 20 percent tariff. The producer must now sell his car at the world price of $20,000, but the steel that he uses to produce it will cost him $12,000 ($10,000 plus 20 percent), leaving only $8,000 for value added. Thus although the tariff on automobiles is 0, the overall impact of the tariff policy on the automobile producer is a 20 percent *fall* in value added (a decline from $10,000 to $8,000). Industries are affected not only by the tariffs on goods that they produce, but also by the tariffs on all intermediate goods that they purchase.

The Effective-Rate Formula

The *effective rate of protection* measures the overall effect of a tariff structure on an individual industry. To see how it is measured, let us continue with our automobile-steel example and let P_A and P_S denote the world prices of automobiles and steel, respectively, and suppose that the amount of steel used in the production of a single automobile is denoted by a. Then, at *world* prices, the value added v in a single car is

$$v = P_A - P_S a. \tag{8.1}$$

Suppose that automobile imports are subject to the tariff rate t_A and steel imports to the tariff rate t_S. Then, at *domestic* prices, the value added v' is

$$v' = P_A(1 + t_A) - P_S(1 + t_S)a. \tag{8.2}$$

Now, the *nominal* rate of protection (that is, the tariff) on automobiles is equal to the proportion by which the domestic price exceeds the world price:

$$t_A = \frac{Q_A - P_A}{P_A},$$

where $Q_A = P_A(1 + t_A)$ is the domestic price. The *effective* rate of protection, by analogy, is defined as the proportion by which value added at domestic prices exceeds value added at world prices:

$$e_A = \frac{v' - v}{v}, \tag{8.3}$$

where e_A denotes the effective rate of protection on automobiles. We can obtain a formula with which to measure e_A by substituting (8.2) and (8.1) into (8.3) and rearranging:

$$
\begin{aligned}
e_A = \frac{v' - v}{v} &= \frac{[P_A(1 + t_A) - P_S(1 + t_S)a] - [P_A - P_S a]}{v} \\
&= \frac{[P_A - P_S a] + [P_A t_A - P_S t_S a] - [P_A - P_S a]}{v} \\
&= \frac{P_A t_A - P_S t_S a}{v} = \frac{P_A t_A - P_S a t_A + P_S a t_A - P_S t_S a}{v} \\
&= \frac{[P_A - P_S a]t_A}{v} + \frac{P_S a[t_A - t_S]}{v},
\end{aligned}
$$

or

$$e_A = t_A + [t_A - t_S]\frac{P_S a}{v}. \tag{8.4}$$

This formula leads to a number of observations. First, if the automobile industry uses no intermediate goods ($a = 0$), then the effective rate equals the nominal rate ($e_A = t_A$). This is as expected, for in this case the full price of the car goes toward value added. Second, if all goods have the same tariff rate (so that $t_A = t_S$), then the effective rate again equals the nominal rate. Thus effective-rate calculations become interesting when tariff rates differ across commodities. In the above numerical example, if the 20 percent tariff on automobiles and the 20 percent tariff on steel *both* hold, then the domestic price of a car is $24,000 and the cost of steel is $12,000, leaving value added at $12,000, which is just 20 percent above what it would be at world prices ($10,000).

Formula (8.4) implies, third, that if the tariff rate on the final good exceeds that on the intermediate good (so that t_A exceeds t_S), then the effective rate exceeds the nominal rate (e_A is larger than t_A). Finally, the gap between the nominal and effective rates is larger the more important the intermediate goods are in the production of the final good (that is, the larger is $P_S a$ relative to v).

Use of Effective Rates

Why use a formula such as (8.4) to calculate effective rates of protection? There are two basic reasons. The effective rates measure the impact of the tariff structure as a whole upon individual *industries* rather than goods. Suppose one is interested in income distribution in the short run when factors are specific to the industries in which they are employed. Then the effective rates are the indicators to look at because value added is what these factors receive. Industry lobbyists care about the effective protection they receive rather than about the nominal protection. Government officials engaged in tariff bargaining with foreign countries use effective-rate calculations to discover the effects of proposed tariff changes on special interests and industry pressure groups.

The second reason has to do with resource allocation. The presumption is that the impact of any tariff structure is to cause resources to flow from industries with low effective rates of protection to industries with high rates because value added is what resources earn in an industry. Economists, therefore, look at the set of effective tariff rates of a country if they wish to obtain some idea of how that country's tariff structure has influenced its allocation of resources among the various industries.

For some purposes nominal rates are more relevant than effective rates. The relative price of a commodity indicates the opportunity cost of producing more of it as well as the value of more of it to consumers, regardless of how important intermediate goods are in the final stage of that commodity's production. Because of this, nominal tariff rates—which indicate the effects of protection on prices—are relevant to our earlier discussions of such things as the production and consumption costs of protection and the optimum tariff. Effective rates are not necessary for these important topics.

Since the mid-1960s, many economists have made calculations of the effective tariff rates of many countries. One feature that has been given prominence by these studies is the *cascading* nature of the developed countries' tariff structures. These countries typically levy higher nominal tariffs on goods at more advanced levels of processing so that raw materials have relatively low tariffs and finished goods produced from those materials have relatively high tariffs. Formula (8.4) shows that if the nominal tariff on a good exceeds that on its intermediate input, the effective tariff exceeds the nominal tariff. Thus the cascading nature of the industrial countries' tariffs results in relatively high effective protection of the later stages of production. One study revealed, for example, that although the nominal U.S. tariff on woven wool fabrics was 20.7 percent, the effective rate of protection of the activity of weaving the fabrics was 60.9 percent. Table 8.2 shows overall average nominal and effective rates of protection for the industrial countries as a group. The first column shows how nominal tariffs rise as the stages of production become more advanced, and the second column shows the resulting high effective rates for the more advanced processes. Spokesmen for the LDCs point to such calculations as indications that the DCs' tariff policies constitute a

TABLE 8.2 **Average Rates in All Industrial Countries at Various Stages of Production**

Stage of processing	Nominal rate (%)	Effective rate (%)
1	4.6	4.6
2	7.9	22.6
3	10.2	29.7
4	22.2	38.4

SOURCE: United Nations Conference on Trade and Development, *The Kennedy Round Estimated Effects on Tariff Barriers* (New York: United Nations, 1968).

much more serious obstacle to industrialization than the moderate nominal tariff levels would appear to suggest. Industrialization in the LDCs could involve advancing their production to later stages, thus replacing some of their exports of rudimentary goods with the export of more finished goods. But it is these stages of production that are highly protected in the developed countries. The tariff structures of the latter thereby tend to lock in the LDCs to the earlier stages.

Another prominent feature is the high degree of effective protection afforded industrial activities in many LDCs with import substitution policies. A country might wish to develop an automobile industry, for example, and attempt to do this by giving both high protection to finished automobiles and low protection to many intermediate goods such as parts. As a result, the share of total cost accounted for by value added is low relative to the share of intermediate goods (because few are produced in the local industry), and the tariff on automobiles substantially exceeds that on inputs. Then, formula (8.4) implies that the effective rate could be much higher than the nominal rate. Many studies have revealed an extensive tendency for LDCs to shelter industrial activities behind effective tariffs that greatly exceed the (frequently high) nominal tariffs. As an extreme example, Anne Krueger's study of Turkish policies revealed that superphosphate fertilizer, with a nominal tariff of 27 percent, was accorded an effective tariff rate of 925 percent.

Problems

8.11 Suppose that shoes have a 25 percent nominal tariff rate, leather a 15 percent rate, and two-thirds of the cost of a pair of shoes is due to the leather they contain and one-third to value added. What is the effective rate of protection of the activity of making shoes from leather?

8.12 Suppose that, in a refinery, a_O barrels of crude oil, a_C tons of coal, and a_M units of materials are combined with value added to yield b_G gallons of gasoline and b_A gallons of aviation fuel. If P_O, P_C, P_M, P_G, and P_A denote the world prices of oil, coal, materials, gasoline, and aviation fuel, respectively, and if t_O, t_C, t_M, t_G, and t_A denote the corresponding nominal tariff rates, derive a formula, analogous to (8.4), for the effective rate of protection of refining, e_R.

8.13* Consider the example of steel and autos in the text. *Gross* output, denoted X_A and X_S for autos and steel, respectively, refers to the total output of an industry. *Net* output (Y_A and Y_S) refers to gross output less that part of output used as an input in other industries (that is, that part of gross output available for consumption or export). Thus, $Y_A = X_A$ and $Y_S = X_S - aX_A$. Chapter 1 showed that relative commodity prices equal the marginal rate of transformation between any two goods that are produced. Show that this refers to the *MRT* between *net* outputs. Will the ratio of values added per unit equal the *MRT* between *gross* outputs? Why? What do you conclude about the significance of effective rates of protection?

6. SUMMARY

1. Tariffs can be imposed to influence a country's relations with the rest of the world and to influence the domestic economy. International motives include the optimum-tariff argument, production shifting, profit shifting, and limiting trade for noneconomic reasons.

2. A tariff is usually a first-best way of attaining an international objective, at least if one takes a nationalistic—as opposed to a cosmopolitan—point of view.

3. Domestic motives include raising government revenue, countering domestic distortions, the infant-industry argument, noneconomic objectives, and changing the domestic distribution of income.

4. The tariff is usually a second-best tool for these purposes because it introduces distortions of its own, which more direct methods would not do.

5. The effective rate of protection measures the excess of actual value added per unit in an industry above what it would be if calculated at international prices. Effective rates differ from nominal rates when intermediate goods and final goods are subject to different tariffs, and the effective rates measure the direct impacts of a tariff structure on factors employed in the various sectors.

SUGGESTED READING

Baldwin, R. E. "Trade Policies in Developed Countries." In *Handbook of International Economics*. Vol. 1. Edited by R. W. Jones and P. B. Kenen. Amsterdam: North-Holland, 1984. A useful survey.

Corden, W. M. *The Theory of Protection*. Oxford: Oxford University Press, 1971. Effective protection.

———. *Trade Policy and Economic Welfare*. Oxford: Oxford University Press, 1974. The tariff as a policy tool.

Greenaway, D. *Trade Policy and the New Protectionism*. New York: St. Martin's, 1983. A survey of theory and practice.

Johnson, H. G. *Aspects of the Theory of Tariffs*. London: Allyn & Unwin, 1974. The traditional approach.

CHAPTER 9

How Nations Restrict Trade

> A protective tariff is immoral and dishonest, because its sole pur-
> pose is to increase prices artificially, thereby enabling one citizen to
> levy unjust tribute from another. —CORDELL HULL

This chapter discusses how commercial policy is actually conducted. First,
we seek to uncover those circumstances that determine whether protection is
granted or not. Then, we look at commercial policy in action.

1. THE POLITICAL ECONOMY OF PROTECTION

The motives for tariffs discussed in Chapter 8 do not, on the whole, make
a strong case for protection. In nearly all cases, the tariff is second-best—dominated by some other policy tool. The optimum-tariff argument is first-best,
but only from a narrow nationalistic point of view. In any event, the argument
is relevant only to countries that occupy a special place in the world economy.
This holds for production shifting and for profit shifting also. Trade limitation
for noneconomic reasons is unambiguously a first-best use of a tariff, but the
argument really reduces to protection for its own sake. How, then, do we explain the substantial protection characteristic of both past and present?

Fallacious Arguments for Protection

The most natural way to proceed is first to examine the arguments advanced by protectionists. Our discussion of various motives noted the times
and places when they were so used. But, in addition, one finds many invalid
arguments reflecting a misunderstanding of the theory of international trade.

Perhaps the most common is the *cheap foreign labor* argument, the asser-
tion that, because wages in many parts of the world are only a small fraction
of wages at home, free trade must result in massive domestic unemployment
or massive real wage cuts. The argument is a fundamental misunderstanding
of the principle of comparative advantage.

Sometimes factors other than labor occupy center stage, as when attention is directed to modern, efficient foreign plants (cheap foreign capital), and the argument has been carried to its extreme to assert that each product should be accorded protection equal to the excess of the domestic cost of production above the foreign cost, regardless of the source of this difference. This principle, sometimes called that of the "scientific tariff," was actually written into U.S. law in 1922, and the Tariff Commission was given the thankless task of measuring cost differences as a basis for tariff revision (few rates were actually changed in this way).

Another common fallacy is found in the *keep the money at home* argument: imports should be restricted because the necessity of paying for them results in a loss of the nation's money to foreigners. This reflects an ignorance of international equilibrium: imports are paid for by the sale of exports and assets to foreigners to the mutual benefit of both parties.

Tariffs and Pressure-Group Politics

Thus far we have looked at the motives advanced for tariffs. An alternative is to examine who benefits and who loses on the presumption that self-interest governs political behavior. A tariff always hurts some individuals and benefits others, so there is always a group with a vested interest in protection. But, except when there is a substantial terms-of-trade improvement, the losses always exceed the gains so that free trade would attract the majority of "dollar votes" if given the chance. Thus we must examine the political aspect in more detail.

Theories of the economic behavior of representative government have been described by Anthony Downs, Mancur Olson, and Albert Breton. From this perspective, the central relevant fact about protection is that its costs are diffused over many people while the benefits are concentrated on relatively few. Consider, for example, the case of a textile industry in a developed country. If the industry is faced with severe competition from imports, a tariff could mean the difference between having a job and losing it for textile workers, and between solvency and bankruptcy for textile firms. Thus people in the industry have a vital stake in the tariff question. Protection for textiles would harm many more people, but each person would be affected only slightly. All consumers would have to pay more for textiles, but such purchases account for only a small part of consumers' budgets. Export industries will also be harmed because factors will be bid away by textile producers and because foreign countries will ultimately have to buy fewer goods from this country if they are forced to reduce their sales to it. But these costs are long-term and will be spread over all export industries so that individual exporters will perceive little effect.

The implication of this asymmetry is that the economic gains from the tariff, though smaller than the economic losses, will translate into a larger political impact. Because the gainers have a vital interest, they have a strong incentive to organize and exert whatever influence they can. Their decision on whether to support elected officials will likely be determined by the officials' positions on the tariff issue. Those who will lose from the tariff are large in number, but since they are not greatly affected individually, they have less incentive to organize or even to keep informed about the issue. Their decision on which elected officials to support will be determined by the positions of those officials on other public questions. Moreover, those who gain from a tariff would find it easier to organize than would the losers since the gainers are more likely to come in contact with each other because they are in the same business or because they are more geographically concentrated. Such concentration would also make their support more important for politicians from the same region.

Notice that this *pressure group* argument is related to individuals' time horizons and the degree to which factors are specific to industry, as discussed in section 3 of Chapter 8. If the time horizon is short and factors are highly specific, the gains from a tariff will be concentrated on those actually located in the industry rather than on the industry's intensive factor wherever located. This strengthens the pressure-group argument.

This connection between politics and economics goes both ways. If tariff protection is important in a country, those industries that most markedly possess the characteristics described above will be the industries most likely to obtain protection and to prosper. Thus the country will tend to develop an industrial structure with these characteristics. Similarly, if the ability to benefit members by obtaining tariff protection is important to the appeal of trade associations and labor unions, groups organized on an industry basis and appealing to individuals with a short-term horizon would be most likely to prosper because they would appeal most to the people who care most. Thus we would expect to see such pressure groups adopt a short-run, industry-specific view of tariff matters, even if the general population does not.

Characteristics of Protected Industries

Do protected industries in fact possess the characteristics that the above discussion suggests would likely lead to protection? Let us look at the limited available evidence.

1. There is evidence that the industrial nations tend to protect most heavily industries that make intensive use of unskilled labor. David Stafford Ball found that the tariff structure of the United States in 1962 tended to give higher effective rates of protection to industries with lower average wage rates. Richard Caves and Ronald Jones, likewise, showed that in the late 1960s U.S. tariff rates, both nominal and effective, were higher in industries where wage rates were lower. Similar evidence has been marshaled for Western European countries by M. Constantopoulos and others. All of this is

consistent with the pressure-group theory because unskilled workers typically find it most difficult to find a new job after losing an old one due to import competition; thus their interest in protection should be high. Also, workers are voters. On the other hand, we saw in Chapter 6 that in the industrial countries wages tend to be lower in import-competing industries and, more generally, that these countries tend to have a comparative disadvantage in goods that intensively use unskilled labor. Since it is the import-competing industries that are protected in any case, one might expect to find a negative correlation between tariffs and wage rates regardless of what actually determines protection. A different question was addressed by John Cheh. He found that in international tariff negotiations in the mid-1960s, the United States reduced tariff rates the least in those industries with the highest labor-adjustment costs (the costs of moving to a new job), and the extent of unskilled labor was a determinant of those costs. James Riedel failed, however, to find similar evidence for West Germany.

2. A few studies have related tariffs to the concentration-diffusion characteristics emphasized in the pressure-group theory. A study of the U.S. Tariff Act of 1824 by J. J. Pincus found that high protection tended to go to those industries that were most concentrated, where communication among producers was easiest, and that had a presence in a sizable area. Richard Caves examined the 1963 Canadian tariff structure and compared the ability of alternative theories to explain it: a majority-vote theory predicting that tariffs would be high when a majority of voters benefit, an industry-size theory predicting that the highest protection would go to the industries that are the largest, actually or potentially, and a pressure-group theory predicting that protection would be highest in those industries where producers were the most concentrated and buyers the least concentrated. The last theory performed the best.

3. Some investigators have looked directly at the tariff-making process rather than the resultant tariffs. The political scientist E. E. Schattschneider wrote a classic account of the passage of the U.S. Tariff Act of 1930. Robert Baldwin has performed a statistical test of congressional voting on the 1974 U.S. Trade Act. He found that protectionist votes were positively related to political-party membership (because of party loyalty—the bill was sponsored by a Republican administration), the prominence of protectionist industries in congressional districts, and the receipt of campaign contributions from protectionist unions. The presence in congressional districts of industries opposed to protection seemed to have no effect.

4. The tendency, noted in Chapter 8, of the tariff structures of industrial countries to offer greater protection at more advanced stages of production is clearly consistent with the pressure-group theory. Producers of intermediate goods sell to the industries that use them so that buyers as well as sellers could be concentrated. Producers of final goods, on the other hand, sell to consumers in general so that buyers are likely to be far less concentrated than sellers.

Problems

9.1 List the characteristics likely to be possessed by industries with substantial protection. What specific industries seem to have these characteristics? Find out how protected those industries are.

9.2 On the basis of this section's discussion of what determines relative tariff rates in a country, speculate about what national characteristics should distinguish high-tariff countries from low-tariff ones. How do your speculations stack up against actual policy differences across countries?

---

2. *CASE STUDY:* THE TARIFF HISTORY OF THE UNITED STATES

A brief overview of U.S. tariff history will illustrate the points made in Chapter 8 and also set the stage for a discussion of current policy issues. Table 9.1 shows the average U.S. tariff rate in selected years since 1821.

The Early Period

In colonial times the individual colonies pursued their own commercial policies, and after the Revolution they passed their own tariff laws. These were intended to raise government revenue, but the protection of local industries soon became a significant motive as well. Conflicts between the states naturally arose, and attempts at coordination and at using state tariffs as a source of needed national revenue came to naught.

TABLE 9.1 Average U.S. Tariff Rates *(total duties as a percentage of total dutiable imports)*

Year	Average tariff (%)		Year	Average tariff (%)
1821	45		1925	38
1830	62		1932	29
1835	40		1940	36
1850	27		1946	25
1861	19		1950	13
1865	48		1960	12
1893	50		1970	10
1900	49		1980	6
1910	42		1991	5
1920	16			

SOURCE: *Statistical Abstract of the United States.*

With the adoption of the Constitution, tariff policy became the exclusive responsibility of the new national government, which needed revenue. In April 1789 James Madison introduced a bill in Congress for a moderate tariff. Madison's purpose was simply to raise *revenue*. (He hoped to hit the spring imports, already on the high seas, with a tariff when they arrived!) But protectionist sentiment soon surfaced and influenced the measure that was eventually adopted. Pennsylvania interests obtained protection for their young steel industry, which had been nurtured by local duties before the adoption of the Constitution. Logs began rolling, as the support of interests harmed by some aspects of the bill were enlisted by the addition of protectionist features for their own benefit. This was indicative of subsequent years. The most common rationale for this protection was the *infant-industry argument,* voiced by Alexander Hamilton and others. Nationalist sentiment, especially resentment of the British—important exporters to the United States—also played a role. The level of protection that emerged, little more than 5 percent overall, was nevertheless modest by later standards, as Table 9.1 reveals.

Economic relations with Europe were interrupted by the Napoleonic Wars, by Jefferson's embargo of trade with France and England (in retaliation for interference by those warring nations with U.S. shipping), and especially by the War of 1812, during which the Royal Navy blockaded the coast. This amounted to protection of a very high order indeed! The close of hostilities was followed by new tariffs to protect war-nurtured industries—a pattern consistently followed after later wars. Protection was generally favored by the Northeast, the home of import-competing industries and owners of capital, a relatively scarce factor. Interests in the South and West, where people owned land and produced exports, tended to oppose tariffs. The former were on balance dominant, and protection became more intense, culminating in 1828 with an act called the Tariff of Abominations. This produced a dramatic fusion of the tariff issue with that of states' rights when South Carolina vainly tried to nullify the tariff.

The Respite

The coming of Jacksonian democracy reflected a shift in the balance of political power that soon resulted in tariff reductions. This process was also facilitated by a spirit of compromise and by a surplus in the federal budget, for which the tariff was the principal revenue source. Tariffs by and large fell steadily between the 1820s and the Civil War, coinciding with liberal trends in Europe. But the trend was never as strong in the United States and ended sooner so that the country continued to be relatively protectionist.

The Age of High Protection

In any event liberalism ended with the Civil War. Secession shifted political power to Northern interests, who had been protectionists all along. The exporting South, which had enjoyed heavy cotton sales to Britain, had favored free trade. Also, the need to finance the war resulted in increased tariffs, as did the desire to use tariffs to put foreign goods on the same footing as heavily taxed domestic goods.

The end of the war witnessed, in familiar fashion, a continuation of the high-tariff policy. The protectionist era was to continue for over seventy years. Tariff rates fluctuated, a modest downward revision was attempted when Grover Cleveland was president, and there was a real respite in Woodrow Wilson's administration.

Throughout the nineteenth century, the tariff was the major source of federal revenue. This ensured that protection was intimately related to questions of national taxation and the role of the central government as well as to struggles between economic interests and to debate over the wisdom of industrialization. The tariff was the major political issue of the century, eclipsed only by slavery when that was an open question.

The Wilson administration brought about a large reduction in protection with the Underwood Tariff of 1913, which abolished tariffs on some important products such as raw wool, iron, and coal. But the liberal respite ended with the usual reaction after the First World War and with the return of the Republicans to power. Tariffs rose during the 1920s, culminating in the Smoot-Hawley Act of 1930.

During the election campaign of 1928, the Democrats had abandoned their traditional opposition to high tariffs and embraced protection in their platform. The original purpose of the tariff bill that the Republicans introduced was to aid agriculture. The important agricultural commodities that were heavily exported could not be helped much by tariffs, and, although many agricultural duties were substantially raised, a proposal for export subsidies for farm products was defeated. But a logrolling avalanche resulted in a large general rise in tariffs on manufactures. The need for revenue and the infant-industry argument, both so prominent in the nineteenth century, were no longer significant motives. The desire to *benefit special interests,* with a generally nationalistic sentiment and the 1929 stock-market crash for background, was the driving force. During the congressional debate, thirty-six foreign countries protested that they would be seriously hurt by the proposed changes, and over one thousand American economists signed a petition against the bill. The petition had little apparent effect, although Senator Smoot complained that opponents of his bill resided "in American schools of economics, and in the cloistered halls of theoretical universities," while Senator Shortbridge described himself as "not overawed or at all disturbed by the proclamation of the college professors who never earned a dollar by the sweat of their brow by honest labor—theorists, dreamers." In any event, the resultant act raised American tariffs to historic highs, comparable to the Tariff of Abominations of a century before.

The result was little short of catastrophic. Within two years, sixty foreign countries had instituted tariff increases of their own. These countries were concerned both with retaliating against the United States and with stimulating domestic employment in the face of the deepening world depression. The mutual increases in protection canceled each other out, and the resulting dramatic shrinkage in world trade simply made the Depression worse for all. By 1932 American imports were only 31 percent of their 1929 level, and exports collapsed in even greater proportion.

The Liberal Period

The new Roosevelt administration soon saw the need to revive world trade and hoped to assist American recovery by increasing exports. The result was a landmark in U.S. tariff history—the reciprocal Trade Agreements Act of 1934.

This act authorized the president to enter into bilateral agreements to reduce (or increase) U.S. tariffs by up to 50 percent in exchange for reciprocal foreign concessions. The act (technically an amendment to the Smoot-Hawley tariff, which remains the basic U.S. tariff act to this day) was originally valid for only three years, but it was renewed many times into the 1960s.

The Trade Agreements Act was a turning point in two ways. It was, first, intended to break with the old policy of high protection. Second, it transferred tariff-making initiative from the legislative branch, highly subject to the logrolling of sectorial interests, to the executive branch, with a relatively more national outlook. (Earlier tariff laws had contained provisions for executive flexibility, but, as intended, they had not been widely applied and not in a liberalizing direction.)

By the Second World War, the United States had reached twenty-one agreements with foreign nations, and the Smoot-Hawley tariff levels were moderately reduced as a result. The liberal period continued after the war, the first major conflict in U.S. history followed by a reduction of protection instead of an increase. We shall examine postwar experience presently. As is clear from Table 9.1, present U.S. tariff rates are far below the basic Smoot-Hawley levels, and low in historical perspective.

3. *CASE STUDY:* EUROPEAN COMMERCIAL POLICY

In the early nineteenth century, Europe exported manufactures to the United States for primary products. Now let us look at policy from the other side of the ocean.

As Britain emerged from the industrial revolution and the Napoleonic Wars, its rising entrepreneurial class challenged the landed aristocracy for both political and economic power. The political struggle culminated in the Reform Bill of 1832, while the economic conflict centered on the Corn Laws, which protected agriculture. These duties were finally repealed in 1846 as Tory prime minister Sir Robert Peel executed a historic about-face that shattered his own party. During the next fifteen years Britain repealed the Navigation Acts (which, since the mid-seventeenth century had funneled through England most materials produced in British colonies) and dismantled most of its tariffs. For over eighty-five years the country embraced a free-trade policy that was a foundation stone of the *Pax Britannica* and was supported by both political parties and challenged by no major public figure until Joseph Chamberlain did so near the turn of the century.

This trend toward free trade was not confined to Britain. Liberalization had taken place in the United States from the 1830s to the Civil War, as we have seen, and was extended to Continental Europe by a series of commercial treaties between the major powers. But toward the end of the century a reverse trend set in. The United States was highly protectionist from the Civil War, and Russia had remained so. Rising protectionism on the Continent stemmed from emerging nationalism and imperialism, which embraced commercial

---

The Most-Favored-Nation Clause

The most-favored-nation clause is an agreement between two nations to apply tariffs to each other at rates as low as those applied to any other nation. Thus if a country reduces tariffs on goods from some other country, it also applies these new lower rates to goods from all other countries that have MFN status with it. Thus bilateral agreements have multilateral effects. For example, the United States–United Kingdom trade agreement of 1938 provided for a reduction of U.S. duties on about 47 percent of U.S. imports from the United Kingdom. Because of the MFN clause, duties were also reduced on about 9 percent of U.S. imports from France, 13 percent of those from the Soviet Union, and 14 percent of those from Ireland.

The MFN clause has always been prominent during liberal periods. Thus the European commercial treaties of the 1860s relied upon it, and use of the MFN clause was a central part of the U.S. reciprocal trade agreements strategy adopted in 1934. By contrast, during its highly protectionist period, the United States did not employ the MFN clause as described above but, instead, used a much weaker "conditional" version that provided only for negotiations on the extension of tariff reductions granted third countries. When countries with (unconditional) MFN agreements became more protectionist, they often sought to escape by adopting narrow definitions of commodities in tariff legislation. An example quoted in generations of textbooks was provided by the German tariff law of 1902, which established a separate duty for "brown or dappled cows reared at a level of at least 300 metres above sea level and passing at least one month in every summer at an altitude of at least 800 metres." The purpose was obviously to isolate the duties on Swiss cattle from the MFN clause by defining them to be a distinct commodity.

The United States currently extends MFN status to nearly all countries.

policy as a weapon, and from labor migration and reductions in transportation costs, which gave the newly settled temperate zones a comparative advantage over Europe in food, even in Continental markets. France and Germany succumbed to the agrarian interest and, in contrast to earlier British behavior, imposed high duties on agricultural imports.

Despite the growing protectionism, tariffs on average remained low, by historical standards, before the First World War. But after that conflict, the trend to protection resumed at an accelerated pace, as war-weary nations turned inward. The Depression and the Smoot-Hawley tariff in the United States gave the process a gigantic boost. Country after country erected barriers to escape from the world slump, to export their own unemployment, or to retaliate against new barriers abroad. Britain abandoned free trade in 1932. The form of protection changed as well as its extent. Before the First World War, commercial policies had relied almost exclusively upon tariffs. Now nontariff barriers became important. France adopted an extensive system of import quotas, and other countries followed. Many types of controls, direct and indirect, were instituted.

4. *CASE STUDY:* CANADIAN TARIFF HISTORY

Canadian policy is of special interest because the country was for so long caught between the geographical proximity of the large U.S. economy and the political connection with Britain. Table 9.2 shows average Canadian tariff rates in selected years.

Prior to Confederation, in 1867, the separate colonies were allowed to levy their own tariffs—in addition to those set by Britain—even on trade among themselves. In 1791 the former French possessions were split into two parts that were allowed separate tariffs (but not on each other's goods) until

TABLE 9.2 Average Canadian Tariff Rates *(total duties as a percentage of total dutiable imports)*

Year	Average rate (%)	Year	Average rate (%)
1850	15.6	1900	27.7
1855	13.7	1913	26.1
1867	19.6	1929	24.4
1870	20.9	1939	24.2
1880	26.1	1946	21.2
1890	31.0	1953	18.6

SOURCE: J. H. Young, *Canadian Commercial Policy* (Ottawa: Royal Commission on Canada's Economic Prospects, 1957).

1840. These duties were the most important sources of revenue for the colonial governments and tended to be highest in those colonies with the greatest need for government revenue.

The crucial Canadian exports in those days were wheat and timber, which received preferential treatment in the British market. Trade with Britain exceeded that with the United States. But Canada's position changed after England abolished the Corn Laws in 1846; with goods from all countries admitted free of duty, Canada no longer had a preferential position in the British market. The colonies ended preferences on British goods and began to look south. The Reciprocity Treaty of 1854 established free trade in agricultural products between the United States and the British colonies in North America.

At this time, *revenue* was the primary motive for tariffs, which accounted for about two-thirds of all government revenues. A fall in these revenues as a result of an 1857 recession (and the reciprocity with the United States, which also reduced revenues) led to rate increases in the Cayley-Galt tariffs of 1858–1859. These duties also had a protectionist intent, as sentiment for the protection of Canadian manufacturing began to be significant at this time. Partly in response to these tariffs, but also because of U.S. ill will toward England resulting from the Civil War and because of a general U.S. shift toward protection, that country abrogated the Reciprocity Agreement in 1866.

Confederation in 1867 implied a single national tariff policy. But that policy was at a crossroads. Continued British commitment to free trade and the U.S rejection of reciprocity precluded a preferential Canadian position in either major export market. Sentiment for a protectionist policy continued to grow, but the first choice of the public was still for reciprocity with the United States, a policy that both the Liberal and Conservative parties continued to advocate for thirty years. But the United States consistently turned a deaf ear, so Canada chose protection. The country adopted a national policy of attracting scarce capital and immigrants, building up a manufacturing sector, and giving that sector a domestic market enlarged by westward expansion. A key part of the program was the protectionist National Policy tariff law of 1879. This set the tone of Canadian tariff policy for about sixty years.

At the close of the century Canada granted preferences for British goods, even though Britain refused to abandon free trade to reciprocate. By 1904 preferences of one-third were extended to most of the British Empire. One motive for this policy was to prevent the rapidly growing trade with the United States from dominating Canada's international transactions. The Canadian tariff structure consisted of three parts: the General Tariff, having the highest rates; the Intermediate Tariff, applying to countries with MFN status with Canada; and the Preferential Tariff, applying to the empire. Since the United States and Canada did not grant each other MFN status, tariffs on trade between these countries were high by world standards.

In 1911 Canada and the United States concluded a second reciprocity agreement, but the Canadian parliament refused to approve it even though the country had tried for so many years to obtain just such a pact. The manufacturing sector's desire for a general policy of protection had become too strong.

The Depression struck Canada via a decline in the foreign demand for Canadian exports. Also the U.S. Smoot-Hawley tariff caused much resentment, and the result was more Canadian protection in response. Britain abandoned its policy of free trade, and the Ottawa Conference of 1932 established a new system of Imperial Preferences.

The shift in U.S. policy marked by the Trade Agreements Act of 1934 resulted in a Canadian-U.S. trade agreement in 1935 and again in 1938. These agreements, the first between the two countries since reciprocity in 1854, involved a mutual duty reduction and extension of MFN status.

5. *CASE STUDY:* NORTH AMERICAN FREE TRADE?

There has been considerable progress toward establishing free trade on a regional basis in North America. The United States, Canada, and Mexico have concluded a series of trade agreements, of which three stand out.

The U.S.-Canada Automotive Agreement

A free-trade pact is one possible strategy for liberalizing trade. An alternative is to free trade sector by sector, as with the 1965 automotive agreement between the U.S. and Canada, mentioned in Chapter 2. This provided for free trade in motor vehicles and parts at the manufacturer's level (but not for consumers). In addition there were floors imposed on the manufacturers for their Canadian production and for the Canadian content of cars sold in Canada.

The agreement has succeeded in producing an internationally integrated automobile industry with large gains in efficiency. Before the agreement, automobile prices in Canada were about 10 percent higher than in the United States, wages were about 30 percent less, and the return to capital was about the same. The agreement enabled the automobile firms to specialize their Canadian operations to a few models, reaping economies of scale. Two-way trade expanded dramatically. Within a few years the price gap had shrunk to just a few percent, and the difference in wages narrowed by a large amount.

During the 1980s some problems began to emerge. The domestic content requirement on cars sold in Canada remained a cost disadvantage. This gave Asian manufacturers an edge in competing in the Canadian market. Tariffs had gradually come down, so the free-trade advantage given to North American producers by the agreement was less significant (and Korean cars were free from tariffs because of preferences given to LDCs). Japanese and Korean firms began planning to set up Canadian operations. Since they were not part of the agreement, they would not be subject to the domestic content limitations and so would be free to use large quantities of parts imported from their home factories. In any event the agreement has allowed a large Canadian automobile industry to exist. Workers and other pressure groups in the United States complain that it has exported automobile jobs to Canada. However, the U.S.-Canada free-trade pact preserved the automotive agreement.

The U.S.-Canada Free Trade Agreement

Trade between the United States and Canada dominates Canada's international transactions, is the largest single component of U.S. trade, and is by a considerable margin the largest bilateral trade flow in the world. As we have seen, sentiment for liberalizing this exchange has waxed and waned over the years.

During the 1970s the Canadian government, concerned about the nation's "cultural identity," had taken a restrictionist stance and tried to promote trade with other parts of the world. But attitudes changed in the 1980s, both within the government and among the public. In the United States, the Trade and Tariff Act of 1984 authorized the president to negotiate trade agreements with Israel or other countries, and a free-trade pact with Israel was reached. Heartened by this, the leaders of Canada and the United States agreed to begin negotiations for bilateral free trade.

The issue is much more important to Canada than to the United States for two reasons. First, since in size the Canadian economy is only a small fraction of the U.S. economy, bilateral trade is much more important relative to Canada's economy. Second, Canada has higher average tariffs than does the United States and imposes them on a larger fraction of imports, so a larger adjustment is under consideration. This is because Canadian manufacturing is inefficient relative to the rest of the industrial world: the protectionist policy causes a large assortment of goods to be produced at low scales of operations. Thus potential gains from liberalization are large, as indicated by the estimates discussed in Chapter 7.

Negotiations began in May 1986. In the fall of 1987, about two weeks before a negotiating deadline set by the U.S. Congress, the talks collapsed. This made front-page headlines in Canada but attracted only modest attention in the United States—an indication of the relative importance to the two countries of their mutual trade. After feverish high-level telephone calls, resumed negotiations reached agreement just hours before the deadline. The pact eliminates bilateral tariffs and many nontariff barriers over a ten-year adjustment period, and a mechanism to settle trade disputes was set up. The pact has been controversial in Canada, with opponents associating it with all the country's economic problems.

The North American Free Trade Agreement

While Canada is the largest trading partner of the United States, Mexico is the third largest (after Japan). As had been true with Canada, the issue of free trade with the United States followed a fundamental change in Mexican attitudes toward international trade. For years Mexico had been highly suspicious of its huge northern neighbor and had followed inward-looking policies, with high barriers to trade and an emphasis on import substitution. The nation even refrained from joining the GATT (see below). For some years Mexico experienced healthy growth, and this was maintained through the 1970s by new oil discoveries, the dramatic oil-price increases, and heavy borrowing from abroad. The bubble burst in 1982, when Mexico found that it could not continue to service its foreign debts, and ushered in the international debt crisis (which we will examine in detail later in this book).

After another crisis in 1985, Mexico began a series of outward-oriented economic reforms. These included reductions in tariffs and import licensing, with tariffs being cut by over a half. In 1986 Mexico joined the GATT. During this period of reform, Mexico reached several bilateral trade accords with the United States. But President Salinas of Mexico wished to go much further, hoping for a free-trade agreement to consolidate the reform effort and to stimulate foreign investment in the Mexican economy. In 1990 the United States agreed to participate in negotiations for such a free-trade area. Canada, anxious that its own agreement with the United States not be undercut, also came on board so that when actual negotiations began in 1991 all three countries were involved. On August 12, 1992, representatives of the three countries successfully reached agreement on a North American free trade area (NAFTA). Ratification of the agreement quickly became a contentious political issue in Canada and the United States.

Like Canada, Mexico has an economy much smaller than that of the United States, so its trade with the United States is relatively much more important for Mexico than for the United States. The NAFTA is accordingly a much more prominent issue there. It is not a much more contentious one, though, because it is not so much a change in policy as the culmination of a Mexican policy shift that occurred in the 1980s. Moreover, Mexico's position differs from Canada's in that its economy is much different in structure from that of the United States: Mexico is much less developed than its northern neighbor and possesses quite different factor endowments. U.S. free trade with Mexico could well imply more specialization and disruption across sectors than has free trade with Canada, so it is not surprising that it could be more controversial in the United States.

Economists have not been reluctant to calculate predictions of the effects of a NAFTA. For example, Gary Hufbauer and Jeffrey Schott of the Institute for International Economics have estimated that such an agreement could by 1995 raise U.S. imports from Mexico by $7.7 billion and U.S. exports to Mexico by $16.7 billion so that the U.S. balance-of-trade surplus with Mexico would increase by $9 billion. Mexico's overall balance-of-trade surplus is expected to fall by $12 billion—the $3 billion rise in the U.S. surplus plus an increase of $3 billion in Mexican imports of intermediate goods from third countries. This Mexican trade deficit would be financed by international borrowing, with foreign capital attracted by the vibrant Mexican economy.

Indeed, the capital began flowing even as a NAFTA was being negotiated, partly in response to the Mexican reforms of the 1980s and partly in anticipation of a NAFTA. Hufbauer and Schott also estimate that 112,000 U.S. workers would lose their jobs but that 242,000 new jobs would be created, a net gain of 130,000 jobs for the United States. Mexico would on balance create 609,000 jobs.

6. COMMERCIAL POLICIES AFTER THE SECOND WORLD WAR

As the Second World War drew to a close, the United States and other Allied nations grappled with the problem of devising an international order free from the mistakes of the past. The most prominent result was the United Nations, but also international institutions were created to deal directly with the postwar economy. The guiding principles, reflecting American attitudes, were *liberalism* (minimal restrictions on international transactions) and *symmetry* (all nations should be treated the same). Two of these institutions, the International Bank for Reconstruction and Development (IBRD) and the International Monetary Fund (IMF), will be discussed in subsequent chapters. A conference at Havana in 1948 adopted a complex charter for the third institution, the International Trade Organization (ITO), which was to deal with commercial policy. But the ITO was stillborn since the charter was never ratified by national governments. Instead, an interim arrangement, the General Agreement on Tariffs and Trade (GATT), has by default become the international body dealing with trade matters.

The GATT

As its name implies, the GATT is technically an agreement rather than an organization (thus participating nations are *contracting parties* rather than member states). But it has acquired a physical form as well, with a small permanent secretariat in Geneva and a Council of Representatives. The GATT is not a treaty; American adhesion was via an executive agreement, and Congress has never passed on the matter.

There are three aspects to GATT. The *first* is the *agreement* itself, establishing standards for the commercial policies of the contracting parties. Two standards are fundamental: quotas are prohibited, and each nation must observe the MFN clause with all contracting parties. There are exceptions to each of these rules; for example, quotas are allowed for dealing with temporary balance-of-payments problems, and customs unions (which depart from the MFN clause) are permitted.

The *second* aspect of GATT is its role in the *settlement of trade disputes* between nations. GATT has no enforcement machinery, but it does provide an impartial recourse that has been of considerable use in the past, notably during the 1960s. Furthermore, GATT procedures help ensure that the interests of third countries are taken into account by the parties directly involved in any dispute.

The *third* aspect of GATT is its *sponsorship of tariff reductions.* These reductions have been accomplished in a series of multilateral negotiations, or rounds.

The GATT Rounds of Multilateral Tariff Negotiations

There have, thus far, been eight major tariff-cutting rounds. They are logical extensions of the United States' reciprocal trade agreements in the sense that each participating country "trades" tariff concessions (that is, reductions) for concessions from its partners, and the MFN clause applies. But there is one important difference: the GATT rounds are *multilateral,* whereas the earlier trade agreements involved *bilateral* negotiation between the United States and a single foreign nation. Since the MFN clause implies that a bilateral agreement will have direct multilateral consequences, the multilateral approach to negotiation is much more efficient.

The first two GATT rounds, held during 1949–1951 as the ITO was dying its slow death, substantially lowered tariffs. This success probably indicated that special interests were not very sensitive to tariff cuts at that time: the United States had a very strong position, whereas the weakened European industries were sheltered by quotas and other direct controls. However, trade was further liberalized when these quotas were eliminated in the late 1950s. The liberalization achieved by GATT is relevant mainly to trade in manufactures between the industrial countries. The more than one hundred nations that either belong to GATT or accept its provisions include many LDCs in addition to the principal industrial nations, and most of the formerly communist states either belong or intend to join. But the LDCs generally continue to follow protectionist policies.

The next three rounds achieved only modest success, as protectionist pressures began to mount. The sixth (1964–1967), known as the Kennedy Round because it resulted from an initiative by the Kennedy administration in the United States, was a more ambitious effort designed to prevent the emergence of the European Common Market from dividing the industrial world into exclusive trade blocs. In the end, tariffs on manufactures were slashed by an average of one-third, the largest reduction in any single round, but then the EEC went on to develop a highly protectionist Common Agricultural Policy (see Chapter 18).

The Kennedy Round also witnessed changes in American policy. American participation in the first five GATT rounds had been under the authorization of extensions of the reciprocal Trade Agreements Act of 1934. This act was not renewed for the Kennedy Round, with Congress instead passing the Trade Expansion Act of 1962. This measure gave the president increased negotiating authority and introduced a new feature into American policy: Trade Adjustment Assistance (TAA), which provides for unemployment compensation and retraining assistance for workers and firms injured by import competition. Instead of resisting the reallocation of resources implied by a movement toward comparative advantage, that reallocation should be accepted and rendered as harmless as possible. From an economic point of view, factors that are specific in the short run should be compensated for their losses and also rendered less specific. From a political point of view, opposition to trade liberalization should be bought off.

The seventh GATT negotiating session, the Tokyo Round, concluded in 1979. The Tokyo Round Agreement chopped a further one-third, on average, off tariffs on manufactures. Also, success was achieved in dealing with *non-tariff barriers*. Codes of conduct were agreed upon in various areas: governmental procurement; customs valuation procedures; technical regulations for safety, health, national security, the environment, and so forth; government subsidies; safeguards or "escape clauses"; dumping. The codes specify, in varying degrees of detail, appropriate government policies and procedures, and each code provides for a GATT committee to help resolve international disputes in its respective area. The codes are not amendments to the GATT itself; they need not be subscribed to by all GATT members, and countries that have not signed the GATT may subscribe to the codes.

7. THE URUGUAY ROUND AND OUTSTANDING TRADE ISSUES

The GATT negotiations have reduced the industrial countries' tariffs on manufactures to relative insignificance by historical standards. Other issues now seem more pressing. These were addressed in the most recent GATT round, the Uruguay Round (so named because the preliminary meeting was held in Punta del Este, Uruguay, in 1986).

1. *Trade in Agricultural Goods.* The central focus here was on the highly protectionist Common Agricultural Policy (CAP) of the EEC. This policy, a descendant of the decision in the late nineteenth century by Continental countries to protect their agricultural sectors, is currently the most important economic function of the European Economic Community. By contrast, the United States, with its strong comparative advantage in temperate-zone agricultural products, sees the CAP as a unilateral denial to America of a major export market. Indeed, because of export subsidies, the Community has become a major agricultural exporter. Thus the issue is a major sore spot in Atlantic relations and promises to remain one for some time.

The United States took an aggressive position on agricultural trade in the Uruguay Round negotiations, insisting on the abolition of export subsidies. Europe resisted. The American position reflected the country's interest in agricultural trade, but it was also intended to enlist the support of other agricultural exporters for other issues in the negotiations. The talks were scheduled to conclude in 1990; instead they broke down in December of that year over an American-European impasse over agriculture. Talks resumed in February 1991 and concluded in December 1993, after a compromise on agriculture.

2. *Trade in Services.* This includes tourism and transportation, insurance, telecommunications, banking, construction, and so on. Also important is income earned from foreign investment (the income is the fee paid for the services of the invested capital). Commodity trade has traditionally been regarded as much more important than services trade, but the latter has grown more rapidly for over a decade and is now prominent. Figures are hard to come by, but it is thought that the annual value of trade in services now approaches $1 trillion. This trade has not been covered by international agreements, so national barriers abound. The United States, as a large supplier of services, would like them brought into the GATT fold. Other industrial nations seem increasingly inclined to agree, but many LDCs are reluctant. The U.S. Trade and Tariff Act of 1984 gave the president, for the first time, authority to negotiate international agreements to lower barriers to trade in services.

The Uruguay Round negotiations featured a separate negotiating group for services trade. LDC skepticism abated, and the negotiations enjoyed some success.

3. *Counterfeit Goods.* Everyone knows about fake copies of Rolex watches and designer jeans. But counterfeiting is much more prevalent than that: there are bogus versions of everything from automobile and aviation parts to drugs, fertilizers, and medical equipment. Pirated copies of books and computer software are readily produced in countries that do not subscribe to (or enforce) international copyright agreements. (Pirated versions of this text exist; I hope you are not reading one.) Trade in counterfeit goods has grown rapidly in recent years. Sometimes the fakes are shoddy goods trying to pass for quality products. Sometimes they are quality goods trying to avoid a royalty or license fee, or trying to acquire status. In any event, producers of legitimate goods see both their sales and public images threatened by the counterfeiters. While the latter exist in most countries, a disproportionate share of counterfeit exports seems to come from industrializing countries—Taiwan is probably the largest single source. These countries have the ability to produce efficiently but not to innovate. They have a comparative advantage in counterfeiting! When the United States was young, its people behaved similarly: nineteenth-century English authors complained bitterly that their books were pirated by American publishers. But now American concern has become great. The Trade and Tariff Act of 1984 provided for retaliation against countries tolerating such behavior, and the United States has persuaded several countries to tighten up their laws and enforcement efforts. An international code of conduct is being negotiated.

4. *Nontariff Barriers.* Tariffs have been the dominant form of protection historically. But in recent decades nontariff barriers have been of steadily increasing importance, and by the 1970s most observers regarded them as at least as significant overall as tariffs. This trend is due in part to the fact that

the repeated reductions in tariffs have rendered the latter relatively less important. But two other influences are also at work. First, GATT restrictions ensure that protectionist pressures find outlets in nontariff barriers. Second, the increased role of government in the economies of the industrial countries has created new nontariff barriers, made existing ones more significant, and created new opportunities for the employment of such barriers. For example, a preference for domestic firms over foreign rivals in government purchases becomes more significant as the size of the government grows.

5. *The LDCs.* The GATT tariff reductions have centered on the manufactures exchanged among the industrial countries. Those cuts have also applied to LDC exports because of the MFN clause, but the goods involved have not been of central importance to the LDCs. Increased attention has, accordingly, been given to LDC trade. A new Part IV, for improving LDC trade, was added to the GATT in 1965, and during the 1970s the industrial countries adopted systems of tariff preferences for LDC manufactures. But benefits are modest. The retarded state of LDC trade is due in good part to the LDCs themselves, who have adopted protectionist policies and have refrained from aggressive participation in the GATT rounds. Demands for a new international order lose something in credibility when they come from those who are not fully exploiting the existing order. But the DCs have indicated by their deeds that any substantial increase in LDC competition with DC manufacturing industries will meet protectionist resistance. The tariff preferences exclude some sensitive industries, such as textiles, that are in fact the most important for LDC development.

In fact, international negotiations (such as the Uruguay Round) have been much less important for LDCs than their own attitudes toward policy. The spectacular success of countries with outward-oriented trade policies has induced policy reform in many countries, with import substitution giving way to increased trade. The transformation of policy in Mexico was discussed above. The wholesale decision of most formerly communist nations to become market economies has also provided a powerful demonstration effect.

You can get some idea about current tariff rates from Table 9.3. (These figures are not comparable to those in Tables 9.1 and 9.2, which divided revenues by dutiable imports rather than by all imports.) Note that in Table 9.3 the rates are higher for the LDCs than for the DCs. Of course, these figures take no account of nontariff barriers.

8. THE "NEW PROTECTIONISM"

Protectionism since World War II

The progressive tariff reductions in the years since the Second World War have, paradoxically, been accompanied by a gradual resurgence of protectionism. Successive extensions of the reciprocal Trade Agreements

TABLE 9.3   **Average Tariff Rates of Selected Countries, 1989** *(receipts from international trade taxes ÷ total imports)*

Country	Rate (%)
Canada	3.3
India	45.2
Japan (1985)	2.1
Korea	7.0
Mexico	6.2
Sweden (1983)	0.9
United States	3.4

SOURCES: International Monetary Fund, *Government Finance Statistics Yearbook; International Financial Statistics.*

Act during the 1950s were obtained only at the price of concessions to protectionists. The executive branch of the government, to be sure, has retained a relatively liberal outlook on trade, and the Republican party is less protectionist than before the Second World War. But Democratic legislators have become steadily less liberal, and the labor movement—important to Democratic politicians—has gradually abandoned its support of free trade. Labor supported extensions of the Trade Agreements Act and the Trade Expansion Act of 1962, but in the 1970s most major unions had become protectionist. Organized labor supported the abortive Burke-Hartke bill, which would have reversed forty years of American trade policy and restored high protection. The Trade Act of 1974 was a liberal counterattack but was passed with many concessions. Further concessions were required to obtain the enabling legislation necessary for the United States to adhere to the codes negotiated during the Tokyo Round. The Trade and Tariff Act of 1984 contained many protectionist features (but not as many as had been feared), and the number of protectionist bills before Congress has greatly increased in recent years.

One can only speculate about the reasons for the weakening free-trade position. Perhaps economic recession in the 1970s, together with the decline and redistribution of real incomes implied by the historic rise in oil prices, strengthened the determination of special-interest groups. A second factor would be the threat that transitional LDCs will capture the world markets for certain sensitive manufactures such as textiles, shoes, steel, and automobiles. The great postwar expansion of trade among the DCs, with those countries' economic structures becoming similar, has involved an expansion of intra-industry trade rather than industrial specialization. The DCs have, accordingly, largely been spared the disruption involved in reallocating factors of production from one industry to another. A rapid expansion of trade with the transitional LDCs, with their distinctive economic structures, does not promise to be nearly as painless. Finally, a large U.S. trade deficit since the mid-1980s has threatened many tradable-goods industries.

The actual protectionist measures adopted in the industrial countries have not, by and large, involved the simple application of new tariffs and quotas in violation of the GATT. Nor have they often utilized GATT-sanctioned measures such as the escape clause, which would require compensating concessions (the escape clause is discussed below). Instead, importing nations have bypassed the GATT entirely by negotiating trade-limitation agreements with exporters directly. For example, exports of color television sets to the United States from Korea and Taiwan (and, from 1977 to 1980, from Japan) are limited by "orderly marketing agreements" between the respective governments. Exporters enter into such agreements because of the threat that, otherwise, importers would impose even more stringent limitations. Occasional explicit quotas make the threat credible: thus in 1976 the United States imposed quotas on specialty steel imports from the EEC after concluding a bilateral agreement with Japan. Other "voluntary" agreements, numerous in the last twenty years, include a multilateral arrangement governing cotton, woolen, and synthetic textiles, a shoe quota, and the restraints on Japanese automobile exports discussed in Chapter 7.

Steady erosion has afflicted the principle, fundamental to both the U.S. trade-agreements policy and to GATT, that tariff liberalization should involve reciprocal concessions extended to all nations via the MFN clause. Some of this erosion has been consistent with, or accommodated by, the GATT: customs unions and tariff preferences for LDC exports. Note that the latter violates reciprocity as well as the MFN clause. There have also been outright violations of the GATT, such as the 1965 agreement between the United States and Canada establishing free trade in automobiles and parts by the major manufacturers. Finally, outside the GATT entirely, the "voluntary" export quotas are both nonreciprocal and discriminatory.

Dynamics of Contemporary Trade Policy

The evolution of trade policy in the modern world economy can be viewed as the result of four central forces, often acting in conflict.

1. *Multilateralism.* This is the most important force. It is represented by the GATT and its rounds of multilateral negotiations which have resulted in historically low barriers to the exchange of manufactures among the industrialized countries of the world.

2. *Regionalism.* This refers to the formation of regional trading blocs, such as the European Union and the NAFTA. Regionalism has emerged as a countervailing tendency to multilateralism, and some fear that the industrial world might evolve into a collection of several regional blocs with high barriers between them. The growth of regionalism is in part a reaction to slowing progress on the multilateral front, but the fear is that it may itself contribute to the slowdown. However, it is not inevitable that regionalism impede multilateralism: the successful Kennedy Round was in part a reaction to the formation of a trade bloc in Europe.

3. *The New Protectionism*, or "unilateralism." This refers to trade restrictions, like those just discussed, undertaken by a single nation or done by bilateral negotiation as a result of one nation's initiative. The most important example is the voluntary export restraint. The trade restrictions are usually protectionist, but sometimes they involve a country trying aggressively to expand its exports, such as the semiconductor agreements, discussed below, between the United States and Japan intended to expand the share of U.S. firms in the Japanese market for computer chips.

4. *Policy Reform by the "Outsiders."* This could turn out to be the most important of all in historical perspective. It includes economic reform in many LDCs, moving away from import substitution and state control and adopting outward-oriented policies. It also includes the efforts of formerly central-planned states to develop market economies and to participate fully in the international trading system.

9. TOOLS OF THE NEW PROTECTIONISM

There are four major, explicit trade-policy tools, consistent with the GATT, that the United States may employ, or threaten to employ, to obtain a "voluntary" export quota from another nation. Many similar tools are used by other industrial nations.

1. *The Escape Clause (Safeguard Provisions).* Since 1947, American trade agreements have included the provision that concessions could be withdrawn if they produced unforeseen injury to a domestic industry. Other nations use similar clauses, and they are consistent with the GATT and the subject of one of the codes negotiated in the Tokyo Round. Countries injured by such a withdrawal may retaliate if they do not receive mutually acceptable compensating concessions. Under American law, an injured industry may petition for relief to the International Trade Commission (ITC—known as the Tariff Commission until the 1974 Trade Act). The ITC then defines the scope of the industry and determines whether the industry so defined has suffered or will suffer serious injury due to increased imports—as a result of the 1974 Trade Act, the increase in imports need not be traced to a tariff concession. If such injury is found, the ITC recommends specific action to the president. This can include adjustment assistance or import protection in the form of higher duties, quotas, or marketing agreements. The president may modify or reject the recommendations, but Congress can then overrule him. The escape-clause machinery has been used many times, although it has not usually resulted directly in increased protection. From 1948 to 1953, fifty-one applications to the commission resulted in action in only three minor cases. Since then, the law has been tightened, and the commission has become more aggressive. In recent years the escape clause has become an important implicit influence leading to orderly marketing agreements—the president has an in-

centive to negotiate such agreements to placate Congress and the ITC, and foreign countries face implementation of the harsher ITC recommendations if they do not reach agreement with the president.

2. *Antidumping Duties.* These may be imposed on foreign goods dumped in the American market (sold in America at a price below the price in the country of origin or below the cost of production or below both). Such duties, to eliminate the price differential, have long been provided for in the laws of many nations and are the subject of one of the codes negotiated in the Tokyo Round. Under American law, the Commerce Department investigates complaints to determine if goods are being dumped, and, simultaneously, the International Trade Commission investigates the extent of injury to domestic interests. If dumping is found and the injury is not immaterial and is due to the dumped imports, the Commerce Department assesses duties.

Until recently in other countries as well as the United States, these procedures seldom resulted in actual duties. Investigations were protracted, and the authorities often failed to rule that dumping was taking place, even in the face of substantial evidence; firms were accordingly reluctant to file and pursue complaints. But this has changed in recent years. The law has been tightened, and administration has been shifted to the Commerce Department from the Treasury, with the former expected to be more zealous than was the latter. As a result, use of the antidumping law has greatly increased, and the statute has become a principal protectionist tool.

But why do countries have antidumping laws at all since the opportunity to buy goods at a low price would seem to be a good thing? No doubt our earlier discussion, of why commercial policies in general are widely used despite the gains from free trade, applies here. But there are also several arguments for singling dumping out for special treatment. Dumping could indicate that a foreign firm has a monopoly over both foreign and domestic markets because a monopoly would charge each market the price it would bear. If demand is more elastic in the domestic (importer's) market, the monopolist will charge a lower price here than in the foreign market as long as the monopolist is able to separate the two markets. There are sound economic reasons for measures to deal with monopoly and to prevent such price discrimination. But simply forcing the monopolist to charge us a *higher* price, as the antidumping law attempts to do, makes no sense from a national point of view.

A second argument is that a foreign oligopolist might temporarily dump its products in the domestic market to crush domestic competition or force it to adhere to an international cartel. Prices would be increased once the objective was attained. Antidumping laws are thus defended as a way of preventing such tactics. This possibility often figures in public discussions, and in the early part of this century many countries did adopt antidumping laws because of fear about the behavior of large American and German firms. But contemporary incidents of this sort are rare; such an aggressive foreign oligopolist would, after all, be employing an expensive strategy to attain an advantage it could not realistically hope to keep for long.

A third possibility is that periodic dumping could be the response of foreign firms to recessions, new competition, or other events. These firms might prefer to sell for a time at a price below long-run average cost, rather than closing down completely or even making large layoffs. The American steel industry accused European firms of doing this in 1979–1980. If dumping is used in this way to smooth out production fluctuations, foreign workers enjoy more secure job prospects and foreign firms presumably need pay a lower wage than they would if they offered less secure jobs. Antidumping laws would thus prevent foreign firms from using the domestic market as a buffer in this way.

An antidumping law differs from the measures analyzed in Chapter 7 in that it is a *rule* for a tariff to be imposed in certain circumstances rather than a tariff itself. This distinction can be important, especially in imperfectly competitive markets where firms do not passively react to prices. For example, a foreign exporter, knowing that such a law is on the books and is being enforced, might export less and charge a higher price in order to reduce the chance that antidumping duties will be imposed in the future. And the existence of such a law makes it more attractive for domestic firms to compete vigorously with foreign rivals in domestic markets: the home firms know that, if they reduce prices, foreign firms will be more reluctant to follow suit or will be more likely to be subjected to antidumping duties if they do. This last possibility is one way in which such a law could conceivably benefit consumers, who on most counts seem to be losers.

3. *Countervailing Duties.* These may be imposed on imports that have received subsidies from the government of the exporting country, with the duties set so as to cancel out the subsidy. Many countries have such laws, which are the subject of one of the GATT codes. The American law, like the antidumping statute, is administered by the Commerce Department. Government subsidies are ubiquitous these days, so severe application of such laws could conceivably strangle trade. However, as with antidumping laws, countervailing duties were seldom imposed until a few years ago. But usage has greatly increased; for example, about 40 percent of U.S. imports from India have been subject to countervailing duties.

4. *Unfair Trade Practices (Section 301).* The president may exclude from the country goods that have been marketed with unfair import practices, such as an attempt to monopolize trade in the United States. Section 301 of the Trade Act of 1974 provides for retaliation against countries that unfairly restrict their markets to U.S. *exports*. Affected firms may file complaints with the U.S. trade representative, who investigates and makes recommendations to the president. He can then impose penalties, which might include quotas or tariffs on goods from the offending nation. The Trade and Tariff Act of 1984 allows the administration itself to initiate complaints, taking some of the burden off private firms. Section 301 has been employed increasingly in recent years. For example, Canada's refusal to allow tax deductions to Canadian companies for their commercials on U.S. television resulted in a similar U.S.

refusal. Section 301 differs from the other instruments we have looked at in that the trade restrictions that it provides for are not intended to give protection to import-competing firms; rather they are bargaining chips, or threats, to be used to eliminate foreign restrictions on our exports. They have a political purpose as well: to defuse domestic demands for protection.

In addition to these four major protectionist tools, various minor provisions are available. The *national security clause,* for example, provides for increases in protection for threatened industries important to national security; tariffs and quotas may be imposed on *agricultural imports* if necessary to preserve the effectiveness of a domestic agricultural program. *Trade Adjustment Assistance* basically provides a type of insurance for the import-competing sector and not for the rest of the economy, so its long-term effect is to subsidize that sector, thereby reducing trade.

These tools are used in pursuit of two distinct strategies. The most important has been *import protection* to accommodate domestic special-interest groups. Sometimes the tools themselves are used for this purpose, and sometimes the tools (or the implicit threat to use them) are used in conjunction with negotiation with foreign governments to induce them to limit exports. This has resulted in the system of voluntary export restraints, described in the following case study.

The second strategy has been an *active trade policy* to expand foreign market access for domestic exports. A good example of this is the U.S. effort to expand sales of computer chips in Japan, discussed in a subsequent case study. Section 301 is the tool often used (or threatened to be used) in this regard. Recently there has been talk of altering the approach used in active trade policy to a *results-oriented* one. This means that in dealing with foreign authorities our negotiators would no longer try to induce them to eliminate specific trade barriers or perceived procedures to which we object, but would instead negotiate a specific market share for exports and leave it to them to decide how to achieve this. Such an approach is at odds with the basic philosophy of the last half-century of trade liberalization, which has been to remove trade barriers and let markets decide what happens. A results-oriented approach substitutes haggling among politicians for the haggling of the market. It becomes tempting only if we are sufficiently optimistic about the judgments of politicians and sufficiently pessimistic about our ability to identify the true trade barriers.

Problem

9.3 Find out about recent U.S. trade policy actions by reading the latest *Annual Report of the Trade Agreements Program* and recent reports of the International Trade Commission. Interpret these actions in the light of the discussion in section 1.

10. *CASE STUDY:* THE VER SYSTEM

The most prominent way to implement protectionist initiatives in the industrial world is the voluntary export restraint (VER), an arrangement whereby a government (or firms) protects an industry by persuading the authorities (or firms) in a trading partner to restrict exports. This allows the country to avoid violating existing international agreements (such as the GATT) and sometimes its own trade laws as well, and also to avoid the danger of retaliation posed by unilateral action, at the cost of the revenues that could be raised were tariffs or import licensing employed instead.

Over one hundred VERs now manage more than 10 percent of world trade, and in some sectors such arrangements are far more prominent than this. Most of world trade in textiles and apparel is now covered, as is over one-third of Japan's export of manufactures to other industrial countries. Chapter 7 discussed a prominent example: Japan's voluntary export restraint of automobiles to the United States. The following features distinguish such arrangements from standard tariffs.

VERs are invariably sector-specific. However, they operate within frameworks that can vary sector by sector. The framework might be multilateral (the MultiFiber Arrangement in textiles) or isolated and bilateral (Canadian lumber exports to the United States). There might be a series of independent arrangements linking a single exporter to diverse importers (Japanese automobile exports), a single importer to several exporters (United States imports of machine tools), or several exporters to several importers (steel).

VERs are bilateral. Regardless of the framework in which the VERs operate, the key negotiations and agreements are between a single importer and a single exporter.

The restrictions are quantitative. That is, the trade is subject to quota rather than tax, although taxes may be present as well.

The restrictions are largely voluntary on both sides of the market. This is essential because a primary reason to resort to such measures is to circumvent the spirit of the GATT in specific areas, without bringing down the entire GATT structure, by ensuring that no nation involved has a motive to complain. This need not require industry interests in both countries to welcome the arrangement: it will be negotiated, at least to a significant degree, by government officials who may be willing to sacrifice something in one sector for a quid pro quo elsewhere, or even without a quid pro quo, in order to preserve a relationship that is in the national interest overall. This should be kept in mind. Nevertheless, there must be a strong presumption that industry interests are not hurt, or at least not hurt too much: these agreements are typically negotiated in a politically charged atmosphere that draws the attention of the interests concerned and that induces them to exert themselves to the utmost politically. And the negotiations are sector-specific.

The restrictions are temporary (at least in original intent) responses to established import positions that have harmed import-competing interests. It is true that management arrangements often seem to linger for quite a while, and in textiles and apparel, at least, they became almost a permanent fixture. But actual agreements are invariably for short periods, and usually the original intent is not to renew them many times. The original agreement itself is almost always the response to a large, established import presence (usually a recently established or recently enlarged one), not to the prospect that such a presence may come about. No doubt this is partly a matter of political economy: being able to point to a recently large volume of imports makes it easier to enlist the sympathy of fellow citizens for restrictions. But it is also a reflection of the voluntary element in these arrangements: for us to offer importers significant rents from their share of our market, they must have a significant share of that market. Finally, there must be a significant import-competing interest adversely affected by the imports. This interest is the source of the political pressure to manage trade.

The restrictions are discriminatory. This is a major way in which VERs violate the spirit of the GATT. It implies that an analysis of such trade should consider the roles played by at least three distinct groups of firms: import competitors, restrained exporters, and unrestrained exporters. As noted above, unrestrained exporters can usually be expected to benefit from a VER and so not pressure their government to protest its formation. The activities of such firms have been central to how many such agreements have in fact functioned, and in some industries they have played a dominant role in the evolution of trade management (for example, textiles and steel). Discrimination is a vital property of the VER system.

Discrimination also implies a fourth potential group of firms: import competitors that are not part of the arrangement. In reasonably competitive markets characterized by constant costs, these firms are unlikely to be affected very much by trade management in which they do not participate. But significant economies of scale raise the possibility that restrained exporters may divert production from the newly restricted markets to compete in countries not within the arrangement. For example, the negotiation of the VER on Japanese automobiles sold in the United States aroused fears in some countries that the Japanese would be induced by the agreement to compete more fiercely in those countries in order to maintain production levels. Thus there is a part of the global industry that is threatened by such arrangements, and this holds the potential for defeat of the basic goal of bypassing the GATT by ensuring that no one will file a protest. But this does not happen. Perhaps unprotected import competitors require significant diversion, not just the threat of such diversion, to be roused to effective action. Probably more important is a desire on their part to acquire managed trade of their own, regardless of whether diversion takes place or not. They would then not be likely to agitate for legal challenges to a VER since that would make it more difficult for them to acquire a VER of their own. The response by other importers of Japanese cars to the VER on Japanese exports to the United States was not to challenge that agreement formally; it was to negotiate VERs of their own with Japan.

11. *CASE STUDY:* POLICY AND INTERNATIONAL TRADE IN SEMICONDUCTORS

Policies of several nations have been controversial for years in the international semiconductor industry. Furthermore, the industry well illustrates many of the points raised in this chapter.

From the invention of the transistor at Bell Laboratories in 1947 until the 1970s, the semiconductor industry was largely the domain of a relatively small number of American firms. This was a result of both the strong American comparative advantage in high technology and, in the early years, large purchases of semiconductors by the U.S. military. During the 1960s the American firms began setting up assembly operations in Mexico and Asia, but the "high tech" remained in the United States.

Targeting and Protection

Both the Japanese and European governments protected their semiconductor industries with tariffs and other barriers such as quotas, preferential procurement policies, and so on. Their intent was to target their small semiconductor industries for development. Possible reasons for targeting this industry can be seen once the nature of semiconductor production is understood.

Semiconductor production essentially consists of placing tiny circuits on small silicon chips. Technical progress is rapid, with the regular introduction of new types of chips or of more powerful versions of existing types. Several sorts of scale economies are prominent in this production. The first is the cost of building a chip-producing facility; this has increased rapidly over the years as chips have become more sophisticated and their production more intricate. Another is the cost of the research and development necessary to introduce a new chip. These scale economies are both *static:* the costs are incurred once before production begins and are then averaged over all chips produced. Thus, the larger the production, the smaller their contribution to average costs. Another scale economy is *dynamic*, being cumulatively experienced as long as a chip is produced. When a new chip is introduced, production costs are typically high largely because many of the chips are faulty and must be thrown away. But as it produces more chips, the firm learns how to do it better, failure rates fall, and costs decline dramatically. This process has been repeated with the introduction of each new chip, and it is fairly predictable. Still another dynamic scale economy extends across generations of chips: producing one type of chip apparently enhances the ability of firms to develop and produce future generations of chips. (This effect is much more difficult to measure, however.) All of these scale economies are *internal* to the individual chip producer: they depend on what that producer does, not on what the whole semiconductor industry does, and they influence the costs of that producer, not the costs of others.

Other economies of scale are *external* to the individual chip producer. Semiconductors are intermediate goods, used in the production of computers, consumer electronics, capital goods and a host of other products. The process of developing and producing chips generates valuable knowledge useful to other chip producers and to developers of the products that use chips. This knowledge is an externality to the extent that it spills over from the chip producers to these other firms that can use it. This spillover inevitably occurs because of contacts between individuals in the industry, the mobility of workers between firms, and all sorts of other forms of observation. As you might expect, these externalities are in practice virtually impossible to measure. But most observers and industry participants believe them to be important.

We know from Chapter 8 that circumstances such as these may generate motives for protection. The internal economies of scale imply that perfect competition is unlikely to prevail permanently in the semiconductor industry, and, in fact, it has been oligopolistic from the beginning. This means that *profit shifting* could have been a motive: the Europeans and Japanese may have protected their industries so that the oligopolistic profits captured from the sale of semiconductors in their economies would go to their own firms rather than to American firms.

The external economies imply that *production shifting* may also have been a motive: the Europeans and Japanese may have protected their industries so that the knowledge spillovers from semiconductor production would flow to their own firms. If the externalities are *international,* such protection was unnecessary because their firms would have benefited from spillovers from American production as well as from local production. But even though a portion of the externalities in semiconductor production is international, most industry participants believe there is a strong *national* component as well. Thus production shifting could have been a motive.

The European and Japanese Semiconductor Industries

Both Europe and Japan were successful in fostering semiconductor industries. However, this happened in different ways in the two places.

Europe. American firms, finding it difficult to export to Europe because of the trade barriers, began setting up local production facilities in the late 1960s. That is, they undertook what is called *direct investment* in Europe. (Direct investment will be discussed in detail in Chapter 11.) This resulted in a European semiconductor industry that was, in substantial degree, American-owned.

Evaluation of European Policy. If profit shifting was the object of European policy, it failed. Any profits would have gone to a large extent to American firms even though these firms were producing in Europe. Also, Europe never became a significant exporter of semiconductors, so, again, the policy was a failure to the extent that it was intended for infant-industry protection.

Since Europe did develop a semiconductor industry, it presumably profited from national spillovers to its computer industry, and so forth. But since its semiconductor industry did not become internationally competitive, as evidenced by its inability to export and by the continuing protection it received, firms using semiconductors must have had to pay a penalty in terms of higher prices and, perhaps, less availability. This would have inhibited the development of these other industries, thus preventing them from generating spillovers of their own. Neither the increased spillovers from the semiconductor industry nor the reduced spillovers from the semiconductor-using industry can be measured, so we do not know whether, in this respect, European policy was a success or a failure.

Europe did follow a protective policy, and it did succeed in developing a semiconductor industry. But probably that policy was a mistake and, on balance, costly for Europe.

Japan. In the 1960s and 1970s American firms tried to set up production facilities in Japan, as they were doing in Europe. But the Japanese government actively restricted direct investment, and only one American firm, Texas Instruments, was persistent enough to succeed. The other firms, unable to export to Japan and unable to invest there, exploited that market in the only other way possible: they licensed (for a fee) Japanese firms to use their technology.

The Japanese semiconductor industry developed during the 1970s. The Japanese government eliminated its formal trade barriers by the middle of the decade, and it eliminated its restrictions on direct investment by the end. Nevertheless, American firms were unable to obtain more than a small share of the Japanese market even though at that time they were offering superior products at lower prices. The Japanese industry went on to make dramatic gains in the 1980s. They challenged American firms in world markets for some kinds of chips, and by the end of the decade Japanese firms together had a larger share of the world semiconductor market than American firms together. The Japanese success was most dramatic in the market for RAM (random-access memory) chips, where they overtook the Americans as early as 1982. By 1986 they dominated the market, forcing most American firms to cease producing RAM chips completely.

Evaluation of Japanese Policy. The Japanese government targeted its semiconductor industry for development, and that industry subsequently enjoyed spectacular success. This much is clear. Two questions arise: (1) Was the Japanese policy responsible for this success, or would it have happened anyway? (2) Was this a good thing for Japan (and not just a good thing for the Japanese semiconductor industry)?

Japanese government policy consisted of three elements: protection against imports, restrictions on direct investment, and subsidies for the development of new technology. As noted above, the first two were eliminated fairly early, and the subsidies were never very large. Japanese spokesmen accordingly contend that government policy had little to do with the industry's success. This has been challenged on two grounds.

The first notes that an infant-industry strategy involves government aid only during the initial stages, before the industry can grow and compete on its own. Perhaps the modest Japanese policy measures provided the critical difference between success and failure early on and were then withdrawn. This seems unlikely in view of the small subsidies and the fact that protection ceased well before the industry became internationally competitive.

In any event, critics mainly emphasize their second point—that even after *formal* protection ended, Japanese firms declined to purchase more attractive American products, indicating that *informal* protection continued, perhaps at the instigation of the Japanese government. Japanese retort that American products were not purchased because they were less suitable for Japanese needs. To understand this debate it is necessary to understand the structure of the Japanese industry.

The American industry consists of computer firms (notably IBM) that produce chips for their own use and sell few to other firms, and semiconductor firms (like Intel) that mainly produce chips and sell most of them on the market. Japanese firms, by contrast, are large, vertically integrated producers (for example, Hitachi and NEC) of a wide range of electronic products who both use the chips they produce and also sell many on the market. In addition, the Japanese semiconductor firms are members of *keiretsu*, gigantic combinations of diverse Japanese firms. *Keiretsu* members own shares in each other (making it difficult for an outsider to come along and acquire one) and buy each others' products (often making it difficult for an outsider, whether foreign or Japanese, to sell to one of these firms in competition with a fellow member). Also, a *keiretsu* will often contain a large bank, easing the members' access to capital.

It is easy to see how foreign firms would find it difficult to penetrate such an industrial structure, especially if the Japanese government tacitly encouraged its firms, as has been alleged, to "buy Japanese." American critics complain that the whole arrangement makes for informal protection, regardless of how involved the Japanese government might be behind the scenes. In any event, it seems that the success of the Japanese semiconductor industry was due in large part to a combination of industrial structure and government policy, with the latter probably playing only a small part.

Was this a good thing for Japan? The policy clearly had costs since for years Japan had to make do with inferior semiconductors at high prices. Consider now whether the policy also had benefits. As regards profit shifting, the policy was a failure since, although the Japanese greatly increased their market share since the 1970s, they do not appear to have found it very profitable, with one exception that we will discuss presently. Oligopolistic rivalry has been intense in this market.

Because of their vertical integration, the Japanese firms themselves must have captured many of the spillovers from their semiconductor activity. Other benefits would have accrued to their *keiretsu*. The same holds true for the negative spillovers—that is, those spillovers never realized because of the slower development of semiconductor-using activities due to the inability to get the best semiconductors at the best price. (Although these firms came to dominate the world market for RAM chips, they failed to become internationally competitive in many types of computers.) For this reason, these spillovers should probably be considered, in the Japanese case, as *internal* rather than *external*. Thus, while we cannot hope to measure the true extent of these spillovers, they must have been largely captured by those generating them and so not a justification for a costly government policy. Note that this is just another aspect of the previous argument concluding that formal government policy may not have been that important for protecting the industry.

A bottom-line best guess on the Japanese policy of targeting the semiconductor industry: formal government policy probably contributed to the successful development of the Japanese semiconductor industry, but this contribution is unlikely to have been large; the policy probably imposed net costs on Japan (and so was socially mistaken), but the costs may not have been very big.

U.S.-Japan Semiconductor Trade Agreements

The success of the Japanese firms alarmed the American producers. Not only had the Americans lost a significant share of their global market, but they feared that the large Japanese firms would be better able than they themselves to afford the ever-more expensive plants required for the increasingly sophisticated chips. In 1985 they filed a *Section 301 petition* and *antidumping petitions* against the Japanese. Antidumping actions were aided by the widespread practice in the semiconductor industry of *forward pricing:* since costs predictably fell dramatically over the lifetime of a chip, firms would initially sell below cost, knowing that the subsequent fall in costs would allow them to recoup their losses. (This practice was initiated by the American firm Texas Instruments.) The petitions precipitated negotiations between the U.S. and Japanese governments that, in 1986, resulted in an agreement on semiconductor trade.

The agreement called for the U.S. petitions to be withdrawn, for the Japanese firms to refrain from dumping, and for the Japanese government to encourage Japanese purchases of semiconductors from foreign firms. The U.S. Commerce Department would monitor the production costs of individual Japanese firms, who would keep their export prices above these costs. In a separate letter, the Japanese government mentioned 20 percent as a five-year target for the foreign share in the Japanese semiconductor market.

This was the first U.S. high-tech trade agreement. Three unusual features should be noted. First, it did not simply try to protect the U.S. industry, but also tried to improve foreign *market access* for U.S. firms. Second, the market-access provisions included a specific market-share target instead of calling for the elimination of specific trade barriers (as we have seen, the formal barriers had already been eliminated). That is, it was *results-oriented*. Third, antidumping aspects tried to take into account the interests of firms that use semiconductors, and not just the interests of the producers. It did this, first, by tying the export prices of Japanese firms to their costs so that if a firm lowered its costs, it could lower its price (this would still leave the firm unable to match forward-pricing rivals). Second, it also applied to the prices the Japanese charged in third markets so that a U.S. computer firm, for example, would not have to pay more for Japanese chips than a European computer maker (it would also inhibit the ability of Japanese semiconductor firms to compete with American firms in third markets).

The agreement has been regarded with mixed feelings by American firms. Japanese firms have made real efforts to increase their purchases of American semiconductors, and American sales in Japan have indeed been rising, but American firms have been disappointed at the slow rate. American officials have repeatedly pressured the Japanese, so American policy has consisted not only of negotiating the agreement, but also of a steady stream of threats, bluster, and so on during the agreement's implementation. On the whole, American semiconductor firms have done well since the agreement came into place. They have increased sales to Japan, opened Japanese offices and production facilities, increased their worldwide market share, initiated some joint ventures with Japanese firms, and some American firms have even reentered the market for RAMS. This sort of thing may have happened even without the agreement; the earlier Japanese success was obviously consistent with the convergence of comparative costs between the two countries that has occurred over the years. But it seems clear that the agreement and the continuing government pressure have helped U.S. semiconductor producers to at least some degree.

If U.S. semiconductor firms have been cautious in their reaction, U.S. firms using semiconductors have been downright hostile because of the agreement's attempt to prevent Japanese dumping. Soon after the agreement went into effect, the prices of Japanese RAMs began to rise. In 1987–1988 prices were high, Japanese supply was severely restricted, and U.S. firms found it impossible to get the chips they needed. Japanese firms increased their U.S. profits by over $4 billion at this time, a rare occasion of high profits. Recall Chapter 7's discussion of the VER on Japanese automobiles, when American attempts to protect the domestic industry generated record profits for the Japanese. In this case, it is not clear that the agreement was the cause: Japanese firms were much more dominant in the world market for RAMs than in the world automobile market, so perhaps they would have colluded in the absence of an agreement. But the latter at least contributed, and many U.S. buyers of chips blamed it entirely.

While the net effects of the agreement on U.S. and Japanese firms are ambiguous, two consequences are clear. First, it had little effect on U.S. exports to Japan: the increased American sales of chips were actually supplied by American plants in various other countries. Second, Korean manufacturers of semiconductors clearly benefited. The agreement's attempt to keep Japanese prices up worldwide and to increase the foreign market share in

Japan gave the Koreans the opening they needed to penetrate the semiconductor market. Recall from Chapter 7 how the VER on Japanese automobile exports to the United States also helped the Korean automobile industry.

The agreement expired in 1991 but was replaced with an extension. The new agreement actually incorporated a goal of a 20 percent foreign market share by the end of 1992 (it never got much above 14 percent under the old agreement), although it stated that the target was "neither a guarantee, a ceiling nor a floor on the foreign market share." Also, in a concession to the negative views of U.S. users of semiconductors, the Commerce Department no longer collects cost data on Japanese producers.

As 1992 drew to a close, it appeared that the 20 percent goal would not be reached. American officials threatened Japan with unspecified dark sanctions for the country's failure to fulfill a commitment that the Japanese denied even existed and that, in any case, was arbitrary to begin with. The bizarre situation was defused when, to everyone's relief and amazement, the foreign market share in Japan jumped to above 20 percent in the final quarter of 1992. The American reaction was to suggest new goals.

12. *CASE STUDY:* DOES JAPAN PLAY FAIR?

During the 1980s the United States developed a large excess of imports over exports in its trade with Japan, this deficit rising to over $50 billion in 1986. Import-competing industries demanded protection, and exporters complained that they could not sell their wares in the Japanese market. The previous section discussed one example in detail.

American pressure was brought to bear on the Japanese, who restricted some of their exports to the United States. Chapter 7 discussed in detail the most prominent of these: the restraints on automobiles, and we just discussed semiconductors. But frustration over the perceived inability of American firms to sell in Japan mounted as the bilateral trade deficit remained huge. Many Americans came to feel that Japan was taking advantage of them. "Japan bashing" came into vogue, with legislators outdoing each other in denunciations of Japan and with numerous trade bills introduced into Congress that were thinly disguised attempts to strike back at that country. The U.S. administration strongly pressured Japan to open its markets to foreign (that is, American) goods. The Japanese responded with promises to reduce import barriers, but the trade imbalance did not respond. American frustration increased. In Japan, too, resentment developed: people began to think that Americans were blaming Japan for their own problems. Trade issues threatened the alliance itself.

Does Japan play fair? To answer this question, we must first distinguish between the overall trade imbalance between the United States and Japan, on the one hand, and the structure of trade between the two countries, on the other. With regard to the overall imbalance, two points should be kept in mind. First, the United States has been running a large deficit relative to the rest of the world as a whole (not just Japan), and Japan has had a surplus relative to the rest of the world. These are determined by macroeconomic policies and behavior, not by trade policies. Such things are discussed later in this book. Second, we saw in Chapter 1 that a bilateral deficit could be consistent with multilateral balance and that this seems relevant to U.S.-Japanese trade.

So consider the structure of trade between the United States and Japan. Chapter 1 described the nature of this trade, and Chapter 6 discussed the trade of both countries from a factor-endowments perspective. It appears from this that Japan's trade is, in broad terms, determined by economic fundamentals such as comparative advantage rather than by conscious policy. At least Japan is no worse than other countries in this regard.

We can look instead at attempts to influence the country's trade pattern by policy measures. Japan has participated in the GATT rounds of tariff reductions, and Japanese tariffs on manufactures are, accordingly, low. Indeed, their average tariffs on manufactures—depending on how such averages are calculated—may well be lower than those of other industrial countries, including the United States! We have seen also that nontariff barriers have become relatively more important in today's international economy. Here, again, Japan does not seem to be particularly guilty, relative to other industrial countries; the most prominent Japanese nontariff barriers restrict exports, not imports, in response to external pressure.

If Japan in fact has relatively low formal tariff and nontariff barriers, what is all the fuss about? Perhaps it is easier to look abroad for the source of one's troubles than to correct them oneself. Also, it is only natural that the success of many Japanese exporters should arouse the resentment of their foreign competitors. Many American manufacturers have suffered from Japanese competition, and there do not seem to be many current tales of successful industrial exporting to Japan, especially by American manufacturers of consumer goods. Indeed, Japan spends a smaller fraction of its income on foreign manufactured goods than does any other developed country. In any event, many Americans view the trade imbalance as unjustified and believe that it is basically the result of Japanese practice.

Two perceived aspects of that practice receive particular attention. The first consists of *government policies* other than trade policies, which still have an effect on trade. Americans often suggest that these may be worthy of emulation. The second aspect consists of *informal trade barriers*. These are regarded as unfair and deserving of retaliation.

Japanese government policies that receive the most attention include the following: (1) government *subsidies and tax incentives* that benefit export industries; (2) government *targeting* of specific promising potential export industries for further development, said to be done through informal persuasion as well as by government loans that signal private investors which industries are favored; and (3) government encouragement or acquiescence for *joint research and development* projects, whereby the cooperating Japanese firms can achieve faster progress at a lower price than U.S. firms, which are usually not allowed to behave in this way.

Many commentators have pointed to these policies as the secret of Japan's success and have urged the United States to adopt an "industrial policy" along these lines. But the evidence suggests that these measures are relatively unimportant or that they simply compensate for other defects of the Japanese economy. For example, tax incentives in Japan are modest relative to those of other countries, and few government subsidies actually go to export industries. Government targeting substitutes for the lack of developed markets for equities and venture capital, and cooperative research projects compensate for the restricted mobility of trained professionals and the limited communication between them.

The issue of informal trade barriers is far more emotional. The claim here is that, despite the low tariff and nontariff trade barriers, the Japanese economy simply makes it too hard for foreign firms to sell their products there. The previous section described one example. The cumbersome and expensive distribution system makes it difficult for new firms to enter the market; elaborate, irrational and unstated product standards exclude foreign goods; Japanese firms establish long-term relations with their suppliers and are reluctant to allow new suppliers a chance at their business; Japanese customers simply refuse to buy foreign products, even when they are cheaper and better than Japanese ones. These are the accusations. The Japanese acknowledge that there are problems, but they claim that they are the same sort of social and linguistic barriers that their own exporters had to overcome with hard work and patience: foreign firms wishing to develop markets in Japan should also pay their dues.

Who is right? The question cannot be answered categorically; "informal" barriers just cannot be measured. To be sure, anecdotal evidence in support of the accusations abounds. American producers of baseball bats were for years thwarted in their efforts to market a superior product in Japan; Nippon Telephone and Telegraph has been notoriously reluctant to give American firms an even chance at supplying telecommunications equipment. Such stories have been repeated again and again. Often these cases have resulted in official American pressure on the Japanese government, Japanese promises to reform, and then a tortuously slow pace of change that infuriates both sides. With such disputes repeatedly in the public eye, they influence disproportionately the public perception of what U.S.-Japanese trade is really like, and they generate the suspicion that there are many other cases that have simply not yet come to receive publicity. Nonetheless, the aggregate amount of trade at issue in these cases is tiny relative to the overall volume of trade between the two countries, and there is no evidence of a systematic distortion of the pattern of that trade.

Thus far we have examined trade in manufactured goods since that gets the lion's share of attention. But the evidence of Japanese trade barriers is in fact far more striking with regard to trade in agricultural products. All industrial countries, including the United States, protect their agricultural sectors.

In Chapter 5 we saw how world trade in wheat is distorted by such policies, and we discussed the Common Agricultural Policy of the EU (which is described in more detail in Chapter 20). Thus Japan is by no means the only sinner. But it does seem to be one of the worst. Japan protects its agriculture more than does either the United States or the EU, and only some Scandinavian countries are as bad. For example, Japan is closely identified with the production of rice, but foreign growers can produce the crop at about one-fifth the Japanese cost and would certainly develop a large export market there if given the chance. The overall effect of Japanese policies influencing trade is clearly to protect agriculture at the expense of manufacturing. Thus, with the overall size of the trade balance determined by macroeconomic behavior and policy, a general liberalization of Japanese trade would likely *increase* Japan's surplus of manufactured exports over manufactured imports!

This protection is very costly for the Japanese consumer. Food is expensive in that country, as travelers can attest. Also, Japan is scarcely endowed with useful land, relative to its population. With much of this land devoted to the protected agricultural sector, the supply of residential land is tight. As a result, its price—and, therefore, the price of housing—is extremely high. This has a profound effect on the quality of life in Japan.

The large U.S.-Japanese trade imbalance has produced much controversy and acrimony, and not a little misleading public debate. But some basic conclusions can be drawn.

1. The trade imbalance is not due to either country's trade policy, but to national savings behavior and macroeconomic policies (which we discuss later in this book).
2. Japan's tariffs and nontariff barriers are low relative to those of other countries.
3. Controversy abounds over alleged informal import barriers thrown up by Japanese society. But it seems clear that individual foreign firms have been stymied by such barriers and that the total amount of trade involved is small relative to total Japanese trade.
4. The basic pattern of Japanese trade in manufactured goods seems mostly determined by economic fundamentals, not by Japanese policies.
5. The net effect on trade of Japanese policy is to protect agriculture at the expense of manufacturing as a whole.

13. SUMMARY

1. Tariff structures in industrial countries are often seen as reflections of pressure-group politics within those countries. But evidence linking protection to industry characteristics is ambiguous.

2. Postwar tariff deductions under GATT have reduced to historically low levels tariffs on trade in manufactured goods among the DCs. Nontariff barriers, agricultural trade, and the trade of the LDCs remain serious problems, while counterfeit goods and restrictions on trade in services have become major issues. The Tokyo Round established codes regarding nontariff barriers, but their effectiveness is not yet determined.

3. The Uruguay Round ambitiously addressed trade in services and agricultural trade, but it stalled because of U.S. and European disagreement over agriculture.

4. Contemporary international trade policy features a basic tension between multilateralism (the GATT), regionalism (NAFTA, EU), and the new protectionism (VERs).

5. Major contemporary tools of trade policy include escape clauses, anti-dumping duties, countervailing duties, and provisions for dealing with unfair trade practices. These tools are employed directly, and the threat to use them often results in orderly marketing arrangements (that is, negotiated quotas) between countries.

SUGGESTED READING

Baldwin, R. E. "The Political Economy of Postwar U.S. Trade Policy." *The Bulletin,* New York University Graduate School of Business Administration (1976). Mentioned in the text.

Ball, D. S. "United States Effective Tariffs and Labor's Share." *Journal of Political Economy* (Apr. 1967). Cited in the text.

Bauer, R. A., I. D. S. Pool, and L. A. Dexter. *American Business and Public Policy.* 2d ed. Chicago: Aldine-Atherton, 1973. The political system and the tariff.

Breton, A. *The Economic Theory of Representative Government.* Chicago: Aldine, 1974. Cited in the text.

Caves, R. E. "Economic Models of Political Choice: Canada's Tariff Structure." *Canadian Journal of Economics* (May 1976). An empirical investigation of what determines the tariff.

Caves, R. E., and R. W. Jones. *World Trade and Payments.* 3d ed. Boston: Little, Brown, 1981. See pp. 242–45.

Cheh, J. H. "United States Concessions in the Kennedy Round and Short-Run Labor Adjustment Costs." *Journal of International Economics* (Nov. 1974). Cited in the text.

Constantopoulos, M. "Labour Protection in Western Europe." *European Economic Review* (Dec. 1974). Cited in the text.

Downs, A. *An Economic Theory of Democracy.* New York: Harper & Row, 1957. Cited in the text.

Ethier, W. J. "Dumping." *Journal of Political Economy* (June 1982). Dumping and employment.

Hillman, A. L. *The Political Economy of Protection.* Chur: Harwood Academic Publishers, 1989. A useful survey.

Krueger, A. "Some Economic Costs of Exchange Control: The Turkish Case." *Journal of Political Economy* (Oct. 1966). Cited in the text.

Olson, M. *The Logic of Collective Action: Public Goods and the Theory of Groups.* Cambridge: Harvard University Press, 1965. Cited in the text.

Pinchin, H. McA. *The Regional Impact of the Canadian Tariff.* Ottawa: Economic Council of Canada, 1979.

Pincus, J. "Pressure Groups and the Pattern of Tariffs." *Journal of Political Economy* (July 1975). Cited in the text.

Riedel, J. "Tariff Concessions in the Kennedy Round and the Structure of Protection in West Germany: An Econometric Assessment." *Journal of International Economics* (May 1977). Cited in the text.

Schattschneider, E. E. *Politics, Pressures and the Tariff.* Englewood Cliffs, N.J.: Prentice Hall, 1935. The classic account of the passage of the Smoot-Hawley tariff.

Stanwood, E. *American Tariff Controversies in the Nineteenth Century.* Boston: Houghton Mifflin, 1903. One of the two basic treatments of U.S. tariff history.

Taussig, F. W. *The Tariff History of the United States.* New York: Augustus M. Kelley, 1967. The other.

Tyson, Laura D'A. *Who's Bashing Whom? Trade Conflict in High-Technology Industries.* Washington: Institute for International Economics, 1992. The case for an active trade policy; interesting case studies.

Viner, J. *Dumping: A Problem in International Trade.* Chicago: University of Chicago Press, 1923.

Yeats, A. J. *Trade Barriers Facing Developing Countries.* New York: St. Martin's, 1979.

Young, J. H. *Canadian Commercial Policy.* Ottawa: Royal Commission on Canada's Economic Prospects, 1957.

CHAPTER 10

International Factor Movements

Where wealth and freedom reign, contentment fails,
and honour sinks where commerce long prevails.
—OLIVER GOLDSMITH

We have so far examined the international exchange of commodities and ignored international movements of productive factors. Indeed, the classical theory and its modern descendants see international factor immobility as the basic cause of international trade.

But international factor movements are prominent in modern economic life. Trillions of dollars are invested in foreign nations, and our world has been shaped by the great migrations of history. This chapter investigates such factor movements and relates them to international trade. The first three sections discuss the basic theory applicable to all factor movements. We then study issues specifically related to *labor* mobility and to *capital* movements, respectively.

1. THE BASIC THEORY: ABSOLUTE ADVANTAGE VERSUS COMPARATIVE ADVANTAGE

We can obtain a feel for the role of factor mobility by returning to the simple Ricardian model used to elucidate the first principles of international trade. Table 10.1 reproduces Table 1.1.

TABLE 10.1 A Simple Ricardian Model: Labor Required in Each Country to Produce One Unit of Each Good

	Butane	Apples
France	6	2
Germany	1	1

TABLE 10.2   **Changes in Production**

(a) If France produces one less unit of butane, Germany one more, and the countries trade.

	Butane	Apples
France	−1	+3
Germany	+1	−1
World	0	+2

(b) If France produces one less unit of butane and the labor moves to Germany.

	Butane	Apples
France	−1	0
Germany	+1	+5
World	0	+5

Recall that if both countries initially produce both goods, world production will become more efficient if France shifts labor from butane production to apple production, if Germany does the reverse, and if France trades apples to Germany for butane. Table 10.2(a) shows that each unit of butane produced in Germany rather than France allows the world to have 2 additional bushels of apples. Table 10.2(b) shows what would instead be achieved if labor were to become internationally mobile. If France again produces 1 less unit of butane, the 6 workers that then become available now migrate to Germany instead of to the French apple industry. In Germany the 6 workers can produce the needed butane plus 5 bushels of apples. World production becomes more efficient if factors move from countries where their productivity is low to countries where it is high. Note that factor mobility raises world production more than does trade and specialization: trade is basically a (second-best) substitute for factor mobility.

Beneficial trade is a consequence of *comparative* cost differences—in this case, the fact that 6/2 exceeds 1/1. But beneficial factor movements result from *absolute* productivity differences—6 exceeds 1, and 2 exceeds 1. In this simple example, all production should take place in Germany, where labor is absolutely more productive in both industries.

Problems

10.1 In the simple Ricardian example of Table 10.1 and Table 10.2, is it meaningful to talk of the French and German production possibility frontiers once labor becomes internationally mobile? What about the world frontier? Draw such a curve, if you can, and compare it with Figure 1.2(a). (Assume, as in Chapter 1, that, initially, France has 600 workers and Germany 500.)

10.2 Our discussion of the simple Ricardian model tacitly assumed that French and German laborers were identical and that the productivity differences in Table 10.1 reflected differences in climate. Suppose, instead, that Table 10.1 shows each country's labor productivity at *home,* but that 3 French laborers are always required to do the same work that could be done in the same country by 1 German worker (thus 2

German workers can produce 1 unit of butane in France and so forth). Derive the world production possibility frontier in this case. Describe who produces what and where at various points along this curve.

10.3 In Problem **10.2,** suppose that everyone in the world always consumes equal amounts of apples and butane. Fully describe international equilibrium.

2. THE BASIC THEORY: FACTOR MOBILITY AND THE FACTOR-ENDOWMENTS THEORY OF TRADE

To proceed further we must leave the simple Ricardian world. The Heckscher-Ohlin-Samuelson model of Chapter 5 is a logical next step since it views trade as due to differences in relative factor endowments.

Figure 10.1—like Figure 5.1—shows the relation between relative commodity costs and relative factor rewards. Since this relation is purely technological, it is, therefore, common to all countries sharing the technology. In the figure, butane is relatively labor-intensive. Suppose that Germany is relatively labor-abundant and that France and Germany have similar tastes so that in autarky Germany has a lower wage-rental ratio. German relative autarkic factor prices are *OG* in the figure, and the French are *OF*. Thus German relative autarkic commodity prices equal *OB*, and the French equal *OA*.

Now suppose that France and Germany freely trade apples and butane but that capital and labor remain immobile internationally. Then a common world price will be established between *A* and *B*—say, equal to *OP*. If both countries continue to produce both goods, they will have equal factor prices, as indicated by *W*.

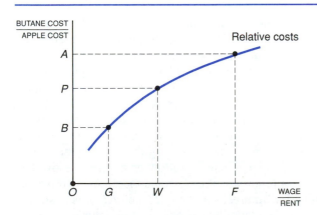

FIGURE 10.1 **Relative Factor Prices and Relative Commodity Costs** With constant returns to scale, the relation between relative factor rewards and relative costs is purely technological and so is not affected by factor movements.

But suppose, alternatively, that capital and labor can freely move between the two countries while apples and butane are not traded. Since there is now a single world labor market, the wage in France equals that in Germany because no one would willingly work for a wage below that available elsewhere. Similarly, capital's rent is the same in both countries. Suppose the common relative factor price is OW. Then relative commodity prices equal OP in both countries, even though goods are not traded.

Once again, factor movements and commodity trade are substitutes. If factor endowments are close enough so that trade leads to factor-price equalization, the two types of international economic intercourse are perfect substitutes. Otherwise, trade is again a second-best substitute for factor mobility; if trade incompletely equalizes factor prices, the introduction of factor mobility would lead each factor to migrate from the country where its (absolute) marginal productivity was lower to where it was higher, to the benefit of world productive efficiency.

World Efficiency

The efficiency argument is depicted another way in Figure 10.2. If factors are initially immobile, each country has a given production possibility frontier. Sliding one country's frontier along that of the other traces out the world production possibility frontier, illustrated by TT' in Figure 10.2. This shows the possible combinations of apples and butane available to the entire world if the two countries efficiently specialize and trade but factors do not move internationally. Between A and B France and Germany both produce both goods so that factor prices are the same in the two countries. Suppose, again, that apples are capital-intensive. Between T and A, the capital-abundant country—say, France—specializes in apples; between B and T', Germany specializes in butane. Thus France has higher wages and lower rents than Germany along TA and BT'. (The more nearly identical France and Germany are, the larger the segment AB. If both countries have the same endowment of capital per worker, A coincides with T and B with T'. If, on the other hand, France has sufficiently more capital per worker than Germany, the segment AB shrinks to nothing and is replaced by a kink where both countries specialize and factor prices are not equalized.)

In reality, some factors are relatively mobile internationally while others are not. We can represent this by allowing one factor—say, capital—to move freely between France and Germany while supposing that labor remains immobile. The segment AB will not be affected by allowing capital to move between countries because factor prices are already equal there. The two factors are equally productive in both countries. But along TA and BT' it is desirable to shift capital from capital-abundant France, where the factor's marginal productivity is low, to Germany. This will, in fact, happen because capital receives a lower rent in France than in Germany along TA and BT'. Thus these two portions of the world production possibility frontier shift outward when capital becomes mobile and, consequently, more productive. The new frontier

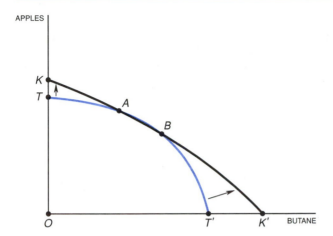

FIGURE 10.2   World Production Possibility Frontiers   If a factor becomes internationally mobile, the world production possibility frontier expands, except where trade itself causes factor-price equalization.

is *KK'*. This shows the menu of possible combinations of apples and butane available to the world if the two countries efficiently specialize and trade goods and capital.

Capital's rent is equalized along the entire frontier *KK'* because there is now a single world capital market. There are two disjoint national labor markets, but in fact the wage must be the same in both countries. If the wages were not equal, the country with the higher wage could not compete in either commodity market because producers in that country would have to pay just as much for capital and more for labor than would producers in the other country, and technology is the same in both countries. Thus both factor prices are equal everywhere along *KK'*, and the international immobility of labor is of no consequence.

Factor Movements and Income Distribution

Since factor mobility and commodity trade tend to substitute for each other, it should come as no surprise that the two have similar effects on the internal distribution of income. Suppose that France is freely trading with the rest of the world, that both factors are initially immobile internationally, and that trade has not completely equalized factor prices. Now suppose that one factor—say, capital—becomes mobile. If France is initially capital-abundant and so has a lower rent than the rest of the world, capital will now flow out of France until the French rental rises to equal that abroad. Thus the income of French capitalists rises. Because capital has left France, labor has become relatively more abundant in that country, and the French wage accordingly falls.

Thus capital mobility, like commodity trade, redistributes income from a country's relatively scarce factor to the relatively abundant one.

Factor mobility must make a country as a whole better off because the ability to exchange factors, like the ability to trade goods, widens opportunities. But a country with monopoly power in world factor markets can potentially make itself even better off, at the expense of the rest of the world, by exercising that power and limiting factor mobility.

Problems

10.4 Figure 5.6 used the Rybczynski theorem to show the effect of economic growth on international trade. In similar fashion, depict the effects of international factor movements on international trade.

10.5* How is our discussion of international factor mobility and the Heckscher-Ohlin-Samuelson model affected if, before either factor is internationally mobile, the two countries are separated by a factor intensity reversal?

10.6* Discuss how our treatment of factor mobility and the Heckscher-Ohlin-Samuelson model changes if technology is different in the two countries.

10.7* Suppose two countries, each resembling the specific-factors model, engage in free trade. Discuss the results, for factor-price equalization and other possible properties, if the *intersectorally* mobile factor, labor, also becomes *internationally* mobile. What happens if, instead, one of the sector-specific factors becomes internationally mobile (but remains intersectorally immobile)? Discuss how international factor mobility can substitute for intersectoral factor mobility.

3. FACTOR MOVEMENTS AND TRADE: SUBSTITUTES OR COMPLEMENTS?

To the extent that countries trade to economize on scarce factors, trade should substitute for factor mobility. Suppose France exports capital-intensive commodities. The production of these goods for export will increase the demand for capital in France and so cause the rental there to rise relative to what it would have been without the trade. Now if France exports these goods because France is capital-abundant, the country would have a low rent in autarky. Thus the increase in capital's rent brought about by trade causes the rent in France to move *toward* that in the rest of the world, thereby reducing the incentive for capital to flow abroad. Trade has substituted for capital mobility.

But, as we found in Parts One and Two, countries may trade for reasons other than to economize on scarce factors. In these cases trade and factor mobility could be *complements*.

Intraindustry trade furnishes an example of this complementarity. Recall from Chapter 2 that countries may trade to enlarge the division of labor and to increase product diversity. This *intraindustry trade* is related to factor mobility in a way different from *interindustry trade* (the exchange of apples for butane). Suppose that endowments in the two countries differ greatly and that France specializes in apples and Germany in butane. Then intraindustry trade cannot take place; all trade is interindustry. Now suppose factors become internationally mobile and interindustry trade declines as factor movements substitute for it. Both countries will eventually begin to produce both goods, and then intraindustry trade will become possible. Thus, while factor mobility is a substitute for interindustry trade, it is *complementary* to intraindustry trade.

Return to the Heckscher-Ohlin-Samuelson model, and suppose that autarky factor rewards—and, therefore, commodity prices—would be the same in France as in Germany so that there is no reason to trade. Now suppose that France develops a more efficient apple technology but that Germany does not. This establishes a basis for trade: France should export apples to Germany for butane. Then the increased French production of (capital-intensive) apples for export will cause the French rent to rise. In this case, it will be moving *away* from that in the rest of the world. Capital will flow into France. Commodity trade causes the factor-reward disparity that induces factor mobility. Thus trade and factor mobility are complements.

Note that in this case a mindless application of a Leontief-type calculation would appear to confirm the Heckscher-Ohlin theorem. The capital-abundant country is exporting capital-intensive goods. But the latter is not caused by the former; both are due to a third cause: the French advantage in apple technology.

The general result is the following. If countries trade because of different relative factor endowments, as in Heckscher-Ohlin theory, trade and factor mobility substitute for each other. But if trade is due to technological considerations (*other than* factor endowments), trade and factor mobility will likely complement each other. Chapter 6 showed that, while there is good reason to think that factor endowments are important in determining trade, the question of just how important they are remains unanswered and controversial. So the extent to which trade and factor mobility complement or substitute for each other must likewise remain an open question.

Does it really matter? Yes, a lot. Many important international economic policies are in fact based on a firm implicit belief that trade and factor mobility are substitutes. In the past Canada maintained a high tariff (described in Chapter 5) partly in hopes of inducing foreign capital to be invested there. This hope was based on the belief that capital mobility would substitute for denied trade. One reason the United States wants low trade barriers with Mexico (as in NAFTA) is to lower the pressure of Mexicans trying to migrate north. An important argument for Western Europe to encourage trade with the former communist countries of Central and Eastern Europe is that this should lower migration from those countries. Both of these motives are based squarely on the belief that trade will substitute for labor migration.

Problem

10.8 Suppose that France and Germany are as in the standard Heckscher-Ohlin-Samuelson model *except* that they have identical factor endowments *but* different tastes: France has a greater relative preference for butane than does Germany, which has a greater relative preference for apples. What will happen if there is free trade but no factor mobility. Discuss the possible consequences of also allowing factors to migrate. Are trade and factor mobility substitutes or complements in this case?

4. LABOR MIGRATION

Thus far we have looked at factor mobility in general terms. The remainder of this chapter focuses on problems peculiar to individual factors. Start with labor.

The massive eighteenth- and nineteenth-century migrations from Europe to the Western Hemisphere and Australia certainly constituted a significant international factor movement to which the theory of section 1 applies. For example, when settlement in the new temperate-zone regions and a fall in transport costs caused Western Europe to develop a comparative disadvantage in grain, the imports of the latter drove much of the rural Continental population first into the cities and then to overseas emigration. The relation between trade and factor mobility was also illustrated by the late nineteenth-century response of many Continental countries: tariffs on agricultural imports to reduce rural depopulation.

But what unique considerations attach to labor? Most obviously, the role of productive factor is but one facet of human existence. Thus the decision to migrate hinges on an overall comparison of the quality of life in the prospective destination with that at home, and not merely on a comparison of wage rates. Labor might, therefore, not respond to wage differentials, and migration could be a result of political or social upheavals not related to wage rates. Perhaps all this is partial justification for the classical theory's assumption that labor is simply immobile internationally. Still, the purely economic motive, in the form of wage differentials, is an important determinant of migration.

Migration involves the movement of both a factor of production and of the owner of that factor so that the source country loses its claim to the factor's earnings. An export of capital, by contrast, implies that the source country will receive the earnings of that capital. A migrant, however, might repatriate some of her earnings for the benefit of relatives left behind or to accumulate a nest egg for her future return. But she is not obligated to do so. The fact that migrants are people also complicates the evaluation of policy. Migration often affects the welfare of the migrants themselves in different ways than it affects the welfare of people left behind or of those already in the host country. Thus

the effect of migration policy, in either country, on "national welfare" could be sensitive to whether migrants are counted as part of the nation or not.

The consequences of migration also reflect labor's unique character. The distributional and efficiency implications discussed in section 1 are important, but so are the social and cultural implications. Opposition to immigration is often, in part, a response to the latter's effect on the real wage, but it usually also reflects fears about the disruptive effects of a large influx of foreigners. We now look in detail at contemporary issues involving labor mobility.

Guest Workers

In many parts of the world, the *temporary* migration of largely unskilled workers is an important phenomenon. Prominent examples include the employment of migrant Latin American labor in United States agriculture and light industry, large numbers of south European and North African workers in the labor-intensive industries of northern Europe, and the extensive reliance of oil-rich Middle Eastern countries on labor from elsewhere in the Middle East and from southern Asia. At times migrants have constituted over one-quarter of the Swiss labor force, for example.

These migrations are subject to diverse legal arrangements. The European Economic Community provides for *unrestricted factor mobility* among members so that Italians are free to take jobs in Germany, for example.

Migrant labor movements into northern Europe, aside from this intra-EU mobility, are generally subject to *guest-worker* systems: the host-country government issues temporary permits to foreign workers to enter the country and take jobs. By controlling the number of permits, the host country can adjust the flow of migrant workers in response to changing economic and social conditions. Such systems govern the extensive employment of Bosnians, Serbs, Turks, and North Africans in France, Switzerland, and Germany (and of Italians in Switzerland, which is not a member of the EU).

Migrant labor has two basic effects on host countries. The workers are unskilled and are willing to accept wages that are low by the host country's standards and jobs that native workers would not want at viable wage levels. Travelers to northern European cities such as London immediately notice how many chambermaids, transit conductors, and so forth are foreign. Labor-intensive industries that would not be able to compete on world markets if they had to pay native wages can survive by hiring cheaper migrant workers. Since these industries also employ some domestic factors, painful adjustments are avoided. Thus the Florida vegetable growers who complain about the competition of cheap Mexican tomatoes themselves hire migrant Mexican workers. This is, of course, another case of factor mobility substituting for international trade. Instead of exporting textiles to Europe, North Africa receives an income for the labor it "exports." If Europe increases the tariff on textiles, North African firms become less able to compete in Europe, but

guest workers in the European textile industry benefit, and North African remittances from emigrants rise.

Guest workers also increase the ability of the host country to deal with macroeconomic disturbances. The country can keep average aggregate demand high and use the guest workers as a buffer against fluctuations. During boom periods the authorities issue more permits to foreign workers. When demand falls, guest workers are sent packing, and native workers suffer no unemployment. The home country essentially "exports" the business cycle to foreign workers. During the boom years of the 1960s, northern Europe attracted record numbers of guest workers, many of whom were sent home during the recessions of the 1970s.

Arrangements like these can potentially benefit all concerned. Workers in the prosperous host country obtain insulation from the effects of business fluctuations by "trading" them to foreign guest workers, who in return receive higher wages than they could earn at home.

Migrant workers also cause problems for host countries. Although these workers typically take jobs that most native workers do not want, there are inevitably some groups of host-country unskilled workers that do compete with the foreign laborers and who, therefore, suffer because of such migration. The United Farm Workers in California oppose the admission into the country of migrant workers from Mexico. Also the presence of such workers in significant numbers or for extended periods or both can produce serious social tensions. Continued reliance on foreign workers has, for this reason, been a prominent political issue in Switzerland.

The countries from which the migrants come likewise receive both benefits and costs. On the plus side, part of the population (the migrants themselves) receive employment offers better than they can apparently find at home, and the remittances of these workers benefit the rest of the source country. For some LDCs, these remittances are significant. For example, in 1979 Pakistan's remittances from its workers abroad were fully 77 percent as high as the country's earnings from commodity exports. Furthermore, the export of workers into the DC labor-intensive industries is an indirect way to penetrate markets from which the LDCs are significantly excluded by DC protection. Labor emigration can also be an important safety valve to release tensions in an LDC with a large supply of unemployed labor. It is partly for this reason that Mexico has sometimes urged the United States to admit more migrant workers.

On the negative side, source countries may find themselves faced with more severe business fluctuations. A recession in the DC host country will send unemployed guest workers returning home at the same time that domestic export industries find demand drying up in their DC markets. When these workers do return, they often bring with them alien tastes and habits acquired abroad. Sometimes they even refuse to accept at home the kind of jobs they held abroad. Also the migrant workers are sometimes relatively highly skilled by LDC standards, so that what looks like an influx of unskilled migrant workers to a host DC could appear to be a brain drain to the source LDC.

Finally, concern about the treatment that guest workers receive can sometimes involve the host and source countries in conflict.

Illegal Immigration

Immigration laws are often difficult to enforce, so sufficiently strong economic incentives might well induce migration even if it is not legal. The strong pull of high U.S. wages on abundant labor pools south of the border causes considerable illegal immigration. In recent years this has been of the same order of magnitude as legal immigration, and how to deal with it has been a major policy issue. Some parts of the U.S. economy have become dependent on the labor of illegal workers, and some parts of source-country societies have become dependent on sending such migrants abroad. About a quarter of the Mexican labor force is employed in the United States, much of it illegally.

For many years Europe, implementing guest-worker systems to deal with labor shortages, did not worry about illegal immigration. But in the 1970s it proved difficult to deal with migrants when their services were no longer needed. One implication of this was a rising concern with illegal immigration in the form of "overstays": people who had entered the country legally and subsequently lost the right to stay but had not left. Thus, whereas authorities in the United States typically worried about how to keep illegal immigrants from entering, European authorities were more often concerned with compelling them to leave.

But this dichotomy is no longer as sharp as it once was. U.S. law has been changed to attempt to reduce the heavy reliance on enforcement at the border (this is discussed in the following section). In Europe, the prospect of large-scale immigration from the former communist countries has by contrast produced new concern over entry. Germany, for example, has revised its law to make it less easy for prospective immigrants to gain entry by claiming refugee status.

Illegal immigration usually involves unskilled labor and most often is temporary, at least in original intent. Skilled workers are much more likely to be accommodated legally; when they are not, they are less willing to move anyhow if that means enduring illegal status. Illegal immigrants are more likely to find themselves driven abroad by economic necessity rather than by a desire no longer to live in their homeland. Also their illegal status makes it more difficult to put down roots in the host country.

Problem

10.9 In Chapter 8 we saw that a small tariff would improve the welfare of any country large enough to influence its terms of trade. How is this argument affected if the importable sector is relatively intensive in the use of unskilled (migrant) labor and if the incomes of such migrants are not counted as part of national welfare?

5. *CASE STUDY:* REFORM OF U.S. IMMIGRATION LAW

For years illegal immigration into the United States has been regarded there as a serious economic issue, and successive administrations have attempted to deal with it. The problem acquired new urgency in the 1980s, when deteriorating economic conditions in Mexico and some other Latin American countries accelerated the flow of would-be migrants. Apprehensions at the border of individuals attempting to enter the country illegally increased from about 300,000 in 1979 to a yearly rate of over 2 million in just six years. Though many are caught, many others get through; some try repeatedly until they make it. Some even go back and forth almost regularly, working in the United States but living just outside. The feeling gradually arose that the country had lost control of its borders.

Estimates of the number of illegal immigrants residing in the United States vary greatly (they do not stand up to be counted), with official numbers ranging from 3.5 million to 7 million. They account for a significant part of the nation's pool of unskilled labor, and some industries depend heavily upon them. We tend to think of these people as working in southern agriculture or as domestic help. Although they are important in these occupations, many more of them are employed in other industries and services in all sections of the country.

Various proposals to deal with illegal immigration involved different combinations and variants of four possible specific measures: (1) *Beefed-up enforcement at the border* to try to reduce the number of migrants entering illegally. (2) *Employer sanctions,* or penalties for people or firms who employ illegal immigrants, in an attempt to eliminate the jobs that attract the migrants in the first place. (Although illegal immigrants have no right to be in the country, it was legal to employ them if they were, in fact, present; and they were also entitled to certain public services and forms of assistance.) (3) *A guest-worker system* to accommodate those sectors that rely heavily on such labor. (4) *Amnesty* for migrants who have become part of American society even though they do not have legal status.

Reform is difficult because any specific change will affect different groups in different ways. For example, firms that employ illegal immigrants or that employ unskilled workers whose wages are bid down by competition with such immigrants would presumably oppose any effective reform, whereas legally resident unskilled workers should be among the most ardent supporters. Also the latter should especially prefer employer sanctions since these sanctions promise to protect directly the jobs of that group and to offer protection against competitors already illegally present in the economy as well as those attempting to enter. But it is just these workers who are most likely to resemble the illegal immigrants in terms of education, ethnic background, and so on. Thus they can expect to suffer if sanctions induce employers to discriminate against anyone who "looks suspicious." More generally, questions of civil liberties necessarily arise.

Efforts at reform have also been hampered by our ignorance about illegal immigration. Not only do we not know how many there are, it is also not clear how directly they compete for jobs with native workers. There is also controversy about whether such migrants pay more in taxes than they consume in public benefits, and many other questions.

Despite these difficulties, a compromise immigration measure, the *Immigration Reform and Control Act of 1986* was passed by Congress and signed into law by President Reagan on November 6, 1986. The act contained versions of the measures described above. It is no longer legal to employ illegal immigrants, and firms have to verify the status of new employees within twenty-four hours. Employers found to be using illegal immigrants face fines of $250 to $10,000 for each illegal alien hired. An amnesty provision offered legal residence—and eventual citizenship—to those who could demonstrate that they had been continually residing in the country since before January 1, 1982.

This reform of the immigration laws is of major historical significance, and it is having effects on many facets of American life. But whether it has achieved the primary goal of significantly reducing illegal immigration is not yet clear.

6. INTERNATIONAL CAPITAL MOVEMENTS

Important as the international migration of labor is, it receives much less attention than cross-country investment. Accordingly, we next consider the international movement of capital.

What Are International Capital Movements?

By an international capital movement we do *not* mean the sale by one nation to another of capital equipment such as tools, machines, or building supplies. This is international *trade*. International capital movements refer to borrowing and lending between countries. An example would be a French sale of bonds in Germany. The French can use the proceeds of the bond sale to purchase equipment and thereby increase their stock of capital; by purchasing French bonds, German savers reduce the volume of savings that can be used for investment in Germany. Thus the French capital stock increases and the German falls, relative to what would have happened without the bond sale, producing the international reallocation of real capital studied in section 1. Alternatively, the French might simply spend the proceeds on high living—that is, borrow in order to enjoy today at the expense of tomorrow.

Such a transaction is variously described as a French *capital inflow,* an *international sale of assets* (the bonds), or *international borrowing*. The opposite side of the transaction (that is, the German point of view) is, likewise, described by the synonyms *capital outflow, purchase of foreign assets, foreign lending*.

Walras's Law

If it cannot borrow, a nation must pay for its imports with exports: $pM \equiv X$. This was assumed in the first six chapters of this book. International capital mobility allows a country to pay for imports by selling either goods (exporting) or assets (borrowing). Furthermore, if the country owns foreign assets such as bonds, it will be receiving interest payments from abroad, and this interest can also be used to pay for imports. Thus

$$pM \equiv X + C + E. \tag{10.1}$$

Here C denotes the net international sale of assets (total assets sold to foreigners minus total assets bought from foreigners), expressed in units of exportables, and E denotes net interest payments from abroad (interest received from foreigners minus interest paid to foreigners), also expressed in units of exportables. C and E are not directly related because the former describes *present* asset exchanges, whereas the latter is determined by *past* borrowing and lending. But the two are related over time: if C rises now, we are selling more assets on which we must subsequently pay interest, so E will be reduced in the future.

Rearranging Walras's Law (10.1) allows us to display, in Figure 10.3, the classification of a nation's international transactions. The *trade balance,* or excess of the value of exports over imports, is added to net receipts of foreign investment income to obtain the *current-account balance*. E can be interpreted as the sale of capital services: if we receive interest from abroad because we have purchased a bond, that interest is, in effect, the fee that foreigners are paying to us for the use of the principal value of the bond. Thus the current-account balance can be regarded as the net sale of goods and services to the rest of the world. The capital-account balance is likewise the net sale of assets to the rest of the world. These two balances are really two

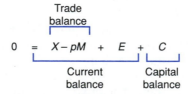

FIGURE 10.3 **International Transactions Balances**

ways of describing the same thing because by Walras's Law one always equals minus the other.

Capital Movements in Perspective

In the latter part of the nineteenth century, Great Britain was by far the world's most significant capital exporter, with British loans financing the construction of railroads the world over. Just before the First World War, about one-quarter of British national wealth consisted of foreign assets, and the interest from these assets accounted for about one-tenth of British national income. Because of this, the country was simultaneously able to import more than it exported and still acquire additional net foreign assets; in Figure 10.3, E was sufficiently large and positive so that $X - pM$ and C could both be significantly negative at the same time.

Piracy and the Wealth of Nations

Back in the sixteenth century, Elizabeth I invested a portion of her share of the swag from Francis Drake's voyage of discovery in the *Golden Hind* in a company that formed the basis of England's foreign investment. John Maynard Keynes, looking back from the twentieth century at her pirated investment, was fond of pointing out that, if one assumed a reasonable rate of return on it and also assumed that about half of the investment income was reinvested abroad (as was actual British performance about the turn of this century), a compound interest calculation would show a time path of accumulation of Elizabeth's original investment roughly similar to the actual course of British foreign investment holdings.

The Rise and Fall of the United States As World Lender

The United States was a net debtor throughout the nineteenth century: the great transcontinental railroads were financed with foreign capital and built by migrant labor. By the end of the century, the country was on balance acquiring assets from the rest of the world and about the time of the First World War became a net creditor. Europe sold off the bulk of her foreign assets to finance two world wars. The United States became the most important creditor nation. Table 10.3 shows the American position. Panel (a) summarizes the international transactions in 1993, while panel (b) shows the international investment position as of the end of that year. The numbers in panel (a) are *flows,* the transactions taking place during the year, whereas panel (b) shows *stocks,* the accumulated total of all past transactions at a particular time (the end of 1993).

TABLE 10.3 **American Capital Movements and Position (billions of dollars)**

(a) International transactions, 1990		(b) International investment position, end of 1990	
Current balance	−103.9	U.S. ownership of	
(Of which: net		foreign assets	2,370.4
investment income)	(3.9)	Foreign ownership of	
Capital balance	−103.9	U.S. assets	2,926.4
		Net U.S. international	
		investment	−555.8

SOURCE: *Survey of Current Business.*

We said the United States had become the largest creditor nation in the world, but panel (b) of Table 10.3 shows the country actually to be in debt on balance. This is because huge current-account deficits in the 1980s wiped out the U.S. net investment position and in a few years transformed the country from the largest creditor to the largest debtor (see Table 10.4).

The United States reached a peak as a creditor in 1982, with a net position of over $379 billion. And, indeed, the country has continued to acquire foreign assets at a steady pace since, as the first row of Table 10.4 shows. But the rapid increase in the sale of assets to foreigners, financing a large current-account deficit, caused the net position to turn negative by 1987. The country has now become the largest debtor in the world. This despite the fact that it seems clear that the United States is also one of the most capital-abundant countries in the world.

Types of Capital Movements

Capital transactions differ in three ways, summarized in Figure 10.4. The first basis is the identities of the individuals exchanging assets. *Official capital movements* are those undertaken by a country's official monetary authority

TABLE 10.4 **U.S. International Investment Position (billions of dollars)**

Year	1979	1982	1983	1987	1990	1993
U.S. ownership of foreign assets	729.9	1,119.4	1,225.0	1,625.4	2,086.9	2,370.4
Foreign ownership of U.S. assets	450.0	740.2	866.6	1,648.2	2,318.3	2,926.2
Net U.S. international investment	342.9	379.2	358.4	−22.8	−251.4	−555.8

SOURCE: *Survey of Current Business.*

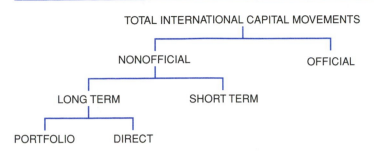

FIGURE 10.4   Types of International Capital Movements

such as a central bank. Such movements are a result of the authority's management of the nation's money, and we shall study them when we turn to international monetary economics. In this chapter, we confine our attention to *nonofficial movements*. The latter are, in turn, classified by time to maturity. An international capital movement is an exchange of assets, and an asset is a promise to pay interest and, at some date, to mature—that is, to be redeemed for money. *Short-term* capital movements are those involving assets whose original time to maturity was less than a year; other capital movements are *long term*. Short-term assets include demand deposits and cash (which are already matured), as well as treasury bills, commercial paper, and so forth. Long-term assets include equity and real estate (which never mature), and bonds, notes, mortgages, and so forth.

Short-term and long-term transactions are separated to distinguish capital movements that finance international trade or involve speculative flyers from those that accommodate the international transfer of means of production, as treated in sections 1 through 3. This chapter predominantly concerns the latter. Note that this attempt at separation is imperfect because there is nothing to prevent someone from turning a treasury bill over and over as it matures, or from selling a share of common stock the day after it is purchased, or from buying a twenty-year bond in the secondary market one week before its date of maturity.

Long-term capital movements are themselves further classified according to whether the purchaser of the asset has operating control over the issuer of the asset. If so, the movements are termed *direct;* if not, they are *portfolio* investments. If you buy shares of common stock in a corporation, you become part owner and can vote at annual meetings. Buy enough shares and you can acquire control. But if you instead purchase bonds issued by that corporation, you have no share of ownership and no right to help make decisions, no matter how many bonds you own. This is essentially the distinction between direct and portfolio investment. Of course, the ownership of a single share of common stock gives no real control. Thus, to be classified as a direct investment, a

TABLE 10.5   **The U.S. Foreign Investment Position, end of 1993**

	U.S. foreign assets	Foreign U.S. assets	Net U.S. position
Private long term	1,234.7	1,503.9	−269.2
Direct	716.2	516.7	199.5
Portfolio	518.5	987.2	−468.7
Other	1,135.7	1,422.3	−286.6
Total	2,370.4	2,926.2	−555.8

SOURCE: U.S. Department of Commerce, *Survey of Current Business.*

single individual or entity must own a minimum share of the foreign firm. Sometimes this minimum is 25 percent; for U.S. statistics it is, in practice, 10 percent. Direct investment generally consists of national corporations setting up foreign subsidiaries or buying substantial shares in foreign firms.

British foreign investments before the First World War were largely portfolio, but American investments are significantly direct. Table 10.5 gives a detailed breakdown of the U.S. foreign investment position summarized in Table 10.3(b).

Problems

10.10 For each of the following transactions, tell, from the point of view of each country, whether the transaction contributes to the current balance or the capital balance and, if the latter is the case, what type of capital movement it is.

   a New Yorkers use checks drawn on a New York bank to buy bonds from a Canadian corporation.

   b Russia sends oil to Germany in exchange for oil-drilling equipment.

   c Russia, in exchange for oil-drilling equipment, promises to send Japan 100 million barrels of oil from the new well in five years.

   d An American firm issues six-month commercial paper in London to finance the purchase of a British department store.

   e You use a check drawn on a Philadelphia bank to buy a vacation home on the Mediterranean.

10.11 In section 4 we saw that remittances from natives working abroad are important sources of income for some countries. How do you think that such payments fit into the scheme of Figure 10.3?

7. INTERTEMPORAL TRADE

If a country runs a capital-account surplus, it is selling assets to foreigners, or *borrowing* from the rest of the world. In the future it will have to pay the loans back with interest. In other words, the country is consuming goods now at the expense of the future. Thus capital movements are a way for countries to trade over time: the country with a capital-account surplus (or capital inflow) is in effect trading future goods to the rest of the world in exchange for present goods. Looking at capital movements in this way gives valuable insights and also permits a direct application of the theory developed in Part One.

Autarky Equilibrium

Begin by considering an economy—call it France—in economic isolation from the rest of the world. Figure 10.5 shows its production possibility frontier, which, as usual, depends on French resources. But the axes no longer represent different goods that can be produced today, but rather the same good available at different times: present goods and future goods. That is, the curve shows production possibilities *over time*. If the French produce at *A*, for example, they will have the quantity *OP* of present goods to consume today, and tomorrow (or the next year) they will be able to consume the quantity *OF* of future goods. If the French cut back present consumption by *AG* (thus consuming only *GF* today), they can invest the resources that would have been used to produce *AG* to expand their productive capacity instead, allowing them to increase tomorrow's production by *GH*. The frontier is bowed outward because the best investment projects are undertaken first; additional investment in the form of present sacrifices yields less future payoff. The curvature

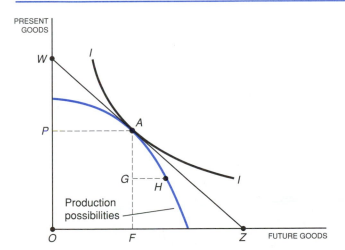

FIGURE 10.5 Autarky Equilibrium At the autarky equilibrium *A*, France consumes the quantity *OP* of goods today. In the future the quantity *OF* will be consumed. *OZ/OW* indicates the relative price of present goods in terms of future goods, or 1 plus the rate of interest.

of the production possibility frontier, therefore, indicates *opportunities to invest* in France.

Figure 10.5 also shows an indifference curve, labeled *II*, reflecting French tastes for consumption now versus consumption tomorrow. That is, the indifference curve indicates French *impatience* to consume. Autarky equilibrium occurs at the point on the production possibility frontier that attains the highest indifference curve—that is, at a point of tangency such as *A* in the figure. The common slope reflects the autarky price of future goods in terms of present goods. The distance *OW* measures the value, in terms of present goods, of the total French production (and consumption) pattern over time. We can call this France's *wealth*.

If none of France's wealth were consumed today, but instead the entire amount *OW* invested at the going rate of interest, *i*, it would be worth *OW* $(1 + i)$ tomorrow. This is *OZ* in the figure. Thus *OZ/OW* indicates $1 + i$, 1 plus the autarky rate of interest in France.

International Equilibrium

It should be clear that we can now use the full apparatus of Chapters 1 and 4 to talk about a comparative advantage in present goods relative to future goods, to derive import demand and export supply curves, and so on. Such curves are shown in Figure 10.6.

The vertical axis measures $1 + i$, the price of present goods in terms of future goods. The downward-sloping line through *F* is France's demand

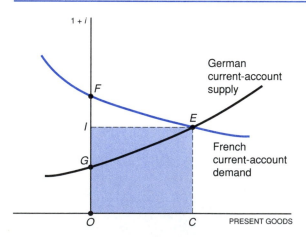

FIGURE 10.6 **International Equilibrium** At the equilibrium *E*, France runs a present current-account deficit (capital-account surplus) of *OC*. In the future France will have a current-account surplus of *OIEC*.

curve for imports of present goods, and the upward-sloping line through G is Germany's supply curve of exports of present goods. These are derived in exactly the same way as the analogous curves in Chapter 4. If France imports present goods, it must pay for them with future goods. That is, an import of present goods is also an export of promises to pay in the future: a *capital-account surplus*. Thus the French demand curve for imports of present goods can also be thought of as a demand curve for a capital-account surplus or for a current-account deficit.

Autarky equilibrium is at F for France and at G for Germany. Thus France has the higher autarky rate of interest and so a comparative advantage over Germany in future goods relative to present goods. If free international capital mobility is allowed, a single world rate of interest (equal to $OI - 1$) will be established with equilibrium at E. Thus France develops a current-account deficit (capital-account surplus) of OC, and Germany develops a corresponding current-account surplus. When the future eventually arrives, France will have to pay this back with interest: $OC(1 + i)$ in total. Thus the *future* French current-account surplus is given by the area $OIEC$.

The movement from autarky to free capital mobility can be thought of as follows. Since the autarky interest rate is higher in France, the marginal opportunity to invest must also be greater there. Thus when capital mobility is allowed, investors increase their investment in France (shift production from present goods to future goods) and do the reverse in Germany. As the interest rate in France falls to the international level, consumers there are less tempted to postpone gratification, so the demand for present goods rises and that for future goods falls. The reverse happens in Germany. Thus France develops an excess demand for present goods and an excess supply of future goods.

Problems

10.12 Draw Figure 10.5 as it would appear if France were in the international equilibrium depicted in Figure 10.6. Do the same for Germany.

10.13 Suppose that Figures 10.5 and 10.6 are generated by the Heckscher-Ohlin-Samuelson model of Chapter 5, where labor and land are the two primary factors, present goods are relatively labor-intensive, and (as in the HOS model) both of these primary factors are immobile internationally. Discuss the meaning of the four basic HOS theorems in this context. Contrast this with the conclusions reached in section 1 of this chapter, where one of the primary factors was internationally mobile, and both goods were "present" goods.

10.14* What happens to the equilibrium in Figure 10.6 if France imposes a tariff on the import of German goods and spends the proceeds on future goods? Does it matter if France taxes exports instead? Suppose it taxes the sale of assets to foreigners? The payment of interest to foreigners?

8. *CASE STUDY:* AN INTERTEMPORAL INTERPRETATION OF THE DETERIORATION OF THE U.S. CURRENT ACCOUNT

The U.S. Current-Account Deficit

We saw above that the United States developed a strong creditor position during this century and then quickly dissipated that position with large current-account deficits in the 1980s. While there are complex questions associated with this experience, interpreting it in terms of the theory presented in section 7 sheds light on one aspect.

In the early 1980s a large federal budget deficit developed as a result of a tax cut, an increase in defense spending, and only modest cuts in other spending programs. Table 10.6 shows the U.S. experience.

The increase in the federal budget deficit can be interpreted as an increase in the government's demand for present goods. To the extent that it was not accompanied by an increased private desire to save—and it appears not to have been—this constitutes a shift in national demand from future goods to present goods.

Figure 10.7 illustrates the situation. The *ROW* line is the rest of the world's excess supply curve of present goods, and the line labeled *US* is what the U.S. excess demand curve for present goods would have been if the earlier experience had continued. Equilibrium is at *B,* with the United States running a current-account surplus of *CO.*

The shift in demand from future goods to present goods is represented by a rightward shift of the *US* curve to that labeled *US'.* If the economy were closed, the new equilibrium would be at *A* and imply a large increase *AE* in the rate of interest. Although interest rates were in fact high (after accounting for inflation), there was no dramatic rise. This is accounted for by the existence of an international capital market. With the U.S. economy open, equilibrium is instead at *B',* so the interest rate rises only by *DD'.* At the same time, the modest current-account surplus is transformed into the large current-account deficit of *OC'.*

The U.S.-Japan Trade Imbalance

The largest and most visible part of the U.S. current-account deficit has been the bilateral deficit with Japan. This has been predominantly a trade im-

TABLE 10.6   The U.S. Budget and the Current Account *(billions of dollars)*

	1980	1983	1985	1990
Federal budget surplus	−72.7	−208.0	−221.6	−220.4
Current-account surplus	1.1	−40.1	−122.3	−92.1

SOURCE: *Budget of the United States; Economic Report of the President.*

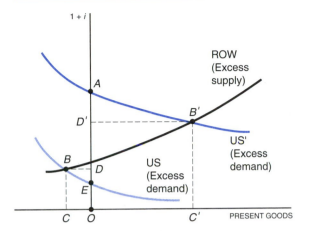

FIGURE 10.7 The U.S. Current-Account Deficit U.S. fiscal policy shifts the demand curve for present goods to the right, transforming a small current-account surplus into a large deficit. The interest rate also rises but much less than it would in a closed economy.

balance, exceeding $43 billion in 1992, which has generated intense debate within and between both countries. Much of this debate has centered on whether the trade imbalance is the result of "unfair" Japanese trade policies (discussed in detail in Chapter 9). In this sense all the sound and fury is misplaced: trade policies influence the structure of international trade, not the overall balance.

Our intertemporal analysis offers, by contrast, an appropriate framework to analyze the overall imbalance. To do this in a simple way, focus exclusively on U.S.-Japan transactions, ignoring the rest of the world.

The present analysis directs attention to the impatience to consume and the opportunity to invest in each country. It is clear that the United States and Japan differ much more in regard to the former than in regard to the latter. In recent years net saving in the United States has been barely a percentage point or two of national income, while it has approximated 20 percent in Japan. We have discussed U.S. fiscal policy as a possible contributing factor to the low savings rate (that is, high preference for present consumption) in that country. The unusually high savings rate in Japan (that is, high preference for future consumption)—which has persisted for many years—has excited much speculation. It has been variously attributed to several causes. One is the inherent thrift of the Japanese people. Another is the very high cost of housing, which necessitates much saving to buy a home (if so, this makes Japanese trade policy significantly responsible since, as we saw in Chapter 9, this policy helps explain the high cost of housing). A final possible cause is the Japanese tax system, which—until recently, at any rate—encouraged saving. Whatever the reason, the savings rate in Japan is unusually high.

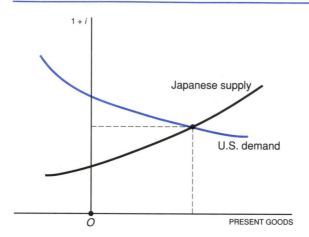

FIGURE 10.8   U.S.-Japan Experience   A high propensity to save in Japan and a low propensity to save in the United States generate an equilibrium with a large U.S. current-account deficit.

The net result is as in Figure 10.8. The Japanese savings behavior implies a net supply curve for current-account imbalances low and to the right; the U.S. net demand curve is high and to the right. Equilibrium features a large U.S. current-account deficit and Japanese current-account surplus.

All this might seem like mere common sense. To understand its true power, remind yourself of the loud public debate that centers on alleged "unfair trade practices" and completely ignores macroeconomic considerations. The present analysis suggests how this public turmoil may be misplaced.

Problems

10.15 Use the HOS model (with present goods and future goods as the two commodities) as a framework to explain the pre-1980s situation in which the United States ran a current-account surplus.

10.16 The current-account imbalance at point B' in Figure 10.7 could be eliminated if the United States shifted its curve back. But U.S. authorities urged the rest of the world (in particular, Germany and Japan) to adopt more expansionary policies. Compare the results of these two possible responses, using both Figure 10.5 and Figure 10.7.

9. SUMMARY

1. In Ricardian theory, factor mobility raises world production more than does trade and specialization. Beneficial trade is a consequence of comparative cost differences, whereas beneficial factor movements are a consequence of absolute productivity differences.

2. In factor-endowments theory, factor movements are perfectly substituted for by commodity trade if trade leads to factor-price equalization. With incomplete factor-price equalization, factor mobility will lead to migrations from low marginal product areas to high marginal product areas.

3. Factor mobility, like commodity trade, redistributes income from a country's relatively scarce factor to the relatively abundant factor.

4. Trade and factor mobility are substitutes when the trade is due to factor endowments but complementary if the trade is due to some other technological cause.

5. Guest workers accept low wages in host countries and increase the ability of the host country to deal with fluctuations in the demand for labor. The host country exports business cycles to foreigners.

6. International capital movements (borrowing and lending between countries) allow countries to pay for imports by selling assets—that is, by promising to export in the future.

7. There are three types of capital movements: official, nonofficial short term, and nonofficial long term. The latter are divided between direct and portfolio (long term) investments.

SUGGESTED READING

Feis, H. *Europe: The World's Banker, 1870–1913.* New York: Norton, 1966. A historical account of capital movements before the First World War.

MacDougall, G. D. A. "The Benefits and Costs of Private Investment from Abroad: A Theoretical Approach." *Economic Record* (Mar. 1960).

Markusen, J. R. "Factor Movements and Commodity Trade As Complements." *Journal of International Economics* (May 1983). Are they substitutes or complements?

Mundell, R. A. "International Trade and Factor Mobility." *American Economic Review* (June 1957). A basic theoretical treatment.

Ohlin, B. *Interregional and International Trade.* Rev. ed. Cambridge: Harvard University Press, 1967. Stresses the relation between trade and factor mobility.

Piore, M. J. *Birds of Passage.* Cambridge: Cambridge University Press, 1979. Migrant labor in the modern world economy.

Thomas, B. *Migration and Economic Growth.* Rev. ed. Cambridge: Cambridge University Press, 1972. The great migrations to the Western Hemisphere.

CHAPTER 11

The Multinational Firm

> If the rivalry of first-class powers for the control of foreign markets, whether for the sale of goods or the investment of capital, has proven itself a menace to the peace of the world (and that such is the case, no one will care to deny), the explanation must be sought in the arrested development of political relations rather than in the underdevelopment of industrial conditions. The integration of political control has not kept pace territorially with the expansion of commercial interests.
> —HENRY C. ADAMS

The theory of Chapter 10 applies to both direct and portfolio capital movements. This chapter discusses the distinctive questions associated with direct investment. Direct investment consists of the acquisition by domestic firms of foreign subsidiaries and (wholly or partially owned) affiliates. Such investment has grown rapidly since 1945, and this has thrust into prominence the multinational corporation—a giant enterprise spanning many countries, arranging its operations on a global scale. This phenomenon has been the subject of an enormous literature, both popular and academic. Some see such firms as harbingers of a new dawn, diffusing modern technology and capital into dark corners of the globe; others see our future dominated by faceless corporate bureaucracies with loyalties only unto themselves.

1. DIRECT INVESTMENT AND THE MULTINATIONAL CORPORATION

Multinational firms operate production facilities in a number of different countries; the term does not apply to companies that merely export from a single country, no matter how large the exports. The precise definition of a multinational enterprise (MNE) differs from writer to writer. Depending upon the definition, there are 250 to 750 of these firms, about half of them based in the United States; a few of the others are state-owned. The 50 largest multinationals are, together, at least as sizable as all others combined. About one-fifth of world GNP is produced by MNEs, with the fraction exceeding one-third for some individual countries. About one-fourth of world trade now consists of trade between subsidiaries and branches *within* MNEs.

While thinking about these patterns, it is important to realize that direct investment need not imply an actual movement of capital. Suppose that an American firm purchases a subsidiary in the United Kingdom with funds raised in the United States. This act of direct investment does constitute a movement of capital because the United States has on balance acquired foreign assets (the subsidiary). But suppose that the subsidiary had been purchased with funds the American firm acquired by selling bonds in London. In this case there has been no capital movement—the United States and the United Kingdom simply traded assets (the subsidiary for bonds). A direct-investment outflow from the United States has been offset by a portfolio-investment inflow. This sort of thing is, in fact, important because MNEs do raise a significant amount of capital locally in host countries. The phenomenon was apparent in Table 10.5, which showed that the United States is a heavy creditor in terms of direct investment but a debtor with regard to other types of capital flows.

The distinctive feature about direct investment, then, is *not* that one country is on balance acquiring the assets of another—this may or may not be true. The distinctive feature is that firms in one country are acquiring control of business operations in another country.

International capital movements have been prominent for a long time, but MNEs have become so only since the Second World War. Why this rapid recent growth? One immediately thinks of modern advances in communications and information processing. Efficient global management requires efficient global communications. The first American plant in Europe—a Singer sewing-machine factory in Scotland—was opened in the 1860s, soon after the first transatlantic cable was laid.

But it is also true that a little historical perspective makes the MNE seem like less of a distinctly modern animal than contemporary discussions imply. American foreign investment has always been predominantly direct, while European foreign investments have tended more to portfolio. Thus the emergence of the United States as the major source of capital would, by itself, greatly increase the role of direct investment in the world. As Table 11.1 shows, American foreign investment in 1914 was largely direct, just as in 1980. The difference is that in 1914 the country was a net debtor to the rest of the world. But even then, the United States had a net-creditor position with respect to direct investment alone! British popular publications in the early years of this century, with a strangely modern flavor, decried the takeover of local businesses by American firms—even as Great Britain was by far the world's dominant capital exporter!

An additional perspective on the postwar surge of direct investments is afforded by recognition of the role of the Depression, which caused foreign investment to dry up. The Second World War followed, so that direct invest-

TABLE 11.1   The U.S. Foreign Investment Position, 1914

	U.S. assets abroad	Foreign assets in United States	Net U.S. position
Private long term	3.5	6.7	−3.2
Direct	2.6	1.3	1.3
Portfolio	0.9	5.4	−4.5
Other	—	0.5	−0.5
Total	3.5	7.2	−3.7

SOURCE: *Statistical Abstract of the United States.*

ment did not resume until after 1945, when it had a lot of catching up to do. From this point of view, the heavy postwar direct investment is not a new phenomenon so much as a return to the long-term trend. The stock of U.S. foreign direct investment in 1980 had about the same relationship to U.S. GNP (8 percent) as it did in 1914.

Although a historical perspective erodes the popular impression of MNEs as distinctly recent phenomena, significant changes have occurred. The diffusion of direct-investment sources has already been noted. The character of MNEs also has evolved. Before the Depression, the majority of American-based MNEs dealt with natural resources: *mining, agriculture, and petroleum.* The expansion since the war has been concentrated in *manufacturing.* Thus while in 1914 less than 20 percent of U.S. foreign direct investment was in manufacturing, over 40 percent is now. Likewise, about 40 percent of foreign direct investments in the United States involve manufacturing. Since the 1980s, furthermore, foreign direct investment in *services* has become increasingly prominent, just as services have acquired an increasing role in international trade. The share of services in the outward direct investment of both the United States and the United Kingdom, for example, increased from about one-quarter in the 1970s to over one-third in the 1980s. Services have also become more important in the inward direct-investment flows of LDCs, where highly specialized services tend to be scarce and expensive. Finally, direct investment tends to be most prominent in the more innovative and technologically sophisticated areas of the world economy. For example, multinational firms tend to do significantly more research and development (R&D) than do firms in general.

Industrial organization has also changed. Formerly, most MNEs were *vertically integrated:* the divisions of the firm form a succession of stages along which products pass for further processing. Such an organization is most likely for firms dealing with natural resources and has characterized the large oil companies for years. But now *horizontal integration,* where similar products are simultaneously produced in different countries, has become more important (for example, in Heinz and other food-processing firms).

TABLE 11.2   The Big Ten: Largest Multinational Corporations, Ranked by Assets, 1990

Name	Home	Industry	Assets ($ billion)	Sales ($ billion)	World employment	Foreign/ world assets	Foreign/ world sales	Foreign/ world employment
General Motors	United States	Motor vehicles	180.2	122.0	767,200	.29	.31	.33
Ford Motor	United States	Motor vehicles	173.7	97.7	370,383	.32	.48	.51
General Electric	United States	Diverse	153.9	57.7	298,000	.11	.14	.21
Royal Dutch/Shell	United Kingdom/Holland	Oil	106.4	106.5	137,000	.65	.44	.72
Exxon	United States	Oil	87.7	115.8	104,000	.59	.78	.63
IBM	United States	Computers	87.6	69.0	373,816	.52	.61	.45
Mitsubishi	Japan	Trading	73.8	129.3	32,417	.23	.35	?
Fiat	Italy	Motor vehicles	66.3	47.5	303,238	.29	.44	.22
Matsushita	Japan	Electronics	62.0	46.8	210,848	?	.45	.32
Mitsui	Japan	Trading	60.8	136.2	9,094	.25	.35	?

SOURCE: United Nations.

2. *CASE STUDY:* THE GIANTS

Four of the five largest corporations in the world produce either petroleum or motor vehicles, when ranked by dollar value of assets.

For perspective, these sales figures are sometimes compared to the gross national products of individual countries. In 1990 the GNP of the United Kingdom was $924 billion; of Switzerland, $219 billion; and of Greece, $60 billion. That of Uruguay, $8 billion, was less than the total sales of each of all but two of the fifty largest corporations! But these common comparisons are misleading because GNP is a measure of *value added* (output minus intermediate inputs), whereas total sales is not. Nevertheless, these corporations are gigantic.

Five of the six largest firms are based in the United States. Note that the three largest all have a larger share of employment than of assets located abroad, with the share of foreign sales somewhere in between. This suggests that these firms may be supplying foreign markets from foreign operations that are more labor intensive than their home operations. IBM, on the other hand, makes a larger fraction of its sales abroad than of either its assets or its employment, suggesting that exports from the United States are relatively more important for this firm.

3. WHY DO MULTINATIONAL ENTERPRISES EXIST?

The reason MNEs exist is not obvious because neither international trade nor international capital movements require that firms also be international. Some firms choose to go multinational, and some do not. Those that do generally possess some distinctive attributes that they wish to exploit: trademarks, patents, reputation, managerial ability, the knowledge of how to exploit markets for particular product groups, and so forth. Firms set up foreign operations in order to apply these firm-specific *ownership* advantages and capture their full value—that is, in order to earn worldwide monopoly rents on attributes that are shared with no other firm. If so, MNEs are imperfectly competitive by their very nature. This argument applies most naturally to horizontally integrated MNEs, but often it seems to apply in a reverse sense to vertically integrated firms as well. These firms frequently go multinational by integrating backward to obtain control of sources of raw materials. This is often done for defensive reasons to ensure that the firm will not be cut off from such supplies—that is, so that the raw materials do not become the unique attributes of competitors.

This ownership-advantage approach has casual support in that industries where such characteristics seem most natural have many MNEs, while firms in other industries, such as steel and textiles, rarely go multinational. Furthermore, empirical research in the last twenty years has conclusively shown that MNEs tend to be larger than other firms and tend to devote proportionally more resources to research and development. Both traits are consistent with this story. But such evidence cannot be conclusive: for example, are firms multinational because they are large, large because they are multinational, or both large and multinational because of some other reason?

If we do, in fact, accept the hypothesis that companies go multinational in order to earn monopoly rents on ownership advantages, we then face the question of why they do not earn these rents in some other way. Consider a firm that owns, say, a valuable patent and wishes to obtain the monopoly rent that the patent could earn in a certain foreign market. There are three basic ways of doing this.

1. The firm could produce the patented product at home and export it to the foreign market.
2. The firm could license a foreign firm to produce the patented product in the foreign market.
3. The firm could acquire a subsidiary in the foreign market to produce the patented product.

These methods are sometimes combined. For example, a foreign subsidiary is often set up to assemble parts manufactured in the home country; this is a combination of methods 1 and 3. Or the home firm might attempt to enter the foreign market by combining with firms from other countries; such a *joint venture* is essentially a combination of methods 2 and 3.

Any of these methods can capture the full monopoly rent of the patent. Method 2 does this directly by charging a monopoly fee for use of the patent, while the other methods do it indirectly by selling the patented product at a monopoly price. Why, then, should the firm go multinational—that is, choose method 3? Note that this is the same problem that arose in section 4 of Chapter 6, which discussed the possibility of exporting a patented product, method 1, to exploit a comparative advantage in R&D.

Sometimes *locational* considerations can narrow the choices. Perhaps method 1 is ruled out because production costs for the patented product are lower in the foreign market or because transportation costs, tariffs, or foreign tax breaks make foreign production more attractive. But these considerations give no basis for choosing between methods 2 and 3. Also, we have seen that direct investment is heaviest between the industrial countries, where cost conditions are relatively similar and trade barriers relatively low.

The choice between licensing and establishing a foreign subsidiary involves a choice of how much reliance to place on market transactions and the price system as opposed to administrative decisions within the firm. If the patent is licensed to a foreign producer, the technology is transferred between countries via a market at a market price (the licensing fee). But if, instead, a foreign subsidiary is acquired, the technology transfer is *internalized* within the firm, and no market mechanism is used. Market transactions and internal administration are both costly. The choice between these two methods will presumably hinge upon which costs less. Such an explanation of firm size was advanced many years ago by Ronald Coase.

To summarize, MNEs will tend to develop in industries with three characteristics. First, the firms in the industry must possess *unique ownership advantages* that can be exploited in different countries. *Locational characteristics* must be such that, second, efficient exploitation of these characteristics entails production of goods and services in a number of different countries. Finally, it must be *cheaper to internalize* the transfer of these attributes between countries than to do so through markets.

This story is great as far as it goes, but it does not go far enough. For one thing, we want a theory with concrete predictions of when direct investment will take place: For example, is it more likely between similar economies or between dissimilar economies? Such predictions allow us to test a theory by examining the facts. As discussed in Parts One and Two, this process has had a powerful effect on the development of trade theory. Again, we want a theory that tells us what all this means for welfare: Do host countries, source countries, both, or neither gain from direct investment? What should policy be? This is why we care about these questions in the first place. Having had a brief look at the giant multinationals in our world, we next examine specific theories of the multinational firm. We then confront these theories with the evidence.

Why Are There Universities?

The distinction between internal administration and market transactions is nicely illustrated by the university. Universities exist to conduct research and disseminate its results through teaching. But individual faculty members independently undertake research projects and design and teach courses. Thus there could, in principle, be much more extensive use of market transactions. For example, individual professors could set and charge tuition fees for their courses and issue individual "diplomas." A student would then acquire a college education by dealing directly with professors and earning a few dozen diplomas. Instead, all this is internalized within the university to which the student pays a lump-sum fee. What do you think are the "costs" of the decentralized system that results in there being universities instead? What advantages would the decentralized system have?

Problems

11.1 Give an example of a vertically integrated MNE in a natural-resource industry. Why is it "natural" for firms in such industries to integrate vertically? Can you explain this in terms of our general theory of why firms go multinational?

11.2 Suppose that you are an executive in a firm with a valuable patent to be exploited in a foreign market. You must choose whether to do so by setting up a foreign subsidiary or by licensing the patent to a foreign firm. What concrete factors would you consider?

11.3 Many years ago, IBM decided to close down its operations in India, rather than complying with a law requiring substantial local ownership. Can you think of any reasons why IBM would prefer doing no business at all to participating in a joint venture?

4. INTERNATIONAL TRADE THEORY AND THE MULTINATIONAL FIRM

The previous section described the circumstances under which direct investment is likely to take place. But we want to be able to answer more fundamental questions. Which types of countries are likely to undertake direct investment? To receive it? Are multinational firms good or bad for the world? Who gains and who loses? To come to grips with these questions, we employ the theory of international trade developed in Parts One and Two.

Recall that international trade can be due to comparative advantage, economies of scale, or imperfect competition. Start with comparative-advantage trade.

Comparative-Advantage Trade Theory

Comparative-advantage trade theory has nothing explicit to say about direct investment. With constant returns to scale and perfect competition, it does not matter how big firms are or who controls them: two separate firms have exactly the same production opportunities as would a single firm formed by combining them, and all firms always maximize profits. The firm's size and extent, including its possible extension across national borders, are indeterminate but also inconsequential. Thus the theory is consistent with direct investment but tells us nothing about it.

But direct investments are examples of international capital movements, which Chapter 10 introduced into the Heckscher-Ohlin-Samuelson model. If we treat the conclusions of that chapter as applicable to direct investment, the following appear as immediate normal implications of the theory.

Direct investment should be stimulated by differences in factor endowments.

Differences in factor endowments (and, from the factor-price equalization theorem, *large* differences if there is free trade in goods) generate the differences in factor rewards that induce international factor movements.

International trade and direct investment should be negatively correlated.

This is because commodity trade and factor movements should be substitutes, as discussed in Chapter 10.

These are important implications, but they need to be taken with a grain of salt. This is because, although direct investments are themselves international capital movements, they may be offset by other movements in the opposite direction, so that no net international movement of capital takes place. For example, if an American firm finances a direct investment in Europe by borrowing in Europe, our two implications do not apply. This qualification is important in practice.

In terms of the previous section, we have examined *locational* considerations (that is, international differences in factor prices) but have not introduced *ownership* or *internalization* considerations. Also, the comparative-advantage approach assumes away economies of scale and imperfect competition, both of which seem centrally relevant to real MNEs.

Economies of Scale and Imperfect Competition: Multinational Monopolistic Competition

Now consider economies of scale and imperfect competition. To be more concrete, suppose that these features are present in a manufacturing sector characterized by monopolistic competition, as discussed in Chapter 3. Recall that there are two countries and two goods, call them food and manufacturing, with food labor-intensive and manufacturing capital-intensive. The manufacturing sector in each country is composed of many firms producing differentiated products. Each firm employs capital together with labor to produce its unique variety, subject to increasing returns to scale. Consumers have a preference for variety that allows the existence of many manufacturing firms in equilibrium. Since each firm is the only producer of its particular variety of manufactured good, it can control its price, which it duly manipulates to obtain maximum profit. But the existence of significant profits attracts new firms, each producing its own new, unique variety, and this keeps profits low for all firms. Review Chapter 3 now if your memory is unclear.

Assume that all factors, including capital, are internationally immobile but that manufacturing firms can operate in either country. Interpret capital not as physical capital, but as the input to research that can be conducted at a distance from the workers that utilize it. That is, each firm can produce manufactures by combining its capital with labor located in any country. Research costs are spread over every unit the firm produces at every location; thus manufacturing production entails increasing returns to scale. These are *international* economies of scale *internal* to the firm. Research also is what enables the firm to produce a unique variety, and so is the source of the firm's *ownership advantage*.

Suppose that the two countries are identical and allow trade and direct investment. Direct investment takes place when a manufacturing firm with capital (and, therefore, research) in one country employs labor in the other country to produce some or all of its output.

If the two countries are identical, there is no basis for the interindustry trade of food for manufactures, and factor prices will be the same in both countries. This means there is no motive for direct investment: nothing can be gained by employing foreign labor instead of home labor if they both must be paid the same wage. International exchange will consist only of the *intraindustry* trade of manufacturing varieties produced by national firms in both countries.

Now let endowments differ slightly, with the home country relatively capital-abundant. Then it will export capital-intensive manufactures; with world manufacturing production more concentrated at home, there are fewer varieties to import. Thus *interindustry* trade displaces some intraindustry trade. Since modest endowment differences still cause trade to equalize factor prices across countries, direct investment does not take place: foreign labor must be paid the same as domestic labor, so there is no reason for a manufacturing firm in either country to employ workers in the other country.

Larger endowment differences would prevent trade from itself equalizing factor prices. Foreign wages would fall below home wages, and at least one country would specialize. The lower foreign wage would induce home manufacturers to hire foreign labor and become multinational firms. Foreign manufacturers remain national, if some foreign capital remains in the manufacturing sector. If home firms employ labor in both countries, wages must be equal; direct investment will have prevented factor-price disparities. But if the endowment difference is sufficiently pronounced, home manufacturers will employ only capital at home, and factor prices will diverge.

Direct investment is, in effect, a proxy for real international capital mobility.

Endowment differences stimulate direct investment, which cannot occur when trade alone would equalize factor prices.

The formation of multinationals is associated with a decline in intraindustry trade: trade and direct investment are negatively correlated.

Two-way direct investment can never take place.

The bottom line to all this is that, with economies of scale and imperfect competition, we still have the same two predictions that we teased out of comparative-advantage trade theory. In terms of the discussion of the previous section, we now have both *locational* considerations (factor-price differences) and *ownership* advantages (the ability of firms to produce unique varieties), but *internalization* considerations have not been introduced.

5. THE EVIDENCE

This section takes a look at actual patterns of direct investment. One objective is to see how useful the theory described in section 4 actually is in understanding this investment.

About half of all MNEs, and eleven of the largest fifteen, are based in the United States. Indeed, nearly half of all direct investment once came from the United States, as Table 11.3 shows. The table also shows that the capital-abundant part of the world is, in fact, the dominant source of direct investment. Between 1976 and 1992 the four countries listed modestly reduced their share of world investment from 73 percent to 60 percent; but more dramatic is the fall in U.S. direct investment relative to that of the other three countries, notably Japan. Transitional LDCs such as Brazil, Hong Kong, and Mexico are now acquiring significant direct investments, and the former communist countries have established foreign operations.

Table 11.4 shows where direct investments have been made. Two features stand out. Most direct investment is located in the relatively capital-abundant part of the world, so that direct investment flows have not, typically, been from capital-abundant to capital-scarce countries.

The largest part of world direct investment is that among the developed countries themselves, rather than between these countries and the less developed.

Second,

Direct investment is, by and large, heaviest between those areas that trade the most with each other (that is, between the DCs).

This is also apparent in the location of U.S. foreign direct investments: nearly one-quarter are in Canada, over one-third are in Western Europe, and Latin America is the most important LDC area. Thus trade and direct investments

TABLE 11.3 **Sources of Accumulated Stock of Direct Investment *($ billions)***

Source country	1976		1992	
United States	137	(48%)	474	(24%)
United Kingdom	32	(11%)	259	(13%)
Japan	19	(7%)	251	(13%)
Germany	20	(7%)	186	(10%)
World total	287	(100%)	1,949	(100%)

SOURCE: United Nations Economic and Social Council, United Nations Conference on Trade and Development.

TABLE 11.4   **Location of Accumulated Stock of Direct Investment, 1991**

Host region	Stock ($ billion)		
Developed countries	1,370	(80%)	
Western Europe			702
North America			544
Developing countries	339	(20%)	
Asia			174
Latin America/Caribbean			129
Total	1,709	(100%)	

SOURCE: United Nations Conference on Trade and Development.

are broadly *complementary.* This contrasts sharply with the analysis concluding that trade and factor movements are *substitutes.*

The ownership patterns are, however, becoming more diversified. Foreign MNEs have been growing faster than American so that the American share of world direct investment has declined. Foreign direct investment in the United States has also recently grown at a significantly faster pace than American direct investment abroad, although the latter is still larger than the former. In the 1960s and 1970s direct investment was dominated by U.S. investment abroad, as revealed in Table 11.3. But with the increased European investment in the United States and Japanese investment in the United States and in Europe, direct investment is now dominated by the *triad* of the United States, the European Economic Community, and Japan all investing in each other (though direct investment into Japan is still relatively modest).

Direct investment increasingly consists of two-way direct investment between DCs.

On balance, however, the DCs are heavy creditors of the LDCs in direct investment.

Direct investment by the DCs in the LDCs is many times greater than direct investment in the opposite direction.

Table 11.5 looks at direct investment in a different way, showing the *flows* of direct investment that constituted additions to existing stocks and that took place each year, on average, from 1987 to 1991. (New direct investment surged in the late 1980s, slowed abruptly in the early 1990s, and then recovered again.)

Compare Table 11.5 with Table 1.4. The dominant entry in each table refers to exchanges of the DCs *with each other.* Recall from Chapter 1 that the largest part of world trade has become the exchange of similar goods between similar countries, whereas comparative advantage appears to emphasize the

TABLE 11.5 **Patterns of International Direct Investment, 1987–1991**
(average annual flows in $ billions)

Flows to	Flows from		Total
	DCs	LDCs	Total
DCs	$148 (80%)	4 (2%)	152 (82%)
LDCs	32 (17%)	2 (1%)	34 (18%)
Total	180 (97%)	6 (3%)	186 (100%)

SOURCE: Estimated from data from United Nations Conference on Trade and Development, *Programme on Transnational Corporations.*

trade of dissimilar goods between dissimilar countries. This situation directed attention to "newer" trade theories emphasizing economies of scale and imperfect competition. The same sort of situation has arisen (with a lag of 10 to 15 years) with respect to direct investment. The largest part of world direct investment is two-way direct investment between similar (industrial) countries. (Indeed, this dominance is even more pronounced than is its analog for international trade.) In contrast, existing theories emphasize one-way direct investment between dissimilar countries. Interestingly, this is true even when direct investment has been added to the "new" trade theories explicitly developed in response to the analogous situation in international trade!

These broad suggestions from the data have also been demonstrated in a more formal way in a statistical analysis by S. Lael Brainard of MIT. Brainard used data on sales by foreign affiliates as measures of multinational activity and found that such activity was not explained by differences in relative factor endowments. Indeed, she found that *similarities* in factor endowments promoted intraindustry affiliate sales.

6.* *EXPLORING FURTHER:* NEW-NEW THEORIES OF THE MULTINATIONAL FIRM

The desire to reconcile theory and fact draws attention to three specific topics involving multinational firms.

Internalization

The theory discussed in section 4 dealt with *ownership* and *locational* considerations but assumed *internalization.* That is, we supposed that, if a home firm had a distinct product—designer beazelbulbs, say—that was profitable to produce in a foreign country, the firm itself would produce beazelbulbs abroad instead of subcontracting some foreign firm to produce them or licensing or selling to some foreign firm the right and the know-how to produce and market beazelbulbs. In fact, each of these methods is often used, and we wish to discover what determines which will be chosen. That is, when will the firm go multinational by internalizing the foreign production (by establishing or investing in a foreign affiliate), and when will it remain national by arranging for foreign production at arm's length from itself (by subcontracting or licensing or selling its ownership advantage)? There are many facets to this internalization question, but we can say something about two of them that are important.

1. *Expropriation and Defection.* Suppose that our firm goes multinational, establishing—or investing in—an affiliate in the foreign country to produce and market beazelbulbs. A major concern of the firm will be the fear that, once it has invested in the affiliate and given to it the means of producing and marketing beazelbulbs, it will be deprived of that affiliate, who will become a competitor rather than an ally. For example, the host-country government might simply *expropriate* the affiliate. This possibility is a real threat to multinational firms, especially with regard to investments in less developed countries. Even if the affiliate is not expropriated, there is always the danger that its key employees, once they learn the secrets of beazelbulbs, will defect and produce and market them on their own.

The potential multinational firm can take some steps to help prevent such a catastrophe. For example, it might withhold key technology or equipment from its foreign affiliate to lower the chances that the latter could be a viable operation on its own. Another deterrent to defection or expropriation is the threat that a defecting affiliate would face fierce competition in world markets from its former parent. This threat would not mean much if the affiliate enjoyed much lower production costs than the parent—perhaps the (locational) reason for setting up the affiliate in the first place. But if production costs do not differ much between parent and affiliate, the threat would be a potent one.

The more similar the home and foreign countries, the smaller the differences in production costs between the parent and its affiliate. For example, if the two countries' relative factor endowments are sufficiently similar, the parent and affiliate will face identical factor prices. In this case the parent's ability to punish a defecting affiliate with fierce competition would be the strongest, so the former would be most likely to establish an affiliate, confident that the threat of strong punishment would suffice to prevent expropriation or defection. If relative endowment differences between the countries become larger, the parent's ability to compete diminishes, the chances of expropriation or defection accordingly increase, and the parent will become reluctant to establish an affiliate in the first place. The bottom line is that the formation of multinational firms is promoted by *similarities* between countries in factor endowments and is retarded by dissimilarities.

2. *Incomplete Contracts.* Suppose that our firm has decided to do the design work and early production stages of beazelbulb manufacture in its home country but that, due to locational considerations, the final production stages would be performed abroad. The firm must decide whether to establish (or to invest in) a foreign affiliate to do the final production (that is, to become

itself a multinational firm) or to establish some arm's-length arrangement with an independent foreign firm to do the production for it. In the latter case, the home and foreign firms would negotiate a contract calling for the home firm to deliver, on certain dates, certain quantities of unfinished beazelbulbs of specified quality, calling for the foreign firm to complete the manufacturing process in certain ways, to make specified payments to the home firm, and perhaps calling for other actions as well.

Negotiating such a contract with a foreign firm is simpler than establishing and operating a foreign affiliate. But it has its drawbacks. The most important drawback is the fact that the future is inherently uncertain, and no contract, no matter how long and detailed, can account for every conceivable (or inconceivable) event that might occur. If something unforeseen should happen, a multinational firm can respond by giving its foreign subsidiary new instructions, but a national firm bound by a negotiated contract with a foreign firm will still be responsible for fulfilling that contract even if, with hindsight, it now seems highly disadvantageous.

If this sort of possibility does not matter much, the firm may as well go ahead and negotiate a contract, sparing itself the trouble of establishing and operating an affiliate in a foreign land. But if the possibility appears important, it would be better for the firm to become multinational. When will such a possibility seem likely to matter? It will matter most in those industries that, first, are most subject to unforeseen events, and in which, second, unforeseen events are likely to involve large consequences for what the firm wants to do.

Standardized industries, where familiar products are produced in well-understood ways, are the least subject to surprising developments, whereas *innovative* industries, in which there is a lot of R&D involved in developing new products and new production methods, are the most subject. In fact, firms that do a lot of R&D are more likely to be multinational than those that produce standardized goods.

Other things being equal, unforeseen events are less likely to involve large consequences for the firm the more *dissimilar* the home and foreign economies are to each other. Suppose, for example, that our firm is designing a new beazelbulb that it intends to produce in three stages. The first stage, involving a lot of engineering work, will be done at home, and the second and third stages, using less skilled labor, will be done abroad. The firm, therefore, arranges for production facilities abroad—by negotiating a contract with a foreign firm, let us say. Now suppose that the design work turns up some unexpected advantages to having the second stage performed in proximity to the first stage. If the home and foreign countries are quite different, with unskilled labor much cheaper and engineers much scarcer than at home, the cost advantage to having the second stage produced abroad will be the dominant consideration, and the firm will not wish to have the work done at home, despite the new-found advantages to proximity. Thus in this case a contract requiring the firm to have the second stage done abroad would not be a hindrance. But if the two countries were more alike so that having the second stage done abroad would confer only modest cost savings, the firm might value the advantages of proximity more highly and wish to do the second stage at home instead. In this case the contract would be a hindrance, and the firm would have been better off retaining control by establishing an affiliate abroad.

If two countries differ a lot—say, in their factor endowments and factor prices—this difference will pretty much determine how a firm should divide its operations between the two countries, and this division is unlikely to be influenced by subsequent surprises (even if the firm's profits are influenced). In this case the firm might as well employ the simpler strategy of negotiating a contract with an independent foreign firm. But if the countries do not differ much, subsequent surprises are much more likely to determine how the firm wants to allocate activities between the two countries. In this case the firm will establish a foreign affiliate so that it can retain more subsequent control.

The two aspects of internalization that we have considered—the threat of expropriation or defection and the fact that contracts cannot cover all contingencies—both lead to the same conclusion. As far as internalization is concerned, direct investment is more likely between countries with similar endowments than between countries with different endowments. Thus internalization considerations might account for actual patterns of direct investment, if they are sufficiently important relative to ownership and locational considerations.

Transfer Costs to Trade

The international trade of commodities involves certain distinct costs: transportation costs (sometimes related to geographic distance), tariffs and other trade taxes, and administrative expenses involved in shipping goods across national borders. These *transfer costs* are important in reality: there is considerable evidence that countries trade the most with those countries from which they are separated by the least "economic distance," with the latter formulated to relate to some or all components of transfer costs.

If high transfer costs make it expensive for a firm to supply a foreign market by exporting, the firm might seek to avoid these costs by establishing a foreign affiliate to produce its goods in the foreign market. Thus transfer costs might induce direct investment. Note that this is a specific example of locational considerations.

To see how this might work, recall the discussion of multinational monopolistic competition in section 4 of this chapter. There are two countries and two goods, food and manufacturing, with food labor-intensive and manufacturing capital-intensive. The manufacturing sector in each country is composed of many firms producing differentiated products. Each firm employs capital at home together with labor in either country to produce its unique variety, subject to increasing returns to scale. All factors, including capital, are internationally immobile, but manufacturing firms can operate in either country. Consumers have a preference for variety that allows the existence of many manufacturing firms in equilibrium. Each firm can control its price, which it manipulates for maximum profit. Significant profits attract new firms, each producing its own new, unique variety, and this keeps profits low for all firms. If the home and foreign countries have sufficiently similar endowments, trade in goods will equalize factor prices so that manufacturing firms in one country have no incentive to become multinational by employing labor in the other country. If factor endowments differ sufficiently, trade will not equalize factor prices so that manufacturing firms in the high-wage country will become multinational, employing labor in the low-wage country. Thus direct investment occurs only between countries whose endowments differ sufficiently so that trade cannot equalize factor prices, and two-way direct investment never occurs.

Now introduce transfer costs to trade in manufactures. Manufacturing firms in the high-wage country still have an incentive to go multinational in order to utilize cheaper foreign labor. But now firms will establish foreign operations even if wages are equal in the two countries in order to avoid the transfer costs. Furthermore, manufacturing firms in the low-wage country will also have an incentive to go multinational, provided that the difference in wage rates in the two countries is sufficiently small relative to the transfer costs. Thus adding transfer costs to the model of multinational monopolistic competition introduces the possibilities of direct investment between similar economies and of two-way direct investment.

Transfer costs are important in practice, and taking them into account makes the model perform more like the real world. But there are still reasons to doubt whether transfer costs are in fact an important cause of direct investment. One problem is that while transfer costs are important in reality, so are the costs of establishing and managing from a distance a foreign operation. These "multinationalization" costs are likely to depend in part on the same sort of "economic distance" as do transfer costs (although some, such as the fixed cost of opening another plant, do not). The two types of costs will tend to cancel each other out so that transfer costs could induce direct investment only in industries where they are large relative to multinationalization costs.

Another problem is that direct investment induced by transfer costs is a *substitute* for trade in goods. While there are cases where this is true (Japanese automobile plants in the United States were, to at least some extent, a response to actual and feared trade barriers), trade and direct investment seem on the whole to go together. S. Lael Brainard, in the study referred to in the previous section, found that intraindustry affiliate sales and intraindustry trade are positively correlated, indicating that the two are complements rather than substitutes.

Services

Services are accounting for an increasing share of output in industrial economies and for an increasing share of international trade. And, as we have seen, direct investment has in recent years increasingly involved the service sector. This direct investment has tended to come from firms doing a lot of R&D and supplying sophisticated services. Supplying services to foreign markets often requires direct investment: you cannot service your foreign customer from a distance—you need to go where the customer is.

Sometimes trade in goods and trade in services go together. If you are selling a customer a sophisticated beazelbulb, say, you may have to customize it—preferably on the spot—to the purchaser's requirements, train her employees how to use the beazelbulb, and be available for maintenance and modifications as needed. Thus the desire to export beazelbulbs would lead you to go multinational in order to be able to supply foreign customers with the services they demand. Thus trade in services complements trade in goods, and since exporting services requires direct investment, direct investment *complements* trade in goods.

To see how this might work, return once again to our model of multinational monopolistic competition. Ignore transfer costs and multinationalization costs. But now the producer of each differentiated manufacture must employ labor, located in the same country as his customers, in order to provide services to the buyers of his product. So each exporter of manufactured goods must become a multinational firm. Thus direct investment will be large when trade in manufactures is large. And if the home and foreign countries become more similar so that they conduct a lot of intraindustry trade in manufactures, they will also experience two-way direct investment.

To sum up, if direct investment is introduced into the basic models of international trade—those based on economies of scale and on imperfect competition as well as those based on comparative advantage—direct investment appears most likely between countries that differ most in factor endowments, and two-way direct investment appears most unlikely. These implications of the theory are dramatically at odds with reality. But implications consistent with the facts can emerge if account is taken of some or all of three additional considerations, each of practical relevance in itself: internalization issues, transfer costs, services.

7. PUBLIC POLICY TOWARD THE MULTINATIONAL ENTERPRISE

This section deals with how the governments of source and host countries view MNEs and the policies they employ.

The MNE and National Sovereignty

Perhaps the most serious issues involving MNEs stem from the fact that they constitute a degree of integration of business enterprise not matched by political integration. This generates three sorts of problems involving political-economic interaction.

1. An MNE spans several countries, which might each wish to influence the firm's behavior in contradictory ways. With the source country pressuring the parent in one direction and the host country pressuring the subsidiary in another, the firm is caught in the middle. For example, on several occasions American pressure through the parents has prevented French subsidiaries of American firms from selling advanced products and technology to the French government and French firms. Again, the U.S. government sometimes succeeded in preventing foreign subsidiaries of American MNEs from trading with communist nations even though the host countries wished to encourage such trade. A dramatic example of this occurred in 1982 with regard to disagreements between the United States and some European countries over policy regarding the construction of a natural-gas pipeline by the Soviet Union. These examples involve the source country influencing the subsidiary via the parent. Sometimes, though less often, the host country attempts to influence the parent via the subsidiary, as some Arab governments have tried to do to limit trade with Israel.

2. MNEs can also influence governments in both host and source countries. Thus the firm might try to shape relations between the two. For example, in the early 1970s, the International Telephone and Telegraph Company, whose Chilean subsidiaries were having trouble with the government of leftist President Allende, tried to induce the U.S. government to pursue a strong anti-Allende policy.

3. To the extent that MNEs can shift operations between subsidiaries in different countries, national governments lose influence over firms within their borders. Both direct controls and "moral suasion" become less compelling when the firm to which they apply can simply pack up and leave.

In summary, the commercial integration represented by MNEs has outstripped political integration and thereby eroded national sovereignty and furnished new channels for a government of one country to influence events in another: a recipe for political conflict. In principle, these effects are symmetrical between source and host countries; in practice, the latter seem to lose the most sovereignty. Thus this question of the erosion of national sovereignty is a much more serious issue in host countries.

Source-Country Issues

Two issues figure prominently in discussions within source countries.

1. *Taxation.* Two provisions of current tax laws have caused intense debate in the United States. American MNEs must pay corporate income taxes on their global profits, but they may deduct from their U.S. taxes any taxes paid to foreign governments. The reason for this is to avoid double taxation of foreign subsidiaries, and it is done in such a way as to give the host country first crack at taxing them. This is common international practice, but it works to the disadvantage of source countries. The parent MNE cares only about after-tax earnings, but to the source country as a whole tax revenues also mat-

Transfer Prices

This is an especially prominent example of how MNEs can cause trouble for national policy. *Transfer prices* are those that the various divisions of an MNE charge each other; for instance, the price that Ford pays to its Italian subsidiary for cylinder heads imported into America by the parent to use in Escorts produced in New Jersey. From a global viewpoint, transfer prices are simply what the MNE charges itself. The firm has an incentive to set these prices artificially to minimize its global tax bill. For example, if corporate profits are taxed less in Italy than in America, Ford can lower its total tax bill by increasing the transfer price of the cylinder heads, thereby reducing the profits of the parent and increasing those of the Italian subsidiary in equal amounts. Such behavior can potentially undermine the ability of governments to fashion their own tax systems. Governments, therefore, frown on the use of artificial transfer prices, so it would be risky for Ford to charge itself a price dramatically different from what it charges outside customers for the cylinder heads. But what if there are no outside customers, or what if the transfer price is, say, a licensing fee for a patent whose true "value" we can only guess about? After all, the theory in section 3 suggested that an important reason MNEs exist in the first place is to internalize transactions not easily priced. But there is an incentive for firms to refrain from deliberately setting false transfer prices: the need for efficient global management. Using "wrong" prices can cause managers to make "wrong" decisions, and artificially shifting profits around makes it very difficult to judge executive performance. One way out of this is to keep two sets of books: one for the tax authorities and one for management.

---

ter. Thus the effect of this provision is to redistribute part of MNE gross earnings from source to host countries. In 1977 foreign tax credits of $26 billion reduced total U.S. corporate taxes by almost one-third. The provision also invites abuse. Some Arab countries have called the payments that they exact from oil companies "taxes," rather than royalty fees for drilling or sale prices for oil. As taxes, the total payments can be deducted from the companies' U.S. tax liabilities; as fees or prices they could only be used to reduce taxable earnings. In 1977 oil companies claimed about 70 percent of the $26 billion in foreign tax credits. IRS regulations were tightened in 1980 in an attempt to end this behavior.

A second controversial provision is that U.S. taxes on the profits of foreign subsidiaries need not be paid until those profits are actually repatriated to the United States. Thus by reinvesting the earnings in the subsidiary, the MNE can defer taxation and in effect put the taxes to work for itself; continual reinvestment allows indefinite deferral. In 1979 total U.S. earnings on foreign direct investment were almost $38 billion, of which over $18 billion was

MNE Taxation Example

Suppose a home-based MNE is considering an investment of $5 million, which it can make either at home or abroad. The investment would be equally productive in each place, yielding a pre-tax annual return of $1 million. The home tax rate is 50 percent, and the foreign rate is 25 percent. The U.S. tax liability on the firm's earnings will be $500,000. If the MNE invests abroad, it will incur a foreign tax of $250,000. But this can be deducted from its U.S. taxes so that after-tax earnings will be $500,000 regardless of where the investment is made. The absence of double taxation is globally efficient: the MNE perceives the alternatives as equivalent, and they are equally productive ($1 million) to the world as a whole. But they are not equally advantageous to the home economy because total domestic earnings (domestic tax revenues plus MNE after-tax earnings) would be $1 million if the investment is made at home and only $750,000 if it is made abroad. Now suppose that the MNE plans to reinvest all earnings indefinitely wherever the investment is made. In this case, U.S. taxes can be deferred indefinitely if the investment is abroad. This does not alter total home-country earnings of the two alternatives, but the MNE's after-tax earnings of the foreign alternative rise to $750,000. Thus the MNE perceives the foreign investment as superior even though it remains equivalent to the domestic alternative from a global point of view and inferior from a domestic point of view.

Comparison of Home and Foreign Investments

	Abroad	*At home*
Pre-tax earnings	$1,000,000	$1,000,000
Foreign tax liability	$250,000	—
Home tax liability	$250,000	$500,000
After-tax earnings of MNE	$500,000	$500,000
Total home-country earnings	$750,000	$1,000,000
After-tax earnings of the MNE if not repatriated	$750,000	$500,000

reinvested abroad by corporations. Of course, since the subsidiaries cannot defer host-country taxes unless specifically allowed to, this provision makes no difference if the host-country tax rate is at least as high as the U.S. tax rate: there would be no U.S. tax liability in any case. But when the host-country rate is lower, this regulation increases the return to foreign investment relative to home investment and gives the MNE an incentive to reinvest its foreign earnings abroad.

2. *Labor.* Organized labor in the United States generally opposes foreign direct investment by American firms and has supported proposals to

limit it, such as repeal of the above tax provisions. Labor's argument is that American jobs are "exported" when MNEs set up foreign subsidiaries instead of expanding at home. Defenders of MNEs retort that direct investment generates more American jobs than it eliminates, in part because the alternative to foreign subsidiaries, which themselves import from America, is a loss of markets to foreign firms. Who is right?

Note, first, that the total number of jobs available in America depends primarily on macroeconomic conditions and policies rather than on the allocation of capital. But there are still two senses in which labor may have a case. Chapter 10 showed that an outward movement of capital could redistribute domestic income from labor to capital. The country as a whole would gain (except possibly if the capital flow is in response to artificial distortions such as the tax laws), although this need not be much consolation to labor. But recall that direct investment need not coincide with real capital movements, and, as MNE defenders point out, foreign direct investment does seem, on the whole, to be complementary to domestic exports. Second, organized labor's bargaining position is weakened when a corporation can threaten to shift operations abroad. Unions could in principle go multinational themselves and bargain on a global scale. But this has not happened, although there has been some increase in international labor communication. One potential problem is that a multinational union would absorb within itself the inherent conflicts of interest between its national branches. (The Canadian part of the United Automobile Workers split off from its U.S. parent even as the automobile industry itself was becoming more integrated.) An MNE, concerned itself only with global profits, might still be able to play one branch off against another. In any event, MNEs have in the past refused to bargain with international labor federations.

Host-Country Issues

Host countries have displayed ambivalent attitudes toward direct investment. Sometimes they entice MNEs with tax breaks and other inducements; at other times they subject these firms to hostile propaganda, severe restrictions, and even outright nationalization of subsidiaries. This ambivalence reflects the fact that these countries perceive both benefits and costs. On the plus side, MNEs are seen as sources of outside capital, advanced technology, modern business methods, and jobs—the latter the flip side to American labor's attitude. How important are these advantages? In general, they can be realized without the MNE, as we saw in the preceding section: capital movements need not take the form of direct investment, new technology can be embodied in imports or licensed directly, and even managerial ability can be hired. But the MNE may help. Tax laws may cause capital to flow more readily through the firm, and firm-specific attributes such as patents may be transferred exclusively, or at least more cheaply, within the MNE. LDCs in particular often find direct access to capital and technology difficult to come by.

Host-country complaints are that MNEs are too restrained in conferring these benefits, that they lead to a loss of national sovereignty as discussed above, and that they exploit the host country. Let us look at these in detail.

1. *Exploitation.* Host countries often charge that the subsidiaries of MNEs earn excessive profits, and these subsidiaries are, indeed, frequently more profitable than their parents. If the profits reflect high seller concentration within the host country, then the problem is to reduce this concentration, whether it is in domestic or foreign hands, and *not* simply to transfer it from the latter to the former by restricting direct investment. If, on the other hand, the MNE is exacting a monopoly price for a unique attribute that it is bringing to the host country, then the latter can obtain for itself some of this monopoly rent by bargaining with the MNE over terms of entry. LDCs often charge that oil and mineral extraction operations are much too profitable to MNEs. Exploration rights naturally fetch a modest price when no one knows what, if anything, will be found; charges of exploitation are sometimes the result of looking only at the high returns to those projects that pay off while ignoring the counterbalancing losses from those that fail. Other times the charge is that a corrupt (previous) regime, for personal gain, disposed of the nation's birthright at too low a price. This involves the MNE in domestic politics.

2. *Inadequate Transfer of Capital and Technology.* The complaints here are that MNEs do not bring enough new capital into host countries and that they tend to make the host country technologically dependent upon the firm. It is true that MNEs raise much capital locally and that they typically concentrate R&D in the source country. But the basic problem is not so much that MNEs retard these transfers as that host countries want more. Another charge is that technology is often not transferred in an efficient way, that techniques are not sufficiently adapted to distinctly local conditions or are made unnecessarily obscure (so that the MNE would continue to be indispensable). The evidence is mixed on such charges.

Host-Country Policies toward Direct Investment

The combination of a generally hostile attitude toward MNEs and a consciousness of the benefits they can bring ensures ambivalent and variable host-country policies. LDC attitudes vary greatly from country to country and from regime to regime, although foreign direct investment is almost always restricted in some ways. Some countries, such as Mexico, have prohibited foreign majority control. The industrial nations have generally been more liberal, but all restrict direct investment in some way. Except for the United States and Germany, all have applied formal screening procedures to new investments, with the screening ranging from pro forma in Italy's case to stringent in Japan's.

Attitudes can change dramatically over time. During the 1960s and 1970s many governments seemed most sensitive to the dangers that multinational firms may pose, and by the early 1970s about fifty foreign affiliates were being expropriated per year by host governments. But since the late 1970s governments have become much more concerned with the benefits multinational firms may confer, and expropriations have become rare.

8. *CASE STUDY:* CANADIAN POLICY TOWARD FOREIGN DIRECT INVESTMENT

Canadian policy is of special interest because of the dominant position of foreign direct investment in Canada's industry and because more U.S. direct investment has been directed to Canada than to any other single country.

Like the United States, Canada was a heavy borrower in the nineteenth century. Britain was the primary source: by 1900 Britain held about 85 percent of outstanding Canadian international debt. Most of the rest was held by the United States, which, though still a net debtor overall, had begun to acquire substantial foreign assets.

Relative to GNP and also in per capita terms, foreign investments in Canada peaked during 1900–1914, when prairie settlement generated a boom and a large demand for capital, about a third of which was satisfied from abroad. Since 1914 Britain's importance has declined and that of the United States has increased, with the latter overtaking the former in the 1920s as the largest creditor. Today the United States accounts for more than 80 percent of outstanding foreign investment in Canada, with the rest about evenly divided between the United Kingdom, on the one hand, and all other countries, on the other.

Significant direct investment in Canada goes back to Confederation in 1867, but portfolio investment was the overwhelmingly dominant form before the First World War. After the war, the relative importance of direct investment rose, and in the 1950s the total stock of outstanding foreign direct investment in Canada overtook that of portfolio investment.

As the economy grew and became more capital abundant, Canada relied less and less upon foreign investment for new capital and even began to acquire substantial foreign investments of its own. But, unlike the United States, Canada did not cease to be a net borrower. In recent years Canadian direct investments in the United States have increased, making Canada the third-largest foreign direct investor in that country. Indeed, Canadian per capita holdings in the United States exceed U.S. per capita holdings in Canada, but in view of the size disparity, Canada is a heavy net debtor vis-à-vis its southern neighbor. Canada, like the United States, is actually *acquiring* direct investments in the rest of the world, essentially financing the purchases by selling other assets. Since 1975 new Canadian direct investments abroad have exceeded new foreign direct investments in Canada (however, Canadian figures ignore reinvested earnings). But the country's situation differs from that of the United States in two ways: in terms of total *stocks* of outstanding direct investment Canada remains a debtor, and the recent increase in net new direct investment abroad is in part a response to Canadian public policy.

Canada displays the host-country ambivalence toward direct investment that we discussed in the preceding section. The country has encouraged capital inflows, including direct investment, to spur development. The National Policy Tariff of 1879, for example, induced direct investment in Canada by foreign firms who could no longer export competitively to the Canadian market in the face of higher protection. Also protection tended to raise the reward of relatively scarce Canadian capital and so attract foreign investment. But during the 1920s Canadians began to have substantial doubts about direct investment as the country became aware of the prominence foreign firms were acquiring in Canadian industry. These doubts grew with the rapid expansion of foreign investment in Canada following the Second World War. The Gordon Report of 1958 and the Gray Report of 1972 emphasized the costs of such a situation, and restrictive policy measures followed. At the same time, some foreign investments were still encouraged. Almost three-fifths of Canadian industry is foreign-controlled (over 80 percent of foreign direct investment in Canada is from the United States).

In the 1970s Canada adopted major policy measures to limit foreign investment. The Foreign Investment Review Act of 1973 required all new foreign direct investments in Canadian industry to be reviewed to obtain government approval. The review agency in fact approved most applications, but it tended to become more exacting over time. The Canada Development Corporation invested in important sectors of the economy thought likely otherwise to attract foreign capital. Also, the National Energy Program, announced in October 1980, had as one of its goals the "Canadianization" (at least 50 percent Canadian ownership) of the oil and natural-gas industry. Direct investment is also limited by a number of minor measures, such as laws that do not allow Canadian companies tax deductions for advertising in Canadian editions of foreign-owned publications or in foreign television stations with a Canadian audience. These measures caused resentment in the United States.

In the 1980s Canada reversed its policy. Review of foreign investment was ended, and such investment was once again welcomed. These changes have been embodied in the free-trade pact negotiated between Canada and the United States in 1987 and in the subsequent NAFTA. Thus can attitudes change.

Problem

11.4 In view of the discussion in this chapter, what do you think are the pros and cons of foreign direct investment for a country such as Canada? Should Canada discourage such investment or welcome it?

9. SUMMARY

1. MNEs exist when (1) there are firm-specific attributes that can earn monopoly rents in a number of countries; (2) locational considerations indicate costs can be lowered by producing in different countries; and (3) the internalization of some international transactions within firms is cheaper than the use of markets.

2. Although the DCs have made large direct investments in the LDCs, the dominant component of world direct investment is two-way direct investment among the industrial countries composing the triad of the United States, the EU, and Japan.

3. Actual patterns of direct investment might be explained by the relative importance of internalization considerations, transfer costs to trade, services.

4. Host countries have long had ambivalent attitudes toward foreign direct investment, hoping to receive capital and technology from multinational firms but fearing exploitation by them. In recent years many countries have begun extending a warmer welcome than they previously had.

SUGGESTED READING

Barnet, R. J., and R. E. Muller. *Global Reach: The Power of the Multinational Corporations.* New York: Simon & Schuster, 1974. A detailed but popular critical discussion.

Behrman, J. N. *National Interests and the Multinational Enterprise.* Englewood Cliffs, N.J.: Prentice Hall, 1970. The sovereignty problem.

Brainard, S. Lael. "An Empirical Assessment of the Factor Proportions Explanation of Multinational Sales." Sloan School of Management, Massachusetts Institute of Technology, Working Paper #3624-93-EFA, Nov. 1993. International differences in factor endowments do not explain multinational activity.

Caves, R. E. "International Corporations: The Industrial Economics of Foreign Investment." *Economica* (Feb. 1971). Imperfect competition and the MNE.

Christelow, D. B. "National Policies toward Foreign Direct Investment." Federal Reserve Bank of New York, *Quarterly Review* (Winter 1979–80). A survey of such policies.

Coase, R. H. "The Nature of the Firm." In *Readings in Price Theory.* Edited by G. J. Stigler and K. E. Boulding. Homewood, Ill.: Irwin, 1952. Coase's theory of the firm, cited in the text.

Crichton, M. *The Rising Sun.* New York: Knopf, 1992. Ignore the half-baked economics; enjoy the story and observe it as an example of anti-Japanese paranoia.

Ethier, W. J. "The Multinational Firm," *Quarterly Journal of Economics* 101 (Nov. 1986): 805–833. [Reprinted in *Imperfect Competition and International Trade, 1992.* Edited by G. Grossman. Cambridge: The MIT Press.] Internalization and the theory of the multinational firm.

Foreign Direct Investment in Canada. Ottawa: Government of Canada, 1972. A policy-aimed discussion: the Gray Report.

Helpman, E., and P. R. Krugman. *Market Structure and Foreign Trade.* Cambridge: The MIT Press, 1985. See Chapters 12 and 13 for theories of the multinational firm based on ownership and locational considerations.

Hood, N., and S. Young. *The Economics of Multinational Enterprise.* London: Longman, 1979. An extensive survey of the earlier literature.

Servan-Schreiber, J. J. *The American Challenge.* New York: Atheneum, 1968. An influential European polemic.

Part Four

Monetary Mechanics

National sovereignty gives international economics much of its distinctive character. A notable example is the fact that different countries have different monetary systems, with international transactions complicated accordingly. When you travel across the United States, you see prices quoted in the same dollars that you carry in your wallet, that you make other payments with, and in which your paycheck is denominated. But when you visit Germany, you find prices quoted in marks and face the problem of making sense of, say, a price of DM 50 for a haircut. At the same time, a German brewery exporting beer to the United States is concerned with how many marks it will get for the $100,000 it is being paid for the beer—a consideration absent from German sales. Questions like these are answered by the *exchange rate:* the price of one country's money in terms of that of another. For example, if the U.S.-German exchange rate is DM 2 per dollar, that haircut will set you back $25, and the brewery will receive DM 200,000 for its beer.

Now if we could be sure that the exchange rate would always be DM 2 per dollar, the difference in monies would be no more than a nuisance, just as the fact that in the United States length is measured in feet and inches whereas Europeans use meters and centimeters. But exchange rates are neither units of measurement nor laws of nature. They are prices and as such are subject to change. The table shows how much of various currencies could be purchased for 1 U.S. dollar at the end of certain time periods. For example, at the end of 1985, 1 U.S. dollar would have bought 200.5 Japanese yen (1 yen would have bought .005 [= 1 ÷ 200.5] dollars); at the end of 1980, the French-German exchange rate was 2.305 (= 4.516 ÷ 1.959) francs per mark. The two bottom currencies illustrate the great diversity of behavior: while the Liberian-U.S. exchange rate remained fixed at unity, the Argentine-U.S. rate changed enormously.

Exchange rates are facts of life to international travelers and business-people. *Balance of payments* surpluses and deficits, by contrast, do not touch most people directly, although they do sometimes grab headlines.

What determines exchange rates and payments imbalances? What difference does it make what happens to either? What is the balance of payments anyway? This is the first set of questions addressed by international monetary theory. A second set asks: How does macroeconomic policy work in an open economy? What is the relation between internal economic objectives and external ones? Between macroeconomic policy in one country and performance in another?

But before we can tackle questions like these, we need to understand exactly what it is that we are dealing with here. Part Four is devoted to this preliminary task. Chapter 12 explains what the balance of payments is, and Chapter 13 describes the international financial markets in which exchange rates are determined. With these necessary *monetary mechanics* out of the way, Parts Five and Six will then give answers to our two sets of questions.

Selected Exchange Rates *(national currency per U.S. dollar, end of period)*

Currency	1970	1975	1980	1985	1993
U.S. dollar	1.0000	1.0000	1.0000	1.0000	1.0000
Canadian dollar	1.0112	1.0164	1.1947	1.3975	1.3240
Japanese yen	357.6500	305.1500	203.0000	200.5000	111.8500
French franc	5.5200	4.4855	4.5160	7.5610	5.8950
Deutsche mark	3.6480	2.6223	1.9590	2.4613	1.7263
Pound sterling	0.4178	0.4942	0.4193	0.6923	0.6751
Argentine peso*	4.0000	60.9000	1,992.5000	11,757,344.0000	144,725,023,600.0000
Liberian dollar	1.0000	1.0000	1.0000	1.0000	1.0000

*There were monetary changes in Argentina over this period; the table is in terms of old pesos.
SOURCE: International Monetary Fund, *International Financial Statistics*.

CHAPTER 12

The Balance of Payments

Well, I don't give a [expletive deleted] about the lira.
—RICHARD M. NIXON

This chapter concerns balance-of-payments accounting procedures. The purpose is to make the basic statistics in the rest of this book understandable.

1. THE NATIONAL BUDGET IDENTITY

The budget identity (or *Walras's Law*) is a basic economic concept applying to any individual or group of individuals, whether a person, a family, or a nation: the act of buying something is by definition an act of selling something of equal value in return.

Well, then, what is it that we as a nation are buying? First of all are all the *goods and services* that we are importing from the rest of the world; call the total of these M, and measure it in terms of our currency. Next come the *assets* that we are buying from the rest of the world: stocks, bonds, foreign real estate, foreign money, and so on. Call the total of all these C_B (for *C*apital assets *B*ought), and measure it in terms of our currency.

The next two items are a little more subtle. First, if foreigners have invested in our country by buying our stocks, bonds, and so forth, we must pay them the interest, dividends, and so forth that their investments have earned—that is, we are buying the services of their investments, and we must pay for those services. Denote by E_P the total, in domestic currency, of investment *E*arnings that we must *P*ay the rest of the world. So far we have considered payments that we must make to the rest of the world for things we have received from it. But there are also payments made for their own sake. For example, some of us might send money or gifts to relatives still in the "old country." Or perhaps pensions are owed to people who are now foreign residents. Or perhaps the government is paying for foreign economic aid or for foreign military aid or for foreign bribes. Denote the total of such obligations by U_P, for Unilateral Payments transferred abroad, and measure it, too, in terms of domestic currency.

Thus the total, in terms of domestic currency, of all our purchases abroad and transfers there is $M + C_B + E_P + U_P$.

How are we paying for all this? First of all, by the *goods and services* that we are exporting to the rest of the world; call the total of these X, and measure it in terms of our currency. Next come the *assets* that we are selling to the rest of the world: stocks, bonds, foreign real estate, foreign money, and so on. Call the total of all these C_S (for Capital assets Sold), and measure it in terms of our currency. Next, if we have invested abroad by buying foreign stocks, bonds, and so forth, we will receive from them the interest, dividends, and so forth that our investments have earned—that is, we are selling the services of our investments, and we must be paid for those services. Denote by E_R the total, in domestic currency, of investment Earnings that we are Receiving from the rest of the world. Finally, there are also unrequited payments received from the rest of the world. Denote the total of such payments by U_R, for Unilateral Receipts transferred from abroad, and measure it, too, in terms of domestic currency.

Thus the total, in terms of domestic currency, of all our sales abroad and transfers received from there is $X + C_s + E_R + U_R$. Thus the national budget identity—that total sales to the rest of the world plus transfers received from there must equal total purchases from the rest of the world plus transfers made there—can be written

$$X + E_R + U_R + C_S \equiv M + E_P + U_P + C_B. \tag{12.1}$$

Subtracting the right-hand side from the left-hand side gives the following equivalent formulation:

$$T + E + U + C \equiv 0, \tag{12.2}$$

where

$$T = (X - M) \qquad \text{balance-of-trade surplus}$$
$$E = (E_R - E_P) \qquad \text{net investment earnings}$$
$$U = (U_R - U_P) \qquad \text{net transfers from abroad}$$
$$C = (C_S - C_B) \qquad \text{net sale of assets}$$

Equation (12.2) displays the major categories of a nation's international payments and shows that they are not independent of each other: they must always sum to zero.

2. BALANCE-OF-PAYMENTS ACCOUNTS

The *balance-of-payments accounts* attempt to fill in the national budget identity with actual numbers. More specifically, they record transactions in a specific time interval between national residents and the rest of the world. The time interval is usually a year; some countries, such as the United States, also report quarterly.

KEY CONCEPT

A country's *balance-of-payments accounts* are a record of transactions in a specific time interval between residents of that country and the rest of the world.

Residence

The distinction between domestic residents and foreigners is not on the basis of legal citizenship, but rather "normal" location of residence. Tourists, military and diplomatic personnel, and temporary migrants are treated as residents of the country from which they come; their transactions while abroad result, in principle, in balance-of-payments entries, whereas payments they receive from or make to their home countries do not. A permanent migrant, by contrast, is a resident of the country where she is, even if she still retains the citizenship of the country she has left; in this case transactions in the new country do not involve the balance of payments, but remittances sent to relatives in the old country do. Foreign subsidiaries are regarded as residents of the country in which they are located. Thus sales by a parent firm to a foreign subsidiary result in balance-of-payments entries, even though the transaction takes place within a single corporation.

Double-Entry Bookkeeping: Credits and Debits

There are two general rules to remember in balance-of-payments accounting. The first is to distinguish between *debits* and *credits*. An international transaction involves the sale of some good, service, or asset in exchange for the purchase of an equal-valued good, service, or asset. Thus the total value of all sales always equals the total value of all purchases: this is the national budget identity (Walras's Law). The balance-of-payments accounts reflect this identity by using a double-entry system in which each transaction gives rise to both a credit entry and an equal debit entry. Thus the sum of all credits equals the sum of all debits.

A credit entry results from any action that creates an obligation for a foreign resident to pay a domestic resident: the export of a good or service, the sale of an asset, or the receipt of a unilateral transfer from abroad. A debit entry, then, results from any action that creates an obligation for a domestic resident to pay a foreign resident: the import of a good or service, the purchase of an asset, or making a unilateral transfer abroad.

KEY CONCEPT

Credit entries reflect obligations for foreigners to pay domestic residents; *debit* entries reflect obligations for domestic residents to pay foreigners.

Suppose that Acme Spirits buys 200 cases of whiskey from a Scottish distillery, paying for it with a $25,000 check. This generates for the U.S. balance of payments a $25,000 debit entry under merchandise trade (the *import* of the whiskey) and a $25,000 credit entry under short-term capital flows (the *export* of the $25,000 demand deposit via the check). What are the effects of the transaction on the U.K. balance of payments? On the French balance of payments?

Suppose, for example, that $1,000 worth of wheat is given to some African nation for famine relief. This results in a $1,000 credit entry for merchandise trade (the export of wheat) and a $1,000 debit entry for unilateral transfers (making a transfer to foreigners).

To summarize: *each transaction generates two equal entries, a credit (+) for an export of a good, service, or asset, or for the receipt of a unilateral transfer, and a debit (−) for an import of a good, service, or asset, or for making a unilateral transfer.*

Classification of Transactions

Since the sum of all credits equals the sum of all debits, interest attaches not to the overall balance of payments—always equal to zero—but to its constituent parts. The purpose of the accounts is to reveal the structure of a country's international transactions. The second rule of accounting is, therefore, to put the debits and credits in the proper subaccounts.

The overall balance is divided into the current account $(T + E + U)$ and the capital account (C). But countries disaggregate more than this. Table 12.1 shows how the balance of payments is broken down to a moderate degree. The current account is split up into the constituents labeled 1 through 5. Line 1 shows merchandise trade: exports (+) and imports (−) of goods. Lines 2 and 3 likewise show net trade in services disaggregated into two parts. Unilateral transfers are included in the current account in items 4 and 5, with transfers of the government segregated from the rest.

In the capital account, official reserve transactions are segregated from the rest. These are capital transactions undertaken by the country's official monetary authorities. In most large countries this is the central bank; in the case of the United States, this means the Federal Reserve System. The reason that these transactions are segregated is that, while the other transactions are performed for their own sake by private and government agents, the official reserve transactions are undertaken by the authorities in order to manage the country's balance of payments. How and why the authorities might do this is discussed at length later in this book.

The nonofficial capital account is split into four parts. *Capital transactions* involving the government are segregated into item 6. *Direct investment* (7) includes transactions in which the investor has significant control over the operations of the firm being invested in, such as when a firm in one country buys a foreign firm or invests in a foreign subsidiary. (In practice, "operating control" is taken to mean an ownership share of at least 10 percent.) Thus direct investment records the actions of multinational firms. *Portfolio investment* (8) refers to the exchange of long-term securities in which control is not involved; typical transactions involve bonds issued by governments and private firms. Long-term assets are those whose original term to maturity is at least a year. Many treasury bills, bank loans, commercial paper, and so on have shorter maturities, as does cash (which is always matured). Transactions in such short-term assets are included in item 9.

Item 11 shows the official transactions. It should in principle now equal the total of items 1 through 9. But in practice this will not be so because errors are inevitable in compiling the accounts. An additional entry, called the *sta-*

TABLE 12.1   **Classifications of the Balance-of-Payments Accounts**

1 Merchandise trade
2 Investment income
3 Other services
    Total goods and services (= 1 + 2 + 3)
4   Private unilateral transfers
5 Government unilateral transfers
    Total current account (= 1 + 2 + 3 + 4 + 5)
6 Government capital
7 Direct investment
8 Portfolio investment
9 Other private capital
    Total nonofficial capital account (= 6 + 7 + 8 + 9)
10 Statistical discrepancy
11 Official reserve assets
    Official reserve transactions balance
        (= 1 + 2 + 3 + 4 + 5 + 6 + 7 + 8 + 9 + 10
        = − 11)

tistical discrepancy, is, therefore, added to balance the books. Item 10 is simply the total of the other ten items with the sign reversed. This discrepancy does not measure total errors, because many will cancel out, but only net errors. In particular, if a transaction is missed entirely by the compilers of the accounts, both debits and credits are reduced the same amount. Thus the statistical discrepancy comes from overlooking (or incorrectly measuring) one side of transactions.

Data on merchandise trade come from customs declarations and, for most countries, are regarded as the most accurate part of the accounts. Trade in services, by contrast, is typically estimated by various sampling techniques; errors are likely substantial but not necessarily volatile year by year. Reporting procedures for capital transactions are likewise highly imperfect, and the volume of such transactions is volatile, especially at the short end of the maturity spectrum. Many economists accordingly view the statistical discrepancy as substantially a reflection of unrecorded short-term capital movements.

The *Official reserve transactions balance* is the total of all items except for the transactions of the authorities. It is often referred to as the *balance-of-payments surplus* (if positive) or *deficit* (if negative). Since the national budget identity requires that all items sum to exactly zero, the official reserve transactions balance must equal item 11 with the sign reversed.

Balances of payments are typically presented in greater detail than in Table 12.1, with the format varying from country to country to isolate what is important to individual countries. Ghana, for example, has a separate entry for exports of cocoa beans and products; the United States isolates military and agency sales from other exports and military grants from other transfers.

Problems

12.1 A U.K. distillery sells an American firm 200 cases of whiskey in exchange for a $25,000 check drawn on an American bank. The distillery uses $15,000 of this to buy equipment in France and the other $10,000 to retire bonds it had issued years ago to a group of wealthy Italian investors. Write all the resulting entries in the balance-of-payments accounts of the United States, France, United Kingdom, Germany, and Italy.

12.2 Write all balance-of-payments entries resulting from each of the following transactions.

    a The U.S. Army gives $1 million in pay to American soldiers stationed in Germany.

    b Ford Motor Company (U.S.) pays $1 million to Ford's German subsidiary for automobile parts.

    c An American automobile dealer pays $1 million, by check, to the German firm BMW for automobiles.

    d BMW pays $1 million to the Bundesbank for DM 1.6 million.

e Daring Danny of Denver, sky-diving champion of all Colorado west of the Rockies, pays Lloyds of London $10,000 for a life-insurance policy.

f Lloyds of London pays Daring Danny's widow $1 million in settlement of a life-insurance policy claim.

g A Japanese firm sends Russia $2 million worth of drilling equipment in return for $2 million worth of oil.

h A Japanese firm sends Russia $2 million worth of drilling equipment in return for a promise of $4 million worth of oil in five years.

i You visit Singapore and have $1,000 stolen by a local pickpocket.

j You visit Singapore and lose $1,000 worth of American traveler's checks, for which you receive a refund from the local bank.

3. *CASE STUDY:* THE U.S. BALANCE OF PAYMENTS

Table 12.2 shows the U.S. balance of payments in 1993. The current account is split up into the constituents labeled 1 through 32. Unilateral transfers are included in the current account in items 30, 31, and 32, with two categories of transfers of the U.S. government segregated from the rest. The table shows only the excess of credits over debits (transfers received minus transfers made) for each category: evidently private unilateral transfers made to the rest of the world exceeded those received from abroad by $13.7 billion in 1993. Total credits and debits are listed separately for the other categories of the current account (trade in goods and services and investment income); for all listed categories of the capital account (lines 33–61), transactions involving U.S. assets and foreign assets are listed separately, but for each type only the excess of credits over debits is shown.

At the bottom of the table, under "Memoranda," various subtotals of special interest are displayed, the number for each indicating the excess of total credits over total debits. For example, the current account surplus ($T + E + U$ in equation (12.2)) is shown on line 70. Since the current account was in deficit by $103.9 billion, the total capital account should have been in surplus by an equal amount. But line 63 indicates a statistical discrepancy of $21.1 billion, implying that the reported capital account surplus must have been $21.1 billion less than the reported current account deficit. If we guess that the statistical discrepancy probably reflects mainly errors and omissions in the capital account, the current account deficit indicates that the United States, on balance, borrowed $103.9 billion from the rest of the world in 1993.

The current account balance (line 70) receives a lot of attention in the popular press, where it is sometimes referred to as "the balance of payments." Just about as much attention is also given to line 64, the balance on merchandise trade. This is unfortunate. As you can see from Table 12.2, in 1993 the United States had a deficit on merchandise trade of $132.6 billion. But it also had a *surplus* on services trade (line 65) of $56.9 billion. Thus the total trade deficit (line 66) was a much more modest $75.7 billion. This pattern has been typical of U.S. transactions for years; so focusing on the balance on merchandise trade gives a very distorted picture of the country's actual trade position. Why the misplaced emphasis on merchandise trade? For a long time in the United States, as elsewhere, services have been becoming steadily more important; but many years ago merchandise trade was in fact the major part of total trade. Also, as we have seen, the merchandise trade statistics are more exact than the statistics on services. One result of this is that the services statistics had been released quarterly whereas the trade statistics are released monthly and have, therefore, gotten more attention. In an attempt to redress the balance, the government now also releases services figures monthly.

TABLE 12.2   U.S. Balance of Payments, 1993

		Credits $(+)/$ debits $(-)$
1	**Exports of goods, services, and income**	**−755.5**
2	Merchandise, adjusted, excluding military	456.9
3	Services	184.8
4	Transfers under U.S. military sales contracts	11.4
5	Travel	57.6
6	Passenger fares	16.6
7	Other transportation	23.2
8	Royalties and license fees	20.4
9	Other private services	54.9
10	U.S. government miscellaneous services	0.8
11	Income receipts on U.S. assets abroad	113.9
12	Direct-investment receipts	57.5
13	Other private receipts.	51.3
14	U.S. government receipts	5.1
15	**Imports of goods, services, and income**	**−827.3**
16	Merchandise, adjusted, excluding military	−589.4
17	Services	−128.0
18	Direct defense expenditures	−12.2
19	Travel	−40.6
20	Passenger fares	−11.4
21	Other transportation	−24.5
22	Royalties and license fees	−4.8
23	Other private services	−32.1
24	U.S. government miscellaneous services	−2.3
25	Income payments on foreign assets in the United States	−109.9
26	Direct-investment payments	−5.1
27	Other private payments	−63.2
28	U.S. government payments	−41.6
29	**Unilateral transfers, net**	**−32.1**
30	U.S. government grants	−14.6

31	U.S. government pensions and other transfers	−3.8
32	Private remittances and other transfers	−13.7
33	**U.S. assets abroad, net (increase/capital outflow(−))**	**−147.9**
34	U.S. official reserve assets, net	−1.4
35	Gold	—
36	Special drawing rights	−0.5
37	Reserve position in the International Monetary Fund	0.0
38	Foreign currencies	−0.8
39	U.S. government assets other than official reserve assets, net	−0.3
40	U.S. credits and other long-term assets	−6.0
41	Repayments on U.S. credits and other long-term assets	−6.0
42	U.S. foreign-currency holdings/short-term assets, net	−0.3
43	U.S. private assets, net	−146.2
44	Direct investment	−57.9
45	Foreign securities	−120.0
46	U.S. claims on unaffiliated foreigners reported by U.S. nonbanking concerns	−0.6
47	U.S. claims reported by U.S. banks, not included elsewhere	32.2
48	**Foreign assets in the United States, net (increase/capital inflow (+))**	**230.7**
49	Foreign official assets in the United States, net	71.7
50	U.S. government securities	52.8
51	U.S. Treasury securities	48.7
52	Other	4.1
53	Other U.S. government liabilities	1.7
54	U.S. liabilities reported by U.S. banks, not included elsewhere	14.7
55	Other foreign official assets	2.6
56	Other foreign assets in the United States, net	159.0
57	Direct investment	21.4
58	U.S. Treasury securities	24.9
59	U.S. securities other than U.S. Treasury securities	80.1
60	U.S. liabilities to unaffiliated foreigners reported by U.S. nonbanking concerns	14.3
61	U.S. liabilities reported by U.S. banks, not included elsewhere	18.5
62	**Allocations of special drawing rights**	—
63	**Statistical discrepancy (sum of the above with sign reversed)**	**21.1**
	Memoranda	
64	Balance on merchandise trade (lines 2 + 16)	−132.6
65	Balance on services (lines 3 + 17)	56.9
66	Balance on goods and services (lines 64 + 65)	−75.7
67	Balance on investment income (lines 11 + 25)	3.9
68	Balance on goods, services, and income (lines 66 + 67)	−71.8
69	Unilateral transfers, net (line 29)	−32.1
70	Balance on current account (lines 68 + 69)	−103.9

SOURCE: U.S. Department of Commerce, *Survey of Current Business.*

From lines 44 and 57 the net U.S. position on direct investment is $(-57.9 + 21.4)$ billion, or $-\$36.5$ billion. Thus the United States acquired, net, $36.5 billion of direct-investment assets via the rest of the world. Thus, to a degree, the United States was borrowing abroad to finance direct investments abroad.

The net dealings of U.S. authorities in international reserves are shown in items 34 through 38. International reserves include gold and foreign exchange plus two items (special drawing rights and IMF reserve positions), which we shall study later in this book. The U.S. dollar constitutes foreign exchange for countries other than the United States, and most countries hold a good part of their international reserves in the form of dollars. Authorities use international reserves to influence the value of their national money. For example, U.K. authorities might use some of their dollar reserves to buy pounds, thus forcing up the value of the pound (or preventing it from falling). Similarly, Canadian authorities might sell Canadian dollars for U.S. dollars, forcing down the value of the Canadian dollar. The net effect of both actions is to increase the price of the pound in terms of Canadian dollars.

In 1993 U.S. authorities increased their holdings of international reserves by $1.4 billion (as always, a "purchase" of anything is a debit and a "sale" a credit). This is recorded in line 34, which shows the total sale by U.S. authorities of reserve assets to purchase dollars. The United Sates differs from most other countries in that the U.S. dollar is a reserve asset for foreign countries. Thus the U.S. payments deficit (dollars for sale) can be accommodated either by U.S. sales of international reserves for the dollars or by foreign official purchases of the dollars. The reverse is the case for surpluses. Items 49 through 55 record net foreign official transactions in dollar assets, with increases in foreign holdings recorded as credits (a "sale" of dollars) and decreases as debits.

The official reserve transactions balance (the "balance of payments") is not mentioned in Table 12.2. But we can calculate it from the data that are presented. U.S. official reserve assets ($-\$1.4$ billion) plus foreign official assets in the United States ($71.7 billion) sum to $70.3 billion. This offsets the deficit. Thus in 1993 the United States had a balance-of-payments deficit of $70.3 billion.

Problems

12.3 Generally, only transactions between American residents and foreign residents generate entries in the American balance of payments. But in one case, transactions between two foreigners result in such entries. What is this case?

12.4* Consider Canada's balance of payments.

Canadian Balance of Payments, 1993 *(billions of Canadian dollars)*

Merchandise trade	9.8
Services	−14.2
Goods and services	*4.4*
Private unilateral transfers	0.7
Official unilateral transfers	−0.5
Income	−26.7
Total current account	*−30.9*
Direct investment	−1.6
Portfolio investment	27.1
Other nonofficial capital	11.5
Total nonofficial capital	*37.0*
Net errors and omissions	−6.6
Change in value of reserves	−0.1
Official reserve assets	0.6
Net official reserve transactions	*0.5*

SOURCE: International Monetary Fund, *International Financial Statistics.*

a Discuss each line. In what ways do Canada's payments differ from those of the United States? Why?

b What is the item "Change in value of reserves"? To what is a negative number due?

4. *CASE STUDY:* HOW SHOULD THE ACCOUNTS TREAT THE ACTIVITIES OF MULTINATIONAL FIRMS?

Chapter 11 showed the prominence, in the current world economy, of direct investment and the multinational firm. A large part of the foreign activity of U.S. industry is in fact conducted through foreign affiliates. Most of this is not reflected in the U.S. balance of payments because, as we have seen, foreign subsidiaries of U.S. firms are treated as residents of the countries in which they are located, not as residents of the United States. This is not unreasonable for some purposes, such as indicating the impact of foreign trade on economic activity in the United States. But it does give a distorted picture of the role of U.S. firms in the world economy.

Because of this, several individuals and groups of individuals have proposed that the U.S. balance-of-payments statistics be supplemented (*not* replaced) by an alternative method of calculating transactions involving trade in goods and services. For example, a study panel of the National Academy of Sciences has proposed that trade transactions be compiled on the basis of

TABLE 12.3   **Effects of Alternative Approaches to the Trade Accounts, 1991**
              (billions of dollars)

	Conventional balance of payments	National Academy of Sciences proposal	Alternative residence-based approach
U.S. sales to foreigners	581	816	632
U.S. purchases from foreigners	609	652	608
Balance	−28	164	24

SOURCE: J. S. Landefeld, O. G. Whichard, and J. H. Lowe, "Alternative Frameworks for U.S. International Transactions," *Survey of Current Business* 73 (1993): 50–61.

national *ownership* rather than national *residence.* Thus the transactions of foreign affiliates of U.S. firms with their parents (or with other U.S.-owned firms) would no longer enter the accounts, but their transactions with foreigners would.

Another proposal, an alternative *residence-based approach,* would also include sales by foreign affiliates of U.S. firms to foreigners. But it would deduct from this all payments made to foreigners for labor and so on so that the correction to the usual statistics would basically consist of the earnings of foreign affiliates.

Table 12.3 shows what effects these proposals would have if they were applied to the U.S. balance-of-payments statistics for 1991. The existing statistics show a U.S. deficit on trade in goods and services of $28 billion in 1991. But if the procedure contained in the National Academy of Science's proposal had been followed instead, the United States would have been shown to have run a huge surplus of $164 billion. Even the less radical alternative residence-based approach would have reversed the $28 billion deficit into a $24 billion surplus.

Thus the issue raised by these proposals is significant. The implication of all this is that, in interpreting the numbers generated by an accounting method, one should keep in mind what that method is intended to reveal.

5. SUMMARY

1. The national budget identity requires that, if *all* transactions are accurately measured, total payments to the rest of the world must equal total receipts from the rest of the world.

2. The balance of payments measures economic transactions between domestic residents and foreigners.

3. In the balance of payments, a sale of anything to the rest of the world or the receipt of a unilateral transfer from the rest of the world is recorded as a credit (+); a purchase of anything from the rest of the world or the grant of a unilateral transfer to the rest of the world is recorded as a debit (−).

4. Official transactions in reserve assets are segregated from all other transactions because, unlike the latter, they are undertaken not for their own sake, but in order to manage a country's overall international payments.

SUGGESTED READING

Hooper, P., and C. Mann. "The Emergence and Persistence of the U.S. External Balance: 1980–1987." In *Studies in International Finance*. Princeton: Princeton University Press, 1989. Surveys developments during the 1980s.

Howard, D. H. "Implications of the U.S. Current Account Deficit." *Journal of Economic Perspectives* 3 (1989): 153–65. How the deficits affect national wealth.

International Monetary Fund. *Final Report of the Working Party on the Statistical Discrepancy in World Current Account Balances*. Washington: International Monetary Fund, 1987. The global statistical discrepancy.

Landefeld, J. S., O. G. Whichard, and J. H. Lowe. "Alternative Frameworks for U.S. International Transactions." *Survey of Current Business* 73 (1993): 50–61. Discusses several proposals for different measurements of U.S. international transactions.

Maldonado, R. M. "Recording and Classifying Transactions in the Balance of Payments." *International Journal of Accounting* 15 (1979): 105–33. The dirty details.

Meade, J. E. *The Balance of Payments*. London: Oxford University Press, 1952. Chapters 1 through 3 contain the classic account of concepts of the balance of payments.

CHAPTER 13

International Financial Markets

> How much have these speculators thrown away? . . . Nothing like it
> has been known in the history of speculation—so large and so wide-
> spread. Bankers and servant girls have been equally involved. . . .
> The argument on which bankers bought was the same as the argument
> on which servant girls bought . . . so little do bankers and servant
> girls understand of history and economics.
>
> —JOHN MAYNARD KEYNES

Various financial markets exist so that international transactions may take
place. These include foreign-exchange markets, where national currencies are
traded, and credit markets in which countries borrow and lend to each other.
Also included are the Euromarkets—newer and rapidly growing institutions
that testify to the degree of economic integration that has occurred in the international economy since the Second World War. This chapter is devoted to
these various markets.

1. THE FOREIGN-EXCHANGE MARKET

The currencies of different countries are exchanged for each other on the
foreign-exchange market. *Foreign exchange* is simply the money of a foreign
country: thus French francs are foreign exchange to Americans but not to the
French. The basic purpose of this market is to facilitate international trade
and investment.

There are two aspects to the foreign-exchange market. The *retail* portion
of the market is where firms and individuals who require foreign currency can
buy it, or where they can dispose of any foreign money they may have acquired. Typical transactions include a firm buying foreign exchange from its
bank in order to purchase foreign goods or a tourist exchanging her own
money for foreign money at an airport bureau of exchange.

Suppose, for example, that an American firm, Acme Spirits, wishes to purchase 200 cases of whiskey from a distillery in Scotland. The distillery charges £10,000 for the whiskey; that comes to $16,000 at an exchange rate of $1.60/£. Acme Spirits wishes to pay in dollars, whereas the distillery wants to be paid in pounds: this is where the foreign-exchange market comes in. If the contract between the two firms calls for payment in pounds, Acme Spirits will have to buy £10,000 from its bank; if, on the other hand, the contract calls for payment in dollars, the U.K. distillery will sell $16,000 to its bank. In either case, the British sale of whiskey to the United States requires that some firm buy pounds for dollars from the banking system.

Suppose the contract is in pounds. Then when it comes time to pay for the whiskey, Acme Spirits will go to the foreign-exchange department of its bank—say, bank A in New York—to buy the necessary pounds. Acme Spirits will pay bank A $16,000 and receive in exchange a check for £10,000 drawn against some British bank, say bank B in London. The firm then pays for its whiskey by sending the check to the distillery in Scotland. Figure 13.1 schematically depicts Acme Spirits' transactions.

Where did bank A get the £10,000 it sold to Acme Spirits? This brings us to the second part of the foreign-exchange market, the *interbank market*. It might conceivably be the case that bank A numbers among its customers firms exporting to Britain who acquire pounds that they sell to the bank. If so, the bank could then sell these pounds to Acme Spirits. But it is unlikely that things will exactly balance out in this way. So suppose that the pounds that Acme Spirits and other firms wish to buy from bank A exceed the pounds that are offered to bank A for sale. Then, in order to meet its customers' needs, the bank must acquire additional pounds. It gets them from other banks. It might

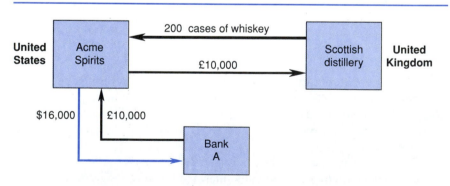

FIGURE 13.1   Transactions Involved in U.S. Importing   If a U.S. firm needs to pay pounds to a U.K. firm to purchase goods, the U.S. firm must also purchase the necessary pounds from its bank.

be able to buy them from another New York bank that finds itself with more pounds than necessary for business. Or bank A could buy the pounds from a British bank—say, bank B in London.

Why should bank B sell pounds—that is, buy dollars? To service the needs of its own British customers who require dollars in order to purchase goods, services, or assets from the United States. Perhaps a British firm, Coagulated Mush, Ltd., has agreed to pay $16,000 to an American exporter for 3,000 bushels of soybeans. Then Coagulated Mush will wish to buy $16,000 from its bank—say, bank B. Figure 13.2 shows schematically the related transactions in commodity and foreign-exchange markets. In real terms, the United States is trading soybeans to the United Kingdom for whiskey. The foreign-exchange market allows this trade to take place between two monetary economies using different monies. Note that, after all transactions have been made, each country's money is still circulating within the country. The £10,000, for example, were paid by Coagulated Mush and received by the distillery, which perhaps keeps them on deposit in bank B. The $16,000 were paid by Acme Spirits and received by the agricultural exporter, who perhaps keeps them on deposit in bank A.

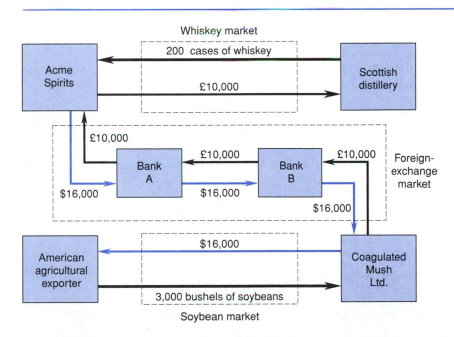

FIGURE 13.2 **International Trade and the Foreign-Exchange Market** In this example the United States is trading soybeans to the United Kingdom for whiskey. The foreign-exchange market facilitates this exchange between two monetary economies with different currencies.

The Interbank Market

Participants in the interbank foreign-exchange market are the international departments of large commercial banks in the major financial centers of the world: London, New York, Zurich, Frankfurt, Paris, Tokyo, Singapore, Toronto, and so forth. There is some activity in secondary centers such as Osaka and San Francisco, and large banks outside these centers often participate via affiliates; small regional banks do not participate, but meet their customers' foreign-exchange needs by dealing with correspondent banks that are in the market (thus Acme Spirits, even if located in Lexington, Kentucky, need not go to New York to obtain its £10,000). Because of its worldwide dispersion, the foreign-exchange market is active twenty-four hours a day, although individual banks by and large observe normal working hours.

A participating bank typically maintains a trading room equipped with computer terminals, telephones, and telex machines over which dealers make and receive price quotations and agree to transactions. The bank will likely communicate directly with the trading rooms of banks in foreign centers but will go through a broker when dealing with other banks in the same center. There are eight such brokers in New York. The trading room of a major New York bank will then be connected, by direct telephone and telex lines, to brokerage offices and to trading rooms in other countries. A bank will make transactions in response to the collective needs of its commercial customers; in addition, many major banks will "make a market" in one or more currencies—that is, they will continuously be prepared to deal on either side of the market. There are several hundred market-makers worldwide.

The foreign-exchange market is made into a unified, worldwide whole by what is known as *arbitrage* (buying cheap and selling dear). Suppose, for example, that a dealer were to discover that a bank in New York was dealing in Swiss francs at the rate of $0.6740/SFr, whereas a bank in Zurich was doing so at $0.6745/SFr. The dealer could then buy Swiss francs from the New York bank and sell them to the Swiss bank, earning a profit of $.0005

Triangular-Arbitrage Example

Suppose that London banks are dealing in dollars at $1.60/£ and in Swiss francs at SFr 2.39/£, whereas in Zurich Swiss francs cost $0.6710 each. Then, by using dollars to buy pounds in London and using these pounds in turn to buy Swiss francs, a bank could obtain Swiss francs in London for $0.6695 (=1.60/2.39) and sell them in Zurich for $0.6710. Such arbitrage would soon make the rates consistent.

per franc. This may not seem like anything to get excited about, but it becomes significant when you realize that even a "small" deal on the interbank market involves multiples of $100,000 and that the transaction would tie up funds for only minutes or seconds. Such arbitrage would quickly drive up the price of Swiss francs in New York, where they are being bought, and drive down the price in Zurich, so that a single world price would be established. In the same way, exchange rates in various centers are made mutually consistent, a process known as *triangular arbitrage*. Arbitrage is part of any market, but it is especially relentless with foreign exchange because of the great communication between participants and the homogeneity and storability of the product (money). Indeed, such arbitrage operations rarely need actually occur anymore: exchange rates seldom get out of line in the first place because everyone knows that massive arbitrage would take place if they did.

The supplies and demands of various currencies by the participating banks are the proximate determinants of exchange rates, which are liable to fluctuate throughout the day. These rates then determine the prices individual banks charge corporate customers. Representative rates are published daily in the financial press; Table 13.1 reproduces a selection of typical quotations in New York.

Among the participants of the foreign-exchange market are central banks. They participate for two reasons. First, they service the foreign-exchange needs of their respective governments, agencies, and government-owned firms, just as commercial banks enter the market in order to serve their customers. But central banks also participate in order to administer a fixed or pegged exchange-rate regime or to manage a float. That is, they intervene in the market to influence exchange rates by altering demand and supply conditions. In the United States such official dealings are performed in the New York market by the Federal Reserve Bank of New York.

Special Role of the Dollar

The U.S. dollar is the world's most important single currency and has a qualitatively distinct role in several respects. The dollar is, first of all, a *vehicle* currency, or medium of exchange in the foreign-exchange market. That is, exchanges between third currencies often take place through dollars rather than directly. If a bank in Norway required Swiss francs, for example, instead of trying to buy the francs directly for Norwegian kroner, the bank would likely buy dollars for kroner in Oslo and then use the dollars to buy francs in Zurich. Because of this, the dollar market is the largest part of the market in foreign centers. Each country is the ultimate source of its own currency. Thus the dollar-pound market is the largest part of the London foreign-exchange market, and London is also the most important center for dollar-pound transactions. The second most important center is New York. Similarly, dollar–Swiss franc exchanges are the largest activity in Zurich. Zurich is the most

TABLE 13.1 **Foreign Exchange Rates** *(New York, Wednesday, March 23, 1994)*

	$ value per unit of foreign currency		Units of currency per dollar	
	Wed.	Tue.	Wed.	Tue.
Brazil (cruzeiro)	0.0012	0.0012	817.2500	802.0000
Britain (pound)	1.4970	1.4893	0.6680	0.6715
30-day fwd	1.4950	1.4873	0.6689	0.6724
60-day fwd	1.4935	1.4860	0.6696	0.6729
90-day fwd	1.4921	1.4848	0.6702	0.6735
Canada (dollar)	0.7332	0.7318	1.3639	1.3665
30-day fwd	0.7336	0.7314	1.3631	1.3673
60-day fwd	0.7342	0.7308	1.3621	1.3683
90-day fwd	0.7347	0.7304	1.3611	1.3692
France (franc)	0.1740	0.1739	5.7475	5.7505
Italy (lira)	0.000601	0.0006	1,664.7500	1,666.0000
Japan (yen)	0.0094	0.00944	106.3800	105.9300
30-day fwd	0.009409	0.00945	106.2800	105.8200
60-day fwd	0.009422	0.009454	106.1300	105.7800
90-day fwd	0.009446	0.009478	105.8700	105.5100
Malaysia (ringgit)	0.3670	0.3676	2.7245	2.7200
Mexico (peso)	0.301477	0.301477	3.3170	3.3170
Pakistan (rupee)	0.0329	0.0329	30.4000	30.4000
Russia (ruble)	0.000581	0.000581	1,722.0000	1,722.0000
Singapore (dollar)	0.6307	0.6299	1.5855	1.5876
Slovakia (koruna)	0.0306	0.0306	32.7300	32.7300
Sweden (krona)	0.1274	0.1275	7.8505	7.8445
Taiwan (New Taiwan dollar)	0.0379	0.0379	26.4000	26.4000
United Arab Emirates (dirham)	0.2725	0.2725	3.6700	3.6700

SOURCE: *New York Times.*

important center for such activity, and New York is second. Because it is second in so many individual markets, New York is overall one of the largest foreign-exchange centers in the world.

Foreign central banks also use the dollar as a vehicle, or *intervention currency.* That is, the Bank of England influences the value of the pound by exchanging pounds and dollars in the London foreign-exchange market, the Bank of Japan exchanges dollars and yen in Tokyo, and so forth. Partly because of this, a large portion of official international reserves are held in the form of dollars (and dollar-denominated assets).

Finally, commercial contracts are sometimes denominated in dollars, and payment is sometimes made in dollars, even when neither party to the contract is American. For example, European countries use dollars to pay for Middle East oil. This practice is most common in raw material and commodity markets, which are unified globally and deal in standardized contracts. The extensive Japanese imports of raw materials from southeast Asia and Australia are largely denominated in dollars. Thus the dollar is in some degree an international money.

Problems

13.1 Figures 13.1 and 13.2 assumed that contracts were in terms of the currency of the exporter. How are the figures changed if contracts are in the importer's currency? If all contracts are in dollars?

13.2 In Figure 13.2, trade between the United States and the United Kingdom was assumed to be in balance. Suppose instead that, at the same prices, Acme Spirits imports 400 cases of whiskey, soybean exports remaining at 3,000 bushels. How is the figure changed?

13.3 The foreign-exchange market described in this section involves bank deposits. But exchanges of *currencies* also take place, though on a smaller scale. For example, a tourist might buy a few pound notes from her New York bank before leaving for London, and she might sell a few pound notes to that bank when she returns. Describe the influence of arbitrage on the relation between the dollar price of pound notes in New York and the pound price of dollars in London. How do you think this influence compares with that of arbitrage in the foreign-exchange market as discussed in the text?

2. *CASE STUDY:* THE FOREIGN-EXCHANGE MARKET AND THE ELECTRONIC AGE

The interbank transactions arranged by foreign-exchange dealers have traditionally been settled by cable transfers of funds. Suppose bank A in New York agrees to buy £1 million from bank B in London for $2 million. At settlement time, bank A credits bank B's account in bank A with a deposit of $2 million, or else it deposits by cable that amount in bank B's account in some other American bank. Similarly, bank A has its London account credited with £1 million.

The interbank market depends upon modern means of communication. When these methods were more primitive, substantial efforts went into arbitrage. "Foreign exchange" consisted of bills and acceptances rather than bank deposits, and exchange rates in different centers could remain apart for some time. In the years between the two world wars, a precautionary payment to a telephone operator was a not-unwise way to try to ensure that a dealer's call to a foreign bank would quickly get through should lines become jammed in a time of crisis.

Technology and business methods continue to evolve. Dealing rooms are now aglitter with monitors displaying up-to-the-minute rates, and some banks are replacing or supplementing verbal quotations with the simultaneous electronic display of current dealing prices. Foreign-exchange brokers are expanding their activities across national borders.

Cable transfers are being replaced by automated electronic payments systems as the means of settling transactions. About three thousand banks now participate in the Society for Worldwide Interbank Financial Telecommunication, popularly known as SWIFT. SWIFT is headquartered in Brussels and consists of three linked operating centers that are, in turn, connected to regional processing centers. A bank wishing to make a transfer sends instructions to such a regional processor via normal telecommunications channels, and then SWIFT takes over.

3. *CASE STUDY:* THE VOLUME OF FOREIGN-EXCHANGE DEALING

In April 1977 the Federal Reserve Bank of New York surveyed forty-four U.S. banks about their foreign-exchange operations. Other surveys (including more banks) were conducted in 1980, 1983, and 1986. Average daily turnover in each month is summarized in Table 13.2.

In March 1986 similar surveys were conducted in London and Tokyo by the central banks of Britain and Japan, with the results shown in Table 13.3. Since London, New York, and Tokyo are the largest centers in the foreign-exchange market, the three surveys together come close to giving a global view.

Since these surveys covered only the three centers shown in Table 13.3 and they did not include all participants in those centers, total daily turnover in the global foreign-exchange market must have considerably exceeded $200 billion per day. This made it the largest financial market in the world.

TABLE 13.2 Average Daily Turnover in the New York Foreign-Exchange Market

Currency exchanged for $U.S.	*Percentage of total turnover*			
	April 1977	*March 1980*	*April 1983*	*March 1986*
German mark	27	32	33	34
Pound sterling	17	23	17	19
Canadian dollar	19	12	8	5
Japanese yen	5	10	22	23
Swiss franc	14	10	12	10
Other	18	13	8	9
Average total dealings ($billion/day)	$5.3	$23.4	$33.5	$58.6*

* Includes $8.5 billion of transactions by nonbanks.

TABLE 13.3 Average Daily Turnover in Three Centers, March 1986

Currency exchange	Percentage of total turnover		
	London	New York	Tokyo
German mark/$U.S.	28	34	
Pound sterling/$U.S.	30	19	
Canadian dollar/$U.S.	2	5	
Japanese yen/$U.S.	14	23	82
Swiss franc/$U.S.	9	10	
Cross-currency	4		
Other	13	9	18
Average total dealings ($billion/day)	$90.0	$58.6	$48.0

Moreover, this turnover was more than twenty-five times as great as the average daily value of world exports of goods and services. Since 1986 the foreign-exchange market has continued its rapid growth, reaching an average daily volume of nearly $700 billion by the early 1990s.

London appears to be the largest center, and Tokyo is now nearly as large as New York. Table 13.2 shows very rapid growth in New York, and that seems to have been the case elsewhere as well. The Tokyo market in particular has expanded enormously in recent years. This is the result of significant liberalization of Japanese restrictions on foreign-exchange trading as well as the large Japanese trade surplus.

Note that nearly all foreign-exchange transactions include the U.S. dollar—in London and Tokyo as well as New York. This illustrates the role of the dollar as vehicle currency. *Cross-currency* transactions (the direct exchange of two currencies other than the dollar) do exist, but the volume is small.

Problem

13.4 Tables 13.2 and 13.3 reveal significant dealings in Swiss francs despite the fact that Switzerland and its economy are small relative to many countries not mentioned in the tables (and, therefore, included in the "Other" category). Can you think of any possible reasons for this? Answer the same question with regard to the Canadian dollar. Explain the relative importance of these currencies in the table summarizing turnover in London.

4. THE FORWARD MARKET

When two banks agree on a foreign-exchange transaction, they also agree on when that transaction shall actually take place. Most common is a *spot transaction,* which calls for settlement two business days (sometimes one day) after the deal is made. But sometimes the banks agree to make the transaction further in the future—say, in thirty, sixty, or ninety days. These are called thirty-, sixty-, or ninety-day *forward* contracts. Table 13.1 included rates for forward contracts in a couple of currencies. An agreement to exchange two currencies in two months is not the same as an agreement to exchange them in two days, so the agreements can be expected to involve different prices. This is reflected in the table. The demand and supply for spot foreign exchange will determine the spot exchange rate; the demand and supply for thirty-day forward foreign exchange will determine the thirty-day forward rate; and so forth.

Why do forward markets exist? Return to the example of Acme Spirits. Suppose the company agrees to buy 200 cases from the Scottish distillery for £10,000. The contract between the two firms will call for the whiskey to be delivered by a certain date and for the pounds to be paid by a certain date. Suppose the latter is in ninety days. By contracting to purchase the whiskey, Acme Spirits has obligated itself to pay £10,000 in ninety days. The firm can easily find out what a pound costs now by opening a newspaper or calling a bank, but it has no way of knowing how many dollars will be required to buy £10,000 in ninety days, when the time comes to pay. If the pound should appreciate in the interval, Acme Spirits could sustain a serious loss. Although there are other risks involved in doing business, this *exchange risk* is unique to foreign trade; it does not arise when Acme Spirits purchases sour-mash whiskey from a Kentucky distillery.

Acme Spirits can escape from this risk by means of forward exchange. When the firm agrees to buy the whiskey and pay for it in ninety days, it can also purchase £10,000 ninety days forward from its bank (bank A). If the ninety-day forward exchange rate is $1.50/£, Acme Spirits would be obligating itself to pay the bank $15,000 in ninety days and then to receive £10,000 in return, which it would pay to the Scottish distillery. In this way Acme Spirits escapes all exchange risk—its future obligation is now in terms of dollars, and the firm need not worry about what happens to the spot exchange rate in the future.

This transaction does not eliminate the exchange risk; it simply transfers it from the company, whose business is liquor, to the bank, whose business is foreign exchange. Bank A is now obligated to come up with £10,000 in ninety days. Since all good bankers abhor risk, bank A will seek to escape it. How? By buying pounds forward from another bank—say, bank B—which has sold dollars forward to customers who have contracted to make dollar payments in ninety days. The forward transactions are exactly the same as the foreign-exchange market transactions illustrated in Figure 13.2. These transactions are agreements to make the indicated payments in ninety days. No market participant is left with any exchange risk. This is a major economic function of the forward exchange market: to allow international trade to proceed unimpeded by exchange risk.

Forward contracts can be readily obtained for the currencies of the major industrial countries for periods of up to a year and, in some cases, up to five years. Forward markets do not exist for most LDC currencies, and forward coverage in any currency is difficult to obtain for many years ahead. This hampers LDC trade and long-term trade agreements.

The Federal Reserve surveys of New York foreign-exchange activity, alluded to in section 3, also reveal the percentage composition of various types of transactions (see Table 13.4).

Interest Arbitrage

The spot and forward markets for any pair of currencies all have their own exchange rates, but these rates are not independent. To see how they are related, consider the position of a trader who has some funds that he will not need for thirty days. Presumably, he wishes to invest the money in the interim. A safe way to do so would be to buy U.S. Treasury bills. If i_{US} denotes the interest rate earned in thirty days, then each dollar invested in the treasury bills will be worth $1 + i_{US}$ dollars when the bills mature thirty days hence. But foreign governments also issue treasury bills of their own, so our trader could also buy, say, U.K. Treasury bills. Suppose the latter earn the rate i_{UK}. The dealer could then compare i_{US} and i_{UK} to see which bill pays more. But such a comparison ignores *exchange risk:* if the dealer buys U.S. Treasury bills, he will have dollars in thirty days, whereas if he buys U.K. Treasury bills, he will have pounds, and who knows how many dollars a pound will then be worth. Like Acme Spirits in the previous example, our trader can use the forward exchange market to escape this risk—that is, he can sell pounds forward at the same time that he buys U.K. Treasury bills. Suppose he does this. How much will each dollar invested in such a fashion be worth in thirty days?

If the spot price of a pound is R_s, each dollar can buy $1/R_s$ pounds (if a pound costs \$2, \$1 buys one-half a pound). If this many pounds are invested in U.K. Treasury bills, in thirty days they will become $(1/R_s)(1 + i_{UK})$ pounds. The trader protects himself by *now* selling this many pounds forward. If R_{30} denotes the thirty-day forward price of the pound, each dollar invested in this way will be worth $(R_{30}/R_s)(1 + i_{UK})$ dollars in thirty days. This term is called the *covered yield,* to distinguish it from the uncovered yield $1 + i_{UK}$,

TABLE 13.4 **The Composition of Foreign-Exchange Transactions**

Type	April 1977 (%)	March 1980 (%)	April 1983 (%)
Spot	55	64	65
Swap*	40	30	33
Outright forward	5	6	2

*A *swap* is a contract to buy a currency at one date and sell it back at a later date.

TABLE 13.5　Covered Interest Arbitrage

If: $(I + i_{US}) < \dfrac{R_{30}}{R_s}(I + i_{UK})$	$(I + i_{US}) = \dfrac{R_{30}}{R_s}(I + i_{UK})$	$(I + i_{US}) > \dfrac{R_{30}}{R_s}(I + i_{UK})$
Then traders:		
(1) redeem U.S. bills	continue as they were	(1) redeem U.K. bills
(2) buy pounds spot	doing	(2) sell pounds spot
(3) buy U.K. bills		(3) buy U.S. bills
(4) sell pounds forward		(4) buy pounds forward
So that:		
(1) U.S. capital-account deficit increases	no change	(1) U.S. capital-account deficit decreases
(2) the above inequality shrinks		(2) the above inequality shrinks

which exposes the trader to exchange risk. The trader compares this covered yield to $1 + i_{US}$ in order to discover whether the U.S. or U.K. Treasury bills are more attractive. If the yields on the two bills differ, traders will move their funds into the higher-paying bill, a process known as *covered interest arbitrage*.

The process is illustrated in Table 13.5. If, for example, $(1 + i_{US}) < (R_{30}/R_s)(1 + i_{UK})$, then the U.K. Treasury bills yield more. Traders will, therefore, simultaneously buy pounds in the spot market, use the pounds to buy U.K. Treasury bills, and sell the proceeds in the forward market. They will do this with whatever liquid funds they have available or can obtain by selling or redeeming U.S. Treasury bills they own. As many dealers do this, i_{US} will tend to rise and i_{UK} to fall, as the U.S. and U.K. treasuries find it respectively harder and easier to sell their bills to the public. Similarly, the increased demand for spot pounds and supply of forward pounds by the dealers causes R_s to rise and R_{30} to fall. As a result, the two yields will be driven together.

If international capital mobility is perfect—that is, if dealers are completely unwilling to hold a treasury bill yielding less than an alternative bill—the yields must be equal so that the middle column of Table 13.5 holds. In this case,

$$\frac{R_{30}}{R_S}(1 + i_{UK}) = 1 + i_{US}. \tag{13.1}$$

This is known as the *covered interest parity* condition. It is sometimes written an alternative way. Divide both sides of (13.1) by $1 + i_{UK}$ and then subtract unity from both sides. This gives

$$\frac{R_{30} - R_S}{R_S} = \frac{i_{US} - i_{UK}}{1 + i_{UK}}. \tag{13.2}$$

The left-hand side of this equation is called the *forward premium* (if positive) or *forward discount* (if negative) on the pound. It measures the percentage return a dealer can obtain by simultaneously buying pounds spot and selling them forward (a *swap* transaction). The right-hand side, called the (discounted) *interest differential,* measures the uncovered international difference in yields. With capital mobility perfect, any departure from covered interest parity would immediately induce enough interest arbitrage to force the interest rates and exchange rates back into line; imperfect capital mobility would allow persistent divergence.

Speculation

Interest arbitrage supplies one theory of the relationship between spot and forward exchange rates: the forward premium should equal the interest differential. Speculation supplies another theory. The dealer in the above example was not a speculator, but an arbitrageur: he always avoided exchange risk by taking a covered position. But other individuals might actually want to incur such risk in the hope of making a killing. The forward market can be used for speculation as well as for eliminating risk.

Suppose, for example, that the thirty-day forward rate for the pound is $1.60 but that a certain trader believes that in thirty days the spot rate will be $1.50/£. If she has the courage of her convictions, the trader will sell pounds forward, hoping to make a profit in thirty days. Suppose that she sells £1 million pounds forward—that is, agrees that in thirty days she will deliver £1 million in return for $1.6 million. By agreeing to deliver pounds that she does not own (taking an *open* position), the trader is assuming exchange risk. If she turns out to be right and in thirty days the spot rate is in fact $1.50, the trader can buy the £1 million in the spot market for $1.5 million and then execute the forward contract, receiving $1.6 million for the pounds. This gives her a profit of $100,000: not bad for a few minutes' work. Of course, if she guessed wrong and the spot rate actually turns out to be $1.80/£, she loses $200,000, but that is the risk one takes to play the game. The economist John Maynard Keynes made a fortune for himself—and for King's College, Cambridge—by foreign-exchange speculation. But earlier he had suffered losses and had had to be bailed out by a loan from a financier who admired his work and by an advance on royalties of *The Economic Consequences of the Peace*.

TABLE 13.6   Speculation

If:	$R_{30} > E_{30}$	$R_{30} = E_{30}$	$R_{30} < E_{30}$
Then:	speculators will sell pounds forward	no reason to speculate	speculators will buy pounds forward
So that:	R_{30} is forced down	no effect on R_{30}	R_{30} is forced up

Table 13.6 indicates the role of speculation. In the table, R_{30} denotes the thirty-day forward rate of the pound in terms of dollars, and E_{30} denotes what people in general believe the spot rate will equal in thirty days. Since speculators buy forward pounds, thereby forcing up the rate when the latter is less than E_{30}, the forward rate is driven to equal the expected future spot rate— that is,

$$R_{30} = E_{30}.$$

Subtracting the current spot rate, R_s, from both sides and dividing R_s into both sides gives

$$\frac{R_{30} - R_s}{R_s} = \frac{E_{30} - R_s}{R_s} \tag{13.3}$$

The left-hand side is, once again, the forward premium on the pound. The right-hand side is the percentage by which people expect the spot rate to appreciate. Thus speculation implies that the forward premium should equal the expected spot appreciation.

Consistency of the Explanations

We thus have two theories explaining the relation between spot and forward rates. If international capital mobility is nearly perfect, we would expect interest arbitrage to exert dominant influence on the forward premium; a strong consensus on expected future appreciation should give speculation a dominant influence. The two theories are by no means inconsistent. With both nearly perfect capital mobility and a strong consensus about expectations, the two theories together imply that the expected spot appreciation should equal the interest differential.

How do forward premiums actually behave? We cannot directly observe the speculation theory because we do not know what people think the future holds in store. But all the variables in the covered interest parity relation (13.2) are observable, as Table 13.7 illustrates with data as of March 1994. In

TABLE 13.7   Ninety-Day Forward Premiums and Interest Differentials, March 1994

	United Kingdom	Canada	Germany	Japan
(1) Interest differential in favor of the U.S. dollar	−1.4	−0.2	−2.1	1.7
(2) Forward premium (+) or discount (−) relative to the U.S. dollar	1.3	−0.8	2.0	−1.9
(3) Difference: (1) − (2)	−0.1	−1.0	−0.1	−0.2

TABLE 13.8   **Ninety-Day Forward Premiums and Interest Differentials, February 1973**

	United Kingdom	Canada	Germany	Japan
(1) Interest differential in favor of the U.S. dollar	−2.5	1.5	0.7	1.3
(2) Forward premium (+) or discount (−) relative to the U.S. dollar	−3.9	1.5	5.7	21.7
(3) Difference: (1) − (2)	1.4	0.0	−5.0	−20.4

this case the interest parity relation holds well. In general, capital mobility between the industrial countries is sufficiently great that interest parity usually exerts a dominating influence, even though there are huge pools of funds able to react to expectations about exchange-rate movements. Interest differentials and forward premiums commonly differ by less than 1 percent, and differences above 2 percent are rare. Nevertheless, occasions do arise when interest differentials and exchange-rate expectations markedly diverge, so that at least one of the two theories must fail.

Consider, for example, Table 13.8, which records the analogous information as Table 13.7 for sometime in February 1973 instead. In this case interest parity works reasonably well for the United Kingdom and Canada but badly for Germany and, especially, Japan. In February 1973 the existing exchange-rate system was in its death throes. Fears were widespread of foreign-exchange crises with exchange controls and the closing of markets. Traders strongly expected the yen and mark to appreciate relative to the dollar (as in fact they did). Under such conditions capital mobility was far from perfect. Spot rates were still pegged, and interest rates were heavily influenced by domestic monetary objectives in the various countries. With imperfect capital mobility, interest arbitrage was inadequate to counter the heavy speculation on appreciation of the mark and yen relative to the dollar. Examples such as this are, however, rare.

Problems

13.5 In the text, Acme Spirits covered itself against exchange risk by buying pounds forward. Another way of accomplishing this would have been to borrow dollars from its bank, use the dollars to buy spot pounds, and deposit the pounds in a British bank until the time came to pay for the whiskey. What would be the cost of this second method? Which method would probably be cheaper and why?

13.6 Suppose that the U.S. interest rate is 8 percent per annum, the U.K. rate is 12 percent per annum, the spot price of a pound is $2.06, and the one-year forward price is $2.00. Describe the interest arbitrage this should induce.

13.7 Suppose in Problem **13.6** that the ninety-day forward price of a pound is $2.02. Describe the interest arbitrage that should be induced.

13.8 Can you think of any reason why capital movements should be less than perfect if all traders are free to buy and sell spot and forward foreign exchange and the treasury bills of all countries?

13.9 Work out the interest-arbitrage argument in the text if instead the trader is British and is concerned about the value of his assets in pounds rather than dollars. Do the same for the speculation example in the text.

13.10* As we shall see, exchange depreciation may cause domestic inflation. Suppose Acme Spirits were confident that, should the dollar depreciate relative to the pound, the American price of scotch whiskey would quickly rise in the same proportion. How should this influence the firm's decision on obtaining forward cover for its obligation to the U.K. distillery? What if Acme Spirits knew that dollar depreciation would raise the U.S. price of the whiskey but was unsure about how much or how soon?

13.11* Between 1973 and 1979 many controls on international capital movements were removed by the United Kingdom and by Germany. Can you discern any effects of this in Tables 13.7 and 13.8? Explain.

5.* *EXPLORING FURTHER:* EQUILIBRIUM IN THE FORWARD EXCHANGE MARKET

The Arbitrage Schedule

Why should capital mobility not be perfect—that is, why should any departure from interest parity not immediately bring about a switch of funds from the lower-yielding to the higher-yielding bill sufficiently massive to restore parity? There are two basic reasons. The first is *transaction cost:* time and expense are involved in selling one asset and assuming a covered position in another. If the difference in covered yields between the two assets is smaller than the transaction cost of switching between them, arbitrage will not ensue. However, this is a minor influence. For one thing, transaction costs are small, considerably less than 1 percent of the value of the transaction. In addition, the assets involved have short maturities (from a few days to up to a year) so that a substantial amount of the total funds committed to the market is always being redeemed; the cost of reinvesting these funds in one asset is the same as in the other so that transaction costs are not an issue. Sustained departure from interest parity cannot be explained by transaction costs.

The more important consideration is *risk*. If the two investments are perceived as risky, traders will want to protect themselves by diversification and so will not arbitrage without limit. The direct *foreign-exchange risk* is met by forward cover, but there are other types of risk. *Default risk* on the treasury bills is negligible since they are the obligations of the governments of wealthy nations. The default risk on the obligations of some governments, such as those of LDCs with large foreign debts, can be significant, but these currencies do not have forward markets. When traders arbitrage the commercial paper issued by U.S. and U.K. corporations rather than treasury bills, default risk is more significant, but only slightly so. There is one other source of default risk. When a U.S. trader invests in U.S. Treasury bills, he has an obligation of the U.S. government alone; but when he invests in U.K. Treasury bills, he has an obligation of the U.K. government (the bill) plus an obligation of a private bank (the forward market). The default risk of the latter must be taken account of. This risk is small although it is not zero: several banks have gone bankrupt during the last decade and defaulted on their forward contracts. *Country risk* is potentially more significant. Conceivably, a crisis might arise that would induce the political authorities to close down the foreign-exchange market, impose exchange controls, or take other measures that might prevent the trader from converting the proceeds of maturing foreign bills into domestic currency. This latter sort of risk was probably the most important reason for the failure of interest arbitrage revealed in Table 13.8.

The above considerations govern the shape of the *arbitrage schedule,* drawn in Figure 13.3. This curve shows how many forward pounds will be demanded by interest arbitrageurs at each value of the forward premium on the pound. The distance OI in each panel measures the interest-rate differential of the United States over the United Kingdom: $\dfrac{i_{US} - i_{UK}}{1 + i_{UK}}$. The arbitrage schedule goes through I because there is no incentive to perform arbitrage when the forward premium just equals the interest differential. When the forward premium is less than the interest differential, such as at point B, arbitrageurs

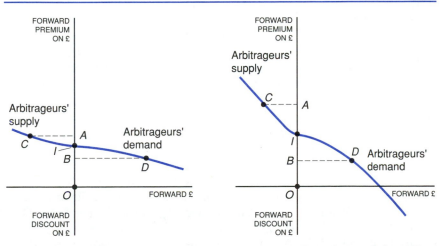

(a) **More nearly perfect capital mobility**   (b) **Less nearly perfect capital mobility**

FIGURE 13.3 The Arbitrage Schedule The arbitrage schedule shows how many forward pounds will be demanded by interest arbitrageurs who wish to sell spot pounds and buy U.S Treasury bills.

switch from U.K. Treasury bills to U.S. Treasury bills, and British dealers, therefore, demand forward pounds in order to cover their dollar investments. The distance *BD* indicates this demand, and it accordingly equals the total amount that British dealers commit to U.S. bills plus interest. When the forward premium exceeds the interest differential, arbitrage proceeds in the reverse direction, and American dealers cover their purchases of U.K. bills by demanding forward dollars—that is, by supplying forward pounds. Thus the forward premium *OA* in the figure causes arbitrageurs to supply the quantity *AC* of forward pounds.

The more nearly perfect is international capital mobility, the more elastic is the arbitrage schedule because a given deviation from interest parity causes a greater amount of interest arbitrage. This is illustrated in Figure 13.3 by the contrast between panel (a) and panel (b). With perfect capital mobility the schedule would be horizontal. The position of the arbitrage schedule depends upon interest rates in the two countries. An increase in the U.S. interest rate increases the interest differential, moves point *I* higher, and shifts the curve up. An increase in the U.K. interest rate has the opposite effect.

The Speculation Schedule

Figure 13.4(a) shows the forward position that will be taken by speculators at each value of the forward premium. The distance *OE* measures the expected appreciation of the spot rate, $\dfrac{E - R_s}{R_s}$. If the forward premium equals *OE,* there is no incentive to speculate. By Table 13.6, when the forward premium exceeds *OE,* speculators will sell forward pounds (for example, they sell *FG* when the premium equals *OF*); when *OE* exceeds the forward premium, speculators will buy forward pounds (they buy *JH* at *OH*). The position of the speculation schedule depends upon the actual spot exchange rate and the expected future rate. An increase in the latter moves point *E* higher and shifts the curve upward; an increase in the actual spot rate produces the opposite effect.

Panels (b) and (c) combine the arbitrage and speculation schedules to determine equilibrium. In panel (b), the interest differential exceeds the expected appreciation of the pound. Equilibrium is at point *B,* and the actual forward premium equals *OA.* Since this is less than the interest differential, arbitrageurs take a position in U.S. Treasury bills and so cover themselves by purchasing *AB* forward pounds from speculators, who are induced to sell this quantity by the fact that the forward premium exceeds the expected appreciation of the pound, *OE.* Panel (c) shows the opposite possibility.

As discussed in section 4, forward exchange will also be demanded by firms engaged in the international trade of goods and services. Figure 13.4 assumes that such trade is balanced in the sense that the demand for forward pounds resulting from U.S. importing equals the supply of forward pounds due to U.K. importing.

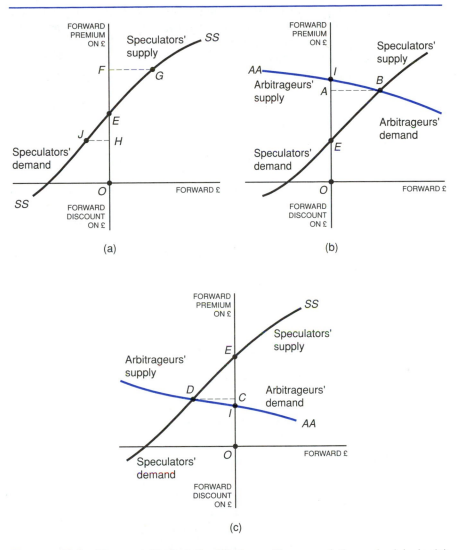

FIGURE 13.4   Forward Market Equilibrium   The speculation schedule in (a) shows how many forward pounds speculators will offer to sell at each forward premium. Equilibrium occurs where the supply of speculators equals the demand by interest arbitrageurs. In (b) the interest differential exceeds expected appreciation, and in (c) the expected appreciation exceeds the interest differential.

Consistency of the Interest Arbitrage and Speculative Theories

Suppose that the interest differential and the expected spot appreciation are unequal. Then the forward premium will be between the two, as shown in

Figure 13.4, and, with nearly perfect capital mobility, it will almost equal the interest differential. Now the consensus expectation *OE* about spot appreciation may actually turn out to be either right or wrong: the future is uncertain. But there is no reason to err in one direction rather than the other, and speculators who consistently guess wrong will lose their shirts. So, over the long term, the consensus expectation *OE* should *on average* equal the amount by which the spot rate *on average* actually does appreciate (more about this in section 11). An individual speculator, though, cannot know what the consensus expectation is because she has no way of probing the minds of her rivals. But Figure 13.4 shows that the forward premium exceeds the consensus expectation whenever the interest differential exceeds the forward premium and is less than the consensus expectation whenever the interest differential is less than the forward premium. Since the consensus expectation turns out, on average, to be correct, this means that a speculator can assure herself of a profit, on average, by selling forward pounds whenever the forward premium is less than the interest differential and by buying forward pounds in the opposite case. If *OE* and *OI* frequently diverge, speculators will become more confident, and, armed with the knowledge that they will gain over the long term, they will become more willing to speculate. That is, the speculators' schedule will become more elastic, as shown in Figure 13.5. With capital mobility nearly perfect and the arbitrage and speculation schedules highly elastic, a small excess of the interest differential over the spot appreciation will induce a very large movement of arbitrage funds from U.K. Treasury bills to U.S. Treasury bills, as shown in Figure 13.6(a). This will put heavy upward pressure on the U.K. in-

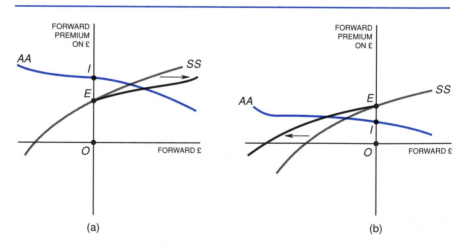

(a)   (b)

FIGURE 13.5   An Increase in Speculators' Confidence The speculation schedule shifts out horizontally if speculators become more confident in their beliefs and thus more willing to speculate.

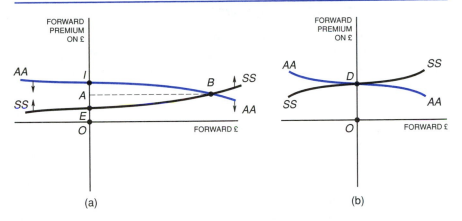

(a)　　　　　　　　　　　　　　　　(b)

FIGURE 13.6　Consistency of Speculative and Arbitrage Theories　As the U.K. interest rate rises and the U.S. interest rate falls, the arbitrage schedule shifts down and the speculation schedule shifts up.

terest rate and heavy downward pressure on the U.S. interest rate and on the spot exchange rate. This tends to shift the arbitrage schedule down and the speculation schedule up so that the market will tend toward the situation depicted in Figure 13.6(b). Thus, with nearly perfect capital mobility, there is heavy pressure on national interest rates and on the spot exchange rate to adjust themselves so that the interest differential, the forward premium, and the expected spot appreciation all remain nearly equal to each other.

Problems

13.12 Show graphically how the forward exchange market would likely react to each of the following events, and describe the consequences in words.

　a An increase in domestic interest rates.

　b An increase in the expected future spot rate.

　c An increased fear that foreign banks may be unable to honor their forward commitments.

Relate this to the situations described in Table 13.8.

13.13 The text assumed that commodity trade between the United States and the United Kingdom was balanced. How would the analysis change if the United States had a large trade surplus with the United Kingdom?

13.14 Show geometrically the result of intervention by the Bank of England to support the spot exchange rate of the pound relative to the dollar. Do the same for intervention to support the forward rate.

6. FOREIGN CURRENCY FUTURES AND OPTIONS

Forward exchange is the traditional means of dealing with changes over time in the values of national currencies. It is also the most important. But the rapid growth in the foreign-exchange market in recent years has involved the introduction of new financial instruments.

Foreign Currency Futures

A foreign currency *future* is a contract for a certain amount of a foreign currency to be delivered at a certain date in the future. Unlike forward exchange, futures contracts are in standard amounts, mature on standard last trade dates at three-month intervals, and are traded on regulated exchanges. The most important exchange is the International Monetary Market (IMM) of the Chicago Mercantile Exchange—a center of commodity futures trading—where regulation is by the Commodity Futures Trading Commission. Another important center is the London International Financial Futures Exchange (LIFFE). The Singapore International Monetary Exchange (SIMEX) has a link with the IMM allowing contracts from one exchange to be traded on the other. Foreign currency futures are also traded on several other exchanges around the world.

On March 23, 1994, the price on the IMM of a futures contract for £62,500 (the standardized quantity for a sterling contract) for delivery on the last trade date in September was $93,125—or $1.4900/£. Suppose that Julie bought two of these contracts. Then she could pay $186,250 on March 23, and subsequently take delivery of £125,000 on the maturity date in September. But in fact Julie would actually have put up only a small fraction (called a *margin payment*) of the value of the contracts. Suppose that this margin was $10,000. Now suppose that the next day the price of these contracts increased $0.02/£. Thus the value of Julie's two contracts rose $2,500 (that is, £125,000 × $0.02/£). Julie would be paid this $2,500 and would be free to take it and spend it as she wished. If the price of the contracts had instead fallen, the resulting loss would have been taken from her margin, and she would have had to pay more if the margin had fallen too low. At the close of each business day, increases and decreases in the value of the contracts would have been settled in this way. If Julie had held on to her contract until the September last trade date, she would have had to take delivery of the £125,000 and pay the balance of the price of the contracts. But it is rare for this to happen. More typically, she would have closed out her position before this by selling the contracts.

Thus buying a futures contract is like making a wager. You put up your stake (the margin), and each day you collect your winnings or pay up your losses until you decide to withdraw your stake by closing out your position. The winnings and losses are the changes in the total value of the futures contract, whereas the margin is only a small fraction of that value. (We say that the activity is a highly *leveraged* one.) Futures trading is, accordingly, a convenient way to speculate or to hedge. It is not a convenient way to arrange for future delivery of a currency, however, unless you just happen to want the currency on one of the four last trade dates per year.

The IMM deals in standardized futures contracts for the British pound, the Canadian dollar, the German mark, the Japanese yen, the Swiss franc, the French franc, and the Australian dollar, as well as the ECU, a basket of European currencies. (The ECU will surface later in this book.) Each contract is for a standardized amount of the respective foreign currency. Thus when futures prices vary, it is the dollar value of the contract that changes, not the foreign-currency value. Orders are executed in a trading pit by floor traders and brokers. There is a clearinghouse that nets out positions and guarantees members against default.

Foreign Currency Options

An *option* gives the buyer a right to make a transaction in the future but does not obligate him to do so. If you purchase a *call* option on the pound, for example, you pay the price of that option now and in exchange receive the right to buy a certain number of pounds at a certain price (called the "strike price") at any time up until a certain date in the future. Buying a *put* option would give you the right to *sell* a certain number of pounds at a certain price at any time up until a certain date in the future. The seller (or "writer") of the options is in an asymmetric position: he receives the price of the option now but has no discretion in the future since he is obligated to accede to your decision on whether to exercise the option or not. With a forward exchange contract, by contrast, both parties are required to consummate the agreement; therefore, each knows this will be done.

Foreign currency options are traded on the Philadelphia Stock Exchange, the London Stock Exchange, and a few other exchanges as well as over the counter. The options described above are sometimes called *American-style* options because they can be exercised at any time up to the expiration date. *European-style* options, which can be exercised *only* on the expiration date, are traded on the Chicago Board Options Exchange.

Options allow one to speculate with limited downside risk. For example, on April 13, 1994, a call option on the British pound at the strike price of $1.525/£ with an expiration date in June could have been bought for $0.005/£. Suppose that Sam, believing the pound was sure to go higher than $1.525, bought options on £125,000 (four option contracts in the standard amount of £31,250 each). These options would have cost him $625 (£125,000 × $0.005/£) plus any necessary brokerage commissions. This would have been the most Sam could lose. If he turned out to be wrong and the pound never went above $1.525 before the expiration date, he would simply not exercise the options and so would lose the $625. But if the spot price of the pound had risen to $1.545 he would have exercised the options, buying £125,000 at the strike price of $1.525 and selling them at the spot price of

$1.545. This would have yielded him $0.02/£ or $2,500, for a net profit of $1,875 (minus brokerage commissions). If he had instead speculated by buying pounds forward or by buying futures contracts, Sam would have exposed himself to unlimited risk.

Foreign currency options offer merchants a direct way to buy insurance against the risk of exchange-rate movements. Suppose that Mary expects to receive a payment of £50,000 from Britain sometime within the next month. If she pays, say, $400 to buy put options on £50,000 at a strike price of $1.50, she is in effect paying a $400 premium to purchase insurance that the exchange rate will not fall below $1.50/£. For if the spot rate does fall lower than this, Mary simply exercises her options when she receives the £50,000 and sells them at the strike price of $1.50/£.

Options on Futures and Futures on Options

As the foreign-exchange market continues to grow, it continues to develop new financial instruments. On the Chicago Mercantile Exchange, it is now possible to buy options on the foreign currency futures that are traded on the IMM. Such a call option, for example, would give the buyer the right to buy a certain number of standardized futures contracts on a certain currency at a certain price up to a certain date. On the LIFFE, contracts are now traded that are essentially futures contracts on options on foreign exchange.

7. THE EUROCURRENCY MARKET

Banks in New York accept dollar deposits and make dollar loans; London banks deal in pounds sterling, and so on. But recent decades have witnessed the rapid development of a new type of banking.

Eurodollars and Eurocurrencies

Eurodollars are dollars deposited in banks outside the United States, and, more generally, *Eurocurrency* deposits are denominated in currencies other than that of the country in which the bank is located. Institutions that accept deposits and make loans in Eurocurrencies are known as *Eurobanks*. Note that the location of the bank is the determining factor: dollar deposits in London are Eurodollars even if the depositor is an American citizen and the bank accepting the deposit is a London branch of an American bank.

The Eurocurrency market is the major international financial innovation of the postwar period. From virtually nothing in the late 1950s, the market grew to over $5 trillion in size in the early 1990s. About two-thirds of the total are Eurodollars; Euromarks and Euro-Swiss francs are the most important other Eurocurrencies, and there are large markets in Eurosterling, Euro-French francs, and Euroyen.

Example: Eurocurrency Mechanics

The best way to understand the phenomenon is to consider an example. Suppose that a German firm—say, Bayer—has acquired $5 million in the form of a demand deposit in an American bank—say, Bank of America. Bayer will not need the funds for thirty days and wishes to earn interest in the meantime. The traditional course of action, as described in section 1, would be to sell the dollars for marks on the foreign-exchange market and to invest the marks. But suppose that Bayer wishes to keep dollars because it anticipates making dollar payments in a month. The firm could invest the dollars in New York, or it could use the Eurodollar market. We shall presently discuss some reasons why the latter might be preferable. Suppose Bayer deposits the money in a London Eurobank—say, Barclays. This means that Bayer pays Barclays $5 million and receives a $5 million deposit in return. Barclays then deposits the money received from Bayer into its own account at a correspondent bank in New York—say, Chase Manhattan. When the payments clear, Bank of America pays Chase Manhattan the $5 million. This situation is depicted in Table 13.9. Chase Manhattan has the $5 million deposit from Barclays; the table assumes a 20 percent reserve requirement in America, so Chase Manhattan holds $1 million in reserves at the FED and loans out the remaining $4 million. Barclays has as a liability the $5 million deposit of Bayer, and its reserves are the $5 million Barclays has on deposit with Chase Manhattan. In this example the Eurodollars may be identified as the $5 million Bayer deposit at Barclays in London.

Table 13.9 is, however, only the beginning of the story. Barclays will not sit on its $5 million but will lend it out to earn interest. Of course Barclays knows that in thirty days it must repay Bayer. But the money can be put to work until then, and in any case new dollar deposits will be constantly coming in. The Eurodollar market is largely unregulated, so Barclays is under no legal obligation to hold reserves against its dollar deposits, as New York banks must do. Suppose that Barclays nevertheless keeps a small reserve—say, $100,000—against an emergency and decides to lend the rest. Perhaps

TABLE 13.9 Initial Creation of Eurodollars

Assets	Liabilities

Reserves:
  $1 million
Loans:
  $4 million
	Deposits:
	  $5 million

(a) **Chase Manhattan in New York**

Assets	Liabilities

Reserves:
  $5 million
	Deposits:
	  $5 million

(b) **Barclays in London**

Coagulated Mush, Ltd. borrows $1.9 million from Barclays to pay for imports from the United States. Barclays then gives Coagulated Mush a check for $1.9 million drawn on Chase Manhattan, and Coagulated Mush pays it to the American firm, National Grain, which then deposits it in its own account in New York. Suppose, for simplicity's sake, that this is at Chase Manhattan. Then Barclays's deposit at Chase Manhattan goes down by $1.9 million and National Grain's deposit increases by that amount.

If Barclays at the moment has no other customers seeking loans, it will lend the remaining $3 million to some other bank that does. Suppose Credit Suisse in Zurich borrows the money because a Swiss customer, Tick-Tock Watch, wants to borrow funds to meet a payroll. Barclays lends the funds to Credit Suisse by opening a deposit of $3 million in that bank and transferring to it $3 million of its own balance at Chase Manhattan (assume that Credit Suisse also uses Chase Manhattan as its New York correspondent). This interbank deposit is shown in Table 13.10. Suppose that Credit Suisse also keeps a $100,000 reserve in New York and sells the remaining $2.9 million on the foreign-exchange market for, say, SFr 5 million, which are loaned to Tick-Tock. The $2.9 million now leave the Eurodollar market; presumably they will largely be used by their purchasers to buy American goods, services, and assets, and the American sellers will likely hold their deposits in American banks—such as Chase Manhattan.

The final position is summarized in Table 13.11. The *gross* size of the Eurodollar market (total deposits of dollars in banks outside the United States) is $8 million. But this does not take into account the fact that $3 million of this total is used only for an interbank loan between two Eurobanks. Subtracting this amount leaves a *net* size of $5 million.

TABLE 13.10   An Interbank Deposit

Assets	Liabilities	Assets	Liabilities
Reserves: $0.1 million (in New York) Loans: $1.9 million (to Coagulated Mush) $3.0 million (to Credit Suisse)	Deposits: $5.0 million	Reserves: $3.0 million (in New York)	Deposits: $3.0 million

(a) **Barclays in London**   (b) **Credit Suisse in Zurich**

TABLE 13.11   Final Position

Assets	Liabilities	Assets	Liabilities
Reserves: $0.42 million	Deposits: $0.10 million (Barclays)	Reserves: $0.10 million	Deposits: $5.00 million
Loans: $1.68 million	$1.90 million (National Grain)	Loans: $1.90 million (Coagulated Mush)	
	$0.10 million (Credit Suisse)	$3.00 million (Credit Suisse)	

(a) **Chase Manhattan in New York**   (b) **Barclays in London**

Assets	Liabilities
Reserves: $0.10 million	Deposits: $3.00 million (Barclays)
Loans: SFr 5 million (= $2.90 million)	

(c) **Credit Suisse in Zurich**

Reasons for the Markets

The Eurocurrency markets developed in response to two basic causes. The first was *political:* some individuals who desired to hold dollars did not want to become involved with U.S. financial markets. This motive figured in the early days of the market. In the 1950s the Soviet Union increased its trade with the West and accordingly began to acquire and use dollar balances. But the Soviets were reluctant to hold their dollars in U.S. banks: they feared that U.S. authorities could monitor their use or could confiscate or freeze them should the Cold War take a bad turn. (The American assets of Communist China had been frozen.) The Soviets found a Paris bank that was able to find dollar borrowers (the cable address of this bank was EUROBANK—hence, the generic term). In recent decades the political motive has again become important as Arab governments have placed in the Eurocurrency market huge amounts of funds earned from oil sales.

The second major impetus to the development of the Eurocurrency markets was furnished by national *controls.* From 1963 until 1974 U.S. exchange controls limited the ability of foreigners to borrow dollars in the United States, and strict U.K. controls seriously limited foreign sterling borrowings until 1978. Such controls had the effect of directing international borrowing and lending toward the Eurocurrency market. National regulation of banking activity has the same effect. All major countries regulate domestic banking in national currencies, but Eurobanking is largely unregulated. U.K. authorities, for example, regulate the sterling activity of British banks because domestic money (sterling) is important to the domestic economy, but they leave British banks essentially free to do what they wish with foreign money (such as dollars) in the belief that such activity has little direct domestic effect but is a source of business for the banking industry. Such regulations often drive a wedge between the rates banks pay depositors and the rates they charge borrowers. The U.S. Fed, for example, requires member banks to hold a portion of their deposits as noninterest earning reserves. Even more significant was Regulation Q, which placed ceilings on the interest rates U.S. banks could pay depositors (for example, interest was prohibited on deposits of less than thirty days). When money was tight and lending rates were high, deposit rates were held down by Regulation Q, and large gaps between the two arose. Eurobanks are basically unregulated and so are not subject to interest rate ceilings or reserve requirements (and what reserves they choose to hold as a precaution earn interest). All this gives Eurobanking a competitive edge over national banking.

To see how that competitive edge works, suppose that domestic banks have a 25 percent reserve requirement. Then domestic bank D may lend out only $75 of each $100 received as deposits. If the deposit rate is, say, 5 percent, bank D must pay $5 interest on the deposit and, therefore, must charge $6^1/_4$ percent interest on the $75 loan just to pay for the deposit ($75 $\times$ $6^1/_4$ percent = $5). If $1^3/_4$ percent is necessary to cover the other costs of banking, the minimum rate that bank D can charge on its loans is 8 percent. Since Eurobank E faces no reserve requirement, it can pay $5^1/_2$ percent on its deposits, thereby luring dollar deposits away from bank D, and charge $7^1/_2$ percent for its loans (thereby luring away borrowers) and still cover its costs.

Regulation of domestic U.S. banks was a crucial factor in the rapid growth the Eurocurrency markets experienced in their formative years during the late 1960s and early 1970s. When U.S. monetary policy tightened in 1969, for example, foreign subsidiaries of U.S. firms switched their deposits from American banks to the Eurobanks, which paid higher interest. At the same time, corporate borrowers also went to the Eurobanks, where loans were more readily available and the terms attractive. American banks responded by opening many foreign branches to participate in the growing Eurocurrency business (about 40 percent of the activity in London has actually been done through the branches of American banks, and in recent years the branches of Japanese banks have also become important). The home offices then borrowed dollars from their overseas branches to lend to their domestic customers.

The location of Eurocurrency markets has been determined by national regulations, with the action naturally gravitating toward those countries with the least restrictions. The market is basically unregulated not because no countries regulate such activity, but because the market stays away from those that do. Thus there is little Eurocurrency activity in either the United States or Germany, each a financial colossus, whereas significant centers are in Nassau, Panama, the Cayman Islands, Luxembourg, and Bahrain. (The prefix "Euro" is evidently obsolete.) Other important centers include Zurich, Paris, Amsterdam, Hong Kong, and Singapore; activity in the latter two centers is sometimes labeled the "Asia-dollar market." But the most important center, where about a third of all business takes place, is London. In the 1950s exchange control prevented London from continuing as the major international financial center that it long had been: specialized institutions and the expertise of the City (London's financial district) were underutilized. Then the Eurodollar market began to develop. The British quickly realized that this offered a way for them to utilize their international banking skills without disturbing domestic monetary arrangements. Accordingly, when in 1958 restrictive regulations were removed, London quickly became the focal point of the new market.

Despite their crucial role in the formative years of the market and their decisive continuing effect on the location of Eurocurrency activity, national controls are no longer of such importance for the total size of the Euromarkets. These markets have become the conduit for a major part of large-scale international credit transactions, and they function efficiently. Their continued existence no longer requires a competitive advantage over national money markets. Also, the national controls have weakened, at least in part, no doubt, because of the increased competition national markets have faced from the Euromarkets. American and British exchange controls have been terminated. In the United States, Regulation Q has been liberalized—for example, there are no longer interest-rate ceilings on large negotiable certificates of deposit, a major competitor of Eurodollar deposits. American banks have been required to hold reserves against the Eurodollars they borrow. In recent years the political motive has been more important, rendering the Euromarkets attractive for deposits of Arab oil earnings.

The Nature of Current Activity

Eurodollar deposits are typically large ($1 million or more) and short-term (overnight to six months), although there are exceptions. Loans are also large and short-term, but there is also much business in medium-term (three to seven years) loans with the interest rate adjusted every few months. The largest of these loans are typically syndicated (made jointly by a number of banks so that even the largest credit needs can be met). Alternatively, banks might lend by purchasing *Euronotes* and *Eurocommercial paper* issued by borrowers; the banks can then sell these obligations on secondary markets if they wish, something that is difficult to do with straight loans. Eurocurrency futures and options are also actively traded on several exchanges.

In the formative years of the market, large corporations were the most important (nonbank) borrowers and lenders. European central banks deposited part of their dollar reserves in the market, and American banks borrowed from it when money was tight. After the rise in oil prices, the governments of oil-exporting countries also became prominent depositors and petrodollars (that is, dollars earned by selling oil) an important source of funds. Governments have also become much more important in recent years as borrowers. The then-communist countries became important borrowers, and many LDCs have borrowed huge sums to finance large payments deficits. Britain, Canada, and Italy have also borrowed Eurodollars to augment their official reserves. A good part of the payments deficits prompting these loans was in fact due to the increases in the price of oil during the 1970s. Thus the Eurocurrency markets played a key role in "recycling" petrodollars from oil exporters to oil importers.

Problems

13.15 Suppose that Bayer acquires $5 million drawn on an American bank and deposits it in the London branch of Chase Manhattan. Chase's New York office then borrows $4 million from its London branch. Show the balance-sheet entries of both the home office and the branch. What are the effects on the sizes of the Eurodollar market and the U.S. and U.K. money supplies?

13.16 The text showed that U.S. reserve requirements gave Eurobanks a competitive edge over domestic banks. But Eurodollars are mostly time deposits, and U.S. reserve requirements for time deposits are low, whereas the requirements for demand deposits are much higher. Would you not, therefore, expect Eurodollars to consist mainly of demand deposits? Why do you think this has not happened?

13.17 The Depository Institutions Deregulation and Monetary Control Act phased out all U.S. ceilings on deposit interest rates by 1986. What do you think were the effects on the Eurocurrency markets?

13.18 Measure what happens to (1) U.S. liabilities to foreign official institutions, (2) German official holdings of dollars, and (3) the size of the Eurodollar market in the following series of transactions:

a The Bundesbank switches $1 billion from its account at Morgan Guaranty New York to Morgan Guaranty London (MGL) in order to obtain a higher interest rate.

b MGL lends $900 million to a German firm (which is facing tight monetary conditions inside Germany). The German firm in turn sells the dollars to the Bundesbank for marks in order to invest in Germany. The Bundesbank deposits the $900 million at MGL.

c Another German firm borrows $810 million from MGL and trades the dollars for marks. In turn, the Bundesbank deposits the $810 million at MGL.

d The Bundesbank lodges a protest with the Federal Reserve Board, complaining that it is impossible to maintain an anti-inflationary policy as long as the United States insists on flooding Europe with excess dollars. How should the Fed reply?

13.19* Suppose that Texaco and British Petroleum each make $500 million payments to the government of Kuwait:

a Texaco makes payment by issuing a draft on its account with Citibank/New York (CBNY).

b BP sells spot sterling for dollars, causing the Bank of England to draw down its dollar reserves held with CBNY by $500 million in order to support the spot rate.

c Kuwait deposits the $1 billion with CB London.

Show how these transactions affect

i The U.S. and U.K. money supplies.

ii The size of the Eurodollar market.

In what way would these transactions tend to influence interest rates in the United States, the United Kingdom, and the Eurodollar market? How might this alter patterns of borrowing and lending?

13.20* During the mid-1960s many observers worried that the Eurodollar system would collapse in the face of widespread speculation against the dollar. Since that time we have witnessed several speculative episodes, and in each instance not only has the Eurodollar market survived, but it has actually increased in size. Explain why this should have been expected by analyzing the impact of the expectation of a dollar depreciation on

a Nonbank demand for Eurodollar borrowing.

b Non(commercial)bank supply of Eurodollar deposits.

8. *CASE STUDY:* THE IRANIAN FREEZE

On November 14, 1979, as part of the deterioration of relations following the Iranian seizure of the U.S. embassy and the holding of embassy personnel as hostages, President Carter ordered the freezing of all official Iranian assets in the United States, estimated to be about $12 billion. Up to half of this amount was not directly in the United States, but consisted of Eurodollar deposits in the overseas branches of American banks. The administration in effect attempted to extend the freeze beyond the United States by virtue of the fact that many Eurobanks are U.S.-owned. This action was strongly resented in the banking community (one poll claimed that two-thirds of international bankers—including Americans—disapproved) on the grounds that it struck at one of the basic attractions of a key financial market, that it would place the branches of American banks at a competitive disadvantage relative to other Eurobanks in the competition for Eurodollar deposits, and that it would induce a shift of funds for Eurodollars to other Eurocurrencies.

Some commentators blamed the subsequent depreciation of the dollar in part on the freeze. Also the fact that different national jurisdictions were involved meant that the U.S. action caused an immense legal tangle to begin to develop. A new law journal was founded just to specialize in issues raised by the freeze. The agreement for the return of the hostages, reached early in 1981, also included measures for releasing the frozen assets and for settling private claims against Iran. Several years later the Eurodollar market proved convenient when several countries (including the United States) wished to sell arms secretly to Iran, which was locked in a bitter war with Iraq.

9. SHOULD THE EUROCURRENCY MARKETS BE REGULATED?

Recommendations that the Eurocurrency markets be regulated are based upon a number of alleged abuses.

1. One alarm is that the rapid growth of Eurocurrencies has created a huge volume of world liquidity in an unmanaged fashion. This is asserted to be highly inflationary. One consequence of the lack of regulation is the absence of uniform reporting requirements for Eurobanks; thus we are highly uncertain about the size and composition of the market. But it is huge. Estimates of its gross size range upward from $6 trillion. The net size of the market is greater than any single country's money supply: the number of Eurodollars is greater than the U.S. money supply, the (gross) size of the Euromark market exceeds the German money supply, and likewise for (gross) Euro-Swiss francs and Switzerland's money supply. These figures are mind-boggling and seem to give great force to the expressed fears. But detailed considerations result in a much calmer view. There is, first, the distinction between gross size and net size noted earlier. Second, total net deposits still contain many deposits from central banks and non-Eurobanks. Total nonbank deposits of the public are perhaps $1 trillion. Third, these deposits are time deposits and thus less analogous to national money supplies than to the much larger totals of commercial bank time deposits, saving and loan shares, and other near-monies. Eurocurrencies are not actually media of exchange. All this makes the problem seem much less ominous. It is still true that the Eurocurrency markets have supplied liquidity services in an unmanaged fashion, but this is a problem with near-monies that central banks have long faced anyway.

2. It has been asserted that the international movement of Eurocurrencies frustrates the attempts of individual countries to control their own money supplies. For example, when the Fed tried to tighten U.S. monetary conditions in the late 1960s, American banks were still able to lend by simply borrowing Eurodollars from their foreign branches. But this alarm also loses much of its force when the actual nature of Eurodollars is closely examined. The above example of Eurocurrency mechanics makes it clear that a bank or corporation that borrows Eurodollars receives not newly created dollars, but already existing deposits in an American bank. Thus when U.S. banks borrowed Eurodollars from abroad, they did not draw new dollar deposits into the system, but merely reallocated existing deposits among themselves. This did not impede the Fed in its efforts to control the total stock of such deposits. Indeed, the Euromarkets contributed to efficiency by allowing credit to be allocated by market-clearing prices (the Eurodollar interest rates) instead of by rationing due to distorted domestic prices. Nevertheless, there is again a kernel of truth to the popular alarm. If the authorities do in fact attempt to influ-

ence the economy by credit rationing, their efforts could be frustrated by domestic borrowing in the Euromarkets. Or if the Eurodollars borrowed from abroad had originally been deposited in the market as the result of central-bank intervention, they could render control of the money supply more difficult, both at home and abroad. But this is really the basic problem of conducting an effective national monetary policy in the face of a high degree of capital mobility. The Eurocurrency markets enter the discussion basically because they are a symptom and a product of highly mobile capital. Only to the extent that they, in turn, foster even more capital mobility are the Eurocurrency markets candidates for regulation on this score.

3. The Eurocurrency markets have been accused of contributing to international financial instability by weakening the pressures on deficit countries to adjust. As we have seen, in recent years many countries, primarily but not exclusively LDCs, have borrowed in the Eurodollar market to help finance balance-of-payments deficits. If these countries had been unable to borrow Eurodollars, they would have been forced to take steps to correct their deficits as their international reserves became depleted. These countries might instead have borrowed from other governments or from the International Monetary Fund; but such lenders, unlike the Eurobanks, would have required corrective action as conditions for the loans. Many LDCs have found it difficult to service or to repay their loans, and this has, in turn, raised fears about the solvency of some major banks (the LDC debt crisis is discussed later in this book). Defenders of the Eurocurrency markets retort that these markets add a desirable degree of flexibility to the world economy and claim that the official borrowing of Eurodollars was an essential part of the "recycling" of petrodollars in response to the large and sudden increases in oil prices. In any event, what is at issue is again the degree of capital mobility.

4. It is often said that the Eurocurrency markets supply a huge pool of liquid capital that can be moved from currency to currency in search of speculative gain. Once again, what is basically at issue is the desirability of a high degree of capital mobility, of which the Eurocurrency markets are symptoms.

5. Eurobanking is often said to be collectively risky because of the absence of regulation. Although the quality of their loans is sometimes criticized, Eurobanks have no reason to be less concerned with the safety of their assets than national banks. But the Eurocurrency system differs in one obvious respect from a national banking system: the latter has a *lender of last resort* (the central bank) that is prepared to supply funds in the event of a crisis to prevent the collapse of the system. It is feared that a serious economic shock could, in contrast, cause the Eurocurrency system to fall apart like a house of cards. If central banks collectively are to supply a lender of last resort to such a market, they must get their act together. They have, in fact, consulted about the problem, and it seems that this issue will be attacked by continued efforts of central banks to reach a consensus on individual responsibilities and not by formal regulation.

The various alleged dangers of the Eurocurrency markets reflect to a large extent misunderstanding about the nature of those markets. There are two serious problems to be faced if Eurocurrency regulation is to be used to deal with the alleged dangers.

First, since the basic problem is capital mobility, regulation will be effective only to the degree that it succeeds in limiting such mobility. We are really talking about exchange control with all its problems here. Second, the prospects of effectively regulating the Eurocurrency markets are questionable.

Can the Eurocurrency Markets Be Regulated?

We saw in the previous section that Eurocurrency activity gravitates to those countries where it is not restricted. Should any country attempt to regulate the activity within its borders, the business will simply go elsewhere. Thus there is a strong incentive for those countries where the Euromarkets are located to continue to leave them unregulated, despite the alleged dangers in doing so. Regulation must be multilateral to succeed. Attempts, thus far unsuccessful, have been made to gain agreement for multilateral regulation, with the United States and Germany relatively more enthusiastic than those countries that have the business. Agreement and successful implementation seem unlikely because they would have to be very comprehensive: the market has already demonstrated an ability to locate in obscure places. Thus meaningful regulation of the Eurocurrency markets probably cannot be achieved without substantial exchange controls by the major nations.

International Banking Facilities

In the United States, Eurocurrency regulation has actually been reduced. Since December 1981 U.S. banks have been allowed by the Federal Reserve to set up International Banking Facilities (IBFs), which are free of reserve requirements and interest-rate ceilings. The IBFs are allowed to deal only with foreigners in either dollars or foreign currency and are excluded from domestic business. The idea is to allow U.S.-based banks to capture part of the business in the Eurocurrency markets.

For years much Eurocurrency business has in effect been conducted in New York but put on the books of Caribbean branches of U.S. banks. Some believed that creating IBFs would cause an illusory gain in IBF business when the Eurocurrency business was transferred to the books of New York IBFs, resulting in large numbers but little practical significance. In fact, there was no rush on the part of U.S. banks to replace their Caribbean "shells" with IBF "shells." IBFs still have some disadvantages relative to the foreign-based Eurobanks: IBF deposits must be for at least two days, and IBFs cannot issue negotiable instruments. However, foreign banks that are prohibited from operating in the Caribbean have set up IBFs instead.

10. THE EFFICIENCY OF THE FOREIGN-EXCHANGE MARKETS

Managed floating has been the exchange regime for key industrial countries since March 1973. Since then *exchange rates have fluctuated.* Wide swings and sharp movements of the rates have produced much consternation and have at times strongly influenced national policies. Jacob Frenkel of the Bank of Israel and Michael Mussa of the University of Chicago have calculated that the dollar/pound, dollar/mark, and dollar/French franc exchange rates each experienced average monthly fluctuations in excess of 2 percent between June 1973 and February 1979. Such turbulence reduces the usefulness of national currencies as money. At the same time, exchange rates have varied much more than relative inflation rates, national economic policies, or other fundamental influences, and so it is not at all clear that this turbulence is simply the price that must be paid to allow individual countries to control their own money supplies. However, we cannot conclude from the pronounced exchange-rate variability that the foreign-exchange markets have not functioned well. The world economy has been subjected to serious shocks since 1973 (for example, oil price increases and decreases), and before that foreign-exchange crises afflicted and ultimately destroyed the adjustable peg system.

An important criterion for judging the performance of markets is that of efficiency. *A market is efficient if its prices fully reflect all currently available information.* Why is it important that the foreign-exchange market be efficient? Individual consumers and producers base decisions on relative prices; those prices equal corresponding marginal rates of transformation, marginal rates of substitution, and so on, and cause individuals to make socially "correct" decisions. Exchange rates are used to compare prices expressed in different currencies; therefore, if the exchange rates do not reflect all available information, the decisions of individual consumers and producers will not be based on all available information and so will not be socially correct.

Interest Arbitrage

Judging the efficiency of a market is fundamentally difficult because we cannot directly observe whether prices do in fact reflect all available information. An indirect way to try to judge efficiency is to look for unexploited profit opportunities: if some information is not reflected in prices, someone should be able to "beat the market" by utilizing the overlooked information. For example, consider the discussion of interest arbitrage in section 4. The interest-parity condition, Equation (13.1) or (13.2), essentially requires that exchange rates (spot and forward) fully reflect the information contained in the interest rates. If this is not so—that is, if interest parity does not hold— you can make a profit by conducting covered interest arbitrage as summarized in Table 13.4. In this case you are exploiting your information about interest rates to beat the market. In fact it is just such activity, or dealers' anticipations of such activity, that will cause the exchange rates to adjust to reflect this information if the markets are in fact efficient.

As Tables 13.7 and 13.8 illustrated, there is a strong tendency toward interest parity, but the tendency is by no means complete. Here we face a problem of interpretation. It is possible that the departures from interest parity reflect a lack of total efficiency in the markets. But it is also possible that these departures reflect information *in addition* to interest rates and are, therefore, in a sense consistent with efficiency. For example, the exchange rates could reflect the risk that a bank might default on a forward contract or that a government might impose exchange controls preventing individuals from repatriating funds placed in foreign assets. We can obtain some perspective on this by examining the activities of Eurobanks, which simultaneously engage in foreign-exchange transactions and Eurocurrency borrowing and lending. Tables 13.7 and 13.8 compared forward premiums with differentials in domestic interest rates. If we were to instead go to, say, the Eurocurrency market in London and compare the forward premium on the mark relative to the dollar with the interest rate differential between Euromarks and Eurodollars, we would find interest parity holding almost exactly. Indeed, interest arbitrage is so pervasive in the Euromarkets that dealers routinely use the interest-parity formula to determine quotes. Why this difference between Euromarkets and national markets? In the former case the risk factor largely washes out. A Eurobank in London could conceivably default on forward contracts, but it would likely do so on both mark and dollar contracts; neither dollars nor marks constitute British money, so the chance of British exchange controls on Eurobank activities in the two currencies is slight and common to both. Also, the Eurocurrency markets are subject to less existing regulation. In summary, *interest arbitrage is virtually complete in the Euromarkets and is strong, but not complete, between national markets.*

Figure 13.7 shows the virtual identity between the Euromark interest rate and the covered interest rate of Eurodollars. The figure also shows how controls influence the relation between Eurocurrency markets and domestic markets. Germany had exchange controls from 1971 through 1973 that limited foreign purchases of German assets and allowed the domestic (interbank) interest rate to remain considerably above the Euromark rate. When many of these controls were terminated in 1974 the two rates quickly converged, as is shown in the figure.

Speculation

Interest arbitrage in the Euromarkets furnishes some evidence for market efficiency. The evidence cannot be decisive, however, because interest rates constitute only a portion of all the information that exchange rates should reflect. For example, forward exchange rates should reflect all available information about future spot rates—that is, the forward rate should be the "best" available forecast of what the spot rate will be. If the market is not efficient in this sense, individuals can utilize the unexploited information to conduct profitable speculation, as described in section 4.

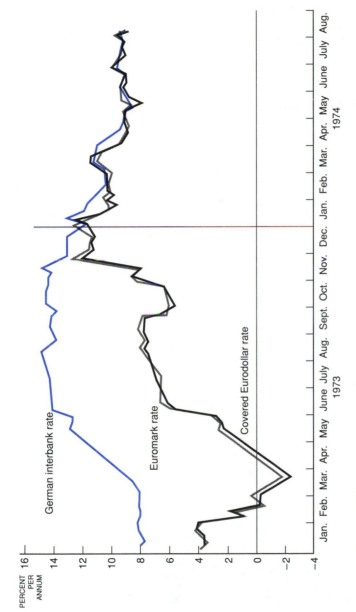

FIGURE 13.7 Interest Arbitrage in the Eurocurrency Markets (January 1973–August 1974) The near-coincidence of the Euromark and covered Eurodollar interest rates shows covered interest parity in the Euromarkets. Prior to 1974, German controls allowed interest rates in Germany to diverge, but the removal of these controls established covered interest parity for these rates as well.

SOURCE: Money Manager for Euromark rate; Federal Reserve Board for all other interest and exchange rates.

How good a forecast is the forward rate? Not very good in the sense that the forward premium generally differs from the spot appreciation that subsequently takes place, and often by large amounts. But the errors may not be systematic; thus a speculator need not be able to make money simply by betting against the forward rate in a mechanical way. Figure 13.8 depicts a hypothetical but typical relationship between the thirty-day forward premium at various dates and the appreciation of the spot rate that actually happens in the thirty days after each date. If the forward rate were a perfectly accurate forecast of the future spot rate, the circle at each date would coincide with the cross at that date. The crosses do not predict the circles well, but they are not biased in any way either. Many economists have investigated the ability of the forward rate to forecast the future spot rate, and these investigations together indicate that *the forward premium is an inaccurate but almost unbiased predictor of the future spot appreciation.*

Formal investigations do cast doubt on whether the forward rate is completely unbiased. For example, Lars Hansen and Robert Hodrick of Carnegie-Mellon University presented data showing that, for several currencies in the 1970s and in the 1920s, the expected return from speculation was not necessarily zero. Other researchers have consistently obtained similar results. *Forward premiums generally exhibit some (small) bias as predictors of future spot appreciations.*

By using information not incorporated into the forward rate, is it possible to find a predictor that is not only unbiased, but also more accurate than the forward rate? A number of economists have investigated this possibility with mixed results. The forward rate is often better, and never much worse,

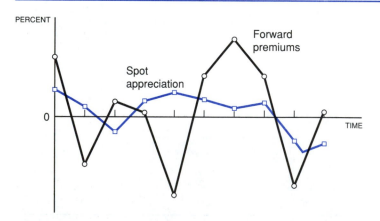

FIGURE 13.8 Hypothetical Forward Premiums and Subsequent Spot Appreciation   In this example, the forward premiums are not close to the subsequent spot appreciations, but they do not differ in a systematic way.

than proposed alternatives, but there are indications that a modest improvement on the forward rate is possible. In recent years a number of firms have gone into the business of forecasting exchange rates and selling their predictions to banks and corporations. That these forecasting firms can earn a profit is interesting because their customers can presumably learn current forward quotes with a simple telephone call. The periodical *Euromoney* concluded that corporate treasurers utilize the services of forecasting firms not to obtain forecasts so much as to obtain other market information provided by forecasters. It is difficult to know what to make of this. Richard Levich of New York University has studied the performance of the forecasters and has found that they may offer some modest benefits relative to forward rates. Overall, research to date indicates that *the forward rate is almost the best available forecast of the future spot rate, but the jury is still out on whether it is in fact the best.*

Why It Is So Hard to Test Market Efficiency

Economists often try to test for the efficiency of foreign-exchange markets by comparing forward rates and subsequent spot rates—for example, the thirty-day forward rate might be compared to the spot rate that actually prevails thirty days later. Such tests are really investigating a joint hypothesis that (a) individuals use all available information in trying to predict the future behavior of spot rates (for example, the hypothesis might be that people do not know what the future spot rate will actually be, but they do discover the probability law that governs its behavior) and that (b) the forward rate equals what people expect the future spot rate to be—that is, their "best" guess. There are two fundamental difficulties. The first is that we cannot test (a) and (b) separately because we cannot observe individuals' predictions. Thus if a test should reject the joint hypothesis that (a) and (b) hold, we would not know whether the rejection is due to the fact that (a) is false, that (b) is false, or that both are false. The second problem is that we do not know whether (a) and (b) are in fact necessary for the foreign-exchange markets to be efficient (in the general sense that exchange rates rationally reflect all available information). For example, under some circumstances it might be necessary in equilibrium to pay traders a *risk premium* in order to induce them to hold a currency perceived as unusually risky. In such a case hypothesis (b) need not hold, but the market could still be efficient: the difference between the forward rate and the expected future spot rate would furnish the required risk premium. Under this interpretation, the empirical evidence that the forward rate is not quite an unbiased predictor of the future spot rate indicates that (small) risk premiums do exist. Efforts to explain these premiums empirically have not yet been conclusive.

It is costly to acquire information, and the value of the information can only be guessed at beforehand. Thus hypothesis (a) need not hold if people believe that it is not worthwhile to acquire information that is available at a price, but the market could still be efficient. It is a difficult theoretical problem to delineate precisely the circumstances under which (a) and (b) characterize efficiency, and it is a difficult empirical problem to decide when those circumstances actually hold.

The Effect of New Information

To the extent that exchange rates do fully reflect all current information, the appearance of new information should immediately cause changes in exchange rates as the market absorbs the news. Any reader of the financial press is aware of the frenetic reception the market accords significant and unexpected news items. Short-term fluctuations in exchange rates seem to be dominated by the receipt of new information because these fluctuations are much larger than what can be explained by continuing influences such as differences in national inflation rates or interest rates. Over longer periods of time the transient information effects tend to cancel each other out so that the latter continuing influences become more important.

Day-to-day movements in forward rates tend to be accompanied by almost identical day-to-day movements in current (not future) spot rates. One reason for this is interest arbitrage, which, as we have seen, links spot and future rates together in the interest-parity relationship. But the receipt of new information would also produce such behavior. Suppose, for example, that some development implying a weakening of the pound relative to the dollar suddenly becomes publicly known. The spot pound/dollar exchange rate will adjust quickly as the market absorbs the news. Now the forward rate is a bad forecast of the future spot rate, but it may be largely an unbiased one. The news item is the *only* change that has taken place and so is the only reason to change the (admittedly bad) forecast of the future spot rate. The forward rate, therefore, responds in basically the same way as the current spot rate.

In summary, available evidence indicates a high degree of efficiency in foreign-exchange markets, and those markets accordingly seem sensitive to new developments. But the evidence also indicates departures from complete efficiency.

Problem

13.21 German exchange controls on capital inflows were relaxed on January 30, 1974, but Figure 13.7 shows that the Euromark and German interbank interest rates actually moved together a few months *earlier.* Can you think of any reason for this?

11. INTERNATIONAL CREDIT MARKETS

International borrowing and lending has increased enormously in the last quarter of a century. Commercial banks are the typical sources of short-term loans, with much of this international lending done by Eurobanks. We saw in section 7 that the Eurocurrency markets also supply medium-term (three to seven years) credit in the form of loans with an interest rate that adjusts every few months. This is how much of the LDC debt, that is now so difficult to service or repay, was contracted.

Long-term international borrowing is typically done not from banks, but by the sale of bonds to the public. Foreign corporations and governments can borrow American funds for up to twenty-five years by selling bonds in New York, for example.

Foreign bonds are the traditional means of long-term credit. Suppose, for example, that Coagulated Mush, Ltd. wishes to borrow £100 million for twenty years for a plant expansion program. The firm decides to raise the funds in New York. To do so, Coagulated Mush issues $150 million of bonds, assuming the exchange rate is $1.50/£, and sells them in New York (through a New York underwriter). The firm may use some of the dollar proceeds of the bond sale to buy equipment in the United States, but probably the dollars will be sold on the foreign-exchange market for pounds. Coagulated Mush will have to pay interest on the bonds in dollars and will eventually have to redeem them for dollars upon maturity.

From the point of view of the lenders (in this case the Americans who purchased Coagulated Mush's bonds) there is little difference between foreign bonds and domestic bonds. Both are sold in the local market, are denominated in the local currency, and are subject to local regulations (though sometimes some regulations for foreign bonds differ). The main difference is that the foreign bond is the obligation of a foreign resident. But from the borrower's point of view foreign bonds differ in that they establish a long-term obligation to make payments in foreign currency. Coagulated Mush is obligating itself to make dollar payments for twenty years; had the money been raised locally by selling domestic bonds in London, the obligation would have been in pounds.

New York is a major market for foreign bonds. Canadian firms and governments annually raise billions of dollars by selling U.S. dollar-denominated bonds in New York. Other major centers are in Switzerland (where non-Swiss borrowers sell bonds denominated in Swiss francs), in Germany (mark bonds), and more recently in Japan (yen bonds). (Foreign dollar-denominated bonds issued in New York are often called *Yankee bonds;* foreign yen-denominated bonds issued in Tokyo are frequently referred to as *samurai bonds.*) Both the size of the foreign bond market and its distribution among the centers vary greatly from year to year in response to credit conditions. The general trend in recent years has been a declining role for the U.S. market relative to foreign bond issues in Switzerland and Germany. Since the 1980s the largest volume of foreign borrowing has in fact been in Switzerland. So has the largest volume of foreign lending: for the most part, foreign bonds sold in Switzerland are purchased not by the Swiss themselves, but by other foreigners. Switzerland is just the place where foreigners lend to each other, and the Swiss franc is just the currency in which they measure those loans.

In recent decades international bond markets witnessed an innovation analogous to the Eurocurrency markets in international banking. In addition to the traditional foreign bonds, we now have *Eurobonds*—international bonds denominated in a currency other than that of the country or countries in which they are sold. If Coagulated Mush had wished to go this route, it would have sold its dollar-denominated bonds in London or, perhaps through an international syndicate, in London, Paris, and Amsterdam simultaneously. The purchasers of the bonds would have paid dollars for them, and they would have received dollars for interest. In 1985 about $136 billion of new Eurobonds were issued. During the late 1960s over 90 percent of Eurobond issues were denominated in dollars, but this proportion has declined over the years. Eurobonds are denominated in many different currencies; there has, for example, been an issue in Kuwaiti dinar. Some Eurobond issues are "currency cocktails," denominated in terms of a basket of different currencies. The European Currency Unit (ECU) is an important example.

Political motives and national regulations were important in the development of Eurobonds, just as they were with Eurocurrencies. The market received a big boost in 1964 when the United States imposed the Interest Equalization Tax on foreign bond sales (except for bonds issued by Canadians). That tax has been repealed, but national regulations still matter. For example, an issue of dollar-denominated Eurobonds would not subject the borrower to the disclosure requirements of the Securities and Exchange Commission that would apply were the bonds issued in New York. Also, individuals buying the Eurobonds could more easily preserve anonymity (for sundry nefarious purposes). Eurobonds are usually *bearer* bonds (your only proof of ownership is physically possessing the bond, as with currency) rather than *registered* bonds.

We saw that such regulations were no longer crucial to the survival of the Eurocurrency markets, which have matured to the point that they can compete on equal terms with national markets. The same is not true of Eurobonds. Markets for these bonds are thin, especially the secondary markets, so that a bondholder who wishes to sell out before maturity may have difficulty. Also underwriting costs are higher in the Eurobond markets than in the national markets, and borrowers typically must pay a premium.

In 1989 total issues of new international bonds amounted to $259 billion. Nearly half of these were denominated in U.S. dollars

Euroequity consists of shares in corporations. Like Eurobonds, Euroequity issues are handled by syndicates of banks that sell the shares simultaneously in different centers around the world. But since the shares of the issuing firms are listed on the national stock exchanges of the countries in which the firms are located (and where most of their shareholders live), subsequent trading tends to take place there. External trading in these shares has been growing rapidly in recent years, however, especially in the shares of companies from countries with small national stock markets. London is the center of this activity. Thus shares in firms such as Sweden's Volvo and the Netherlands' Philips are actively traded in the London Euroequity market in addition to the exchanges in Stockholm and Amsterdam, respectively.

While relying on issues of bonds and equity for long-term borrowing, firms have traditionally met short-term credit needs with bank loans, as discussed above. But in recent years issues of short-term securities in the Euromarkets have been relied on increasingly, instead of bank loans, for this purpose. Thus there is a *Eurocommercial paper* market in which firms sell short-term obligations to investors. Many other types of short-term instruments now also exist. Eurobanks, either individually or in syndicates, are usually involved in the issue of these instruments, sometimes only as dealers and sometimes as underwriters (who promise to buy themselves any securities for which buyers cannot be found at a guaranteed price).

The Euromarkets are growing rapidly not only in terms of size, but also in terms of introducing new techniques and instruments. This is because the markets are competitive: the largest banks from around the world participate. Of course, these banks also participate in their respective national markets. The growth of the Euromarkets and deregulation in many national markets (partly in response to competition from the Euromarkets) are causing the distinctions between the two sets of markets gradually to evaporate.

12. SUMMARY

1. The monies of different countries are exchanged for each other in the foreign-exchange market, which exists to facilitate the international exchange of goods, services, and assets.

2. Spot foreign-exchange transactions are settled within two business days; forward transactions are settled at some specified date in the future. Forward markets furnish a way for firms dealing in international markets to escape exchange risk.

3. Two theories explain how spot and forward rates are linked. Covered interest parity asserts that the forward premium equals the interest-rate differential, whereas the speculative theory claims that the forward premium equals the expected appreciation of the spot rate.

4. Eurodollars are dollars on deposit in banks outside the United States. The Eurodollar market has grown from nearly nothing in the 1950s to its present gigantic size because of the competitive edge over national markets resulting from the lack of Eurodollar regulation and because of the desire of some governments holding dollars to stay clear of the United States.

5. The foreign-exchange market is efficient if exchange rates fully reflect all available information. Research has not yet concluded whether the foreign-exchange markets are in fact fully efficient.

6. Foreign bonds are domestic currency bonds issued in domestic credit markets by foreign firms or governments. Eurobonds are denominated in a currency other than that of the market in which they are issued.

SUGGESTED READING

Andrews, M. A. "Recent Trends in the U.S. Foreign Exchange Market." Federal Reserve Bank of New York, *Quarterly Review* 9 (1984): 38–47. Recent developments.

Bank for International Settlements. *Annual Report*. Basle (published each June). The standard source for information on the Eurocurrency markets.

Bryant, R. C. *International Financial Intermediation*. Washington: Brookings Institution, 1987. Regulating international capital markets in an interdependent world.

Einzig, P. *The History of Foreign Exchange*. New York: St. Martin's Press, 1962. Foreign exchange through the ages.

Erdman, P. *The Billion Dollar Sure Thing*. New York: Hutchinson, 1973. An entertaining novel featuring details of the foreign-exchange markets; written while the author was in a Swiss jail.

Frenkel, J. A., and M. L. Mussa. "The Efficiency of the Foreign Exchange Market and Measures of Turbulence." *American Economic Review* 70 (May 1980): 374–81. An interpretation of market behavior.

Froot, K. A., and R. H. Thaler. "Anomalies: Foreign Exchange." *Journal of Economic Perspectives* 4 (1990): 179–92. Good discussion of market efficiency.

Frydl, E. J. "The Debate over Regulating the Eurocurrency Markets." Federal Reserve Bank of New York, *Quarterly Review* 4 (1979–80): 11–20. The pros and cons.

Grabbe, J. O. *International Financial Markets*. 2d ed. New York: Elsevier, 1991. Good treatment.

Hansen, L. P., and R. J. Hodrick. "Forward Exchange Rates As Optimal Predictors of Future Spot Rates: An Econometric Analysis." *Journal of Political Economy* 88 (Oct. 1980): 829–53. Empirical study cited in text.

Keynes, J. M. *A Tract on Monetary Reform*. London: Macmillan, 1923. Section 4 of Chapter 3 is the classic description of the forward market.

Kubarych, R. M. *Foreign Exchange Markets in the United States*. New York: Federal Reserve Bank of New York, 1978. A good description of the contemporary foreign-exchange market.

Levich, R. M. "Empirical Studies of Exchange Rates: Price Behavior, Rate Determination and Market Efficiency." In *Handbook of International Economics*. Vol. 2. Edited by R. W. Jones and P. B. Kenen. Amsterdam: North Holland, 1985. A useful survey.

McKinnon, R. I. "The Eurocurrency Markets." Princeton University, *Essays in International Finance* 125 (1977). A good description and analysis.

Roll, R., and B. Solnik. "A Pure Foreign Exchange Asset Pricing Model." *Journal of International Economics* 7 (May 1977): 161–79. A theoretical treatment.

Part Five

International Monetary Economics

Now that we have examined the mechanics of how the balance-of-payments statistics are compiled and how international financial markets work, it is time to step back and analyze the operation of the international monetary system. The basic problem is this: How can different countries, whose citizens wish to make economic transactions with each other, come to grips with the fact that each country uses a different money for its transactions?

There are in principle two distinct methods of doing this. In one, called *floating exchange rates,* the authorities in each country concern themselves only with their own country's monetary situation. The U.S. Fed, for example, looks after the supply of dollars, and the German Bundesbank looks after the supply of marks. The exchange rate (the price of a mark in terms of dollars) will then be determined by the foreign-exchange market, described in the previous chapter, and this rate will then be used for transactions between the United States and Germany. Under this method, each country completely controls its own money supply, but the exchange rate between them is determined by the vagaries of the market. This method is studied in detail in Chapter 14.

In the other method, called *fixed exchange rates,* the authorities in the two countries prevent the exchange rate from varying, even if this requires them to alter their money supplies. Under this method, the authorities maintain a stable exchange rate, but they lose the ability to conduct their monetary policies independently. We study this in Chapter 15.

Although there are *in principle* but these two methods to operate an international monetary system, there are *in practice* much more complicated methods than this might suggest. There are several reasons for this. (1) How each method works depends on institutions and markets, and these change from country to country and from time to time. (2) In practice countries almost never rely on one method in its pure form but instead combine the two methods, and the way they combine them differs from country to country and from time to time. (3) Sometimes countries are reluctant to trust their international transactions entirely to any monetary system and instead attempt to control those transactions directly to some degree. The extent to which they do this also differs from country to country and from time to time. After Chapters 14 and 15 present the basic theory, Chapter 16 looks at actual international monetary arrangements and how they have worked.

CHAPTER 14

The Exchange Rate

> What, then, has determined and will determine the value of the franc? First, the quantity, present and prospective, of the francs in circulation. Second, the amount of purchasing power which it suits the public to hold in that shape. —JOHN MAYNARD KEYNES

This chapter focuses on exchange rates: how they are determined and what happens if they change. As the table on page 431 reveals, exchange rates often change.

The basic idea of exchange-rate adjustment has been shared by many economists in many lands and at many times. But it is appropriate to associate it with the American economist Frank Taussig, who early in this century developed a basic analysis that his students then used in empirical studies.

1. MONEY

An international monetary system determines how different national monies relate to each other. So our first order of business is to understand money itself. Now, if you are like most people, you would reply, when asked, that, although you cannot describe or define money precisely, you know it when you see it. Probably you are half right. This section describes what money does, what money is, and what determines a nation's overall demand for money.

FRANK W. TAUSSIG (1859–1940)

Frank Taussig's father migrated from Prague to the U.S. Midwest and became a merchant, medical practitioner, mayor, judge, tax collector, banker, bridge builder, and railroad president. Taussig was only an economist. He spent his career on the Harvard faculty and lived in Cambridge, Massachusetts, for over sixty years. He became the foremost American applied economic theorist, his *Principles of Economics* was for many years the leading text, and he edited the *Quarterly Journal of Economics,* a prominent professional journal, for forty years. The increasing specialization of the field is indicated by the fact that Taussig was the first major economist to specialize in the subfield of international trade. In 1917 Taussig became the first chairman of the Tariff Commission (now called the International Trade Commission, discussed in Chapter 9), and as economic adviser to President Woodrow Wilson he attended the Versailles peace conference after the First World War. His daughter Helen became a medical researcher and helped devise the operation to treat "blue babies," those with congenital heart defects.

What Money Does

The most important thing money does is serve as a *medium of exchange.* That is, people accept it as payment for what they have to sell and use it to purchase what they buy. Typically, an individual in a modern economy will work for (that is, supply labor to) a firm in exchange for a paycheck, which she will then use to buy the different goods and services that she purchases from different places. A firm will sell its products for money, which it uses to pay its workers and to pay for different materials from different sources. And so on. Without a medium of exchange, all this would require direct barter. Thus the worker would have to go to her grocer, her hairdresser, her hardware store, and so on, and somehow strike deals with each to work a certain amount of time in exchange for their products. Firms likewise would need to strike thousands of barter deals with workers and suppliers. One's mind can scarcely comprehend the enormity of the task. Even primitive economies find a medium of exchange useful; a modern economy, with its elaborate division of labor, could not exist without one.

A second function of money is to serve as a *unit of account.* That is, money is the measuring rod for the prices of everything else. Obviously, it is extremely convenient to have a single common denominator for this so that each commodity need have but one price (its money price) rather than a multitude of prices (its price in terms of each and every other commodity) and so that the prices of different commodities can easily be compared. Maybe we should not add apples and oranges, but we can add their prices.

Finally, money is also a *store of value.* That is, if you put some of your wealth into money today, next week you will be able to use that money to buy goods: the money will have retained value. The importance of this aspect of money is subtle. On the one hand, it is absolutely critical because money could not serve as a medium of exchange if it were not also a store of value: no one would accept money as payment if it instantly became worthless. But money is not an especially important store of value because there are many others: savings accounts, bonds, stocks, real estate—any asset.

What Money Is

No one really knows. Currency is obviously money because it has the three properties just described. Most people would also regard demand deposits (that is, checking-account balances) as money for a similar reason. But then things become less clear. For example, savings deposits are not a medium of exchange, but in many cases they can easily be turned into demand deposits (in some cases more easily than in others!); so if they are not money, they substitute for it very well. Other assets also substitute to varying degrees because they can also easily be turned into money (we say they are "highly liquid"). And what about credit cards, bank cards, and overdraft protection on checking accounts? There are many different ways of measuring a country's money supply, depending on what you classify as money. The relative sizes and usefulness of these measures are important in monetary economics. But for the purposes of this book, you will not go far wrong if you simply think of a nation's money supply as the sum of its currency in circulation plus demand deposits.

The Demand for Money

Now that we know what money does, we can analyze what determines the demand for it. Since money is a medium of exchange, people need to hold it (that is, they *demand* it) between the time that they sell whatever they have to sell and the time that they then buy whatever they decide to buy. Thus what matters is (1) the time between transactions and (2) the amount (that is, the value) of transactions.

The amount of transactions in a country depends on the level of economic activity there. There are various ways of measuring this activity, but we can get a good grip on it by taking *national production* as our measure. If y is an index of national production and P is an index of producer prices, then Py measures the value of national production. So, if the amount of money that a country wishes to hold is proportional to the value of its transactions and if the latter is indexed by Py, we can write the demand for money, L, as

$$L = kPy,$$

where k denotes the factor of proportionality. The value of k depends on the amount of time money is held between transactions: the more time, the larger k has to be.

What determines the time between transactions? When we are holding money between transactions, we are using it as a store of value, and, as we saw above, there are many stores of value besides money. Money is a poor store of value in the sense that it pays little or no interest. Currency, of course, earns no interest at all, and checking accounts pay very little. Certificates of deposit, bonds, stocks, and so on all pay more. The more they pay, the greater the incentive to minimize the time between transactions. For example, if these other stores of value pay a high rate of interest, we will be tempted to invest or deposit our paychecks and other receipts in them as soon as we are paid and then to cash them in when we have to make payments, so that we actually hold money for only a little while. But if this rate of interest is not high it just does not make sense to go to all the bother. Thus the larger the rate of interest, the shorter the time between transactions and, therefore, the smaller the value of k. Since there are many alternative stores of value, there are many interest rates to consider, but we can think of them all as indicated by the interest on government bonds, denoted i.

We can indicate the dependence of k on i by writing $k = k(i)$, which simply means that "k is determined by i." The preceding argument implies that as i goes up, k goes down, and as i goes down, k goes up. Taking all this into account, the national demand for money is

$$L = k(i)Py.$$

Increases in P and y raise the demand for money, L, and increases in i lower it.

The *supply* of money—that is, the total currency in circulation plus the amount of demand deposits in the banking system—is determined by a country's central bank, such as the U.S. Federal Reserve. The way in which a central bank does this and the problems it might run into in the process will be discussed later. For now, suppose that the central bank sets the money supply somehow. The national money market will be in equilibrium when the demand for money, L, equals the supply, which we denote G.

$$G = k(i)Py$$

Problems

14.1 Suppose that the money market is in equilibrium and that the central bank then increases the supply, G. If i and y do not change in response, what must happen to the price level P?

14.2 Suppose that the money market is in equilibrium and that the economy experiences a growth in production, y. If the central bank does not change the money supply, G, and if P does not change in response, what must happen to the rate of interest i?

14.3 Suppose that the money market is in equilibrium and that the central bank then increases the supply, G. If P and y do not change in response, what must happen to the rate of interest i?

14.4 Suppose that the money market is in equilibrium and that the country experiences an inflationary rise in the price level P. If the central bank does not change the money supply in response and if i does not change, what must happen to output y?

2. INTERNATIONAL MONETARY EQUILIBRIUM

Now we can turn to monetary arrangements between a country and the rest of the world, with which it trades goods. Suppose two countries, the United States and Germany: The United States produces apples and exports them to Germany, which exports butane to the United States. Suppose that there are no nonofficial international capital movements between the United States and Germany: their citizens trade only goods. The American money supply consists of a fixed quantity G^{US} of dollars, and the German money supply consists of a fixed quantity G^G of marks. The authorities in each country hold international reserves and control the size of their country's money supply. The American exchange rate, R, is the price of a mark in terms of dollars.

International reserves consist of an asset the central banks themselves cannot create. For example, they might consist of gold, created by nature, or of pounds, created by a third country (the United Kingdom). By contrast, dollars are created by the American central bank and marks by the German central bank.

Money Prices and the Exchange Rate

P_A, the world money price of apples, is also the U.S. price level since the United States produces just apples: P_A is the number of dollars required to purchase an apple. Similarly, P_B, the money price of butane, or the German price level, is measured in marks. For these two prices to be comparable they must be expressed in a common currency, and the exchange rate is used for this. For example, the price of butane in terms of dollars is RP_B. (What is the price of apples in terms of marks?) The relative price of butane in terms of apples is $p = RP_B/P_A$. The equilibrium value of p is determined in international commodity markets, the subject of Parts One and Two of this book.

National Monetary Equilibrium

Suppose that y^{US} denotes total American output (production of apples) and that y^G denotes total German output (production of butane). Now apply the discussion of the previous section to the United States and to Germany individually. The demand for money in the United States will accordingly equal the supply when

$$G^{US} = k(i_{US})P_A y^{US}. \qquad (14.1)$$

Here, i_{US} denotes the U.S. interest rate. Similarly, if i_G denotes the German interest rate, the demand for money in Germany will equal the supply when

$$G^G = k(i_G)P_B y^G, \qquad (14.2)$$

where y^G denotes total German output measured in terms of butane. If we multiply both sides of this equation by R, we can express it in terms of dollars and so make it comparable to (14.1):

$$RG^G = k(i_G)(RP_B)y^G. \qquad (14.3)$$

The Equilibrium Exchange Rate

For the world to be in equilibrium the demand for each type of money must equal the supply—that is, (14.1) and (14.3) must hold. Dividing (14.1) into (14.3),

$$R\frac{G^G}{G^{US}} = \frac{k(i_G)[RP_B]y^G}{k(i_{US})P_A y^{US}} = p\frac{k(i_G)}{k(i_{US})}\frac{y^G}{y^{US}}. \qquad (14.4)$$

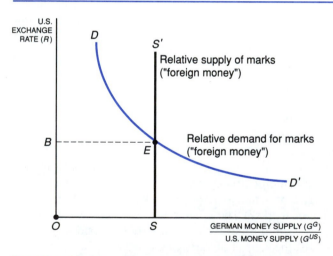

FIGURE 14.1 International Monetary Equilibrium The equilibrium exchange rate is determined by the intersection of the demand curve for foreign money relative to home money with the supply curve.

The expression on the right is determined by the terms of trade p, given by commodity markets, the two interest rates i_{US} and i_G, determined by borrowing and lending in the two countries, and the national production levels, y^{US} and y^G. All of these might relate to monetary conditions in subtle ways, which we address later in this book. But there is no need to go into all that to grasp the essentials of how an international monetary system functions. So suppose for now that the terms of trade, the rates of interest, and national outputs have all been determined elsewhere. Thus the right-hand side of (14.4) is exogenously given.

Then (14.4) says that the product of the exchange rate, R, and the relative money supplies, G^G/G^{US}, must be constant for the world to be in equilibrium. This is illustrated in Figure 14.1 by the curve DD'. This curve (an example of what is called a "rectangular hyperbola") shows for each value of the exchange rate R the ratio G^G/G^{US} that would be demanded in equilibrium. The area $OBES$ in the figure equals the magnitude of the right-hand side of (14.4), and this is true of any rectangle formed by taking as a corner any point, such as E, on the curve DD'. If OS measures the actual relative supply of the two monies, the world must be somewhere on the line SS', so that equilibrium is at E, the intersection of the demand and supply curves. Thus OB measures the equilibrium exchange rate.

Problems

14.5 Suppose that whiskey costs £120 per case, that wheat costs $90 per bushel, and that the relative price of whiskey in terms of wheat is 2 bushels per case. What is the U.S. exchange rate, the price of a pound in terms of dollars? What is the dollar price of whiskey? The pound price of wheat?

14.6 Suppose that the United States produces 1,000 bushels of wheat, Europe produces 600 bolts of cloth, 5 wheat exchange for 1 cloth in equilibrium, k equals $\frac{1}{2}$, the U.S. money supply consists of $2,000, and the European money supply consists of £3,000. Describe international monetary equilibrium and illustrate with a diagram analogous to Figure 14.1. Suppose the U.S. money supply were to rise to $4,000; calculate the effect on your answer and illustrate the change in your diagram. Do the same if the terms of trade were to alter so that 5 wheat exchange for 3 cloth.

14.7 In the discussion in the text, how will the American equilibrium exchange rate be affected by

   a an improvement in the American terms of trade?

   b a growth of German income relative to American?

   c an increase in the American rate of interest?

14.8 Suppose that the dollar becomes worth fewer marks (so R rises). What will be the direct impact of this on American and German firms if they pursue the following alternative pricing policies:

   a Each firm holds the domestic currency price of its product fixed and adjusts the foreign currency price.

b Each firm holds constant in foreign currency the price of its product and adjusts the domestic currency price.

c Each firm holds constant *both* the domestic currency price at which it sells in domestic markets and also the foreign currency price at which it sells in foreign markets.

What consequences would likely develop in each case for the respective firms? Can you think of any reason why firms might respond in one way rather than in others?

14.9 Show the effects of an increase in the American money supply in Figure 14.1. What happens to the equilibrium exchange rate if the Americans increase their money supply by 25 percent each and every year? What happens to the money prices of both goods?

3. EXCHANGE-RATE ADJUSTMENT

Suppose that, in Figure 14.2, equilibrium is at E but the actual exchange rate is OC so that the world is at E'. The origin of such a disequilibrium is not what concerns us now. We ask: What will be its consequences?

Payments Imbalances and Exchange-Rate Adjustment

With the actual exchange rate at OC, the demands and supplies of the two monies do not match. The relative demands corresponding to the ex-

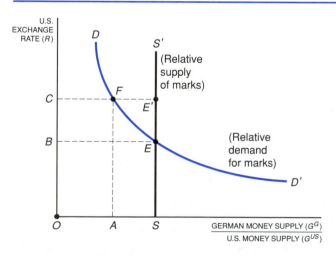

FIGURE 14.2 A Disequilibrium Exchange Rate If equilibrium is at E but the actual exchange rate is OC, a reduction in the relative foreign money supply from S to A depreciates the equilibrium exchange rate from OB to OC and establishes equilibrium.

change rate OC are indicated by F: demand OA is less than the actual supply OS. The exchange rate corresponding to the relative supply OS is indicated by E, and SE falls short of SE'.

Thus the American exchange rate (the price of marks) is too high and/or the supply of German money (marks) too high. One could equivalently say that the German exchange rate (the price of dollars) and/or the supply of American money (dollars) are too small. The monetary authorities in the United States and Germany could react in either of two distinct ways.

They could, *first,* maintain the value of their currencies by freely exchanging them with the public for international reserves. This is shown in Figure 14.3(a). In this case the exchange rate is held fixed at OC. The American authorities increase the number of dollars in circulation, and the German authorities lower the number of marks in circulation. With the American money supply rising and the German falling, the world would move from E' toward equilibrium at F. How do the authorities change the two money supplies? Simple. Since the public wants more dollars and fewer marks, the public goes to the central banks offering to sell marks in exchange for dollars, and the central banks oblige the public by exchanging the two currencies at the price OC. It is just this willingness of the authorities to deal without limit at this price that maintains the exchange rate. Now, if the public buys newly printed dollars from the U.S. central bank for marks, the U.S. authorities have no use for the marks they have acquired, so they sell them to the German central bank for international reserves. If, on the other hand, the public buys dollars from the German central bank, the German authorities have to get the dollars somehow since they cannot print them. They get the dollars by selling international reserves to the U.S. central bank.

On balance, the world's public acquires more dollars and fewer marks, the American central bank acquires more international reserves, and the German central bank loses reserves. The U.S. experiences a balance-of-payments surplus and Germany a balance-of-payments deficit, according to the official reserve transactions balance described in Chapter 12.

Alternatively, the authorities could refrain from buying and selling the two currencies and thus keep the respective money supplies fixed but alter exchange rates instead. In this case G^G/G^{US} would remain equal to OS. If the exchange rate fell from OC to OB in Figure 14.3(b), the world would move from E' to E and reach equilibrium; people would be willing to hold the existing supplies of the two currencies, and payments imbalances would not arise. Thus there is an alternative method of adjustment: variations in exchange rates.

These two distinct methods of international adjustment might in practice be combined in various ways. Figure 14.3(c) shows one possibility. The authorities could initially fix the exchange rate, thereby moving from E' to H. They could then alter the exchange rate from OC to OG. This would eliminate much of the disequilibrium but not all of it; the payments imbalances would continue until the world moved from K to J. The new equilibrium at J would differ from that at E' in both relative money supplies and the exchange rate.

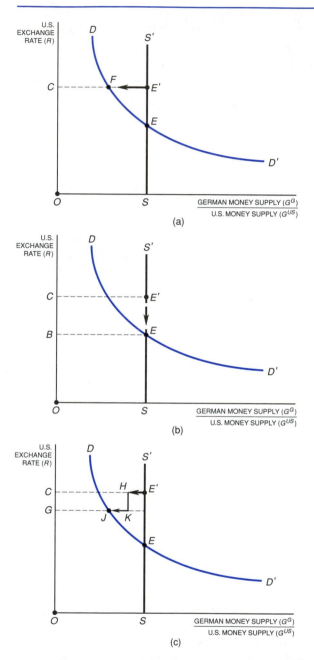

FIGURE 14.3 Adjustment to International Monetary Equilibrium We see three alternative responses: (a) adjustment through payments imbalances, which brings the world to *F;* (b) adjustment through exchange-rate variations, which brings the world to *E;* and (c) adjustments through both, which bring the world to the intermediate position, *J.*

Implications of Exchange-Rate Adjustment

There are two broad implications of exchange-rate adjustment. *First,* balance-of-payments deficits and surpluses can be corrected or prevented by variations in exchange rates. This would reduce or eliminate the need for central banks to buy or sell international reserves.

Second, exchange-rate variations allow individual countries to control their own money supplies. Suppose the American and German monetary authorities desire money supplies in the ratio *OS* in Figure 14.3. If the exchange rate is fixed at *OC,* the world moves from *E'* to *F,* so relative money supplies move away from the desired ratio *OS* toward *CF.* But if the exchange rate is altered to *OB,* the world will move to *E* and the authorities will be able to maintain the desired ratio.

A currency is said to *depreciate* if it becomes worth less in terms of foreign currencies—that is, if more domestic currency is required to buy a unit of foreign currency. Similarly an *appreciation* is an increase in the value of domestic currency in terms of foreign currency: less home money is needed to buy a unit of foreign money. In Figure 14.3(b) a change in the exchange rate from *OC* to *OB* constitutes an appreciation of the dollar and a depreciation of the mark.

Problems

14.10 In Problem **14.6,** what cumulative payments imbalance would result if the exchange rate were held fixed after the increase in the U.S. money supply? What exchange-rate adjustment would be required if the U.S. money supply were maintained at $4,000? What would happen if, after the initial increase in the U.S. money supply to $4,000, the authorities decided not to let it subsequently fall below $3,000?

14.11 Suppose that German real income y^G grows by 10 percent each year but that American real income y^{US} remains constant. What happens to international equilibrium if the Americans increase the supply of dollars by 5 percent a year and Germany increases the supply of marks by 10 percent per year?

14.12 In the last two columns of the table on page 340 "Selected Exchange Rates," which currencies are shown to have appreciated and which to have depreciated relative to the U.S. dollar? Relative to the franc?

4. EXCHANGE-RATE REGIMES

An exchange-rate regime is the arrangement used by a group of countries to settle payments among themselves and to determine their exchange rates. There are basically five distinct regimes. The present chapter has described two different methods of international adjustment. Exclusive reliance on one or the other of these methods gives us two possible exchange regimes. There are also two hybrid regimes that combine the two methods in different ways. The fifth regime involves dispensing with both methods in favor of direct government controls over international monetary transactions. Let us briefly describe each regime.

1. *Fixed Exchange Rates.* The authorities in each country freely buy and sell the national currency for international reserves at a permanently fixed price. Chapter 15 will describe this regime. In terms of Figure 14.3, disturbances to demand and supply result in horizontal adjustments, as shown in panel (a).

2. *Floating Exchange Rates.* The authorities never exchange national money for international reserves; therefore, each country's overall balance of payments is never in deficit or surplus. Exchange rates freely adjust in private markets to equilibrate demands and supplies of national monies. In terms of Figure 14.3, disturbances to demand and supply conditions result in vertical adjustments, as in panel (b).

3. *Adjustable Peg.* In this, the first hybrid regime, authorities buy and sell the national currency for international reserves at a fixed price (the peg), but that price can be adjusted from time to time if payments imbalances are large.

4. *Managed Floating.* In this regime, as with floating exchange rates, the authorities do not fix a price for the national currency, but they may nevertheless buy and sell it to influence the exchange rate.

5. *Exchange Control.* This regime differs from all others in that the authorities directly administer exchanges of national monies. For example, citizens who acquire foreign currency by selling goods, services, or assets to foreigners may be required to sell that currency to the authorities for domestic money, and citizens who wish to buy goods, services, and assets from abroad may need to apply to the authorities for the foreign currency they require. If the authorities simply bought and sold foreign exchange on demand at a price that kept receipts equal to sales, this regime would be identical to floating exchange rates except for the authorities serving as a clearinghouse. But they do not do this. Instead, their willingness to deal with domestic citizens and the terms on which they deal vary according to the identity of the citizen, the nature of the commodity the citizen wants to buy or sell, and the foreign country he wants to deal with. For example, the authorities might be willing to sell foreign exchange to citizens to import goods from country A but not to import the same goods from country B. Or a food importer might be able to obtain foreign exchange from the authorities at a low price, whereas a bicycle importer has to pay a higher price for a limited amount of foreign exchange and a would-be automobile importer is denied foreign currency altogether. In this way exchange control is used to manipulate international trade and investment as well as to adjust the balance of payments and exchange rates.

Problems

14.13 Two implications of exchange-rate adjustment were indicated in section 3 of this chapter. Discuss how these implications apply to each of the five basic regimes discussed in this section.

14.14 Discuss reasons why a country might prefer one regime over another.

14.15 Using the source material described in Appendix II, find examples of countries employing each of the five regimes discussed in this section. Describe in detail the specific arrangements of each country. Do they illustrate the possible reasons you gave in your answer to Problem **14.14**?

5. EXCHANGE REGIMES IN PRACTICE

Present exchange-rate arrangements are complex. This is because different countries have different regimes. The European Union (EU) nations have formed the European Monetary System (EMS) and (except for Greece, Italy, and Britain) maintain adjustable pegs vis-à-vis each other. Other industrial countries, by and large, have managed floats. Thus the French franc is pegged to the German mark and Belgian franc but floats, with management, relative to the U.S. dollar and the Japanese yen.

Many LDCs maintain adjustable pegs relative to the U.S. dollar, and some peg to the French franc, U.K. pound, Spanish peseta, or South African rand. A few of these pegs are unadjustable—that is, fixed. The relation of these currencies with each other is determined by the relations between the currencies to which they are pegged. For example, the Panamanian balboa is fixed in terms of the dollar, Botswana pegs its pula to the dollar, and the Gambia pegs its currency, the dalasi, to the U.K. pound. Thus, indirectly, the balboa and the pula are pegged to each other and in a managed float against the dalasi. Still other countries peg to a basket of currencies rather than a single one. Thus Saudi Arabia pegs the riyal to a basket consisting of specified amounts of dollars, marks, and so on. The riyal might appreciate against the dollar, say, if that appreciation is offset by a depreciation relative to other currencies in the basket. Finally, exchange control is widespread. Most European countries had extensive controls until 1958 and still sometimes impose limits on their citizens' freedom to exchange assets with foreigners. For example, some controls were imposed after a 1992 crisis. The United States had controls on capital movements in the late 1960s and early 1970s, and Britain retained various restrictions until the late 1970s. But, by and large, exchange controls in the DCs are isolated measures aimed at specific limited purposes and not representative of the basic character of the exchange regimes. This is not true of the LDCs and the former communist states, where exchange control is pervasive.

A second reason for the complexity of contemporary practice is that individual countries typically rely on combinations of regimes. The isolated use of exchange controls by DCs has already been cited. Countries that peg their currencies seldom do so completely. Instead they typically establish a band around the peg in which the exchange rate floats (with or without management), and pegging consists of preventing the exchange rate from leaving the band. For example, in December 1986 the French franc was pegged to the German mark in the EMS at Fr 3.256/DM. On January 12, 1987, the peg was

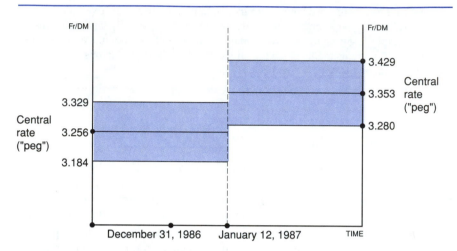

FIGURE 14.4 **The Franc/Mark Exchange Rate in the EMS** The authorities intervene to prevent the exchange rate from leaving a band around its pegged value. Sometimes the peg is changed, moving the band with it.

adjusted by 3 percent to Fr 3.353/DM. But the upper and lower limits of intervention were 2.25 percent on each side of the peg—that is, the authorities were in fact obligated to keep the exchange rate within a 4.5 percent band, centered on the peg. Figure 14.4 illustrates the situation. The width of the band can also be changed. This happened in the early 1990s, when the band around most EMS parities was widened dramatically to 30 percent.

Pegging involves keeping the market rate in the band, within which it floats, perhaps with management. Thus countries with an adjustable peg also typically float to some extent. Still another combination is a *dual exchange market,* which has been utilized by Belgium, Italy, and some other countries. In Belgium, for example, citizens who require foreign currency to purchase foreign goods must buy the currency at the *commercial* foreign-exchange rate, while citizens who wish to buy and sell financial assets must use the *financial* rate. The commercial rate is pegged (Belgium is in the EMS), and the financial rate floats. The system is thus a combination of three regimes: exchange control, adjustable peg, and floating. A dual exchange market is a special case of *multiple exchange markets,* used by many LDCs. Foreign-exchange dealings are segmented into a number of separate markets, and a citizen must use a specific market depending upon the reason she wants to buy or sell foreign currency. Arrangements often differ between markets, with a pegged rate in one market, a floating rate in another, and complete reliance on administrative controls in yet another.

Still another source of complexity is the fact that different countries often use a single regime in markedly different ways. Methods of exchange control differ enormously from country to country. The degree of management of a managed float can vary. American authorities, for example, have typically practiced light management, whereas the Japanese have often intervened on a large scale, sometimes to the extent of, in effect, pegging the yen. The adjustability of an adjustable peg can vary from country to country. A number of Latin American countries routinely adjust their pegs each month. By contrast, throughout the 1950s and 1960s the DCs were reluctant ever to adjust their pegs, even in the face of large payments imbalances. Malaysia has pegged its ringgit to a basket, but the composition of the basket has been a secret.

Complexity also arises from the fact that countries often alter their exchange regimes or their ways of administering regimes. Methods of exchange control are often varied; many countries have stopped pegging to the dollar and begun pegging to currency baskets. Some countries have switched from an adjustable peg to a managed float or vice versa; the extent of management of a float has varied from year to year or from month to month; and so on. For example, after following a basically passive policy, U.S. authorities announced in late 1978 that they would actively attempt to limit depreciation of the dollar. But in early 1981 the authorities announced that the United States would not intervene at all (that is, shift from managed floating to free floating), except under extraordinary circumstances such as the immediate aftermath of an attempted assassination of President Reagan. As another example, a European pegging arrangement (called the "snake") was in existence for five years before the start of the EMS in 1979, and during those years participation in the scheme varied greatly. Current arrangements are indicated in Table 14.1.

Advantages and Disadvantages of the Various Regimes

Exchange control is a method of influencing international trade and investment, as well as the payments mechanism. Thus it possesses the advantages and disadvantages of other means of protection, discussed in detail in Part Three. The regime is attractive to governments that want to pursue economic or political goals at odds with free-market behavior; therefore, exchange control is most likely to appeal to those nations that generally try to manipulate the economy. This is why the regime is common in LDCs and former communist countries. The disadvantages are those that pertain to economic controls generally: distortions, inequities and inefficiencies, and a tendency for black markets and other evasive practices to develop and for bureaucratic control to grow in response.

The great advantage of fixed exchange rates is that each nation's currency becomes more useful as money. The basic economic roles of money, you will recall, are medium of exchange, store of value, and unit of account. When foreign currency has a fixed value in terms of domestic currency, it becomes a simple matter to make sense of foreign-currency prices of foreign goods; travelers are likely to find foreigners willing to accept the travelers' money as payment; and no one need worry about which currency is the safer form of holding liquid balances. Both domestic and foreign currencies are

TABLE 14.1 Exchange-Rate Arrangements as of June 30, 1994

Currency pegged to					Limited flexibility		More flexibility		
U.S. dollar	French franc	Other currency	SDR	Other basket	Informal peg to U.S. dollar	EMS	Adjusted according to a set of indicators	More management	Less management
Antigua and Barbuda	Benin	Bhutan (Indian rupee)	Libya	Algeria	Bahrain	Belgium	Chile	Angola	Afghanistan, Islamic State of
Argentina	Burkina Faso	Estonia (deutsche mark)	Myanmar	Austria	Qatar	Denmark	Nicaragua	Belarus	Albania
Bahamas, the	Cameroon	Kiribati (Australian dollar)	Rwanda	Bangladesh	Saudi Arabia	France		Cambodia	Armenia
Barbados	C. African Rep.	Lesotho (South African rand)	Seychelles	Botswana	United Arab Emirates	Germany		China, P.R.	Australia
Belize	Chad	Namibia (South African rand)		Burundi		Ireland		Colombia	Azerbaijan
Djibouti	Comoros	San Marino (Italian lira)		Cape Verde		Luxembourg		Ecuador	Bolivia
Dominica	Congo	Swaziland (South African rand)		Cyprus		Netherlands		Egypt	Brazil
Grenada	Côte d'Ivoire	Tajikistan, Rep. of (Russian ruble)		Czech Republic		Portugal		Greece	Bulgaria
Iraq	Equatorial Guinea			Fiji		Spain		Guinea	Canada
Liberia	Gabon			Hungary				Guinea-Bissau	Costa Rica
Lithuania	Mali			Iceland				Honduras	Croatia
Marshall Islands	Niger			Jordan				Indonesia	Dominican Rep.
Micronesia, Fed. States of	Senegal			Kuwait				Israel	El Salvador
Nigeria	Togo			Malta				Korea	Ethiopia
Oman				Mauritania				Lao P.D. Rep	Finland
Panama				Mauritius				Malaysia	Gambia, the
St. Kitts and Nevis				Morocco				Maldives	Georgia
St. Lucia				Nepal				Mexico	Ghana
St. Vincent and the Grenadines				Papua New Guinea				Pakistan	Guatemala
Suriname				Slovak Republic				Poland	Guyana
Syrian Arab Rep.				Solomon Islands				São Tomé and Principe	Haiti
Turkmenistan				Thailand				Singapore	India
Yemen, Republic of				Tonga				Slovenia	Iran, I.R. of
				Vanuatu				Somalia	Italy
				Western Samoa				Sri Lanka	Jamaica
								Sudan	Japan
								Tunisia	Kazakhstan
								Turkey	Kenya
								Uruguay	Kyrgyz Rep.
								Venezuela	Latvia
								Viet Nam	Lebanon
									Macedonia, F.Y.R. of
									Madagascar
									Malawi
									Moldova
									Mongolia
									Mozambique
									New Zealand
									Norway
									Paraguay
									Peru
									Philippines
									Romania
									Russia
									Sierra Leone
									South Africa
									Sweden
									Switzerland
									Tanzania
									Trinidad and Tobago
									Uganda
									Ukraine
									United Kingdom
									United States
									Zaire
									Zambia
									Zimbabwe

Financial Wizardry in the Third Reich

During the Depression many governments resorted in desperation to exchange controls, the practice attaining a perfection of sorts in Hitler's Germany with an elaborate system devised by economics minister Horace Greeley Hjalmar Schacht (his father had lived for a time in America and had acquired an admiration for the famous journalist). Experience with the system was described by Douglas Miller in a book review in the *American Economic Review* (December 1943, pp. 923–25).

New decrees were published so rapidly that American government representatives could not keep pace in translating and dispatching them to Washington. . . .

When the text of new laws and decrees was published, printed copies were piled on the floor beside the desk of the unhappy translator, higher than the top of his desk. In ordinary trade practice there is a normal lapse of several weeks or months between the placing of an order for foreign goods and the final shipment to the customer. During this period so many changes in regulations could and did take place that business men became discouraged and were unwilling to make new contracts. . . .

Dr. Schacht's cynicism about Germany's financial integrity went so far that he even seemed to take pleasure in the distress of foreign creditors, and he enjoyed the sensation of confusing and bewildering them. . . .

. . . It became well known in Berlin that successful applications for exchange permits should be accompanied by tangible rewards. Sometimes these ran into high figures. Curiously enough, in many cases small gifts of rare articles were very successful in obtaining needed official documents. It was reliably reported that the standard bribe of two cartons of American cigarettes would usually insure the granting of exchange permits in doubtful cases, when there was no substantial objection. Some of the German officials had acquired the un-German habit of smoking American cigarettes with their characteristic flavor and could no longer be satisfied by the domestic brands. The exchange and tariff regulations brought the cost of an ordinary 15-cent packet to the price of 6 marks in tobacco stores and 9 marks plus 10 per cent tax in hotels and night clubs. This price raised them to the status of real luxuries, presents fit for a Nazi bigshot. .

more useful as money than either would be if the exchange rate were liable to fluctuate. You can easily appreciate this point if you imagine for a moment that New York and New Jersey each had its own money, with a flexible exchange rate between the two. Consider the plight of a New Jersey commuter working in New York. She would be paid in New York dollars but would have large obligations, such as a mortgage, in terms of New Jersey dollars and so would be unsure about how much of her salary would be required for these obligations. And, in addition to her New Jersey bills, she would make some New York purchases (for example, lunches) and so would always have to keep some of each currency on hand. Many consumer items could be bought in either New York or New Jersey, so she would be constantly trying to compare prices expressed in terms of the two currencies. Finally, the consumer would need to worry about whether it would be safer to keep her savings account, bonds, and so forth in terms of New York dollars or New Jersey dollars.

As this example makes clear, the basic advantage of fixed exchange rates is also the basic disadvantage of floating rates. The converse is also true. The great advantage of floating exchange rates is that they allow individual countries to control their own money supplies, whereas with fixed rates national monetary policies are inextricably linked.

Chapter 16 will look in detail at the efforts of the countries of the world to fashion an efficient international monetary system. These efforts involve much debate about the alleged advantages and disadvantages of the various exchange regimes. Such debate really consists only of elaboration of the basic points just discussed, and applications of the basic theory contained in this and the next chapter.

Problems

14.16 This section gave reasons why a country might wish to peg its currency rather than to float. But why might it want to peg to a currency basket rather than to some individual currency? What considerations might influence the decision of which currency or currency basket to peg to?

14.17 With a pegged exchange rate the authorities usually establish a band around the peg within which the exchange rate is allowed to float, perhaps freely, perhaps not. Under the gold standard a similar band was common, not because of policy, but because of the cost (shipping, insurance, and forgone interest) of transporting gold from one country to another. Suppose that in Paris the French authorities freely exchanged gold and francs at the rate of Fr 100/ounce, while in Berlin the German authorities bought and sold gold for DM 50/ounce. Suppose it cost the equivalent of one-tenth of an ounce of gold to transport each ounce between Paris and Berlin. Calculate the band within which the franc price of a mark must fall.

6. INTERNATIONAL CAPITAL MOVEMENTS: INTERTEMPORAL TRADE

So far, we have considered only international trade in commodities. If the authorities attempt to influence the exchange rate, they will also trade international reserves. But nonofficial capital movements have not yet entered the picture. The international monetary system basically exists to facilitate trade in goods, but trade in assets is actually much larger and has a dominant effect on how well the international monetary system works. So we turn now to international capital movements.

Three distinct features of capital movements are important for international monetary economics. We will take things gradually, incorporating the three features one at a time in this and following sections. The first, and most fundamental, feature is that *international capital movements constitute intertemporal trade.*

When a country sells a bond, it is borrowing: the country acquires present goods and services (what it uses the proceeds of the bond sale for) in exchange for a promise to supply goods and services in the future (when it pays interest on the bonds and ultimately redeems them). That is, it trades over *time.* This section focuses squarely on this intertemporal aspect of capital movements.

Intertemporal Equilibrium

Since introducing time will complicate things, let us compensate with a simplification. Instead of two commodities, apples and butane, suppose that there is only one, called *goods.* To introduce time in as simple a way as possible, suppose that there are two periods, the *current* and the *future.* Both producers and consumers must choose between goods currently available and goods to be available in the future. If firms produce fewer current goods, they can invest their resources in productive capacity in order to be able to provide more future goods. If consumers consume more current goods, they will save less and, therefore, be able to consume fewer future goods.

If current goods and future goods are alternatives, what is their relative price? A consumer might either consume a current good now or save what it costs. If she saves it, the savings will be worth $1 + i$ in the future, where i is the rate of interest. Thus sacrificing one current good will "buy" $1 + i$ future goods: the price of current goods in terms of future goods is just $1 + i$.

Figure 14.5 shows the international trade of current goods for future goods. The horizontal axis measures quantities of current goods, and the vertical axis measures their price $1 + i$. The downward-sloping curve measures the excess of the American demand for current goods over their supply. This curve intersects the vertical axis at U: if $1 + i$ equals OU, the American demand for current goods will just equal the American supply. This indicates what the American interest rate, i_{US}, would be in autarky if the United States could not trade current goods for future goods with Germany or if there were no international borrowing or lending—that is, no international capital mobility.

Why does the American curve have a negative slope? Suppose the interest rate declines. Businesses will now find investment more attractive since interest is what they must pay to borrow funds for investment. Thus investment rises—that is, fewer resources are used to produce current goods, and more are devoted to developing the capacity to produce future goods. In other words, the supply of current goods falls. On the other hand, the lower interest rate means consumers are rewarded less for saving, so they will save less or consume more now. Thus the demand for current goods rises. Since a reduction in the rate of interest reduces the supply of current goods while increasing the demand for them, it must raise the excess of demand over supply. (If you need more detail on what's behind intertemporal trade, you should review Chapter 10, especially sections 7 and 8.)

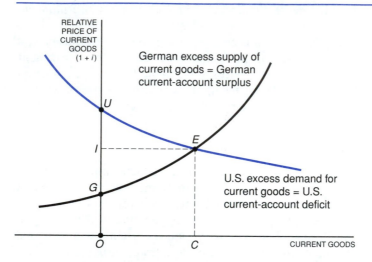

FIGURE 14.5 **Intertemporal Equilibrium in the Goods Market** A country's opportunity to invest and impatience to consume determine its excess demand or supply curve for current goods. The intersection of the United States' excess demand curve for current goods and Germany's excess supply curve determines the international rate of interest (*OI* minus 1) and the current-account (capital-account) imbalance *(OC)*.

The other curve shows the excess of German *supply* of current goods over *demand*. It slopes up for similar reasons. In autarky, point G measures one plus i_G, the German interest rate.

Now allow free international capital mobility—that is, allow the United States and Germany to trade current goods for future goods. A single world rate of interest (equal to $OI - 1$) will be established with equilibrium at E. The United States buys the quantity OC of current goods from Germany in return for promises to supply goods in the future—that is, the United States develops a *current-account deficit* (or a *capital-account surplus*) of OC, and Germany develops a corresponding *current-account surplus* (or *capital-account deficit*). When the future eventually arrives, the United States will have to pay this back with interest: $OC(1 + i)$ in total. Thus the *future* American current-account surplus will be the area $OIEC$.

The Exchange Rate

Now we examine the behavior of the exchange rate over time. Suppose that the demand for money in each country is proportional to the current consumption of goods in that country. Then the analog of equation (14.4) for the current period is

$$R^c \frac{G^G}{G^{US}} = \frac{k_G^c (RP_G^c)\, y^G}{k_{US}^c (P_{US}^c)\, y^{US}} = p^c \frac{k_G^c}{k_{US}^c} \frac{y^G}{y^{US}} = \frac{k_G^c}{k_{US}^c} \frac{y^G}{y^{US}}. \qquad (14.5)$$

In this expression R^c denotes the *current* value of the exchange rate, and y^{US} and y^G denote American and German demand for current goods, and the k^cs and P^cs denote the current values of k and P in each country. (Since American current goods are the same as German current goods, they must sell for the same price: $p^c = 1$.) In a similar way we can look at money market equilibrium in the future:

$$R^f \frac{G^G}{G^{US}} = \frac{k_G^f (RP_G^f)\, z^G}{k_{US}^f (P_{US}^f)\, z^{US}} = p^f \frac{z^G}{z^{US}} = \frac{z^G}{z^{US}}. \qquad (14.6)$$

In this expression R^f denotes the *future* value of the exchange rate, and z^{US} and z^G denote American and German demand for future goods. (Since American future goods will be the same as German future goods, they will sell for the same price: $p^f = 1$. We have also assumed for simplicity that in the future k^f will have the same value in Germany as in the United States.)

Figure 14.6 shows the current demand curve, labeled DD', and the future demand curve, labeled FF'. It is clear from Equations (14.5) and (14.6) that, if k^c has the same current value in Germany as in the United States, the cur-

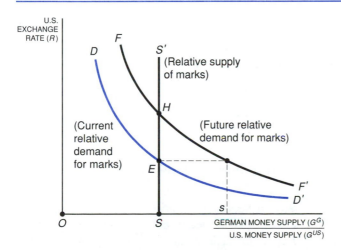

FIGURE 14.6 Intertemporal Behavior of the Exchange Rate and Equilibrium in the Money Market If Americans consume relatively more current goods than Germans compared to future goods, there will be a relatively greater demand for dollars now and a relatively greater demand for marks in the future. This means the dollar will depreciate over time.

rent demand curve will lie inside the future one, as is illustrated in the figure, if $z^G/z^{US} > y^G/y^{US}$ or if $y^{US}/z^{US} > y^G/z^G$—that is, if American consumption is biased toward current goods relative to German consumption. Figures 14.5 and 14.6 together show full intertemporal equilibrium in both the commodity markets and the money markets.

If the authorities in both countries hold money supplies unchanged over time, the supply curve SS' will stay fixed, as is shown in the figure. Thus equilibrium will move from E to H as the world goes from the current to the future: the dollar will depreciate. If $y^{US}/z^{US} > y^G/z^G$, a relatively large part of current world consumption is taking place in the United States, so there is a large current need for dollars, whereas in the future a relatively large part of world consumption will take place in Germany, so there will be a larger future need for marks. If the authorities instead peg the exchange rate at its current level, there will be a future American balance-of-payments deficit and German balance-of-payments surplus, moving the relative money supplies from S to s.

Problems

14.18 Suppose that the United States and Germany move from autarky to the situation shown in Figures 14.5 and 14.6. Describe in detail the effects on firms and consumers in both countries and the effects on money market equilibrium.

14.19 The discussion in the text assumed a single world rate of interest was established. Suppose instead that in the current period everyone believes that the German government will in the future impose a tax on interest income received from abroad. How does this affect international equilibrium?

14.20* The equilibrium depicted in Figures 14.5 and 14.6 calls for the dollar to depreciate in the future. But if people realize that this is going to happen, they will want to take care that, when the future arrives, they are holding few dollars and many marks. How would this consideration affect the analysis in the text?

7. *CASE STUDY:* THE DETERIORATION IN THE U.S. CURRENT ACCOUNT

The United States developed large current-account deficits in the early 1980s. At the same time, the dollar experienced a dramatic and prolonged appreciation relative to most major currencies. This was puzzling to many observers in light of the large deficits. Then in 1985 the dollar began a big decline. While this experience is complex, our theory is illuminating.

In the early 1980s a large U.S. federal budget deficit developed. To the extent that it was not accompanied by an increased private desire to save—and it appears not to have been—this can be interpreted as a shift in national demand from future goods to current goods.

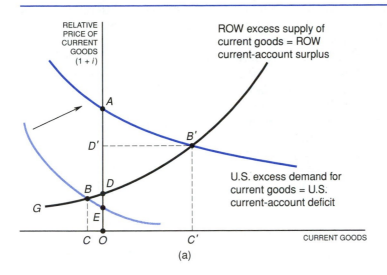

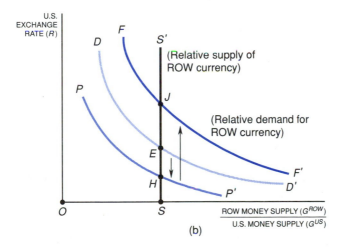

FIGURE 14.7 The U.S. Current-Account Deficit U.S. fiscal policy shifts the demand curve for current goods to the right, transforming a small current-account surplus into a large deficit. The exchange rate appreciates in the current period but will depreciate in the future.

Figure 14.7 illustrates the situation. The ROW line in panel (a) is the rest of the world's excess supply curve of current goods, and the U.S. line through points B and E is what the U.S. excess demand curve for current goods would have been if the earlier experience had continued. Equilibrium is at B, with the United States running a current-account surplus of CO.

The shift in demand from future goods to current goods is represented by a rightward shift of the U.S. curve. If the economy were closed, the new equilibrium would be at *A* and imply a large increase *AE* in the rate of interest. With the U.S. economy open, equilibrium is instead at *B'*, so the interest rate rises only by *DD'*. At the same time, the modest current-account surplus is transformed into the large current-account deficit of *OC'*.

Panel (b) shows the effect on the exchange rate. *DD'* is what the demand curve would have been before the demand shift, assuming that both countries consume current and future goods at a constant rate. But the U.S. demand shift toward current goods shifts *DD'* down to *PP'* in the current and out to *FF'* in the future. Thus current equilibrium moves from *E* to *H,* and in the future it will move from *H* to *J.* The dollar *appreciates* now, though subsequently it must depreciate.

Thus the theory explains the simultaneous current-account deficit and strong appreciation of the dollar. Many observers at the time thought the appreciation *caused* the deficit (by making U.S. prices higher in terms of foreign currency and foreign prices lower in terms of dollars), and they were puzzled that the dollar was becoming even stronger while the current account was so weak. The present theory offers an explanation and suggests that *both* the deficit and the depreciation were due to a *common cause:* a change in U.S. time preference.

Expectations

The dollar began a substantial depreciation in 1985, a depreciation that was particularly large relative to the Japanese yen and German mark. Our theory might seem to explain this as well: Figure 14.7 clearly calls for a big depreciation in the future. But here the model's simplicity begins to be a handicap. Figure 14.7 shows both the dollar depreciation and the turnaround in the current-account deficit taking place in the future period; but when the dollar actually began to depreciate in 1985, there was no sign of any improvement in the deficit. Our simple model, with the "future" represented by just one period, cannot possibly deal with a complex reality where different events occur at different times as the future gradually unfolds. Nevertheless, it is suggestive.

Suppose that the shift depicted in Figure 14.7 takes place, and the current appreciation of the dollar occurs. The theory now predicts a depreciation in the future, and anyone who understands what is happening will know this to be so. Such a person will not want to be holding any more dollars than necessary when the depreciation takes place and so will attempt to sell them before that. Thus, in terms of the figure, the shift of the demand curve from *PP'* toward *FF'* should occur before the actual reversal of the current-account deficit. How much before? Our typical individual presumably realizes that others also expect a future depreciation and so wants above all not to be one of the last to sell dollars. He is weighing this fear of being too late against the usefulness of dollars for current transactions. Any sign that others are attempting to unload dollars will prompt him to do so. So will any events that signal that a depreciation may not be too far off: attempts to deal with the current-account imbalance, indications that central banks are about to intervene to force a dollar depreciation, and so on.

Problems

14.21 In response to the large federal budget deficits, the United States enacted the Gramm-Rudman Law mandating the elimination of that deficit over a period of several years, with spending cuts automatically triggered by insufficient progress. Analyze the effects of such a law in terms of Figure 14.7.

14.22 In response to the current-account imbalance, U.S. authorities urged the rest of the world (in particular, Germany and Japan) to adopt more expansionary policies. Discuss this in terms of Figure 14.7.

14.23* The U.S. current-account deficit shown in Figure 14.7 has its counterpart in a capital-account surplus: the United States is selling assets to foreigners. Suppose that these assets are dollar-denominated bonds and that there are also bonds denominated in foreign currency. What is the relation between the interest rates on these bonds and the interest rate shown in panel (a) of the figure? What does the text's discussion of expectations imply about the interest rates on U.S. and foreign bonds?

14.24* What should U.S. monetary policy have been if the authorities wished to prevent the exchange-rate fluctuations shown in Figure 14.7? If the authorities wished to prevent U.S. interest rates from rising too much?

8. INTERNATIONAL CAPITAL MOVEMENTS: EXPECTATIONS

Section 6 introduced international trade in assets by treating the assets as claims to future *goods*. But, you will recall from our investigation of international financial markets in Chapter 13, real-world assets generally pay *money*, not goods. A bond, for example, is a promise to pay so much money as interest each year up to a certain date and then to repay the principal, also in money. So if you buy a foreign bond, you receive the promise of *foreign* money. Of course, some assets, such as common stock or real estate, confer ownership of objects other than money. But investing in such assets abroad does generally involve receiving foreign money in the future. Suppose, for example, you buy a condo in Paris. True, you now own a condo rather than a pile of francs (a big pile of francs). But the rents you receive for the use of your condo will be in francs, and when you sell it on the Paris real-estate market, you will get francs for it.

To see what difference this makes, suppose now that U.S.-issued assets are dollar bonds and that German-issued assets are mark bonds rather than claims to future goods. People will need to compare yields on American and German bonds to decide which to buy. Although this still involves comparing the interest rates, i_{US} and i_G, now more is involved. *Expectations* about the future course of the exchange rate influence the relative attractiveness of dollar bonds and mark bonds. Suppose, for example, that people expect the dollar to depreciate by d percent (that is, they expect the mark to appreciate by d percent). Consider an American investment adviser, Marie, wondering how to invest her clients' wealth. If she invests in American bonds, she earns the American rate of interest, i_{US}. If she invests in German bonds, she will earn the German rate of interest i_G. But in the latter case her investments will be in the form of marks, and the mark is expected to increase in value by d percent relative to the dollar. Thus the net return to Marie's clients for investing in German bonds is $i_G + d$. In deciding where to put her entrusted wealth, Marie will compare i_{US} to $i_G + d$. If Marie now comes to expect the dollar to depreciate by more than she had previously thought—that is, if d rises—then German bonds become more attractive relative to American bonds and she will be led to buy the former and to sell the latter.

In this case, i_{US} and $i_G + d$ must be equal because no one would be willing to hold any of the bond with the lower return (thus forcing up its interest rate). Thus $d = i_{US} - i_G$.

KEY CONCEPT

Yields on foreign bonds and domestic bonds are equal when expected exchange-rate changes are related to differences in interest-rate levels by *interest parity:*

(IP)   (expected depreciation) = (domestic interest rate) −
                                                          (foreign interest rate).

This relationship expresses the idea that the expected rate of depreciation of a nation's currency cancels out international differences in interest rates. Interest parity is sometimes referred to as *uncovered interest parity* (UIP) since it does not analyze the possibility that people take steps to protect themselves from (that is, to *cover*) exchange-rate risk. Such possibilities were considered in Chapter 13. For example, an American purchaser of German bonds might sell marks *forward;* in this case he need not worry about what the future spot price of the mark will be. But in practice such forward cover is difficult to obtain for more than one year ahead or for currencies other than the major ones.

How does all this affect our analysis? Simple. Figure 14.8 shows what Figures 14.5 and 14.6 look like when assets are bonds rather than promises to

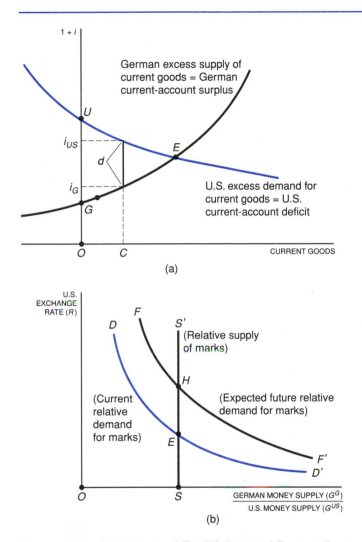

FIGURE 14.8 **Intertemporal Equilibrium and Expectations** The U.S. interest rate exceeds the German interest rate by the expected depreciation of the dollar relative to the mark *(d = HE/ES)*.

pay future goods. In panel (a), the U.S. current-account deficit is shown by *OC*, and the U.S. interest rate, i_{US}, exceeds the German interest rate, i_G, by *d*, the expected future depreciation of the dollar. In panel (b), *DD'* still represents the current relative demand curve for marks, and *FF'* represents what the relative demand curve is expected to be in the future. Thus the U.S. exchange rate is expected to depreciate from *ES* to *HS*, a change in the proportion *HE/ES*. Therefore, *d* in panel (a) equals *HE/ES* in panel (b).

Problems

14.25 If the U.S. rate of interest is 6 percent and the comparable U.K. interest rate is 9 percent, what is the consensus view about the likely future course of the dollar-sterling exchange rate if interest parity is to hold?

14.26 The formula for interest parity given in the text applies *instantaneously* for assets that are about to mature. The formula varies slightly for different maturities. Suppose, for example, that r denotes what a dollar invested in the United States will earn in interest over the next three months, that r^* is the number of pounds sterling a pound invested in the United Kingdom would earn over the next three months, that R is the current U.S. exchange rate (the number of dollars required to buy £1 now), and that E denotes what this exchange rate is expected to be in three months. Then interest parity will hold if $(1 + r) = (1/R)(1 + r^*)E$. Explain why. The formula can also be written

$$\frac{E - R}{R} = r - \frac{E}{R} r^*.$$

Derive this expression. The term on the left is the expected depreciation of the dollar relative to the pound over the next three months. Newspapers will quote three-month interest rates on an annualized basis. To obtain r from such a quote, divide the latter by 4 (to change it from an annual basis to a three-month basis), and then divide it by 100 (to change it from a percentage to a decimal). Thus a three-month interest rate of 12 percent corresponds to a value of r of .03. *(The above formula converges to the one in the text as the time to maturity becomes arbitrarily small.)*

14.27 Suppose that the present exchange rate is $1.50/£ and that in the United States the three-month, six-month, and one-year interest rates are respectively 12 percent, 10 percent, and 8 percent on a yearly basis. The corresponding U.K. interest rates are 6 percent, 10 percent, and 10 percent. Describe what the market must expect the future course of the exchange rate to be if interest parity holds.

9. INTERNATIONAL CAPITAL MOVEMENTS: IMPERFECT CAPITAL MOBILITY

Thus far we have looked at two features implied by international capital movements: trade in assets is *intertemporal* trade; *expectations* about the future course of the exchange rate influence the relative rates of return on assets denominated in different currencies. Now we look at the third: the implications of the *degree of international capital mobility*. The international exchange of assets is often limited by regulation, by the lack of international financial markets, or by an unwillingness on the part of citizens of one country to acquire the assets of another. In practice capital mobility varies widely. Bonds issued by multinational corporations and the governments of industrial states have international markets, whereas the obligations of smaller entities tend to be traded only locally. Some governments severely restrict the freedom of their residents to trade assets with foreigners. Some countries are viewed as so risky that they can sell few if any of their assets. Canadian firms and governing bodies regularly float bond issues in New York, but many LDCs can sell few bonds and must borrow largely from banks.

KEY CONCEPT

Perfect international capital mobility means that domestic and foreign bonds are regarded as equivalent by the market, so they must have the same yield. With *no international capital mobility,* national bonds cannot be traded between countries, so there is no direct pressure to equalize interest rates. The intermediate possibility of *imperfect international capital mobility* encompasses all cases where national bonds can be traded internationally but are not fully equivalent: a reduction in the domestic interest rate relative to the foreign rate will make domestic bonds less attractive but will not cause everyone to refuse to hold any of them.

With *perfect international capital mobility,* residents of each country treat the bonds of all countries as perfect substitutes and so always buy the one with the highest yield.

Figure 14.9 illustrates different degrees of international capital mobility. The horizontal axis measures the rate of interest i_{US} on American bonds. The portfolio curve of American residents relates this to the fraction of their total bond holdings that they wish to keep in the form of American bonds. This fraction, b, is measured on the vertical axis.

If there is *no international capital mobility,* this fraction must be 1 for every value of the American interest rate: the portfolio curve is horizontal. At the other extreme, with perfect capital mobility American residents will wish to hold only the bond with the higher expected yield. Thus when i_{US} is less than $i_G + d$, they wish to hold only German bonds so that the portfolio curve is flat with a value of 0. When i_{US} exceeds $i_G + d$, they wish to hold no German bonds at all, so the portfolio curve is flat with a value of 1. At interest parity, American residents do not care what combination of bonds they own, so the portfolio curve is vertical.

With *imperfect capital mobility,* American residents are more reluctant to acquire (or are prevented from acquiring) German bonds, but a reduction in the American rate of interest will induce them to acquire more. The portfolio curve,

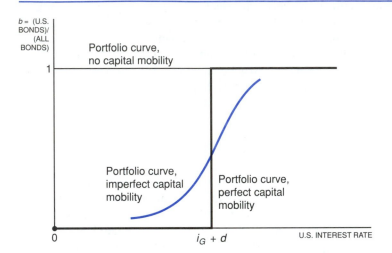

FIGURE 14.9 The Degree of International Capital Mobility   If there is no international capital mobility, American residents always hold only American bonds; with perfect mobility, they hold only the bond with the higher yield; imperfect capital mobility implies that the proportion of bond holdings devoted to domestic bonds falls as the domestic interest rate falls below the interest-parity level.

therefore, slopes up, as indicated. The slope of this curve as i_{US} falls below the interest-parity level can be thought of as an index of the degree of capital mobility: the steeper the curve, the closer we are to perfect capital mobility.

Illustration of Interest Parity

The degree to which interest parity holds may be a measure of the degree of international capital mobility, but we cannot look within the hearts and minds of individuals to discern their expectations about the future. For example, the middle column of Table 14.2 shows the amount by which the interest rates in various countries exceeded that in the United States in January 1994. The right-hand column shows the *actual* depreciations (at annual rates) of the respective currencies over the next three months. The columns would coincide if interest parity were exact. There is in fact little indication of interest parity; only Canada comes close, and in four cases the two entries do not even have the same sign. But there is a basic reason why this can indicate nothing about the degree of capital mobility: we have no idea of how successful people had been in forecasting the actual depreciations before they took place. We would expect that, over time, errors in one direction would tend to cancel out errors in the other direction so that interest differentials and exchange

TABLE 14.2   Interest Differentials and Depreciation, January 1994

Country	Interest differential* over U.S.	Actual subsequent depreciation relative to dollar
Canada	0.61	1.0
France	3.24	−0.9
Germany	2.55	−1.1
Italy	5.85	−1.5
Japan	−0.72	−1.6
United Kingdom	1.83	−0.2

*Money-market rates for Italy and Japan; interbank rates for France and Germany; treasury-bill rates for Canada and the United Kingdom.
SOURCE: International Monetary Fund, *International Financial Statistics.*

depreciations would more nearly match on the average over the long run. Table 14.3 shows average interest differentials over 1993 as a whole and average subsequent depreciations relative to the dollar. The correspondence between the two is somewhat closer than in Table 14.3. Nevertheless, quantification of the importance of interest parity is basically prevented by the fact that people's expectations are not observable.

Figure 14.10 shows international equilibrium with less-than-perfect capital mobility. In order to run a current-account deficit, the United States in the figure needs to pay an interest rate that exceeds the German rate of interest by more than the expected rate of depreciation of the dollar. The high U.S. interest rate (and low German interest rate) results in a smaller current-account imbalance than would occur with perfect capital mobility.

TABLE 14.3   Average Interest Differentials and Depreciation, 1993

Country	Average interest differential* over U.S.	Actual subsequent depreciation relative to dollar
Canada	1.82	2.5
France	5.39	1.1
Germany	4.18	0.9
Italy	7.15	0.2
Japan	0.04	−2.8
United Kingdom	2.16	0.4

*Money-market rates for Italy and Japan; interbank rates for France and Germany; treasury-bill rates for Canada and the United Kingdom.
SOURCE: International Monetary Fund, *International Financial Statistics.*

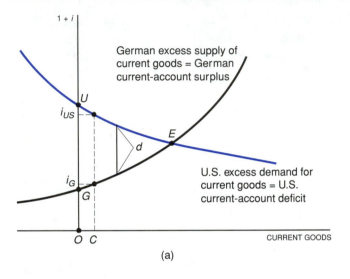

(a)

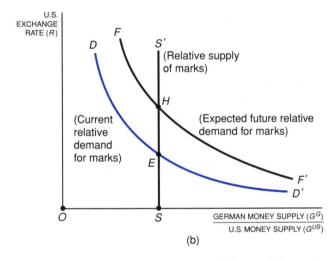

(b)

FIGURE 14.10   Intertemporal Equilibrium and Imperfect Capital Mobility
The U.S. interest rate exceeds the German interest rate by more than the expected depreciation of the dollar relative to the mark $(d = HE/ES)$.

10. MONETARY POLICY AND EXCHANGE RATES

Suppose the U.S. central bank undertakes an expansionary monetary policy. The most common way to expand the money supply is with open-market operations: the central bank buys bonds from the public in exchange for money. Thus more money circulates, and the public owns fewer dollar-denominated bonds. So the total supply of dollar-denominated assets does not change but becomes more liquid, with some bonds replaced by money.

Figure 14.11 shows the effect of such an increase in the U.S. money sup-

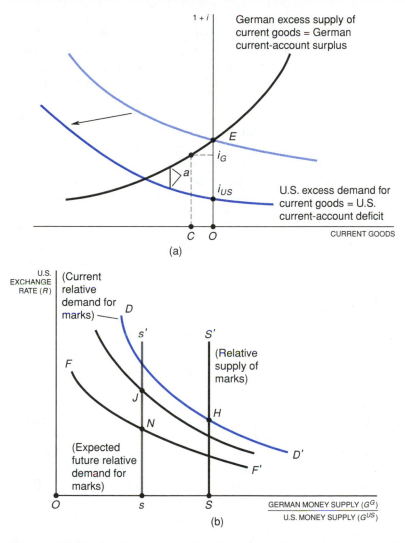

FIGURE 14.11 An Increase in the American Money Supply An American open-market purchase of bonds shifts the relative demand curve for marks and the U.S. excess demand curve for current goods to the left. This causes the dollar to depreciate, generates a U.S. current-account surplus, and lowers interest rates worldwide, with the U.S. interest rate falling relative to the German interest rate.

ply. For simplicity, suppose that the initial equilibrium, at E and H in panels (a) and (b), respectively, features a zero current-account imbalance, a zero expected depreciation of the dollar, and equality between the U.S. and German interest rates. (The DD' curve in panel (b) is both the original current relative demand curve for marks and what the curve is originally expected to be in the future; SS' denotes the original relative supply curve.)

Now the U.S. Fed conducts an open-market purchase of bonds. By increasing the supply of dollars, this shifts the relative supply curve in panel (b) to the left—from SS' to ss'. By lowering the supply of dollar bonds, this operation also shifts to the left in panel (a) the U.S. excess demand curve for current goods (which is also the U.S. excess supply curve of bonds).

In panel (a), the shift of the U.S. curve produces an American current-account surplus (capital-account deficit). Evidently, the Fed's purchase of bonds from the U.S. public in effect induces the public to purchase bonds from abroad. Interest rates fall in both countries, but the U.S. rate falls relative to the German. In panel (b), the shift of the relative supply curve causes a depreciation of the dollar, but this depreciation of the dollar is moderated by a leftward shift of the current relative demand curve. The latter shift is due to the fact that the fall in the U.S. interest rate relative to the German interest rate causes the value of the U.S. k to rise relative to the value of the German k. Finally, the emergence of an American current-account surplus means that, relative to Germany, the United States is pushing consumption into the future, so the future relative demand curve for marks will now be expected to be below the new current relative demand curve, as is also shown in panel (b). Thus the dollar is expected to appreciate from sJ to sN. The expected appreciation of the dollar is indicated by a in panel (a), so $a = JN/sN$. Thus the expansion in the U.S. money supply causes the dollar to depreciate, but it also generates the expectation that this depreciation will be reversed by a subsequent appreciation.

If you compare this analysis of the effects of an increase in the money supply with the discussion in section 3, you will notice two important differences. First, there is considerably less variation in the exchange rate. Obviously, R would have increased more in Figure 14.11 if the DD' curve had not also shifted, and this reflected the role of bond markets. An open-market operation changes the composition of dollar assets between money and bonds; it does not change the composition of world assets between those denominated in dollars and those denominated in marks.

Second, the presence of international bond markets has eroded the ability of national authorities to conduct independent monetary policies with a floating exchange rate. The increase in the American money supply has lowered interest rates in Germany. Each country can still directly control its own money *supply,* but monetary *conditions* in each country depend in part on actions in the other.

Problems

14.28 Repeat the analysis of this section for the case of no international capital mobility. Show how your analysis is consistent with the discussion in section 3.

14.29 What would be the effect on the analysis of this section of an *increase* in the degree of international capital mobility?

11. *CASE STUDY:* EMPIRICAL ESTIMATION OF EXCHANGE-RATE MODELS

This chapter has discussed determinants of the exchange rate. As we have seen, many industrial countries have not had pegged rates since the early 1970s. The subsequent decade or so gives us experience that can be used to test empirically theories of the exchange rate.

The theory that we have discussed in this chapter suggests that, in a floating exchange-rate regime, the exchange rate is determined by relative money supplies, relative income levels, and interest-rate differentials:

$$R = \phi(G/G^*, y/y^*, i - i^*) \tag{14.7}$$

This expression simply means that the value of the exchange rate R (and the change in R, since its past value is known) depends upon the ratio of the home money supply to the foreign (G/G^*), the ratio of home income to foreign (y/y^*), and the excess of the home rate of interest over the foreign $(i - i^*)$.

Price levels might also be used in the equation. Furthermore, alternative theories claim that the exchange rate—and changes in the exchange rate—also depend upon home and foreign trade balances and upon the difference between what the home inflation rate is expected to be and what the foreign inflation rate is expected to be. Part Six will discuss why these other variables might influence the exchange rate.

Empirical work has used data on these variables to estimate a specific relationship like (14.7). Other work has also incorporated price levels, expected inflation differentials, and trade balances to estimate alternative versions of (14.7). This work has led to various results, but two seem especially prominent.

First, these studies have generally yielded reasonably good fits. That is, when actual data are used to estimate a curve, most observations lie close to the resulting curve. This means that variations in the exchange rate appear to be accounted for by variations in the other variables considered.

The *second* result is more disconcerting. Richard Meese of the University of California at Berkeley and Kenneth Rogoff of Princeton University have shown that these estimated relationships do not perform well out of sample. For example, if data from 1973–1980 are used to estimate a relationship such as (14.7) and if this estimated relation is then used to explain what the exchange rate did in 1981, the resulting estimation is not good. In particular, such an estimate is typically no better than that derived from the simple hypothesis that the percentage change in the exchange rate is a random variable. Furthermore, this is true of all the alternative estimated versions of (14.7), using different collections of the variables mentioned above. Estimated models of the exchange rate perform badly with data outside the sample used to obtain the estimates.

This work seems to indicate that existing simple models of the exchange rate are too simple. More complicated models, incorporating more economic structure as well as additional variables, appear to be necessary.

What is not clear is whether the exchange rate can in fact be forecast—that is, whether any model not too complex to be tractable will be able to explain the exchange rate any better than the simple hypothesis that that rate follows a random walk.

12. SUMMARY

1. The equilibrium exchange rate is determined by the condition that the relative demands for home and foreign monies equal the relative supplies.

2. A disequilibrium exchange rate can be corrected in two basic ways: (1) by allowing payments imbalances to alter relative money supplies until the actual exchange rate becomes an equilibrium one (automatic adjustment process); (2) by altering the exchange rate to its equilibrium value. In practice these two methods are usually combined in various ways, and sometimes countries attempt to avoid them by resorting to direct controls.

3. Exchange-rate adjustments have two basic implications: they can eliminate payments imbalances, and they allow individual countries control of their own money supplies.

4. Fixed exchange rates make national monies more useful as money. Flexible rates give individual countries control over their own money supplies but do not eliminate international economic interdependence.

5. Uncovered interest parity holds when the excess of the domestic interest rate over the foreign interest rate is equal to the expected depreciation of the home currency.

6. International capital mobility implies a role for: (1) intertemporal trade; (2) exchange-rate expectations; (3) the degree of capital mobility.

7. Empirical estimates of simple exchange-rate models yield reasonably good fits but do not perform well out of sample.

SUGGESTED READING

Cooper, R. N. "Monetary Theory and Policy in an Open Economy." *Scandinavian Journal of Economics* 78 (1976): 146–68. This issue contains other papers concerned with asset markets and the exchange rate.

Frenkel, J., and H. Johnson, eds. *The Economics of Exchange Rates*. Reading: Addison-Wesley, 1978. A collection of papers stressing asset markets.

Jones, R. W., and P. B. Kenen, eds. *Handbook of International Economics*. Vol. 2. Amsterdam: North-Holland, 1985. Especially relevant to this chapter are Chapter 14 by Jacob Frenkel and Michael Mussa (exchange rates and asset markets) and Chapter 18 by Maurice Obstfeld and Alan Stockman (exchange-rate dynamics).

Meese, R. A., and K. Rogoff. "Empirical Exchange Rate Models of the Seventies: Do They Fit Out of Sample?" *Journal of International Economics* 14 (1983): 3–24. The answer is "no."

Razin, A., and L. E. O. Svensson. "The Current Account and the Optimal Government Debt." *Journal of International Money and Finance* 2 (1983): 215–24. A geometric analysis of intertemporal questions.

Taussig, F. W. *International Trade*. New York: Macmillan, 1927. Part 3 contains Taussig's treatment of the causes and effects of exchange-rate changes.

CHAPTER 15

The Automatic Adjustment Process

Suppose four-fifths of all the money in Great Britain to be annihilated in one night, . . . what would be the consequence? Must not the price of all labour and commodities sink in proportion . . . ? What nation could then dispute with us in any foreign market . . . ? In how little time, therefore, must this bring back the money which we had lost, and raise us to the level of all the neighboring nations? Where, after we have arrived, we immediately lose the advantage of the cheapness of labour and commodities; and the farther flowing in of money is stopped by our fulness and repletion. . . . Now, it is evident, that the same causes . . . must for ever, in all neighboring nations, preserve money nearly proportionable to the art and industry of each nation.
                                                              —DAVID HUME

This chapter investigates those problems that arise simply from the existence of money. Unlike Chapter 14, exchange rates now will be *fixed*. The key idea is that of the automatic adjustment process of the balance of payments, the exposition of which is generally credited to David Hume and, sometimes, to Richard Cantillon.

1. INTERNATIONAL MONETARY EQUILIBRIUM

We follow the same strategy as in Chapter 14: first, the basic ideas in a simple framework, and then various extensions and applications. As before, imagine that the world consists of two countries, the United States and Germany, with the United States exporting apples and Germany exporting butane.

DAVID HUME (1711–1776)

One of the preeminent eighteenth-century thinkers, Hume, like his close friend and fellow Scot Adam Smith (and like John Stuart Mill but unlike Richard Cantillon and David Ricardo), was a philosopher who also made important contributions to economics—and to history, politics, aesthetics, sociology, and psychology. For Hume all these concerns were aspects of a single system of philosophy. His economic thought focused on the underlying causes of industrial progress and was one of the principal predecessors of the work of Adam Smith, whose *Wealth of Nations* was published the year that Hume died.

RICHARD CANTILLON (1680–1734)

Like Ricardo, Cantillon was an economist who accumulated a fortune through financial dealing. He was from an Irish family of sympathizers of the Stuart pretenders to the English throne and for years lived in Paris, where many Stuart sympathizers took refuge. While he was there, he understood the defects in a financial scheme being masterminded by John Law. Although this earned him the hostility of Law and his friends, when the scheme collapsed Cantillon had his fortune. A mistake in labor relations, however, was to cost him his life. While he was living in London, he fired his cook, who then set fire to the house, taking care that Cantillon was in it at the time.

Money Supplies and Money Prices

For starters, assume that money consists of gold coins and nothing else. There is a fixed number G of such coins, so that if G^{US} is the money supply in the United States and G^G that in Germany, $G = G^{US} + G^G$. The GG' line in Figure 15.1 shows the various ways that the total world money supply can be distributed between the two countries. The length of OG ($= OG'$) measures the total number of gold coins; at point E, for example, the German money supply is equal to OA and the American to OB.

P_A is the world money price of apples (the number of gold coins needed to buy 1 apple), and P_B is the money price of butane. The relative price of butane in terms of apples, $P = P_B/P_A$, is determined by demand and supply, as discussed in Parts One and Two. But the pure theory cannot determine the two *money* prices.

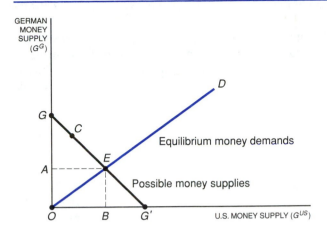

FIGURE 15.1 **International Monetary Equilibrium** The equilibrium distribution of the world's money supply is determined by the intersection of the demand and supply curves.

As before, we start with a rudimentary version of the demand for money. The demand for dollars will equal the supply when

$$G^{US} = k(i_{US}) P_A y^{US},$$ (15.1)

where y^{US} stands for American national income measured in units of apples, i_{US} is the American rate of interest, and $k(i_{US})$ denotes the number of dollars that the Americans wish to hold for each dollar of income. Similarly, the demand for money in Germany will equal the supply G^G of marks when

$$G^G = k(i_G) P_B y^G,$$ (15.2)

where y^G denotes German income in terms of butane. The theory can be used to determine two things: the equilibrium distribution of the world money supply between the United States and Germany, and absolute money prices.

Equilibrium Distribution of the World's Money

For the world to be in equilibrium, the demand for money in each country must equal the supply—that is, (15.1) and (15.2) must hold. Dividing (15.1) into (15.2)

$$\frac{G^G}{G^F} = \frac{k(i_G)P_B y^G}{k(i_{US})P_A y^{US}} = p\frac{k(i_G)}{k(i_{US})}\frac{y^G}{y^{US}}.$$ (15.3)

The right-hand side of (15.3) depends upon the relative price p, determined in goods markets, and on the interest rates, determined in the credit markets. Thus (15.3) tells us what the ratio of the two money supplies must be in equilibrium. This is depicted in Figure 15.1 by the line OD, whose slope (EB/OB) equals $p\,[k(i_G)/k(i_{US})]\,[y^G/y^{US}]$.

The world must be on the GG' line in Figure 15.1 for the money supplies in the two countries to total the world stock of gold coins, and it must be on the line OD for equilibrium. Thus the intersection E depicts the equilibrium money supplies in the two countries: G^{US} should equal OB, and G^G should equal OA.

Money Prices

Commodity markets determine p, the ratio of P_B to P_A, but not the absolute values of P_B and P_A. This is a task of the quantity theory. Adding together (15.1) and (15.2), the quantity equations for the two countries, gives a world quantity equation that equates the total world supply of money to the total world demand:

$$G^{US} + G^G = G = k(i_{US})\,[P_A y^{US}] + k(i_G)\,[P_B y^G]$$

$$= P_A[k(i_{US})\,y^{US} + pk\,(i_G)y^G]. \qquad \textbf{(15.4)}$$

Everything on the extreme right-hand side of (15.4) except P_A is determined; thus (15.4) says that P_A is proportional to G. The world stock of money determines the absolute price of apples and, hence, the absolute price of butane as well since $P_B = pP_A$.

Problems

15.1 Suppose that America and Europe trade, America specializing in and exporting wheat and Europe specializing in and exporting cloth. American wheat production equals 1,000, and European cloth production 600. In equilibrium, 5 wheat exchange for 1 cloth. The world money supply consists of 2,000 gold coins, and in each country $k = 1/2$. Describe international monetary equilibrium, and illustrate it with a diagram analogous to Figure 15.1. Suppose that the world money supply increases to 4,000 gold coins; calculate the effect on your answer and illustrate the change in your diagram. Do the same if the terms of trade were to alter so that 5 wheat exchange for 3 cloth.

15.2 The discussion in the text supposed that k had the same value in both countries. Show in detail how the argument would change if k were different in Germany than in the United States. How would your answer to the first part of the above problem change if k were to fall to $1/4$ in America but remain at $1/2$ in Europe?

15.3 Assume that in equilibrium the German supply of butane is 111 and its supply of apples is 21, that the United States exports 70 apples to Germany for 30 units of butane, and that American production is 100 apples. Suppose that the world money supply consists of 1,520 gold coins and that k equals 2 in each country. Find the equilibrium money supplies in the two countries and the equilibrium money prices of the two goods.

15.4* England has 100 labor units, of which 5 are required to produce either a cask of wine or a bolt of cloth. The English always consume equal quantities of the two goods. Portugal has 100 labor units with 1 required to produce a cask of wine and 4 to produce a bolt of cloth; the Portuguese always consume equal-valued quantities of wine and cloth. The world money supply consists of 150 gold coins, and k equals 1. Describe and illustrate international monetary equilibrium. Show what happens if England's labor force increases to 1,000.

15.5* Show how the discussion of this section changes if, instead of remaining fixed, G constantly *increases* at the rate of 10 percent per year.

2. THE AUTOMATIC ADJUSTMENT PROCESS

The previous section described international monetary equilibrium. But one point has been left dangling: the existing supply of gold coins requires the world to be somewhere on the line GG' in Figure 15.1, but is there any reason to think that it will be at point E? This is the subject of the automatic adjustment process, the key idea of this chapter.

The Balance of Payments

If the citizens of a country, say the United States, wish to import the quantity M of butane, they must pay $P_B M$ in money (gold coins) to do so; similarly, their exports X of apples will yield them $P_A X$ in return. Thus the American *trade balance* $P_A X - P_B M = B$, or *balance-of-payments surplus*, equals the net amount of money the Americans are receiving from abroad. Alternatively, if the Americans wish to increase their money holdings and if the total number of gold coins in existence does not change, the only way they can do so is by exporting a larger value of goods to Germany relative to their imports. (Note that this is an application of Walras's Law to a world with three markets: apples, butane, and gold coins. Because there are no assets other than money, the terms C and E in equation (12.2) on page 342 have dropped out.) If the world is in equilibrium, the apple and butane markets are in equilibrium, and each country's exports are equal in value to its imports so that their balances of payments are zero. This is reflected on the monetary side by the fact that at point E in Figure 15.1 each country's demand for money is equal to its supply.

Overview of the Adjustment Process

What if the world's money is not distributed in the equilibrium fashion? Suppose, for example, that we are at point C in Figure 15.1 rather than at E. Then the German money supply exceeds its equilibrium level while the American supply falls short. The Germans use their excess money to purchase more apples from the United States and to consume more of their own butane, thereby exporting less. Thus German imports exceed exports in value; Germany runs a balance-of-payments deficit. The American money supply, on the other hand, is deficient, so the Americans decrease their purchases of German butane (cutting imports) and of American apples (freeing more for export); the United States runs a balance-of-payments surplus. The German deficit and corresponding American surplus mean that on balance Germany is selling gold to the United States for goods. The American money supply is increasing, and the German money supply is falling. In Figure 15.1 the world is moving along the GG' line from C toward E. This continues until the supply of money in each country equals the demand—that is, until E is reached.

This is the essence of the automatic adjustment process. Note that it contains three basic ingredients. (1) Monetary theory determines the equilibrium allocation of the world's money supply between countries. (2) A nonequilibrium distribution of the world's money causes balance-of-payments deficits and surpluses. (3) These deficits and surpluses redistribute money between countries. The first ingredient was studied in section 1. The explicit mechanics behind point (2) will be examined in detail in Part Six. The essential requirement of point (3) is that a country with a balance-of-payments deficit should have a contracting money supply and a country with a payments surplus an expanding money supply, a requirement sometimes called the "Rules of the Game." This is trivial in the present context, where a payments surplus and an increase in the money supply are really just two different names for the same thing. But this is not true with the more elaborate financial arrangements that exist in the world. Therefore, we shall return to the Rules of the Game in section 6 of this chapter.

KEY CONCEPT

The Rules of the Game: A balance-of-payments deficit should be fully reflected in a reduction in the supply of money, and a surplus should be fully reflected in an increase in the supply of money.

Implications of the Automatic Adjustment Process

The classical automatic adjustment process has two broad implications. *First,* balance-of-payments deficits or surpluses are both the symptoms of an international misallocation of money and the means by which such misallocations are corrected. Thus payments imbalances are transitory and beneficial and no cause for alarm.

Second, the adjustment process ensures that the world has a single international monetary system in which individual countries cannot pursue independent monetary policies (except transitorily). This is illustrated in Figure 15.2(a). Suppose the Americans create sufficient money to double their money supply so that the world moves from E to H and the GG' line shifts to G_1G_1', the length EH measuring the American money creation.

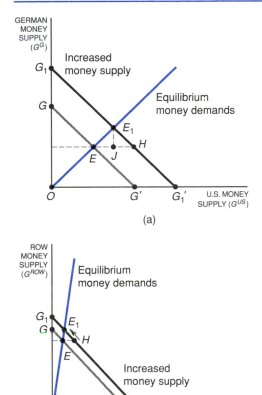

FIGURE 15.2 **American Money Creation** (a) Despite the creation of *EH* new money, the Americans have managed to increase their money supply by only *EJ*. (b) The possibility of the Americans increasing their own money supply diminishes further when the United States is only a modest part of a big world.

(Perhaps the Americans find this much gold in a cave, or they discover the philosophers' stone and turn this much base metal into gold, or, better yet, they print this much paper money and are able to convince everyone that it is just as good as gold.) The equilibrium is at E_1. With the world at *H*, the United States develops a payments deficit and Germany a surplus; this continues until the American money supply has shrunk and the German money supply has expanded sufficiently to reach E_1. Despite the creation of *EH* of new money, the Americans have managed to increase their money supply only by *EJ*, and they have been able to do this only by increasing Germany's money supply in the same proportion. Thus the automatic adjustment process ensures that a country can have nontransitory control over its money supply only by controlling that of the entire world. This point has even more force when we realize that a single country, even a relatively large one, will be small compared to the rest of the world. Suppose, for example, that the Umited States is one-twentieth of the world in the sense that in equilibrium the American money supply will equal 5 percent of world money. Then in order to increase their money supply any specified amount, the Americans would have to create twenty times that amount of new money; nineteen-twentieths of any money created will flow out of the country in balance-of-payments deficits. This is illustrated in Figure 15.2 (b). Even if the Americans are undaunted by this and try to wag the tail by swinging the dog, other countries are unlikely to remain passive and allow the United States to determine their monetary policies. Thus the classical automatic adjustment process effectively implies that individual countries lack control over their money supplies, except transitorily. Or, equivalently, independent national monetary policies require that the automatic adjustment process be aborted.

We have examined a purely *monetary* disturbance—an increase in the American money supply. The process can be further illuminated by examining the consequences of a *real* shock. Suppose, for example, that people's tastes change from American goods toward German goods or from apples toward butane so that the equilibrium relative price p of butane in terms of apples rises. In Figure 15.3 the line OH shifts to OH' so that E_1 is the new equilibrium. With the world initially at $E,$ an American balance-of-payments surplus—and German balance-of-payments deficit—now emerges. These payments imbalances are due to changes in the commodity markets, not to changes in monetary policy in either country. The imbalances persist until the world moves from E to the new equilibrium at E_1.

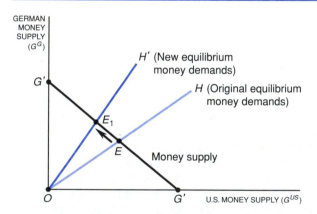

FIGURE 15.3 A Real (Goods) Disturbance A real disturbance shifts the demand curve, so equilibrium moves along the supply curve.

Problems

15.6 As in Problem **15.1**, America produces 1,000 wheat, Europe 600 cloth, and in equilibrium 5 wheat exchange for 1 cloth. Initially, the world money supply consists of 2,000 gold coins, and $k = \frac{1}{2}$. Now suppose that the world money supply increases to 4,000 coins, with the increase taking place in America. Calculate the cumulative payments imbalances necessary to restore equilibrium.

15.7 In Problem **15.6**, suppose that the American money supply remains equal to 2,000 gold coins but that economic growth in America raises wheat production to 2,000 units. Calculate the cumulative payments imbalance necessary to restore equilibrium.

15.8 Suppose that, in Problem **15.4***, Portuguese tastes permanently change so that each Portuguese now always spends one-fourth of her income on cloth and three-fourths on wine. Find the new monetary equilibrium, and calculate the cumulative payments imbalances that are necessary in order to reach this new equilibrium from the old one.

15.9* Show how the discussion of this section changes if the Americans, instead of doubling their money supply just once, double it every year forever.

3. MONETARY SYSTEMS

So far we have assumed a rudimentary monetary system. It is time to consider more complex and realistic systems.

Alternative Standards

The Gold Standard. The monetary units (francs, marks, lire, dollars, and so on) of the countries adhering to a gold standard are all defined in terms of gold. So far in this chapter we have assumed that money consists solely of gold coins so that the only difference between American and German money is the symbol appearing on the coins. This is a special example of the gold standard, called the *gold-coin standard*. Such a system has never really existed in pure form, perhaps the closest modern example being Egypt in the days of the British Empire, where British gold sovereigns formed the main medium of exchange.

A realistic historic description would be as follows. Money consists of both gold coins and paper notes (and perhaps also of demand deposits). The government mint will accept gold to be struck into coins and vice versa, as under a gold-coin standard. The central bank would also be prepared to redeem paper money for gold on demand. Thus all of the country's money would be valued in terms of gold, although gold need not form a large part of the actual circulating medium.

Indeed, gold coins might be dispensed with entirely. Ricardo advocated a *gold-bullion standard* in which gold would not be minted into coins so that money would consist only of paper notes (and deposits), which the central bank would exchange on demand for gold bars.

The central feature of the gold standard was the direct fixing of the *value* of a country's money in terms of gold. Thus the monies of any pair of countries on a gold standard were fixed in value relative to each other, regardless of whether they consisted of identical physical objects, as under a gold-coin standard. In the latter case a government had little monetary responsibility beyond the operation of a mint to strike coins as required. In the other forms of the gold standard the central bank must hold *reserves,* a stock of gold that can be used to redeem paper money. It was the willingness of the central bank to sell from its reserves in exchange for paper money or to add gold to its reserves by buying it with newly created paper money that maintained the value of the nation's money in terms of gold.

Gold-Exchange Standard. A country can tie the value of its money to gold not only directly, by standing ready to exchange its money for gold, but also indirectly, by standing ready to exchange its money for that of some other country that is on a gold standard. This is called a *gold-exchange standard.* The central bank of a country on such a standard would hold its reserves not in gold (although it might still own some), but in the money of some gold-standard country or else in bonds or bills denominated in that money. For example, in the years before the First World War, India held its reserves in the form of assets denominated in British sterling and maintained the value of the rupee in terms of the pound. Since Britain was on the gold standard, this served indirectly to maintain the value of the rupee in terms of gold.

Other Metallic Standards. Other metals might play the role of gold in the above discussion. Copper has been used for money, and silver long served as a medium of exchange along with, or instead of, gold. Thus we can think of various types of silver standard analogous to the versions of the gold standard. The *bimetallic standard* fixes the value of money in terms of both gold and silver and thus also fixes the relative price of the two precious metals.

Convertible Paper. A country might also tie the value of its money to that of another country that is not on the gold standard; the first country would then hold its international reserves in the form of assets denominated in the currency of the latter country. The monies of a group of countries tied together in such a way would be fixed in value relative to each other.

Inconvertible Paper (Flexible Exchange Rates). The above monetary standards all share one crucial property: the relative values of the monies of all countries on a standard are fixed. That is, they imply *fixed exchange rates* (an exchange rate, you will recall, is the relative price of one money in terms of another). It is also possible that central banks might just issue fiat money and *not* stand ready to redeem it at a fixed price for some commodity (such as gold) or some foreign money. In this case exchange rates would not be fixed but would be determined by market conditions, as are the prices of other assets and goods. International adjustment through the balance of payments, the topic of this chapter, would be replaced or supported by adjustment through exchange-rate variations. Such adjustment was the topic of the previous chapter.

The Automatic Adjustment Process under Various Standards

The discussion of the automatic adjustment process was conducted on the assumption of a gold-coin standard. It applies, however, to all the systems described in this section except for flexible exchange rates. The automatic adjustment process consists of three basic ingredients, of which the first two, the equilibrium allocation of world money and the payments imbalances generated by a misallocation, depend crucially upon fixed exchange rates. These are common to all the standards. Let us consider, therefore, the third ingredient: the Rules of the Game.

Suppose that the United States is experiencing a balance-of-payments deficit and Germany a surplus. Then the Germans are selling more goods and nonmonetary assets to the United States than they are buying and are, therefore, acquiring American money. Under a gold-coin standard the Germans acquire American gold coins. These can be circulated in Germany, or they can be melted down and struck into German coins by the German mint. The institutional arrangement inevitably implies that the American money supply decreases and the German increases by the amount of the payments imbalance.

Suppose, then, that one of the other standards (except for flexible exchange rates) holds and that the Germans acquire American notes rather than gold coin. The Germans require German money rather than American money. Therefore, they redeem their American notes with the American central bank for gold (gold standard) or for some other money (gold-exchange standard or convertible paper), which they then sell to the German central bank for marks. The American central bank sells international reserves and buys dollars in an amount equal to the payments deficit, and the German central bank acquires reserves and sells marks in a like amount. Thus the payments imbalance reduces the American money supply and increases the German, just as under a gold-coin standard. Indeed, it might even have a greater effect now, if the loss of reserves by the American central bank causes it to contract the note issue or if the monetary assets purchased by the American central bank served as the base for a private banking system.

Monetary Standards in Practice. Gold and silver served as the basis for most monies until well into the nineteenth century. During that century gold gradually displaced silver until, during the quarter century or so before the First World War, the major nations were joined in a gold standard. India and Austria-Hungary participated via gold-exchange standards. The war brought about the collapse of this system, but afterward there was an attempt to restore the gold standard. Because of wartime inflation, however, and because the United States had acquired many assets, including gold, during the war, people feared that there was a shortage of gold elsewhere. Thus when the gold standard was restored, Britain adopted the gold-bullion form (dispensing with the need for gold for coinage), and some other countries adopted a gold-exchange standard (dispensing with the need for gold reserves). The British return to the gold standard (at the prewar price of gold) in 1926 was criticized by Keynes (notably in a pamphlet entitled "The Economic Consequences of Mr. Churchill"—Winston Churchill was chancellor of the exchequer at the time) on the grounds that it would necessitate unemployment. At any rate the British economy stagnated. The Depression occasioned a widespread abandonment of the gold standard and cases of both convertible and inconvertible paper. After the Second World War a gold-exchange standard was established in which the United States assumed the responsibility of fixing the value of the dollar in terms of gold, and other countries undertook to fix their currencies in terms of dollars. During the 1960s the U.S. responsibility gradually eroded, and the system came more closely to resemble a paper (dollar) standard. In the 1970s the major industrial countries ceased to commit themselves to maintain the values of their currencies relative to any common standard; the system of fixed exchange rates ended. However, most LDCs continue to fix the values of their currencies in terms of some major currency or composite of currencies (so there is a group of countries on a dollar standard, and so on), and a varying group (the "snake") of European countries has undertaken to maintain the values of its currencies relative to each other. Also, the major industrial countries have continued to buy and sell reserves even though they no longer accept obligations to maintain fixed exchange rates.

4. *CASE STUDY:* THE GOLD STANDARD OF 1880–1914

Several features of the period of the gold standard are noteworthy. *First,* this was a time of relatively free trade and substantial international capital mobility, although some countries were quite protectionist and nationalism became increasingly prominent. *Second,* the major countries remained on the system without major difficulty—that is, the gold standard worked. *Third,* Britain played a central role. London was the major international financial center, and Britain was a large-scale lender of long-term and short-term capital. *Fourth,* because of London's role as a financial center, the Bank of England was able to influence substantially short-term capital flows by changes in interest rates and was thereby able to manage with relatively small gold reserves. Other countries maintained larger reserves and experienced swings in them. *Fifth,* the major countries experienced boom and bust together, and there appear to have been no large adjustments of relative prices. *Sixth,* there were large current-account deficits and surpluses financed by large-scale long-term capital movements, with Britain, France, and Germany the main lenders.

Economic historians have often noted that price movements apparently did not take place to bring about international adjustment. It is natural to try to explain this in terms of other channels of adjustment. We noted above that capital movements played a role. Adjustments through variations in incomes and employment and in the public's desire to hold money have also been offered as explanations. Further, the absence of sizable price movements does not imply that price adjustment was not relevant. If price elasticities are large, only small or incipient price changes are necessary to induce adjustment.

The simplest explanation is pure luck: perhaps things just happened to work out in those years so that adjustment was not necessary. A more sophisticated version of this explanation would note that the collection of countries participating in the gold standard was not determined at random: individual countries elected to adopt the standard when they viewed participation as feasible and advantageous. This self-selection process would imply that adjustment problems would be much more likely to arise between countries on the standard and those off it rather than among the countries adhering to the gold standard.

Although the gold standard worked, the countries on it experienced much boom and bust together. Also the disastrous attempt to restore the standard after the First World War gave it a bad name for many years. But some of President Reagan's advisers wanted to bring it back, and a commission was appointed to study the issue as part of an investigation into the role of gold.

5. THE BALANCE OF PAYMENTS AND THE DOMESTIC BANKING SYSTEM

A hypothetical example profitably illustrates the mechanics of payments imbalances with actual modern banking systems. Suppose that the French and German central banks hold international reserves in the form of U.S. dollars ($). The French central bank will buy or sell reserves for francs (Fr) at the rate of Fr 4 per dollar. The German central bank likewise maintains the value of the deutsche mark (DM) at two per dollar. Thus Fr 2 will always exchange for DM 1. Table 15.1 shows hypothetical balance sheets for all parties. A balance sheet lists all the assets and liabilities of a party at a particular time. Since net worth is defined as the excess of assets over liabilities, the total value of all assets must always equal the total value of all liabilities plus net worth.

In this example, the assets of the French public consist of Fr 2,500 in demand deposits in French commercial banks plus Fr 1,000 of other assets; the sole liabilities of the public are Fr 2,000 in loans borrowed from the commercial banks. Thus the net worth of the French public is Fr 1,500, the excess of total assets over liabilities.

The demand deposits of the public constitute the liabilities of the commercial banks since a deposit is an obligation to pay the depositor. Suppose that the commercial banks are required to keep reserves at the central bank equal to one-fifth of total deposits, and suppose that the commercial banks hold only this minimum requirement. Then the assets of the commercial banks consist of the required reserves (Fr 500) plus the loans they have made

TABLE 15.1 Hypothetical Initial Situation

(a) The French public

Assets	Liabilities, net worth
Demand deposits: Fr 2,500	Loans: Fr 2,000
Other assets: Fr 1,000	Net worth: Fr 1,500

(b) French commercial banks

Assets	Liabilities
Reserves: Fr 500	Demand deposits: Fr 2,500
Loans: Fr 2,000	

(c) The French central bank

Assets	Liabilities
Government bonds: Fr 300	Commercial bank reserves: Fr 500
International reserves: Fr 200 [$50]	

(d) The German public

Assets	Liabilities, net worth
Demand deposits: DM 1,500	Loans: DM 1,200
Other assets: DM 500	Net worth: DM 800

(e) German commercial banks

Assets	Liabilities
Reserves: DM 300	Demand deposits: DM 1,500
Loans: DM 1,200	

(f) The German central bank

Assets	Liabilities
Government bonds: DM 200	Commercial bank reserves: DM 300
International reserves: DM 100 [$50]	

to the public. The liabilities of the French central bank are the Fr 500 of reserves deposited there by the commercial banks. Assets consist of French government bonds owned by the central bank plus its stock of international reserves. Suppose that the latter consists of $50, valued, therefore, at Fr 200.

Panels (d) , (e), and (f) of Table 15.1 show the analogous information for Germany. The example supposes that German commercial banks are also required to hold reserves equal to one-fifth of total deposits and that the German central bank owns $50 of international reserves.

Now suppose that France runs a balance-of-payments deficit of Fr 100 (= DM 50) with Germany by buying that value of goods more from Germany than it sells. Table 15.2 shows all the changes in balance sheets resulting from the deficit. The French pay for the extra Fr 100 worth of goods by means of a check drawn on their account with a French commercial bank. Thus the immediate impact of the deficit, labeled (1), is that the French public's demand deposits decline by Fr 100, and this also constitutes a decline in net worth. The German public receives the check, so its net worth increases by DM 50 (= Fr 100) and its assets are augmented by a demand deposit of Fr 100. The German public, however, wants its money in the form of marks, not francs; so in the second stage, denoted (2), the German public sells to the French central bank (either directly or through intermediaries) the Fr 100 check in exchange for $25 of international reserves. The German public then sells the $25 to the German central bank for DM 50, which it deposits in its accounts with the German commercial banks, whose reserves thereby increase by DM 50. When the French central bank clears the Fr 100 check with the French commercial bank on which it is drawn, the latter must pay from its reserves, which, therefore, fall by Fr 100. The final stage, labeled (3) in the table, occurs when the commercial banks adjust to their new reserve positions. The French commercial banks have lost Fr 100 of reserves; with a reserve requirement of one-fifth, this requires a Fr 500 contraction of deposits. Deposits have in fact fallen by only Fr 100, so the banks must call in loans and allow deposits to fall by another Fr 400. The German commercial banks are in just the opposite position.

The final situation is shown in Table 15.3. Note, first, that the payment imbalance of Fr 100 (= DM 50 = $25) has resulted in a flow of $25 of international reserves from the French central bank to the German central bank and a corresponding decline in French net worth and rise in German net worth. This is the analog to the flow of gold coins discussed earlier in this chapter. The reserve flow does not itself constitute changes in money supplies as it does under the simple gold-coin standard. But it does act directly to reduce commercial bank reserves in the deficit country and increase them in the surplus country. This, in turn, causes a contraction of the money supply in the former and an expansion in the latter to a degree determined by reserve requirements. With a requirement of one-fifth, the French money supply has contracted by Fr 500, and the German has expanded by DM 250.

TABLE 15.2 Mechanics of a Fr 100 French Payments Deficit (DM 50 German Payments Surplus)

(a) The French public

Assets	Liabilities, net worth
Demand deposits: (1) −Fr 100 (3) −Fr 400	Loans: (3) −Fr 400
	Net worth: (1) −Fr 100

(b) French commercial banks

Assets	Liabilities
Reserves: (2) −Fr 100	Demand deposits: (2) −Fr 100 (3) −Fr 400
Loans: (3) −Fr 400	

(c) The French central bank

Assets	Liabilities
International reserves: (2) −Fr 100	Commercial bank reserves: (2) −Fr 100

(d) The German public

Assets	Liabilities, net worth
Demand deposits: (1) +Fr 100 (2) −Fr 100 (2) +DM 50 (3) +DM 200	Loans: (3) +DM 200
	Net worth: (1) +DM 50

(e) German commercial banks

Assets	Liabilities
Reserves: (2) +DM 50	Demand deposits: (2) +DM 50 (3) +DM 200
Loans: (3) +DM 200	

(f) The German central bank

Assets	Liabilities
International reserves: (2) +DM 50	Commercial bank reserves: (2) +DM 50

TABLE 15.3 Situation after the Fr 100 Payments Imbalance

(a) The French public

Assets	Liabilities, net worth
Demand deposits: Fr 2,000	Loans: Fr 1,600
Other assets: Fr 1,000	Net worth: Fr 1,400

(b) French commercial banks

Assets	Liabilities
Reserves: Fr 400	Demand deposits: Fr 2,000
Loans: Fr 1,600	

(c) The French central bank

Assets	Liabilities
Government bonds: Fr 300	Commercial bank reserves: Fr 400
International reserves: Fr 100 [$25]	

(d) The German public

Assets	Liabilities, net worth
Demand deposits: DM 1,750	Loans: DM 1,400
Other assets: DM 500	Net worth: DM 850

(e) German commercial banks

Assets	Liabilities
Reserves: DM 350	Demand deposits: DM 1,750
Loans: DM 1,400	

(f) The German central bank

Assets	Liabilities
Government bonds: DM 200	Commercial bank reserves: DM 350
International reserves: DM 150 [$75]	

Problems

15.10 Work through the example in the text if the French reserve requirement is one-tenth rather than one-fifth (keep the German requirement equal to one-fifth).

15.11 Suppose that in Italy the money supply is 300,000 lire while the Spanish money supply equals 60,000 pesetas. In each country money is in the form of paper notes, but the central bank will exchange its money on demand for gold. In Spain the central bank will buy or sell pesetas for 2 ounces of gold each, and the Italian central bank will exchange a half ounce of gold for each lira. Each central bank has 50,000 ounces of gold in its international reserves. Suppose that Italy experiences a balance-of-payments deficit of 40,000 lire, and Spain accordingly has a surplus of 10,000 pesetas. Describe what happens, and calculate the money supplies and international reserve stocks in the two countries after the payments imbalance takes place.

15.12 In Problem **15.11,** suppose that Italian law or custom guarantees that at all times the size of the Italian money supply equals exactly 6 lire for each ounce of gold contained in the international reserves of the Italian central bank. How does your answer to Problem **15.11** change?

15.13 Suppose, in Problems **15.11** and **15.12,** that each central bank initially has a stock of reserves equal to $50,000, that the Italian central bank will exchange 2 lire for $1, and that the Spanish central bank will exchange 1 peseta for $2. How do your answers change?

6. THE RULES OF THE GAME AND MONETARY POLICY

The third ingredient of the automatic adjustment process, the Rules of the Game, is that payments deficits should reduce a nation's money supply and that surpluses should increase it. This is inevitable under a gold-coin standard but not with more realistic monetary systems.

Sterilization

Suppose that France is running a balance-of-payments deficit, with the French central bank selling reserves for (paper) francs and the German central bank correspondingly selling marks for reserves. Then the French money supply is falling, and the German supply is rising. If this is the whole story (and under the gold-coin standard it must be, unless the world gold stock changes), then the payments imbalance is in fact redistributing world money as required for the automatic adjustment process. But this need not be the whole story. For example, the French central bank could further reduce the French money supply by selling bonds for francs, thereby taking the latter out of circulation. In this case the policy *reinforces* the monetary contraction produced by the payments deficit: the Rules of the Game are being followed. But, on the other hand, the French central bank might put new francs into circulation (by buying bonds from the public with newly printed francs). This policy tends to *sterilize* the monetary contraction produced by the payments deficit: the Rules of the Game are being violated. If the French central bank creates money at a rate equal to the payments deficit, the latter is completely sterilized by the former and the French money supply remains constant. Analogously, the German central bank could withdraw marks from circulation (by selling bonds to the public) so as to prevent the German money supply from rising. In such a case the payments imbalance is redistributing international *reserves* from France to Germany, but it is not redistributing *money;* the automatic adjustment process is being aborted.

KEY CONCEPT

A central bank *sterilizes* a payments imbalance (violates the Rules of the Game) if it wholly or partially prevents that imbalance from changing the size of the domestic money supply.

Table 15.4 shows the changes in the balance sheet of the French central bank if it sterilizes the Fr 100 deposit shown in Tables 15.2 and 15.3. The entries in *italics* are the same as in Table 15.2 and show the direct effect of the payments deficit: a reduction in international reserves and in the reserves of the commercial banks, the latter leading to a decrease of the money supply. The other two entries show the sterilization operation: an increase in the holdings of government bonds and in commercial bank reserves. (Sterilization is just like any other open-market operation: the central bank buys bonds from the public with a check drawn on itself; the public deposits the check in a commercial bank, which in turn adds the check to its reserves with the central bank.) On balance, the liabilities of the central bank do not change; therefore, as desired, the money supply is not affected. The only effect of the sterilized deficit is to alter the composition of central-bank assets: government bond holdings increase, and international reserves fall by equal amounts.

In Figure 15.4 point H represents an international monetary misallocation at which France is running a payments deficit and the rest of the world is running a surplus. France is depicted as small relative to the rest of the world, realistic for a single country. If both central banks refrain from interfering with the monetary consequences of the payments imbalances, the world gradually moves from H to equilibrium at E. Central-bank reinforcement of these

TABLE 15.4 Attempted Sterilization of a Fr 100 Deficit

Assets	Liabilities
Government bonds: +Fr 100 International reserves: *−Fr 100*	Commercial bank reserves: *− Fr 100;* +Fr 100

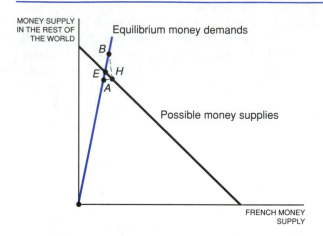

FIGURE 15.4 Sterilization   If countries sterilize their payments imbalances, the latter have no effect on money supplies. Thus a world in disequilibrium at *H* will not be moving toward equilibrium at *E*.

payments consequences speeds up the movement, and partial sterilization slows it down. If both central banks completely sterilize, the world stays put at *H* and the payments imbalances continue unchecked.

Why might a central bank wish to do this? To prevent the internal economic adjustments associated with the correction of the payments imbalance. The reduction of the French payments deficit might well involve reduction in French aggregate demand and perhaps an increase in unemployment; correction of the foreign surplus requires an increase in aggregate demand abroad. A country may prefer to leave payments imbalances uncorrected rather than experience such internal adjustments. For example, the disequilibrium in Figure 15.4 might be due to a shift in tastes away from French goods, which the authorities expect to be reversed in the future. Then they might want to sit out the deficit, rather than adjusting from *H* to *E* and then back again when tastes change. Also, there is the chance that through sterilization a country might force the burden of adjustment onto the rest of the world. Suppose, for example, that France completely sterilizes its deficit but that the rest of the world does not sterilize its surplus, at least not completely. Then the French money supply remains constant, and the foreign money supply gradually increases. In Figure 15.4 the world moves from *H* to *B,* where equilibrium is restored (this is apt to take quite a while since the cumulative French deficit must increase the money supply in the entire rest of the world in proportion to the original excess French money supply). If, on the other hand, the rest of the world sterilizes its surplus but France does not sterilize its deficit, the world moves from *H* to equilibrium at *A*.

Limits to Sterilization

Sterilization is impossible in a pure gold-coin standard. But even in more realistic monetary systems there are two significant factors which limit, in varying degrees, the ability of a central bank to sterilize payments imbalances.

1. *Central-Bank Assets.* Suppose France is running a payments deficit that it completely sterilizes. Then the French central bank is simultaneously selling international reserves for dollars and selling dollars for domestic bonds. Thus on balance the central bank is exchanging international reserves for domestic bonds. This is clear in Table 15.4. Obviously, this process can continue only as long as the central bank possesses international reserves to sell. If nothing is done to correct the payments deficit, sooner or later the central bank will begin to run out of reserves. Then unless the central bank can somehow borrow additional reserves from abroad, the French must choose between two alternatives. They can cease sterilization (that is, stop trying to control their own money supply) and allow the automatic adjustment process to correct the deficit, or they can cease maintaining the value of the franc and stop selling international reserves (that is, abandon fixed exchange rates). If the French completely run out of reserves, only the second alternative is available. A stock of reserves is required to allow the automatic adjustment process to work because the payments deficit will be corrected only gradually; sterilization requires even larger reserves, whereas a policy of reinforcing the monetary consequences of payments imbalances reduces the need for reserves.

2. *International Capital Movements.* Suppose again that the French have a payments deficit that the central bank attempts to sterilize. Then the French central bank is buying domestic bonds from the public in exchange for francs at the same rate that the public is selling francs to the rest of the world through the payments deficit. Then on balance the French public is retaining a constant money supply but losing bonds at a rate equal to the payments deficit—that is, the public's holdings of bonds relative to money is falling. To redress the balance, the public will buy bonds from the rest of the world in exchange for money. This increases the balance-of-payments deficit above what it would have been otherwise, and this increase *offsets* the sterilization operation. The degree of offset depends upon the degree of international capital mobility. If capital is completely immobile, the French public buys no foreign bonds, there is no offset, and the only constraint on the central bank is the size of its stock of international reserves, as discussed above.

If, at the other extreme, capital is perfectly mobile internationally, the French public will simply buy from abroad bonds to replace those sold to the central bank; the bank's attempt to sterilize will be offset by an equal capital-account deficit. The only effect of such a sterilization operation will be to increase the size of the payments deficit and thus the rate at which the bank's stock of international reserves is depleted; the automatic adjustment process will not be affected at all.

If capital mobility is of an intermediate degree, an attempt at sterilization will be partially offset: a portion of the sterilization effort will be nullified by a consequent capital-account deficit, and the remaining portion will add to the French money supply. The degree of offset depends upon the degree of capital mobility. With imperfect capital mobility (and so partial offset), the authorities can still hold the money supply constant and abort the automatic adjustment process. But in order to do so they must conduct sterilization operations on a larger scale than what the payments imbalance would otherwise be because they must also sterilize the monetary consequences of the capital-account deficit induced by the sterilization operation itself. Thus the balance-of-payments deficit and the consequent rate of depletion of international reserves will be increased by sterilization to an extent dependent upon the degree of capital mobility.

Table 15.5 shows the balance-sheet entries for the French central bank if capital flows offset its attempt to sterilize the Fr 100 deficit in our earlier illustration. Panels (a) and (b) show the same four entries as does Table 15.4 for the direct effects of the payments deficit and for the sterilization operation. The additional entries shown in **boldface** result from offsetting capital flows. If capital mobility is perfect, as in panel (a), the public purchases from abroad all the Fr 100 of bonds that have been sold to the central bank, resulting in another Fr 100 deficit. The net effect on commercial bank reserves, and thus on the French money supply, is the same as if no sterilization had been attempted. The only effect has been to double the size of the payments deficit and of the resulting loss of international reserves.

If, on the other hand, there is no capital mobility—that is, if domestic residents are unwilling or unable to sell bonds to foreigners or to buy bonds from them—there will be no offset to sterilization. Table 15.4 still applies.

Panel (b) of Table 15.5 shows the offset in an intermediate case, where international capital mobility exists but is not perfect. This illustration assumes that French citizens purchase enough foreign bonds to replace three-fourths of the domestic bonds sold to the central bank. In this case the sterilization operation succeeds in limiting the decline in commercial bank reserves to Fr 75 rather than Fr 100 but at the cost of a balance-of-payments deficit and international reserve loss of Fr 175 rather than Fr 100. Panel (c) makes the same assumption about international capital mobility and shows what happens if the central bank perseveres and conducts open-market operations on a scale sufficient to prevent the money supply from falling. This requires a payments deficit and international reserve loss fully four times as great as that which would occur with no attempt at sterilization.

In general, then, the ability of a country to sterilize the monetary effects of a payments imbalance depends both upon the size of its stock of international reserves and other assets and upon the degree of international capital mobility. In addition, some central banks simply do not have the ability to make extensive sterilization attempts. For example, the facilities for large-scale open-market operations are often lacking.

TABLE 15.5   Sterilization and Offsetting Capital Flows

(a) Perfect capital mobility

Assets	Liabilities
Government bonds: +Fr 100 International reserves: −Fr 100 **−Fr 100**	Commercial bank reserves: −Fr 100 +Fr 100 **−Fr 100**

(b) Imperfect capital mobility and partial sterilization

Assets	Liabilities
Government bonds: +Fr 100 International reserves: −Fr 100 **−Fr 75**	Commercial bank reserves: −Fr 100 +Fr 100 **−Fr 75**

(c) Imperfect capital mobility and complete sterilization

Assets	Liabilities
Government bonds: +Fr 400 International reserves: −Fr 100 **−Fr 300**	Commercial bank reserves: −Fr 100 +Fr 400 **−Fr 300**

Sterilization in Practice

Since the Second World War, governments and central banks have accepted a responsibility for maintaining desirable internal aggregate economic conditions. Before the First World War, by contrast, central banks interpreted their basic responsibility as maintaining the external value of the national currency. Thus one would expect sterilization to be more prominent in the more recent period.

Studies by Arthur Bloomfield and by Ragnar Nurkse have nevertheless revealed that in the period before the First World War—the heyday of the gold standard—and also in the interwar period, central bank transactions in domestic assets violated the Rules of the Game more often than not. Since the Second World War, sterilization has been common. A number of important industrial countries have routinely sterilized the monetary effects of all payments imbalances so as to allow the discretionary component of monetary policy to be aimed unambiguously at internal objectives.

Throughout the last quarter century or so the principal industrial economies have become more integrated, and, as an inevitable consequence, the degree of capital mobility between them has increased. One would expect, therefore, that sterilization has steadily become more difficult. Recent decades have seen numerous instances where central banks have abandoned fixed exchange rates to maintain control over their money supplies.

Does Sterilized Intervention Work?

Suppose that the French and German central banks are conducting intervention operations, the French buying francs and the German selling marks. (This was in fact being done on a massive scale in the autumn of 1993.) The purpose of this intervention is to influence the exchange rate—to prevent the price of the mark in terms of francs from rising or, perhaps, to induce it to fall. If the Rules of the Game are being followed—that is, if the intervention is not being sterilized—the French money supply will be contracting and the German money supply will be expanding. This will presumably contribute toward the objective.

But if the intervention is being sterilized—that is, if the French central bank is also buying franc bonds with francs, and the German central bank is selling mark bonds for marks—the two money supplies will not be changing at all. Instead, the public's holding of franc bonds will be falling and its holding of mark bonds expanding. This is the basic difference between unsterilized intervention and sterilized intervention: whether payments deficits alter money supplies or whether they alter stocks of national bonds.

KEY CONCEPT

Unsterilized intervention increases the money supply of a surplus country and reduces the money supply of a deficit country. *Sterilized* intervention increases the supply of bonds denominated in the currency of a surplus country and reduces the supply denominated in the currency of a deficit country.

Is sterilized intervention effective in influencing exchange rates? The question is important because, as we have seen, most intervention is in fact sterilized: countries are simply not willing to surrender the ability to control their money supplies. But the evidence is not encouraging. Most studies by economists indicate that sterilized intervention actually has little effect on exchange rates.

Problems

15.14 In Problem **15.11,** suppose that the Italian central bank sterilizes completely the Italian deficit and that there is no offset. How do your answers to that problem change? What are the changes in the bond holdings of the Italian public? The Italian central bank? How do your answers change if the Spanish authorities also fully sterilize the Spanish surplus?

15.15 Suppose, in Problem **15.14,** that the Italian authorities completely sterilize and the Spanish do not sterilize at all. Suppose also that one-half of any Italian sterilization is offset by a purchase of foreign bonds: whenever the Italian central bank buys 2 lire worth of bonds from the Italian public, the public then buys 1 lira's worth of bonds from abroad. How do your answers to Problem **15.14** change? How do they change if, instead, three-fourths of any sterilization is offset?

15.16 Sterilization is simply monetary control motivated by the balance-of-payments; thus any method of monetary control can be used for sterilization. The text discussed open-market operations; alternative methods are changes in reserve requirements and in discount rates, which you studied in your introductory economics course. How would the latter two be used to sterilize the effects of a deficit? Rework the example of Tables 15.4 and 15.5 if the French authorities try to sterilize by changing reserve requirements rather than by open-market operations.

7. *CASE STUDY:* GERMANY IN THE 1960s AND 1990s

The 1960s

The problems that the automatic adjustment process poses for national monetary policy are well illustrated by the experience of Germany in the 1960s. Richard Herring and Richard Marston of the University of Pennsylvania studied international financial markets in the period and estimated an empirical model of the monetary sector of the German economy. They used their estimated model to simulate the effects of various hypothetical policy measures and events. Table 15.6 shows the simulated effects of a hypothetical attempt by German authorities, in the first quarter of 1964, to increase the German money supply by purchasing DM 250 million worth of bonds from the public (there are other ways of influencing the money supply, but for convenience we describe them all as purchases and sales of bonds).

As discussed in the previous section, this attempt would induce the public to purchase bonds from abroad and so generate a capital-account deficit. This would require the central bank to purchase marks and sell international reserves, thereby offsetting the initial attempt to increase the money supply as well as depleting the central bank's stock of international reserves. The bank could attempt to sterilize this offsetting effect of the deficit by purchasing more bonds from the public. This would further increase the offsetting capital-account deficit and require further sterilization, and so on. The table shows the total simulated outcome. The first row of the table shows the effects that are simulated to occur in the quarter in which the initial purchase is made; the second row includes two years of subsequent repercussions. The third column shows that the total purchase of bonds (the initial DM 250 million plus all the sterilization operations) is DM 803 million in the initial quarter. The first col-

TABLE 15.6 **Simulated Effects of a Hypothetical Purchase of DM 250 Million Worth of Bonds from the Public by the German Authorities in the First Quarter of 1964** *(millions of DM)*

	(1) Total reduction of international reserves	*(2) Sterilization*	*(3) Total purchase of bonds from public [(2) + 250]*	*(4) net effect [(3) − (1)]*
Current quarter	603	553	803	200
After two years	784	720	970	186

SOURCE: R. Herring and R. Marston, *National Monetary Policies and International Financial Markets* (Amersterdam: North Holland, 1977).

umn shows that DM 603 million of this—fully 75 percent—would have been offset by an induced capital-account deficit, thereby reducing international reserves by that amount. The authorities would then typically have sterilized the effects on the money supply of this sale of international reserves to the extent of DM 553—or 92 percent. The remaining DM 50 million would be unsterilized so that the net effect on the public—the total purchase of bonds from the public minus the total sale of international reserves to the public—was DM 200 million, or 80 percent of the original DM 250 million.

This is a picture of determined sterilization overcoming a high degree of international capital mobility to maintain substantial control of the money supply. By sterilizing 92 percent of offsetting capital flows, 80 percent of the initial operation is made to stick in the current quarter. But to do this, the central bank is forced to accept a loss of international reserves more than three times the size of the net effect on the public.

When two years of repercussions are added in, the effects are even more pronounced. The fraction of bond sales to the public that are offset by international capital movements rises from 75 percent to 81 percent. With the authorities still typically sterilizing 92 percent of these offsetting movements, the net effect on the public falls to DM 186 million, or 74 percent of the initial operation. And the total loss of international reserves (DM 784 million) is now more than four times the size of the net effect on the public.

The 1990s

In the early 1990s a newly reunified Germany was spending huge sums in the former East Germany. To limit the inflationary consequences of this public expenditure, the Bundesbank restrained monetary growth and allowed German interest rates to rise. The rest of Europe was more concerned about recession. European currencies were linked in the EMS's pegged exchange rates. In the autumn of 1992 massive payments imbalances developed, with Germany running a huge surplus. The crisis was defused only when the British pound and Italian lira were allowed to float. These two countries quickly adopted less restrictive monetary policies.

In the autumn of 1993 another crisis erupted, centering on the franc-mark exchange rate. Again, massive intervention took place, with Germany in surplus and France in deficit. This time, the crisis ended only when the intervention bands around the EMS pegs were widened dramatically—the bands had been ±2.25 percent for most currencies and were widened to ±15 percent for most currencies. This amounted in effect to a constrained float.

The lessons seem to be twofold. (1) Sterilized intervention is not that effective in controlling exchange rates. (2) When it comes to the crunch, the ability to control the money supply is more important to countries than adhering to an exchange-rate peg.

8. RESERVE CURRENCIES

The key institutional feature behind the automatic adjustment process is fixed exchange rates, which ensure that the monies of different countries are substitutes for each other. As we saw in section 3, many possible monetary arrangements incorporate this feature. In several of these arrangements, such as a gold-exchange standard or convertible paper, some countries might hold their international reserves in whole or in part in assets denominated in the currency of some other country. In this case the latter country is in a unique position. This can be seen by comparing two examples.

Suppose that international reserves consist of gold and of dollars. In the first example, France is running a balance-of-payments deficit with Germany, and the two countries have neither deficit nor surplus with the rest of the world. France must be losing international reserves—gold and/or dollars—in an amount equal to its deficit, and Germany must be acquiring them in an amount equal to its surplus. If neither country sterilizes, the French money supply is falling and the German money supply is rising.

Now suppose that the United States is running a deficit and Germany (or the rest of the world) a surplus. Since the dollar is the American currency, U.S. international reserves consist only of gold. The German central bank is selling marks and acquiring dollars. If the Germans simply add the dollars to their reserves, German international reserves have increased by the amount of the German payments surplus, just as in the first example, but the American reserves have not fallen at all. Instead, the American authorities have increased their liabilities to the German authorities (because dollars are a liability of the U.S. central bank). Only if the German central bank sells some or all of the dollars it has bought to the American authorities for gold or if the Americans sell gold directly to the public will the U.S. stock of international reserves be depleted by the deficit. Similarly, an American balance-of-payments surplus would not increase the U.S. stock of international reserves to the extent that the rest of the world financed its deficit by selling dollar reserves to the public. The conclusion is that a country with a reserve currency need not be restrained by the size of its international reserves.

All this is illustrated by Table 15.7. The top entry shows the cumulative U.S. balance-of-payments deficit for the fifteen years 1963–1977. The United States was in deficit during most of this time, and the cumulative total was large. But only a small part of this deficit was financed by a sale of U.S. reserve assets; most of it took the form of increased U.S. liabilities to foreign authorities— that is, of increased holdings of dollar reserves by foreign officials.

The bottom three entries of Table 15.7 illustrate a second implication of a reserve currency. In our example, when the German central bank accumulated reserves by adding to its stock of dollars, it also increased the world total of reserves: German reserves rose, but U.S. reserves did not fall. That is, the deficits or surpluses of a country with a reserve currency change the total supply of reserves in the world. Most of the large increase in world reserves that occurred between 1963 and 1977 was accounted for by increases in foreign-exchange reserves (reserves in the form of reserve currencies—the dollar and a few others).

There is a third way in which countries with a reserve currency may differ from others. In the above example, suppose that Germany does add the dollars acquired from its payments deficit to its reserves. It would be foolish for the Germans to hold these dollars in the form of money, which earns no interest. Instead, they will hold the dollars in the form of dollar-denominated interest-bearing assets such as treasury bills or bonds. Thus, when the German authorities purchase dollars for marks as a result of their payments surplus, they then sell the dollars for dollar-denominated assets: the U.S. deficit is sterilized.

TABLE 15.7 **Cumulative Totals of U.S. Deficits and World Reserves,**
1963–1977 *(billions of dollars)*

U.S. balance-of-payments deficit	118	
Sale of U.S. reserve assets		6
Increased U.S. liabilities to		
foreign official institutions		112
Increase in world reserves	256	
Increase in foreign-exchange reserves		224
Increase in other reserve assets		32

SOURCE: International Monetary Fund, *International Financial Statistics.*

The combined effect of the two German operations is to sell marks to the public in exchange for dollar-denominated assets so that the public's holdings of dollars do not change. The U.S. payments deficit is automatically sterilized by the German central bank without the need for any U.S. action.

In sum, a country with a reserve currency differs from other countries in three ways *if* the other countries respond to surpluses or deficits by adding to or subtracting from their official holdings of the reserve currency. To the extent that the latter takes place, payments imbalances of the reserve-currency country (1) do not change that country's stock of international reserves; (2) do change the total world stock of international reserves; (3) are automatically sterilized.

The U.S. dollar is now the most important reserve currency, and these three features have applied to American payments imbalances. Several other currencies have a limited reserve role, and the three features have a limited relevance to them. The British pound, formerly an important reserve currency, now has but little significance; the French franc is a reserve currency for some former French colonies; and several other currencies have gained a reserve role in recent years.

Problems

15.17 In the text we showed that imbalances of a reserve-currency country could be automatically sterilized. But sterilization will be offset, to some degree, if capital is internationally mobile. Suppose that foreign central banks hold reserves only in the form of U.S. dollars. What does this imply about a U.S. balance-of-payments deficit if there is partial mobility of capital between the United States and the rest of the world? If capital is perfectly mobile? How do your answers change if foreign central banks always hold half of their international reserves in the form of dollars and half in the form of gold?

15.18 In Figure 15.4, suppose that the U.S. supplies a reserve currency for the rest of the world. Show what happens if the Americans increase their money supply and the rest of the world sterilizes its own imbalances. If the rest of the world does not sterilize. If the rest of the world tries to increase its money supply.

---

9. SUMMARY

1. The automatic adjustment process of the balance-of-payments is the heart of the classical international monetary contribution.

2. The process has three central ingredients: (1) monetary theory determines the equilibrium allocation of the world's money among countries; (2) nonequilibrium allocations cause payments imbalances; (3) the Rules of the Game assure that payments imbalances redistribute money to attain the equilibrium allocation.

3. The two basic implications of the process are (1) payments imbalances are temporary; (2) individual countries cannot control their own money supplies.

4. The key requirement for the automatic adjustment process is fixed exchange rates. The process is relevant to any monetary system once this requirement is met.

5. Those who believe that the automatic adjustment process takes a long time to work are more concerned with what happens as the process occurs and give less emphasis to the self-correcting nature of payments imbalances or the ultimate lack of national monetary control.

6. Countries sometimes attempt to retain control over domestic monetary policy by sterilizing payments imbalances. Their ability to do so is limited by their holdings of international reserves and by the degree of international capital mobility.

7. If sterilization becomes too difficult, countries must choose between controlling exchange rates or controlling money supplies.

8. A country with a reserve currency differs from other countries in three ways if other countries change their holding of the reserve currency in response to surpluses and deficits. Payments imbalances of the reserve-currency country (1) do not change that country's stock of international reserves; (2) do change the total world stock of international reserves; (3) are automatically sterilized.

SUGGESTED READING

Bloomfield, A. *Monetary Policy under the International Gold Standard.* New York: Federal Reserve Bank of New York, 1959.

Dornbusch, R. *Open Economy Macroeconomics.* New York: Basic Books, 1980. See Chapters 7 and 10.

Emminger, O. "The D-Mark in Conflict between Internal and External Equilibrium." *Princeton Essays in International Finance* 122 (1977). An account of German experience by the former head of the central bank.

Frenkel, J., and H. G. Johnson, eds. *The Monetary Approach to the Balance of Payments.* Toronto: Toronto University Press, 1976. A collection of basic papers.

Herring, R., and R. Marston. *National Monetary Policies and International Financial Markets.* Amsterdam: North Holland, 1977.

Hume, D. "Of the Balance of Trade." In *Essays, Moral, Political and Literary.* London: Longmans Green, 1898. The classic reference.

International Monetary Fund. *The Monetary Approach to the Balance of Payments.* Washington: IMF, 1977. A collection of papers by IMF staff members.

Nurkse, R. *International Currency Experience.* Geneva: League of Nations, 1944.

Samuelson, P. "A Corrected Version of Hume's Equilibrating Mechanisms for International Trade." In *Flexible Exchange Rates and the Balance of Payments.* Edited by J. S. Chipman and C. P. Kindleberger. Amsterdam: North Holland, 1980. A recent statement of the classical process.

Viner, J. *Studies in the Theory of International Trade.* New York: Harper & Brothers, 1937. Excellent discussion of the development of classical thought.

Weber, W. E. "Do Sterilized Interventions Affect Exchange Rates?" *Federal Reserve Bank of Minneapolis Quarterly Review* (1986): 14–23. Nope.

Yaeger, L. *International Monetary Relations: Theory, History, and Policy.* 2d ed. New York: Harper & Row, 1976. Discusses the history of different international monetary systems.

CHAPTER 16

The International Monetary System

> The doctor found, when she was dead,
> Her last disorder mortal.
>
> —OLIVER GOLDSMITH

We saw in Chapter 14 that the present international monetary system—if system is the word—is a confusing arrangement with prominent use of managed floating and adjustable pegs. The present chapter discusses how this state of affairs came about and the policy issues that it raises. We first describe the development of the international monetary system since the Second World War. In addition to explaining how we got where we are, this discussion will expose the basic problems that need to be faced to fashion a workable system. We then will examine current proposals for international monetary reform.

1. THE BRETTON WOODS SYSTEM

As the Second World War drew to a close, the Allied powers set about planning a new international order that culminated in the United Nations. The postwar economic system was not ignored in this process. Negotiations over a new international monetary system were centered largely between the United States and Britain, with the former the relatively more influential participant. Final agreement on the new system was reached in 1944 at Bretton Woods, New Hampshire, in a conference of the Allied nations. The resulting international monetary arrangement is accordingly often called the Bretton Woods system.

Planning for the new system focused on ways to deal with the policy dilemmas described in the preceding section. The planners were concerned, in particular, with how to reconcile internal and external balance and with how to limit international policy conflict.

The Bretton Woods Conference

In July 1944 over 300 representatives of 44 Allied nations met for three weeks at the hamlet of Bretton Woods, New Hampshire, to reach final agreement on details of the postwar international monetary system. The conference was held at the Mt. Washington Hotel, a huge, old-style White Mountains resort that, like the system whose birth it witnessed, fell upon bad times in the 1970s. The British delegation was headed by Keynes and the American by Treasury Secretary Morgenthau and his deputy, Harry Dexter White, later a victim of the McCarthy period. Preceding the conference, there had been several years of preparations and negotiations, notably between the United States and Britain, whose respective positions had been embodied in plans drafted by White and Keynes. The American position reflected the interests of a creditor nation and the British those of a debtor nation, natural in view of the roles the countries would play after the war. The conference adopted an agreement much closer to the White Plan than to the Keynes Plan, but developments in later years were to move in the direction of the latter (just as the United States developed a persistent deficit position).

The Bretton Woods System in Outline

Two international economic institutions were founded. The International Bank for Reconstruction and Development (IBRD—better known as the World Bank) provides loans for the purposes indicated in its name. The International Monetary Fund (IMF) was designed as the centerpiece of the new international monetary system and will figure prominently in this chapter. Postwar planners subsequently designed a third institution, the International Trade Organization, to deal with commercial policy, but the ITO never came into being.

Many of the people who helped design the new system had in mind two earlier experiences—or at least caricatures of these experiences. One was the international gold standard in the generation preceding the First World War. This was viewed as a successful international monetary system, although national governments had not pursued economic policies for domestic macro-economic goals, as they were expected vigorously to do in the postwar world. The second experience was that of the 1930s, when national policies were by contrast formulated with domestic goals paramount—but at the expense of the international economy. The experience was perceived to have been characterized by extensive trade and payments restrictions, competitive exchange depreciations, and unstable floating exchange rates. The problem in designing a new system was to capture the international harmony and stable exchange rates associated with the gold standard while allowing individual countries the freedom to pursue their own macroeconomic policies. This basic problem remains very much with us today.

The planners tried to solve this problem with an exchange-rate compromise between floating and fixed rates: an *adjustable peg* system. Countries would normally intervene to keep their exchange rates within a narrow band of their pegs; at the same time, domestic policies would presumably be directed toward maintaining desirable macroeconomic conditions. Should a country find that its balance of payments was in "fundamental disequilibrium"—a term never defined—it would be able to adjust its peg instead of undergoing a severe deterioration of internal conditions in order to maintain the old peg.

The International Monetary Fund

The IMF is a specialized agency of the United Nations and has 178 member states, nearly all the nations of the world. The IMF was intended to play two fundamental roles. First, the Fund was to discourage aggressive exchange-rate behavior by members and help them to manage their balances of payments efficiently and in ways conducive to international harmony. Members accepted general principles, obligations, and rules of conduct by joining the Fund and signing its Articles of Agreement. Chief among these obligations was to maintain an adjustable peg and to allow free convertibility of the national currency for current-account transactions—that is, to allow individuals freely to exchange domestic money for foreign money in order to buy and sell goods and services with the rest of the world. (Countries were to be allowed, as a tool of balance-of-payments policy, to attempt to control foreign-exchange dealings associated with capital-account transactions.) Also, the Fund itself was to oversee and influence member policies (for example, large cumulative peg adjustments required IMF approval), to consult periodically with members, and to render members technical advice. To do this, the Fund was given a staff of international civil servants—currently about 1,500 in number—at its headquarters in Washington, D.C. The Fund is managed by an executive board and a managing director (presently Michel Camdessus of France), with ultimate authority resting in a Board of Governors, which meets annually, representing the member countries.

The second fundamental role assigned the IMF was to supply credit to member states. The Fund received contributions subscribed from members and was to use these resources to lend international reserves to countries with balance-of-payments difficulties. Countries would thereby be better able to finance temporary payments deficits without imposing unwelcome contractionary policies or changing their pegs than if they had to rely solely on their own international reserves.

IMF Credit Facilities. Each member country has a quota whose size reflects the relative international economic importance of the country. (The largest quota, that of the United States, is over 7,600 times the size of the smallest, that of Micronesia.) Its quota equals the subscription payment each country has made to the Fund and also determines its borrowing privileges from the Fund. In addition, voting power in the IMF is proportional to the quotas, in sharp contrast to the "one country, one vote" principle used by the United Nations and its other agencies. Quotas are reviewed every three to five years and have been increased several times in order to enlarge Fund resources; sometimes relative quotas are adjusted to reflect changes in relative country sizes. When new members join the Fund, they receive their own quotas, thereby increasing the aggregate total.

Quota subscription payments are generally made 75 percent in the member's own currency and 25 percent in international reserve assets. The latter payments were originally in gold, but now they are in Special Drawing Rights (SDRs)—an international reserve asset created by the IMF in 1969 (SDRs are more fully described below). At present the total of all members' quotas is almost SDR 145 billion, worth over US$205 billion in late 1993. The Fund may also enlarge its resources by borrowing, has profitably sold gold to the public, and receives fees when members borrow from it.

The Fund operates several borrowing facilities.

a. *Basic Credit Facility.* A member technically draws on this facility by using its own currency to purchase from the Fund other currencies or SDRs in order to finance payments deficits. The loan is repaid when the member repurchases its own currency with other currencies or SDRs. Any member may unconditionally borrow in this way until the Fund's holdings of the member's currency equal the member's quota; such unconditional borrowing rights, called the *reserve tranche,* thus originally equal 25 percent of the quota (they can come to equal more than this, if other members borrow a member's currency and so reduce the Fund's holdings to less than 75 percent of the quota). Because reserve tranche positions are unconditional borrowing rights, nations usually count them as part of their international reserves. This means that a country does not lose reserves when paying its subscription to the IMF: the reserves it pays just equal the reserve tranche position it acquires. Borrowing beyond the reserve tranche may be made under four *credit tranches,* each equal to 25 percent of the quota. Such borrowings are conditional, with the member required to implement (increasingly significant) policies to deal with its payments imbalances. If a member fully utilizes the five tranches of the basic facility, it will have borrowed 125 percent of its quota and the Fund's holdings of the member's currency will equal 200 percent of that quota.

b. *Extended Credit Facility.* This provides for additional conditional borrowings beyond the basic facility, up to 140 percent of the quota, for countries with severe problems.

c. *Structural Adjustment Facility.* This provides loans to low income developing countries undertaking structural adjustment policies and experiencing protracted balance-of-payments problems.

d. *Enhanced Structural Adjustment Facility.* A newer program intended to supplement the Structural Adjustment Facility.

e. *Special Facilities.* The IMF has two arrangements to aid countries (chiefly LDCs) with payments problems due to fluctuations in export earnings.

Such countries may borrow from the *compensatory facility* to finance payments deficits and from the *buffer stock facility* to finance contributions to buffer stock arrangements for the stabilization of primary product prices.

f. *Systemic Transformation Facility*. This is intended to aid formerly central planned economies that are becoming market economies and are experiencing balance-of-payments problems during the transition.

The Special Role of the Dollar

It was recognized from the beginning that the United States would play a special role, primarily because of the size of the American economy and the devastation in Europe but also because the United States owned the bulk of the world's stock of gold reserves. One important aspect of this special role had to do with the adjustable pegs. Each currency was given a par value in terms of gold, thereby defining parities between every pair of currencies. Each country except the United States was obligated to buy and sell its own currency in its own foreign-exchange market so as to keep its dollar exchange rate within a band of at most 1 percent on either side of its dollar parity (the "peg"). The dollar was an *intervention currency*—the currency most countries exchanged for their own when intervening. The United States, by contrast, was not obligated to intervene in the exchange market, although it occasionally did so, but was instead obligated to exchange gold for dollars with other central banks on demand, at the par value. (Thus the Bretton Woods system was an example of a *gold-exchange standard*.)

Example: Bretton Woods Obligations

From 1951 to 1967 the gold parity of the U.K. pound was £12.5 per ounce and that of the U.S. dollar was $35 per ounce, so that sterling's dollar parity was $2.80/£ (=[$35 per ounce]/[£12.5 per ounce]). The Bank of England was thus obligated to exchange dollars for pounds on the London foreign-exchange market in whatever quantities necessary to keep the dollar-pound exchange rate between $2.772/£ and $2.828/£—1 percent below and above $2.80. (In practice the exchange rate was kept within the narrower band of $2.78 to $2.82.) The U.S. Fed was obligated to sell gold at $35 per ounce (plus a small handling charge) to the Bank of England for any dollars acquired through intervention and to buy gold at $35 per ounce (minus the handling charge).

If every country that acquired dollars through intervention always redeemed them for gold with the United States and if every country selling dollars first acquired them by selling gold to the United States, all payments imbalances (including those of the United States) would be fully reflected in gold movements between central banks. But it was realized that countries would in fact wish to hold some part of their international reserves in the form of dollars (and a few other currencies). Thus the dollar was also a *reserve currency,* as discussed in Chapter 15.

Special Drawing Rights

Under the Bretton Woods system, countries' international reserves could consist of three assets: gold, IMF reserve tranche positions, and reserve currencies. In 1969 the First Amendment to the Articles of Agreement of the IMF provided for a fourth reserve asset, Special Drawing Rights. Physically, SDRs are simply bookkeeping entries at the IMF in accounts for member countries and the Fund itself. SDRs can be exchanged for national currencies with other central banks and the Fund. If, for example, the Bank of England were to use SDRs to purchase dollars from the U.S. Fed, the Fed would pay the dollars to the Bank of England; at the same time, the U.S. SDR account would be increased by an appropriate amount, and the U.K. account decreased. The IMF can create new SDRs from time to time in response to global need for additional international reserves; the newly created SDRs are allocated among member nations in proportion to their IMF quotas. When a member's SDR balance falls below its total allocation, it must pay the IMF interest on the difference; members are paid interest by the Fund on SDR holdings in excess of allocations.

The SDR was initially defined as equal in value to one-thirty-fifth of an ounce of gold, which at the time made SDR 1 worth $1. But since 1974 the SDR has been valued on the basis of a currency basket; at present the basket is composed of the currencies of the world's five largest exporting countries. Currently, SDR 1 has the value of a basket consisting of US$0.572, DM 0.453, Fr 0.8, ¥ 31.8, and £0.0812. This value is calculated daily on the basis of market exchange rates.

SDRs were created and allocated in 1970, 1971, 1972, and again in 1979, 1980, and 1981. There are now SDR 21.4 billion in existence, worth $30.4 billion as of October 11, 1993.

Although there have been proposals to allow private individuals and organizations to hold SDRs, they are now held by and exchanged among only central banks, the Fund, and a few other agencies. However, the SDR is used to some extent by others as a unit of account—for example, some commercial bank deposits are valued in SDRs, although they cannot consist of SDRs. The IMF intends to have the SDR become the principal international reserve asset, the Fund using the SDR as its unit of account. IMF quotas, for example, are now set in terms of SDRs.

Problems

16.1 On April 11, 1994, the dollar exchange rate of the German mark was $0.58, of the French franc $0.17, of the Japanese yen $0.01, of the pound sterling $1.47, and of the Italian lira $0.0006. What was the price of SDR 1 in terms of U.S. dollars? In terms of French francs? In terms of Italian lire?

16.2 Until the creation of SDRs, there were three international reserve assets under the Bretton Woods system. The rapid growth of the world economy and of the volume of international transactions during the years that this system existed made for a substantial increase in the world's need for international reserves. How reasonable do you think it would have been to expect this increased need actually to have been met by increases in each of the three reserve assets?

16.3 In view of the intervention obligations of the Bretton Woods system, what is the maximum percentage by which the market value of the dollar could fluctuate relative to any other currency? What is the maximum percentage by which any two (nondollar) currencies could fluctuate relative to each other?

2. THE BRETTON WOODS SYSTEM IN OPERATION

The previous section described how the Bretton Woods system was supposed to work. But it never functioned quite that way.

The Postwar Transition, 1947–1958

The IMF and IBRD were formally set up at the end of 1945, and the IMF commenced operations in 1947. But the Fund assumed a basically passive attitude for some years. It was not, for example, a significant source of international credit until the late 1950s; this role was instead played by direct dealings between national governments, as with the American Marshall Plan and later foreign-aid programs. The Fund also passively approved the initial par values proposed by members, although it did come to be accepted that exchange rates were of international concern, and adjustable pegs were generally adopted. A realignment of exchange rates took place in 1949, resulting in a substantial appreciation of the dollar.

It was regarded as unrealistic to expect weakened countries quickly to abandon wartime controls and allow current-account convertibility. Britain, under American pressure, was unsuccessful when it attempted to restore convertibility in 1947. Thus nations were allowed a transitional period of grace before accepting their convertibility obligations. Except for the United States and a few Central American states, all IMF members exercised this option. This transitional period was at first expected to last no more than five years, but it was not until the beginning of 1959 that most industrial nations had restored current-account convertibility; to this day only about one-third of the

178 IMF members have accepted this obligation, with exchange control remaining pervasive among the LDCs.

The Posttransitional Years, 1959–1973

The postwar transition had definitely ended by 1959: the IMF had found itself, its operations had become significant, and a quota increase had bolstered its resources; the currencies of the major industrial countries were convertible for current-account transactions; the days of "dollar scarcity," or fragile European payments positions, were over; European recovery from the war was accomplished; GATT (the General Agreement on Tariffs and Trade) was established; and DC tariff barriers had been significantly reduced. The Bretton Woods system was basically in full swing during the 1960s. But these years were hardly calm. Recurring balance-of-payments crises, each more serious than the last, culminated in the 1971 crisis, which ended the official gold convertibility of the dollar, and the 1973 crisis, in which the Bretton Woods system finally collapsed. The industrial nations responded to these crises with reforms of the system, some within the IMF and some independent of it. These crises were a reflection of the basic nature of the Bretton Woods system, and their causes can best be analyzed in terms of two essential features of that system: the gold-exchange standard reserve-asset arrangement and the adjustable peg exchange-rate regime.

Reserve Assets. As we have seen, there were originally three types of reserve assets: gold, IMF reserve tranche positions, and reserve currencies. National incomes have grown rapidly since the war, and trade volumes even more so. Also, capital has become much more internationally mobile. Consequently, the view has been widely shared that the world has needed a growing stock of international reserves. Consider, then, the possibilities of increasing each of the three reserve assets. Gold reserves were limited by the physical amount of the metal in existence. There was some chance of increasing gold reserves by new mining and by coaxing some out of private hoards, but this was limited, especially with the price of gold held fixed in an inflationary world. The value of gold stocks could have been increased by a general devaluation (that is, an increase in the price of gold in terms of all currencies). Some economists did recommend such a move, and the French favored it; but most officials were dead set against it. Partly this was for the same reasons that militated against adjustments in exchange-rate pegs, reasons to be examined presently. Also, a rise in the price of gold would substantially benefit the principal gold exporters, who just happened to be South Africa and the USSR.

IMF reserve tranche positions could be increased by raising IMF quotas, and this was done a number of times. But this could not by itself increase the world stock of international reserves—whenever a quota increase boosts a nation's IMF reserve tranche position, its subscription payment reduces its stocks of other reserve assets by an equal amount.

Thus international reserves could in fact be increased only if reserve-currency holdings (in effect, dollar holdings) could be increased, and this is what happened, as is apparent from the first three columns of Table 16.1. This process, in turn, required American balance-of-payments deficits—as we saw in Chapter 15, international reserves will be increased by the payments deficits of reserve-center countries, provided that other countries accumulate the reserve currency. This caused two sorts of problems.

The first, diagnosed by Robert Triffin and sometimes called the *confidence problem,* is the simple result of the need for increased reserves: the dollar was as good as gold because the United States would exchange dollars for gold at a fixed price with central banks on demand; the world needed a continually increasing stock of reserves that could be supplied only by continual U.S. payments deficits; if this continued long enough, foreign central banks would eventually have more dollars than the United States had gold. Everyone would then know that all the dollars could not possibly be redeemed for gold, and the United States would be viewed as a country with a chronic deficit. The dollar would thus eventually cease to be attractive. This is an inherent defect in a reserve-currency system because the only alternative would be not to increase reserves and so strangle world commerce.

The second problem is the *asymmetric position of the reserve-center country.* As we saw in Chapter 15, such countries do not lose international reserves as a result of payments deficits as long as surplus countries are willing to accumulate the reserve currency. This means that reserve centers are free of the pressure to correct payments deficits faced by other countries, which must worry about running out of reserves. This is apt to be resented by these other countries.

During the 1950s the persistent American deficits were generally welcome: the U.S. gold stock was huge, the dollar was at least as good as gold, and the weak European economies faced a "dollar shortage"—they needed reserves. But this changed in the late 1950s and 1960s. The dollar shortage was over, but the U.S. deficits did not disappear. Table 16.2 shows the inter-

TABLE 16.1   International Reserves, End of Year *(billions of dollars)*

	1949	1969	1973	1993
World reserves*	46	78	178	1,087
Gold*	34	39	36	44
IMF positions	2	7	8	45
Foreign exchange	10	32	123	977
SDRs	—	—	11	20
U.S. reserves*	26	17	30	75

*Gold is valued at the official price.

SOURCE: International Monetary Fund, *International Financial Statistics.*

TABLE 16.2   U.S. Balance of Payments, Selected Years *(billions of dollars)*

	1961	1966	1971	1972	1973	1980	1985	1993
Merchandise trade	5.6	3.8	−2.3	−6.4	0.9	−25.5	−122.1	−132.6
Services trade	−1.4	−0.9	1.0	1.0	1.0	6.1	0.1	56.9
Current account	3.8	3.0	−1.4	−5.8	7.1	2.3	−125.4	−103.9
Government and long-term capital	−3.5	−6.7	−8.0	−4.5	−7.9	−2.9	67.7	−51.9
Private short-term capital	−0.7	3.1	−10.8	1.0	−2.6	−33.3	39.2	64.4
Statistical discrepancy	−1.0	0.6	−9.8	−1.9	−2.7	25.4	23.4	21.1
SDR allocation	—	—	0.7	0.7	—	1.2	—	—
Official reserve assets	1.4	−0.1	29.2	10.4	6.2	7.3	−5.0	70.3
Balance-of-payments surplus	−1.4	0.1	−29.2	−10.4	−6.2	−7.3	5.0	−70.3

SOURCE: Department of Commerce, *Survey of Current Business.*

national payments experience of the United States since 1960. The remaining American gold stock no longer looked huge compared to the dollar holdings of foreign central banks. During the 1960s the latter overtook the former, and all the world knew that the United States could not redeem all those dollars for gold even if it wanted to. "We'd better not ask, then," was the inevitable next thought. The dollar would continue to be worth one–thirty-fifth of an ounce of gold only as long as the United States did not actually have to make good on its promise to sell gold at that price.

Any large-scale attempt to redeem dollars for gold would have forced the United States to repudiate its obligation, thereby leaving foreign central banks stuck with devalued dollars. Thus those central banks were loath to precipitate a run on the dollar by trying to redeem their dollar holdings or by refusing to accept new dollar balances in settlement of payments deficits, thereby making the problem even worse. By and large during the 1960s the American obligation to maintain central-bank gold convertibility of the dollar ended de facto, although it continued de jure. More and more, the gold-exchange standard became a dollar standard.

The United States tried to persuade and induce foreign central banks to hold dollar balances instead of demanding gold in exchange and imposed various capital controls in an attempt to stop the outflow. The former was by and large successful, but the latter was not. What the United States did not do was adjust monetary and fiscal policies to improve the balance of payments. American macroeconomic policies were used for internal objectives. That the country was able to do this was partly due to the relatively closed nature of the American economy compared to other industrial nations; but no doubt it was also partly due to the reserve-currency role of the dollar and the fact that the de facto erosion of the gold-convertibility obligation eliminated the basic source of pressure on the United States to cure a payments deficit.

Naturally, many Europeans took a dim view of this. Countries with a persistent surplus, such as West Germany, had an increasingly difficult time sterilizing the effects of those surpluses, especially when the American deficit worsened in the late 1960s in response to the Vietnam War inflation; this German experience was examined in Chapter 15. From this point of view, the American deficits looked as though the United States was using its special position in the international monetary system to export its inflation instead of curing it. Other Europeans pointed out that the persistent American deficits meant that the United States was acquiring goods, services, and assets from the rest of the world for dollars that the latter had no option but to accept. To such individuals, America's privileged position allowed her to force Europe to finance both the Vietnam adventure and the acquisition of European industry by American corporations.

To many Americans, the U.S. position seemed like anything but a privilege. The fact that the United States had persistent deficits meant that other countries on balance had persistent surpluses. If those countries chose not to eliminate those surpluses by currency revaluation or other measures, it must be that the surpluses were actually welcome. When country A complained that America should reduce its deficit, country A did not mean, so the argument went, that its own surplus should be reduced, but rather that the surpluses of countries B, C, D, and so on, should shrink, thereby making the dollars acquired by country A more attractive. Under this interpretation the United States was in the unique position of having no direct control over its own balance of payments, which was determined by the aggregate desire of foreign central banks to acquire dollars and/or run surpluses. As we have seen, a dollar devaluation (gold price rise) was rejected as a possible policy. Even if it happened, a devaluation, by showing that the gold value of the dollar was indeed subject to change, would make both central banks and private individuals less willing to hold dollars. It, therefore, would simply make things worse, unless the devaluation caused a sufficient depreciation of the dollar relative to other currencies to cure the American deficit. But dollar devaluation would not produce dollar depreciation if other countries also devalued, and many others presumably would; if they had not revalued on their own, their exchange rates must already be at desired levels. The basic reality was that exchange rates were determined by the intervention policies of countries *other than* the United States.

Two significant reforms attempted to rectify the reserve-asset problems of the Bretton Woods system. In the late 1960s confidence in the dollar eroded sufficiently so that private individuals increasingly tended to hoard gold; central banks then had to increase gold sales to the private market in order to maintain the $35/ounce price. Thus central-bank gold holdings started to fall. To stop this, the central banks of the major industrial countries agreed in 1968 to suspend dealings with the private gold market and to exchange the metal only among themselves. This created a two-tier gold market with one price for central-bank gold (the official price of $35/ounce) and another price on the disjoint private gold market.

The second, and potentially more significant, reform was the creation of SDRs. The basic idea was to establish a new asset whose quantity could be consciously adjusted in response to the world's need for international reserves. Thus reserve currencies would no longer be needed for this purpose, and the confidence problem and the asymmetric position of reserve centers could be addressed. But the creation of SDRs was not accompanied by provision for exchange-rate adjustment or other measures to deal directly with the American deficit, and when SDRs actually began to be allocated in 1970 they turned out to be but a drop in the bucket of liquidity provided by massive U.S. payments deficits.

Adjustable Peg Regime. The confidence problem and the asymmetric role of reserve centers were inherent in the original reserve-asset arrangement of the Bretton Woods system. But they need not have been fatal to that system: in principle the problems could have been dealt with by sufficient exchange-rate adjustments, perhaps supplemented by the extensive use of the SDR. That this did not in fact happen is due to a second, more fundamental, defect: the inherent deficiency of an adjustable peg system. At bottom, that deficiency is due to the fact that there is always a latent contradiction among (a) constant exchange rates, (b) autonomous national macroeconomic policies, and (c) international capital mobility. We saw in Chapter 15 that (a) and (b) are inconsistent in the long run and that an increased degree of international capital mobility renders the long run more immediate. When capital becomes sufficiently mobile, the latent contradiction becomes a painfully real one. A basic goal of the Bretton Woods system was to sidestep this problem by providing countries with the means of delaying this contradiction until it disappeared or, if it proved so inhospitable as to stay around, to eliminate it by exchange-rate adjustments. But in the end, the adjustable peg system could not sidestep the problem. Instead, it aggravated it.

As we saw in Chapter 14, individuals' decisions on how to allocate wealth between assets denominated in different currencies—say, the franc and the mark—are sensitive to the difference between the German interest rate i_G and the French interest rate minus the expected depreciation of the franc relative to the mark, $i_F - d$. If capital is highly mobile, a modest change in the difference between these rates of return can generate a large portfolio shift and, therefore, a large payments imbalance. The essence of an adjustable peg system is that the peg should be changed by significant amounts on isolated occasions in response to a "fundamental disequilibrium." Thus if things are working smoothly and there is no reason to expect a parity change, d should equal zero or, more accurately, be constrained by the intervention band about the peg. But consider what happens if things are not working smoothly. Suppose, for example, that France runs a payments deficit that persists long enough so that individuals suspect a fundamental disequilibrium. If the market begins to expect a downward adjustment of the French peg, d could become huge. Suppose that, say, a 10 percent devaluation is expected within a week. Expressed as an annual rate of return, d equals 520 percent—since there are fifty-two weeks in the year—a magnitude sufficient to dwarf any conceivable difference between i_F and i_G. This would induce individuals to try to get out of francs before the devaluation—that is, it would cause a flight of short-term capital from France, thereby worsening the French payments deficit and making the devaluation even more likely to take place. An inhibiting consideration is the fact that devaluation is not certain; if the French payments position unexpectedly improves, individuals may not realize their 520 percent profit from switching from francs to marks. But they will not lose much either: the franc will certainly not be revalued. The adjustable peg system thus presents the market with a *one-way option* in a payments crisis: the market does not know for certain whether or not the peg will be adjusted, but it does know in which direction any adjustment will be.

Instead of allowing the exchange rate to adjust constantly in response to market pressure, the adjustable peg system requires a currency's parity to be defended until it becomes obvious to everyone that a change in some direction is called for and then to make the change all at once. People will realize this and attempt to protect themselves by selling a currency that is expected to be devalued and buying a currency that is expected to be revalued. If capital is sufficiently mobile, these precautionary capital flows will cause the fulfillment of the expectations upon which they are based. Thus parity changes in an adjustable peg system will be associated with balance-of-payments crises.

The economics of an adjustable peg system also generates a political climate that adds instability. When officials are attempting to defend the peg of a currency associated with a serious payments imbalance, they have little choice, if capital is highly mobile, but to proclaim publicly their confidence that the peg will be maintained. Any expression of doubt will induce capital movements destructive toward defending the parity. (Even if officials know that a parity change is imminent, they must lie through their teeth until the last moment.) Once officials have nailed the flag to the mast for a given parity, it becomes even more important to them that the parity be defended. If officials change the parity after public declarations that such a thing will never happen, not only will their words be given less credence in the future, but, more ominously, their policy will have failed its own publicly proclaimed test. Richard Cooper of Harvard noted that within a year of the devaluation of their currencies, nearly 60 percent of the finance ministers lost their jobs. As a result of this political climate, parity adjustments will tend to be avoided as long as possible: the adjustable peg will not be very adjustable after all, and such adjustments as do occur will happen only as climaxes to serious crises. Furthermore, with peg adjustments made only under the gun of major crises, devaluations are more likely than revaluations because deficit countries, who need worry about running out of reserves, are more vulnerable than surplus countries. With depreciations relative to the dollar more common than appreciations relative to the dollar, the dollar will, over time, tend to appreciate relative to other currencies in general. This could worsen the U.S. payments position and help eventually to bring about a dollar crisis.

During the 1960s, parity adjustments took place only in response to currency crises. These crises were recurrent and became steadily more massive as capital became more mobile. In response, the major industrial nations, increasingly conscious of thralldom to a common system, came more and more to cooperate and consult. Major currency crises were met with "rescue operations" in which governments not directly involved jointly extended loans to the central banks of countries with currencies under attack; central bank officials of the major nations met monthly in Basel, Switzerland, to compare notes. It is ironic that the deficiencies of the Bretton Woods system did result in the concrete embodiment of one of that system's major goals: general acceptance of the view that exchange rates are a matter of international concern rather than of nationalistic prerogative.

This cooperation naturally tended to center on the major nations most crucially involved. These came to be organized as the Group of Ten (G-10)—the United States, Canada, Great Britain, Japan, Sweden, France, Germany, Italy, Belgium, and the Netherlands; Switzerland, not in the IMF, is a de facto eleventh member of the G-10. Negotiations within the G-10 have often upstaged the more broad-based IMF, which has sometimes been reduced simply to ratifying agreements reached by the smaller group. In 1962 these countries established the General Arrangements to Borrow, under which the G-10 nations stand ready to lend to each other—through the IMF—international reserves to deal with actual or potential payments crises. This agreement has often been utilized.

Problems

16.4 Discuss how each of the following might be interpreted as evidence in the debate over whether U.S. payments deficits were *supply-determined* (due to a failure of the United States to adopt measures to eliminate its deficit) or *demand-determined* (due to the failure of foreign countries to eliminate their surpluses):

    a The United States improved its current-account position in the early and mid-1960s, but the overall payments deficits continued.

    b Even as the IMF was allocating a new reserve asset, in the early 1970s the American deficit exploded.

16.5 The text discussed the role of speculative capital movements with an adjustable peg. How would this discussion change in the presence of each of the following alternative exchange regimes: free floating, managed floating, fixed exchange rates.

3. *CASE STUDY:* THE 1969 DEVALUATION OF THE FRANC

The French franc was strong during the early 1960s, but confidence in the currency was shattered by the student-worker strikes in May 1968 and by the subsequent wage settlements, viewed as inflationary. The balance of payments went into deficit, and speculative outflows increased during the autumn. The government tightened price controls, imposed temporary exchange control, and then raised taxes. Middle-class French citizens began taking suitcases full of currency to Switzerland for conversion into Swiss francs. It was generally expected that at a November 1968 meeting the franc would be devalued and the mark revalued, but President de Gaulle surprised everyone by announcing that national honor made it unthinkable that the franc would ever be devalued. Exchange controls were imposed, a $2 billion credit from the Group of Ten was arranged, and the crisis abated, although the basic position of the franc did not change. In July 1969 the new president, Pompidou, apparently decided that a devaluation was necessary after all, but he kept the decision a secret from all but a few close advisers, and the existing parity was supported in public. A few weeks later the franc was devalued by 11.1 percent, with the surprise announcement made on a weekend—when the exchanges were closed—in August, when all France goes on vacation (*le grand départ*). In 1970 the balance of payments improved dramatically.

4. COLLAPSE OF THE BRETTON WOODS SYSTEM

Although the persistent American deficit was a problem, attention was dramatically focused on recurring crises of other currencies. In fact, the American current-account position improved in the early 1960s. But by the end of the decade there was a widespread feeling that the dollar was overvalued. The dollar appreciation implied by the devaluations of other currencies and the American inflation generated by the deficit financing of the Vietnam War caused America's competitive position to deteriorate. The current account went into deficit in 1968, and in 1971 the United States recorded a merchandise trade deficit for the first time in this century.

The 1971 Crisis

The weakness of the American competitive position was briefly masked in 1970, when a combination of an American recession and high economic activity in Europe restored a surplus to the U.S. current account. But relatively loose American monetary policy contributed to a capital outflow, and the payments deficit of $9.8 billion was the largest ever up to that time. Then economic activity began to abate in Europe, the United States began to emerge from recession, and it became clear that American officials had no intention of aborting the recovery. A flight from the dollar began. In the spring of 1971 the crisis centered on strong currencies especially in demand by individuals selling dollars. Germany and Holland were forced to suspend support of their parities and allow their currencies to float upward; Switzerland and Austria revalued. By summer, the crisis clearly centered on the dollar, as one foreign currency after another came to be demanded by sellers of dollars. Foreign central banks began to redeem with the United States some of the huge dollar balances they were acquiring.

On August 15, 1971 (the 202nd birthday of Napoleon Bonaparte), President Nixon announced that the United States would no longer redeem dollars from other central banks. A domestic price and income freeze was also announced, and a temporary 10 percent surcharge was levied on imports. In thus "closing the gold window," the United States was not merely responding to the run on the dollar and to recent dollar redemptions by foreign central banks. After all, the window had already been almost shut anyway, and if the United States had wished to complete the closure in a way consistent with its earlier behavior, it would have simply offered central banks increased incentives to hold dollars and/or told them in private that dollars would not be redeemed. Instead, the window was slammed shut in as public and dramatic a manner as possible. The deed was aggressive: the United States had decided on the necessity of new international arrangements, including a realignment of exchange rates, and was determined to force the rest of the world to acquiesce. The president's announcement would greatly increase the flight from the dollar and thereby require any country wishing to maintain its parity to buy huge quantities of dollars publicly proclaimed as officially inconvertible into other assets. Interbank foreign-exchange markets were mostly closed for a week—much to the discomfort of many American tourists—and when they opened, the major currencies were allowed to float. Only Japan, the industrial nation with the most effective controls on international transactions, attempted to maintain its dollar parity; but before the month of August was out the Japanese, too, were forced to give up and release the yen from its peg. The import surcharge could be defended on the grounds that similar measures had been employed during the 1960s by other countries with balance-of-payments problems. But actually the surcharge was another American weapon, a measure that would be ended once concessions had been gained.

During the autumn of 1971 the currencies of the major industrial nations were allowed to float—with management—while negotiations on reform proceeded. These negotiations culminated in an international conference at the Smithsonian Institution in Washington, D.C., on December 17 and 18. The United States dropped its import surcharge, and a realignment of exchange rates was worked out, with the dollar depreciated by an average of about 10 percent. This was done partly by a devaluation of the dollar (to $38 per ounce of gold) and partly by revaluation of various other currencies. But the dollar price of gold was now a nonprice at which the United States would neither buy nor sell gold, for it was widely accepted that America would not resume its convertibility obligation. The deficit of 1971 had itself been more than twice the size of the total American stock of reserve assets.

The Smithsonian Agreement also provided for a widening of intervention bands from 1.00 percent on either side of parity to 2.25 percent, and the IMF later established a group, known as the Committee of 20, to develop proposals to reform the international monetary system. But basically the Bretton Woods system was patched together again. The principal formal change, the end of official dollar convertibility, simply made explicit what had been largely implicit since the late 1960s. President Nixon described the Smithsonian accord as "the most significant monetary agreement in the history of the world." It was to endure for almost fifteen months.

The 1973 Collapse of the Bretton Woods System

During 1972 the Smithsonian parities were defended, and the Committee of 20 began its work. A spate of bad economic news in Britain ushered in another crisis for the pound in June, and the United Kingdom abandoned its parity and resumed a managed float.

In February 1973 another major dollar crisis suddenly materialized, and interbank foreign-exchange markets were closed. Another exchange-rate adjustment was agreed upon. But by the end of the month the exchanges were in crisis once more, and in March the major industrial countries abandoned their new dollar parities. This was the end of the Bretton Woods system. At first many people hoped that adjustable pegs might once again be resurrected as soon as the markets calmed down. But these hopes gradually faded with the passage of time, especially after the dramatic oil-price increases of 1973–1974 and the subsequent steep world recession.

Present Arrangements

Meanwhile, the Committee of 20 was deliberating. It soon became apparent that international agreement on major reforms would not be forthcoming, and realization gradually spread that managed floating was not temporary. Thus when the committee finished its work in July 1974, it presented no major reform proposals but instead concluded that international monetary reform must be a matter of evolution. Some relatively minor changes were made, and the IMF established an Interim Committee (to be replaced by a permanent Ministerial Council upon alteration of the Articles of Agreement) to oversee the reform process.

The first order of business was to amend the Articles to allow managed floating since the actual state of affairs was still illegal. The major stumbling block to such an amendment was a disagreement between the United States and some Europeans—notably, France. The latter wished to retain a role for gold and to provide for the ultimate return of an adjustable peg system; the

United States was opposed to both ideas and wished to minimize official intervention. In November 1975 a summit meeting at Rambouillet resolved the issue, accepting the essentials of the American position. Agreement was formalized at an Interim Committee meeting in Jamaica during January 1976, and the Second Amendment of the IMF Articles of Agreement was subsequently ratified and entered into force on April Fool's Day, 1978. This amendment finally legalized the managed float. In fact, it legalized practically anything except a gold peg, innocuously describing the international monetary system to be "the kind prevailing on January 1, 1976."

Bretton Woods Retrospective

How successful was the Bretton Woods system? While the actual date of its demise might have been influenced by exogenous events such as the Vietnam War, there is little doubt that the system carried within itself the seeds of its own destruction. Depending on how it is defined, the Bretton Woods system lasted for fifteen to twenty-seven years, a lifetime roughly comparable to that of the gold standard at the turn of the century. This lifetime was punctuated by recurrent international financial crises. But still there was an unprecedented steady growth of world income and trade and a great liberalization of international transactions between the industrial nations. That the system's inherent flaws ultimately proved decisive was to a large extent the result of that system's own success in fostering (or at least permitting) this great expansion of multilateral economic activity. The repeated crises were troublesome, to be sure, but even that cloud has proven to have had its silver lining: the habits and institutions of official international consultation and cooperation, developed in response to the crises, still remain and are of great importance in our present unstructured world. Indeed, the timing of the system's death was itself fortuitous since adjustable pegs could not possibly have handled the oil shock and subsequent events as well as did the more flexible arrangement actually in place.

The Bretton Woods system is history's only example of an international monetary order created largely by conscious human decision rather than evolution. The creation was fatally flawed but served its purpose at least adequately. Its flaws gathered strength as a result of the system's basic success, and they ultimately shattered that system just as it was about to become seriously inappropriate to changed circumstances.

Problem

16.6 The Smithsonian negotiations included considerable debate over whether the depreciation of the dollar should involve a dollar devaluation or just the revaluation of other currencies. Can you think of any reasons for this since everyone knew that the United States would not restore official gold convertibility in any case?

---

5. INTERNATIONAL MONETARY REFORM ISSUES

The international monetary system continues to evolve, and proposals for substantive reform continue to be debated. These can best be discussed relative to the two features so crucial in the breakdown of the Bretton Woods system: reserve assets and the exchange-rate regime.

Reserve Assets

With freely floating currencies, international reserves are unnecessary. Therefore, it might be thought that the substitution of widespread managed floating for the adjustable peg system would reduce the need for reserves. But the huge American payments deficits of 1970–1973 greatly expanded international reserves so that, when the Bretton Woods system collapsed, world reserve-currency holdings were nearly $120 billion, of which about 85 percent were U.S. dollars. These were referred to as the *dollar overhang:* huge holdings of inconvertible dollars that central banks presumably did not want but could not dispose of without cataclysmic effect on the exchange markets.

As it turned out, however, management of the float has been sufficiently intensive so that the overall amount of intervention since 1973 has not been greatly different from before. Also, since 1973 total international reserves other than gold have grown more slowly than the value of total world exports. Thus there is no longer much concern that total world reserves are excessive. Policy issues instead center upon the *composition* of those reserves and relate in particular to the role of currency reserves and the asymmetric position of the United States as a reserve center. The world faced just these problems under the Bretton Woods system, and our discussion of them in section 2, therefore, remains relevant to the present day. Additional present-day issues can be discussed by looking separately at various reserve assets.

Gold. For over two decades the French advocated a monetary role for gold, and today some advocate greater reliance on the metal. The dominant attitude, however, shared by the IMF and the United States, has been to phase out gold as a reserve asset. Recent actions have been consistent with this goal. The IMF will no longer accept gold in Fund transactions, and gold has generally been displaced by the SDR for IMF purposes. The two-tier system has been abolished so that central banks may deal in gold with private markets, and the amended Articles of Agreement do not allow currencies to be pegged to gold (thus there is no official gold price; the United States still values its gold stock at $42.22 per ounce, but this is only a national accounting convention). Aside from the gold transactions just described plus some gold that members of the European Monetary System subscribed to that organization, there have been few central-bank gold dealings in recent years. The metal is basically an inactive asset.

SDRs. We discussed above how the IMF wished the SDR to become the principal reserve asset. But, as Table 16.1 shows, SDRs accounted for less than 2 percent of world reserves at the end of 1993. For the SDR to become the principal reserve asset, it is necessary that the role of reserve currencies be formalized and limited.

A proposed move in this direction is the establishment of an IMF *substitution account*. Such an account would accept dollar deposits from central banks and in return issue an equivalent amount of SDRs. Ideally, this would both deal with the dollar overhang and expand the role of the SDR. Consideration of such an account was recommended by the Interim Committee at the 1979 IMF annual meeting in Belgrade, but at present the proposal is in limbo.

Reserve Currencies. The role of the dollar has been at issue since the Second World War. Discussions since 1973 have focused on ways to make the dollar more like other currencies—that is, to moderate the asymmetrical position of the United States. The proposed substitution account could, under certain circumstances, contribute toward this end. So, too, could proposals for *multicurrency intervention* (various plans under which a basket of currencies would, in effect, replace the dollar as principal intervention currency). These proposals and others have made little headway. But while debate on these issues has continued, actual practice has quietly been changing. Central banks have been diversifying their holdings of foreign exchange away from nearly exclusive reliance upon dollars. Dollars declined from almost 87 percent of official foreign-exchange holdings at the end of 1976 to barely 59 percent at the end of 1980. These figures should be qualified in two ways. First, when the European Monetary System (EMS) was created, the member states contributed gold and SDRs and received in return European Currency Units (ECUs). This will be discussed in greater detail in Chapter 21. The point is that national reserve holdings count as part of international reserves, whereas EMS holdings do not. Thus the creation of the EMS necessarily reduced the dollar's share in total foreign currency reserves by adding another (nondollar) currency: the ECU. Second, most of the remaining decline in the dollar's relative importance is due to the decisions of a small group of countries, mainly oil exporters, to diversify the currency composition of newly acquired liquid holdings.

But these considerations cannot nullify the trend. The "small group of countries" is part of the world, and the ECU was inaugurated, in part, expressly to reduce the dollar's role. Furthermore, in recent years there has been some increase in the use of nondollar currencies for intervention purposes; many nations now peg to currency baskets rather than to the dollar; and the SDR has in effect displaced the dollar within the IMF in a technical sense.

Thus there is a definite, if modest, tendency for the dollar increasingly to share its hitherto unique position with other currencies. The dollar's role in international reserves greatly exceeds the United States' current role in the world economy. In this sense the tendency is natural. But is it desirable? Two arguments say no. The first claims that, for politico-economic reasons of obscure origin, an efficient international monetary system requires a dominant currency to take a leadership role. This was done by the pound under the gold standard, by the dollar under the Bretton Woods system, and by no one during the terrible 1930s. This view may have its merits, but the dominant theme in international monetary negotiations since 1944 has been that the international monetary system is a matter of collective concern.

The second argument is that diversification of official foreign-exchange holdings is destabilizing because central banks will dump their reserve holdings of currencies they expect to depreciate in exchange for currencies they expect to appreciate. Why should central banks act in a more destabilizing way than alternative private holders of the same currencies? Perhaps they should not, if only economic motives matter. But political motives also count, especially once official agencies become involved. The 1979 American freeze of Iranian dollar assets was prompted at least in part by the fear that the Iranians were about to dump their dollars on world markets. What is not clear, however, is whether such dangers are increased by diversification of the currency composition of those holdings.

The Exchange-Rate Regime

It was not by conscious design that the world abandoned the adjustable peg system for widespread managed floating; the former had ceased to be feasible. Of the unstable triumvirate of pegged exchange rates, autonomous national macroeconomic policies, and extensive international transactions, nations are unwilling to dispense with the second and have not wished (fortunately) to impose the Draconian controls necessary to nullify the effects of the third. Thus the first must go. This has come to be widely recognized, and debate is no longer significantly concerned with whether a general system of adjustable pegs should be reintroduced or with the general merits of fixed versus floating rates (there has, however, been much discussion about whether specific countries or groups of countries—such as the EU members —should peg). Instead, debate has centered over whether, and how, intervention ought to be internationally regulated in a world of managed floating. Recall that a fixed exchange-rate system has two basic advantages: national monies are more useful as money when they can be exchanged for each other at fixed prices, and countries are prevented from aggressively manipulating their exchange rates for nationalistic purposes. Proposed rules attempt to salvage some of these gains by limiting exchange-rate fluctuations and by subjecting national intervention to international guidelines. The Second Amendment to the IMF Articles of Agreement gave the Fund a vague responsibility for surveillance of members' intervention, and the Fund has on two occasions made general statements on the subject. But debate continues. Most of the discussion has centered on three types of norms for behavior.

1. *Leaning against the Wind.* The basic idea here is that central banks should intervene to resist, but not neutralize, market forces: exchange-rate fluctuations should be reduced, but long-term trends should be dictated by the market. Some central banks, such as the German Bundesbank, have described

their intervention policies as leaning against the wind (or the correction of "disorderly" market conditions). Much actual intervention since 1973 seems to have been of this sort. The principal reason for this prominence is probably the large exchange-rate fluctuations that have been experienced with managed floating.

The most common complaint about such a policy is that countries might lean too heavily and prevent needed exchange-rate adjustments. The Japanese have often been criticized on this score, and in 1977 a number of American officials—in a resurrection of the pre-1971 complaint that only the United States lacked control over its exchange rate—expressed the view that excessive European and Japanese intervention was preventing a desirable (to the Americans) depreciation of the dollar. It is even possible that countries might not merely defend inappropriate rates, but actually use monetary policy, news leaks, and so forth to induce changes in directions that are desired for nationalistic reasons—and then defend the new rates.

2. *Targets.* A second idea is that target values should be set for the various exchange rates and that the authorities should then intervene to move rates toward these targets. This approach has been favored by some individuals who would like a return to adjustable pegs but realize that that is not practicable. The targets are not to be interpreted as pegs that must be maintained, and different advocates of this approach have different views of how forcefully central banks should attempt to attain their targets; the use of targets could involve either more intervention or less than a general policy of leaning against the wind. Indeed, some proposals have provided for targets to be altered or abandoned, should they entail too heavy a degree of intervention.

There have been isolated instances of coordinated intervention, when central banks have been in agreement about the desired future course of exchange rates. A notable example was the Plaza Hotel agreement for coordinated intervention that was reached in September 1985 when officials in most major countries agreed that the dollar was valued too highly relative to other currencies. Also, in late 1986 there were reports in the press that U.S. and Japanese officials had agreed to try to keep the exchange rate within the band of ¥ 150–155/$. And in February 1987 seven major industrial nations agreed, at a meeting at the Louvre in Paris, to coordinate their macroeconomic policies. Apparently, they also established target zones for their exchange rates and procedures for adjusting the targets. Exchange-rate volatility was modest for some months, but then the dollar depreciated sharply around the time of the stock-market crash on October 19, 1987 ("Black Monday"). We will return to this experience below.

3. *Objective Indicators.* Some individuals have recommended that countries be required to alter their intervention policies when objective indicators signal the presence of substantial disequilibrium. Several indicators have been suggested, such as the net amount of intervention in one direction in a specified time interval. A country would be required to cease leaning against the wind, or to alter its exchange-rate target, once the total of such interven-

tion reaches a pre-set limit. The use of objective indicators was strongly advocated by American negotiators in the early 1970s, but foreign governments did not agree.

Problems

16.7 Under what circumstances could the existence of a substitution account lessen the asymmetric position of the United States?

16.8 Discuss the likely consequences of a unilateral U.S. return to the gold standard, assuming that other major countries do not follow suit and that the IMF's rules and policies are not altered.

16.9 Suppose that the fluctuations of some exchange rates consist of random deviations from a constant equilibrium value. If a central bank undertakes to lean against the wind, would its intervention on balance serve to move the exchange rate toward equilibrium or away from it? Answer the same question if the exchange-rate fluctuations consist of random deviations from a *moving* equilibrium.

6. EXPERIENCE SINCE THE END OF BRETTON WOODS

The bottom line of the previous section is that, while there has been much discussion over many years of many proposals for reform of the international monetary system, very little has in fact been done. Thus individual countries have been left to make their own exchange-rate arrangements, and, as we saw in Chapter 14, they have done so in a variety of ways. But the most important feature—the feature characteristic of the present age in international monetary history—is the managed float among the three most important currencies: the U.S. dollar, the Japanese yen, and the German mark (with other European currencies linked, in various and changing ways, to the latter). This section reviews experience with the managed float.

The experience has many facets, but three are especially important: (1) changing U.S. attitudes about managing the float; (2) international coordination of economic policies; (3) European efforts toward monetary integration. Throughout the period of the float, the major exchange rates have indeed fluctuated, exhibiting major and prolonged swings.

Changing U.S. Attitudes

These attitudes changed with the philosophies of the individuals in power and with macroeconomic circumstance. In the early years of the float the United States took a basically hands-off view: the exchange rate was best left to the dictates of the market. In the late 1970s the Carter administration took a more activist approach. But attitudes were reversed again in the early 1980s, when the Reagan administration decided that intervention should not be used to influence exchange rates, just to maintain "orderly market conditions" during times of crisis. At the same time, the Federal Reserve pursued a tough anti-inflationary policy, keeping U.S. interest rates high, and the administration adopted an expansionary fiscal policy, generating a large government budget deficit and a deficit on the current account. (This experience was analyzed in Chapter 14.) These circumstances conspired to produce a prolonged appreciation of the dollar during the early 1980s. The governments of the major industrial economies became convinced that exchange rates were seriously misaligned and that the misalignment was damaging their economies. In 1985 an international agreement for coordinated intervention signaled a reversal of the U.S. attitude against attempting to manage the exchange rate.

Target Zones and International Policy Coordination

At the Plaza Hotel in New York, the Group of Five (the United States, Japan, West Germany, Great Britain, and France) announced on September 22, 1985, a policy of coordinated intervention to depreciate the dollar. The announcement was clearly taken seriously by the markets, and subsequent monetary policy actions of the governments involved appeared supportive. The dollar began a prolonged decline, especially against the mark and yen.

By 1987 several governments had concluded that the decline had gone too far. Japan and Germany, concerned that the appreciation of their currencies was hurting their firms in world markets, intervened to support the dollar but to no avail. The United States, which had done little to deal with its budgetary deficit, was concerned about its continuing current-account deficit and urged a reluctant Germany and Japan to stimulate their economies. Fears arose that countries, working at cross purposes, were beginning to manipulate exchange rates for selfish ends, thereby running the risk of currency chaos. A new dose of international cooperation seemed to be needed. The United States began to intervene in support of European and Japanese attempts to support the dollar.

At the Louvre in Paris on February 22, 1987, officials from the Group of Six (the United States, Japan, West Germany, Great Britain, France, and Canada) agreed on a coordinated effort to support the dollar. Apparently, they did a lot more than this, establishing target zones for the yen-dollar and mark-dollar exchange rates, with 5 percent bands. But the target zones were not publicly announced. Many traders interpreted this as a lack of confidence by the governments on their ability to achieve the targets. If so, this lack was well placed since several months later the dollar depreciated outside of the zones. Later in the year, currency markets were further disrupted after the stock-market collapse in October. New target zones have apparently been negotiated since that time, but, once again, they have not been publicly announced.

European Monetary Integration

The target zones initiated by the Louvre agreement are, however, modest compared with what the European Union has been attempting to do. These attempts will be described in greater detail later in this book when we examine international economic integration. For present purposes, the important thing to know is that in 1979 the European Community established the European Monetary System (EMS), which involved pegging many of the European currencies to each other (that is, to the German mark). This worked reasonably well throughout the 1980s, so that attempts to manage the float of the mark relative to the dollar and yen in effect amounted to managing the float of much of Europe relative to the dollar and yen. But in the early 1990s the system ran into trouble, with Britain and Italy dropping out of the pegging arrangement and most other exchange rates being constrained only within huge 30 percent bands.

Overview

The world has not adopted formal rules for managed floating, and IMF surveillance has apparently not had substantial impact. But, despite disagreements and other incidents, the central banks of the industrial countries have not waged international currency war with each other. The sense of common interest in the system and the Bretton Woods legacy of international cooperation and consultation have thus far proved sufficient.

The major nations have worked with policy coordination and target zones: less formally in the Louvre accord, more formally in the EMS. The general experience seems to have been that these zones are maintained when it is to the advantage of all the participating nations and abandoned when this is not so. Perhaps this is the best we can reasonably hope for: a permanent, global system of target zones is not likely to work well when the incentives for international cooperation are subject to such change. The main disadvantage of the more ad hoc approach is that, when such incentives are weak, there is nothing formal to restrain national governments. But, thus far at least, this has not produced major problems.

7. SUMMARY

1. After the Second World War the international financial order, the Bretton Woods system, featured a modified gold-exchange standard in which countries maintained adjustable pegs vis-à-vis the U.S. dollar, while the United States undertook to exchange gold for dollars with foreign central banks at a fixed price. A new institution, the International Monetary Fund, was founded as part of the system.

2. The Bretton Woods arrangement was subjected to recurrent crises and finally collapsed in March 1973. The system was flawed by a contradiction, latent in an adjustable peg framework, between constant exchange rates, autonomous national macroeconomic policies, and international capital mobility.

3. The IMF articles have been amended to legalize present practices and to allow countries wide discretion in exchange practices. The major industrial countries basically have managed floats relative to each other, except for the adjustable pegs of the European Monetary System, while the majority of LDCs peg to a currency or to a basket of currencies.

4. Since the Plaza Hotel agreement of 1985, the major industrial nations have practiced intermittent coordinated intervention. Since the Louvre accord of 1987, this has involved (secret) target zones for the dollar/mark and dollar/yen rates.

SUGGESTED READING

Coombs, C. A. *The Arena of International Finance*. New York: Wiley, 1976. An insider's account of central-bank policy in the Bretton Woods years.

Cooper, R. N. "Currency Devaluation in Developing Countries." *Princeton Essays in International Finance* 86 (June 1971).

Destler, I. M., and C. R. Henning. *Dollar Politics: Exchange Rate Policymaking in the United States*. Washington: Institute for International Economics, 1989. Politics and exchange rates.

Dornbusch, R., and J. Frankel. "The Flexible Exchange Rate System: Experience and Alternatives." In *International Finance and Trade*. Edited by S. Borner. London: Macmillan, 1988. Experience with the managed float.

Gardner, R. N. *Sterling-Dollar Diplomacy*. 2d ed. New York: McGraw-Hill, 1969. The formation of the Bretton Woods system.

IMF. *The International Monetary Fund: Purposes, Structure and Activities*. A descriptive pamphlet available free of charge from the Fund.

————. "Supplement on the Fund." *IMF Survey,* annually in September. Useful descriptions of the Fund.

McKinnon, R. I. "Private and Official International Money: The Case for the Dollar." *Princeton Essays in International Finance* 74 (Apr. 1969).

Plumptre, A. F. W. "Exchange-Rate Policy: Experience with Canada's Floating Rate." *Princeton Essays in International Finance* 81 (June 1970).

Solomon, R. *The International Monetary System, 1945–1976: An Insider's View.* New York: Harper & Row, 1977.

Triffin, R. *Gold and the Dollar Crisis*. New Haven: Yale University Press, 1960. Triffin's diagnosis of the Bretton Woods system.

Williamson, J. *The Failure of World Monetary Reform, 1971–1974*. New York: New York University Press, 1977. A perceptive account of the negotiations accompanying the collapse of the Bretton Woods system.

Yeager, L. B. *International Monetary Relations: Theory, History, and Policy.* 2d ed. New York: Harper & Row, 1976. Chapters 19 through 32 give an excellent history of the Bretton Woods system.

Part Six

Open-Economy Macroeconomics

Thee are two ways to adjust to an international monetary disequilibrium. Such a disequilibrium will induce payments imbalances at the existing exchange rate. The authorities can allow exchange rates to adjust in response. This will alter the *values* of national money supplies to accommodate what is demanded and thereby prevent or eliminate the payments imbalances. Alternatively, the authorities can intervene to maintain the existing exchange rates and thereby alter the *supplies* of national monies to accommodate what is demanded. In the former case the individual countries are able to control independently their money supplies but must be prepared to suffer exchange-rate volatility. In the latter case the reverse holds. In practice, both methods are combined in various—and varying—ways. Part Five gave an overview of how all this works.

Now we apply a microscope to the critical element of this: the way in which monetary disequilibrium induces payments imbalances and the way in which exchange-rate variations can eliminate or prevent them.

There are three *channels of adjustment* through which this can happen. They involve adjustments, respectively, in *incomes, prices,* and *international capital movements.* Each receives its own chapter.

CHAPTER 17

Incomes and Adjustment

> For every problem, economists have an answer. Simple, neat and
> wrong.
> —H. L. MENCKEN

This chapter looks at incomes in the adjustment process. The economics of
John Maynard Keynes is central here.

1. BASIC INCOME-EXPENDITURE THEORY

We begin with a review of the elementary macroeconomics of a country
in autarky. To put matters in clear relief, suppose that prices remain fixed.
Thus we can speak unambiguously of the total output of all goods, or gross
national product. This will depend upon the extent to which the economy's
resources are actually employed.

Equilibrium

An economy is in equilibrium if the demand for the nation's output
equals supply. Let Y denote total national output of all goods (since relative
prices are fixed, they can be used to make the outputs of distinct goods, such
as apples and butane, commensurable). Then Y is both the supply of goods
and the level of national income. Demand has two components. First is the
demand for goods for consumption, denoted C. Consumption depends upon Y
because if output increases, then so does income and part of the increase will
be devoted to consumption. The second component, denoted I and called investment, is autonomous demand: private investment and government expenditure. Thus for supply to equal demand,

$$Y = C + I.$$

JOHN MAYNARD KEYNES (1883–1946)

The foremost economist of this century was, like John Stuart Mill, the son of an economist who, like Cantillon and Ricardo, made a fortune in financial speculation. After a brilliant career at King's College, Cambridge, Keynes joined the India office and, in addition, became a major figure in the Bloomsbury group (which included the literary figures Virginia and Leonard Woolf, the historian Lytton Strachey, and the art critic Roger Fry). He served in the Treasury during the First World War and was the Treasury's representative at the Versailles peace conference, which Taussig also attended. His denunciation of the settlement in *The Economic Consequences of the Peace* was an influential popular success. Between the wars, Keynes was a prominent critic of economic policy but, as a member of the minority Liberal party, removed from power. He also pursued many outside activities, continued his financial speculation, and conducted a prominent academic career at Cambridge. The latter culminated in *The General Theory of Employment, Interest and Money,* the classic work of the Keynesian revolution. During the Second World War he was an adviser to the government, and he negotiated with the United States over war finance and the structure of the postwar international monetary system.

This can also be written $Y - C = I$. Now $Y - C$ is that part of income not spent on consumption—that is, national savings and taxes, and so is denoted S. Then the equilibrium condition can also be expressed

$$S = I. \qquad (17.1)$$

In this form the condition says that total injections I (that is, expenditure not due to income) must exactly replace total leakages S. Equilibrium is depicted in Figure 17.1. Y_0 indicates the value of Y that solves Equation (17.1). Since I does not depend on Y, it is the horizontal line through A and B. The S curve, on the other hand, slopes up because part of an increase in income will normally be saved. The slope is called the *marginal propensity to save (MPS)*. Thus in Figure 17.1, $MPS = BC/AB$.

Thus far nothing has been said about full employment output—that is, the value that Y would have if all resources were employed at desired levels. If this is greater than Y_0, such as Y_1 in Figure 17.1, the economy must have unemployed resources. If, on the other hand, it is less than Y_0, the economy cannot actually produce Y_0, at least not for long, and inflationary pressures will build up.

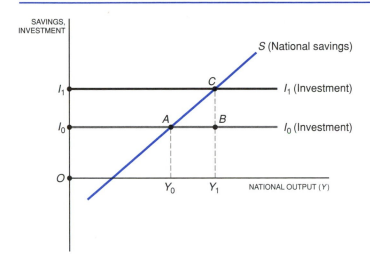

FIGURE 17.1 **Equilibrium National Output** The equilibrium level of national output is that which equates savings to investment.

KEY CONCEPT

The *marginal propensity to save* is the fraction of an additional unit of income that a country will save.

The Multiplier

Suppose now that I is increased in the amount $I_1 - I_0$ in Figure 17.1— that is, the I_0 line shifts to I_1. Then the intersection moves from A to C, and national output is increased by $Y_1 - Y_0$. Now from the figure it is apparent that $(I_1 - I_0)/(Y_1 - Y_0) = BC/AB = MPS$. Thus

$$Y_1 - Y_0 = \left(\frac{1}{MPS}\right)(I_1 - I_0).$$

The number $1/MPS$ is called the *multiplier* because the initial change in I is multiplied by it to find the resulting change in Y.

We can look at this in another way, less direct but more illuminating. Suppose that firms increase their investment in a new plant by $I_1 - I_0$. Then there will be a "first round" increase in Y in the amount $I_1 - I_0$ in order to meet this demand. Thus the total wages, profits, rents, and so forth increases by $I_1 - I_0$. Of this increased income, $(MPS)(I_1 - I_0)$ will be saved and the rest, $(1 - MPS)(I_1 - I_0)$, will be spent on consumption, giving rise to a "second round" demand for this much additional output. This, in turn, generates a

---

KEY CONCEPT

The *investment multiplier* is the amount by which a unit increase in investment will increase equilibrium national income.

"third round" demand in the amount $(1 - MPS)(1 - MPS)(I_1 - I_0)$, and so forth. The total demand for new output, including all successive rounds, is thus

$$Y_1 - Y_0 = (I_1 - I_0) + (1 - MPS)(I_1 - I_0) + (1 - MPS)^2(I_1 - I_0) + \ldots$$
$$= [1 + (1 - MPS) + (1 - MPS)^2 + \ldots](I_1 - I_0).$$

Now the term $[1 + (1 - MPS) + (1 - MPS)^2 + \ldots]$ is an example of a *geometric series* and equals $1/(1 - (1 - MPS)) = 1/MPS$, which is the multiplier.

Problems

17.1 Suppose in England that consumption equals 100 units plus three-fourths of the English income. What is the English multiplier? What is the English income if investment equals 200 units? How much does income increase if investment increases to 300? Answer this by the method of successive rounds, calculating the increase in income after 6 or 7 rounds.

17.2* We can investigate the *stability* of the equilibrium in Figure 17.1. Suppose that investment is OI_0 but that income is OY_1 so that saving exceeds investment. Since some output is not being sold, so we would expect firms to cut back production. This suggests the disequilibrium hypothesis: Y is falling when S exceeds I and rising when I exceeds S. Is the equilibrium in Figure 17.1 stable? Draw an unstable equilibrium. What is the stability condition?

---

2. THE DEMAND FOR IMPORTS

Suppose now that the autarkic economy begins to trade with the rest of the world. How do things change?

To answer this we need to describe the international environment. We can keep our discussion as close as possible to that of the preceding section by supposing initially that the following four assumptions are true.

1. The price of each good is fixed in terms of the currency of the country in which the good is produced. Thus the price of French apples is fixed in terms of francs, the price of German butane is fixed in terms of marks, and so on. This just extends to all countries the assumption made in the previous section for a single closed economy.

2. The authorities maintain a fixed exchange rate. This ensures that the prices of foreign goods also remain fixed in terms of domestic currency so that the prices of all goods are fixed in all countries.

3. There are no (nonofficial) international capital movements. Thus the balance of payments will coincide with the balance of trade (except if we wish to consider transfers).
4. The authorities in each country completely sterilize all payments imbalances. This implies that balance-of-payments deficits and surpluses will not have feedback effects on monetary conditions in any country.

These assumptions are chosen to focus our analysis and not for their realism. Assumption 2, as we have seen, is relevant to some countries and times but not to others. Assumption 3 enables us to abstract from international capital movements until we are ready to tackle them head on. Assumptions 1 and 4 make our analysis mainly a short-run one; these assumptions become more unrealistic the more time people have to respond to economic events.

Equilibrium

Equilibrium still requires that the demand for national output equal its supply or that total injections equal total leakages. Now exports constitute an injection of demand for domestic output just as does investment, and expenditure on imported goods constitutes a leakage from expenditure on domestic goods as does saving. Thus the equilibrium condition (17.1) must be revised to read

$$S + M = I + X. \qquad (17.2)$$

If trade is balanced—that is, if $X = M$—(17.2) is equivalent to (17.1) and the open-economy situation is just like the closed-economy one. But this is not so if there is a trade imbalance. Because of assumption (3), the *trade balance* $X - M$ also equals the balance-of-payments surplus.

Import Demand

What determines $X - M$? The demand for domestic exports is the same thing as the foreign demand for their imports. Thus we need know only what determines M—the same principles applied to the rest of the world will explain exports.

The demand for imports, like that for any good, depends upon prices and income. But prices are constant, so national income assumes the strategic role. Figure 17.2 depicts a curve showing the demand for imports at various levels of Y, if all other determinants (such as relative prices) do not change. The curve slopes up because as income increases consumption increases and part of the increase will normally be spent on foreign goods.

Propensities and Elasticity

The import curve is a crucial link between the domestic and foreign economies. Thus its properties are important. The term "average propensity

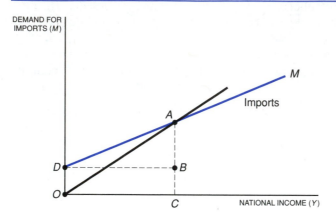

FIGURE 17.2   **The Demand for Imports**   With prices fixed, the national demand for imports is determined by national income.

to import" (*APM*) refers to *M/Y*. In Figure 17.2 the *APM* at point *A* is thus *AC/OC*. The *APM* at any point on the import curve is equal to the slope of a line through that point and the origin.

The "marginal propensity to import" (*MPM*) is the slope of the import curve. Thus at *A* in Figure 17.2 the *MPM* equals *AB/DB* (= *AB/OC*).

The "income elasticity of imports" (η) is the elasticity of the import curve; $\eta = MPM/APM$. Thus in Figure 17.2 the value of η at *A* is $(AB/OC)/(AC/OC) = AB/AC$.

KEY CONCEPT

The *average propensity to import* is the fraction of total national income that is spent on imports. The *marginal propensity to import* is the fraction of a unit increase in national income that would be spent on imports. The *income elasticity* of imports is the percentage by which the demand for imports would increase if national income increased by 1 percent.

Problems

17.3 Suppose that English imports always equal 50 units plus one-fourth of English income. Draw the English import function, and calculate *MPM, APM,* and η.

17.4 Portugal always spends one-half of its income on imports. Draw the Portuguese import curve, and calculate *MPM*, *APM*, and η.

3. *CASE STUDY:* MEXICO, FRANCE, AND OTHER COUNTRIES

Some examples can clarify the above concepts. The contrast between Mexico and France is instructive.

Mexico has a large, fairly underdeveloped economy, and so the foreign sector is not very large: in 1978 about 8 percent of Mexican gross domestic product was devoted to imports—that is, *APM* = .08. But these imports include capital goods, necessary for growth, and "luxury" consumer goods, the demand for which is sensitive to income. In 1978–1979 the increase in Mexican imports was 16 percent of the increase in income. If this is taken as indicative of the *MPM,* their *MPM* = .16 and η = .16/.08 = 2—that is, each percentage increase in Mexican income was accompanied by a 2 percent increase in imports.

France, on the other hand, is an open economy with more extensive trading relations. In 1977 the French *APM* = .19—that is, almost one-fifth of national income was spent on foreign goods. In 1977–1979 the increase in French imports was about 19 percent of the increase in French income. If this is taken as indicative of the French *MPM,* then *MPM* = .19 and η = .19/.19 = 1. Thus while the French *APM* is about two and one-half times as large as the Mexican, Mexico appears to have almost as large an *MPM* and a larger elasticity. It, therefore, appears more open on a marginal criterion. These properties are reflected in the curves in Figure 17.3.

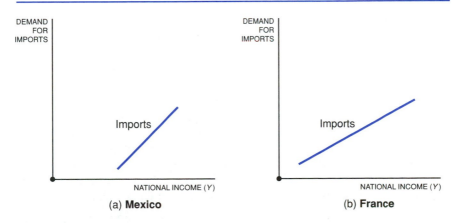

(a) **Mexico**   (b) **France**

FIGURE 17.3 Imports and Incomes Mexico's import curve is more elastic than France's, but it also shows a lower *APM* at low levels of national income.

TABLE 17.1   **French Imports and Income**

	1978	1979	Change from 1978–79
(1) Imports (billions of francs)	369	455	86
(2) Income (GNP in billions of francs)	2,140	2,445	305
(3) Imports at constant prices	369	411	42
(4) Income at constant prices	2,140	2,437	297
(5) (1) ÷ (2)	0.17	0.19	0.28
(6) (3) ÷ (4)	0.17	0.17	0.14

SOURCE: International Monetary Fund, *International Financial Statistics.*

Estimation

These back-of-the-envelope type of calculations are helpful in under-standing the concepts involved. But they should be used with care. There is no problem with the *APM:* one simply divides observed imports by observed income. But *MPM* and η are more difficult. They refer to import changes that would result from income changes with *other things constant.* Our calculations, however, involved actual changes during a period when other things, including relative prices, were indeed changing.

A good example of these difficulties is seen in Table 17.1, which shows the relevant data for France in 1978 and in 1979.

The oil-price rise in 1979 inflated the value of imports relative to income because the French import oil. Thus we see that the *APM* in 1979 was 0.19 if actual imports are divided by actual income, but 0.17 if the data are adjusted for the price changes. Which measure is correct? They *both* are. The *APM* depends upon the units of measurement, and the two numbers differ because these units have changed; with accurate price indices, either number can be converted to the other. If we now try to estimate the *MPM* as above by dividing observed import changes by observed income changes, the contrast is even greater; we obtain a value of 0.28 when actual data are used and 0.14 with price-deflated data. Which is correct? Neither. The first number is much larger than the second because the rise in oil prices inflated imports relative to income. But the relative price change caused the French to alter their spending patterns; the import curve shifted down. Thus both numbers reflect a combination of a shift in the curve with a movement along it; consequently, neither is a good indicator of the *MPM,* which refers only to the movement along the curve.

Some Estimates of Income Elasticities

A study by the economists H. S. Houthakker and S. P. Magee contained estimates of income elasticities. Several of these are presented in Table 17.2.

TABLE 17.2   Income Elasticities of the Demand for Merchandise Imports

Country	η
Australia	0.9
Japan	1.2
United States	1.7
United Kingdom	1.5
Canada	1.2

SOURCE: H. S. Houthakker and S. P. Magee, "Income and Price Elasticities in World Trade," *Review of Economics and Statistics* 2 (1969).

North American Experience

The United States has a large self-sufficient economy and, thus, a relatively low *APM*. Also, as the economy developed during the nineteenth and twentieth centuries, it became less dependent on foreign imports, so the *APM* tended to fall. From a value of 0.1 near the beginning of this century, it steadily declined to about 0.03 after the Second World War. But recent behavior has been different. The *APM* has been rising for some time and in 1993 was about 0.11. Note that the estimate of the U.S. income elasticity in Table 17.2 is above unity. This estimate is also the largest in the table, so that the United States seems open by this criterion, although the *APM* of 0.11 is relatively low.

Since we have looked at both Mexico and the United States, a few words about Canada will complete a cursory survey of North America. Canada, unlike the United States, did not become a relatively closed economy as it developed: in 1993, about 31 percent of Canadian GNP was spent on imports. The elasticity estimate in Table 17.2 is, however, less than that for the United States. But the estimate does exceed unity, and, indeed, the Canadian *APM* has tended to rise in recent years.

Problems

17.5 Describe the effect of each of the following on a country's import curve:
a The country imposes a tax on imports from abroad.
b The country's residents decide to save less, thereby boosting income and imports.
c The country establishes an import quota, prohibiting imports in excess of a certain amount, M_0.
d The rest of the world imposes a tax upon its imports from this country.

17.6 Using the 1993 U.S. *APM* of 0.11 and the estimate of the U.S. η shown in Table 17.2, calculate an estimate of the U.S. *MPM*. Calculate the actual increase in U.S. imports for 1993–1994 as a fraction of the actual U.S. increase in GNP (see Appendix II for data sources). Compare the two results. List all the reasons you can think of why they might differ from each other and from the true *MPM*. Do the same for Canada.

4. THE SIMPLE FOREIGN TRADE MULTIPLIER

Equilibrium

Let us now once again consider a country—say, France—trading with Germany. Using Equation (17.2), French equilibrium income is determined by

$$S + M = I + X. \tag{17.3}$$

Now French exports X are simply German imports, which depend upon German income. From the French point of view, German income is exogenous, and thus so is X. Therefore, the right-hand side of (17.3) is exogenous; the left-hand side depends upon Y. The equilibrium level of income is that which equates the left-hand side to the right-hand side. This is shown in Figure 17.4.

The parallel with Figure 17.1 should be obvious; the picture is the same, only the labels have been changed. The distance OD now represents the sum of investment and exports; and the upward-sloping line shows how savings plus imports depend upon income. Its slope, BC/AB, thus equals $MPS + MPM$. Equilibrium French income is DA, determined by the intersection of the two curves.

Foreign Trade Multiplier

Suppose that French investment plus exports increase, say, by the amount DE in Figure 17.4. This could be an increase in I, or in German imports, or any combination of the two. Then equilibrium moves from A to C, and French income increases by AB.

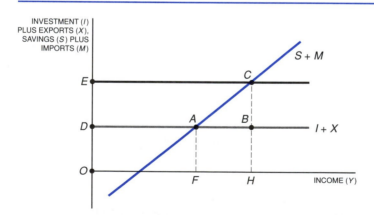

FIGURE 17.4 Equilibrium French Income   Equilibrium national income is that level which equates savings plus imports to investment plus exports.

Thus the increase in income AB is related to the increase DE in autonomous expenditure by

$$AB = \left(\frac{1}{MPS + MPM} \right) DE.$$

The term $1/(MPS + MPM)$ is called the foreign trade multiplier because it must be multiplied by the increase in autonomous expenditure to find the resulting increase in income.

KEY CONCEPT

The *foreign trade multiplier* is the amount by which the equilibrium national income of an open economy will be raised by a unit increase in investment or in exports.

A slightly different picture of equilibrium is also useful. Rearranging (17.3), we obtain

$$S - I = X - M. \qquad\qquad \textbf{(17.4)}$$

The left-hand side is the excess of saving over domestic investment; in a closed economy, it must be zero. The right-hand side is the *trade balance*, or excess of exports over imports. Each side of Equation (17.4) is graphed in Figure 17.5. $S - I$ has a positive slope because an increase in income raises S and leaves I untouched; $X - M$ slopes down because the income increase raises M but not X. Equilibrium is at point T. This graph has the advantage of explicitly showing the two major variables that are determined in equilibrium: national income (equal to OH here) and the trade balance (TH).

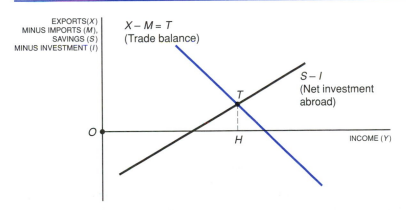

FIGURE 17.5 Equilibrium Income and the Trade Balance National income and the balance-of-trade surplus are jointly determined.

Several important conclusions emerge from our discussion of the foreign trade multiplier.

First, the multiplier is smaller than if the economy were closed because the denominator has increased by *MPM*. An increase in *I* will thus cause a smaller increase in income than if foreign trade were absent. This is because some of an increase in demand leaks onto foreign goods. This may not matter much for the United States, which spends only a small fraction of extra income on foreign goods, but it is crucial for an open economy such as Belgium, which spends over half its GNP on imports.

Second, the international sector now becomes another source of distur-

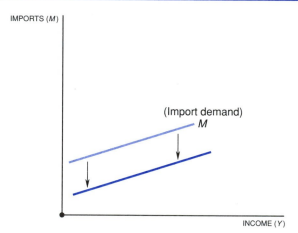

(a) **A reduction in import demand causes...**

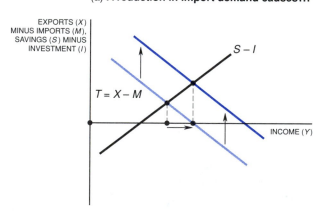

(b) **...an increase in national income**

FIGURE 17.6   A Shift in Import Demand   The downward shift of the *M* curve shown in panel (a) corresponds to the upward shift of the *X − M* curve in panel (b). This, in turn, causes a change in equilibrium that increases both national income and the trade-account surplus.

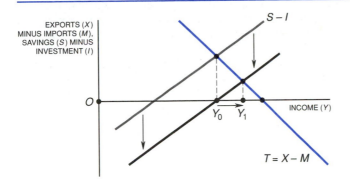

FIGURE 17.7   **An Increase in Investment**   An increase in investment shifts the $S - I$ curve down and thereby causes an increase in national income and a decline in the balance-of-trade surplus.

bances influencing income. An increase in exports causes the same multiplied increase in income as an increase in investment. Also national income can be influenced by changing import demand. The import curve can be shifted downward by tariffs, quotas, or other restrictions on the import of specific goods; with aggregate consumption unchanged, such measures switch demand from foreign goods to domestic goods. This is depicted in Figure 17.6(a). Then the exports-minus-imports curve will shift up by a like amount, producing the increase in national income depicted in Figure 17.6(b).

Third, policies that influence national income will also influence the trade balance, itself frequently a matter of concern for policy makers. Suppose the French increase I, causing income to rise from Y_0 to Y_1 in Figure 17.7. Then the trade balance falls, as the figure shows. Similarly, a reduction in I will increase the trade balance. The implication is that in making expenditure policy, the authorities will wish to consider its effects on the trade balance as well as on national output.

Problems

17.7 Use the method of successive rounds to derive the foreign trade multiplier.

17.8 Find the multiplier for England if consumption equals 100 units plus three-fourths of English income and if imports equal 50 units plus one-fourth of income. What is English income if investment equals 200 units and exports equal 100? If investment increases to 300? Suppose that investment remains at 200 but trade policy is used so that English imports now equal 40 plus one-fifth of English income; calculate the effect on income.

17.9 Suppose that the Portuguese always save one-quarter of their income and spend one-half on imports. Calculate the multiplier. What is Portuguese income if investment equals 50 and exports equal 100?

17.10 Calculate a formula for the term that must be multiplied by a change in I to obtain the effect on the trade balance $X - M$.

17.11 The discussion in the text assumed that autonomous expenditure was all devoted to domestic goods. Suppose instead that the fraction MPM of an increase in I is spent on imports. Calculate the formula for the multiplier in this case. How would your answer to Problem **17.10** change?

17.12 The discussion of trade policy assumed that the reduction in M for any Y was all spent on domestic goods—that is, that trade policy switched expenditure from foreign goods to domestic ones. Suppose instead that the income no longer spent on foreign goods is simply saved. How would trade policy affect income and the trade balance in this case?

5.* EXPLORING FURTHER: GENERAL EQUILIBRIUM

In this section we examine repercussions between two trading economies. The simple foreign trade multiplier expresses the direct link between the domestic and international economies. But there are indirect links as well. For example, an increase in French investment will cause a multiplied increase in French income, and this will increase imports as indicated by the French import curve. This increase in French imports is an increase in German exports, so there will also be an increase in German income as determined by the German foreign trade multiplier. Now the increase in German income will bring about an increase in German imports from France, which will induce a "second round" increase in French income. And so on through successive "rounds."

These repercussions reflect the fact that the French and German incomes are not independent, but are jointly determined. This is explicit in (17.5) and (17.6):

$$S^F + M^F = I^F + M^G \tag{17.5}$$

$$S^G + M^G = I^G + M^F \tag{17.6}$$

Expression (17.5) says that French income depends upon German income (through M^G) and (17.6) that German income depends upon French income (through M^F). Neither can be determined independently of the other.

To see how the two national incomes are jointly determined, we must first see how each depends on the other. Figure 17.8 shows how French income depends upon German income. Suppose German income equals Y_0^G, as shown on the vertical axis in Figure 17.8(b). Then this determines German imports from France, and the French equilibrium income is determined as in section 4. This is shown at point A in Figure 17.8(a) so that French income is Y_0^F. In other words, if German income is Y_0^G, then French income must be Y_0^F; this is recorded in Figure 17.8(b) at point B. Now if German income increases from Y_0^G, to Y_1^G, German imports from France will increase by MPM^G $(Y_1^G - Y_0^G)$. The intersection in Figure 17.8(a) then shifts from A to C, French income increasing from Y_0^F to Y_1^F. This is recorded in Figure 17.8(b) as a

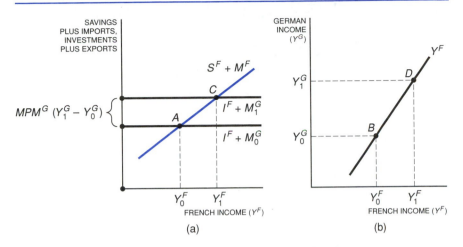

FIGURE 17.8 How French Income Depends upon German Income A rise in German income will increase French exports to Germany (a) and thereby increase French income as well (b).

movement from point B to D. By the foreign trade multiplier the increase in French income must be

$$(Y_1^F - Y_0^F) = \left(\frac{1}{MPS^F + MPM^F}\right) MPM^G (Y_1^G - Y_0^G).$$

The curve Y^F in Figure 17.8(b), then, shows what French income must be for each level of German income; it has a slope of $(MPS^F + MPM^F) / MPM^G$.

In similar fashion a curve Y^G can be derived showing what German income must be for each level of French income. This curve is depicted in Figure 17.9. To test yourself, show exactly how this curve is derived, and demonstrate that it must have a slope of $MPM^F/(MPM^G + MPS^G)$. The Y^F curve, then, shows all combinations of French and German incomes for which the demand for French output equals the supply, and the Y^G curve shows all combinations for which the demand for German output equals the supply. Equilibrium will be given at the intersection, point A, for only here will French and German incomes be mutually consistent.

Suppose now that there is an increase in French investment. Then for each value of German income, French income will increase by an amount equal to the change in investment times the simple French foreign trade multiplier, as discussed in section 4. This is depicted as the shift in the Y^F curve in Figure 17.10, and the "first round" increase in French income is given by the distance AB. This increases French imports from Germany, which then causes German income to increase in the amount BC. This increases German imports from France, thus inducing a "second round" increase in French income of CD. And so on. Final equilibrium is at E. Thus the increase in French invest-

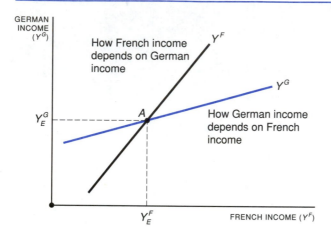

FIGURE 17.9 **General Equilibrium**   Since each country's income depends upon that of the other, equilibrium requires both to be mutually consistent, as at point *A*.

ment has caused an increase of *AF* in French income and an increase of *FE* in German income.

One can now calculate more complex multipliers giving the total effect (direct effect plus repercussions) of various disturbances on national incomes. For example, there are the four multipliers expressing the effect of a change in investment in each country on income in each country. And there are multipliers relating to a shift in import demand. The mind boggles at such vast

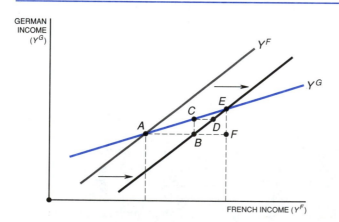

FIGURE 17.10 **Effects of an Increase in French Investment**   An increase in French investment shifts the French income curve to the right, causing equilibrium to move out along Germany's curve. Income rises in both countries.

opportunities for algebraic manipulation. But the purpose of this discussion is simply to emphasize the interdependence between income determination in the separate countries.

Problems

17.13 Show how the Y^G curve in Figure 17.9 is derived, and demonstrate that it must have a slope of $MPM^F/(MPM^G + MPS^G)$.

17.14 Using the method of successive rounds, derive the multiplier that relates changes in Y^F to changes in I^F when all repercussions are accounted for.

17.15 Using the method of successive rounds, derive the multiplier that relates changes in Y^F to changes in I^G when all repercussions are accounted for.

17.16 In England consumption equals 100 units plus three-fourths of GNP, and imports equal 50 units plus one-fourth of GNP. England trades with Portugal, where savings are one-fourth of GNP and imports are one-half of GNP. Calculate multipliers for each country. What is each country's GNP if English investment equals 200 units and Portuguese investment equals 50 units? Calculate the effects of each of the following:

    a an increase in English I to 300

    b an increase in Portuguese I to 100

    c a shift in the English import curve to 40 units plus one-fifth of GNP

Show how your answers illustrate the use of the formulas you derived in Problems **17.14** and **17.15**.

6. INCOME ADJUSTMENT

We now inquire into the implications, for the exchange rate and for the balance of payments, of the Keynesian theory of national income. We will start our discussion with the balance of payments and will continue to assume that the exchange rate is fixed. But then we will begin relaxing the assumptions listed in section 2.

The Balance of Payments

Figure 17.11 shows our initial full equilibrium. Income equals OE and $X - M = O$ so that there is no payments imbalance. Now consider a doubling of the money supply. The easier monetary conditions decrease $S - I$. Let us elaborate.

Recall that, in Chapters 14 and 15, the demand for money in an economy equaled the supply, G, when

$$G = k(i)Py, \tag{17.7}$$

where k denotes the amount of money residents wish to hold for each dollar's worth of income, P is the national price level, i is the rate of interest, and y is

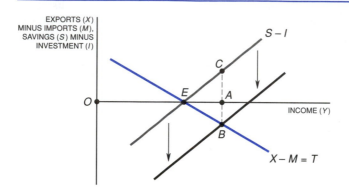

FIGURE 17.11 **Increase in Investment** An increase in the money supply lowers interest rates and so stimulates investment and depresses saving. The resulting downward shift in $S - I$ raises national income and reduces the trade surplus.

real national product. If G now doubles so that (17.7) ceases to hold, something has to give. It cannot be P because we continue to suppose that prices are rigid. So it must be either k or y.

One possibility is *dishoarding*. With an excess supply of money—that is, with the left-hand side of (17.7) greater than the right-hand side, residents begin to spend some of the excess on goods. In other words, savings, S, fall. When production begins to rise in response, y will increase, tending to bring (17.7) back to equality.

The second possibility involves investment. As we saw in Chapter 14, individuals can hold their wealth in the form of money or in other forms, such as real estate, equities, or bonds, that earn interest. The more interest that these other assets earn, the more reluctant will people be to tie their wealth up in the form of money: k will be negatively related to the rate of interest. If G increases, (17.7) can be brought back into equality by an appropriate rise in k. This will come about if the rate of interest falls. That is, when the authorities create more money, the rate of interest paid by other assets will be forced down to induce the public to hold the additional money.

The fall in the rate of interest will stimulate investment, I. This is because businesspeople finance their investment spending by borrowing (or by not lending extra funds). When the interest rate falls, it, therefore, becomes cheaper to borrow to invest. Some projects that would not be profitable when a firm has to borrow at 10 percent to finance them will become profitable if the interest rate falls to 5 percent.

In sum, the increase in the money supply will lower S and/or increase I. In Figure 17.11 the $S - I$ curve shifts down by the amount CB, producing a multiplied increase in income from E to A. As income increases, imports do likewise. There has been no increase in the foreign money supply and, accordingly, no stimulus to foreign $S - I$ so that domestic exports do not change. Thus we develop a balance-of-payments deficit of AB.

This is the same as Figure 17.7: monetary policy is just one form of expenditure policy. As long as the exchange rate remains fixed and the payments deficit is sterilized, this situation will continue. But now suppose the authorities become concerned about the loss of international reserves. They can change the exchange rate and/or they can cease sterilizing. Consider the latter possibility. That is, we now drop assumption 4 and suppose that the balance-of-payments deficit is not sterilized. Then the automatic adjustment process is off and running.

As the deficit continues, the consequent flow of money abroad tightens monetary conditions at home and loosens them abroad. This erodes the initial stimulus to domestic income and begins to stimulate income abroad, reducing the payments imbalance. The payments imbalances cease when the world reaches the new equilibrium. Both home and foreign incomes have now increased in the same proportion as the world's money supply.

Now we consider the role of exchange-rate changes. Suppose that the authorities, instead of ceasing to sterilize the balance-of-payments deficit, attempt to reduce it by a depreciation of the currency. That is, we now relax assumption 2. Suppose that, in Figure 17.12, France has a payments deficit of *AE* and that the franc now depreciates relative to the mark.

Because of assumption 1, the price of French goods is unchanged in terms of francs, and the price of German goods is unchanged in terms of marks. But the depreciation of the franc implies that more francs are required to buy a mark. Thus the price of German goods *rises* in terms of francs. French buyers switch from German goods to French goods: *M* falls. Also the price of French goods *falls* in terms of marks. German buyers also switch from German goods to French goods: *X* rises. Thus depreciation shifts the

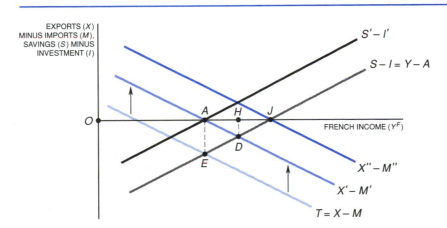

FIGURE 17.12 Depreciation and National Income Depreciation makes domestic goods more competitive with foreign goods and so shifts $X - M$ up. This increases the balance-of-trade surplus, but it also stimulates national income, which in turn stimulates imports and so limits the increase in the trade surplus.

$X - M$ curve up; this is shown by the shift to $X' - M'$ in the figure. At unchanged income, the depreciation is just sufficient to eliminate the initial trade deficit, AE. But income increases by AH, and consequently the trade deficit is merely reduced, from AE to HD. A larger depreciation—one sufficient to shift $X - M$ all the way to $X'' - M''$—is needed to eliminate the payments deficit entirely. In such a case the new equilibrium is at J.

   If the authorities do not intervene at all, a *floating exchange rate* will adjust to prevent payments imbalances from developing. Suppose, for example, the French economy is initially at A, the intersection of $S' - I'$ and $X' - M'$. Now suppose that an expansionary French expenditure policy shifts $S' - I'$ to $S - I$. With a fixed exchange rate the new equilibrium would be at D, and a French balance-of-payments deficit of HD would emerge. But a floating exchange rate adjusts to prevent this: the franc depreciates enough so that $X' - M'$ shifts to $X'' - M''$, and equilibrium moves from A to J. The payments deficit remains equal to zero, but French national income rises by AJ.

The Absorption Approach

   The initial level of employment is important for the success of depreciation in generating a trade surplus or preventing a deficit. If resources are initially fully employed, there is no way for the economy to produce the additional exports made possible by a rise in R, the price of foreign money. The following point of view is instructive.

   The balance-of-trade surplus B is by definition the excess of exports over imports:

$$B = \text{exports} - \text{imports}. \qquad (17.8)$$

In addition to exports the economy also produces goods that it does not export, but uses itself. Since the quantity of such goods that is produced coincides with the quantity that is used, we can rewrite (17.8) as

$$B = (\text{exports} + \text{production of goods not exported}) - \\ (\text{imports} + \text{use of goods not imported}). \qquad (17.9)$$

The first term on the right, exports + production of goods not exported, necessarily equals the total production of goods, or income, denoted Y. The second term, imports + use of goods not imported, is the total quantity of goods used by the economy. This total is often called *absorption* and denoted A. Then (17.9) can also be written

$$B = Y - A. \qquad (17.10)$$

   This identity is just another way of writing (17.8), but it is useful because it looks in another way at the balance of trade, which it describes in macroeconomic terms. Expression (17.10) makes clear the basic point that the trade balance B can be increased only by increasing Y or reducing absorption A. If the economy is at full employment to begin with so that Y cannot be further increased, then it is necessary to reduce A in order to increase B. A rise in p that merely *switches* expenditure from foreign goods toward domestic goods will be ineffective because a *reduction* in expenditure, or absorption, is what is called for.

This reduction in absorption could be brought about in other ways, such as restrictive monetary and fiscal policies. Or the depreciation could itself reduce A. For example, the increase in R could raise p and so switch expenditure toward domestic goods. With the home economy already at full employment, it would be impossible to supply the additional demand for domestic goods. This could force their price up—that is, generate domestic inflation. This inflation would increase the demand for money above the supply, as indicated by (17.7), and thereby cause domestic residents to accumulate additional money by cutting back expenditure—that is, by lowering A. As (17.10) reveals, this will improve the balance of trade.

At this point we are relaxing assumption 1 and allowing prices in each country to respond to macroeconomic conditions there. Suppose, for example, the economy was initially fully employed at point E in Figure 17.12, before depreciation shifted $X - M$ to $X' - M'$. Then income cannot be raised by AH, and the upward shift in $X - M$, therefore, produces an excess demand for domestic goods in the amount AE. This forces domestic prices up, making domestic goods more expensive relative to foreign goods and shifting the $X - M$ schedule back down. This continues until the $X - M$ line returns to its original position: depreciation has had no effect on the trade balance and has only raised prices. Elimination of the trade deficit requires $Y - A$ also to shift up. If both schedules shift as indicated in Figure 17.12, their new intersection is at A, where the deficit has been eliminated and income is unchanged.

Problems

17.17 How does the discussion of Figure 17.11 in the text change if the home country is so small that the flow of money abroad brought about by the home balance-of-payments deficit has no significant effect on the rest of the world? Show the final equilibrium in Figure 17.11.

17.18 Suppose that domestic residents suddenly decide to save more than before at each level of income. Discuss the consequences. Do the same if domestic goods become more attractive to foreigners so that exports rise.

17.19 Suppose the French suddenly acquire an enhanced taste for German goods. Analyze how the exchange rate must adjust to maintain balance-of-payments equilibrium.

17.20 Suppose that a country is initially at full employment and levies a tariff. Discuss the effects on the balance of trade and on aggregate demand, at the initial exchange rate. How must the exchange rate be altered to keep the balance of trade unchanged?

17.21 Does it matter whether the axes in Figure 17.12 are measured in terms of domestic currency or foreign currency? Why?

17.22* Must the discussion of Figure 17.12 be altered if the demand for imports is price-inelastic?

7.* *EXPLORING FURTHER: IS-LM* ANALYSIS IN AN OPEN ECONOMY

Many readers will have learned about *IS* and *LM* curves while studying macroeconomics. The same tools can be used to analyze an open economy.

To make things simple, focus on a country relatively small in that its behavior has only a negligible effect on foreign prices, interest rates, and incomes, which we take as fixed. For the home country to be in equilibrium, two conditions must be met: the demand for the country's output must equal its supply and the country's demand for money must equal the supply. Each condition is described by a separate curve, which we examine one at a time. A third curve describes circumstances under which the balance of trade is zero.

The *IS* Curve

This curve shows the combinations of output (y) and the rate of interest (i) for which the demand and supply of the country's output are equal. The curve corresponds to a given price level. The demand for national output will equal the supply when $X - M = S - I$; this is illustrated in Figure 17.13(a). Now exports X are just foreign imports, and these are determined by prices and foreign incomes, which are fixed; thus X is fixed. But autonomous spending I includes investment, which depends upon the rate of interest i: low values of i will cause firms to invest more because the cost of borrowing to finance investment is low. Autonomous spending also includes government expenditures, which we can denote g. So autonomous spending $I = I(i, g)$, which simply means that I is determined by i and by g. Presumably, I is increased by decreases in i and by increases in g.

The trade balance $T = X - M$ depends on home income y and the price of foreign goods relative to home goods: $RP^*/P = p$, where R is the exchange rate, P^* is the foreign price level, and P is the domestic price level. Foreign income y^* also matters, but we are taking that as fixed. Thus $T = T(p, y)$, which simply means that T is determined by p and by y. Presumably, T is increased by increases in p and by decreases in y. The condition that the demand for domestic output equal the supply can thus be written

$$S(y) - I(i, g) = T(p, y). \qquad \textbf{(IS)}$$

Suppose that i is equal to the distance OA in Figure 17.13(b). This determines the level of investment—call it I_A—and, therefore, the position of the

$S - I_A$ curve, which is drawn in panel (a). Thus y will equal OF, marked off in each panel, and point C in panel (b) is a combination of i and y for which the demand and supply of home output are equal. Suppose that the interest rate were to fall—say, to OB. This would cause domestic investment to rise—say, by the amount DE in panel (a). Thus y rises by the amount FH, indicated in both panels. Point D in the latter is accordingly another combination of r and y for which the demand and supply of output are equal. The IS curve is the collection of all points, such as C and D, for which this is true. We have just demonstrated that this curve has a negative slope.

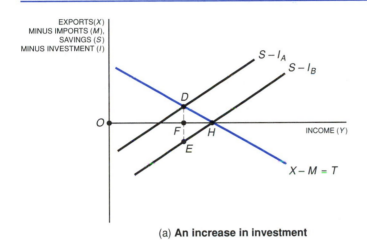

(a) **An increase in investment**

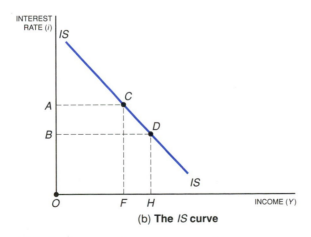

(b) **The *IS* curve**

FIGURE 7.13 **Derivation of the *IS* Curve** The *IS* curve shows combinations of the interest rate and national income for which aggregate demand is in equilibrium. Its position depends upon the price level and the exchange rate.

The *IS* curve is drawn for a specific domestic price level and a specific exchange rate. Thus a change in either will *shift* the curve. Suppose domestic prices fall. This makes domestic goods more competitive relative to foreign goods and so increases the demand for domestic output: $X - M$ shifts up in Figure 17.13(a). Thus for any level of investment I (that is, for any values of i and of g), the equilibrium y increases: the *IS* curve shifts to the right. Analogously, a rise in domestic prices shifts the *IS* curve to the left.

The *LM* Curve

This curve shows the combinations of output (y) and the rate of interest (i) for which the country's demand for money equals the supply:

$$G = k(i)Py. \tag{LM}$$

The curve corresponds to a given level of the country's money supply as well as a given level of the country's prices. Higher levels of income require more money for transactions. Thus an increase in y increases the demand for money. If i goes up, people would sacrifice more interest income by holding their wealth in the form of money, which earns no interest, rather than in the form of assets that do earn interest. Thus they would be more tempted to economize on money holdings: an increase in i reduces the demand for money, so an increase in i would lower the value of k. Suppose that at point C

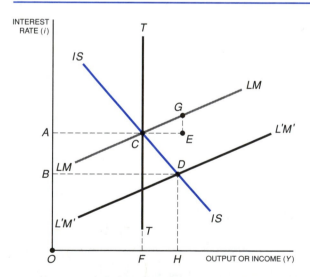

FIGURE 17.14   *IS-LM* Analysis   In full equilibrium the commodity market is in equilibrium (*IS*), the money market is in equilibrium (*LM*), and there is no payments imbalance (*T*).

in Figure 17.14 the demand for money is equal to the supply. If y increases but i remains unchanged, as in a move from C to E, the demand for money will rise and, therefore, exceed the fixed supply. To make demand once again equal to supply, and thereby to get back on the LM curve, the rate of interest must rise. This is illustrated by the movement from E to G. The LM curve consists of all points, such as C and G, for which the demand for money equals the given supply; as we have just demonstrated, the curve has a positive slope.

The LM curve is drawn for a specific domestic money supply and a specific domestic price level. A change in either will shift the curve. Suppose, for example, that the domestic money supply increases. Then the demand for money must rise in order to equal the supply once again. Since a rise in y and/or a fall in i will increase the demand for money, the LM curve must shift downward and to the right.

The *T* Curve

$$T(p, y) = 0. \tag{T}$$

This curve shows the combinations of y and i for which the balance of trade is in neither surplus nor deficit. The curve corresponds to a given level of p. An increase in y will increase imports and decrease the balance-of-trade surplus, while a change in i has no effect. Thus T is vertical, and points to the right of it correspond to trade deficits, points to the left to trade surpluses.

Monetary Expansion, Fiscal Expansion, and Exchange Depreciation

To see *IS-LM* analysis in action, suppose the domestic money supply is suddenly increased. This will shift the LM curve downward and to the right— say, to the curve $L'M'$. The new equilibrium is at D. Since D is to the right of the T curve, there is a balance-of-trade deficit. Thus Figure 17.14 illustrates in comprehensive fashion the effects of the monetary disturbance.

A fiscal expansion is an increase in g. This increases I, shifting the IS curve up and moving equilibrium along the LM curve. This is not shown: you should draw it yourself. If you do so correctly, you will see that i rises, y rises, and equilibrium moves to the right of the T curve, implying a balance-of-trade deficit.

Now consider the effects of a depreciation of the exchange rate. Suppose that the economy is initially at point A in Figure 17.15 and that the trade balance equals zero. Consider a once-and-for-all depreciation of the domestic currency. This increases p and so shifts the IS curve to the right, to $I'S'$ in the figure, so that equilibrium moves from A to B. Depreciation thus increases national income. The rise in p also shifts the T curve to the right so that B is to the left of it: the trade account is now in surplus. The increase in y tends to limit the improvement in the trade balance, but it does not reverse it.

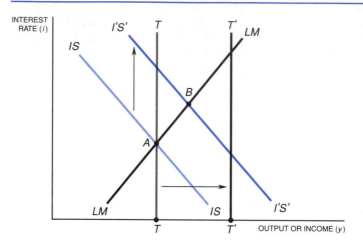

FIGURE 17.15 **Exchange Depreciation** Depreciation shifts the *IS* and *T* curves. Short-run equilibrium is on the *IS* and *LM* curves and so not on *T*, implying a balance-of-trade surplus.

Problems

17.23 How does a rise in the domestic price level affect the *LM* curve?

17.24 How is each of the curves affected by a rise in the foreign price level?

17.25 Analyze the effects of a permanent improvement in the terms of trade (due, say, to a shift in tastes from foreign goods toward domestic goods).

17.26 Analyze the effects of a more expansionary fiscal policy with a fixed exchange rate and with a floating rate.

17.27 Use *IS-LM* analysis to discuss the effects of an increase in the money supply with complete sterilization of all payments imbalances.

17.28 Analyze in detail the effects of an increase in the domestic money supply if the authorities adjust the exchange rate to prevent a balance-of-payments deficit.

17.29 The discussion in the text on the long-run consequences of depreciation assumed that the money supply remained constant—that is, that all payments imbalances were completely sterilized. How must the discussion change if there is no sterilization at all?

8. SUMMARY

1. The Keynesian multiplier in an open economy is reduced by the propensity of expenditure to leak abroad onto foreign goods.

2. Variations in exports supply an additional source of autonomous disturbances.

3. Imports constitute an additional source of leakage from income to expenditure.

4. In an open economy, autonomous changes in home spending affect foreign demand, and autonomous changes in foreign spending affect home demand.

SUGGESTED READING

Alexander, S. "Effects of a Devaluation on a Trade Balance." In *Readings in International Economics*. Edited by R. E. Caves and H. G. Johnson. Homewood: Irwin, 1968. The absorption, or income, approach.

Branson, W. H. "Causes of Appreciation and Volatility of the Dollar." In *The U.S. Dollar—Recent Developments, Outlook, and Policy Options*. Kansas City: The Federal Reserve Bank of Kansas City, 1985. U.S. experience in the early 1980s.

Dornbusch, R. "Exchange Rate Economics: Where Do We Stand?" *Brookings Papers on Economic Activity* (1980): 143–206. A useful statement and discussion.

———. *Open Economy Macroeconomics*. New York: Basic Books, 1980. See in particular Chapters 9, and 11 through 14.

Goldstein, M., and M. S. Khan. "Income and Price Effects in International Trade." In *Handbook of International Economics.* Vol. 2. Edited by R. W. Jones and P. B. Kenen. Amsterdam: North Holland, 1985. Estimates of the income elasticity of import demand.

Helliwell, J. F., and T. Padmore. "Empirical Studies of Macroeconomic Interdependence." In *Handbook of International Economics*. Vol. 2. Edited by R. W. Jones and P. B. Kenen. Amsterdam: North Holland, 1985.

Meade, J. E. *The Balance of Payments*. London: Oxford University Press, 1951. See Parts 2 and 3.

CHAPTER **18**

Prices and Adjustment

In the long run we are all dead.

—JOHN MAYNARD KEYNES

The previous chapter introduced relative price changes when we interpreted exchange depreciation—that is, a rise in R, as an increase in p, the price of foreign goods relative to domestic goods. This chapter examines the role of price changes in greater depth. There are two sources of influence on price formation in an open economy: domestic macroeconomic conditions and price linkages with the rest of the world. We will first look at each source, which reveals three distinct ways in which price changes influence international adjustment. We will then look at each in turn.

1. THE AGGREGATE DEMAND CURVE

Assumption 1 from Chapter 17, that prices are fixed in each country, is not unreasonable in the short run. Many prices are stipulated in contracts, and firms often find it costly or inconvenient to change prices. But eventually contracts will expire and can be renegotiated; the longer firms allow their prices to remain out of line, the more costly it becomes *not* to change them. Thus, with a longer-run perspective, assumption 1 becomes less realistic.

IRVING FISHER (1867–1947)

The greatest American economist thus far spent his career on the faculty of Yale University, where he had done (brilliantly) both his undergraduate and graduate studies, though he did take three years off around the turn of the century to recuperate from tuberculosis, which had earlier killed his father, a minister. Fisher was instrumental in introducing mathematical methods to economic theory and to empirical economics. He made fundamental contributions to the development of general equilibrium, the theory of capital and interest, monetary theory, macroeconomics, and the theory and use of index numbers. Price adjustment was central to all this. But Fisher was no doubt much better known to the public for his views on the stock market: he announced, just before the 1929 crash, that stock prices had reached a permanently high plateau. Unfortunately, he had put his money where his mouth was, losing a fortune (which he had acquired by an invention).

Instead, we would expect price changes to respond, eventually, to the state of aggregate demand. When demand for a country's products is high relative to the country's productive capacity, firms can sell all they want and know that they can get away with price rises. Workers know that firms are anxious to employ them so they demand higher wages, which firms are more likely to grant, believing they can pass along the higher labor costs by raising prices. Thus high aggregate demand will eventually put upward pressure on prices and wages in a country. By analogy, low aggregate demand will eventually generate downward pressure.

An aggregate demand curve shows what the aggregate demand for a country's output will be at each value of that country's price index. Figure 18.1 shows the aggregate demand curve for the French economy that we have been illustrating in Figures 17.11 and 17.12. Figure 17.11 was drawn, you will recall, on the assumption that prices were fixed, as was the exchange rate. Suppose that the fixed price level was P^0, which is depicted in Figure 18.1. Initial equilibrium was at point E in Figure 17.11, so that French aggregate demand was OE. This distance is reproduced as OE in Figure 18.1. This gives us point D on the aggregate demand curve; it shows that the aggregate demand for French goods will be OE when the French price level is P^0.

To find the other points on the aggregate demand curve we need to know what demand will be at other price levels. Suppose, for example, that the French price level is the lower one indicated by P' in Figure 18.1. To deduce what aggregate demand will now be, we need to find out how Figure 17.11 responds to the change in price levels. This will be easy if we first divide both sides of Equation (17.7) by the price level, P:

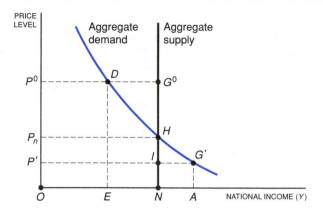

FIGURE 18.1 **Macroeconomic Equilibrium** At any value of the national price index, national income is given by the corresponding point on the aggregate demand curve. If this is not also on the aggregate supply curve, prices will sooner or later begin to change.

$$\frac{G}{P} = k(i)y. \qquad (18.1)$$

Equation (18.1) says that the supply of *real balances, G/P,* should equal the demand for them. The supply of real balances is simply the money supply deflated by the price level. Now it is obvious from (18.1) that a fall in the price level, *P,* must have the same effects as a rise in the money supply, *G.* If prices fall 10 percent, each dollar is worth 10 percent more in real terms; it is the same as if there were 10 percent more money.

This means that a fall in the price level can be analyzed in the same way as we earlier analyzed an increase in the money supply. That is, the $S - I$ curve shifts down, as in Figure 17.11. Equilibrium moves from E to B so that aggregate demand increases.

A fall in the price level produces an additional effect in an open economy. With the exchange rate and foreign prices held constant, domestic goods become cheaper in world markets relative to foreign goods. This is exactly what happened in the previous chapter when the exchange rate depreciated. Thus the $X - M$ curve shifts up, just as in Figure 17.12. Again, aggregate demand increases.

The fall in the price level thus raises aggregate demand for two reasons. The total increase is recorded in Figure 18.1, which gives point G' on the aggregate demand curve. In this way we can deduce what aggregate demand will be at each price level and trace out the entire curve. The curve must slope down, as shown in the figure, because, as we have seen, a fall in the price level stimulates aggregate demand.

Macroeconomic Equilibrium

The distance *ON* in Figure 18.1 measures what national income would be if all of the country's resources were employed to the desired degree. This determines the vertical aggregate supply curve. The intersection of these two curves, at *H,* is the long-run equilibrium corresponding to the macroeconomic policies and the exchange rate reflected in the aggregate demand curve. If the price level is P_n, aggregate demand will be *ON* and there will be no pressure on the price level to change.

At the higher price level P^0 aggregate demand is given by *D* so that national income is only *OE*. This leaves a *deflationary gap* of DG^0 between what the economy is producing and what it can produce. As long as prices remain rigid, the economy stays at *D;* eventually, however, the depressed conditions will put downward pressure on prices. Prices will fall and output will rise as the economy gradually moves down the aggregate demand curve from *D* toward *H*.

At the lower price level *P'* aggregate demand is given by *G'* so that there is an *inflationary gap* of *IG'*. If the economy is capable of producing at most *ON,* then that will be national income. But perhaps the economy can, for a while at least, produce more by having laborers work overtime, by using equipment more intensively than recommended, and so on. If so, national income will be *OA* or something between *ON* and *OA*. As long as prices remain rigid, the economy stays there, but the boom conditions will put upward pressure on prices. Prices will rise, as the economy moves up along the aggregate demand curve from *G'* toward *H*. Output will also gradually fall, if it was above *ON*.

Expenditure Policy and the Exchange Rate

We can test our understanding of the aggregate demand curve by using it to repeat the previous chapter's discussions of the effects of a change in expenditure policy and of a change in the exchange rate. Since the aggregate demand curve was derived for a given expenditure policy and a given exchange rate, a change in either will shift the curve.

Panel (a) of Figure 18.2 shows the effect of a more expansionary expenditure policy such as an increase in the money supply. We know that, at a given price level, such a policy will be expansionary—that is, the aggregate demand curve shifts right. Suppose that the economy was originally at *A*. In the classical world of the automatic adjustment process, examined in Chapter 15, output remains at the full employment level and prices are flexible. The economy, therefore, moves from *A* to *C*. If trade was initially balanced, the higher domestic price level now causes a balance-of-payments deficit. If the deficit is not sterilized, money flows out of the economy, the aggregate demand curve begins to shift back to the left, and the economy gradually moves back down from *C* to *A*. The balance-of-payments deficit ultimately evaporates when prices have returned to the initial level.

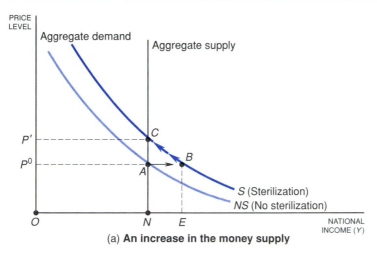

(a) **An increase in the money supply**

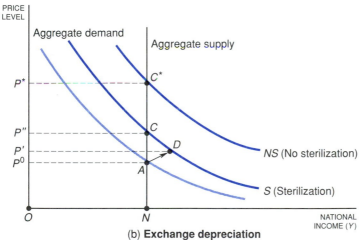

(b) **Exchange depreciation**

FIGURE 18.2 Shifts in Aggregate Demand An increase in the money supply shifts the aggregate demand curve to the right; equilibrium moves from *A* to *B* in panel (a). A depreciation of the exchange rate likewise shifts the aggregate demand curve to the right but also raises the price level; equilibrium moves from *A* to *D* in panel (b). In each panel, *S* indicates the long-run aggregate demand curve with sterilization and *NS* the curve with no sterilization.

The Keynesian world is different. With prices rigid, equilibrium moves instead from *A* to *B*. If the economy can produce the extra output, income increases by *NE*. A balance-of-payments deficit will emerge; but if it is sterilized, it will have no effect on the aggregate demand curve. Sooner or later, prices begin to rise in response to the high demand. The economy moves along the aggregate demand curve from *B* toward *C*, with prices rising and output falling. If the authorities find it impossible or inadvisable to continue completely sterilizing the payments deficit, the resulting fall in the money supply will shift the aggregate demand curve down.

Panel (b) shows what happens if, instead of increasing the money supply, the authorities depreciate the exchange rate. At a given price level, depreciation is expansionary, so the aggregate demand curve again shifts to the right. But with foreign prices also rigid, the depreciation of the currency makes foreign goods more expensive in terms of domestic currency. Since import prices are part of the price index, depreciation must also raise the price index directly. Thus it moves from P^0 to P' in the figure. The net result of the depreciation is, therefore, to move the economy from A to D. If trade was initially in balance at A, the country has a payments surplus at D. Sterilization of this surplus will prevent the aggregate demand curve from drifting even more to the right.

Sooner or later, the boom conditions will cause prices to begin to rise, and the economy will begin moving toward C. Prices rise, and output falls. Eventually, the economy reaches C, where output is back to the predepreciation level. The balance-of-trade surplus is still positive. The depressing effect of the higher price level and the stimulative effect of the trade balance just offset each other so that aggregate demand at C is the same as at A.

If the authorities cease to sterilize the payments surplus, the resulting increase in the money supply will begin shifting the aggregate demand curve toward the right, eventually producing more price rises. This does not come to an end until the domestic price rise has just matched the amount of depreciation so that domestic goods lose their competitive advantage and the trade surplus disappears. Thus the long-run equilibrium, without sterilization, is at C^*, and the price level is P^*. The payments surplus, while it lasted, will have increased the domestic money supply in the same proportion as the depreciation; thus the increased price level and increased money supply just offset each other in their effects on aggregate demand.

Inflationary Pressures in the International Economy

We have used the aggregate demand curve to describe how inflationary pressures are generated in an open economy. We can now summarize what we have learned and extend it to consider explicit interactions between countries. Figure 18.3 shows possible states of aggregate demand in France and Germany, given the exchange rate and expenditure policies in both countries. N^F shows the level of French aggregate demand corresponding to the intersection of the French aggregate demand and aggregate supply curves, and N^G does the same for Germany. Thus if the world is at N in the figure, no pressure will develop on the price index of either country. The line labeled OT shows positions where the pressure on French prices is the same as on German prices. Thus if outputs in the two countries remain at a point on OT below N, eventually the French and German price levels will begin to fall together, so they will not change *relative* to each other. Above N they both rise together.

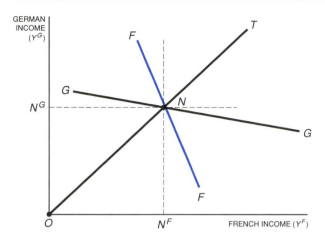

FIGURE 18.3 Inflation in the Open Economy   Along *FF* there is no pressure on the French price level to change, along *GG* there is no pressure on the German price level, and *OT* shows combinations of demand where the pressure on French prices is the same as on German prices.

At points above the *OT* line German prices will eventually begin to rise faster than French prices, and below the line the opposite is the case.

Each country's price index depends in part on import prices and so is sensitive to aggregate demand conditions abroad as well as at home. The line labeled *FF* shows all positions where there is no pressure on the French price level, and *GG* does the same for Germany. If the economies were completely closed so that each price level was oblivious to foreign conditions, *FF* would be the vertical line through *N* and *GG* would be the horizontal one. If, instead, the two economies were completely integrated so that they shared the same price index, *FF* and *GG* would coincide. To the right of *FF*, the French price level will eventually begin to rise, and to the left it will eventually begin to fall. The German price index will eventually rise if the world stays above *GG*, and it will eventually fall if the world stays below.

Problems

18.1 Use the aggregate demand curve to discuss the effects of a fall in the price of oil, assuming a fixed exchange rate. How does your analysis change with a floating rate? In each case discuss how monetary policy might be used to respond to the price fall.

18.2 What happens to the balance-of-trade surplus as we move down and to the right along a country's aggregate demand curve? Explain your answer.

18.3 The three lines in Figure 18.3 divide the plane into six regions. Describe how the economy will behave in each of these regions.

2. INTERNATIONAL PRICE LINKAGES

The previous section discussed how a country's price level is sensitive to macroeconomic conditions in that country. But prices in an open economy are subject also to a second, distinct, influence: international price linkages. These arise because firms are aware, when they set their prices, that they are competing with foreign firms and so must take the prices charged by those firms into account.

Suppose, for example, that aggregate demand is high and a country has an inflationary gap. We argued above that sooner or later inflation would begin to accelerate in such a case as firms realized they could raise prices and pass on wage increases. But if these home firms are competing with foreign firms who produce in a country without an inflationary gap, they will realize that price increases will mean lost sales. The home firms will be more reluctant to raise prices and more resistant to wage demands than they would be without the foreign competition. Or suppose that the dollar depreciates sharply against the yen, as it did in 1993. Since the depreciation raises the dollar price of Japanese cars, U.S. auto producers will have more freedom to

---

The Law of One Price

If the exchange rate is initially Fr 2 per mark and if German firms sell butane for DM 100, butane sells for Fr 200 in France and thereby competes on equal terms with butane sold by French producers for Fr 200. If the franc depreciates by 50 percent so that Fr 3 are now required to buy a mark, the German butane will sell for Fr 300 in France. There is no reason why anyone should buy German butane at this price when identical French butane can be had for Fr 200. Thus French firms can raise their prices, and German firms must lower theirs. A reduction in German prices to DM 75 and an increase in French prices to Fr 225 would restore equality. This is an example of the *Law of One Price:* within a single market identical goods must sell at identical prices.

A related but more demanding proposition is that the relative price of *different* goods is determined by real considerations independently of the exchange rate. In the above example, suppose that France also produces apples that are sold in the French market for Fr 400 per bushel. Thus 2 units of butane initially sell at the same price as 1 bushel of apples. Now suppose, as above, that the franc depreciates and that the price of 1 unit of butane rises to Fr 225. Thus apples have become cheaper relative to butane so that buyers will tend to shift their purchases from butane toward apples, and firms will tend to do the opposite with their production. This puts upward pressure on apple prices and downward pressure on the prices of (both French and German) butane. If the price of apples rises to Fr 450, the predepreciation relative prices will be restored.

raise the prices of their own competing products. And Japanese firms will be under pressure to accept a *lower* yen price to prevent the dollar price from rising too much.

Suppose that the prices of Japanese goods, in yen, are rising at 2 percent per year and that the dollar is depreciating relative to the yen at an annual rate of 3 percent. Then, in terms of dollars, the prices of Japanese goods are rising at 5 percent. Thus if the dollar prices of U.S. goods also rise at a 5 percent rate, the relative price of Japanese and U.S. goods will not change—they will both rise at 5 percent in terms of dollars and at 2 percent in terms of yen.

The key step in this chain of reasoning is the idea that relative prices can be fixed (by nonmonetary considerations) so that the depreciation of the dollar equals the difference between the rise in the U.S. price level and the rise in the Japanese price level. The proposition that the depreciation of a nation's currency is equal to the difference between the rise in that nation's price level and the rise in foreign prices is known as *purchasing power parity* (*PPP*). If this holds, the purchasing power of domestic currency remains constant relative to the purchasing power of foreign currency; hence the term *purchasing power parity.*

KEY CONCEPT

A currency maintains its purchasing power parity if it depreciates by an amount equal to the excess of domestic inflation over foreign inflation:

(PPP) (depreciation) = (domestic inflation) − (foreign inflation)

It is important to realize that *PPP* relates exchange rates and price levels without saying anything about cause and effect. The inflation rate in a large country like the United States is probably due mainly (but not entirely) to internal considerations, so that on balance changes in U.S. inflation tend to influence depreciation of the dollar rather than vice versa. For small countries the reverse is much more true. In general, inflation and depreciation are interdependent and jointly determined.

Note that when the exchange rate does not vary (if it is fixed or pegged, for example), *PPP* asserts that inflation rates are equal across countries. Inflationary pressure originating in one country is dissipated throughout the world by the competitive nature of international markets.

At bottom, *PPP* asserts that relative prices are determined independently of macroeconomic conditions so that international price linkages force changes in inflation rates and exchange rates to cancel out. This is a proposition that need not hold in reality. There are two fundamental ways it might fail. The first is simply that relative prices might need to change. Resources, technology, and preferences can all alter and influence equilibrium relative prices. *PPP* will have to fail if relative national price levels are to adjust. A second basic reason for the possible failure of *PPP* is that international price linkages might be weak. In fact, some prices are more sensitive to international competition than are others. It is useful to classify goods into three categories for this purpose.

1. *Standardized, Internationally Traded Goods.* This category includes goods that enter into international trade and for which one firm's product is virtually indistinguishable from that of another firm: raw materials, intermediate goods such as steel and chemicals, and so forth. The tendency toward *PPP* is strongest for these goods, with the Law of One Price most compelling. If a certain chemical produced by a U.S. firm is identical to the same chemical produced by a British firm, why should any customer buy from a more expensive source? A depreciation of the pound relative to the dollar will result in great pressure on the U.S. firm to lower its dollar price so as not to lose all its customers to the British rival. If the latter is initially operating at full capacity and thus unable to accept more customers, it will be sorely tempted to raise its pound price and expand profits.

2. *Differentiated, Internationally Traded Goods.* In some cases, such as many consumer goods, the products of competing firms are viewed as distinct by purchasers. An increase in the price of a German Audi automobile relative to a French Peugeot, for example, will cause the former to lose some customers to the latter, but certainly not all potential Audi buyers will switch. Many will be content to pay a higher price for the characteristics unique to the now more expensive product. A depreciation of the franc relative to the mark, then, while putting some pressure on Peugeot to raise prices and on Audi to lower them, would be unlikely to result in the same strong tendency toward *PPP* as with standardized traded goods.

3. *Nontraded Goods and Services.* Many goods and especially services do not compete in international markets at all and, therefore, need display no direct tendency toward *PPP*. A barber in Brockton, Massachusetts, will not be unduly concerned to learn that a depreciation of the pound has made haircuts in Bristol, England, relatively cheaper.

With the Law of One Price treated as a law for some goods, a mere guideline for other goods, and irrelevant to yet others, *PPP* is necessarily inexact. It also depends on our time horizon: the more time firms have to adjust to changes, the more completely they will do so. These points are illustrated by a hypothetical example in Table 18.1.

Each row of the table shows the behavior of a particular price index over time. The first column is what we suppose the situation to be before a hypothetical 50 percent depreciation of the dollar. (This depreciation is shown in the first row of the table.) Suppose initially that the average price of each of the three types of U.S. goods is $100 and that the dollar prices of foreign goods competing in world markets with U.S. traded goods are also $100. (No foreign goods compete with nontraded U.S. goods.) The U.S. price index is an average of the prices of the three types of U.S. goods, weighted equally for

TABLE 18.1 **Hypothetical Responses to a 50 Percent Depreciation of the Dollar *[Real exchange rate = 100 × (price of foreign currency) ÷ (U.S. price index)]***

	Before the depreciation	Short-run response	Medium-run response	Long-run response
Price of foreign currency	$1.00	$1.50	$1.50	$1.50
Standardized traded goods				
U.S.	100	150	150	150
Foreign	100	150	150	150
Differentiated traded goods				
U.S.	100	125	139	150
Foreign	100	150	150	150
Nontraded goods				
U.S.	100	100	125	150
U.S. price index	100	125	138	150
Real exchange rate	1.00	1.20	1.09	1.00
Price of traded goods relative to nontraded	1.00	1.44	1.18	1.00

illustration, and so is also initially $100. The *real exchange rate* adjusts the exchange rate for inflation; initially it is 1.00.

Now the 50 percent depreciation of the dollar occurs: the price of a unit of foreign currency rises from $1.00 to $1.50 and stays there. Suppose that foreign firms do not react at all and never change the foreign-currency prices of their goods. This simplifies matters and allows us to focus on U.S. responses. It implies that the dollar prices of foreign goods rise to $150 and remain there.

How do the various U.S. firms react? First, producers of standardized traded goods observe that the prices of foreign competing products are now 50 percent higher in international markets. Thus they can raise their own prices by 50 percent without losing customers. If the markets are competitive, they have no incentive to raise prices by less since they can sell what they want by meeting the going price. So the price of U.S. standardized traded goods also rises to $150. This is the Law of One Price at work. The $50 price rise all goes into fattening profit margins since costs have not changed.

Next, producers of differentiated traded goods also observe the price of competing foreign products rising to $150. This presents them with a choice: they can either raise their own prices, thereby enlarging profit margins, or they can refrain from doing so, thereby luring customers from foreign competitors.

Most likely they will try a little of both, and Table 18.1 shows them raising prices to $125, implying a $25 increase in profit margins and a $25 price advantage over the competition. The Law of One Price is a little wobbly here.

Finally, U.S. producers of nontraded goods observe no direct effect from the depreciation. They have no reason to adjust prices at all.

The overall price index of U.S. goods increases to $125. With a 50 percent depreciation, a 25 percent home inflation, and no foreign inflation, *PPP* has not held but there has been a tendency in that direction. This is reflected in the real exchange rate, which has depreciated by 20 percent. If *PPP* had held exactly, the real exchange rate would have remained at 1.00; if there had been no tendency toward *PPP,* the real exchange rate would have depreciated just as much as the nominal exchange rate, 50 percent.

Notice that the depreciation of the dollar has caused three types of U.S. price changes. First, there has been U.S. *inflation,* with the price level rising. This will cause the economy to move up and to the left along its aggregate demand curve. Next, there has been a fall in the *price of U.S. traded goods relative to foreign goods.* This should shift world demand from foreign goods toward U.S. goods, shifting the aggregate demand curve to the right. Finally, there has also been a rise in the *price of traded goods relative to nontraded goods,* as shown in the bottom row of the table. This should cause U.S. consumers to shift demand from traded to nontraded goods. Also, U.S. producers, observing profit margins, will want to shift production from nontraded goods to traded goods. *(Note: the relative price of traded goods in terms of nontraded goods is often called the "real exchange rate"; we use that term for the exchange rate deflated by the national price index.)*

We have not yet reached the end of the story. Labor unions and other suppliers of productive inputs have experienced a rise in the cost of living and have observed the swelling of firms' profit margins. Wages, and production costs generally, will begin to rise. Suppose they rise enough to cover the full 25 percent increase in the U.S. price index. Producers of nontraded goods will pass these increases on to their customers: these firms compete only with other firms experiencing the same rise in costs. Thus the third column shows the price of nontraded goods rising to $125. But producers of traded goods will find themselves in a bind. A firm producing standardized traded goods, for example, experiences the 25 percent rise in costs but must hold its price to $150, or its customers will desert it for foreign rivals. Thus this firm has no choice but to absorb the entire cost increase in lower profit margins. Producers of differentiated traded goods do have some room for maneuver. The table shows them raising prices to $139, thereby losing some sales and also experiencing an $11 shrinkage in profit margins. The Law of One Price is becoming more effective, with the prices of U.S. goods moving closer to those of foreign goods. The real exchange rate has begun to appreciate back to where it started.

But costs have still not kept pace with prices since the price index is now $138. Thus wages and other costs will continue rising. This will eventually bring about the long-run situation described in the fourth column. Here, the Law of One Price reigns supreme: both types of U.S. traded goods sell for the same price as their foreign counterparts. Also, *PPP* holds: the real exchange rate is back to its initial value of 1.00. Note in addition that only one of the three types of price changes remains: U.S. inflation. Both relative price changes have been reversed eventually.

Thus far we have looked at exchange-rate changes, but the discussion is relevant to any disturbance that threatens to alter prices in one country relative to those in another. For example, suppose that an expansionary monetary policy ignites home inflation, putting upward pressure on costs and prices. Producers of standardized traded goods will be unable to follow suit and will have to watch their profit margins shrink as costs rise. Producers of differentiated traded goods will pass along some of the cost increase in the form of higher prices, and producers of nontraded goods will be able to pass it all along.

How important is *PPP* in reality? Table 18.2 summarizes the recent experience of several countries.

The first column of the table shows the total percentage change in each country's price level between 1985 and 1990 minus the change in the U.S. price level. Thus Canadian prices rose 3 percent more than did U.S. prices in this period, and Japanese prices rose 15 percent less. The second column shows the total depreciation of each country's currency relative to the U.S. dollar. If *PPP* held exactly, the two columns would be identical. This is certainly not the case, though there are significant tendencies in this direction. The smallest inflators, Japan and Germany, experienced the sharpest appreciations. But, on the other hand, there are substantial differences between depreciations and inflation differentials for all the countries. The table shows that these indications differ from country to country, and further examples

TABLE 18.2   **Relative Inflation Rates and Depreciation, 1985–1990**

Country	(1) National inflation less U.S. inflation	(2) Depreciation relative to U.S. dollar	(3) National inflation less German inflation	(4) Depreciation relative to German mark
Australia	25	−34	39	−5
Canada	3	−17	17	22
France	−5	−32	9	7
Germany	−14	−39	0	0
Italy	10	−33	24	6
Japan	−15	−33	−1	6
Korea	9	−20	22	19
United Kingdom	12	−25	26	14
United States	0	0	14	39

SOURCE: International Monetary Fund, *International Financial Statistics*.

would show that they also differ substantially from year to year. The table shows the dollar depreciating against most currencies during 1985–1990, even after allowing for differences in inflation. But before 1986 the dollar had appreciated sharply relative to many of these same countries: extending the table back would make a large difference. Columns (3) and (4), which show a similar calculation for Germany, appear much closer to *PPP* for a majority of the countries in the table. Overall, there are ample indications of both *PPP* and departures from *PPP*.

As part of the International Comparison Project, an extensive effort to render key economic variables comparable across countries, Irving Kravis of the University of Pennsylvania and Robert Lipsey of Queens College made detailed investigations of price behavior. They found departures from *PPP* to be more marked for nontraded goods than for traded goods, but violations of the Law of One Price were extensive and remained significant even when great care was taken to compare actual prices of goods as identical as possible. Other researchers have obtained similar results. This suggests a wide relevance for our discussion of differentiated internationally traded goods. Kravis and Lipsey also found evidence that exchange depreciation tends to lower the prices of nontraded goods relative to traded goods and to lower the prices of domestically produced goods relative to foreign goods.

Table 18.3 examines the U.S. exchange-rate experience in greater detail. The seven rows show how seven different measures of the dollar's exchange rate performed during the 1980s. To facilitate comparison, each measure is scaled to have an average value of 100 during 1980, the base year.

The first four rows show *bilateral* exchange rates of the dollar relative to the currencies of Canada, Japan, and West Germany, three major trading partners of the United States, and South Korea, an important newly industrializing country. Thus the number of Canadian dollars that could have been bought, on average, for US$100.0 during 1980 cost only US$97.6, on average, during 1981. The U.S. dollar appreciated by about 2.4 percent relative to the Canadian dollar during 1980–1981.

TABLE 18.3 **The U.S. Dollar in the 1980s *(period averages)***

	1980	1981	1983	1985	1986	1988	1990
Canadian $	100	97.6	94.9	85.7	84.2	95.1	100.3
Japanese ¥	100	102.8	95.5	95.1	134.5	175.8	156.2
West German DM	100	80.6	71.4	61.9	83.6	103.1	112.2
South Korean W	100	98.2	78.3	69.8	68.9	83.0	85.8
EFFECTIVE	100	91.2	79.4	71.4	89.0	108.3	109.8
REAL	100	88.9	79.3	74.0	93.6	119.0	128.7
MERM	100	88.7	75.1	66.6	77.4	92.1	88.9

SOURCES: International Monetary Fund, *International Financial Statistics;* Morgan Guaranty Trust Company, *World Financial Markets.*

The table shows a steady appreciation of the U.S. dollar relative to the Canadian dollar through 1986. Relative to the Japanese yen, the dollar appreciated sharply early in the 1980s, held steady for several years, and then depreciated even more sharply. Relative to the German mark, there was an early sharp appreciation, followed by several years of steady appreciation, and then followed by a depreciation that, though dramatic, did not restore the 1980 position in 1986, but had done so by 1988. There was also a sharp initial appreciation, followed by several years of steady appreciation, relative to the Korean won, but in this case the subsequent turnaround had not restored the initial position by 1990.

The bottom three rows of Table 18.3 show the behavior of different overall, or *average,* measures of the dollar's exchange value. The *effective* exchange rate is a weighted average of the dollar value of fifteen other currencies, with each weight proportional to the volume of trade between the United States and the respective country. This shows that the dollar, on average, appreciated sharply early in the 1980s, experienced a steady appreciation for several years, and then depreciated sharply. Note that the effective exchange rate is always within the range of values of the four bilateral rates.

The *real* exchange rate is a weighted average of bilateral rates, like the effective exchange rate, but in this case each of the bilateral rates is adjusted for the difference in inflation in the United States and in the respective country. Thus it corresponds to the real exchange rate in Table 18.1. If *PPP* held exactly between the United States and each of the other fifteen countries whose currencies contributed to the average, the real exchange rate would have remained constant at 100. Clearly, it did not do that. Indeed, during 1980–1983 the real rate appreciated more than the effective rate, indicating that, on average, inflation differentials were accentuating the effects of exchange-rate changes rather than moderating them. This appreciation must have produced strong relative price effects. But then *PPP* began to assert itself, and by 1986 the effective dollar appreciation of 11 percent translated into a real appreciation of 6.4 percent. Inflation differentials neutralized almost a half of the appreciation, on average. Then, when the dollar reversed course in 1986–1990, we again see indications of strong relative price effects.

When we calculate a weighted average of bilateral exchange rates, we choose weights in the light of the purpose the average is supposed to serve. The effective and real rates in Table 18.3 used bilateral trade flows—the most common practice—in order to obtain averages that would indicate the importance of exchange-rate changes for the international trade of the United States. But for this purpose we can be more ambitious than merely to use bilateral trade. The dollar-yen rate, for example, affects the U.S. trade position not merely because it affects the U.S. trade balance with Japan, but also because it affects U.S. trade with other countries where U.S. exporters compete with Japanese firms. Also, some large bilateral trade flows may not be sensitive to changes in exchange rates. An alternative to using bilateral trade flows as weights is to estimate empirically the responses of the U.S. balance of trade to changes in individual exchange rates, and to base the weights upon those estimates. This is how the third average in Table 18.3, the MERM rate, was calculated. (The name derives from the fact that the weights used were obtained from the *Multilateral Exchange Rate Model,* constructed by the International Monetary Fund.)

One might expect that the real and effective rates would place relatively more weight on the Canadian dollar because of the very large volume of U.S.-Canadian trade and that the MERM rate would give more emphasis to the yen and mark since Germany and Japan compete with the United States as sellers of manufactures. It is interesting to note that the MERM rate appreciated even more strongly, during 1980–1985, than did the real rate. On the other hand, the depreciation of the MERM rate in the latter part of the period is clearly weaker than that of the real rate even though it is the yen and mark that are appreciating and not the Canadian dollar.

Problems

18.4 What will Table 18.1 look like if the initial disturbance is cost inflation in the United States rather than a depreciation of the dollar? That is, suppose that initially all prices are $100 and both exchange rates are $1.00, and that the price of foreign currency remains $1.00 throughout. Instead, an increase in the U.S. money supply, for example, causes a 50 percent rise in all wages and costs, but there is no similar change abroad. Indicate the responses, and explain your answer.

18.5 In Table 18.3, calculate the 1986 average values of four bilateral exchange rates for South Korea. Calculate the South Korean effective exchange rate, using the following weights: yen, 50 percent; U.S. dollar, 30 percent; deutsche mark, 10 percent; Canadian dollar, 10 percent. Using data in Table 18.2 to approximate inflation differentials, calculate the South Korean real exchange rate.

18.6 This section discussed changes in three types of price indices: the overall price index; the price of home-produced traded goods relative to foreign goods; and the price of traded goods relative to nontraded goods. On the basis of Table 18.3, speculate how each of these behaved in the United States during 1980–1990.

3. RELATIVE PRICE ADJUSTMENT: THE ELASTICITY APPROACH

The previous section identified several different types of price changes in an open economy. It is easier to examine separately their roles in international adjustment. We start with changes in the price of home-produced traded goods relative to foreign goods since section 1 has already said something about their effects. This section elaborates.

The Marshall-Lerner Condition

Consider first the effects of depreciation. In order to concentrate on relative price changes, suppose that all firms hold their prices fixed in terms of their own currency. Thus, in terms of a common currency, all home-produced goods become cheaper relative to all foreign-produced goods—there is no tendency toward purchasing power parity. With home goods now more attractive to purchasers than foreign goods, the $X - M$ curve will shift up, and the aggregate demand curve will shift to the right. What determines how big these shifts are?

The balance-of-trade surplus, measured in home currency, equals $P_h X - RP_f M$, where P_h is the domestic currency price of (home-produced) exports and P_f is the foreign currency price of (foreign-produced) imports. We are supposing that neither of these changes. The depreciation is an increase in R, and this produces a rise in X and a fall in M. The net effect on the trade balance depends on the size of these three changes.

Consider a 1 percent depreciation—that is, a 1 percent rise in R. By itself, this *worsens* the trade balance since it increases the cost of what we are importing by 1 percent. But it also causes the volume of those imports to decline. By how much? That depends on how responsive our demand for imports is to a change in the relative price of those imports. This responsiveness is measured by the *elasticity of import demand,* denoted e. Formally, e is defined as the percentage fall in import demand resulting from a 1 percent rise in the relative price of imports. A 1 percent depreciation therefore reduces the volume of imports by e percent but increases the cost by 1 percent. Thus the total reduction in spending on imports is $e - 1$ percent.

KEY CONCEPT

The *elasticity of import demand* is the percentage increase in the demand for imports resulting from a 1 percent decline in their relative price.

Depreciation also affects export receipts, $P_h X$. The price is not changing, but the volume X is. Our exports are the rest of the world's imports, and the depreciation makes those imports relatively cheaper in the rest of the world. If e^* denotes the foreign elasticity of import demand, a 1 percent depreciation will increase foreign demand for imports—and, therefore, our exports—by e^* percent.

Thus a depreciation of 1 percent increases export receipts by e^* percent and reduces import payments by $e - 1$ percent. The total improvement in the balance of trade is the sum of these two effects, and so it is proportional to $e^* + e - 1$.

The larger the elasticities e and e^*, the greater the impact of depreciation—that is, the greater the shift in the $X - M$ and aggregate demand curves. If $e + e^*$ is not much greater than 1, depreciation will have a negligible effect. Indeed, if import demand in the two countries is so inelastic that $e + e^*$ is less than unity, depreciation will actually worsen the balance of trade. The increase in X and the reduction in M are too anemic to compensate for the fact that it takes more of a depreciated home currency to buy the original assortment of imports.

That price elasticities are crucial should not be surprising. Since we are investigating the role of relative price changes, the sensitivity of the world economy to those changes must be important, and elasticities measure that sensitivity. The Marshall-Lerner condition, $e + e^* > 1$, tells us how much sensitivity is required.

KEY CONCEPT

A reduction in the price of home-produced traded goods relative to foreign goods will increase the balance-of-trade surplus if the *Marshall-Lerner condition* is satisfied:

$$e + e^* > 1.$$

We have been looking at depreciation, but elasticities play a similar role with regard to other disturbances. Suppose, for example, that an increase in the home money supply causes home prices to rise and that the exchange rate remains fixed. Again, we have a violation of purchasing power parity, with home-traded goods rising in price relative to foreign goods. If the Marshall-Lerner condition holds, this will cause the trade balance to deteriorate—that is, the $X - M$ curve will shift down.

The Aggregate Demand Curve with a Floating Exchange Rate

The downward slope of the aggregate demand curve reflects the fact that, at a given exchange rate and foreign price level, a decline in the home price level will stimulate aggregate demand. But, as we saw in section 1, the effect on the trade balance is ambiguous: higher aggregate demand tends to worsen the balance while the reduction in home prices relative to foreign prices tends to improve it. Price elasticities are crucial here. If the Marshall-Lerner condition fails, the relative price change will also tend to worsen the trade balance, so $X - M$ must fall as we move down the aggregate demand curve. But if the price elasticities, e and e^*, are large enough, the relative price change will be sufficiently powerful to ensure that $X - M$ rises as we move down the curve. That is, a movement down and to the right along an aggregate demand curve corresponds to an increase in the balance-of-trade surplus if price elasticities are sufficiently large and to a decrease if they are small.

The aggregate demand curve in Figure 18.1 was derived for a specific value of the exchange rate. Variations in that rate shift the curve. We can also derive an aggregate demand curve for a country with a *floating exchange rate* that always adjusts to keep the balance-of-trade deficit equal to zero. This is done in Figure 18.4.

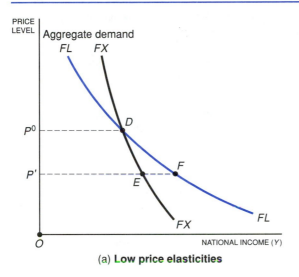

(a) **Low price elasticities**

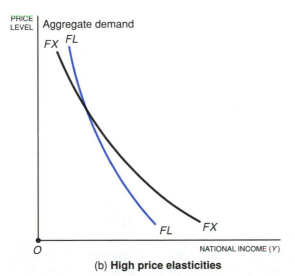

(b) **High price elasticities**

FIGURE 18.4 The Aggregate Demand Curve with a Floating Exchange Rate
FL denotes the aggregate demand curve with a floating exchange rate and *FX* that with a fixed rate. When elasticities are low, *FX* is steeper than *FL* because, with a fixed rate, part of the increase in aggregate demand induced by a price decline leaks into imports. With low elasticities the increase in aggregate demand is magnified by an increase in net exports.

The curve labeled FX in each panel is the aggregate demand curve corresponding to some specified value of the exchange rate. This is the same curve as in Figure 18.1. In panel (a), price elasticities are small, so moving down this curve causes the balance-of-trade surplus to fall. Suppose that it reaches zero at D, when the price level is P^0. Then D must also be on the aggregate demand curve corresponding to a floating exchange rate. Now consider the lower price level P'. If this lower price level is attained with the same exchange rate as at D, the corresponding level of aggregate demand is that given by E on the FX curve. But E must involve a balance-of-trade deficit since it is lower on FX than D, where the deficit is zero. Thus for the deficit to remain zero, P' must involve an exchange rate depreciated relative to that at D. This will stimulate the economy; so F, where the balance of payments is zero at the price level P', must lie to the right of E. Finding all such points for all price levels traces out FL—the aggregate demand curve with a floating exchange rate.

In panel (b), elasticities are large, so that reducing P generates a trade surplus if the exchange rate remains fixed. Then a zero deficit will require an appreciated currency with less aggregate demand. In this case FL must be steeper than FX.

Both FX and FL are drawn for a particular expenditure policy. A change in that policy, such as a monetary expansion, will shift both curves. Along FX the exchange rate is fixed, but the balance of payments varies; a change in the exchange rate will shift the curve. Along FL the balance of payments is fixed (at zero), but the exchange rate varies; a change in the balance of payments will shift the curve.

The *J* Curve

As we saw in the previous section, the U.S. dollar experienced a sharp depreciation in 1985–1990, and this depreciation was not offset, to a large degree, by inflation differentials. But the balance-of-trade deficit continued to widen, and in the 1990s observers were still waiting for the promised turnaround. What happened?

Our discussion in this section suggests two possibilities. One is that, even though foreign price *levels* appear not to have fallen much relative to U.S. prices, the foreign *relative* price of traded goods might have fallen. That is, perhaps the basic assumption of this section did not hold. There were in fact indications that foreign exporters did allow their foreign currency prices to decline along with the dollar, in part and for a while. But this does not seem to have been pervasive enough to offer a full explanation (and even if it were, it would not imply that depreciation should not have improved the balance of trade, only that it would not have done so in the manner discussed in this section).

A second possibility is low elasticity. If the Marshall-Lerner condition did not hold, depreciation would have been expected to worsen the trade balance, not improve it. Some economists are pessimistic that elasticities are large enough for powerful relative price effects, but the evidence does not indicate that they are low enough for the Marshall-Lerner condition to fail. And this is not suggested by experience during the first half of the 1980s, when the dollar appreciated.

In fact it is typical for a depreciation to cause the trade deficit to widen initially and then to narrow after some delay. This is known as the *J curve* effect since a graph of the trade surplus will resemble a *J* if this happens. We saw that a depreciation causes quantity effects (raising X and lowering M) and a value effect (raising the domestic currency cost of imports). In practice the value effect, which worsens the trade balance, is likely to occur before the quantity effects, which are where the improvement comes from. This is because contracts that were signed before the depreciation will determine what trade actually takes place for some time thereafter. More often than not, these contracts are denominated in the currency of the exporter.

Consider, for example, a depreciation of the U.S. dollar. The goods exported from the United States will, for some time, be those that were ordered before the depreciation. With the prices of these goods set in dollars at the time they were ordered, export receipts will not immediately respond to the depreciation. Imports are also goods ordered before, but the prices of many of these will have been set in terms of foreign currency. Thus their *dollar* cost rises as soon as the dollar depreciates. Only after some time passes and new contracts are signed will X and M begin to respond to the change in the exchange rate. There will be even more delays if it is inconvenient or otherwise costly to change sources of supply or to acquire customers, for then businesspeople will wait to see whether the depreciation is permanent before they do anything.

Problems

18.7 When the California gold rush began, the prices of ordinary consumer goods and services were driven to very high levels in the mining regions. After a while these prices fell to more normal levels. Discuss this phenomenon in terms of the automatic adjustment process.

18.8 Suppose that Italy's income is 10,000 olives, Spain's is 4,000 goats, the equilibrium terms of trade equal 2 olives per goat, and $k = 2$. Initially, Spain's money supply is 80,000 gold coins, and Italy's is 100,000 gold coins. Whenever the relative price of goats in terms of olives increases by 1 olive, the Spanish respond by increasing their imports from Italy by 1,800 olives and the Italians purchase 900 fewer goats from Spain. Suppose that the Spanish money supply increases by 72,000 gold coins. Describe in detail the resulting adjustment.

18.9 Suppose, again, that Italy produces 10,000 olives, Spain 4,000 goats, 2 olives exchange for 1 goat in equilibrium, $k = 2$, and Spain's money supply consists of 80,000 pesetas and Italy's of 100,000 lire. Suppose that the peseta depreciates by one-half of its equilibrium value and that the lira price of olives and the peseta price of goats are unchanged. What happens?

18.10 Chapter 15's discussion of the price-specie flow mechanism assumed that the demand for money in each country is proportional to that country's *production* of goods. Sometimes it is argued instead that money demand is proportional to *demand* for a country's goods. Can you think of any reason for one to be the case rather than the other? To see what difference it makes, suppose that each country consumes only the other country's products—that is, the French consume only butane and the Germans only apples. Then French demand for money will be proportional to (py^G) rather than to y^F, and German money demand will be proportional to (y^F/p) instead of to y^G. What difference does this make to the automatic adjustment process?

18.11 Use the aggregate demand curve to discuss the effects of an increase in the money supply with a floating exchange rate.

18.12* The text pointed out that a 1 percent depreciation increased export receipts by $e*$ percent and reduced import expenses by $e - 1$ percent. These were then added to conclude that the total improvement in the trade balance would be proportional to $e + e* - 1$. Actually, this addition gives only an approximation that becomes less accurate the larger the initial trade imbalance. Why is this? Derive the true expression.

4.* *EXPLORING FURTHER:* NONTRADED GOODS

The preceding section examined the consequences of changes in the price of home-produced traded goods relative to foreign goods. This is one type of relative price change an open economy is subject to. This section investigates the other type: changes in the price of traded goods relative to nontraded goods. To focus on this aspect, assume that relative prices of traded goods do not change. Then traded goods can be aggregated, and in Figure 18.5 they are measured on the vertical axis. The nontraded goods are measured on the horizontal axis, and TT' denotes the country's production possibility frontier.

Panel (a) of Figure 18.5 shows an initial balance-of-trade deficit. The slopes of the budget lines FL and CL reflect the relative price of traded goods in terms of nontraded goods. Firms, therefore, produce at A, and national income is reflected in the distance from the origin of FL. Since we are looking at a case where the country is running a balance-of-payments deficit, total spending (or absorption) must be greater than income. It is reflected in the distance from the origin of the consumption budget line, CL. Consumption takes place at point B, where CL is tangent to a community indifference curve. If the nontraded goods market is to be in equilibrium, B must be directly above A so that the demand for nontraded goods will equal the supply. The distance BA measures the excess demand for traded goods. This can be satisfied by importing them from abroad. Thus BA is the balance-of-payments deficit.

Now suppose that depreciation causes the price of traded goods to rise relative to nontraded goods. This is shown in panel (b), where the budget lines FL and CL have been replaced by the flatter FL' and CL'. Production

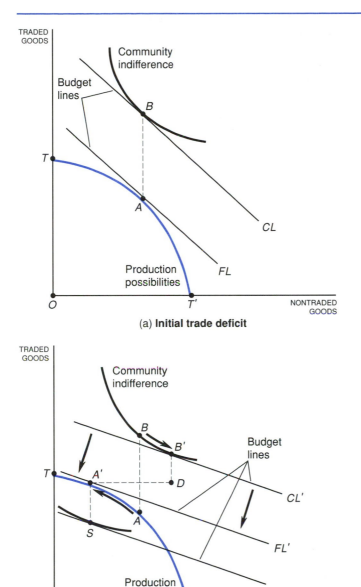

(a) **Initial trade deficit**

(b) **Depreciation**

FIGURE 18.5 **Depreciation and Nontraded Goods** Depreciation causes production to shift from nontraded goods to traded goods and demand to shift in the reverse direction. This narrows the payments deficit and sets off further adjustment to clear the market for nontraded goods.

shifts from A to A' as firms respond by producing more traded goods and fewer nontraded goods. Consumers, of course, react in the opposite way, with consumption moving from B to B'. Since the country is now producing more traded goods and consuming fewer, the balance-of-trade deficit has shrunk to the distance DB' in the figure.

However, this is not an equilibrium. The market for nontraded goods is now out of balance, with the economy demanding more than is being produced. Since these goods are nontraded, this excess demand cannot be satisfied by importing the excess from abroad.

The depreciation has in effect transformed the initial excess demand for traded goods into an excess demand for goods in general. Sooner or later, this will drive up prices and costs in this country, as discussed in section 2. The increase in the price level moves the economy up along its aggregate demand curve, so aggregate demand shrinks. This is reflected by a shift of the consumers' budget line CL' toward the origin. This continues until the demand for nontraded goods comes into line with the supply. In panel (b), this is shown as happening at point S, so that the depreciation has actually generated a trade surplus of SA'.

Problems

18.13 How does the analysis of this section change if, instead of a depreciation, the exchange rate remains fixed but the domestic money supply is increased?

18.14 How does the analysis of this section change if the exchange rate is allowed to float and the domestic money supply is increased?

5. HOARDING AND DISHOARDING: THE MONETARY APPROACH

Thus far we have focused on the role of *relative* prices. Now it is time to look at price *levels*. To concentrate on just that, suppose that the economy has only standardized, traded goods and that purchasing power parity holds exactly. It will prove convenient to examine first the effect of an expansion in the money supply under a fixed exchange rate.

Fixed Exchange Rate

Suppose that the money supply is doubled. What will the public do with its extra money? They will spend it, or *dishoard:* spend more on goods than their income from selling goods. This dishoarding will continue until the public has reduced its money balances to the level that it wants—that is, until the supply of money equals the demand. Figure 18.6(a) shows how the public would respond to a divergence between the money it has and the money it

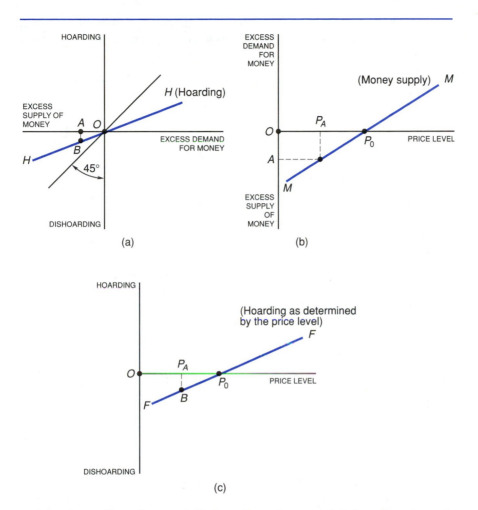

FIGURE 18.6 **Hoarding and Dishoarding** In panel (a), hoarding depends upon the excess demand for money, which in panel (b) is determined by the price level, given the money supply; so in panel (c), hoarding is determined by the price level, given the money supply.

wants by hoarding or dishoarding. At the origin the excess demand for money is zero—the public has just the quantity it wants—so hoarding is zero also. The curve *HH* illustrates how much they would hoard in response to each excess demand or dishoard in response to each excess supply. If supply exceeds demand by *OA*, the public dishoards *AB*.

The response of hoarding to an excess demand, which we call the "propensity to hoard," depends upon how impatient people are to adjust their money holdings. If they are very impatient and, therefore, are willing temporarily to decrease or increase spending in a great amount to hoard or dishoard, the *HH* line will be steep. If this line coincides with the 45° line, any excess money supply will be fully dishoarded at once so that adjustment is immediate. A flatter line indicates slower adjustment.

KEY CONCEPT

A nation spends less than its income in order to *hoard,* or accumulate money. If money holdings exceed demand, the nation *dishoards,* or spends more than its income. Hoarding or dishoarding continues until money demands and supplies come into balance, with the time taken for this determined by the *propensity to hoard.*

Panel (b) of Figure 18.6 shows how the demand for money depends upon the national price level—the *MM* line graphs excess demand, $kPy - L$, against the price level P. Point P_0 shows the price that causes the demand for money just to equal the existing supply. Higher prices raise demand above this supply, and lower prices reduce demand below it, so the curve has a positive slope. An increase in the money supply would shift the curve downward by the amount of the increase.

The *HH* line shows how hoarding depends upon the excess demand for money, which *MM,* in turn, relates to the price level. Thus the two together have the price level determining hoarding, as shown by the *FF* schedule in panel (c). For example, the price P_A generates an excess supply of *OA,* from *MM,* and this excess supply causes hoarding of $-AB$ in panel (a). Thus *FF* shows the price P_A producing this much hoarding.

It is now time to bring France and Germany into the discussion. Suppose that the French money supply is doubled. If the French do succeed in dishoarding—that is, in buying goods with some of their extra money—it is necessary that Germany sell the goods for the money—or hoard. One country's hoarding must always be matched by dishoarding in the other country. Thus when we derive Germany's analog to the *FF* schedule, we reverse ourselves by measuring German *dishoarding* in an upward direction on the vertical axis. In panel (a) of Figure 18.7, *FF* represents the French hoarding schedule, as in Figure 18.6, and *GG* represents the German. This panel corresponds to full international equilibrium. French dishoarding just matches German hoarding at the intersection of the *FF* and *GG* lines. This intersection is at *A* on the horizontal axis, so each country's hoarding is zero: money supply equals demand in both countries.

Now suppose that the French money supply increases. This shifts *FF* downward to *F'F',* as shown in Figure 18.7. Since Germany's money supply is unchanged, *GG* stays put. At the initial price level *OA* the French now want to dishoard *AB*—that is, to buy additional goods worth this much from Germany. But the Germans, at *A,* do not wish to hoard. Thus the world now has an excess demand for goods (excess supply of money), so prices must rise.

If prices rise in the same proportion as the French money supply, so will the French demand for money. For example, if France's money supply doubles, a price rise from *OA* in Figure 18.7(a) to *OC*, where *OA* = *AC*, would leave the country in equilibrium with a desire neither to hoard nor dishoard. But now Germany would be out of balance; the price rise would increase the German demand for money above its unchanged supply, causing the country to want to hoard *CH*. This would constitute an excess supply of goods (demand for money) and would force prices back down. In fact, the price level

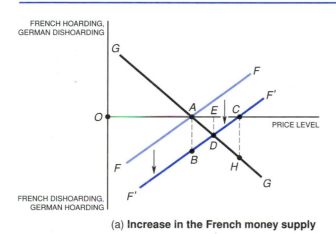

(a) **Increase in the French money supply**

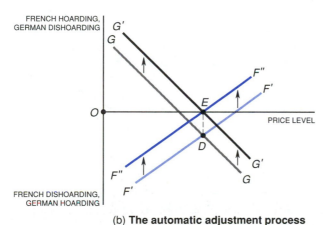

(b) **The automatic adjustment process**

FIGURE 18.7 Response to an Increase in the French Money Supply An increase in France's money supply reduces the French desire to hoard and so shifts *FF* down in (a). This produces a rise in the price level and a French balance-of-payments deficit. The deficit causes the French money supply to fall and the German money supply to rise, so *F'F'* and *GG* shift up in (b).

must rise to *OE,* where French dishoarding of *ED* just matches German hoarding. Thus the increase in *France's* money supply causes temporary inflation in *both* countries and gives France a balance-of-payments deficit and Germany a surplus equal to *ED.*

Note the subtle role of price changes. An increase in one country's money supply generates worldwide inflation but at a rate less than that of the country's monetary expansion. Thus we get an excess supply of money in one country and an excess demand in the other. This brings about the payments imbalances that set the automatic adjustment process in motion. The French deficit of *ED* in Figure 18.7 reduces the French money supply and increases the German money supply in the same amount. These money supply changes shift the *F'F'* and *GG* schedules upward, as shown in panel (b). This shift reduces the payments imbalance and eventually eliminates it completely when the curves have moved to *F"F"* and *G'G',* which intersect on the horizontal axis at point *E.* The demand for money once again equals the supply in each country, and full equilibrium has been restored. The price level now remains constant at this new level, *OE.*

A key parameter is the propensity to hoard. If this is large, the initial payments imbalances are large but the world moves to the new equilibrium with great dispatch. A small propensity implies a modest but long-lived payments imbalance.

Exchange Depreciation

Now we consider the role of the exchange rate. The French hoarding schedule, *FF,* depends upon the size of the French money supply. The German schedule, *GG,* likewise depends on the German money supply, but it also depends on the exchange rate because the Germans hoard marks and measure prices in marks, whereas the axes of Figure 18.8 are measured in francs. (The *GG* schedule is the graph of $RL^G - kPpy^G$.) A 50 percent depreciation of the franc, for example, would shift the *GG* curve away from the origin—upward and to the right—by 50 percent since any mark price and any hoarding of marks would now be 50 percent larger when measured in terms of francs.

Suppose that initially the world is in equilibrium at point *A.* If the franc is depreciated in the proportion *AC/OA,* the *GG* line shifts to *G'G'* in Figure 18.8. The equilibrium is at *B,* where France will develop a payments surplus of *BE* and Germany an equal deficit. The French price level has risen by *AE* in francs, and the German price level has fallen by the mark equivalent of *EC.* Thus the diagram shows how exchange depreciation both improves the payments balance and increases inflation. It has the opposite effect on the country whose currency has appreciated. If the new exchange rate is not altered, the payments imbalances continue until the French money supply rises and the German money supply falls enough so that *FF* and *G'G'* both shift downward to intersect on the price-level axis.

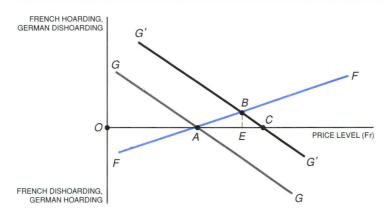

FRENCH HOARDING,
GERMAN DISHOARDING

PRICE LEVEL (Fr)

FRENCH DISHOARDING,
GERMAN HOARDING

FIGURE 18.8 A Depreciation of the Franc   Depreciation of the franc shifts the German schedule out because each quantity of marks corresponds to more francs. Thus equilibrium moves along the French schedule.

Problems

18.15 Suppose that Italy's income is equal in value to 10,000 olives and that Spain's equals 4,000 goats. In equilibrium, 2 olives exchange for 1 goat. If the world money supply consists of 180,000 ounces of gold and if $k = 2$, what are the equilibrium money supplies and money prices? If the Spanish peseta equals 2 ounces of gold and the Italian lira equals ½ ounce of gold, what are the money supplies and money prices in terms of pesetas? In terms of lire?

18.16 Suppose, in the previous problem, that Spain obtained an additional 72,000 ounces of gold from the New World. How must the money prices of goats and olives change if the Spanish excess supply of money is just to equal the Italian excess demand? Suppose that the propensity to hoard of each individual is such that everyone wants to take exactly ten years to adjust money supply to demand, performing one-tenth of the adjustment in each year. What are the Spanish and Italian imbalances in the first year after the Spanish obtain the new gold? What are the new money supplies after one year, and the payments imbalances in the second year? Continue to give answers for succeeding years until the new equilibrium is reached.

18.17 In Problem **18.15**, suppose Spain and Italy have paper currencies, with 100,000 lire and 80,000 pesetas. What are the equilibrium prices and exchange rate?

18.18 Suppose, in Problem **18.17**, that the peseta depreciates, relative to the lira, by one-half of its equilibrium value. If *PPP* holds, what must happen to the money prices of the two goods in the two currencies if the excess demand for lire is to equal in value the excess supply of pesetas?

18.19 The discussion in the text showed that exchange depreciation tends to increase domestic inflation relative to foreign inflation. Suppose that some exogenous event causes the domestic inflation rate to rise but does not influence foreign inflation. What will be the likely effect on the exchange rate, if the latter is free to adjust? What, in turn, will be the consequences of this adjustment? Compare with the effects of increased domestic inflation when exchange rates are fixed.

18.20 Show how Figure 18.8 can be used to analyze a depreciation of the franc if both axes are measured in *marks*.

18.21 The text described the response to a *monetary* disturbance: an increase in the French money supply. Suppose instead that the disturbance is *real*—say, economic growth in Germany in the form of an increase in y^G. Analyze the response using diagrams such as Figure 18.7.

18.22* How do your answers to Problems **18.15** and **18.16** change if the Spanish obtain an additional 72,000 ounces of gold not just once, but each and every year?

6. SUMMARY

1. An *aggregate demand curve* displays the level of equilibrium aggregate demand corresponding to each value of the national price level.

2. When aggregate demand exceeds aggregate supply, the price level will eventually begin to increase and the country will move up along its aggregate demand curve.

3. In an open economy the price level responds to international competitive conditions as well as to domestic macroeconomic conditions.

4. The *Law of One Price* is that similar goods must sell for the same price in different countries when expressed in a common currency. *Purchasing power parity* holds when exchange-rate variations and differences in national inflation rates cancel each other out so that national price levels do not change relative to each other when expressed in a common currency. Empirical evidence indicates that the Law of One Price is not inviolate and that departures from purchasing power parity are not uncommon.

5. Variations in exchange rates or expenditure policies alter the price of home-produced goods relative to foreign goods, the price of traded goods relative to nontraded goods, and the overall price level.

SUGGESTED READING

Dornbusch, R. "Devaluation, Money, and Nontraded Goods." *American Economic Review* 63 (1973): 871–80. The monetary approach.

———. *Open Economy Macroeconomics.* New York: Basic Books, 1980. See in particular Chapters 9, and 11 through 14.

Goldstein, M., and M. S. Khan. "Income and Price Effects in International Trade." In *Handbook of International Economics.* Vol. 2. Edited by R. W. Jones and P. B. Kenen. Amsterdam: North Holland, 1985. Estimates of the price elasticity of import demand.

Kravis, I., and R. Lipsey. "Price Behavior in the Light of Balance of Payments Theories." *Journal of International Economics* 8 (1978): 193–246. This issue contains additional papers dealing with purchasing power parity.

Mundell, R. A. *International Economics.* New York: Macmillan, 1968. Chapters 11, 12, 16, 17, and 18 are especially relevant.

————. *Monetary Theory*. Pacific Palisades: Goodyear, 1971. See Chapters 8 through 11 and 14 through 16.

Neary, P. "Non-Traded Goods and the Balance of Trade in a Neo-Keynesian Temporary Equilibrium." *Quarterly Journal of Economics* 3 (1980). An advanced treatment.

Robinson, J. "The Foreign Exchanges." In *Readings in the Theory of International Trade*. Edited by H. S. Ellis and L. A. Metzler. Homewood, Ill.: Irwin, 1950. The elasticities, or relative price, approach.

Swan, T. "Longer-Run Problems of the Balance of Payments." In *Readings in International Economics*. Edited by R. E. Caves and H. G. Johnson. Homewood, Ill.: Irwin, 1968. Internal and external balance.

Tsiang, S. C. "The Role of Money in Trade-Balance Stability: Synthesis of the Elasticity and Absorption Approaches." *American Economic Review* 51 (1961): 912–36. An algebraic treatment of aspects of the commodity-flow view.

CHAPTER 19

Capital and Adjustment

It is clear enough in principle that private owners of wealth have no right to the liberty to move funds around the world according to their private convenience, and it is clear that, in the uneasy conditions of modern times, no conceivable international currency system can survive for long if that liberty is granted.

—JOAN ROBINSON

Part Six began with four strong assumptions. So far we have relaxed three of them, but we have yet to allow nonofficial international capital movements. Capital mobility was discussed in detail in Chapters 14 and 15, and it is time to consider it again. We do so in the context of a comprehensive treatment of macroeconomic policy in an open economy.

1. INTERNAL AND EXTERNAL BALANCE UNDER FIXED EXCHANGE RATES

We will consider fixed and floating exchange rates separately. This section assumes fixed rates and supposes again that domestic prices are fixed.

In Figure 19.1 the vertical axis measures the interest rate, determined by monetary policy. Suppose that the authorities are able and willing to sterilize payments imbalances so as to exercise independent monetary policy for a prolonged period. The horizontal axis measures the government's budget deficit, a reflection of fiscal policy. Suppose that at A aggregate demand is as desired by the authorities. If government spending rose and increased the budget deficit by AB, national income would be stimulated and aggregate demand would exceed the desired level. An increase in the interest rate would reduce private investment and thereby bring aggregate demand back down. Suppose that an increase from B to C would just do the trick. Then C, like A, indicates a policy combination corresponding to internal balance: aggregate demand equals the target of the authorities. The IB line indicates all such policy combinations. We have just shown that it has a positive slope.

JAMES MEADE (b. 1907)

James Meade was educated at Oxford, and he served on the faculty at Oxford, the London School of Economics, and Cambridge. He was among the group of young economists who helped develop the ideas behind Keynesian economics, and he was also very active in the behind-the-scenes economic work resulting in the development of the post–World War II international economic order. As an academic, Meade was primarily concerned with the theory of economic policy, to which he made fundamental contributions in many areas. He is no doubt most well known, however, for his 1951–1955 work *The Theory of International Economic Policy,* which addresses, in separate volumes, both the balance of payments and trade policy. International capital movements are important in both volumes, and the first volume is much concerned with the relation between internal and external balance. This work basically created the way in which international economic policy was conceived for several decades. In 1977 Meade shared a Nobel prize with Ohlin.

Now consider external balance. Suppose that foreign interest rates, prices, and incomes are not appreciably affected by what happens at home. An increase in the government deficit, by stimulating income and, therefore, imports, will increase the balance-of-payments deficit. An increase in the interest rate will decrease the payments deficit for two reasons. By reducing national income, it reduces imports and so decreases the balance-of-trade deficit; a higher interest rate also makes domestic assets more attractive relative to foreign assets and so generates a capital-account surplus, provided that capital is internationally mobile.

Suppose that the policy combination indicated by *A* results in external balance (a balance-of-payments deficit equal to zero or to whatever the authorities wish). If the government deficit increases by *AB,* the trade account will increase its deficit. To restore external balance, the interest rate must rise. If it rises by *BC,* national income will fall back to what it was at *A* and, therefore, imports and the trade balance will do likewise. If capital is immobile internationally, the balance of trade coincides with the balance of payments and *C,* like *A,* indicates a policy combination corresponding to external balance. But if capital is internationally mobile, the increase in the interest rate from *B* to *C* will induce a capital-account surplus. Since the balance of trade is the same at *C* as at *A* and the capital-account surplus is greater, the balance of payments must have a larger surplus at *C* than at *A.* To restore external balance, the payments surplus must fall—that is, the interest rate must decline to somewhere between *C* and *B.* Suppose that the movement from *C* to *D* will accomplish this. Then *D,* like *A,* indicates a policy combination corresponding to external balance. The *EB* line shows all such combinations. We have

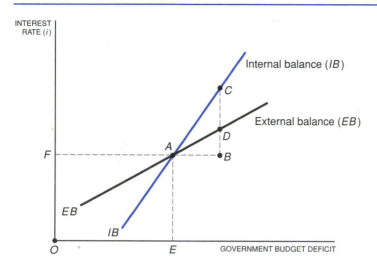

FIGURE 19.1   Internal and External Balance   Fiscal policy and monetary policy have different effects on internal and external balance, so the appropriate mix of policies can achieve both goals.

shown that this line slopes upward and that it is less steep than the *IB* line, provided that capital is not completely immobile internationally.

Since the *IB* and *EB* lines have different slopes, they must intersect. The intersection is illustrated by *A*. This corresponds to the single policy combination giving both internal balance and external balance. By setting the budget deficit equal to *OE* and the interest rate equal to *OF* the authorities can simultaneously hit their targets for the balance of payments and for aggregate demand: there is no conflict between internal balance and external balance. The two *targets* can both be met by the proper use of the two *instruments*.

This happy escape from our policy dilemma is due to international capital mobility, which causes the two instruments to have differential effects. If capital is immobile internationally, monetary and fiscal policy are simply two different ways of manipulating a single instrument: expenditure policy. To see this, note that if capital were not mobile, points *C* and *D* in Figure 19.1 would coincide—that is, the *IB* and *EB* lines would have the same slope. If the target for national income happened to be the level that caused imports to equal exports, all would be well. The *IB* and *EB* lines would coincide, and any combination of the interest rate and budget deficit on this common line would do. But if targeted income caused imports not to equal exports, the *IB* and *EB* lines would be distinct and parallel: they would never intersect. The authorities could attain one target or the other but not both (unless they came up with yet another policy instrument).

As capital becomes mobile, the *EB* line becomes flatter than the *IB* line and the two intersect. If capital is perfectly mobile, the domestic interest rate must always equal the foreign interest rate so that the *EB* line becomes horizontal. That is, it coincides with the *FAB* line. In this case monetary policy is useless to attain internal balance because nothing the authorities can do will influence the interest rate and thereby affect expenditure. Any attempt to alter the money supply will be quickly neutralized by payments imbalances; the automatic adjustment process prevents the country from pursuing an independent monetary policy. Fiscal policy is, however, an effective way to control internal balance. With external balance taken care of by the automatic adjustment process, economic policy reduces to simply setting the budget deficit equal to the level at which the *IB* line intersects the horizontal *EB* line.

Our policy conclusions depend crucially on the ability of the interest rate to influence the balance of payments *independently* of its influence through aggregate expenditure, and this independence follows from the fact that an increase in the interest rate generates a capital-account surplus. But Chapter 14 showed that a permanent change in the interest rate had only a temporary effect on the capital account. Thus our conclusions are strictly short run. This means that we have found only a temporary escape from the internal balance–external balance dilemma, unless the authorities are prepared to intensify progressively their policies again and again in order to obtain a succession of short-run effects. In addition, policy changes could be hard to implement because a lot of time is often required to change fiscal policy: spending changes must be planned, and frequently laws must be altered. Thus if the authorities change both fiscal and monetary policy at the same time, the short-run effect on the capital account could be over before fiscal policy even begins to do its thing.

In addition to this short-run effect on the capital account, two other consequences of a change in interest rates could be important. If the economy is growing in the sense that residents are steadily saving and accumulating new assets, they will continually be putting some of their new savings into foreign assets and the proportion of savings devoted to foreign assets will be sensitive to interest rates. If the domestic interest rate falls, residents will increase their purchases of foreign bonds as they continue to save. Thus monetary policy could have some permanent effect on the capital account after all. In the long run, interest rates will also influence the *current* account (in addition to its effect on the trade balance through expenditure), and this must be considered once we go beyond a short-run horizon. An increase in domestic interest rates *reduces* net interest income received from abroad, both because we must now pay more interest on our bonds held by foreigners and because foreigners own more of our bonds as a result of our temporary capital-account surplus.

Problems

19.1 The *IB* and *EB* lines in Figure 19.1 divide the plane into four zones. What is the interpretation of each of these zones in terms of policy goals?

19.2 Suppose that savings are small so that the increase in the capital-account surplus caused by a rise in the domestic interest rate almost entirely disappears after the short run. Show what the relative positions of the *IB* and *EB* schedules in Figure 19.1 look like in both the short run and the long run. What do you conclude about policy?

19.3 Suppose that the economy is initially in external balance at point *D* in Figure 19.1 and, in order to attain internal balance also, that the interest rate is reduced by *BD* and the budget deficit by *AB*. Show in the diagram what happens after the short-run change in the capital account disappears, assuming that both the continuing effect on the capital account and the long-run effect on net interest income are small enough to be ignored. Show what additional policy measures the authorities must take in order to preserve internal and external balance.

19.4* The intersection of the *IB* and *EB* lines in Figure 19.1 gives a specific policy description (point *A*). But in actual situations we will have at best only a hazy idea of the shape and position of these curves and so will not know where *A* is. It is, therefore, useful to have simple rules for adjusting the targets to "grope" toward *A*. One simple rule would be to assign each instrument to one target. For example, if the interest rate were assigned to internal balance and the budget deficit to external balance, one would reduce the interest rate whenever the economy was in a recession and reduce the budget deficit whenever there was a balance-of-payments deficit. An alternative assignment would be monetary policy to external balance and fiscal policy to internal balance. Discuss the relative merits of these two assignments as means to attain point *A*.

---

2. AGGREGATE DEMAND MANAGEMENT WITH FLOATING EXCHANGE RATES

We now consider how monetary and fiscal policy operate in an open economy with a floating exchange rate. Since the major advantage of such an exchange-rate regime is that it gives an individual country control over its monetary policy, let us consider that first.

Monetary Policy

Suppose that the authorities expand the domestic money supply through open-market operations (buying bonds from the public). The easier monetary conditions will force down the domestic interest rate and stimulate aggregate demand. Lower interest rates make domestic assets less attractive relative to foreign assets, and, therefore, at the original exchange rate a capital-account deficit would emerge. Also, the expansion of aggregate demand would involve an increased demand for imports so that a trade-account deficit would also develop. Now, with floating exchange rates the authorities do not sell international reserves, so the exchange rate must adjust to prevent these deficits from emerging and to keep the overall balance of payments equal to zero. Thus, *an expansionary monetary policy causes the exchange rate to depreciate*. This depreciation will make domestic goods more attractive to consumers, relative to foreign goods, and thereby increase aggregate demand still more. *With a floating exchange rate, expansionary monetary policy stimulates aggregate demand.* Note also that inflationary pressures rise: the increase in aggregate demand, of course, tends to stimulate inflation; in addition, exchange depreciation is itself inflationary, as we saw in Chapter 18. Recall that with fixed exchange rates a country has only transitory control over its money supply; indeed, the previous section showed that, if capital is perfectly mobile, monetary policy has no effect at all on aggregate demand. Thus monetary policy is more effective under floating rates than under fixed rates.

The Role of Capital Mobility. The above conclusions do not depend upon the degree of international capital mobility. But that degree is still important. This can be seen most clearly by contrasting the cases of no mobility and perfect mobility. This is done in Figure 19.2. With no capital mobility, the increased money supply is free to force down the domestic interest rate without causing a capital-account deficit; this stimulates investment and so shifts the curve $S - I$ downward to $S' - I'$ in Figure 19.2(a). At the initial exchange rate this would shift equilibrium from A to C so that aggregate demand y would rise from OA to OB. But this would cause a trade deficit—and, therefore, balance-of-payments deficit—equal to BC. To prevent this, the exchange rate depreciates, shifting the $X - M$ line up to $X' - M'$. The equilibrium is at D, where aggregate demand has increased from OA to OD and where trade is balanced. In fact, monetary policy has been just as potent as it would have been in a closed economy.

If, in contrast, international capital mobility is perfect, domestic interest rates cannot diverge from foreign interest rates, and so monetary policy cannot produce a shift of the $S - I$ line in Figure 19.2(b): the bonds purchased from the public are replaced by new purchases abroad. But this means a capital-account deficit. Suppose that this deficit equals AB in the figure. Since the overall balance of payments cannot be in deficit, the exchange rate must depreciate enough to generate a trade surplus just equal to AB. This will be accomplished by a depreciation that shifts the $X - M$ line up to $X' - M'$. New equilibrium is at C so that aggregate demand has increased from OA to OD.

In both cases monetary policy succeeds in raising aggregate demand, but it does so in different ways and, accordingly, has different results. In panel (a) the new equilibrium involves balanced trade and no net capital flows, but with perfect capital mobility the new equilibrium in panel (b) features a trade surplus and a capital-account deficit. This means that the new equilibrium is only *temporary:* once domestic citizens have bought enough bonds from abroad to replace those sold to the authorities, the capital-account deficit will cease and the economy will revert back to A. In order to maintain permanently the higher level of aggregate demand, the authorities must continue their expansionary monetary operations and not merely conduct them once, as would be sufficient with no capital mobility. Thus, *the greater the degree of international capital mobility, the more temporary the stimulative effects of a monetary expansion.*

Even more important is the difference in international repercussions. In panel (a) the foreign economy is not affected through the capital account by

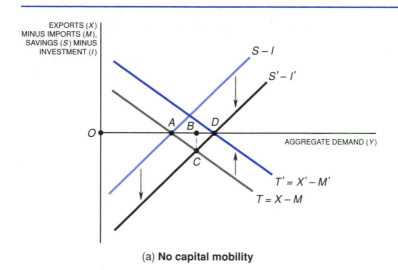

(a) **No capital mobility**

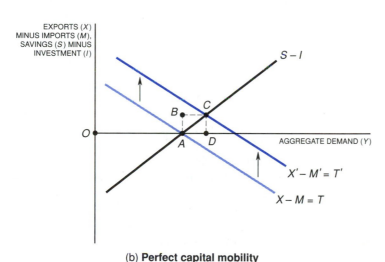

(b) **Perfect capital mobility**

FIGURE 19.2 Expansionary Monetary Policy With no capital mobility, monetary policy in an open economy with a floating exchange rate works just like in a closed economy. Capital mobility prevents interest rates from falling and implies a capital-account deficit and so a trade surplus.

domestic monetary policy because there is no capital mobility by assumption. There are no effects through the trade account either because trade is balanced in both the new equilibrium and the old. Thus domestic monetary policy has limited macroeconomic effect abroad. (It may have microeconomic effects, however, if the exchange depreciation alters relative prices abroad. Thus it is not correct, even with no capital mobility, to say that domestic monetary policy has no foreign repercussions in a floating-rate regime.) But with perfect capital mobility the new equilibrium features a balance-of-trade surplus so that the foreign country has a trade deficit and, therefore, a lower level of aggregate demand. That is, monetary policy stimulates the domestic economy by depressing the rest of the world. (If the home economy is large enough, domestic monetary policy might change both domestic and foreign interest rates together and thereby also influence the foreign economy in that way.) Thus, *the greater the degree of international capital mobility, the greater the perverse foreign repercussions of domestic monetary policy.*

Fiscal Policy

Recall that fiscal policy can be used under fixed exchange rates to control aggregate demand even if capital is perfectly mobile. The easiest way to evaluate the effectiveness of fiscal policy with floating rates is to consider separately the two extreme cases of no capital mobility and perfect mobility. This is done in Figure 19.3.

Suppose first that capital is completely immobile and that the authorities increase government spending—that is, they raise autonomous expenditure I. This would shift the $S - I$ curve downward and stimulate aggregate demand. Now as aggregate demand rises, citizens require more money because of the higher number of transactions. But the money supply is unchanged because monetary policy is not being used. Thus the domestic interest rate is forced up (remember, there is no international capital mobility). This rise in the interest rate reduces private investment so that I actually rises by less than the increase in government spending—the latter partially "crowds out" private spending. The net effect is to shift $S - I$ down to $S' - I'$ in Figure 19.3(a). (Of course, $S - I$ would shift even more if the authorities were to supply the needed additional money and prevent the interest rate from rising—monetary and fiscal policy together would be more potent than fiscal policy alone.) This implies a trade deficit (equal to BC) at the initial exchange rate, so the latter depreciates enough to shift $X - M$ upward to $X' - M'$. New equilibrium is at D, and fiscal policy successfully increases aggregate demand from OA to OD. Again, there are no macroeconomic effects on the rest of the world. (Note that Figure 19.3(a) is just like Figure 19.2(a).)

Now suppose that capital mobility is perfect. Expansionary fiscal policy again shifts $S - I$ downward; but in this case the domestic interest rate cannot rise above the foreign interest rate, so $S - I$ shifts down by the full amount of the increase in government spending. Thus this increase equals AE in Figure 19.3(b). Now as aggregate demand begins to rise, citizens again demand more money. But with perfect capital mobility, any tendency for the domestic interest rate to rise attracts enough foreign capital to prevent the rise. This capital-account surplus must be matched by a trade-account deficit, so the exchange rate appreciates. How far must the exchange rate appreciate? Far enough so that the trade-account deficit equals the increase in government spending. For in that case there is no net effect on aggregate demand so that

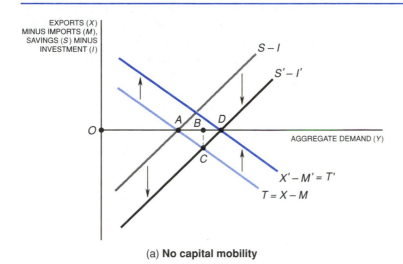

(a) **No capital mobility**

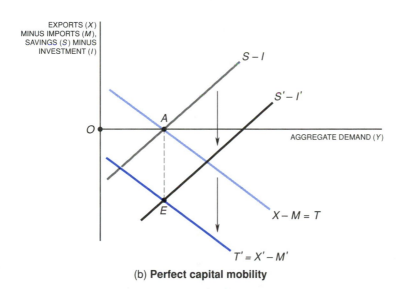

(b) **Perfect capital mobility**

FIGURE 19.3 **Expansionary Fiscal Policy**   Without capital mobility, fiscal policy works like monetary policy. Capital mobility makes fiscal policy ineffective
since it results in a trade deficit that absorbs the fiscal stimulus.

citizens still demand the unchanged supply of money. This is illustrated by
the shift of $X - M$ to $X' - M'$ in Figure 19.3(b). Fiscal policy is totally ineffective—any increase in government spending simply flows abroad through
the balance of trade. (All this can be described in another way. To finance its
increased spending, the government must sell bonds to the public. With per-

fect capital mobility, these bonds are all sold to foreigners, and, in order to prevent the balance of payments from going into surplus, the exchange rate must appreciate enough to generate a trade deficit equal to this bond sale— that is, equal to the increase in government spending.) Although fiscal policy, unlike monetary policy, is powerless to influence aggregate demand, with floating rates and perfect capital mobility, it nonetheless also has foreign repercussions. But there is a difference: whereas expansionary domestic monetary policy depresses the rest of the world, expansionary fiscal policy stimulates the foreign economy. In effect, fiscal policy can influence the domestic economy only to the extent that the policy is huge enough to influence the entire international economy. In summary, *with flexible exchange rates, the greater the degree of international capital mobility, the less effective fiscal policy over domestic activity and the greater the international repercussions of that policy.*

This section has examined both monetary policy and fiscal policy, with both high capital mobility and low capital mobility, when the exchange rate floats. Earlier, we examined these cases with a fixed rate. All these results are summarized for convenience in Table 19.1.

As we have seen, the principal advantage of floating exchange rates is that they allow individual countries to control their own monetary policies. But they do not prevent international repercussions to domestic economic events, and the repercussions of policy can become large with a high degree of international capital mobility. Floating exchange rates do not eliminate international economic interdependence. When the DCs were on an adjustable peg system, there were constant debates about the relative advantages of fixed and floating exchange rates. Most of these debates were based on positions developed in the 1950s and early 1960s, when the degree of international capital mobility was fairly low. But when adjustable pegs were abandoned in the early 1970s, the degree of mobility had greatly increased. Many people were accordingly surprised by the amount of policy interdependence that still remained.

TABLE 19.1 **Effects of Alternative Policies under Alternative Exchange-Rate Regimes**

Exchange regime	Policy	Low capital mobility		High capital mobility	
		Domestic effect	*Foreign repercussion*	*Domestic effect*	*Foreign repercussion*
Fixed rates	Monetary	Substantial (temporary)	Substantial	Slight	Substantial
	Fiscal	Substantial	Substantial	Substantial	Substantial
Floating rates	Monetary	Substantial	Slight	Substantial (temporary)	Substantial (temporary)
	Fiscal	Substantial	Slight	Slight	Substantial

Problems

19.5 Suppose that France and Germany have a floating exchange rate, and suppose that there is an exogenous increase in the German desire to consume French goods. What will be the results? How does your answer depend upon the degree of capital mobility? Contrast your answer with what would happen under fixed rates.

19.6 Suppose that France and Germany have a floating exchange rate and that there is an exogenous increase in the German desire to own French bonds. What will happen? How does your answer depend upon the degree of capital mobility? Contrast your answer with what would happen with fixed rates.

19.7 The text showed that, with floating exchange rates and perfect capital mobility, monetary policy could influence domestic aggregate demand but the influence would be temporary. Fiscal policy would have no influence. Is this lack of influence of fiscal policy also temporary? Explain.

19.8* How are our conclusions about the temporary effect of monetary policy in the presence of capital mobility altered when account is taken of (a) the fact that there will be continuing capital flows in a growing world with positive net saving and (b) international payments of interest income?

3. *CASE STUDY:* U.S. EXPERIENCE IN THE 1980s

In the early 1980s the United States reduced federal tax rates and increased defense spending, leading to large federal budget deficits. Large current-account deficits followed, as shown in Table 19.2. In just a few years the country was transformed from the largest creditor nation in the world to the largest debtor nation.

Table 19.2 shows the current-account deficit equal to about 35 percent of the federal budget deficit for the period as a whole. This proportion tended to rise and was well above 50 percent in the later years. (For a while, Japan alone was financing about a third of the U.S. budget deficit by purchasing U.S. securities.) We can regard the U.S. experience as a response to an expansionary fiscal policy in an open economy without an accompanying expansionary monetary policy. (The actual stance of monetary policy was a matter of some controversy at the time, in part because of regulatory changes that were implemented. But we will ignore this.)

TABLE 19.2 Cumulative U.S Federal Budget Deficits and Current-Account Deficits, 1981–1985 *(billions of dollars)*

Federal budget deficit *(fiscal years)*	$797.32
Current-account deficit *(calendar years)*	$273.60

SOURCE: International Monetary Fund, *International Financial Statistics.*

We have a world with a high degree of capital mobility and exchange rates that are floating—with management. The previous section's discussion of expansionary fiscal policy with perfect capital mobility seems a natural starting point for analysis. That discussion concluded that the current-account deficit would just equal the budget deficit and so have no effect on aggregate demand. The current-account deficits in Table 19.2 may be striking, but they are not that striking. Probably this indicates that capital mobility, though high, is not perfect. But also the United States is not a small country, so it cannot indefinitely borrow large amounts without influencing world interest rates. Moreover, the U.S. current-account position probably would not have been zero without the policy change.

Figure 19.4 illustrates the effect of the U.S. budget deficit. Initial equilibrium is at *A*, with a modest current-account surplus. The budget deficit is *AD*. This shifts the *S − I* curve to *S′ − I′*. This goes through *B* rather than *D* because the government borrowing to finance the deficit makes world interest rates higher than they otherwise would be and so crowds out some private investment. With a floating exchange rate, the currency must appreciate enough to generate a current-account deficit equal to the capital-account surplus resulting from the sale of bonds to foreigners. With perfect capital mobility and a clean float, *X − M* would have to shift down until it passed through *B*. But this is limited by three factors. First, with capital less than perfectly mobile there is a smaller capital-account surplus to offset. Second, since the float is managed, there will be some central-bank intervention to restrain the dollar's appreciation; this means that part of the capital-account surplus will be offset by a balance-of-payments deficit. Finally, since the United States is not small, as

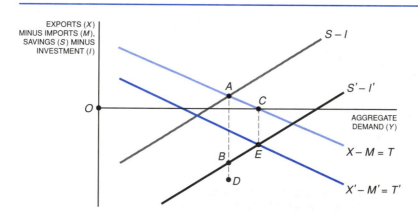

FIGURE 19.4   The U.S. Federal Budget Deficit   The budget deficit shifts *S − I* down, generating a capital-account surplus, as the government sells bonds abroad. The exchange rate must appreciate to shift *X − M* down and generate the corresponding current-account deficit.

the dollar begins to appreciate and the rest of the world develops a trade surplus, these economies will expand and they will demand more U.S. imports.

The net result is that $X - M$ shifts down only to $X' - M'$, which goes through E. The budget deficit of AD has generated a current-account deficit of CE, an appreciation of the dollar, and an expansion of U.S. aggregate demand to C. In addition, foreign aggregate demand has expanded because of the U.S. trade deficit.

The theory seems able to explain nicely U.S. experience in this period. However, we also saw earlier that the dollar then depreciated sharply in 1985–1986. Trying to explain this also is useful because it forces us to think more about limitations and extensions of the theory. Two possible explanations of the depreciation suggest themselves.

One possibility is that central-bank intervention caused the depreciation. That is, that the degree of management of the float increased. Alarmed by the huge U.S. trade deficit and believing that the dollar's appreciation had done too much violence to purchasing power parity, perhaps the authorities decided it was time to force the dollar down. This would shift $X - M$ up. But the U.S. federal budget deficit would still have to be financed. If the foreign-exchange intervention forcing down the dollar was substantial, that would help finance the deficit: a balance-of-payments deficit allows a capital-account surplus, or sale of bonds to foreigners. But intervention does not seem to have been of that order of magnitude. An increase in aggregate demand could generate additional savings to absorb the bonds used to finance the government's deficit: this is what happens as the shift of $X - M$ moves equilibrium along $S - I$. But as aggregate demand rises above aggregate supply, inflation will emerge and this will shift $X - M$ back down. Alternatively, if capital is not too mobile to prevent it, interest rates will rise as aggregate demand increases. This will shift $S - I$ up, moderating the rise in aggregate demand.

The words and actions of authorities in 1985 give some plausibility to the possibility that intervention caused the depreciation of the dollar. Notable was a September 1985 meeting at the Plaza Hotel in New York of the finance ministers of the Group of Five (United States, Japan, West Germany, France, and Great Britain), which, you will recall from Chapter 16, produced a statement that their countries would coordinate their policies to prevent the dollar from being too high. *Expectations* are important here. If people begin to believe that the dollar will depreciate in the future perhaps because they expect intervention or other policy changes, they will take steps to see that they are not holding dollars when that day comes. That is, they will sell dollars *now*, and that selling could bring about the depreciation well before any policy actions take place.

The second possible explanation suggested by our model for the dollar's depreciation is a change in U.S. fiscal policy that would reverse the shift shown in Figure 19.4. In fact, no such change took place in 1985–1986. But there were reasons to think the changes might be forthcoming. For example, the Gramm-Rudman Law mandated a return to a balanced federal budget, and

U.S. authorities became increasingly vocal in urging foreign governments to adopt more expansionary policies. So people may have come to expect such measures, and thereby to expect a dollar depreciation.

Problems

19.9 When large federal budget deficits began to develop in the early 1980s, many commentators expected them to ignite a burst of inflation. But this did not happen. In fact, the inflation rate fell. Explain in terms of our theory.

19.10 How is the discussion of intervention in this chapter sensitive to whether that intervention is sterilized or not?

19.11* Chapter 14 gave an alternative intertemporal explanation of the experience discussed in this section. How consistent are the two explanations? Do you prefer one to the other?

4.* *EXPLORING FURTHER: IS-LM-BP* ANALYSIS

This section adds capital movements to Chapter 17's discussion of the *IS-LM* model. We again focus on a country that is relatively small in the sense that its behavior has only a negligible effect on foreign prices, interest rates, and incomes, which we take as fixed. For the home country to be in complete equilibrium, three conditions must be met: the demand for the country's output must equal its supply, the country's demand for money must equal the supply, and the balance of payments must be in neither deficit nor surplus.

The *IS* curve, showing combinations of the interest rate i and income y for which the demand for output equals supply, and the *LM* curve, showing combinations for which the demand for money equals the supply, are the same as in Chapter 17. Recall that they can be represented by the following expressions:

$$S(y) - I(i, g) = T(p, y). \qquad \textbf{(IS)}$$

$$G = k(i)Py. \qquad \textbf{(LM)}$$

These curves are drawn in Figure 19.5.

With capital movements now being considered, the balance-of-payments surplus B no longer coincides with the balance-of-trade surplus T but must also account for net earnings from abroad E and the capital-account surplus C. That is, $B = T + E + C$. The trade balance T we already know about. Net earnings E depends upon international borrowing and lending that was done in the past and the terms on which those loans were negotiated. So we can regard E as simply given by history. Consider, then, the capital-account surplus C.

C measures the net sale of assets to foreigners at the present time. We will be selling assets to foreigners (that is, we will be borrowing from them) if our outstanding indebtedness to the rest of the world is currently less than our desired indebtedness, and we will be buying assets from the rest of the world if the reverse is the case. Let K denote our outstanding net indebtedness to the rest of the world. Like E, this is a product of history. Let k denote the desired level of indebtedness. This depends upon the home rate of interest i and upon the foreign rate of interest i^*, so write it as $k = k(i, i^*)$. Presumably, k is increased by increases in i and by decreases in i^*: if interest rates are high at home relative to the rest of the world, it is tempting to take advantage of this by borrowing abroad. The actual rate at which we are selling assets (that is, the size of C) depends on the gap between desired indebtedness k and actual indebtedness K:

$$C = C(k(i, i^*) - K).$$

Increases in the gap $k - K$ increase C, so increases in i increase C while decreases in i^* or in K decrease C. Putting it all together, we can write the balance of payments surplus B as

$$B(y, i; p, i^*, K) = T(p, y) + E + C(k(i, i^*) - K).$$

The *BP* Curve

This curve shows the combinations of y and i for which the balance of payments is in neither surplus nor deficit: $B(y, i; p, i^*, K) = 0$. The curve corresponds to a given level of foreign indebtedness K, a given foreign interest rate i^*, a given exchange rate, as well as a given level of both home and foreign prices. An increase in y will increase imports and increase the balance-of-payments deficit by increasing the current-account deficit. An increase in i,

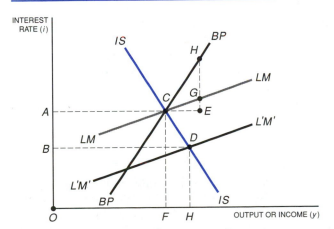

FIGURE 19.5 *IS-LM-BP* **Analysis** In full equilibrium the commodity market is in equilibrium (*IS*), the money market is in equilibrium (*LM*), and there is no payments imbalance (*BP*).

on the other hand, will make domestic assets more attractive relative to foreign assets. The capital-account surplus will accordingly increase and, therefore, the balance-of-payments surplus as well.

Suppose that at point C in Figure 19.5 the balance of payments is in neither surplus nor deficit. An increase in y at unchanged i (represented by a movement from C to E) would produce a balance-of-payments deficit by stimulating imports. To eliminate this deficit, the interest rate i must rise so as to generate a capital-account surplus (the rise in i is represented by a movement from E to H). Thus point H, like C, represents a combination of y and i for which the balance of payments is in neither surplus nor deficit. The BP curve consists of all such points; as we have just seen, this curve must have a positive slope.

The slope of the BP curve will be sensitive to the degree of international capital mobility. If capital is perfectly mobile internationally, the domestic interest rate must equal the rate of interest in the rest of the world; otherwise there would be no demand for the assets of the country paying the lower rate of interest. Thus the BP curve is a horizontal line with a height equal to the rate of interest in the rest of the world. If, on the other hand, capital is immobile, the balance of payments will coincide with the balance of trade. The BP curve will be vertical with a distance from the i axis equal to that of y which causes imports to equal the given level of exports. In general, the greater the degree of international capital mobility, the flatter the BP curve.

The BP curve is drawn for a specific level of foreign indebtedness, a specific exchange rate, and a specific domestic price level. A change in any of these will shift the curve. Suppose, for example, that domestic citizens lose some foreign assets (an increase in foreign indebtedness). At the initial rate of interest, domestic residents were previously buying or selling foreign assets at the rate they wished. Since they now suddenly find themselves with fewer of these assets, they will wish to buy them at a faster rate: the capital-account deficit will rise and, therefore, the balance-of-payments deficit as well. This deficit can be eliminated by a rise in i (making domestic assets more attractive relative to foreign assets) and/or by a fall in y (reducing imports and thereby increasing the trade-account surplus). Thus an increase in foreign indebtedness shifts the BP curve upward and to the left. Analogously, a reduction in foreign indebtedness will shift the curve downward and to the right.

Equilibrium

The economy is in *complete* equilibrium at a common intersection of all three curves, such as point C in Figure 19.5. To see *IS-LM-BP* analysis in action, suppose the domestic money supply is suddenly increased. This will shift the LM curve downward and to the right, say to the curve $L'M'$. The new equilibrium is at D. Since D is below the BP curve, there is a balance-of-payments deficit; the reduction in i (from OA to OB) will tend to generate a capital-account deficit, and the increase in y (from OF to OH) will tend to generate a balance-of-trade deficit. Thus the diagram illustrates in comprehensive fashion the effects of the monetary disturbance.

However, *D* does not represent a permanent equilibrium. The balance-of-payments deficit will cause the domestic money supply to fall (the Rules of the Game) and, therefore, gradually shift the *LM* curve back up and to the left so that *D* will begin to move up along the *IS* curve. Also, the capital-account deficit will increase the ownership of foreign assets and, therefore, cause the *BP* curve to shift down and to the right, while the increase in *y* from *OF* to *OH* will stimulate domestic inflation. The resulting rise in the domestic price level will shift the *IS* curve to the left. These shifts will continue until the three curves once again have a common intersection, when the home economy will again be in equilibrium.

Depreciation

Now we examine the effects of a depreciation of the exchange rate. Suppose that the economy is initially at point *A* in Figure 19.6 and that the trade balance and capital-account balance each equals zero. Consider a once-and-for-all depreciation of the domestic currency. This shifts the *IS* curve to the right, to *I'S'* in the figure, so that equilibrium moves from *A* to *B*. Depreciation thus increases both national income and the interest rate. The trade and capital accounts are also in surplus, with point *B* above *B'P'*, the new external balance line. The increase in *y* tends to limit the improvement in the trade balance, but it does not reverse it. The rise in *i*, on the other hand, makes domestic assets more attractive and so affects the capital account.

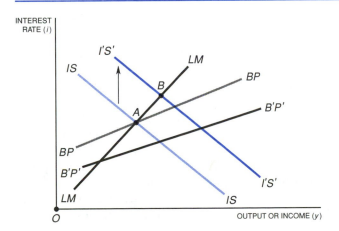

FIGURE 19.6 Exchange Depreciation Depreciation shifts both the *IS* and *BP* curves. Short-run equilibrium is on the *IS* and *LM* curves and so not on *BP*, implying a balance-of-payments surplus.

Point *B* does not represent a permanent equilibrium. Once domestic residents sell to foreigners the quantity of assets they wish, the capital-account surplus will come to an end and the *BP* curve will shift upward. Furthermore, the depreciation will generate domestic inflation, and this will be intensified by the increase in *y* involved in the movement from *A* to *B*. This rise in the domestic price level causes the *BP* and *LM* curves to shift upward and *I'S'* to shift to the left. These shifts will eventually come to an end when the three curves once again intersect in a new long-run equilibrium at some point directly above *A*.

Problems

19.12 How does a rise in the domestic price level affect the *BP* curve?

19.13 How does a rise in the foreign interest rate affect the *BP* curve?

19.14 How does a rise in the level of foreign indebtedness affect the *BP* curve?

19.15 Analyze the effects of a more expansionary fiscal policy with a fixed exchange rate and with a floating rate.

19.16 Use *IS-LM-BP* analysis to discuss the effects of an increase in the money supply with complete sterilization of all payments imbalances.

19.17 Analyze in detail the effects of an increase in the domestic money supply if the authorities adjust the exchange rate to prevent a balance-of-payments deficit.

19.18 Use *IS-LM-BP* analysis to discuss the influence of the degree of international capital mobility on the effectiveness of monetary and fiscal policy.

5. REVIEW OF INTERNATIONAL ADJUSTMENT

We have identified three distinct channels of international adjustment under either fixed or floating exchange rates: income, prices, and international capital movements. The various aspects of exchange-rate adjustment identify different key parameters. The relative importance of the various channels then determines the relative importance of the different parameters, but it is also true that the sizes of the parameters help determine which aspects are more important. For example, consider the degree of *price flexibility:* if prices are flexible enough to respond promptly to exchange-rate changes, the latter will not cause significant changes in relative prices. Thus purchasing power parity and international capital movements must be the important aspects. Different views of which aspect is important result in different views of the role of the exchange rate: the latter is likely to be regarded as an important policy variable by someone who thinks income adjustment is dominant.

Commodity-Flow and Asset-Market Theories of the Exchange Rate

Price flexibility is closely related to yet another pair of divergent interpretations of the role of the exchange rate. Inflexibility implies that relative price changes and income adjustments are important: the exchange rate is linked to *commodity* markets and *flows* of demands and supplies of goods. In this view the mark of an equilibrium exchange rate is its ability to reconcile these demands and supplies and to produce an equilibrium balance of trade. It will do this because it directly influences relative commodity prices.

A high degree of price flexibility, on the other hand, gives prominence to the hoarding and dishoarding of monies and to the international exchange of assets denominated in various currencies. The exchange rate is linked to *asset* markets. In this view the mark of an equilibrium exchange rate is its ability to equilibrate the demands and supplies of *stocks* of various assets. It can do this because it is the relative price of two assets: home and foreign money.

An Eclectic View

Since prices are neither completely flexible nor totally inflexible, both of these very divergent views of the exchange rate are valid. One might wonder how a single exchange rate can adjust to equilibrate commodity markets and to clear asset markets simultaneously. The reason is that the exchange rate does not have to do either job by itself; partial flexibility of commodity prices helps in the flow markets, and interest rates adjust stock demands and supplies. But while an eclectic view is certainly called for, there is much disagreement over the relative importance of the various aspects of adjustment as well as uncertainty about how the different views fit together.

One prominent description of how the commodity flow and asset market roles of the exchange rate come together asserts that in the short run asset markets primarily determine the exchange rate. The reason is that asset markets seem to adjust quickly. The value of the exchange rate determined in the asset markets then influences commodity markets, where prices adjust slowly. This influence affects the balance of trade, the level of national income, and rates of price changes. All this then feeds back into the asset markets. For example, money supplies may change in response to the trade balance if the authorities intervene to prevent a pure float of the exchange rate. Demands for money and assets will be influenced by changing prices, the trade balance, and the level of employment as well as by how the markets expect the authorities to react to all these. The changed asset market conditions then alter the exchange rate, and so on.

6. *CASE STUDY:* EXCHANGE-RATE VOLATILITY

One attractive feature of the previous section's description of the relation between the two views of the exchange rate is that the exchange rate is hypothesized to behave in the short run like an asset price. That is, it should fluctuate a lot in response to new information, just as stock prices on Wall Street react dramatically to news reports. The reason this is attractive is that

TABLE 19.3 **Mean Month-to-Month Absolute Percentage Changes, June 1973–July 1979**

Country	Consumer prices		Exchange Rate relative to $U.S.	Stock market
	National	National relative to United States		
United States	0.7	—	—	3.7
United Kingdom	1.2	0.7	2.1	6.6
France	0.9	0.3	2.0	5.4
Germany	0.4	0.4	2.4	3.0

SOURCE: J. Frenkel, "Flexible Exchange Rates, Prices, and the Role of 'News': Lessons from the 1970s," *Journal of Political Economy* 89 (1981).

since 1973 exchange rates have fluctuated much more than would be necessary to respond to changes in prices or likely changes in underlying equilibrium conditions.

Jacob Frenkel of the Bank of Israel has compared exchange-rate volatility with that of price indices. The first column of figures in Table 19.3 shows, in percentages, the mean month-to-month change in the consumer price indices of four countries, and the second column does the same for each country's index relative to that of the United States. Thus the French consumer price index on average changed by three-tenths of 1 percent relative to the United States' consumer price index each month during the period. The third column of figures shows that exchange rates varied much more. This large variability is to be expected of a stock market, as indicated by the last column. The fact that exchange rates varied less than stock prices could indicate the presence of some commodity-flow role for the former, or it could indicate the presence of intervention. Frenkel presented evidence that the variations in exchange rates were linked to receipt of new information (reflected in unexpected interest rate changes).

7. FLOATING EXCHANGE RATES

We can further investigate the relation between the different views of the exchange rate by studying a floating rate in more detail. Figure 19.7(a) shows the equilibrium exchange rate determined by the intersection of the demand and supply curves. The ray through the origin in Figure 19.7(b) shows what the equilibrium exchange rate must be for each value of the ratio of the home price level (P_h) to the foreign price level (P_f).

We know that $p = RP_f/P_h$, or $R = p(P_h/P_f)$, where the equilibrium relative price p is determined by real considerations. Thus R is related to P_h/P_f by a straight line with slope equal to p. The world must be somewhere on this

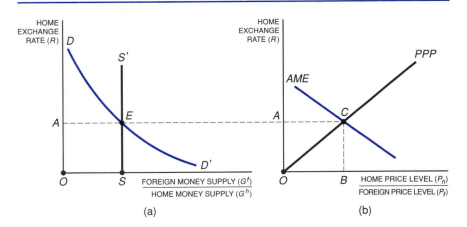

FIGURE 19.7 **Long-Run and Short-Run Equilibrium** In the short run, prices are sticky, and the exchange rate is determined in the asset markets. In the long run, purchasing power parity holds.

line in equilibrium; the money supplies determine exactly where. With the foreign money supply relative to the home money supply equal to OS in Figure 19.7(a), equilibrium is at C in Figure 19.7(b). If R and P_h/P_f move together on this line, the relation between them will not change: purchasing power parity will be exactly preserved. Thus the line is labeled *PPP*.

The world must be on the *PPP* line for long-run equilibrium. In the short run, asset markets determine the exchange rate. The *AME* (asset market equilibrium) line shows what the exchange rate will be for any ratio of the price levels. Since C is an equilibrium, *AME* must intersect *PPP* at that point. If the world will eventually get to long-run equilibrium and if people have at least a rough idea of how the exchange rate will change, *AME* must have a negative slope. For suppose the actual exchange rate is above its long-run equilibrium value of OA in Figure 19.7(b). Then people expect that R will fall—that is, that the home currency will appreciate. This makes home-currency–denominated assets more attractive than foreign-currency–denominated assets, so the home interest rate must be relatively low to compensate. But low home interest rates would cause the home demand for money to exceed the fixed supply of home currency. This can only be prevented if the home price level is also relatively low, implying a lower demand for money. Thus if R is above its long-run equilibrium value, P_h/P_f must be below: *AME* has a negative slope.

Now suppose that the home authorities increase their money supply. This lowers the ratio G^f/G^h, shifting the supply curve SS' to the left, as indicated in Figure 19.8(a), so that the new long-run equilibrium is at E', corresponding to C' in panel (b). *AME* shifts to $A'M'E'$ through C'.

Somehow, the world economy must move from C to C'. One possibility would be for R and P_h/P_f to rise together so that the movement is along the

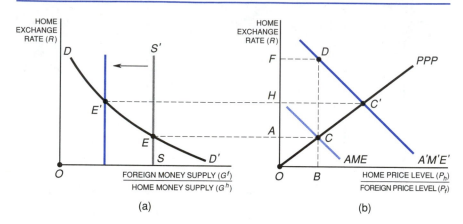

FIGURE 19.8 **Adjustment to a Monetary Shock**   A monetary shock is one that shifts the asset market equilibrium curve. Since prices are sticky in the short run, the exchange rate overreacts to compensate.

PPP line. In this case purchasing power parity would always hold exactly, there would be no relative price changes and no real effects, and we would have a purely monetary theory of the exchange rate. But we have seen that purchasing power parity does not in fact work in this relentless way. So suppose instead that commodity prices react slowly; initially P_h/P_f does not rise, but remains equal to *OB*. Since the world must be on $A'M'E'$ for asset market equilibrium, the exchange rate must rise by *DC*, giving a new short-run equilibrium at *D*. Thus the increase in the home money supply produces a large depreciation. This also involves a departure from purchasing power parity, with home goods now cheaper relative to foreign. A trade surplus develops—and a corresponding capital-account deficit—and home aggregate demand is stimulated. The reverse takes place abroad.

Eventually, P_h/P_f must begin rising. The world moves along $A'M'E'$ from *D* toward C'. This movement violates purchasing power parity, but that is necessary to compensate for the opposite violation in the movement from *C* to *D*. When the world arrives at the new long-run equilibrium at C', purchasing power parity will have been verified in the long-run sense of a comparison of *C* and C', although the movement from one to the other involved sharp departures from *PPP* in opposite directions. Also the adjustment process will have involved much volatility of the exchange rate: first it increased from *OA* to *OF*—overshooting its long-run equilibrium value of *OH*—and then gradually fell part way back.

We have looked at the consequences of a monetary disturbance, so let us now consider a real one. Suppose that consumers shift their tastes from foreign goods toward home goods. This means that the equilibrium value of *p* must

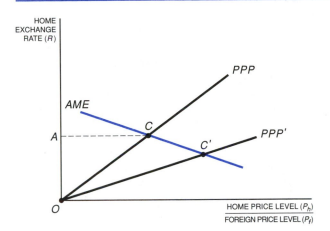

FIGURE 19.9 Adjustment to a Real Disturbance A real disturbance is one that shifts the *PPP* line. Equilibrium moves along *AME*, with the exchange rate and price level both adjusting gradually.

fall. This is indicated by the shift of the *PPP* line to *PPP'* in Figure 19.9. The new long-run equilibrium is at *C'*, and the world must get there from *C*. How?

At the initial prices and exchange rate, the shift in tastes toward home goods produces a trade surplus (and thus a corresponding capital-account deficit). This tends to stimulate income. Also, people know that, with the world at *C* but long-run equilibrium at *C'*, the home currency must appreciate. This makes home-denominated assets more attractive, so asset market equilibrium requires that the home interest rate fall to compensate. This further stimulates aggregate demand. The foreign economy experiences the reverse of all this.

Eventually, the higher demand for home goods and lower demand for foreign goods start to force P_h/P_f up. Then *R* must fall to preserve asset market equilibrium: the world moves from *C* to *C'* along *AME*.

This adjustment in response to a real shock has differed in two ways from the earlier adjustment to a monetary shock. First, *PPP* has been violated not only during the transition, but also in terms of the long-run comparison of *C* and *C'*. This must be so because a real shock changes equilibrium relative prices. Second, the adjustment from *C* to *C'* involved no more volatility of the exchange rate than of commodity prices: even though we still assumed that the latter must adjust slowly, the exchange rate did not overshoot. Instead, interest rates were volatile: the home interest rate initially dropped abruptly relative to the foreign and then gradually moved back into alignment. The prices of securities—linked to the interest they pay—were the volatile elements. With a real shock the exchange rate behaved like commodity prices and not like asset prices, whereas the opposite was the case with a monetary shock.

Problems

19.19 Can the different responses of the exchange rate to monetary and real shocks help explain why in Table 19.3 exchange rates were more volatile than commodity prices but less so than asset prices?

19.20 The monetary shock analyzed in this section was an unanticipated increase in the home money supply. Suppose instead that the home authorities announce that in one year they will increase the money supply by a certain amount, that everyone believes them, and that they then do so. Discuss the likely consequences.

19.21* The discussion of the slope of the *AME* line assumed that people expected the exchange rate to move toward its long-run equilibrium value. Suppose instead that they expect any departure from that value to be accentuated, at least for a while. How might this affect the slope of the *AME* line and the subsequent analysis?

8. POLICY DILEMMAS

Internal and External Balance

National authorities who are concerned simultaneously with aggregate demand (internal balance) and the balance of trade (external balance) face a dilemma: adjusting expenditure policy to influence one of the targets will also influence the other. Escape from the dilemma requires a second policy tool or instrument. Section 1 showed that, when notice was made of active capital movements in response to interest-rate differentials, monetary and fiscal policy no longer had identical relative effects on internal and external targets. Thus the two policies became distinct tools and could, in principle, be used together to attain simultaneous internal and external balance. The disadvantage of this escape from the dilemma was its temporary character.

A second possible escape from the dilemma arises if we forgo fixed exchange rates. A floating exchange rate would automatically attain external balance in the sense that the overall balance of payments would always be zero, so that monetary and fiscal policies could be concentrated on internal balance. Part Five showed that such policies could in fact control aggregate demand with a floating exchange rate. Managed floating and a (truly) adjustable peg could also work: once the exchange rate is treated as a second instrument and adjusts (or is adjusted) to take care of external balance, the dilemma disappears.

International Policy Interdependence

Will the use of the exchange rate as a policy tool eliminate policy conflicts between countries? One might think so because a floating exchange rate eliminates trade imbalances, and a prime cause of conflicts is the international transmission of policy effects through the balance of payments. But the answer is not that simple: the previous chapter showed that domestic policy had foreign repercussions even with floating exchange rates. Figure 19.10 shows the possible situations that a pair of countries could conceivably face. France experiences inflation above the *FF* line and deflation below. Germany experiences inflation above the *GG* line and deflation below. Thus *D* represents the joint target and divides all possibilities into four zones. If the world were in zone I, for example, authorities in both countries would wish to reduce aggregate demand; in zones II and IV the two countries have opposite desires.

Suppose first that expenditure policy is the tool of each country and that the world is in quadrant I. Then both countries decrease autonomous spending, and these actions are mutually reinforcing. Similarly, if the world is in quadrant III, France will increase autonomous spending I^F and Germany will increase I^G, and each country's action will reinforce that of the other. But in quadrants II and IV the goals of the two countries conflict. One will increase I while the other reduces it, and each country's action will frustrate the other. In a perfect world the two countries could simply adopt the values of I^F and I^G that would allow both to reach their desired incomes. But in reality the authorities can never be sure of what result will follow from their policies or even of what policy will actually follow from their attempts, and these attempts cannot be smoothly altered. Thus the possibility of policy conflict is real.

A change in investment in any country constitutes a change in world investment and stimulates all countries. International trade is the mechanism for transmitting the stimulus from country to country. Likewise for a decrease

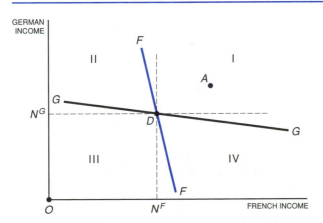

FIGURE 19.10 Possible Policy Conflicts In zone I both countries experience inflation, and in zone III both are in a recession. But in zones II and IV the two countries have opposite problems.

in investment. Thus the Great Depression spread from the United States to the rest of the world. American recessions and booms greatly influence our major trading partners, and most other countries are affected indirectly as well as directly. For example, an American recession will produce a deflationary effect in Australia by reducing the American demand for imports of Australian goods. But it will also reduce demand in Japan, a major trading partner of the United States; since the Japanese import much from Australia, this will, in turn, reduce Australian demand also.

Suppose instead that France and Germany use trade policy. That is, each country attempts to shift its import schedule $M(Y)$ by changing quotas and taxes on trade. As we have seen, manipulation of the exchange rate can also be used for this purpose. Then in quadrant I each country will attempt to shift its import curve up to reduce aggregate demand. But this will stimulate demand in the other country. Likewise in quadrant III, each country's attempt to solve its own problem will make things worse for the other. Quadrants II and IV now represent the cases where policy actions in France and Germany are mutually reinforcing.

A change in trade policy in any country switches aggregate world demand from the products of one country to those of another. Thus during the Great Depression many countries tried to stimulate their economies at the expense of their partners by restricting imports with tariffs and quotas. Such attempts are sometimes called "exporting unemployment" and the policies used to implement them "beggar thy neighbor" policies. To the extent that several nations all attempt this at once, whether for offensive or defensive purposes, their efforts will tend to cancel; but world trade will shrink, with accompanying inefficiency. That is what happened in the 1930s.

Now suppose that France and Germany have a floating exchange rate, and that they find themselves in zone I—say, at A. Then both countries will adopt contractionary monetary and fiscal policies. With the two countries acting in tandem, there would on balance be little effect on the exchange rate and no tendency toward policy conflict. But it is important to note that this conclusion requires both countries to use expenditure policy for internal balance and to leave the exchange rate to take care of external balance. If instead the exchange rate were manipulated for internal purposes, conflict would immediately erupt. Both countries would wish to appreciate to reduce aggregate demand, but there is only one exchange rate between them. One argument for fixed exchange rates is that they would prevent such conflict by preventing the use of the exchange rate as a policy instrument for internal balance.

Suppose next that the world is in zone II, so the French adopt expansionary policies and the Germans contractionary ones. The degree of international capital mobility once again becomes important, so let us start by assuming that there is none. The expansionary monetary and fiscal policy will increase aggregate demand in France and decrease it in Germany. The franc will depreciate relative to the mark; this will serve to prevent a trade imbalance from developing. The situation is clearly better than it would be with fixed exchange rates. In the latter case, trade imbalances would cause each country's

policy efforts to frustrate the other country's efforts. By preventing these imbalances, a floating rate "bottles up" each country's policy at home and thereby
eliminates international conflict and renders policy more locally potent.

Now suppose that capital is highly mobile internationally. Monetary and
fiscal policy might have quite different effects, so consider them separately.
Look at monetary policy first. Suppose the French authorities increase the
money supply by buying bonds from the public, and the German authorities
contract the German money supply by selling bonds. Then the French public
buys bonds from the German public. France has a capital-account deficit, the
franc depreciates, and a trade surplus emerges. At the same time, Germany
experiences a capital-account surplus, an appreciated mark, and a trade-account
deficit. Thus there are international repercussions to the national policies. But
these repercussions are not indicative of conflict; indeed, they are the means
by which each country's policy works. The French trade surplus stimulates
the French economy, while the German trade deficit depresses Germany, just
as desired. If, by contrast, there were a fixed exchange rate, each country's
policy would have been frustrated: the French capital-account deficit and
German surplus would have been matched not by trade imbalances with their
consequent desirable effects, but by a movement of international reserves
from the French central bank to the German central bank. Again, floating exchange rates are more conducive than fixed to both international harmony and
national policy effectiveness. Note also that if the authorities tried instead to
manipulate the exchange rate to attain internal targets, this would not now be
a source of conflict. Each country would desire a depreciated franc and an appreciated mark.

Now suppose that fiscal policy is used. The French increase government
spending, and the Germans reduce it. Then the French develop a capital-
account surplus, the franc appreciates, and their trade balance goes into deficit.
The opposite takes place in Germany. This is a very disruptive situation: the
trade imbalance nullifies each country's policy effort. This situation now is
worse than it would be with fixed exchange rates. In the latter case part of
each country's change in government spending leaks abroad and frustrates
the efforts of the other government; the exchange-rate change that now occurs
increases that leakage.

In sum, a floating exchange rate can cause more international conflict
than fixed rates when exchange-rate manipulation is likely to be used for internal objectives by governments whose objectives are similar or when fiscal
policy is used to attain internal balance and capital is highly mobile.
Otherwise, floating rates increase national autonomy and reduce international
conflict.

Monetary and Fiscal Policy for Internal and External Balance

If the exchange rate is available as an instrument of policy, a government
can attain both internal and external balance by using expenditure policy for
the former and the exchange rate for the latter. But governments are often

reluctant to use the exchange rate as an instrument. Instead, they frequently treat it as a policy objective in its own right. There are two reasons for this. First, we have seen that even with floating exchange rates, policy has international repercussions: an exchange-rate change affects other countries. This ensures that the level of the exchange rate has international political implications and thereby makes it an element in the government's calculations of international relations. Second, the exchange rate has distinct domestic implications. Depreciation increases inflation directly not only through its effect on aggregate demand, but also through its influence on domestic relative prices and, therefore, on the domestic distribution of income.

For all these reasons, governments may regard the exchange rate as a target, like aggregate demand, rather than as an instrument, like monetary and fiscal policy. If so, this brings us right back to the discussion of section 1. With capital internationally mobile, monetary and fiscal policies have differential effects on internal and external balance. Only now "external balance" means the attainment of a targeted exchange rate rather than a targeted balance-of-payments deficit.

9. SUMMARY

1. International capital mobility causes fiscal and monetary policies to have differential relative effects on internal and external balance in the short run. This means that, even with a fixed exchange rate, an appropriate mixture of the two policies can achieve both internal and external balance. But the long-run situation is ambiguous.

2. The greater the degree of international capital mobility, the more temporary the stimulating effects of monetary expansion and the greater the perverse foreign repercussions of domestic monetary policy.

3. With flexible rates, the higher the degree of international capital mobility, the less effective fiscal policy over domestic activity and the greater the international repercussions.

4. Because of international spillovers, the exercise of expenditure policy in one country affects other countries. Thus such policy will be disruptive of international harmony when countries are out of phase and mutually reinforcing when they are in phase.

5. Trade policy and exchange-rate policy redistribute expenditures between countries. Thus such policies are disruptive if directed toward internal balance when countries are in phase and mutually reinforcing when they are out of phase.

SUGGESTED READING

Dornbusch, R. *Open Economy Macroeconomics.* New York: Basic Books, 1980. See in particular Chapters 9, and 11 through 14.

Frenkel, J. A. "Flexible Exchange Rates, Prices, and the Role of 'News': Lessons from the 1970s." *Journal of Political Economy* 89 (1981): 665–705.

Frenkel, J. A., and A. Razin. "The Mundell-Fleming Model a Quarter Century Later." *IMF Staff Papers* 34 (1987): 567–620.

Marston, R. C. "Stabilization Policies in Open Economies." In *Handbook of International Economics*. Vol. 2. Edited by R. W. Jones and P. B. Kenen. Amsterdam: North Holland, 1985. Useful survey.

Meade, J. E. *The Balance of Payments*. London: Oxford University Press, 1951. Like most classics, worshiped rather than read.

Mussa, M. "Macroeconomic Interdependence and the Exchange Rate Regime." In *International Economic Policy*. Edited by R. Dornbusch and J. A. Frenkel. Baltimore: Johns Hopkins, 1979. An excellent survey.

Tobin, J., and J. B. de Macedo. "The Short-Run Macroeconomics of Floating Exchange Rates: An Exposition." In *Flexible Exchange Rates and the Balance of Payments*. Edited by J. S. Chipman and C. P. Kindleberger. Amsterdam: North Holland, 1980. Useful.

Whitman, M. "Policies for Internal and External Balance." Princeton University, *Special Papers in International Economics* 9 (1970). A survey of the literature of the 1960s.

Part Seven

The Modern International Economy

The concluding part of this book examines some issues that involve the basic ideas of both trade theory and international monetary theory. These issues largely concern *economic integration:* a reduction in barriers to economic transactions between residents of different nations. In a sense, most of this book has been concerned with economic integration since we have investigated questions such as the welfare consequences of free or liberal trade, the effects of international transactions on domestic macroeconomic policy, and much more. This part, therefore, appropriately closes the book.

Three sets of global issues intimately involve economic integration. Issues confronting the industrial nations in their relations with each other (*North-North* or *West-West* problems) are strongly colored by the consequences of extensive international interdependence. The interdependence between these essentially similar economies has emerged again and again in the course of our study. *East-West* relations concern the evolution of exchanges between nations that in the past traded relatively little with each other because of fundamentally different economic systems (and with less-than-cordial political relations). The dominant consideration in *North-South* debate has, by contrast, been that of distribution: what the North should concede in order to improve the lot of the South. But in recent years emphasis has increasingly turned also to issues much like those found in East-West relations: how to restructure these economies and integrate them more with the industrial world.

This concluding part devotes one chapter to issues involved in *North-North* or in *West-West* integration and one chapter to issues involved in *North-South* and in *East-West* integration.

CHAPTER 20

Economic Integration

> The world has narrowed to a neighborhood before it has broadened
> into a brotherhood. —LYNDON B. JOHNSON

This chapter examines an aspect of integration hitherto ignored in this book: *biased integration,* a reduction of economic barriers among a group of countries but not between those countries and the rest of the world. Examples include the formation of free-trade areas or customs unions such as NAFTA or the EU, the granting of tariff preferences to the LDCs by the DCs, and the GATT-sponsored multilateral tariff negotiations, which reduce trade barriers among the DCs by much more than barriers between the DCs and the LDCs.

Although we will be concerned with only the economic aspects of integration, there is usually a political dimension as well. Often, political integration brings about economic integration, and achieving the latter may be a significant motive for pushing ahead with the former. Such was the case with the adoption of the U.S. Constitution, and in Canada, Australia, and Russia political unification preceded or was accompanied by economic unification. The imperfect political union of the Austro-Hungarian Empire, on the other hand, ultimately failed to derive a successful customs union. More rarely, economic union precedes political union and may be intended to help foster the latter. The creation of the German Zollverein in 1818–1834 preceded by decades the unification of Germany, and the South African customs union also antedated political unification. The promotion of European unity was, in many quarters, a significant objective of the formation of the EEC in 1957.

1. BIASED INTEGRATION IN THEORY

Economic integration could involve a reduction in barriers to trade or to factor mobility, or a unification of economic policies. We discuss each in turn.

Trade Integration

Suppose that France (F), Germany (G), and the rest of the world (R) all initially trade with each other and all have tariffs. F and G then abolish all tariffs on each other's products but maintain their tariffs on goods from R, whose commercial policy is unchanged. What are the effects of such biased integration? The reduction of tariffs between F and G is a move toward free trade, which we might expect to be beneficial. But now goods from R are subject to a tax in F and G, whereas similar goods from G and F, respectively, are not. We would expect this *price discrimination* to be harmful. Thus biased integration has on balance replaced one distortion (the tariff on F-G trade) with another distortion (geographical price discrimination).

Trade Creation. The elimination of tariffs between F and G creates trade between these two countries and generates gains, as discussed in Chapter 1. Each country concentrates more on producing the goods in which it has a comparative advantage relative to the other country, and trade expands, causing marginal rates of transformation and of substitution in F to equal those in G.

Trade Diversion. Since F now levies a tariff when goods are imported from R but not when the same goods are imported from G, residents of F will now buy from G some products that were previously purchased from R. Similarly, G residents will divert their trade from R to F. This trade diversion is necessarily inefficient because if F residents chose to buy from R suppliers when they competed on equal terms with G suppliers, it must be that the former could supply the product more favorably.

Balance of Trade Creation and Trade Diversion. Trade creation is beneficial, and trade diversion is harmful. Which one dominates depends upon circumstances; biased integration may or may not be a good thing. If, before integration, most of F's trade is with G, trade creation will likely dominate because there is not much trade with R to be diverted. Thus the larger the extent of the integration, the more likely it is to be beneficial: integration of the whole world can involve no trade diversion (in the absence of interplanetary trade). If, on the other hand, most of the products that F imports can be produced more cheaply in R than in G, integration with G is likely to be harmful. The situation is reminiscent of the discussion in Chapter 8 of the use of tariffs to cure domestic distortions: one distortion is replaced by another so that the net effect is ambiguous. This is initially counterintuitive: since integration involves a reduction of tariff protection in the world, one would naturally expect it to be beneficial.

The original intuition is partially resurrected when we realize that, when F and G integrate, they also might want to change the tariffs they levy on imports from R. Suppose that they do in fact do this and that they do it in such a way that, after integration, F and G together import and export to R exactly what they together did before integration. In this case there is no net trade diversion, and integration is necessarily beneficial.

All of this is amply illustrated by the EEC. When Britain joined in 1973, the basic economic issue was one of weighing the trade creation, stemming from free trade with the Continent in manufactures, against the trade diversion of replacing agricultural imports from the Commonwealth and America with more expensive food from Europe. The Kennedy Round of multilateral tariff negotiations in the early 1960s was significantly motivated by a desire to reduce tariffs in general to assure that the formation of the EEC would not divide the industrial world into distinct trade blocks. In other words, the aim was to alter tariffs between the EEC and the rest of the world in such a way as to minimize trade diversion.

Trade Modification. Integration most often takes place between economies that are relatively similar. Thus it might be that F imports from G an

---

Example of Trade Diversion

As hypothesized in Table 20.1, suppose Britain initially imposes a tariff of £0.60 on imports of butter, which can be purchased from either New Zealand or Europe. New Zealand is the more efficient producer and so

TABLE 20.1 **A Hypothetical Case of Trade Diversion**

	New Zealand butter	European butter
World price	£1.00	£1.50
British tariff	0.60	0.60
British price (preunion)	1.60	2.10
European tariff	0.60	0.00
British price (postunion)	1.60	1.50

captures most of the British market; only those British consumers who expressly favor the European product would be willing to pay £2.10 for it when New Zealand butter is available for £1.60. Now Britain and Europe abolish tariffs on each other's products. European butter enters duty-free and, at £1.50, is cheaper than New Zealand butter, which is still subject to the tariff. Many British consumers will now shift from New Zealand butter to European butter. This trade diversion is globally inefficient (because New Zealand can give the world butter at a lower real cost than can Europe) and is also harmful to Britain (because the £0.60 tariff on New Zealand butter would not be paid to New Zealand, but retained by the British collectively).

assortment of goods different from those that it would import from *R* under any circumstances. In this case effective price discrimination is unlikely (because *G* and *R* are not competitive suppliers of identical goods to *F* in any case), and trade diversion will probably not be serious. But integration could still cause a general substitution, by consumers in *F,* of *G* products for *R* products if they serve broadly similar purposes. Suppose, for example, that in Table 20.1 New Zealand produces butter as before but that Europe produces only margarine (that is, relabel the right-hand column of the table as "European margarine"). In this case integration does not cause price discrimination because New Zealand and Europe export different goods to Britain. But obviously our earlier conclusions are unchanged because butter and margarine serve basically the same purposes: they are good *substitutes.* Such trade modification might seem, at this stage, to be essentially the same as trade diversion. But this is not so. For one thing, it might work in the opposite way. To see this, suppose that in Table 20.1 New Zealand once again faithfully exports butter, but that Europe exports bread (once again relabel the right-hand column of the table, this time as "European bread"). The difference now is that people do not consume butter *instead* of bread—the relation between butter and margarine—but butter *with* bread. If they have more of one, they will want more of the other; bread and butter are *complements.* In this sense, when integration makes European bread cheaper in Britain and, therefore, increases British demand for bread, it will also cause the British to *increase* their demand for New Zealand butter.

Thus trade modification might mean that integration between *F* and *G* either increases or decreases trade with *R,* depending upon the relative importance of complements and substitutes. But there is a more fundamental difference between trade diversion and trade modification. The former results when integration involves a new distortion: price discrimination. This, by itself, is necessarily bad. Trade modification, by contrast, does not involve the introduction of price discrimination, but rather the substitution of one pattern of world tariffs by another. This might be good or bad.

The distinction is important in the modern world. As we have seen, the most prominent characteristic of post–Second World War commercial policy is the dramatic mutual reduction of DC tariff barriers unaccompanied by any comparable reduction of LDC barriers. Because of the most-favored-nation clause, however, the reductions in DC tariffs also apply to imports of identical goods from the LDCs. Thus price discrimination and trade diversion are of limited relevance here. But the DCs import from each other a significantly different assortment of goods than they import from LDCs, so that trade modification is potentially very significant. An evaluation of the welfare significance of the dominant feature of postwar commercial policy necessarily reduces to weighing trade creation against (or with) trade modification.

Terms-of-Trade Effects. If the partners together are sizable in the world markets in which they deal, integration could alter world prices and thus the terms of trade of partners. There are two aspects to this.

The first involves the trade between the partners, *F* and *G*. We saw in Chapter 1 that a country need not benefit by a movement from limited trade to free trade because it could suffer a significant terms-of-trade deterioration. The same applies here: if *F* and *G* mutually eliminate tariffs on each other's goods, the terms of trade between them could conceivably change radically. Thus, even if we completely ignore trade diversion, one country might gain by more than total trade creation while the other country loses. This could be compensated for by a transfer payment from the gainer to the loser that still leaves both better off since they together have the net benefit of trade creation to divide (remember, we are ignoring trade diversion for now). This sort of thing is not of such practical irrelevance as it might sound: the EU makes transfers through the community budget, financed by members' contributions, which disburses funds for agricultural support and regional development. Negotiations over Britain's entry involved her relation to that budget (as did renegotiations when the country became convinced it had struck a bad deal).

Integration can also alter the partners' terms of trade with the rest of the world, and this might mitigate the harmful effects of trade diversion. Integration between *F* and *G*, which causes those two countries to trade more with each other and less with *R* (trade diversion), could bring about a reduction in the prices demanded by sellers in *R* if *F* and *G* together constitute a significant portion of the total market for *R*'s products. Furthermore, if *F* and *G* together are significantly more important in world markets than either separately, integration would enable the two jointly to exercise more monopoly power.

National Economies of Scale. We saw in Chapter 2 that, in addition to comparative cost differences, scale economies could serve, in different ways, as a basis for international trade. Consider first those national economies that follow from geographical concentration of an industry, such as cost reductions due to the adoption of an efficient plant size. By allowing increased specialization by the partner countries, integration can result in gains via such scale economies. Suppose, for example, that *F, G,* and *R* each initially has its own steel industry and automobile industry, each of which is protected and serves its local market. Suppose that the markets for these products in *F* and *G* are too small to support plants of the most efficient size. If these countries now integrate, they can jointly rationalize the two industries, with a single efficient steel plant located in, say, *G* serving both countries and a single efficient automobile plant doing the same from *F*. These gains are analogous to those of trade creation with reference to comparative costs. There is also an analog to trade diversion: if *R* was initially exporting some steel and automobiles to *F* and *G*, the reduction in those exports could require the industries in *R* to operate at less efficient scales.

The importance of national scale economies is sensitive to country sizes. Large countries are most likely already to have industries composed of firms sizable enough to operate at efficient scales. Gains are accordingly most likely when integration takes place between small countries with inefficiently small plants; furthermore, if the rest of the world is large, it is unlikely to be forced to inefficient scales of operation by a loss of customers. National scale economies have probably not been a significant factor in the EU, whose member states seem large enough to support efficient-sized industries on their own, but those scale economies are central to many proposals for integration between LDCs, especially LDCs that have adopted vigorous import substitution policies in the past.

International Scale Economies and Product Differentiation. Even economies that are initially large enough to support many firms of efficient size in each industry may benefit from scale economies in another way, as we also saw in Chapter 2. Integration between such economies allows the production process within an industry to be further subdivided, with individual firms concentrating on distinct stages of the process, allowing the realization of any external scale economies due to the further division of labor. Also, different firms can concentrate on different versions of one basic product, giving consumers more choice than they had before. When the integration is between similar countries who, therefore, continue to diversify in production, the result will be to expand intraindustry trade: carburetors will be exchanged for cylinder heads, red wine for white wine, and so forth. Such integration may also produce an analog to trade modification as intermediate goods or differentiated products from the rest of the world become more costly relative to those from the integration partner.

International scale economies and product differentiation appear to be important in the EU since European integration was followed by a large expansion in intraindustry trade rather than in interindustry specialization. More generally, the substantial postwar biased integration of the DCs has been accompanied, as we saw in Chapter 1, by the steady increase of intraindustry trade. By contrast, national scale economies are generally thought to be more relevant to potential integration among LDCs. But even here, there is some evidence that those LDCs that have followed liberal trade policies (that is, biased integration with DCs) and some of those LDCs that have attempted integration among themselves have expanded intraindustry trade.

Competitive Effects. Chapter 3 showed that imperfect competition can furnish yet another basis for trade. If national markets are initially characterized by oligopoly or monopoly, integration may increase economic efficiency by subjecting domestic firms to competition with firms in the partner country, thereby reducing market imperfections. Some economists maintain that this has been a significant benefit of the EU. But a form of trade diversion is also possible: imperfections might become worse if integration shields domestic firms from competition with firms in the outside world. Also, the possibility of integration of firms themselves must be considered.

Factor-Market Integration

Countries sometimes mutually eliminate barriers to factor movements between each other; such is one feature of the EU. This introduces effects analogous to trade integration. For example, productive factors will tend to move from that partner in which their absolute productivities are low to the partner in which they are high; this raises the joint income of the integrating countries. There is even an analog to trade diversion: if the formation of the EU allows Italian workers to enter Germany more readily than it does Turkish workers, the former will tend to displace the latter. This will be inefficient if labor's productivity in Germany exceeds its productivity in Turkey by more than its productivity in Italy.

Integration of Macroeconomic Policies

Integration sometimes takes the form of a merging or coordination of national economic policies—notably, macroeconomic policies. This can have the effect of reducing payments imbalances or exchange-rate fluctuations, and the attainment of fixed exchange rates between the partners is a major consideration in such integration.

Recall the basic inconsistency between (a) fixed exchange rates, (b) autonomous national macroeconomic policies, and (c) free international transactions. The sort of integration we are now considering attempts to attain (a) and forsake (b). The issue is not exactly one of removing policy conflicts between nations: we saw in Part Six that such conflicts are not necessarily eliminated by flexible exchange rates and, with highly mobile capital, may even be accentuated. Rather, the problem is to coordinate macroeconomic policy internationally to make fixed exchange rates feasible.

We currently have many examples of countries that peg their own currencies to another currency or currency basket while floating relative to the rest of the world. Some of these countries do accept the loss of autonomy in macroeconomic policy making; a full monetary union of the EU countries is in fact an ultimate goal of the European Monetary System (EMS). (Later in this chapter we will examine the EU's progress toward approaching this goal.) But many LDCs peg their currencies and maintain fully autonomous national policies by reliance on extensive trade and exchange controls; of the inconsistent triumvirate, it is (c), free international transactions, that is sacrificed. This hardly constitutes economic integration.

Monetary integration limits the likelihood of partner countries aggressively manipulating exchange rates for nationalistic purposes since it produces macroeconomic policy coordination, and it may also constitute a vital step toward a political unification desired for noneconomic reasons. But the primary economic benefit is that the usefulness of each country's money is enhanced, as we discussed in Chapter 14. The principal cost is the loss of autonomy in macroeconomic policy. What circumstances most likely render the benefits more important than the costs?

Monetary integration between two countries is likely to be more attractive the more *open* the economies are relative to each other. If residents of one country conduct a large proportion of their economic transactions directly or indirectly with residents of the other country, fixed exchange rates can greatly increase the usefulness of the first country's money. Also, the loss of policy autonomy is not likely to be large because such countries will be interdependent even with a floating exchange rate. A region best suited to an arrangement with fixed exchange rates between countries in the region is sometimes called an *optimum currency area*. Ronald McKinnon of Stanford has emphasized the importance of degrees of openness in the delineation of such an area. Earlier, Robert Mundell, the originator of the concept of an optimum currency area, had stressed the importance of factor mobility. If such mobility is high, factors will move from areas of high unemployment to areas of low unemployment and equalization of factor costs will also tend to equalize inflation rates within the region. Thus there will be little need, and little opportunity, for independent macroeconomic policies by countries within the region. According to this criterion, then, an optimum currency area is defined by the extent of free factor mobility between countries. The EMS would seem to score high relative to both criteria: its member countries are quite open vis-à-vis each other, and the EU has eliminated internal barriers to factor movements.

Problems

20.1 In terms of the concepts discussed in this section, speculate about the consequences for the United States of the formation of the EEC.

20.2 Should the existence of the guest-worker system discussed in Chapter 10 prove a help or hindrance in the effort of the EU to achieve monetary integration?

20.3 Suppose the world is as described in the Heckscher-Ohlin-Samuelson model of Chapter 5, except that there are several countries instead of just two. Is integration more likely to be beneficial to two countries if their relative endowments are similar or if they are different?

20.4 Are those gains from integration that are due to international scale economies and product differentiation more likely to be large if the partners are similar or if they are different?

20.5* Suppose that F and G mutually eliminate tariffs on each other's products and then jointly levy an optimum common tariff on goods from R. Can you say anything about the significance of trade diversion?

2. BIASED INTEGRATION IN PRACTICE

Perhaps the most significant postwar exercise in economic integration is the GATT-sponsored multilateral reduction in DC tariffs on manufactured goods. This reduction has been in the context of the most-favored-nation clause and, therefore, has not introduced price discrimination, but it has brought about biased integration by largely restricting tariff cuts to goods traded, for the most part, among the DCs. As mentioned earlier, this means that trade diversion can be ignored, but trade modification must be considered in addition to trade creation. We also saw in Chapter 1 that this integration has been accompanied by a large increase in intraindustry trade, leading one to suspect that international scale economies and product differentiation could be important considerations.

Discriminatory tariff preferences—with a group of countries reducing, but not eliminating, tariffs vis-à-vis each other while leaving unchanged tariffs against third-country products—violate the MFN clause and hence are inconsistent with the GATT. But the postwar world still offers some significant examples. Commonwealth Preferences, between those nations formerly part of the British Empire, were established before the war and allowed by GATT to continue. The United Kingdom, though, largely turned its back on Commonwealth Preference by joining the EEC. Other examples of this type of integration are the preference schemes for LDC products adopted by most DCs. These schemes, however, do not involve reciprocal preferences by the LDCs. Finally, it is possible that one effect of the Tokyo Round could be to increase significantly the importance of this type of integration. As a result of that round, codes were established for various nontariff barriers. These codes need not be signed by all GATT members and may be signed by nonmembers. Some of these codes have attracted a limited number of signatories, who intend to apply the codes only to each other. To the extent that these nontariff barriers are equivalent to tariffs, the Tokyo Round may, therefore, produce the nontariff equivalent of discriminatory tariff preferences.

Definitions

The following are the principal forms of biased integration:

Biased tariff reduction. A group of countries nondiscriminately reduces tariffs on goods largely traded only among themselves and leaves other tariffs unchanged.

Discriminatory tariff preferences. A group of countries reduces tariffs on each other's products and leaves unchanged tariffs on the products of other countries.

Free-trade area. The member countries eliminate tariffs among themselves, and each member maintains its own tariff schedule on goods from outside countries.

Customs union. The member countries eliminate tariffs among themselves and establish a common tariff schedule on goods from outside countries.

Common market. A customs union with the additional removal of all barriers to factor movements between members.

Economic union. The members integrate all economic policies.

The GATT departs from the MFN principle by explicitly allowing free-trade areas and customs unions. These differ in that the latter involves a common tariff relative to the rest of the world, whereas the former does not. A major drawback to a free-trade area is the need to regulate internal trade despite the abolition of internal tariffs. If this were not done, individual members would be unable to maintain their own tariffs on goods from nonmembers since such goods would enter the free-trade area exclusively through the member with the lowest tariff. Suppose, for example, that Sweden and Finland participate in a free-trade area, with Finland imposing a tariff on steel of $50 a ton and Sweden one of $30 a ton. Then a Finnish steel importer would, if he could get away with it, import his steel through Sweden, paying the Swedish tariff and then shipping the steel duty-free into Finland. This *trade deflection* would make it impossible for Finland to impose effectively its higher tariff and would also cause Finland to lose tariff revenue to Sweden. Trade between Finland and Sweden must be monitored to prevent this sort of evasion, and administration can become complex (for example, suppose Finland imports cars made in Sweden using steel imported from outside the free-trade area).

A customs union avoids the problem of trade deflection by establishing a common external tariff. But this means that individual members lose the ability to conduct independent trade policies and must reach agreement on a common policy. Also the members must agree on how to distribute among themselves the tariff revenues they jointly collect.

There are many examples of attempted free-trade areas and customs unions. LDCs have formed many such arrangements, lured usually by the hope of realizing scale economies. But the arrangements have in fact achieved little real economic integration. The decisive obstacle has been political disagreement between the governments of would-be partners. Two unions have simply dissolved: the West Indian Federation and the integration of Uganda, Tanzania, and Kenya. The largest arrangement, the Latin American Integration Association, LAIA (formerly the Latin American Free Trade Association, LAFTA), including Mexico and most of South America, has made at best modest progress toward the goal embodied in its name. A subgroup, signers of the Andean Pact, had hoped to accelerate integration among themselves and establish a customs union within LAFTA, but they have been balked by political conflicts. The Central American Common Market actually had to endure a 1969 war between two of its members, Honduras and El Salvador, over a soccer game. The LDC union with the most current promise is probably the Association of Southeast Asian Nations (ASEAN), comprising Thailand, Malaysia, Singapore, Indonesia, and the Philippines. It decided in 1976 to try to form a common market.

The most successful attempts have been made in Europe. The 1957 Treaty of Rome created the European Economic Community (EEC) of France, West Germany, Italy, Belgium, Luxembourg, and the Netherlands. The United Kingdom, Denmark, and Ireland joined in 1973, Greece in 1981, and Spain and Portugal in 1986. The European Free Trade Association (EFTA) was formed in 1960 by seven European nations desiring looser integration than the EEC. The EU has established a true common market and the EFTA a true free-trade area (in manufactures). In 1977 these two groups eliminated most tariffs on each other's industrial goods so that the EFTA and the EU together now comprise a large free-trade area. In North America, Canada and the United States negotiated a free-trade pact (CUSTA) in 1987; in 1993 this was in effect superseded by the North American Free Trade Area (NAFTA) comprising Canada, Mexico, and the United States.

Problems

20.6 Why is it necessary for a customs union to negotiate some way of distributing the joint tariff revenues, rather than simply letting each country keep what it collects (hint: consider the geographical position of Luxembourg)?

20.7 Can you think of any reasons why the European attempts at integration were notably more successful than LDC attempts?

20.8 The United States strongly supported formation of the EEC. Why?

20.9 Discuss the implications of the GATT multilateral tariff reduction for the significance of the EEC.

3. *CASE STUDY:* THE EUROPEAN UNION (EU)

As the most prominent postwar example of formal integration, the European Economic Community (EEC)—as the European Union was originally called—has been an invitation to economists seeking to measure quantitatively the effects of customs unions. Techniques and specific results have varied, but the strong consensus is that formation of the EEC resulted in substantially more trade creation than diversion. But international scale economies and product differentiation may have been even more significant: studies by Bela Balassa and others have shown that the formation of the EEC was followed by a significant increase in the amount and relative importance of intraindustry trade among all the partners rather than by an increase in interindustrial specialization.

But the EEC is more than a customs union. It is something between a common market and an economic union—with the latter the ultimate goal. The EEC followed earlier, more limited, integration measures such as the European Coal and Steel Community (ECSC) and was enthusiastically pushed by those who hoped for a federated European state that would finally end centuries of local wars and establish a new superpower. The EEC changed its name to the European Community (EC) and has now started to refer to itself as the European Union (EU). But the federation remains a dream, and the individual countries have not surrendered key aspects of sovereignty such as foreign and defense policies. Still, the EU is not only an agreement over international economic matters. There is a significant bureaucracy, headquartered at Brussels, with over 10,000 "eurocrats," and members of the EU parliament are now chosen by direct election—prompting speculation that that body may become a power center independent of the national governments. The EU now conducts much economic policy beyond its customs union and the dreamed-of monetary union. There are community regulations and policies dealing with competition (antitrust), labor, industry, social affairs, energy, the environment, and consumer issues. But two areas stand out in the community budget: a regional policy aids economically backward parts of the community, and the Common Agricultural Policy (CAP) is now the single most significant activity of the EU.

The Common Agricultural Policy (CAP)

Most industrial countries have policies to protect their agricultural sectors. The CAP, like these other policies, makes little sense economically. It is very complex and expensive, and its net effect is to cause the community to produce food at a much higher cost than it could be obtained from abroad (trade diversion again). The CAP harms the external relations of the EU with those countries, such as the United States, that are thereby deprived of agricultural export markets. It causes even more internal dissension between those countries who see themselves as net losers (the United Kingdom and Germany) and those who are net gainers (France), and also between community agricultural interests generally and those who object to such a large budget for the benefit of that sector. But in spite of all this, the CAP is a concrete integration achievement in a most difficult and sensitive policy area.

Most of the nations that combined into the EEC had long histories of protection and support for their agricultural sectors. They did not wish to end this support, but free trade in agriculture within the EEC was a central part of integration; thus a common policy was called for. Under this policy the authorities purchase agricultural products within the EU as required to maintain prices at target levels. At the same time, the community is protected from world markets, notably by variable-level tariffs on many products, which assure that EU farmers will not be undersold within the community no matter how much world prices drop. When harvests are good, the authorities accumulate huge stocks of products bought at high EU prices (a $14 million "butter mountain," insured with Lloyd's of London, once burned down in the Netherlands). These products are eventually sold abroad at low world prices. This makes the CAP very expensive. This brief description, however, does not begin to do justice to the complexity of the CAP, which uses more than twenty distinct systems of prices.

The CAP has been in operation since 1968. This operation has become more difficult as a result of the increasing currency fluctuations dating from

1969. CAP support prices were set in terms of units of account (defined in varying ways) and translated into national currency prices using exchange rates. If market exchange rates were used for this, the support prices received by a country's farmers and the food prices paid by its consumers would fluctuate directly with the exchange rate. An appreciation of the mark of 10 percent relative to the unit of account, for example, would immediately reduce by 10 percent the mark price of food in Germany. This was politically unacceptable to national governments. As a result, market exchange rates are not used to translate CAP prices into national currencies. Instead, this is done with administratively determined exchange rates—called "green currency" rates—which the authorities adjust gradually from time to time. This has had two effects. First, when the market rates and green rates diverge—and they have diverged by up to 40 percent—food prices differ from country to country. If the green rate is Fr 2/mark while the actual exchange rate is Fr 3/mark, food prices in Germany are 50 percent higher than in France. Under these circumstances, the CAP would quickly be destroyed by arbitrage between countries. To prevent this, border taxes and subsidies called Monetary Compensatory Amounts (MCAs) have been used to cancel out the price differences. The second effect of this system is that the substantial exchange-rate fluctuations experienced under managed floating imply substantial fluctuations in the relation between market rates and the slowly adjusting green rates. This requires quick and substantial changes in the MCAs. Obviously, this system was much easier to administer when the European Monetary System (EMS) succeeded in limiting fluctuations in members' relative exchange rates. This consideration was in fact the single most significant technical motive for proceeding with the EMS's snake arrangement. The EMS will be discussed in a subsequent case study.

1992

The EEC had succeeded in eliminating tariffs on each member's manufactures by 1968. But trade was far from free. International exchanges within the community were hobbled by national differences in regulation, standards, and taxation, by the procurement policies of national governments, and by a lot of red tape. For example, individual countries maintained their own telecommunications monopolies, there was little trade in many services—such as banking and finance—and the shipment of goods across borders within the EEC involved costly and time-consuming formalities.

By the 1980s many Europeans felt that integration was losing steam and feared that the community was in danger of becoming only a bloated bureaucracy administering a monster of an agricultural program. Then in 1985 the European Commission issued a white paper calling for the "completion of the internal market" by January 1, 1993, and containing hundreds of concrete proposals toward that end. The goal was embodied in a 1986 amendment to the Treaty of Rome, the Single European Act (SEA). The goal was to establish a Europe without frontiers in which residents possessed the "four freedoms" to trade, to migrate, to invest, and to conduct business irrespective of national borders. The program became known as "1992" because of its scheduled implementation at the end of that year.

The program aroused two, quite different, concerns. Some people were skeptical that, in the end, 1992 would ever amount to much. They doubted that the individual governments would all be able to make the numerous and detailed legislative and administrative changes necessary to complete the internal market. Others were concerned that 1992 might, in a sense, prove too successful, with Europe protecting its large, newly integrated internal market from U.S. and Japanese competition by erecting new barriers and becoming a "Fortress Europe."

It is too soon to say whether Fortress Europe will emerge or not, but it is clear that the skeptics were too pessimistic: 1992 was basically successful, with much significant progress. Not all the SEA goals were met, to be sure. Passport checks at common EU borders have not completely disappeared, for example; they still are made along the borders of Denmark, Ireland, and the United Kingdom. And some changes, instead of being made all at once, are being phased in: a common market for insurance, EU-wide stockbrokering, and the common acceptance of vocational qualifications, for example.

Dynamics of the EU

The degree of integration achieved by the EU has been steadily evolving along three dimensions. First, the degree of integration among existing members has changed. Second, new members have entered the union. Third, the EU has developed new arrangements for increasing integration with non-members.

Integration among Existing Members. The program to complete the internal market, discussed above, is a good example of this process. So are the attempts to approach monetary union, which will be discussed below.

Addition of New Members. As we saw above, the Common Market expanded from its original six members in 1957 to twelve by 1986. Austria, Finland, Norway, and Sweden have applied for membership and negotiated terms of entry. Expectations are that, at some indefinite times in the future, additional countries in southern and Central Europe will also join.

In negotiating with new applicants, the EU has been willing to discuss things like regional subsidies but has consistently refused to negotiate over basic principles of how the EU is run. Thus new applicants face a take-it-or-leave-it situation. Partly because of this, joining the EU becomes a controversial political issue in countries that have applied and negotiated terms of entry. When Denmark, Ireland, and the United Kingdom joined in 1973, Norway, which had also negotiated to enter, declined to do so after its voters voted no in a referendum. Greenland, which automatically became part of the EU when Denmark joined, subsequently pulled out. The issue of entry is now very controversial with the new applicants.

Integration with Outsiders. The EU has developed preferential arrangements with a number of other countries and groups of countries. The general system of preferences (GSP), discussed in Chapter 4, extends tariff preferences to most developing countries. The Lomé Convention grants further preferences and extends other forms of aid to a group of LDCs that are former colonies of EU members. The free-trade agreement with the EFTA has already been mentioned. On January 1, 1994, this was deepened into the European Economic Area (EEA) to allow free migration, investment, and trade in services in addition to trade in goods among the participants. These include the twelve members of the EU, the four new applicants mentioned above, plus Iceland. Switzerland, also a member of the EFTA, declined to participate in the EEA after a negative result in a 1992 referendum.

The EU has negotiated European Agreements with Czechoslovakia (now two countries), Hungary, and Poland (CHP). These provide for the phasing in of a free-trade area in manufactured goods, preferences for EU direct investment in CHP, and for CHP gradually to adjust a battery of its economic policies to EU standards. Migration is not provided for; indeed, a desire to substitute trade for migration was an important motivation for the EU. In spite of the agreements, the EU has initiated antidumping actions against some CHP products.

4. *CASE STUDY:* THE YUPPIE TRADE WARS THAT WEREN'T

Spain and Portugal joined the EC early in 1986 and so became part of the CAP. The United States had significant agricultural exports to the two countries and became concerned about the trade diversion that was sure to result. This concern focused especially on U.S. exports to Spain of 2.8 million tons of corn and sorghum, worth about $430 million.

Countries in such a situation are entitled, by GATT rules, to compensation in the form of tariff concessions that would allow them to increase exports of other goods. The United States demanded that the EC allow Spain and Portugal to continue to buy up to 4 million tons of grain a year on world markets, expecting that this would raise U.S. grain sales by about 2.8 million tons. In addition, the United States demanded lower EC tariffs on imports of some industrial goods, worth $100 million to $150 million per year. The Europeans responded that the tariff adjustments that had already been made gave the United States all the compensation it was entitled to.

Negotiations to resolve the dispute were unsuccessful, and they became intertwined with simultaneous haggling about the agenda for the forthcoming GATT round of multilateral trade negotiations. The United States threatened to retaliate with new tariffs on European goods. The EC threatened counter-retaliation, and the specter emerged of an escalating North Atlantic trade war that would drag in other countries (whose trade would also be affected by new measures) and scuttle the GATT round.

The outlook became particularly dark in January 1987 when the president instituted a package of retaliatory tariff increases, to go into effect at the end of the month. The package included tariffs of 200 percent on $400 million worth of U.S. imports of such goods as inexpensive European white wine, Belgian endives, French brandy and cheeses, and British gin. This was sure to get the attention of a certain class of U.S. consumer. While hurting these consumers, the package would not help at all the farmers whose welfare presumably was the concern that prompted the conflict: the only possible U.S. beneficiaries would have been producers of goods competing with the affected imports. But the package was carefully chosen for its effect on Europe. Tariffs of this size would likely be prohibitive, or nearly so, and of the goods affected, 47 percent came from France, the most ardent EC supporter of the CAP.

Frantic last-minute negotiations were conducted by telephone between Clayton Yeutter, the U.S. special trade representative, and Willy de Clercq, the EC trade commissioner. An agreement was reached just hours before the U.S. tariffs were to go into effect. The EC agreed that for four years Spain and Portugal would be allowed to purchase up to 2.3 million tons of corn and sorghum on world markets; this was expected to allow about 1.6 million tons of U.S. exports. In addition, EC tariffs were lowered on twenty-six products, including aluminum sheet, silicon wafers, dried onions, and cigars. It was thought that these concessions would increase U.S. exports by $70 million to $100 million.

Then in the early 1990s it was "déjà vu all over again." This time the dispute centered on U.S. objections that EC subsidies on oilseed production were stimulating European output, thereby depriving American farmers of export sales. The United States demanded that the EC reduce oilseed production. The dispute went to a GATT panel, which twice ruled that the EC subsidies violated trade rules. But Europe refused to budge. Negotiations became heated and broke down in October 1992. The Americans prepared a list of punitive tariffs on $1 billion worth of European exports and threatened to impose the tariffs at any moment if progress were not forthcoming. Europe threatened retaliation. Once again, the American threats targeted French products since France was regarded as the prime villain. For example, the list included a tariff of 200 percent on European white wine, which would have wiped out the U.S. market for, say, Chablis. This was precise targeting: the French agriculture minister was also president of the council of the Burgundy wine region.

This new dispute was complicated by the fact that the Uruguay Round of multilateral trade negotiations was in its sixth year and apparently headed toward a climax. Agricultural issues were prominent in these talks, and everyone realized that a U.S.-EC trade war would scuttle the Uruguay Round.

A compromise was reached at the Blair House in Washington on November 20, 1992. The deal covered not only oilseeds, but also other important issues between the United States and the EC concerning agriculture. Thus the accord seemed both to avert the threatened trade war and to clear the way for a successful completion of the Uruguay Round. But the compromise, which was between the United States and the EC as a whole (as represented by the European Commission), was very unpopular in France. Obstreperous French farmers began attacking McDonalds outlets, and the French government threatened to veto the deal. Such a veto would have both torpedoed the Uruguay Round and wreaked havoc within the EC itself. But, after another year of negotiations, the Uruguay Round was successfully concluded in December 1993 (just before the U.S. administration's negotiating authority was about to expire) after some relatively minor concessions persuaded the French to accept the agriculture accord.

These almost–trade wars illustrate several aspects of the link between regional economic blocs and multilateral trade relations. The first episode shows how trade diversion can affect a bloc's relations with the rest of the world. The second episode shows how relations with the rest of the world can affect conditions within a customs union, whose need to maintain a common external tariff requires joint negotiation with outsiders.

5. *CASE STUDY:* THE EUROPEAN MONETARY SYSTEM AND MAASTRICHT

Full monetary union has been a European goal since at least 1969. The strategy for reaching this goal is gradualism. The first step was attempted in 1972, when the EEC established the "snake in the tunnel": a band of exchange-rate fluctuations for members' currencies narrower than the bands adopted by countries in general after the Smithsonian Agreement (see Chapter 14). The arrangement continued after the collapse of the Bretton Woods system in 1973, with the participating countries jointly floating relative to the rest of the world ("the snake out of the tunnel"). But there was no formal structure for the integration or coordination of monetary and fiscal policies, and countries moved into or out of the arrangement as circumstances changed. In the end the snake basically became a mark currency area, with Germany the only large participant.

A Franco-German initiative in 1978 added new momentum, and the European Monetary System was formed in 1979. Member countries temporarily earmarked for the EMS one-fifth of their reserves of gold and dollars, and received in return equal-valued quantities of European Currency Units (ECUs). The ECU is a currency composite, something like the SDR, used for official transactions within the EEC. The intention seemed to be that, in the hazy future, the EMS should become the EEC central bank with the ECU as the EEC currency. The medium-term goal was to set up a European Monetary Fund to issue ECUs and extend credit to member-country central banks. But the main actual accomplishment was a new snake: adjustable pegs were established for the exchange rates of members' currencies relative to each other, and the countries undertook to maintain market rates within 2.25 percent of these pegs. This has been supported by large standby credit arrangements between the banks.

For some years the EMS seemed to be working well. The pegs had to be adjusted a number of times, but no major crisis forced countries to drop out of the snake. It was regarded as a success—one of the rare success stories of monetary integration. Indeed, it seemed to be getting stronger over time: Spain and Portugal were brought into the pegging arrangement; the United Kingdom, which had originally declined to peg, joined the snake; Italy, which originally was committed only to keeping the lira within 6 percent of its peg, adopted the narrower band of ± 2.25 percent. (Greece is the only member never to have participated in the pegging arrangement, and Portugal, Spain, and the United Kingdom have done so with the wider ± 6 percent bands.) The ECU is also a success itself. It has been embraced by the private sector: a significant volume of bond issues and bank transactions are now denominated in ECUs.

The EMS is an example of what political scientists call the "neofunctionalist" approach to integration: countries are tied together in obscure technical ways in the hope that this will induce more meaningful integration. In this case the hope is that the commitment to exchange-rate pegging will help bring about macroeconomic policy coordination and unification. The contrasting integration approach is to attempt at the outset complete merger (in this case, that could have meant agreeing to start the EMS as an EC central bank). This use of the EMS in the monetary sphere is analogous to the strategy followed by Europeans in the larger context: instead of trying directly to set up a unified European state, they established a customs union with the hope (among some) that it would lead to political union.

Impressed with the apparent success of the EMS, an EC committee in 1989 recommended that the community move to form a European Monetary Union with a single currency and a European central bank. Leaders of the individual member countries met at Maastricht, in the Netherlands, in 1991 and agreed on amendments to the Treaty of Rome that would set in motion the transition to such a union and that would also establish significant integration of the members' foreign, defense, and social policies as well as a common citizenship. The transition process was to involve three stages. In the first stage, all members were to join the snake arrangement. At the time, this meant Greece plus any among the four applicants to the EC that eventually joined. In the second stage, originally scheduled to begin in 1994, the margins of intervention were to be gradually shrunk and the macroeconomic policies of the members were to be coordinated and centralized in various ways. Also, a European Monetary Institute (EMI) was to be set up at this point. Apparently, the intention is that the EMI should eventually acquire the responsibilities of a central bank. The final stage, to take place between 1997 and 1999, involves replacing national currencies with the ECU and establishing the European central bank. Stages 2 and 3 are not to involve all member countries, only those whose economic performance meets certain "convergence criteria." At the time the Maastricht Agreement went into effect, only Luxembourg actually met the criteria.

The Maastricht Agreement soon ran into both political and economic problems. On the political side, the agreement became very controversial in a number of countries, and ratification looked doubtful for a while, especially after Danish voters initially rejected it in a referendum. But by the end of 1993 all twelve countries had ratified the agreement, it went into effect, and the EC became the EU. Several countries, however, retained the option not to participate in various parts of the agreement. For example, Britain declined to participate in the integration of social policy.

The economic problems were even more severe and raised serious doubts about whether monetary union will ever be achieved. Chapter 15 described the exchange-rate crises of 1992 and 1993. The net results were that Italy and the United Kingdom left the snake, and most of the intervention margins were widened to ± 15 percent. Thus, even as Maastricht was being approved, foreign-exchange arrangements were changing in a way that was actually the reverse of what was called for in the agreement.

6. SUMMARY

1. Integration can lead to geographical price discrimination, resulting in trade creation among the partners and trade diversion from the rest of the world. Domination of either effect depends on circumstances.

2. Integration can lead to trade modification, which can either increase or decrease trade with the rest of the world, depending on the substitutability or complementarity of the goods traded. This effect involves a change in the pattern of world tariffs rather than price discrimination.

3. Integration can influence the terms of trade between the partners. If the partners are big relative to the world market, integration can also alter the terms of trade of the partners vis-à-vis the rest of the world.

4. Integration can lead to greater specialization among partners, resulting in reduced costs of production if the industry exhibits national economies of scale. It can also lead to increased product differentiation and division of labor, resulting in expanded intraindustry trade if the partners are similar.

5. Monopoly and oligopoly could decrease as integration results in more competition among partners.

6. Integration of macroeconomic policies can lead to decreased payment imbalances or exchange-rate fluctuations or to attainment of a fixed exchange rate between partners.

7. GATT did not lead to price discrimination, but did cause biased integration, implying that trade diversion can be ignored but trade modification and trade creation must be considered.

8. The EEC apparently caused more trade creation than diversion, and, more importantly, it allowed realization of international scale economies and increased product differentiation.

SUGGESTED READING

Balassa, B. *European Economic Integration.* Amsterdam: North Holland, 1975. An assessment of the economic impact of the EEC.

Cooper, C. A., and B. F. Massell. "Towards a General Theory of Customs Unions for Developing Countries." *Journal of Political Economy* (Oct. 1965).

Corden, W. M. "Economies of Scale and Customs Union Theory." *Journal of Political Economy* (Mar. 1972).

———. "Monetary Integration." *Princeton Essays in International Finance* 93 (Apr. 1972).

deMelo, J., and A. Panagariya, eds. *New Dimensions in Regional Integration.* New York: Cambridge University Press, 1993. Relevant to topics in this chapter are Chapters 1 through 4, 6, 7, 9, and 11.

deVries, T. "On the Meaning and Future of the European Monetary System." *Princeton Essays in International Finance* 138 (Sept. 1980).

Flam, H. "Product Markets and 1992: Full Integration, Large Gains?" *Journal of Economic Perspectives* 6 (1992). The reasons for 1992.

Giavazzi, F., and A. Giovannini. *Limiting Exchange Rate Flexibility: The European Monetary System.* Cambridge: MIT Press, 1989. How the EMS works.

Kemp, M. C. *A Contribution to the General Equilibrium Theory of Preferential Trading.* Amsterdam: North Holland, 1969. The pure theory.

Krauss, M. B. "Recent Developments in Customs Union Theory: An Interpretive Survey." *Journal of Economic Literature* (June 1972).

Machlup, F. *A History of Thought on Economic Integration.* New York: Columbia University Press, 1977. Useful summary of the literature.

Swann, D. *The Economics of the Common Market.* 7th ed. London: Penguin, 1988. A description of the EEC.

Vanek, J. *General Equilibrium of International Discrimination.* Cambridge: Harvard University Press, 1965.

Viner, J. *The Customs Union Issue.* New York: Carnegie Endowment for International Peace, 1950. The classic treatment.

CHAPTER 21

The South and the East in Transition

> Rich men's clubs take care of their own members and we are told to fend for ourselves.
> —INDIRA GANDHI

> When you get there, there is no there there.
> —GERTRUDE STEIN

This chapter turns to countries and groups of countries that, economically speaking, are trying to come in from the cold. That is, they are trying to reform their economies—including their international trade and payments—and to join more fully the interdependent economic system of the modern industrial world. These nations conveniently sort themselves into two groups.

The first group comprises the LDCs, countries trying to overcome the legacy of history, the barriers put in their way by the industrial world and their own past mistakes. Issues involving the LDCs have been discussed in detail in Chapters 1 and 4 and elsewhere in this book. Here we pull things together and look at a new issue: the problem of LDC borrowing and debt.

The second group consists of the former communist countries. These states have experienced—and continue to experience—political and economic revolution and are now struggling to restructure themselves. We first examine the old system, which produced the current mess, and then look at what is happening now.

1. CHANGING STRATEGIES FOR ECONOMIC DEVELOPMENT

The economic performance of a large part of the less developed world has been disappointing since the 1950s. The following circumstances typically (but not always) have applied to these countries.

1. *LDCs have imposed extensive state controls of international trans-actions.* Usually this has involved control over other aspects of economic life and, sometimes, a degree of socialist ownership and central planning as well.

2. *Industrial countries have erected barriers to LDC exports.* In a for-mal sense this is not true since, as we have seen, the DCs have given the ex-ports of LDCs preferential treatment with GSPs and have also extended MFN status so that the GATT-round tariff reductions have applied to the LDCs as well. The problem is that the DCs have been most protectionist in just those sectors that offer LDCs the most hope for export expansion: tex-tiles and apparel, shoes, basic industrial materials, and agriculture. The GSPs contain many exceptions in these areas, and, more importantly, Europe's CAP, the Multifiber Arrangement (MFA), and the proliferation of VERs have together been a powerful impediment to increased LDC exports. (You have met most of these acronyms before, but if they now make your head spin, see Appendix III.)

3. *Import substitution policies have been followed.* These were dis-cussed in Chapter 4. Recall also the discussion in Chapter 8 of the infant-in-dustry argument for protection, which has sometimes been used, among other things, to justify import substitution.

4. *Exports have been discouraged.* Often this has been due to export taxes and controls, but often it has also been the result of other policies. For example, circumstance 2 obviously has this effect as does circumstance 3. Why is this? Why can't an LDC *both* discourage imports and promote ex-ports? For two closely related reasons. First, if an LDC were to do so, that would contribute to a current account surplus ($\equiv$capital-account deficit) so that capital would be flowing *out* of the country, just the opposite of what eco-nomic development entails. Second, if a country does succeed in developing import substitution production, the resources for this must come from the rest of the economy, *reducing* its ability to produce goods for export.

The net result of these circumstances is that a large majority of LDCs have been what is called *inward-looking:* they have discouraged international trade (and, often, direct investment from abroad) and have instead tried to in-dustrialize by developing protected domestic manufacturing for the domestic market. Table 21.1 shows how the policies followed by forty-two LDCs could be classified, on the whole, for the years 1963–1973, as representative of the post–World War II period.

Of the four circumstances described above, individual LDCs can them-selves control 1, 3, and 4. Beginning in the 1980s and increasing in the 1990s, many LDCs have been changing their strategies, relaxing controls on interna-tional exchanges and altering their trade policies from an inward toward an outward orientation. There are three main reasons for this change.

First, the collapse of the communist system has given central planning and socialism a bad name almost everywhere. This clearly works against cir-cumstance 1.

TABLE 21.1   Trade Orientation, 1963–1973

Strong outward	Moderate outward	Moderate inward	Strong inward
Hong Kong*	Brazil*	Bolivia	Argentina
Korea*	Cameroon	El Salvador	Bangladesh
Singapore*	Colombia**	Honduras	Burundi
Taiwan*	Costa Rica	Kenya	Chile
	Côte d'Ivoire	Madagascar	Dominican Republic
	Guatemala	Mexico*	Ethiopia
	Indonesia	Nicaragua	Ghana
	Israel	Nigeria	India
	Malaysia**	Philippines**	Pakistan
	Thailand**	Senegal	Peru
		Tunisia	Sri Lanka
		Yugoslavia*	Sudan
			Tanzania
			Turkey**
			Uruguay**
			Zambia

*NIC in Table 1.9.
**NEC in Table 1.9.
SOURCE: World Bank, *World Development Report* (1987). [Taiwan added.]

Second, evidence in recent decades has increasingly indicated that LDCs with outward-oriented policies have done better than those with inward-oriented policies, working against circumstances 3 and 4. Specifically, rapid export growth seems positively related with rapid growth in national income, a relation sometimes described by the words *trade is an engine of growth.*

Recall the discussion in sections 9 and 13 of Chapter 1 of the NICs and the NECs. These are countries that have adopted outward-oriented strategies and achieved rapid growth of exports and incomes. Probably the most prominent examples are the four countries identified in Table 21.1 as strongly outward-oriented (Hong Kong, Korea, Singapore, and Taiwan), known collectively as the *"Gang of Four"* or, alternatively, as the *Asian Tigers.* Hong Kong has consistently employed nonrestrictive policies. Other countries had sometimes followed policies of the sort described above as typical and then achieved rapid export growth after liberalizing those policies. Even now, most of these countries are not liberal relative to the advanced industrial economies, and many, such as Korea, practice high protection in selected sectors. But they are outward-oriented relative to other LDCs.

Third, the LDC debt problem has forced many LDCs to stimulate exports to service their debts, to pay for imports they can no longer pay for by borrowing, and to try to rebuild their credit standings. The debt problem will be discussed in detail below.

In Table 21.1 Turkey and Uruguay are listed as strongly inward-oriented in 1963–1973. Since then they have changed policies in a more outward-oriented direction and were listed as NECs in Table 1.9. Other countries in Table 21.1 that have made dramatic policy reforms and experienced subsequent growth in exports and incomes include Mexico and Chile.

2. *CASE STUDY:* INDIA

Because of their sheer size, the success or failure of China and India will go a long way toward determining an overall assessment of LDC progress. After Maoists lost power in 1976, China began a series of reforms in both the manufacturing and agricultural sectors. Gradualism pertained both to the pace at which reforms were instituted and the portion of the country to which they were applied. The Chinese economy has expanded rapidly since then and has become steadily more open, with trade growing from less than 6 percent of national income to over 16 percent and with foreign direct investment in China accumulating rapidly.

Upon attaining independence after World War II, India adopted the full range of policies described in the preceding section. Tariffs were high, averaging about 300 percent across a wide range of sectors. Not only were they high, they were often bewildering, with the same product subject to dozens of different rates, depending on who wanted to import it and why. In addition, quotas were extensively employed (firms who required imports often built excess production capacity simply to strengthen their case for obtaining import permits). Direct investment into India was limited and controlled, and foreign entities were not allowed majority positions in Indian firms. Industrial activity was subject to extensive government control and shaped by a vast system of licensing requirements (the "license raj"). A huge array of government regulations determined what firms could and could not do. For example, firms cannot shut down plants or go out of business without obtaining government approval, which in fact is never given. (This policy reflects the fact that to lose one's job in a poor country is a personal catastrophe, while ignoring the equally valid fact that for a poor country to waste its resources in an unproductive activity is a social catastrophe.) As a result, firms really desperate to shut down have sometimes bribed all their workers to quit; others have simply stopped paying their utility bills in the hope that they would be shut down when the power was cut off. To top it all off, about 10 percent of industry was accounted for by especially inefficient publicly owned firms, and powerful unions have had the economic and political muscle to preserve extensive inefficient restrictions to maintain gross income inequalities. For example, workers in industry receive wages about six times higher than those outside industry, and much of the public sector (such as railways) pays wages an additional two to three times as great.

Not surprisingly, India traded little and received little foreign investment. The economy exhibited all the signs of import substitution. To take one example, a visitor to India in the late 1980s would have noticed immediately that most automobiles resembled European vehicles of about 1950—the time when Indian policy was put in place. The result of all this was pathetic economic performance: from 1950 to 1980 growth in income barely kept up with growth in population.

Interestingly, some Indian firms made significant direct investments abroad. In some cases this was just to escape the hostile home environment. But other firms had evidently acquired an ownership advantage (recall Chapter 11) in operating in relatively small, highly regulated economies. They have been able to exploit this advantage in other LDCs.

Attempts at reform were made in the mid-1980s, but they ultimately faltered and came to little. Income did grow significantly in the 1980s. Perhaps this was due in part to the reform attempts. But probably it was caused mainly by unsustainable government spending. In any event, by July 1991 the country found itself in a classic crisis: a large government debt, spiraling inflation, and international reserves that had dwindled to the value of just a few weeks' imports. The government went to the IMF for assistance, and this was granted, subject to the country adopting an austerity program (this is typical IMF practice, as we saw in Chapter 16).

The prime minister, P. V. Narasimha Rao, headed a minority government and was generally regarded as a caretaker unlikely to remain in office for long or to accomplish much. Instead, he astonished everyone (or at least your author) by appointing reformers to the major economic posts (notably the finance minister, Manmohan Singh) and then supporting them through several waves of basic economic reform.

Tariffs were slashed, restrictions on direct investment were eased, Indian firms were allowed to raise capital abroad, tax rates were lowered, the system of licenses was dismantled, and the rupee was made convertible for current-account transactions. There were initial fears that such a shock treatment, coupled with the austerity program, might push the economy into a deep slump. But, though investment and income stagnated for about a year, they did not collapse and then began moderate growth. Inflation came down, direct investment into India grew rapidly (IBM and Coca-Cola, driven out years ago, announced plans to return), Indians began repatriating funds they had sent abroad, Indian firms began borrowing in the Eurobond market, the government deficit fell, and international reserves grew rapidly. The IMF loan was repaid ahead of schedule.

But it is still too soon to discern the long-term effects on growth of the reforms already made or whether the reform will be completed. A lot of reform remains: the public firms have not been privatized, a huge array of regulations remains (firms still cannot shut down plants without permission), and government subsidies are still widespread. Tariffs, though much lower than before, remain very high by modern standards: they still average about 65 percent across many sectors.

3. THE LDC DEBT PROBLEM

No doubt the most dramatic aspect of North-South economic relations since the 1980s has been the LDC debt situation with its recurrent crises. A relative shortage of capital is probably what most distinguishes the South from the North, so large borrowing by the former from the latter is both natural and desirable. Indeed, one of the major problems about the debt situation that emerged in the 1980s is that it has inhibited worthwhile lending.

But how did this situation come about? We must look back to the oil price rise of 1973–1974. This caused LDCs to want to borrow more. LDCs that were oil importers wanted to borrow in order to finance the increased cost of oil without cutting back development programs or current consumption; LDCs that were oil exporters, like Mexico and Nigeria, wanted to borrow against the future export earnings that higher oil prices promised to bring. At the same time, OPEC developed huge current-account surpluses to be invested abroad.

The OPEC surpluses were *recycled* to the LDC borrowers by the Western banking system, especially the Eurobanks. OPEC deposited its earnings in the banks, which then made loans to the LDCs. Typically, these loans were made by large syndicates of banks, were short to medium term, and carried an interest rate set above LIBOR (the London Interbank Offer Rate—the rate charged by London Eurobanks in their loans to each other) that was adjusted periodically in response to changing market conditions. There were two basic results, both clear in Table 21.2. First, the LDCs became more heavily indebted. Total debt became much larger than their total annual exports, and required debt service (scheduled interest and repayments of principle) began to claim a large part of export earnings. Second, the nature of the LDCs' debt changed: the large bank loans made that debt more short-term than it had been and made debt service more sensitive to changes in current interest rates.

Nevertheless, the experience of the 1970s was good on balance. The LDCs did not find their new debt burdensome, and the banks did not find it threatening. Most LDCs found the prices of their exports high and rising, and, with the high inflation that developed, the interest rates that the LDCs had to pay were low in real terms, sometimes even negative. The banks succeeded in recycling the OPEC surplus in a smooth manner, and the LDCs were able to avoid painful adjustments.

Then came the second oil price shock in 1980. In view of the successful experience after the first shock, the LDCs wished to borrow again, and the banks were eager to lend. But the large new debts were *on top of* the earlier ones. More ominously, subsequent experience was much different. Instead of rising export prices, the LDCs typically had to contend with falling prices. Instead of low real interest rates, the 1980s saw rates rise to unusually high levels in real terms. And these high rates did not merely make it more costly to borrow more: because their debt had become much more short term in the 1970s, the higher real interest rates increased the service payments required

TABLE 21.2 **The LDC Debt Situation** *(period averages, in percent)*

	1973–74	1975–78	1979–80	1981–82	1983–85
Total debt/exports					
All LDC borrowers	95.8	120.1	115.4	135.7	158.2
15 heavy debtors*	123.9	169.2	173.7	231.3	280.1
Debt service payments/exports					
All LDC borrowers	12.7	16.7	18.1	22.1	23.0
15 heavy debtors*	18.2	28.6	32.0	43.2	42.6
Floating-rate debt/total debt					
All LDC borrowers	21.1	34.7	44.6	51.1	53.6
15 heavy debtors*	31.9	48.7	63.8	70.8	73.5
Short-term debt/total debt					
All LDC borrowers	7.3	14.3	18.6	20.8	15.3
15 heavy debtors*	7.1	13.8	21.7	25.3	15.7

*Argentina, Bolivia, Brazil, Chile, Colombia, Ecuador, Côte d'Ivoire, Mexico, Morocco, Nigeria, Peru, Philippines, Uruguay, Venezuela, and Yugoslavia.

SOURCE: International Monetary Fund, *World Economic Outlook* (1986).

on a large part of the outstanding debt. The dramatic appreciation of the dollar in the early 1980s also made life more difficult for many LDCs since most of their debt was in dollars. Finally, the industrial world went into a serious recession. This substantially reduced the demand for LDC exports, exports crucial for earning the revenues to service their debts.

The first sign of trouble appeared in 1981, when Poland suspended payments of its debt. But this seemed like a special case: Poland was an Eastern European country rather than an LDC, the country had special political problems, and the creditor banks were largely confined to Western Europe. There were fears that other Eastern bloc countries might get into similar trouble, but effective steps were taken and these fears eventually subsided.

The first real crisis began in August 1982 when Mexico suspended payments and began negotiations for aid and to reschedule its debt. The shock made it clear to the banks how exposed they were. For many large banks, loans to Brazil, Mexico, and Argentina exceeded their own capital, so that default would mean bankruptcy. There were fears that, one by one, the major LDC borrowers would be forced into default and that this would trigger a banking collapse in the industrial countries. Intensive negotiations produced a Mexican rescue operation. The United States provided short-term aid, the IMF extended credit after Mexico agreed to an austerity program, and the banks extended new credit and stretched out repayment of the old loans.

In the next several years many other LDCs found themselves in similar trouble (see Table 21.3), and there were many other rescue operations and renegotiations of debt positions. The LDCs were afraid simply to repudiate their debt because they would be unable to borrow in the future, there would

TABLE 21.3 **The Major Debtors** *(gross debt in billions of dollars at the end of 1985)*

Brazil	106
Mexico	97
Argentina	49
Venezuela	38
Philippines	26
Nigeria	20

SOURCE: Morgan Guaranty Trust Company, *World Financial Markets.*

be no financing available for critical imports, their own foreign assets would be subject to seizure (although they were debtors on balance, these countries also had considerable foreign assets, important to parts of their populations), foreign transactions of all types would become difficult, and there was the possibility of retaliation by creditor governments. For their part, the banks realized they had lent too much in the past, but they were afraid that if they did not go along with new arrangements they would never get any of their money back. Some smaller banks would have been glad to write off the earlier loans and lend no more, but they were kept in line by the bigger banks.

The IMF played an important role in these crises. Before extending credit, the Fund required a country to adopt policies intended to correct its situation. Furthermore, the banks usually required such an IMF "seal of approval" before making new loans or rescheduling old ones. This gave the Fund considerable leverage in its dealings with LDC governments, and the latter were quick to blame the IMF for painful austerity measures. Thus the IMF became unpopular in many debtor countries such as Brazil. Sometimes, as in the Mexican crisis, the Fund used its leverage on the banks, pressuring them to provide new credit.

4. THE INTERNATIONAL TRADE OF CENTRALLY PLANNED ECONOMIES

We now examine the attempts of former communist countries to develop market economies and to join the international trading system. But it is impossible to understand how these countries got to where they are now without understanding where they came from. So first we examine how centrally planned, soviet-type economies worked and how they conducted their international trade.

Foreign Trade in Soviet-Type Economies

In soviet-type economies prices were primarily accounting devices and summaries of terms of exchange; only to a very limited degree did they convey information or serve as incentives to allocate resources, as in market economies. These functions were instead subsumed in the planning mechanism. There were two direct implications of this. The first was that such economies could not allow foreigners to deal directly with domestic consumers and enterprises; such transactions would have been harmful since domestic prices did not reflect opportunity costs. For example, the general tendency in such economies was for consumer goods to have artificially high prices and for capital goods to have artificially low prices—a reflection of the planners' priorities. Were foreigners allowed to do so, they would have sold consumer goods and bought capital goods, thereby causing the planned economy to lose by the transaction (and also frustrating the plan objectives that generated the artificial prices in the first place). Thus foreigners were not allowed to buy and sell freely in the economy, nor, for the same reason, could domestic residents buy and sell freely abroad. Instead, international trade was conducted solely through a government foreign trade organization. The second implication was that this foreign trade organization had a difficult time deciding whether to trade or not. It could not simply compare foreign prices to domestic prices to decide whether to buy or sell because domestic prices did not reflect true opportunity costs.

Resource allocation was basically planned, and the planning process centered on achieving *material balances*. In order to attain basic goals, the planners attempted to reconcile aggregate demands and supplies of all key commodities. This balancing process involved considerable give-and-take with lower levels of the economic hierarchy. The natural tendency was to call upon the foreign trade organization to import those goods for which it turned out especially difficult to balance demands with domestic supplies, and to export those goods for which domestic demands were most easily met. Thus trade tended to follow from the dictates of the planning process. As trade became more significant, it could not be left entirely as a residuum, but had to begin to be allowed a more central role in planning. This required some criterion to decide which goods the plan should attempt to provide for export and which to import. To a large degree, such decisions were based on past history, the "sixth sense" of the planners, and international political objectives. But various formulas were also used to determine those goods in which the country had the greatest comparative advantage and those in which it had the greatest comparative disadvantage.

Trade among the Communist Countries

Communist nations did not trade much, compared with Western countries with similar characteristics. This was partly due to economic considerations, international trade being more difficult to manage for planned economies than for market economies, but obviously international politics were crucial. The West shunned trade with the East in varying degrees, and the East showed a decided taste for autarky. (Actually, this was not dramatically different from precommunist practice: Tsarist Russia was highly protectionist, China resisted Western contacts for centuries, and much of Eastern Europe was controlled by the Ottoman and Russian empires.) The proliferation of communist regimes after the Second World War introduced the possibility of international trade among communist states just as the Cold War was precluding the possibility of significant East-West trade. The Council for Mutual Economic Assistance (CMEA or COMECON) was set up in 1949 as an Eastern counterpart to Western cooperative efforts and as an instrument for Soviet control. COMECON apparently had a substantial real influence: at the start considerably less than one-third of its members' trade was with each other; within five years almost three-quarters was.

What did commercial integration between centrally planned economies actually mean? Trade diversion was simple enough: the foreign trade organizations of the various countries simply looked to each other for deals and tried to ignore market economies. But what about trade creation? The essence of integration between market economies is the reduction of differences between those economies in domestic relative prices, with a consequent increase in specialization and trade. But in centrally planned economies domestic relative prices did not reflect opportunity costs and did not guide the actions of foreign trade organizations. Increased specialization and trade had to be planned for. That is, integration meant the integration of national planning procedures. COMECON made several attempts at this, but relatively little was ever achieved. Some goods were assigned to certain countries; for example, Hungary produced all the buses for the East bloc. Overall, it appears that the early growth of COMECON trade consisted mainly of trade diversion.

Trade between centrally planned economies was in two ways actually *more* difficult than trade between such economies and the West. The first problem was to decide what prices to trade at. When the Soviet Union traded with the West, it knew that it could buy or sell at Western market prices, and the only problem (a big enough one, to be sure) was to decide whether to do so. But when the Soviet Union and Czechoslovakia traded, neither country's prices reflected opportunity costs or the terms at which either country was willing to trade. The foreign trade organizations of the two countries could have resolved this problem on a case-by-case basis if they had limited themselves to barter: Czechoslovakia could have agreed to send the Soviet Union so many tractors for so much oil. But such a cumbersome method of trade would have resulted in little trade taking place. If the two countries were to exchange a range of products, they needed prices with which to value those products and the prices had to be consistent with the prices used for trade between the Soviet Union and Bulgaria, and so forth. Thus COMECON needed a set of prices to govern the trade between its members. To its not-inconsiderable embarrassment, it got those prices from the West. COMECON set its internal prices by computing averages of world prices over the preceding five years and then adjusting them in various ways. (Thus many COMECON prices tended to follow world prices with a lag.) This method worked best with standardized products such as raw materials and worst with differentiated goods, for which the similarities between Western products and their COMECON counterparts were inexact.

The second problem was that of conducting multilateral trade. This difficulty was due to the fact that all the Eastern currencies were inconvertible, and they had to be inconvertible to protect the planning process. We saw above that a centrally planned economy could not allow foreigners freely to spend rubles or allow Russians freely to use their rubles to buy foreign currency. This lack of convertibility meant that there was no medium of exchange for intra-COMECON trade. For example, in a nonmonetary economy a barber would have to barter haircuts for cabbages with a grocer, haircuts for taxi rides with a cabbie, and so forth. The existence of money simplifies things enormously and actually makes a detailed division of labor possible. Convertible currencies do the same thing for international trade: the United States does not need to worry that exports to the United Kingdom are paid for with imports from the United Kingdom because the dollars or pounds acquired for the exports can easily be used to buy goods elsewhere in the world. But if Czechoslovakia sold tractors to the Soviet Union for rubles, the rubles could only have been used to buy what the Czechs could convince the Soviet foreign trade organization to sell. Thus they would not want to part with the tractors before arranging to buy something desirable from the Soviet Union in return. Trade within COMECON accordingly tended to be bilateral, with pairs of countries negotiating so as to balance out their mutual trade over a period of five years or so. Studies of intra-COMECON trade patterns generally showed less than 5 percent of this trade to be multilateral. All this reinforced the tendency of COMECON to foster trade diversion rather than trade creation. Multilateral exchanges were actually easier in East-West trade than in East-East trade since in the former case the convertible Western currency could be used. This was in fact common practice, and East-West trade was rarely conducted with Eastern currencies. Centrally planned economies financed their trade with the West by borrowing and lending in the Eurocurrency markets.

The Transferable Ruble

In an attempt to foster multilateral trade, COMECON established a central clearinghouse and created "transferable rubles" for intra-COMECON trade. COMECON trading prices were denominated in transferable rubles, and when one country sold goods to another it received a credit of these transferable rubles that could then be used to buy goods from any other COMECON country. It might seem that COMECON had its medium of exchange so that extensive multilateral trade was possible. But, alas, no. If Czechoslovakia received transferable rubles from the Soviet Union for its tractors, it was true that the rubles could be used to buy goods from any other COMECON country. But Czechoslovakia could not freely shop around in those countries; it had to convince some other foreign trade organization to strike a deal. Thus it still had no way of knowing that it would in fact be able to use the rubles to buy goods valuable enough to justify the sale of the tractors. The transferable ruble was not a true medium of exchange, and there was little success in promoting multilateral trade.

Asymmetric Integration: East-West Trade

About thirty years ago, East-West trade began to increase significantly, partly in response to the large gains that it promised and partly due to realization of the inadequacies of East-East trade noted above. During the 1960s, the USSR and Eastern Europe expanded their trade with the West more rapidly than their trade with each other. As a result, East-West trade came to account for about 45 percent of total Eastern trade. This interbloc trade was much more important, relative to total trade, for the East than it was for the West (since the latter had much more total trade), and it was also more important relative to GNP (since the West had a larger GNP). On balance, the East exported raw materials to the West in exchange for manufactured goods and new technology.

Serious economic obstacles to East-West trade arose from the centrally planned nature of the Eastern economies. These countries found it difficult to expand their exports to the West fast enough to keep pace with their imports and consequently contracted substantial debts. To a degree, this would probably have happened even if the Eastern countries had market economies because the West was relatively capital-abundant and so would have tended to lend. But the tendency was exacerbated by the actual economic systems. The planning process, together with the practice of trading through the medium of foreign trade organizations, gave individual Eastern enterprises insufficient incentive to develop product varieties or quality standards to compete on world markets. Also goods that did become available for export tended to be tied up in advance by bilateral trade agreements with other COMECON members.

East-West trade was also hampered by foreign trade organizations' use of bilateral agreements, although Eastern attempts to get away from this were, as discussed earlier, more successful with respect to East-West trade than with intra-COMECON trade. Also, Western firms proved adaptable to Eastern practices. Multinational enterprises joined with Eastern governments in cooperative arrangements and joint investments, with the MNE typically supplying capital goods, technology, and perhaps management, and the Eastern nations contributing labor and raw materials. These deals—sometimes on a multibillion-dollar scale—were most often to establish Eastern manufacturing facilities or to exploit Eastern reserves of natural resources. Sometimes the deals involved barter, and often the participating MNEs were paid back with the natural resources or output produced by the project itself. An interesting aspect of such transactions was the fact that Western MNEs essentially served as agents "selling" multilateralism to the centrally planned economy. By utilizing their worldwide organizations and contacts, the MNEs arranged for purchases of goods and credit from all corners of the world. For example, Control Data Corporation was able to sell the USSR a computer when it arranged for the Russians to produce Christmas cards and to market them in Britain to obtain the Western currency to pay for the computer.

5. COLLAPSE AND REFORM

Communist regimes in Europe began collapsing in 1989. Since then, they have all gone, East Germany has been reunited with West Germany, and the USSR has dissolved into its constituent republics, many of which are now loosely linked in the Commonwealth of Independent States (CIS). These countries must now restructure their economies in the most fundamental ways, while enduring the shock and turmoil of the transition without sliding into economic and political relapse.

The Elements of Reform

These countries all want to restructure their economies and to participate fully in the modern multilateral world trading system. Reform of economies such as those described in the preceding section involves several distinct elements.

1. *Central planning must be replaced by markets.* This means both that decisions concerning the allocation of resources must be made by decentralized economic agents rather than by bureaucrats and that the prices used in the resulting transactions must be determined in free markets rather than by administration or regulation.

2. *The economy must be privatized.* That is, ownership of the means of production has to be transferred from the government to private agents.

3. *The currency must be made convertible into hard currencies.* That is, individuals must be able to exchange domestic money for dollars and other Western currencies. This is necessary in order to facilitate free international trade and investment and in order for domestic activity to be guided by world prices.

4. *A modern banking and financial sector must be developed.* Banks under the old regime did not perform many of the functions of Western banks and financial institutions.

5. *A proper legal structure must be developed.* Property rights need to be defined, bankruptcy procedures determined, and commercial law in general developed.

6. *An effective means of conducting economic policy must be made available.* The authorities will need to be able to tax and to spend, and to manage the nation's money supply, probably during a prolonged period of public turmoil and hardship, without resort to galloping inflation, regulation, or trade barriers.

The Pace of Reform

By the early 1990s the above goals were widely shared throughout the former communist countries. (Though often they were only imperfectly understood by officials who had grown up under the old regime.) The problem was how to implement them. The basic general question was how fast to go: Should we try "cold turkey," fully implementing all the measures at once, or take a more deliberate approach, introducing one reform gradually after another?

The case for gradualism has both an economic and a political dimension. Economically, the fear is that going too fast will administer a severe shock to the economy and induce a nightmare of a depression. Politically, the fear is that too many people will suffer at once—and have nowhere to turn—so that public support for reform will evaporate.

The case for cold turkey also has both an economic and a political dimension. Economically, the basic point is that the various elements of reform are not independent (if you glance back over the list, you will see that this is so). Thus the prospects of success for reform with respect to one element depend critically on reform with respect to the other elements. Politically, the argument is that commitment to reform depends on the ultimate gainers (presumably a majority of the population) being identified as soon as possible, and this requires that the ultimate reformed system be in place as soon as possible.

The relative merits of these arguments are not immediately obvious, so it is probably not surprising that the pace of reform has varied country by country. The nearest approach to cold turkey was made by East Germany, which was absorbed into West Germany, and by Poland, which undertook a bold program of comprehensive reform. Both experienced large drops in production and employment. This apparently came as something of a surprise in West Germany, where most people seemed in 1990 to believe that reunification would be painless (Chancellor Helmut Kohl pledged that no one would suffer). Observers in Poland had been less sanguine, but developments still had a strong negative effect on public opinion regarding reform. By 1993, however, signs were emerging in both economies that the turnaround was beginning.

At the other extreme, Bulgaria, Romania, and large parts of the former USSR proceeded very slowly with many aspects of fundamental reform. Other countries have been in the middle, with Hungary and Czechoslovakia (now divided into two) the most successful reformers.

The Pain of Reform

The revolution in the former communist world has been accompanied by economic turmoil and pain: unemployment (which had not been allowed under the old regimes), high inflation, depreciating exchange rates, and so on. As markets came into being, modern consumer goods became readily available, in sharp contrast to the former shortage economies, but large parts of the population could not afford to buy. At least in the past they hadn't had to look at what they could not possess. The economic difficulties produced an anti-reform backlash to at least some degree in most countries, and former communists were voted into office in Lithuania, Poland, and Hungary. (However, in no case was their platform to restore the old order.)

There were distinct origins of these problems. They were, first, a *direct consequence* of the reform measures undertaken by a specific country. But in addition they came about as *repercussions to foreign problems*. That is, economic collapse in Russia generated difficulties for Bulgaria, say, and these in turn caused problems for other Eastern countries, including Russia.

To see how reform measures—intended to *improve* economic performance—could cause such problems, consider the example of East Germany. Shortly after reunification, wages in East Germany rapidly rose to levels approximating those in the rest of the country. German officials welcomed this because they feared that the alternative would be massive internal migration. But East German industry, inherited from the old regime, was so inefficient that, at the higher wages, virtually nothing could be produced and sold at world prices without a loss. So large-scale unemployment soon developed, and the payment of unemployment benefits produced a large transfer from the rest of Germany into the east.

Other former communist countries, not reunifying with anyone, did not experience the same massive rise in wages. But their industries were even less efficient than East Germany's, and they found that much of their industry, too, could not compete at world prices without massive wage cuts, wage cuts that no government concerned for its survival would allow. So substantial unemployment typically developed. But (not reunifying with anyone) these countries had no one to transfer to them large sums of unemployment compensation. The temptation, therefore, was to print money to pay to firms to keep them operating, at a loss, and thereby avoid adding further to unemployment. This is a recipe for high inflation, and the inflation produced a depreciation of the exchange rate. In this way the Russian ruble lost well over 90 percent of its value in 1992–1994.

The second source of problems for a particular country is in repercussions from its former partners. If Poland, say, decides to stop buying Icarus buses from Hungary, this depresses activity in Hungary, which causes Hungary to buy fewer Skoda automobiles from Czechoslovakia, and so on. (If this sounds to you like the foreign trade multiplier studied in Chapter 17, you are right.) Why should Poland stop buying the buses in the first place? Either because reform in Poland has produced the kinds of problems described above so that Poland has to cut back and buy fewer buses, or because the collapse of the old system has allowed Poland to buy buses wherever it wants, and it prefers Mercedes or Scania to Icarus.

To understand the most important way such repercussions worked, consider Russia and its trade. In 1989, COMECON decided that, beginning in 1990, its trade would be conducted at world prices and payments would be in hard currency. This implied a massive improvement in the terms of trade of the then-USSR and corresponding deterioration in the terms of trade of its Eastern European trading partners. This is because the USSR exported oil and raw materials, underpriced according to the old COMECON rules, and imported manufactures, overpriced because their quality was much below that of Western counterparts whose prices had been used. (These changes also implied that COMECON had lost its basic function, and it was accordingly disbanded.)

The massive terms-of-trade shock occurred but was less important than many had feared, though only because something even worse took place. This was the economic collapse of the former USSR. The old system of central planning was abolished with nothing taking its place. Russia's production and export of oil and other materials declined steadily after 1989, and Russian enterprises slashed their purchases of goods from Eastern Europe. Overall, trade among the former COMECON members fell by about one-half in volume.

The reform process among the former communist countries has been one calling out for international coordination. One potential exercise of international coordination would be between Eastern countries to deal with the international repercussions just discussed. But there is also East-West potential. Prosperity in the East requires direct investment from the West to transfer modern technology and know-how. But direct investment requires confidence among Western firms that their investments will be secure, and such security requires political stability, which in turn will not be forthcoming until there is prosperity. International agreements promoting and guaranteeing direct investment could cut through this Catch-22 situation. Finally, suggestions have been made for large-scale Western aid to help the East through the transition, softening the pain to prevent the reform efforts from being aborted.

In spite of all this, little international coordination was actually done. A new multilateral institution, the European Bank for Reconstruction and Development (EBRD), was established to aid development of the former communist economies. But, at least in its early years, the EBRD was not a major force. Critics felt that it was primarily concerned with providing itself with an impressive new headquarters.

6. SUMMARY

1. LDCs that have employed outward-looking policies have generally enjoyed faster growth of exports and of incomes than LDCs with inward-looking policies.

2. A debt crisis developed in the 1980s as many LDCs found it difficult to service loans they had begun borrowing in the 1970s.

3. Prices in a soviet-type economy did not determine resource allocation; therefore, foreign trade organizations decided what goods to trade. They also acted as middle agents in carrying out the foreign transaction.

4. Part of foreign trade played the role of absorbing internal deficits and surpluses that arose during the process of material balancing; an increasing percentage was related to comparative advantage as trade played an increasing role in the national economy.

5. The creation of the COMECON led to big trade diversion but not much trade creation. This was due to the inconvertibility of Eastern currencies, which resulted in little multilateral trade and the necessity of deciding trading prices on a contract-by-contract basis.

6. The collapse of communism and the initiation of reform produced a transitional period of economic turmoil, due both to the impact effects of the reform measures and to international repercussions between Eastern economies.

SUGGESTED READING

Cooper, C. A., and B. F. Massell. "Towards a General Theory of Customs Unions for Developing Countries." *Journal of Political Economy* (Oct. 1965).

Desai, P., and R. Martin. "Efficiency Loss from Resource Misallocation in Soviet Industry." *Quarterly Journal of Economics* (Aug. 1983). Empirical estimates.

Hogan, W. "Economic Reforms in Sovereign States of the Former Soviet Union." *Brookings Papers on Economic Activity* (1991). Useful survey of issues.

Holzman, F. D. *International Trade under Communism: Politics and Economics.* London: Macmillan, 1976. An excellent treatment of the basic issues.

Krueger, A. O. "Asian Trade and Growth Lessons." *American Economic Review* 80 (May 1990). The benefits of outward orientation.

McKinnon, R. I. *Money in International Exchange.* Oxford: Oxford University Press, 1979. Chapter 3 offers an excellent discussion of currency inconvertibility and Eastern trade.

Sachs, J. D., ed. *Developing Country Debt and the World Economy.* Chicago: University of Chicago Press, 1989. The debt crisis.

———. *Poland's Jump to the Market Economy.* Cambridge: MIT Press, 1993. An insider's account by a Western adviser to the Polish government.

Wilczynski, J. *The Multinationals and East-West Relations.* London: Macmillan, 1976.

Appendices

Nothing adds such weight and dignity to a book as an Appendix.
—HERODOTUS (MARK TWAIN)

A Survey of the Pure Theory of International Trade

This survey is for readers with a year or two of university-level mathematics, and will be best appreciated by those who have also studied contemporary microeconomics. The corresponding chapter in the main text is indicated in parentheses after the title of each section of the survey for those who wish to coordinate the two. As in the text, an asterisk (*) indicates portions of the appendix—one section and several subsections—that are relatively more advanced and may be skipped without loss on continuity.

A.1 THE NATIONAL INCOME OF A TRADING ECONOMY (CHAPTER 1)

The Transformation Curve

Suppose that the domestic economy can produce two goods, cloth and wheat. Existing technology and factor supplies determine a production possibility frontier, or *transformation curve*, $S_C = T(S_W)$, where S_C denotes supply of cloth and S_W supply of wheat. The curve is shown in Figure A.1. Point C_O shows the supply of cloth if the home country specializes in it, W_O is the analogous specialization output of wheat, and the transformation curve connects these two points. The derivative of this curve, $T'(S_W)$, is negative, indicating that producing more wheat requires producing less cloth.

National Income

Denote world prices of cloth and wheat (in dollars) as P_C and P_W, respectively. Then, if our economy produces S_C and S_W, its income will be

$$y = P_C S_C + P_W S_W. \tag{1}$$

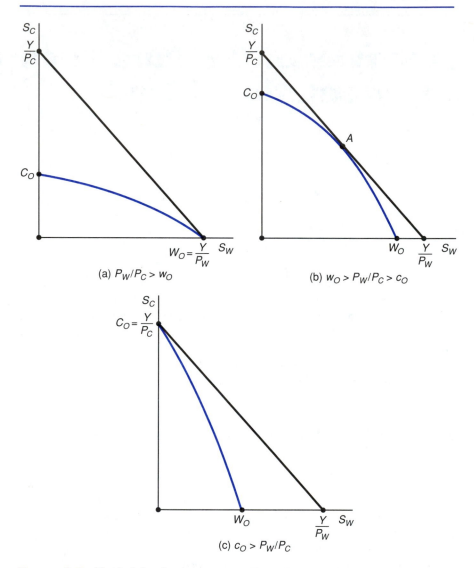

FIGURE A.1 **Maximizing Income**

The collection of S_C and S_W, which, for given P_C and P_W, all yield a particular level of income y in (1), form a straight line with slope $-P_W/P_C$. Such *budget lines* are shown by the black lines in the three panels of Figure A.1. Evidently, increasing P_W relative to P_C makes a budget line steeper, whereas increasing y shifts the line away from the origin. Thus in order to maximize its national income y, a trading economy should produce at that point on its transformation curve that pushes as far from the origin as possible a budget line with a slope reflecting actual world prices. This is shown in Figure A.1.

There are three possibilities. Denote by w_O the slope of $T(S_W)$ at W_O, its steepest spot, and by C_O the slope at C_O, the flattest spot. Then, if $P_W/P_C > w_O$, a budget line will be steeper than every point of the transformation curve, so the country can push its budget line as far out as possible, thus maximizing its income, by producing at W_O. This is shown in panel (a) of Figure A.1. Similarly, if $P_W/P_C < c_O$, the budget line is flatter than $T(S_W)$ at every point and the country should specialize in cloth at C_O. Finally, if $w_O > P_W/P_C > c_O$, the country should produce both goods at that point on its transformation curve just tangent to a budget line, as shown in panel (b).

The *national income function* records the highest income attainable for a country under different circumstances:

$$y\,(P_C, P_W;\,\ldots) = P_C S_C + P_W S_W. \tag{2}$$

As we have just seen, this highest income depends upon world prices plus the shape and position of the transformation curve. Thus y is a function of P_C, P_W, and whatever $(\ldots)$ determines $T(S_W)$.

A Basic Property

Suppose a country is maximizing its national income by producing both goods, as in Figure A.1(b). Then, for a differential movement along the transformation curve:

$$P_C(dS_C) + P_W(dS_W) = 0. \tag{3}$$

Mathematically, (3) is the first-order condition for the solution to the problem of maximizing y subject to $S_C = T(S_W)$. Geometrically, it is obvious from Figure A.1(b), since at point A, where income is maximized, $dS_C/dS_W = T'(S_W) = -P_W/P_C$.

This property tells us something about our national income function. Differentiate (2):

$$\frac{\partial y}{\partial P_C} = S_C + \left[P_C\frac{dS_C}{dP_C} + P_W\frac{dS_W}{dP_C} \right] = S_C \tag{4}$$

by (3). Similarly, $\partial y/\partial P_W = S_W$.

How Income Depends on Prices

In Figure A.2, we arbitrarily fix P_C and let P_W vary, recording how y varies in response. If $P_W < P_C c_O$, then the economy specializes in C so that $y = P_C C_O$, which does not change as P_W changes. If, on the other hand, $P_W > P_C w_O$, the economy specializes in wheat so that $y = P_W W_O$, a straight line through the origin with slope W_O. Intermediate values of P_W imply production of both goods; since we know that $\partial y/\partial P_W = S_W$, y increases as P_W increases, and the slope of the y curve in Figure A.2 shows what S_W is. Thus if $P_W = P_W^A$ in the figure, $S_W = EB/AB$. Furthermore, between $P_C c_O$ and $P_C w_O$,

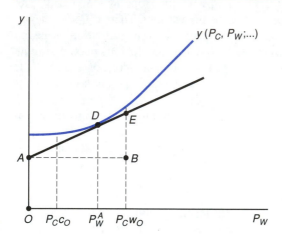

FIGURE A.2 **How Income Depends on Prices**

the y curve increases at an *increasing* rate. This is because $\partial^2 y/\partial P_W^2 = \partial S_W/\partial P_W$, and it is clear from Figure A.1 that an increase in P_W (making the budget line steeper) results in an increase in S_W as the production point moves downward and to the right along the transformation curve.

Suppose that P_W^A is the autarkic equilibrium price so that D shows national income in autarky. The black line tangent to the y curve at D has a slope equal to autarkic production—and, therefore, consumption—of wheat. Thus this line shows how much income is required, at each P_W, to purchase the goods actually consumed in autarky. Note that the y curve lies above this line everywhere (except at the autarky point D), reflecting the gains from trade.

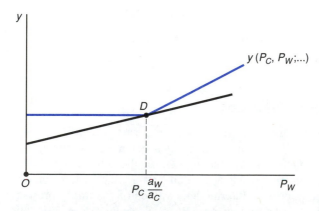

FIGURE A.3 **The Simple Ricardian Model**

The Simple Ricardian Model

In the simple Ricardian model, $C_O = L/a_C$ and $W_O = L/a_W$ where L, a_C, and a_W, respectively denote the national labor supply and the amount of labor required to produce 1 unit of cloth and 1 unit of wheat. $T(S_W)$ is now a straight line, with slope $(-a_W/a_C)$. The national income curve is drawn in Figure A.3. In autarky $P_W = P_C a_W/a_C$, and y is represented by point D, regardless of where on the transformation curve production takes place. The black line through D is drawn with a slope to reflect a hypothetical autarkic S_W.

Problems

A.1.1 Figure A.2 was drawn by holding P_C constant and allowing P_W to vary. Derive an income curve by instead holding P_W constant and allowing P_C to vary.

A.1.2 Equation (4) holds for small (that is, differential) movements along the transformation curve, when both goods are being produced. What can you say about large movements? If only one good is initially produced?

A.2. THE NATIONAL EXPENDITURE OF A TRADING ECONOMY (CHAPTER 1)

Utility

Represent the tastes of an individual or a community by a set of indifference curves, as discussed in section 8* of Chapter 1 and illustrated in Figure A.4. For now, we ignore any difficulties in treating a community in this way. Number the indifference curves in some manner, with curves farther from the origin receiving higher numbers. (For example, draw a ray through the origin, and assign each curve the number equal to its distance from the origin along this ray.) The *utility* $u(D_C, D_W)$ of any consumption combination—the number assigned to the indifference curve passing through (D_C, D_W)—is a measure of the satisfaction derived from the consumption of D_C cloth and D_W wheat. Combinations with higher utility are preferred to combinations with lower utility.

National Expenditure

If the community faces the prices P_C and P_W and consumes the quantities D_C and D_W, its total expenditure is

$$E = P_C D_C + P_W D_W.$$

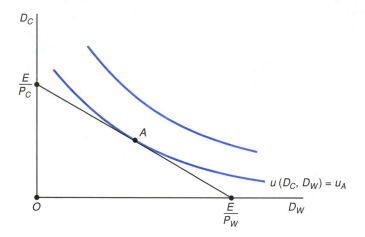

FIGURE A.4   Maximizing Utility—Minimizing Expenditure

Consider the problem of attaining a specified utility level, u_A, with minimum expenditure. Given the commodity prices, the problem is to find that point on the indifference curve $u(D_C, D_W) = u_A$ that pushes a budget line with slope $-P_W/P_C$ as close to the origin as possible. This is at point A in Figure A.4, where the indifference curve and budget line are tangent to each other; the required minimum expenditure is then determined by the intersection of the budget line with either axis.

The *national expenditure function* records the minimum expenditure necessary to achieve various utility levels under various prices:

$$E(P_C, P_W; u) = P_C D_C + P_W D_W, \tag{5}$$

where D_C and D_W are chosen as shown in Figure A.4.

A Basic Property

Suppose that a country is enjoying the utility u_A at minimum expenditure, as shown in Figure A.4. Then, for a differential movement along the indifference curve $u(D_C, D_W) = u_A$,

$$P_C(dD_C) + P_W(dD_W) = 0. \tag{6}$$

This is the first-order condition for the problem of minimizing E subject to the constraint $u(D_C, D_W) = u_A$. This condition is obvious from Figure A.4 since at point A, $dD_C/dD_W = -P_W/P_C$. Now differentiate (5):

$$\frac{\partial E}{\partial P_C} = D_C + \left[P_C \frac{dD_C}{dP_C} + P_W \frac{dD_W}{dP_C} \right] = D_C.$$

by (6). Similarly, $\partial E/\partial P_W = D_W$.

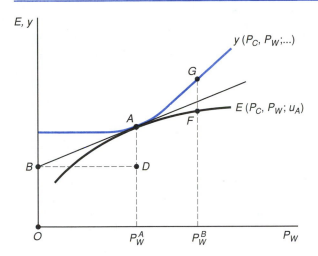

FIGURE A.5   How Expenditure Varies with Price: Autarkic Equilibrium

How Expenditure Depends on Prices

In Figure A.5, we arbitrarily fix P_C, hold u equal to u_A, and let P_W vary, recording how E varies in response. Since $\partial E/\partial P_W = D_W$, E increases as P_W increases and the slope of the E curve always equals the consumption of wheat. Indeed, E increases at a decreasing rate because $\partial^2 E/\partial P_W^2 = \partial D_W/\partial P_W$, and Figure A.4 shows that a rise in P_W, which makes the budget line steeper, reduces D_W and increases D_C. If $P_W = P_W^A$ in Figure A.5, $D_W = AD/BD$.

The Gains from Trade

In Figure A.5, suppose that P_W^A equals the autarkic price of wine, and u_A is the utility enjoyed in autarky. Then the $E(P_C, P_W; u_A)$ curve shows, for each value of P_W, the expenditure necessary to obtain the same utility as that experienced under autarky. The national income function $y(P_C, P_W \ldots)$ shows national income at each price. At the autarkic price P_W^A, of course, $E = y$. Because of the curvature of the two functions, $y > E$ for every other P_W. This shows the gains from trade: at any price, national income is greater (equal at P_W^A) than the amount that must be spent at that price for the country to be as well off as in autarky. The gap is one way of measuring the gains from trade: at the prices P_W^B the country gains GF. Obviously, the gains, according to this measure, are larger the more P_W differs from P_W^A.

Many Goods and Many Citizens*

Suppose that there are n goods. Let $p = (P_1, P_2, \ldots, P_n)$ denote the *vector* of commodity prices. Then $y(p, \ldots)$ can be defined as the national income function analogously to section A.1. It is easily seen that $\sum_{i=1}^{n} P_i(dS_i) = 0$ so that $\partial y/\partial P_i = S_i$ as before. In similar fashion, the expenditure function $E(p, u)$ follows as before, $\sum_{i=1}^{n} P_i(dD_i) = 0$ for given utility, and consequently $\partial E/\partial P_i = D_i$.

Of course, different individuals have different tastes. This means that we should derive an expenditure function for each individual. Suppose that the community consists of m individuals. Let $E^j(p, u^j)$ denote individual j's expenditure function (derived as above) and u^j his utility. Let $U = (u^1, u^2, \ldots, u^m)$ be the *vector* of utilities of the citizens of this community. All citizens face the same commodity prices. Then we can define the community expenditure function.

$$E(p, U) = \sum_{j=1}^{m} E^j(p, u^j).$$

Note that $\partial E/\partial P_i = \sum_{j=1}^{m} \partial E^j/\partial P_i = \sum_{j=1}^{m} D_i^j = D_i$, where D_i^j denotes individual j's demand for good i and D_i denotes the total community demand.

The Gains from Trade with Many Goods and Citizens*

Let p^T denote the vector of free-trade prices, S^T and S^A the free-trade and autarkic vectors of commodities produced, and D^A the autarkic vector of commodities consumed. Then

$$p^T \cdot S^T = y(p^T, \ldots) \geq p^T \cdot S^A$$

because[1] national income is maximized at price p^T when S^T is produced. But $S^A = D^A$ in autarky. Thus $y(p^T, \ldots) \geq p^T \cdot D^A$. This means that the community *as a whole* can afford at free-trade prices to buy what it would consume under autarky. It does not imply that *each* consumer can afford at free-trade prices what she would buy in autarky. But, since the whole community can, there must be some system of lump-sum taxes and subsidies that, if implemented, would enable each individual citizen to purchase under free trade the same goods that she would consume in autarky. This would ensure that no one would be worse off in free trade; such is the meaning of the gains from trade.

---

*An asterisk indicates material that is relatively more advanced and may be skipped without loss of continuity.

[1]Here, $p \cdot S$ denotes the inner product of the vectors p and S: $\sum_{i=1}^{n} P_i S_i$.

The Law of Comparative Advantage

Returning now to an environment of two goods and community indifference curves, point A in Figure A.6 shows autarkic equilibrium, where
$P_W^A/P_C^A = -T'(S_W)$. If the country moves to free trade, it will gain (unless the
free-trade price equals the autarkic price), as we have seen, so that the community's utility will rise—say, from u_A to u_T. This shifts the expenditure function upward, as shown in Figure A.6, with $E = y$ at the free-trade equilibrium.
If the free-trade relative price of wheat exceeds the autarkic price, this equilibrium will be at a point such as B in the figure. At B the y curve is steeper
than the E curve so that $S_W > D_W$—that is, wheat is exported. Also, y is
steeper at B than at A so that S_W has risen: resources have shifted from cloth
production to wheat production. If, on the other hand, the free-trade relative
price of wheat is less than the autarkic price, equilibrium is at a point such as
C and these conclusions are reversed. Finally, note that whatever the home
country exports in equilibrium, the foreign country must import. Thus if the
home country is at a point such as B, the foreign country must be at a point
such as C in the foreign analog to Figure A.6, and vice versa. This implies that the free-trade relative price lies between the autarkic price of the
two countries and that the relative sizes of the latter predict the direction of
trade.

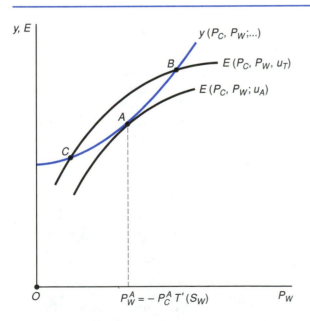

FIGURE A.6 **The Law of Comparative Advantage**

Comparative Advantage with Many Goods*

Once again, allow many goods, but retain community indifference curves (or lump-sum transfers so that no one loses from free trade relative to autarky). Then the vector of commodities consumed under free trade, D^T, yields at least as much satisfaction as obtained under autarky so that $E(p^A, u_A) \leq p^A \cdot D^T$. Now, $E(p^A, u_A) = y(p^A, \ldots) \geq p^A \cdot S^T$. Thus $p^A \cdot D^T \geq p^A \cdot S^T$ so that

$$p^A \cdot (D^T - S^T) \geq 0.$$

But in free trade $p^T \cdot (D^T - S^T) = 0$ so that

$$(p^A - p^T) \cdot (D^T - S^T) \geq 0. \tag{7}$$

$(D^T - S^T)$ is the vector of imports (positive components) and exports (negative components). Letting an asterisk refer to the foreign country, the same logic establishes the foreign analog of (7).

$$(p^{A*} - p^T) \cdot (D^{T*} - S^{T*}) \geq 0. \tag{8}$$

Note that what the home country imports, the foreign country exports: $(D^T - S^T) = (S^{T*} - D^{T*})$. Thus subtracting (8) from (7) gives

$$(p^A - p^{A*}) \cdot (D^T - S^T) \geq 0. \tag{9}$$

Finally, $p^A \cdot S^A = y(p^A, \ldots) \geq p^A \cdot S^T$ and $p^T \cdot S^T = y(p^T, \ldots) \geq p^T \cdot S^A$. Thus

$$(p^A - p^T) \cdot (S^A - S^T) \geq 0. \tag{10}$$

(7) and (8) say that, in each country, imports are positively *correlated* with lower trade prices relative to autarky; (9) says that imports are positively correlated with lower foreign autarkic prices relative to domestic; and (10) says that output reductions are positively correlated with lower trade prices relative to autarky. Thus the basic two-commodity conclusions about comparative advantage hold *on average* in the multicommodity environment. They need not hold on a commodity-by-commodity basis.[2]

An Improvement[3] in the Terms of Trade*

We have seen how free trade is better than no trade. As shown in the text and as we shall see later in this appendix, free trade need not be as good as re-

---

*An asterisk indicates material that is relatively more advanced and may be skipped without loss of continuity.

[2]The basic results of this subsection may be found in A. Deardoff, "The General Validity of the Law of Comparative Advantage," *Journal of Political Economy* 88 (1980): 941–57, and in A. K. Dixit and V. Norman, *Theory of International Trade* (London: Cambridge University Press, 1980), pp. 94, 95.

[3]This subsection depends upon A. Krueger and H. Sonnenschein, "The Terms of Trade, the Gains from Trade, and Price Divergence," *International Economic Review* 8 (1967): 121–27.

stricted trade, from a strictly nationalistic point of view. In what sense does a terms-of-trade "improvement" make a country better off?

Suppose that a country is freely trading at the price vector p^T and that, for some reason, international prices change to $p^{T'}$. We shall call this a terms-of-trade improvement if, at the new prices, the value of the country's original production exceeds that of its original consumption: $p^{T'} \cdot S^T \geq p^{T'} \cdot D^T$. What follows from this? At the new equilibrium, $E(p^{T'}, u_{T'}) = y(p^{T'}, \ldots)$, and, of course, $y(p^{T'}, \ldots) \geq p^{T'} \cdot S^T$. Thus, from our definition of a terms-of-trade improvement,

$$E(p^{T'}, u_{T'}) > p^{T'} \cdot D^T.$$

Thus after the improvement the country can afford what it consumed before and still have something left over. The country must be better off (as always, this means if we drop community indifference curves, that some system of lump-sum transfers can make everyone in the community better off: the gainers gain more in this sense than the losers lose).

Problems

A.2.1 Suppose that a country has the utility function $u(D_C, D_W) = D_C^\alpha D_W^{1-\alpha}$ for some number α between 0 and 1. Derive a formula for $E(P_C, P_W; u)$. Verify the properties discussed in the text.

A.2.2 Derive $E(P_C, P_W; u)$ if consumers *always* demand wheat and cloth in equal amounts. If $u(D_C, D_W) = D_C + D_W$.

A.3. INTERNATIONAL EQUILIBRIUM (CHAPTER 4)

Equilibrium Conditions

Suppose that two countries trade cloth and wheat. Each country's expenditure must equal its income (Walras's Law):

$$P_C D_C + P_W D_W = P_C S_C + P_W S_W, \tag{11}$$

$$P_C D_C^* + P_W D_W^* = P_C S_C^* + P_W S_W^*. \tag{12}$$

Call the home country the one that ends up importing wheat, and accordingly define domestic import demand and export supply as $M \equiv D_W - S_W$ and $X \equiv S_C - D_C$. The foreign country must have the reciprocal trade pattern, so define $M^* = D_C^* - S_C^*$ and $X^* = S_W^* - D_W^*$. Only relative prices count, so define a unit of cloth to be one dollar's worth. This ensures that P_C always equals unity and can, therefore, be dropped, and that P_W—which we now denote simply as P—equals the relative price of wheat in terms of cloth. Making use of the conventions, we can rewrite (11) and (12) as

$$PM = X, \tag{13}$$

$$\left(\frac{1}{P}\right)M^* = X^*. \tag{14}$$

In equilibrium the world demand for each good must equal the world supply, or each country's demand for imports must equal the other's supply of exports:

$$M = X^*, \tag{15}$$

$$M^* = X. \tag{16}$$

Equations (15) and (16) are the equilibrium conditions in the wheat and cloth markets, respectively, but they are in fact redundant: either can be derived from the other by using Walras's Law, (13) and (14). Thus there is only one independent equilibrium condition. This is conventionally expressed by substituting (14) into (15) to obtain

$$PM = M^*. \tag{17}$$

Equation (17) is the algebraic analog to the intersection of demand and supply curves in the geometry of Chapter 4.

Elasticity

By definition, $M(P) = D_W(P,E(P, u)) - S_W(P)$, where $E(P, u) = y(P)$. As usual, demand depends upon relative prices and spending (income) while supply depends upon relative prices. The elasticity of import demand, e, is defined as $-(P/M)\,(dM/dP)$. Differentiate the definition of $M(P)$, noting that $E = y$,

$$\frac{dM}{dP} = \left.\frac{\partial D_W}{\partial P}\right|_E + \frac{\partial D_W}{\partial E}\frac{\partial y}{\partial P} - \frac{dS_W}{dP}, \tag{18}$$

where $\left.\dfrac{\partial D_W}{\partial P}\right|_E$ means that E is kept constant under the differentiation. Now differentiating $D_W(P, E(P, u))$ gives

$$\left.\frac{\partial D_W}{\partial P}\right|_u = \left.\frac{\partial D_W}{\partial P}\right|_E + \frac{\partial D_W}{\partial E}\frac{\partial E}{\partial P}. \tag{19}$$

Substitute (18) into (19), and rearrange to obtain

$$\frac{dM}{dP} = \left[\left.\frac{\partial D_W}{\partial P}\right|_u - \frac{dS_W}{dP}\right] - \frac{\partial D_W}{\partial E}\left[\frac{\partial E}{\partial P} - \frac{\partial y}{\partial P}\right]. \tag{20}$$

The first term in brackets is the *substitution effect*, composed of a demand component and a supply component. As we saw in section A.2, the demand component $\left.\dfrac{\partial D_W}{\partial P}\right|_u = \dfrac{\partial^2 E}{\partial P^2} < 0$, and section A.1 showed that $dS_W/dP = \partial^2 y/\partial P^2 > 0$.

Thus the sign of the substitution effect is unambiguous: it causes the demand for imports to fall as they become more expensive.

The rest of the right hand side of (20) is the *income effect*. We know that $\partial E/\partial P = D_W$ and $\partial y/\partial P = S_W$, so the bracketed portion is just M. Thus the strength and sign of the income effect depends upon the magnitude and direction of trade: near autarky M is almost zero so that the substitution effect necessarily dominates. $\partial D_W/\partial E$ measures how the demand for imports (wheat) increases as expenditure rises. One normally expects this to be positive so that the income effect will work in the same direction as the substitution effect, but it could be negative for some goods (which are called *inferior*). In the latter case the income and substitution effects work at cross purposes. To put (20) in elasticity term, multiply both sides by $-(P/M)$:

$$-\frac{P}{M}\frac{dM}{DP} = \left[-\frac{P}{M}\frac{\partial D_W}{\partial P}\bigg|_u + \frac{P}{M}\frac{dS_W}{dP}\right] + P\frac{\partial D_W}{\partial E},$$

which we can represent as

$$e = c + s + m, \tag{21}$$

where $c = -\dfrac{P}{M}\dfrac{\partial D_W}{\partial P}\bigg|_u$ is the demand substitution elasticity, $s = \dfrac{P}{M}\dfrac{dS_W}{dP}$ is the supply substitution elasticity, and $m = P\dfrac{\partial D_W}{\partial E}$, representing the income effect, is the *marginal propensity to import:* the fraction of an increase in expenditure that is devoted to imports. Note that $1 - m$, the fraction of an increase in spending that is *not* spent on imports (wheat), is the fraction spent on exportables (cloth). Thus if both wheat and cloth are normal, m will lie between 0 and 1; it will be negative if wheat is inferior and greater than 1 if cloth is inferior. (The goods cannot both be inferior. Why?)

Differentiation of (13) yields $\hat{P} + \hat{M} = \hat{X}$, and dividing both sides by $-\hat{P}$ in turn leads to $e - 1 = f$, where $f = -\hat{X}/\hat{P}$, the elasticity of export supply.[4] Thus from (21)

$$f = c + s + (m - 1). \tag{22}$$

The supply elasticity f has the same substitution terms as does e but a different income term. We know that $1 - m$ is the fraction of an increase in expenditure that is spent on exportables. Now any increase in domestic spending on exportables is a *reduction* in exports; thus $m - 1 [= -(1 - m)]$ is the *marginal propensity to export*. Note that if neither good is inferior, income and substitution effects reinforce each other in (21) but work at cross purposes in (22).

Stability of Equilibrium

Let P_O denote the equilibrium prices, or solution to (17),

---

[4] For any variable x, the notation $\hat{x}$ means $(dx)/x$, or $d(\log x)$.

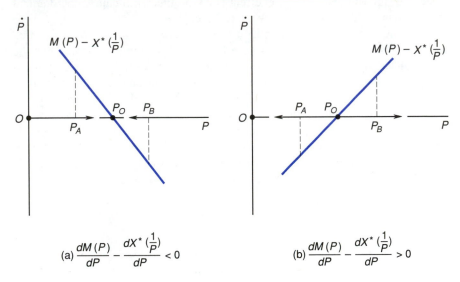

(a) $\dfrac{dM(P)}{dP} - \dfrac{dX^*\left(\frac{1}{P}\right)}{dP} < 0$ (b) $\dfrac{dM(P)}{dP} - \dfrac{dX^*\left(\frac{1}{P}\right)}{dP} > 0$

FIGURE A.7   The Stability Condition

$$P_O M(P_O) = M^*\left(\frac{1}{P_O}\right).$$

We write M^* as a function of $(1/P)$ because the latter is the relative price of cloth, the foreign import. If $P \neq P_O$, markets do not clear; we hypothesize that price is rising whenever demand exceeds supply. This disequilibrium hypothesis can be represented by the differential equation (DH):

$$\dot{P} = M(P) - X^*\left(\frac{1}{P}\right), \tag{DH}$$

where $\dot{P} = dP/dt$, the rate of change of P. If $P = P_O$, $\dot{P} = 0$ so the international economy is stationary. The stability question is whether (DH) will move P toward P_O if it is not there initially. The stability condition that assures this is that a rise of P above P_O reduces excess demand so that in (DH) $\dot{P}$ becomes negative:

$$\frac{dM(P)}{dP} - \frac{dX^*\left(\frac{1}{P}\right)}{dP} < 0. \tag{SC}$$

The role of the stability condition (SC) is demonstrated in Figure A.7. In panel (a), (SC) is satisfied, and in panel (b) it is violated. In the former, P is moving toward P_O whenever, as at P_A or P_B, it is not initially there; in panel (b), P is moving away from P_O when it is not in equilibrium.

We evaluate (SC) at equilibrium P_O and transform it to elasticity terms by multiplying[5] it by $P_O/M(P_O)$:

$$0 > \frac{P_O}{M(P_O)}\left[\frac{dM(P_O)}{dP_O} - \frac{dX^*\left(\frac{1}{P_O}\right)}{dP}\right] = -e - f^*.$$

Since $f^* = e^* - 1$, (SC) can be written

$$e + e^* > 1, \tag{23}$$

which is called the *Marshall-Lerner condition*. We can gain some insight into when the condition is likely to hold by substituting the decomposition (21) into (23):

$$(c + c^* + s + s^*) + (m + m^* - 1) > 0. \tag{24}$$

1. The substitution elasticities are always positive. Thus a greater consumer willingness to substitute between the two goods (high c's) and a greater ease of altering production patterns (high s's) are conducive to stability.
2. A low volume of trade renders the substitution effects dominant relative to the income effects—this is reflected in the fact that M appears in the denominators of the definitions of the c's and s's but does not enter that of the m's. Again, stability is, therefore, more likely.
3. The home and foreign marginal propensities to spend on wheat, the home import, are m and $1 - m^*$. Thus stability is assured if each country has at least as large a marginal propensity to spend on the good it imports as does the other country on that same good ($m \geq 1 - m^*$ or, equivalently, $m^* \geq 1 - m$).
4. In particular, (24) must hold if the two countries have identical tastes in the sense of equal marginal propensities to spend on the same good ($m = 1 - m^*$). This assumption is made in the Heckscher-Ohlin-Samuelson model and other cases where international taste differences are deemed unimportant. Thus the Heckscher-Ohlin theorem derived in this way describes a stable equilibrium.

The relevance for stability of the Marshall-Lerner condition depended upon the disequilibrium hypothesis (DH), and the latter is arbitrary since it was not derived from any detailed theory of how people behave outside of equilibrium.[6] But the condition is useful in another way. It measures the sensitivity of world excess demand to price fluctuations. Thus one would expect

---

[5] Recall that $M(P_o) = X^*\left(\frac{1}{P_o}\right)$ and that $\left(\widehat{\frac{1}{P}}\right) = -\hat{P}$.

[6] However, it can be shown that the Marshall-Lerner condition is also relevant to several alternative disequilibrium hypotheses.

it to be central to an analysis of any problem in which changes in international prices play a significant role. This is indeed the case, as will become apparent when we analyze commercial policy in section A.6.

Problems

A.3.1 Why is it that both cloth and wheat cannot be inferior?

A.3.2 For any variables x and y, show $\left(\widehat{\frac{1}{x}}\right) = -\hat{x}$, $(\widehat{xy}) = \hat{x} + \hat{y}$, and $(\widehat{x/y}) = \hat{x} - \hat{y}$.

A.3.3 Find an explicit solution to the differential equation (DH), and use this solution to derive the stability condition (SC).

A.3.4 Derive the elasticity formulas for an economy with the tastes of Problem **A.2.1** and a Ricardian technology. Derive the elasticity formulas if S_C and S_W cannot be varied at all.

A.4 FACTOR ENDOWMENTS (CHAPTER 5)

Thus far the transformation curve has been simply a datum for each country. We now move on to the 2 × 2 Heckscher-Ohlin-Samuelson production structure discussed in Chapter 5.

Production Costs

Each country has a fixed endowment of capital (K) and labor (L) used to produce the two goods. Firms choose the technique of production that costs

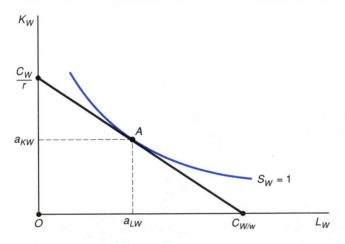

FIGURE A.8   Minimizing Cost

the least at the prevailing wage (w) and rent (r). In Figure A.8 point A on the $S_W = 1$ isoquant depicts the least-cost technique for producing each unit of wheat if the factor prices are as indicated by the slope of the budget line that has been drawn. The technique involves using a_{LW} units of labor and a_{KW} units of capital to produce each unit of wheat at the resulting cost $C_W = wa_{LW} + ra_{KW}$, which can be measured off the diagram as indicated.

The *unit cost function* for wheat records the least cost, determined as above, for producing 1 unit,

$$C_W(w, r) = wa_{LW}(w, r) + ra_{KW}(w, r), \tag{25}$$

and analogously for the cloth industry,

$$C_C(w, r) = wa_{LC}(w, r) + ra_{KC}(w, r). \tag{26}$$

The a's are written as functions of the factor prices because the latter determine what the least-cost technique is, as shown in Figure A.8.

A Basic Property

Suppose that a wheat firm is operating at minimum cost. Then for a differential movement along the isoquant:

$$w(da_{LW}) + r(da_{KW}) = 0. \tag{27}$$

This is the first-order condition for minimizing cost subject to $S_W = 1$ and is obvious from Figure A.8 since at A, $da_{KW}/da_{LW} = -(w/r)$. If we now differentiate (25),

$$\frac{\partial C_W}{\partial w} = a_{LW} + \left[w \frac{\partial a_{LW}}{\partial w} + r \frac{\partial a_{KW}}{\partial w} \right] = a_{LW}.$$

Similarly, $\partial C_W/\partial r = a_{KW}$, $\partial C_C/\partial w = a_{LC}$, and $\partial C_C/\partial r = a_{KC}$.

Isocost Curves

In equilibrium profits are driven to zero so that the price of each good is no greater than its cost. Figure A.9 shows isocost curves for each industry (combinations of w and r for which the minimum cost of production is constant) where cost equals price so that the curves are the graphs of $C_W(w, r) = P_W$ and $C_C(w, r) = P_C$. The slope of such a curve at any point equals minus the capital-labor ratio that that industry would use at the indicated factor prices (proof: the slope of $C_W(w, r) = P_W$ is $(dw)/dr = -(\partial C_W/\partial r)/(\partial C_W/\partial w) = -a_{KW}/a_{LW}$, which is the capital-labor ratio). In panel (a), for each wage-rental ratio—indicated by the slope of a ray through the origin—the cloth curve is steeper than the wheat curve, indicating that cloth is relatively capital-intensive. Panel (b) shows a factor intensity reversal. The cloth curve has the same slope at B as does the wheat curve at D. For wage-rental ratios greater than BE/OE cloth is relatively capital-intensive; at smaller wage-rental ratios wheat is capital-intensive.

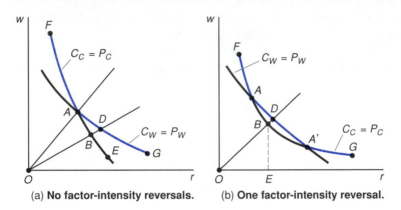

(a) **No factor-intensity reversals.**   (b) **One factor-intensity reversal.**

FIGURE A.9   **Isocost Curves**

Production Equilibrium

If both goods are produced in equilibrium, $P_W = C_W$ and $P_C = C_C$ so that w and r must be given by the intersection of the two isocost curves, as at A in Figure A.9. The slope of each curve at A shows the capital-labor ratio employed in each sector. Now $K = K_W + K_C$ and $L = L_W + L_C$, where K_W is the amount of capital employed in the wheat industry, and so forth. Thus

$$\frac{K}{L} = \frac{L_W}{L_W + L_C}\frac{K_W}{L_W} + \frac{L_C}{L_W + L_C}\frac{K_C}{L_C} = \lambda_{LW}\left(\frac{a_{KW}}{a_{LW}}\right) + \lambda_{LC}\left(\frac{a_{KC}}{a_{LC}}\right), \qquad (28)$$

where $\lambda_{LW} = L_W/L$, the fraction of the total labor force used in the wheat industry, and analogously for λ_{LC}. Clearly, $\lambda_{LW} + \lambda_{LC} = 1$, so that (28) says that the economy-wide capital-labor ratio is a *weighted average* of the two factor intensities.

But what if K/L is not a weighted average of the capital-labor ratios employed in the two sectors at A—that is, if K/L is either larger than the slope of both curves at that point or smaller than both slopes? Suppose that it is smaller and equal to, say, the slope of C_W at D in Figure A.9(a) and the slope of C_C at E. If w and r were as indicated by point E, $P_C = C_C$ but $P_W > C_W$ because E is below the $C_W = P_W$ curve so that cost is less than P_W. This means that E cannot be an equilibrium since wheat producers would earn positive profits. But D is an equilibrium because here $P_W = C_W$ and $P_C < C_C$: the economy specializes in wheat as the unprofitable cloth industry is shut down. In similar manner, high capital-labor endowment ratios result in specialization in cloth, with w and r as indicated by that point (somewhere above A) where the $C_C = P_C$ curve has a slope equal to the endowment ratio.

Thus equilibrium always lies on the portion of the two isocost curves lying farthest from the origin. Such an outer envelope, known as the *factor-price frontier*, is distinguished by colored lines in Figure A.9: *FADG* in panel

(a) and *FADA'G* in panel (b). The frontier consists of smooth segments, where only one good is produced, and a kink, where both industries operate. Factor intensity reversals allow the possibility of multiple kinks.

Factor-Price Equalization

Suppose that the home and foreign countries have identical technologies and free trade so that they also have identical commodity prices. Then the two countries will have the same pair of isocost curves. Assume for a moment that there is no factor intensity reversal. The equilibrium prices that are established for cloth and wheat must imply an intersection of the two isocost curves, otherwise both countries would necessarily specialize in the good represented by the outer curve and the other good could not be produced at all. Thus both countries are represented by a diagram like Figure A.9(a).

If both countries produce both goods, they are both at *A* and so have identical factor prices. If one or both countries specialize, they cannot both be at *A* and must have distinct factor prices. Whether or not both countries are at *A* depends upon whether both have factor-endowments ratios between the slopes of the two isocost curves at *A*.

Factor-price equalization is basically a matter of similarity in factor endowments. The equilibrium commodity prices that are established must be such as to leave one of the countries on the wheat isocost curve at *A* or above and the other country on the cloth curve at *A* or below, otherwise both countries would specialize in the same good and the world would have none of the other. Thus the closer the endowments of the two countries are to each other, the closer the countries must both be to point *A*.

If we never allow factor intensity reversals and turn to Figure A.9(b), the above argument still holds. The only change is that factor-price equalization is no longer identified with nonspecialization in both countries since one country could be at point *A* and the other at *A'* with different factor prices. But note that the two countries must in this case have quite different relative factor endowments, emphasizing the crucial role of similarities in the latter.

The Stolper-Samuelson Theorem

Suppose that a country produces both goods, with factor prices as indicated by point *A* in Figure A.10. Now suppose that the price of cloth, the capital-intensive good, rises from P_C to P'_C. This shifts the cloth isocost curve outward in the proportion of the price rise; thus the figure shows a price increase in the proportion AB/OA. At *B* the C_C curve has the same slope as at *A*, and w, r, and P_C are all greater by an equal percentage so that their relative magnitudes are unaltered.

P_W has not changed, so the new equilibrium is at *A'*. Since the wheat isocost curve slopes down, w is lower at *A'* than *A*: the wage has fallen. Since the cloth isocost curve slopes down, r is greater at *A'* than *B*: the rent has increased by a greater proportion than has P_C. Thus the rent rises relative to the prices of both goods, and the wage falls relative to the prices of both goods.

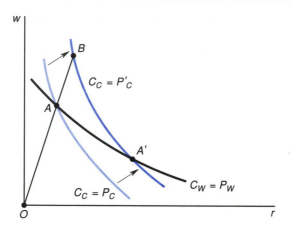

FIGURE A.10   **The Stolper-Samuelson Theorem**

To see the theorem algebraically, set $P_C = C_C(w, r)$ in (25) and $P_W = C_W(w, r)$ in (26), and differentiate both equations:

$$dP_C = (dw)a_{LC} + (dr)a_{KC} + [w(da_{LC}) + r(da_{KC})]$$

$$dP_W = (dw)a_{LW} + (dr)a_{KW} + [w(da_{LW}) + r(da_{KW})].$$

From (27) and its cloth analog, both bracketed terms vanish. Dividing each equation by its respective commodity price and manipulating just a little give

$$\hat{P}_C = \theta_{LC}\hat{w} + \theta_{KC}\hat{r} \tag{29}$$

$$\hat{P}_W = \theta_{LW}\hat{w} + \theta_{KW}\hat{r}, \tag{30}$$

where $\theta_{LC} = wa_{LC}/P_C = wa_{LC}S_C/P_CS_C$, the share of wages in the total earnings of the cloth industry. The θ's are defined analogously so that θ_{KC}, for example, denotes the share of capital rents in the cloth industry. Thus $\theta_{LC} + \theta_{KC} = 1$ and $\theta_{LW} + \theta_{KW} = 1$. Equation (29) then says that $\hat{P}_C$ is a *weighted average* of $\hat{w}$ and $\hat{r}$ and thus lies between the two factor price changes. Equation (30) likewise says that $\hat{P}_W$ is bounded by $\hat{w}$ and $\hat{r}$. It is easy to see that cloth is relatively capital-intensive if $\theta_{KC} > \theta_{KW}$ (or $\theta_{LW} > \theta_{LC}$). Then (29) and (30) imply that

$$\hat{r} > \hat{P}_C > \hat{P}_W > \hat{w}$$

when cloth becomes relatively more expensive ($\hat{P}_C > \hat{P}_W$) and that

$$\hat{w} > \hat{P}_W > \hat{P}_C > \hat{r}$$

when wheat becomes relatively more expensive. A change in relative commodity prices always increases the real reward of the factor intensive in the good whose relative price has increased and reduces the real reward of the other factor.

The Stolper-Samuelson theorem concerns real factor rewards. It says something about income distribution to the extent that different groups in society derive income from different factors. If every individual supplied capital and labor services in the same proportion, the Stolper-Samuelson analysis would be irrelevant to income distribution.

Duality

In section A.1 we wrote the national income function as $y(P_C, P_W \ldots)$ to indicate that income was sensitive to whatever determines the transformation curve. But now that curve is determined by a country's factor endowment, so we have $y(P_C, P_W; K, L)$. Since each factor is paid the value of its marginal product, $\partial y/\partial K = r$ (and $\partial y/\partial L = w$).

Recall that $\partial y/\partial P_C = S_C$. Taking second derivatives,

$$\frac{\partial^2 y}{\partial K \partial P_C} = \frac{\partial r}{\partial P_C} \text{ and } \frac{\partial^2 y}{\partial P_C \partial K} = \frac{\partial S_C}{\partial K}.$$

But $\partial^2 y/\partial K \partial P_C = \partial^2 y/\partial P_C \partial K$ so that

$$\frac{\partial r}{\partial P_C} = \frac{\partial S_C}{\partial K} \tag{31}$$

and similarly for other combinations of factors and goods. A rise in a commodity price produces the same effect on a factor reward as a rise in the endowment of that factor would produce upon the output of the commodity. The relation between goods prices and factor rewards is the turf of the Stolper-Samuelson theorem, whereas the Rybczynski analysis concerns the relation between endowments and outputs. *Reciprocity relations* such as (31) link the two.

We can also now obtain an alternative interpretation of our national income function $y(P_C, P_W; K, L)$. We defined y as the maximum income obtainable when goods that can be produced from K and L are evaluated at P_C and P_W. But y can also be regarded as the minimum that must be spent on K and L if factor prices are to leave commodity costs no lower than P_C and P_W. To understand this, return to Figure A.9(a), and suppose that, for the given P_C, P_W, K, and L, point D denotes equilibrium. Then the slope of the factor-price frontier at D equals $-K/L$. Thus we can think of ourselves as reaching D by pushing a straight line with this slope as close to the origin as possible while still touching the factor-price frontier. In other words, D denotes the combinations of w and r that minimizes $wL + rK$ subject to the condition that w and r not lie below the factor-price frontier—that is, that $C_W(w, r) \geq P_W$ and $C_C(w, r) \geq P_C$.

The Rybczynski Theorem

In equilibrium each factor is fully employed by the two industries:

$$K = a_{KC}(w, r) S_C + a_{KW}(w, r) S_W \tag{32}$$

$$L = a_{LC}(w, r) S_C + a_{LW}(w, r) S_W. \tag{33}$$

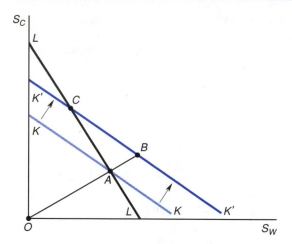

FIGURE A.11   The Rybczynski Theorem

The relations are drawn in Figure A.11 for given wages and rents and, there-fore, fixed a's. The line labeled L is the graph of (33) for the given labor force L and the fixed a's. The slope of this line is $-a_{LW}/a_{LC}$. The K line analogously represents (32), and the fact that the L line is steeper reflects an assumption that cloth is relatively capital-intensive. Point A shows equilibrium outputs of the two goods. (Since both industries are operating, the assumed capital-labor endowment ratio must be between the slopes of the two isocost curves in the pertinent version of Figure A.10.)

   Now suppose that, at unchanged commodity prices, K is increased. If the endowment change is not large enough to induce specialization, w and r will not alter, by the factor-price equalization theorem, and, therefore, the a's re-main fixed. The effect of the increase in K is simply to shift the graph of (32) outward; Figure A.11 shows a rise in K in the proportion AB/OA. If wheat and cloth output were to rise proportionally with K, production would have to shift from point A to B. But instead it shifts to C, the new point of intersec-tion. Since C is above B, the output of cloth, the capital-intensive commodity, has risen in greater proportion than has the stock of capital; since C is to the left of A, the output of wheat has fallen.

   To see the situation algebraically, differentiate (32) and (33), remember-ing that the a's are fixed:

$$dK = a_{KC}(dS_C) + a_{KW}(dS_W)$$

$$dL = a_{LC}(dS_C) + a_{LW}(dS_W).$$

Dividing each equation by its respective factor endowment and manipulating just a little give

$$\hat{K} = \lambda_{KC}\hat{S}_C + \lambda_{KW}\hat{S}_W \qquad (34)$$

$$\hat{L} = \lambda_{LC}\hat{S}_C + \lambda_{LW}\hat{S}_W, \qquad (35)$$

where $\lambda_{KC} = a_{KC}S_C/K$, the fraction of the nation's capital stock used in the cloth industry, and analogously for the other λ's. Note that $\lambda_{KC} + \lambda_{KW} = 1$ so that (34) says that $\hat{K}$ is a weighted average of $\hat{S}_C$ and $\hat{S}_W$ and similarly for (35). As in the previous subsection, we can easily show that, if cloth is relatively capital intensive,

$$\hat{S}_C > \hat{K} > \hat{L} > \hat{S}_W$$

when $\hat{K} > \hat{L}$, and

$$\hat{S}_W > \hat{L} > \hat{K} > \hat{S}_C$$

when $\hat{L} > \hat{K}$.

The Heckscher-Ohlin Theorem

Increases in the wage relative to the rent accompany increases in the relative price of the labor-intensive good, by the Stolper-Samuelson theorem. Thus if two countries are in autarky, share a common technology, and are not separated by a factor intensity reversal, the country with the lower wage-rental ratio must have the lower relative autarkic price of the labor-intensive good. If we define labor abundance to mean a relatively low autarkic wage-rental ratio, this gives us the *price version* of the Heckscher-Ohlin theorem: each country has a comparative advantage in that good relatively intensive in the use of the country's relatively abundant factor. (This is called the price version because factor abundance is defined in terms of autarkic factor prices.)

When can the pattern of trade be predicted on the basis of *physical* factor endowments? Suppose two countries with identical technology and no separating factor intensity reversal enter into free trade. The commodity prices that are established must then yield a situation as illustrated in Figure A.9(a); since both goods must be produced in equilibrium, prices must be such that the two isocost curves intersect and also such that one country produces at A or above and the other at A or below. Suppose, first, that not both countries are nonspecialized—that is, they are not both[7] at point A. Suppose it is because one of the countries is at A or above and specialized in cloth. This must be the capital-abundant country since each point above A has a steeper slope than all points below. Since this country specializes in cloth, it must export it, with the other country exporting wheat. Thus each country exports the good intensive in the country's relatively abundant factor. The argument is similar if we suppose instead that a country is at A or below and specialized in wheat.

Now suppose that both countries produce both goods and are at A. Then factor prices are equalized, and the countries employ similar techniques. If,

---

[7] It could be that one of the countries is specialized but nonetheless at A if its endowment just equals the slope of one of the isocost curves at A. The following argument also applies to such a case.

for example, the home country is relatively capital-abundant in a physical sense, the Rybczynski theorem tells us that $S_C/S_W > S_C^*/S_W^*$. To proceed further, we assume the two countries have similar tastes in the sense that when they face identical prices they consume the two goods in identical proportions— that is, $D_C/D_W = D_C^*/D_W^*$. These ratios, in turn, must equal $(S_C + S_C^*)/(S_W + S_W^*)$ because the world consumption of each good necessarily equals world supply. Thus

$$S_C/S_W > D_C/D_W = (S_C + S_C^*)/(S_W + S_W^*) = D_C^*/D_W^* > S_C^*/S_W^*.$$

The first inequality says that the home country exports cloth and imports wheat, and the last inequality says the opposite about the foreign country. Thus we have the *quantity* version of the Heckscher-Ohlin theorem: a country will export the good intensive in the factor that is (physically) relatively abundant.

The price version has the disadvantage that it requires knowledge of autarkic prices, whereas the quantity version depends upon physical endowments that can be measured in either free trade or autarky. But the price version says nothing about demands, whereas the quantity version requires international similarity whenever endowment differences are small enough to permit factor-price equalization.

Intersectoral Factor Immobility

The Heckscher-Ohlin-Samuelson model has dominated trade theory for most of the last fifty years. But for about seventy years before that economists had put great stress on the degrees of factor mobility between sectors when analyzing the internal effects of international trade. This earlier analysis has now been resurrected and given contemporary expression largely in response to concern about how people actually perceive their interests to be linked to price changes.

The degree of mobility varies between factors and is also sensitive to the relevant time horizon, as pointed out in the text. This variability is often captured in the literature by adding to the HOS model the assumption that one of the factors is sector-specific while the other remains fully mobile between industries. Call the mobile factor labor and the specific factor capital. Since there is still a single labor market, there will be a single wage in each country; but the market for cloth capital is now disjoint from the market for wheat capital, so rents in the two sectors need not be the same. Let r_C denote the rent of cloth capital and r_W that of wheat capital.

The isocost curves in Figure A.12 have the same meaning as before: these curves are derived from isoquants independently of factor mobility. The intersection A will be the equilibrium if the capital-labor ratio lies between the slopes of the two curves at A *and* if the two factors can be allocated as required between the two sectors. We can still regard A as long-run equilibrium, but now we are concerned with a perspective in which intersectoral capital immobility rules A out. Equilibrium will instead be illustrated by a pair of

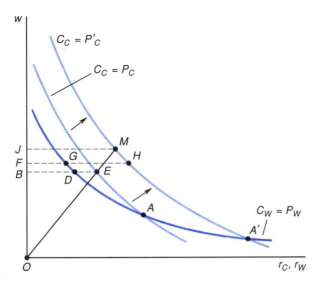

FIGURE A.12   Intersectoral Capital Immobility

parallel points such as D and E. In this case OB measures the common wage, $r_C = BE$ and $r_W = BD$.

How does the Stolper-Samuelson theorem change in this environment? Suppose P_C rises in the proportion EM/OE $(= BJ/OB)$ to P'_C; this shifts the $C_C = P_C$ curve outward, as shown. If labor, like capital, did not move between sectors, the cloth equilibrium would switch from E to M, where w and r_C rise in proportion to P_C while wheat stays at D. But this is impossible because the cloth wage, OJ, would exceed the wheat wage, OB. Thus labor will move from the wheat sector to the cloth sector until a common intermediate wage is established. This is illustrated in the figure by the new equilibrium: G and H.

Because G is necessarily to the left of D, r_W has fallen; because H is to the right of M, r_C has risen relative to P_C; because F is between J and B, w has risen relative to the unchanged P_W but fallen relative to P_C:

$$\hat{r}_C > \hat{P}_C > \hat{w} > \hat{P}_W > \hat{r}_W. \tag{36}$$

A relative price change increases the real reward of the factor specific to the good with the higher price and reduces the real reward of the other specific factor. The reward of the mobile factor rises in terms of one good and falls in terms of the other. Thus the effect on the real wage depends upon how wage income is spent among the two goods and upon just how much the wage changes; the latter depends, in turn, upon the technological details that determine the slopes of the isoquants and thereby those of the isocost curves.

Problems

A.4.1 Geometrically demonstrate how an isocost curve can be derived from a given isoquant. Show how an isoquant can be derived from a given isocost curve.

A.4.2 Show how Figure A.11 may alter in the presence of a factor intensity reversal. Trace out the values of S_C and S_W as K varies from zero toward infinity.

A.4.3 Discuss the Rybczynski theorem if capital is immobile between sectors. What can you say about the factor-price equalization and Heckscher-Ohlin theorems?

A.5 HIGHER-DIMENSIONAL FACTOR-ENDOWMENTS THEORY* (SECTION 9* OF CHAPTER 6)

The Heckscher-Ohlin-Samuelson model has been the mainstay of international trade theory for fifty years. But empirical work during these years has, on balance, been unkind to the model. The basic idea that trade is influenced significantly by relative factor endowments has not fared too badly, but the two-factor, two-commodity HOS model seems decisively inadequate to describe reality. Thus the extension of that model to more goods and factors is the key step in understanding the practical significance of the dominant structure of modern trade theory.

Additional Goods

We start by adding more goods while retaining two factors. A third good brings out the important points; adding still more is straightforward but tedious.

Figure A.13 adds an isocost curve for a third good, deckles, to those of wheat and cloth. For given prices of the latter two goods, the price of deckles, P_D, must just equal that value which will cause the $P_D = C_D(r, w)$ curve to pass through the intersection of the wheat and cloth curves if production of all three goods is to be possible. This is shown in panel (b). Algebraically, if a deckle equation is added to (25) and (26), and if the costs of the three goods are set equal to exogenously specified prices, we have a system of three equations in two unknowns (w and r). This will be overdetermined unless the prices happen to be set just right to make one of the equations redundant.

This would appear to make diversification highly unlikely. So it would if commodity prices were chosen at random. But they are not chosen at random: they must clear markets. The importance of this is apparent upon consideration of autarky, where all three goods must be produced, so that their prices must give a picture like Figure A.13(b).

*An asterisk indicates material that is relatively more advanced and may be skipped without loss of continuity.

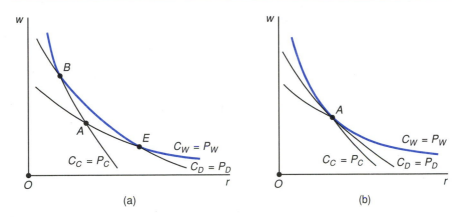

FIGURE A.13   **Factor-Price Frontiers with Three Goods**

Suppose that two countries with the same technology freely trade. It is not now necessary that any individual country be able to produce all three goods, but prices must be such that all three are producible somewhere. This means that the factor-price frontier must include part of each isocost curve—that is, prices cannot be such as to leave any isocost curve entirely below the other two. We have the two possibilities illustrated in Figure A.13. Factor intensity reversals permit additional possibilities, but we assume them away and suppose that deckles are of intermediate capital intensity.

In panel (a), no country can ever produce all three goods at once, and for the world to do so one country must be on the factor-price frontier at point B or above and the other country at E or below: factor-price equalization is impossible. Neither country can have a factor endowment equal to the slope of the curve BE at any point (other than the endpoints). Thus equilibrium prices cannot be such as to yield panel (a) if the two countries have sufficiently similar endowments. The latter require panel (b), which is consistent with both countries producing all goods if they each have an endowment between the slopes of the wheat and cloth isocost curves at A. Thus the factor-price equalization argument is basically unchanged: free trade between countries with sufficiently similar relative factor endowments will equalize factor prices.

Consider next the Heckscher-Ohlin theorem. In Figure A.13(a) one country must be on the frontier at B or above and the other at E or below. It is easy to verify that in this case all the goods exported by the capital-abundant country must be more capital-intensive than all the goods imported, and analogously for the other country, regardless of which country's techniques are used to make the comparison. In panel (b) it is likewise easy to see that the Heckscher-Ohlin predictions continue to hold if one country produces all three goods while the other specializes in either cloth or wheat. But if both countries produce all goods, problems arise. To see why, rewrite (32) and (33) with the addition of a third good:

$$K = a_{KC}(w, r)\, S_C + a_{KW}(w, r)\, S_W + a_{KD}(w, r)\, S_D \tag{37}$$

$$L = a_{LC}(w, r)\, S_C + a_{LW}(w, r)\, S_W + a_{LD}(w, r)\, S_D. \tag{38}$$

For each country, the endowments K and L are given and the a's are determined by the equalized factor prices. Thus (37) and (38) form a system of two linear equations in three unknowns: S_C, S_W, and S_D. The system will likely be underdetermined: if there is one solution with all outputs positive, there must be many such solutions.

A little geometry is useful. In Figure A.14, the *transformation surface* (three-dimensional generalization of the transformation curve) is *AHJGE*. This structure, showing all combinations of the three goods that can be produced from given amounts of the two factors, is a *ruled surface*. It is composed of linear segments, just as an ice-cream cone has its tip connected to its rim by linear segments but is smoothly curved in every other direction on its surface. The three commodity prices determine a *budget plane*. The figure shows the budget plane *BMF*, which reflects relative prices $P_W/P_D = OM/OB$ and $P_W/P_C = OF/OB$. National income is maximized by producing at a point on the transformation surface where the budget plane is as far from the origin as possible. Because the surface is ruled, this occurs not at a unique point of tangency, but anywhere along the line segment *HG*. Now if the foreign country is also producing all three goods, that country can likewise produce anywhere on a linear segment *H'G'* in the foreign analog of Figure A.14.

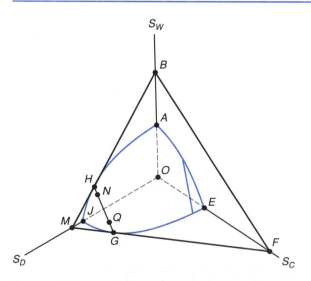

FIGURE A.14   **Transformation Surface with Three Goods and Two Factors**

Because factor-price equalization causes the two economies to use the same techniques, HG and $H'G'$ will be parallel to each other. Thus if the domestic economy were to shift production from, say, N to Q, the foreign economy could switch in exactly the opposite way and world production of all three goods would be unchanged. National production and, therefore, world trade patterns are indeterminate. Neither the Heckscher-Ohlin theorem nor any other statement predicting specific trade flows is valid.

If a country produces just two goods, as at B or E in Figure A. 13(a), the logic of the Rybczynski theorem is clearly unchanged. But if all three goods are produced, the exact effects of endowment changes on outputs must be indeterminate since the outputs themselves are indeterminate both before and after the changes.

With regard to commodity price changes, equations like (29) and (30) hold for all produced goods so that the Stolper-Samuelson theorem continues to hold for changes in the price of all goods (either two or three) that are actually produced.

Additional Factors

Let us now return to two goods but add a third factor, land *(T)*. Then equations (32) and (33) are replaced by

$$K = a_{KC}(w, r, v) \, S_C + a_{KW}(w, r, v) \, S_W \tag{39}$$

$$L = a_{LC}(w, r, v) \, S_C + a_{LW}(w, r, v) \, S_W \tag{40}$$

$$T = a_{TC}(w, r, v) \, S_C + a_{TW}(w, r, v) \, S_W, \tag{41}$$

where v denotes the rent paid for land. Suppose that we are initially in equilibrium and that there is a small change in endowments—say, a slight rise in K. Since T and L do not change, Equations (40) and (41) uniquely determine S_C and S_W for fixed factor prices (except in the special case where (40) and (41) are identical). Thus the increase in K cannot, at the initial factor prices, change the output of either good. But then (39) cannot continue to hold after the rise in K. The conclusion must be that factor prices will change if all factors are to remain fully employed. Thus the factor-price equalization theorem does not hold. The Rybczynski result also runs into trouble because employed endowments *cannot* be changed independently of prices.

We can see this in another way by adding a third factor to Equations (25) and (26):

$$C_W(w, r, v) = wa_{LW}(w, r, v) + ra_{KW}(w, r, v) + va_{TW}(w, r, v) \tag{42}$$

$$C_C(w, r, v) = wa_{LC}(w, r, v) + ra_{KC}(w, r, v) + va_{TC}(w, r, v). \tag{43}$$

If costs are set equal to given commodity prices, we have two equations in the three unknowns w, r, and v. The system is undetermined and cannot be solved without additional information (the factor endowments and their constraints).

If we then differentiate these equations to obtain our version of (29) and (30), we have

$$\hat{P}_C = \theta_{LC}\,\hat{w} + \theta_{KC}\hat{r} + \theta_{TC}\hat{v} \tag{44}$$

$$\hat{P}_W = \theta_{LW}\,\hat{w} + \theta_{KW}\hat{r} + \theta_{TW}\hat{v}. \tag{45}$$

This leaves open the (non–Stolper-Samuelson) possibility that one of the proportional factor-price changes might fall between $\hat{P}_C$ and $\hat{P}_W$. Indeed, in the previous section we had an example where this happened: intersectoral capital immobility. Since cloth capital and wheat capital were distinct, this was a special three-factor, two-good model (special because, although there were in effect three factors in the economy, each sector used only two), and we saw that $\hat{w}$ was necessarily between $\hat{P}_C$ and $\hat{P}_W$.

Many Goods and Factors: Factor-Price Equalization

Let us now turn to the more general case of n goods ($n \geq 2$) and m factors ($m \geq 2$). Consider the factor-price equalization property.

Suppose initially than $n = m$, and let two countries engage in free trade at some equilibrium commodity price *vector p*. If the two countries happen to possess the various factors in identical proportions, they will produce the various goods in identical proportions, have identical factor prices, and use identical techniques (the production sides of such economies will be identical except for scale, and so they will behave identically). Let W be such a common *vector* of factor prices. Then, if we number the goods from 1 to n and the factors from 1 to m,

$$P_i = \sum_{j=1}^{m} W_j a_{ji}(W) \quad i = 1, \ldots, n,$$

or

$$p = WA(W), \tag{46}$$

where $A(W) = \begin{bmatrix} a_{11}(W) \ldots a_{1n}(W) \\ \cdots \\ a_{m1}(W) \ldots a_{mn}(W) \end{bmatrix}$ is the *matrix* of techniques. The problem

is whether factor prices will continue to be identical if relative endowments cease to be. If, in either country, all goods are produced (as they will be with relatively identical endowments),

$$K = A(W)S, \tag{47}$$

where $S = (S_1, \ldots, S_n)$ denotes commodity outputs and $K = (K_1, \ldots, K_m)$ factor endowments. For any non-negative vector S of outputs, Equation (47) gives some non-negative vector K of factors necessary to produce the outputs. Let K_W denote the collection of *all* vectors K that solve (47) for non-negative S's. If both countries have factor endowments in K_W, both can produce all goods at factor prices W. Factor-price equalization will, therefore, be possible, but will it be necessary? Suppose not. That is, suppose that for some other vector of factor rewards, W', the economy can be in equilibrium at the same commodity prices p so that $p = W'A(W')$ and $K = A(W')S'$. Now, $A(W)$ is the cheapest technique to use at factor prices W but is not the cheapest technique at factor prices W' (since $A(W')$ is); therefore,

$$WA(W) = p < W'A(W) \qquad (48)$$

where "$x < y$" means that no component of the vector x is greater than the corresponding component of the vector y and at least one component is strictly less. Exactly analogous reasoning yields

$$p = W'A(W') < WA(W'). \qquad (49)$$

Multiplying both sides of (48) by the vector S yields $WK < W'K$, while multiplying both sides of (49) by S' gives the contradictory result $W'K < WK$. Thus if a country has factor endowments in K_W, that country can have no factor prices other than W.

With an arbitrary number of goods and factors, if the two countries have sufficiently similar factor endowments—that is, both endowments are in K_W—they must have equal factor prices. The factor-price equalization argument survives basically intact in higher dimensions.

If we now allow unequal numbers of factors and goods, the considerations of the previous subsections arise. When $n > m$, the situation does not substantially change; but $m > n$ reduces factor-price equalization to a fluke. The general conclusion is that factor-price equalization can be expected between countries with similar relative factor endowments if there are at least as many goods as factors.[8]

The Stolper-Samuelson Theorem

Suppose that some good—say, the first—is initially produced in equilibrium so that $P_1 = C_1(W)$, that its production requires at least two factors, and let its price rise. In the new equilibrium the cost of production of S_1 must rise at least as much as its price, with $\hat{P}_1 = \hat{C}_1$ if the good continues to be produced and $\hat{P}_1 \leq \hat{C}_1$ if it does not. In either case we must have, as a result of by-now-familiar operations,

$$\hat{P}_1 \leq \hat{C}_1 = \theta_{11}\hat{W}_1 + \ldots + \theta_{m1}\hat{W}_m, \qquad (50)$$

where $\theta_{11} + \ldots + \theta_{m1} = 1$. Thus $\hat{C}_1$ is a weighted average of the $\hat{W}_j$. This means that at least one $\hat{W}_j$ must at least equal $\hat{C}_1$ and, therefore, $\hat{P}_1$ as well: an increase in the price of any good that is initially produced causes some factor reward to rise in at least equal proportion. Now suppose that there is some

[8] The analysis of this subsection depends upon L. W. McKenzie, "Equality of Factor Prices in World Trade," *Econometrica* 23 (1955): 239–57. See also H. Uzawa, "Prices of the Factors of Production in International Trade," *Econometrica* 27 (1959): 448–68; W. Ethier, "Some of the Theorems of International Trade with Many Goods and Factors," *Journal of International Economics* 4 (1974): 199–206; Dixit and Norman, *op. cit.*

other good—say, the second—whose price has not changed, which uses exactly the same factors in its production as does the first good and which is produced after the rise in P_1. Then we must have

$$0 = \hat{P}_2 \geq \hat{C}_2 = \theta_{12} \hat{W}_1 + \ldots + \theta_{m2} \hat{W}_m. \tag{51}$$

Now we know that one of the factor rewards W_j has increased. Thus for (51) to be true, some factor reward must fall: $\hat{W}_i < 0$ for some i. But good 1 uses the same factors that good 2 does. Thus at least one of the $\hat{W}_i$ on the right hand of (50) must be negative; this means that (50) requires some W_i to exceed $\hat{C}_1 \geq \hat{P}_1$. Thus the increase in the price of good 1 must cause the reward of *some* factor to rise in even greater proportion (and, therefore, to rise unambiguously in real terms) and the reward to *some* other factor to fall absolutely (and, therefore, in real terms). The basic requirements are that the good whose price rises actually be produced in the initial equilibrium and that this good use a *nonspecific assortment* of at least two factors in the sense that the factors used to produce this good are precisely the same factors used by some other good that is produced after the price change.

An increase in the price of an initially produced good using a nonspecific assortment of at least two factors necessarily causes some factor reward to rise in even greater proportion and some factor reward to fall.

Thus we have the basic Stolper-Samuelson result that a commodity price change produces *conflict:* some factor has an unambiguously higher real reward, and some factor has an unambiguously lower real reward. This proposition does not depend upon the relative sizes of m and n (if they each exceed 1) and reduces to the standard Stolper-Samuelson theorem when $n = m = 2$. The proposition says nothing about some factors whenever $m > 2$; this is consistent with our earlier conclusion that some proportional factor rewards could be weighted averages of proportional commodity price changes when $m > n$.

The Rybczynski Theorem[9]

Suppose that the endowment of some factor—say, the first—is used in at least two industries and that its quantity is increased. If it is fully employed after the endowment increase, we must have, if factor prices do not change,

$$\hat{K}_1 \leqq \lambda_{11} \hat{S}_1 + \ldots + \lambda_{1n} \hat{S}_n, \tag{52}$$

where $\lambda_{11} + \ldots + \lambda_{1n} = 1$, so that at least one $\hat{S}_i$ must be at least as large as $\hat{K}_1$. Suppose that K_1 is a *nonspecific factor* in the sense that at least one other factor—say, the second—is used in positive amounts by the same sectors that use K_1 and is fully employed initially. Then

---

[9] For more on the topic of this and the preceding subsections, see Chapter 3 of R. W. Jones and P. B. Kenen, eds., *Handbook of International Economics,* vol. 1 (Amsterdam: North Holland, 1984).

$$0 = \hat{K}_2 \geq \lambda_{21}\hat{S}_1 + \ldots + \lambda_{2n}\hat{S}_n. \tag{53}$$

Since at least one of the $\hat{S}_i \geq \hat{K}_1 > 0$, (53) requires *some* $\hat{S}_i < 0$. Then (52) requires *some* other $\hat{S}_i > \hat{K}_1$.

> *At constant factor prices, an increase in the endowment of a nonspecific factor used in at least two sectors that leaves that factor fully employed produces a more than proportional rise in the output of some good and a fall in the output of some other good.*

Once again, this result is independent of the relative magnitudes of m and n. If $n > 2$, some output changes are unaccounted for. This makes the proposition consistent with $n > m$ where outputs are indeterminate: *some* good must increase its output in greater proportion than the factor endowment has risen, but no one can say which.

This proposition applies to cases where factor prices do not change; but we have seen that, if $m > n$, endowment changes *must* generally produce factor-price changes if all factors are to remain fully employed. Thus if $m > n$, our proposition is of practical interest only if unemployment of factors is considered.

Duality

Recall that in the previous section we established the *reciprocity relations*

$$\frac{\partial W_j}{\partial P_i} = \frac{\partial S_i}{\partial K_j}. \tag{54}$$

The proof of these relations was not sensitive to the number of goods and factors and is generally valid, but the application of the relations to our propositions becomes tricky when $n \neq m$. With more goods than factors, terms such as $\partial S_i/\partial K_j$ are indeterminate; with more factors than goods, (54) is derived under the assumption that the economy adjusts to keep all factors fully employed, in contrast to our generalized Rybczynski result. It is still possible to derive some conclusions with unequal numbers of goods and factors, but for simplicity we assume $n = m$.

Note, first, that (54) establishes a duality between those parts of the Stolper-Samuelson and Rybczynski propositions relating to reactions in the *opposite* direction: a change in the price of good i will change the reward of factor j in the opposite direction if, and only if, a change in the endowment of factor j changes the output of good i in the opposite direction. But this duality does not extend to the more-than-proportional reactions in the same direction: $\hat{W}_j > \hat{P}_i$, or $\partial W_j/\partial P_i > W_j/P_i > 0$, implies, from (54), only that $\partial S_i/\partial K_j > 0$; it need not be true that $\partial S_i/\partial K_j > S_i/K_j$.

Second, our Stolper-Samuelson property tells us that a rise in any commodity price reduces the reward of some factor. But is it also true that the real reward of any factor can be changed by the manipulation of just one commodity price? Yes, because the Rybczynski property says that a rise in any factor endowment must reduce the output of some good, and so we can use the duality property (54) to conclude that the reward of any factor can indeed be increased by a fall in some commodity price.

In similar fashion, duality allows us to conclude that the output of any good will fall in response to a rise in the endowment of some factor.

The Heckscher-Ohlin Theorem[10]

We have left the Heckscher-Ohlin theorem for last because, even in the HOS model, this is the most fragile of the four central theorems. The assumptions of no factor intensity reversals and of identical tastes, for example, play little or no role in the other three propositions.

We start with a generalization of the price version. Recall that in the 2×2 case this version made no assumptions about demand but was sensitive to the nature of technology (that is, factor intensity reversals). The same will be true now. Suppose that in free trade a country exchanges the vector $M = D^T - S^T$ of net imports with the rest of the world. Now we know that $p^A \cdot D^T \geq p^A \cdot D^A$, where the superscript A refers to autarky because D^T gives higher utility than D^A, so the country would not have consumed the latter in autarky if it could have afforded the former. Next, let M_K denote the factors of production that were *actually used* to produce M—that is,

$$M_K = \bar{A}M,$$

where the i-th column of $\bar{A}$ is the technique used at home to produce S_i if that good is exported ($D_i^T - S_i^T = M_i < 0$) and is the technique used abroad if the good is imported ($M_i > 0$). Then it must be possible for the country to produce the goods D^T from the factors $K + M_K$ simply by no longer producing imports the same way they are produced abroad. But this technique need not be profitable at autarkic prices:

$$W^A \cdot (K + M_K) \geq p^A \cdot D^T.$$

Thus,

$$W^A \cdot M_K \geq p^A \cdot D^T - W^A \cdot K \geq p^A \cdot D^A - W^A \cdot K = 0.$$

Therefore,

$$W^A \cdot M_K \geq 0. \tag{55}$$

If we apply the same logic to the rest of the world,

$$W^{A*} \cdot M_K^* \geq 0, \tag{56}$$

---

[10] The material of this subsection depends upon A. Deardorff, "The General Validity of the Heckscher-Ohlin Theorem," *American Economic Review* 72 (1982): 683–94; Dixit and Norman, *op. cit.*, 93–102; and J. Vanek, "The Factor Proportions Theory: The N-Factor Case," *Kyklos* 21 (1968): 749–56.

where W^{A*} denotes foreign autarkic factor prices. Now foreign imports are home exports so that $M^* = -M$. Thus $M_K^* = \bar{A}M^* = -\bar{A}M = -M_K$. Substituting this into (56) and subtracting from (55) yields

$$(W^A - W^{A*}) \cdot M_K \geq 0. \tag{57}$$

This says that autarkic factor-price differences are positively correlated with the factor content of imports: countries tend to import (via trade) those factors that are relatively expensive in autarky.

Note two things about this result. First, it is independent of demand, just as is the 2×2 price version. Next, factor content is evaluated according to the *country of origin* of each export instead of using a single country's technique to evaluate all trade flows or using each country's technique for both imports and exports of that country. Of course, if factor prices are equalized, techniques are the same everywhere so that such distinctions do not matter. But otherwise, when countries have substantially different factor endowments, they will use different techniques and the global nature of the technology will begin to matter. We measure factor content the way we do in order to avoid the problems caused by factor intensity reversals and their higher-dimensional analogs. To see this, consider the 2×2 case where a factor intensity reversal separates the two countries. With only two factors, (57) says that each country is a net exporter of its relatively abundant factor. We know that this cannot be true for both countries if each evaluates the factor content of trade according to its own techniques (or if both countries use the techniques of just one country), but it is true when the technique of the exporter is used for each good.

We would expect to have to impose conditions on tastes in order to obtain a general quantity version since this was necessary in the 2×2 case. The two countries will both consume the various goods in similar proportions when facing similar relative prices if the same collection of (n-dimensional) indifference curves can be used to represent tastes in both countries *and* if these curves are radially symmetric—so that all indifference curves have the same slope along the same ray from the origin. In this case, when we assign a utility value to each indifference curve by measuring its distance from the origin along a ray from there, we obtain the same results proportionally no matter which ray is used.

Suppose there are at least as many goods as factors and that countries' endowments are sufficiently similar so that trade equalizes factor prices. Number the m factors in order of decreasing home relative abundance, in the sense that

$$\frac{K_1}{K_1^W} \geq \frac{K_2}{K_2^W} \dots \geq \frac{K_m}{K_m^W}, \tag{58}$$

where K_i^W denotes the total world supply of factor i. Suppose that in free trade home-country income is the fraction g of world income. Then, because of our assumption about tastes, the home country must be consuming the fraction g

of the total world output of each and every good. Because of factor-price equalization, each good is produced by a single technique regardless of how many countries actually produce it. Thus the goods consumed at home must, in the aggregate, require for their production the fraction g of the world en-dowment of each and every factor. Therefore, the net home import of factor i equals $gK_i^W - K_i$. In the chain (58), all factors with ratios greater than g are exported, and all with ratios less than g are imported.

Problems

A.5.1 Show how the presence of factor intensity reversals can alter Figure A.13. Discuss the implications.

A.5.2 Suppose that there are three goods and two factors, that all three goods are being produced in equilibrium, and that the techniques used in the three sectors re-late to each other as follows:

$$\frac{K_C}{L_C} > \frac{K_D}{L_D} > \frac{K_W}{L_W}. \tag{59}$$

Now consider the price change: $\hat{P}_D > 0$, $\hat{P}_C = \hat{P}_W = 0$. What can you say about the consequences for factor rewards and the pattern of production?

A.5.3 Suppose that there are three goods and two factors with relative intensi-ties as in (59) for all wage-rental ratios. If there are two countries, is it possible for one to specialize in deckles in equilibrium? Explain.

A.5.4 How does our general version of the Stolper-Samuelson theorem change if we drop the assumption that the good whose price increases uses a nonspecific as-sortment of factors?

A.5.5 What can you say about the general version of the Rybczynski theorem in the case of more goods than factors if, instead of holding factor prices constant, we fix commodity prices and suppose that all factors remain fully employed?

A.6 TARIFFS (CHAPTER 7)[11]

Tariff-Ridden Equilibria

Suppose, again, that the home country imports wheat from the rest of the world in exchange for cloth but levies an ad valorem tariff at the rate t on wheat imports so that the *domestic* relative price of wheat q is given by

$$q = (1 + t) P. \tag{60}$$

International equilibrium is still given by Equation (17) from section A.3: $PM = M^*$, where P denotes the relative international price of wheat in terms of cloth. Differentiating this expression, we have across equilibria

---

[11] For more detail on the subject of this section, see R. W. Jones, "Tariffs and Trade in General Equilibrium: Comment," *American Economic Review* 59 (June 1969): 418–24.

$$\hat{P} + \hat{M} = \hat{M}*. \tag{61}$$

Now home imports need not equal exports in value at domestic prices. Instead we must have

$$E(q, u_t) = y(q, \ldots) + tPM, \tag{62}$$

where u_t is the level of home utility with the tariff. Total expenditure on wheat and cloth at domestic prices must equal the value of production at domestic prices plus the revenue from the tariff.

The Effects of Tariffs and World Prices on Home Imports

In section A.3 we developed Equation (21), showing how the demand for imports responds to changes in the terms of trade. We wish to do the same now with tariffs and to show how import demand responds to changes in these tariffs. This can be done by repeating the earlier analysis leading to (21) while taking note of (60) and (62), where appropriate. To see where such a procedure would take us, rewrite Equation (20) as follows:

$$dM = \left[\frac{\partial D_w}{\partial P} \Big|_u - \frac{dS_w}{dP} \right] dP - \frac{\partial D_w}{\partial E} \left[\frac{\partial E}{\partial P} dP - \frac{\partial y}{\partial P} dP \right]. \tag{63}$$

This expression, the basic decomposition into income and substitution effects, shows how the economy's agents collectively respond to changes in the relative price they face. To adapt this to cases where tariffs are present, two changes are necessary. First, q must replace P everywhere in (63) because domestic agents respond to domestic prices rather than world prices. Second, tariff revenues must be accounted for: the right-hand side of (62) should replace y in (63). Now the derivative of this right-hand side is

$$\frac{\partial y}{\partial q} dq + dt \, (PM) + PM(dt),$$

so that (63) becomes

$$dM = \left[\frac{\partial D_w}{\partial q} \Big|_u - \frac{dS_w}{dq} \right] dq - \frac{\partial D_w}{\partial E} \left[\left(\frac{\partial E}{\partial q} - \frac{\partial y}{\partial q} \right) dq - PM \, dt - dt \, (PM) \right], \tag{64}$$

where, from (60), $dq = (1 + t) \, dP + P \, dt$. Now we will simplify things by assuming that initially the country has free trade so that $t = 0$ or $P = q$ and that dt accordingly represents the imposition of a small tariff. Making this assumption in (64) and also repeating the same substitutions we made earlier to go from (20) to (21) gives

$$\hat{M} = -(c + s) \, (\hat{P} + dt) - m\hat{P}$$

or

$$\hat{M} = -e\hat{P} - (c + s) \, dt. \tag{65}$$

This expression has a simple interpretation. Imports may become more expensive either because world prices rise ($\hat{P}$) or because a tariff is imposed (*dt*). The former case (a movement along the import demand curve) affects *M* as measured in the usual way by *e* since initially there is no tariff: substitution effects occur because imports are more expensive relative to exports, and the income effect results from the fact that more must now be spent than before the price rise to purchase the same imports. When import prices instead rise because of the tariff (*dt*), the import demand curve shifts. This causes the same substitution effects as would a rise in *P* because imports are relatively more expensive than before in either case. But now there is no income effect because domestic residents collectively "pay themselves" the tariff proceeds; the latter are not paid to foreigners and thereby subtracted from domestic income, as would be the case with a rise in *P*.

A Tariff and the Terms of Trade

Suppose that the home country, initially in free trade, imposes a tariff *dt*. Equation (65) then applies to the home country, while for the foreign country

$$\hat{M}^* = e^*\hat{P}. \tag{66}$$

For equilibrium (61) must hold. Substitute (65) and (66) into (61), and rearrange to obtain

$$\hat{P} = \frac{-(c + s)}{e + e^* - 1} dt. \tag{67}$$

The term $e + e^* - 1$ is necessarily positive if we accept the Marshall-Lerner condition as necessary for stability. Then, since the substitution terms are positive, $\hat{P}$ and *dt* are of opposite sign: a tariff necessarily improves the terms of trade of any country able to influence world prices (if the home country is "small," $e^* = \infty$ so that $\hat{P} = 0$).

A Tariff and Domestic Prices

Equation (67) shows the effect of the tariff on world prices. What about its effect on domestic prices? From (60) we have

$$\hat{q} = \hat{P} + \frac{dt}{1 + t}. \tag{68}$$

Letting $t = 0$ initially, substituting (67) into (68), and rearranging give

$$\hat{q} = \frac{e^* - (1 - m)}{e + e^* - 1} dt. \tag{69}$$

Thus a tariff increases the domestic price of importables if, and only if, the foreign import elasticity exceeds the domestic marginal propensity to spend on the same good (that is, domestic exports). Note that this necessarily holds if the foreign offer curve is elastic. It also holds under the HOS assumption of internationally identical tastes at common relative prices since in that case

$1 - m = m^*$, with initial free trade, so that the numerator of (69) equals $c^* + s^*$. But if $e^* < 1 - m$, we must have the *Metzler Paradox:* a tariff on imports lowers their relative domestic price.

A Tariff and Domestic Welfare

We know that a tariff, as a price distortion, is inefficient for the world as a whole. Its effect on domestic utility can be determined from (62). Differentiating this expression with respect to t gives

$$\frac{\partial E}{\partial q}\frac{dq}{dt} + \frac{\partial E}{\partial u_t}\frac{du_t}{dt} = \frac{\partial y}{\partial q}\frac{dq}{dt} + tP\frac{dM}{dt} + M\frac{d(tP)}{dt}. \tag{70}$$

Recall that $\partial E/\partial q = D_w$, $\partial y/\partial q = S_w$ and note that, from (60), $dq/dt = dP/dt + d(tP)/dt$. Performing these substitutions gives

$$\frac{\partial E}{\partial u_t}\frac{du_t}{dt} = - M\frac{dP}{dt} + tP\frac{dM}{dt}. \tag{71}$$

Recall that $\partial E/\partial u_t > 0$. Thus a tariff influences domestic utility in two ways: a terms-of-trade effect alters what the country must pay for its imports, and a change in import volume alters tariff revenue. The latter has welfare significance because $tP = q - P$, the excess of how much the domestic economy values an import above what it must pay for it. Four conclusions follow from this analysis.

1. If the country initially has free trade, the right-hand side of (71) reduces to $-M(dP/dt)$, which is necessarily positive. Thus a small tariff is better than no tariff for any country able to influence world prices, if foreign retaliation can be ignored.
2. If the country has a prohibitive tariff, $M = 0$ so the right-hand side of (71) reduces to $tP(dM/dt)$. Thus a reduction in t below the prohibitive level increases u_t: a little trade is better than no trade.
3. If the home country levies an optimum tariff—that is, varies t to maximize u_t—the first-order condition is $du_t/dt = 0$ in (71). Thus

$$t = \frac{M\ (dP/dt)}{P\ (dM/dt)} = \frac{\hat{P}}{\hat{M}}.$$

Substituting the equilibrium condition (61) and $\hat{M}^* = e^*\hat{P}$ then gives the formula for the optimum tariff:

$$t = \frac{1}{e^* - 1}.$$

4. At the optimum tariff $du_t/dt = 0$ and dq/dt is positive since $e^* > 1$. Thus from (70), $d(tPM)/dt = tP(dM/dt) + M(d(tp)/dt) > 0$. That is, a further rise in t increases tariff revenue: the optimum tariff is necessarily smaller than the tariff that maximizes tariff revenue.

Problems

A.6.1 Explicitly derive (62).

A.6.2 What will equation (65) look like if we do not assume $t = 0$ initially?

A.6.3 What does the assumption of internationally identical tastes imply about the relative sizes of $\hat{P}$ and $\hat{q}$?

SUGGESTED READING

Bhagwati, J., ed. *International Trade: Selected Readings.* Cambridge: MIT Press, 1981.

Caves, R. E., J. A. Frankel, and R. W. Jones. *World Trade and Payments.* 5th ed. New York: HarperCollins, 1989, pp. 709–63.

Chacholiades, M. *International Trade Theory and Policy.* New York: McGraw-Hill, 1978.

Chipman, J. S. "A Survey of the Theory of International Trade." *Econometrica* (July 1965, Oct. 1965, Jan. 1966). In three parts.

Dixit, A. K., and V. Norman. *Theory of International Trade.* London: Cambridge University Press, 1980.

Jones, R. W. *International Trade: Essays in Theory.* Amsterdam: North Holland, 1979.

Jones, R. W., and P. B. Kenen, eds. *Handbook of International Economics.* Vol. 1. Amsterdam: North Holland, 1984.

Kemp, M. C. *The Pure Theory of International Trade and Investment.* Englewood Cliffs: Prentice-Hall, 1969.

———. *Three Topics in the Theory of International Trade.* Amsterdam: North Holland, 1976.

Mundell, R. A. *International Economics.* New York: Macmillan, 1968.

Takayama, A. *International Trade.* New York: Holt, Rinehart and Winston, 1972.

Woodland, A. *International Trade and Resource Allocation.* Amsterdam: North Holland, 1982.

Source Material in International Economics

Annual Report on the Trade Agreements Program, available from the U.S. Government Printing Office. Describes administration actions with regard to international trade during the previous year: countervailing duties, antidumping actions, and so forth.

Bank of England *Quarterly Bulletin,* published in London in March, June, September, and December of each year. One of the most useful of the central-bank bulletins. Along with British financial data, contains statistics on the London gold market, Eurodollar activity in London, and a selection of exchange rates and external interest rates.

Bank of International Settlements *Annual Report,* published in Basel in June of each year. The standard source for statistics on the Eurocurrency markets. Also contains a useful summary of major financial events in the large industrial countries during the preceding year.

Canada Yearbook, published annually by Statistics Canada in Ottawa. A convenient source for Canadian data.

Canadian Statistical Review, published monthly (with weekly supplements) by Statistics Canada. Contains current data on the Canadian economy plus special articles.

Commodity Trade Statistics, published by the United Nations, gives annual figures on world trade by commodity, by region, and by trading partner.

Direction of Trade, published monthly in Washington by the IMF and the IBRD. Contains a detailed world trade matrix displaying bilateral trade flows among most countries, and also shows trade flows between major country groups. Also a *Yearbook.*

Directory of International Statistics, available in two volumes from the United Nations. Describes statistical publications and machine-readable data bases.

The Economist, published weekly. The most useful of the popular magazines.

Essays in International Finance, published occasionally by the International Finance Section of Princeton University. Nontechnical. The Section also publishes more technical *Studies in International Finance* as well as *Special Papers in International Economics,* which are surveys.

Euromoney, published monthly in London. Features timely articles on developments in the Eurocurrency markets and problems in international lending. Occasionally has special supplements surveying regions that have become the focus of world attention. Statistical section contains an array of national interest rates, Eurodollar rates, and exchange rates.

Federal Reserve Bulletin, published monthly in Washington. Along with domestic U.S. financial data, contains a selection of balance-of-payments statistics, gold statistics, and international money market and foreign-exchange rates. Features invaluable reports on "Treasury and Federal Reserve Foreign Exchange Operations," the only systematic and comprehensive description of official intervention available. (This report is published simultaneously in the *Quarterly Review* of the New York Federal Reserve Bank.)

Foreign Agricultural Trade of the United States, published six times a year by the Economics Research Service of the U.S. Department of Agriculture in Washington. Detailed statistics.

Foreign Statistical Publications, published quarterly in Washington by the U.S. Bureau of the Census. Lists foreign sources, classified by country.

Guide to Foreign Trade Statistics, an annual publication of the U.S. Bureau of the Census. Very useful, especially for those without experience with trade data sources.

Hoel, A. A., K. W. Clarkson, and R. L. Miller. *Economics Sourcebook of Government Statistics.* Lexington, Mass.: Lexington Books, 1983. Description of statistics.

International Currency Review, published bimonthly in London, contains analytical articles of contemporary international financial developments as well as reviews of conditions in approximately twenty of the leading currency markets and the gold market.

International Economic Conditions, issued quarterly by the Federal Reserve Bank of St. Louis. Rates of change in important national and international economic variables for ten major countries.

International Financial Statistics, published monthly in Washington by the IMF. A very useful source with a wealth of data on international and domestic finance for most countries of the world. Also a *Yearbook* and special supplements. Available on computer tape.

International Monetary Fund Annual Report, published in Washington. In addition to a report on Fund activities, contains a discussion of developments in the world economy and the international financial system, with tables and charts.

International Monetary Fund Balance of Payments Yearbook, issued in monthly installments from Washington. Presents annual balance-of-payments data and analytic balances (denominated in SDRs) for all IMF members.

International Monetary Fund Report on Exchange Arrangements and Exchange Restrictions, published annually in Washington. A comprehensive listing of capital controls in each of the member countries.

International Monetary Fund Survey, published monthly in Washington. Timely reports on Fund activities and current issues in international economic policy.

International Trade, published annually by the General Agreements on Tariffs and Trade in Geneva. Developments in international trade, with relevant data.

Journal of Economic Literature, published quarterly by the American Economic Association. Lists current professional journal articles by subject and by journal. Also lists new books and contains book reviews, article abstracts, and review articles.

Journal of International Economics, published quarterly by North Holland in Amsterdam. Scholarly articles on the subject.

Journal of International Money and Finance, published three times a year by Butterworths. Scholarly articles.

MacBean, A. I., and P. N. Snowden. *International Institutions in Trade and Finance.* London: Allen & Unwin, 1981. Useful descriptions and review of the basic institutions.

The Money Manager, published weekly in New York by the Bond Trader. Presents a wide variety of international short-term rates on a timely basis as well as commentary on recent developments. A prime source for nondollar, Eurocurrency rates.

Monthly Bulletin of Statistics, published by the United Nations in New York. Contains basic population and economic data, and detailed analyses of world trade patterns. Also a *Yearbook.*

Monthly Report of the Deutsche Bundesbank, published in Frankfurt in German and English. In addition to German financial data, contains a good selection of international money market rates and exchange rates. Often includes a timely analysis of international economic events.

Organization for Economic Cooperation and Development Financial Statistics, published in Paris once a year with supplements available every two months. A collection of financial data from each member country. Particularly useful as an introduction to individual country sources. Also an important summary of Eurodollar and Eurobond data.

Organization for Economic Cooperation and Development Statistics of Foreign Trade Series A, published monthly, contains detailed trade statistics.

Pick's Currency Yearbook, published annually in New York by Franz Pick. A compendium of unusual financial statistics. Because the data are based solely on personal dealings, this source is less than impeccable; however, nowhere else can one find black-market exchange rates and gold price quotations for virtually every leading financial center.

Review of International Economics, published quarterly by Basil Blackwell. Scholarly articles on the subject.

Statistical Abstract of the United States, published annually by the U.S. Bureau of the Census. A good starting point for information about the United States.

Statistical Sources of the U.S. Government, a publication of the U.S. Bureau of the Budget. Lists and evaluates U.S. sources.

Statistical Yearbook, published annually in New York by the United Nations. A standard statistical source. Available on CD-ROM.

Survey of Current Business, published monthly in Washington by the Department of Commerce. U.S. balance-of-payments statistics are presented in the March, June, September, and December issues, and the U.S. international investment position in October. Information on the activities of foreign subsidiaries of U.S. firms and on particular categories of balance-of-payments flows appears throughout the year.

Trade Yearbook, published annually by the United Nations Food and Agriculture Organization. Contains detailed data on trade in agricultural products. The same organization also publishes a *Production Yearbook.*

Van Meerhaeghe, M. A. G. *International Economic Institutions.* 4th ed. The Hague: Martinus Nijhoff, 1984. Describes international economic organizations.

World Bank Annual Report, published in Washington. In addition to a summary of IBRD activities and a standard array of economic indicators, contains an analysis of international debt outstanding and debt service ratios for developing countries.

World Bank Atlas, published annually by the World Bank. A quick reference for population statistics, per capita GNP, and growth rates for 183 countries and entities.

World Bank Development Report, published annually in Washington by the World Bank. Data on developing countries.

World Debt Tables, published in Washington by the World Bank. A standard source for data on country debt.

World Economic Survey, published annually in New York by the United Nations. Another standard statistical source.

The World Economy, published quarterly in Amsterdam for the Trade Policy Research Center by North Holland. Articles on international economic affairs.

World Financial Markets, published in New York by the Morgan Guaranty Trust Company. Contains trade-weighted exchange rates, Eurobond yields, effective Eurodollar rates, money and bond market rates, and bank lending rates for twenty-eight countries. In addition, there is a good analysis of contemporary financial events. A highly regarded private source.

The Acronyms of International Economics

ACP: Africa, the Caribbean, and the Pacific (or the countries of the Lomé Convention)

ADB: Asian Development Bank

AFDB: African Development Bank

APM: Average propensity to import

ASEAN: Association of Southeast Asian Nations

BIS: Bank for International Settlements

CACM: Central American Common Market

CAP: Common Agricultural Policy (of the EU)

CARICOM: Caribbean Community

CHP: Czechoslovakia (now two countries), Hungary, and Poland

CIP: Covered interest parity

CIS: Commonwealth of Independent States (an organization of most of the republics of the former USSR)

CMEA: Council for Mutual Economic Assistance (now defunct)

COMECON: Another acronym for the CMEA

CRS: Constant returns to scale

CUSFTA: Canada–U.S. Free Trade Agreement

DC: Developed country (or, collectively, the North or the West; unfortunately, DC also sometimes stands for "developing country" and is used as another acronym for LDC)

DM: Deutsche mark

EACM: East Africa Common Market

EBRD: European Bank for Reconstruction and Development

EC: European Community (successor name to the EEC)

ECSC: European Coal and Steel Community (precursor to the EEC)

ECU: European Currency Unit

EEA: European Economic Area (between the EC and the EFTA)

EEC: European Economic Community

EFTA: European Free Trade Association

EMCF: European Monetary Cooperation Fund (of the EMS)

EMI: European Monetary Institute

EMS: European Monetary System

EMU: European Monetary Union

ERM: Exchange-rate mechanism (of the EMS)

ERP: Effective rate of protection

EU: European Union (successor name to the EC)

FDI: Foreign direct investment

FX: Foreign exchange

GATS: General Agreement on Trade in Services (proposed extension of the GATT to trade in services)

GATT: General Agreement on Tariffs and Trade

GDP: Gross domestic product

G–5: Group of Five (France, West Germany, Japan, Great Britain, and the United States)

GNP: Gross national product

G–7: Group of Seven (G-5 plus Canada and Italy)

GSP: Generalized system of preferences (for LDCs)

G–10: Group of Ten (G-7 plus Belgium, the Netherlands, Sweden, and [unofficially] Switzerland)

HO theory: Heckscher-Ohlin theory of international trade

HOS model: Heckscher-Ohlin-Samuelson model of international trade (a subset of the HO theory)

HOV theorem: Heckscher-Ohlin-Vanek theorem (another subset of the HO theory)

IBF: International Banking Facility

IBRD: International Bank for Reconstruction and Development (usually called the World Bank)

IDA: International Development Association

IDB: Inter-American Development Bank

IFC: International Finance Corporation

IMF: International Monetary Fund

IMM: International Monetary Market

IP: Interest parity

IRS: Increasing returns to scale

ISIC: International Standard Industrial Classification (for compiling statistics)

ITC: International Trade Commission (formerly the Tariff Commission)

ITO: International Trade Organization

LAFTA: Latin American Free Trade Association

LAIA: Latin American Integration Association (succeeded LAFTA in 1980)

LDC: Less developed country (or, collectively, the South)

LIBOR: London Interbank Offer Rate (a benchmark rate on Eurodollar loans)

LIFFE: London International Financial Futures Exchange

MCA: Monetary Compensatory Amount (of the CAP)

MERM: Multilateral Exchange Rate Model

MFA: Multifiber Arrangement

MFN: Most favored nation (either the nation, the clause, or the principle)

MIGA: Multilateral Investment Guarantee Agency

MITI: Ministry of International Trade and Industry (in the Japanese government)

MNC: Multinational corporation

MNE: Multinational enterprise (= MNC)

MNF: Multinational firm (= MNE = MNC)

MPM: Marginal propensity to import

MPS: Marginal propensity to save

MRS: Marginal rate of substitution (in consumption)

MRT: Marginal rate of transformation (in production)

MRTS: Marginal rate of technical substitution (of productive inputs)

MTN: Multilateral trade negotiations (that is, the GATT rounds)

NAFTA: North American Free Trade Agreement

NEC: Newly exporting country

NIC: Newly industrializing country

NIEO: New International Economic Order (a set of reforms of the international economy formerly urged by LDCs)

NTB: Nontariff barrier to trade

OECD: Organization for Economic Cooperation and Development (sometimes called the "Rich Men's Club")

OEEC: Organization for European Economic Cooperation (succeeded by the OECD)

OPEC: Organization of Petroleum Exporting Countries

OPIC: Overseas Private Investment Corporation

PPP: Purchasing power parity

QR: Quantitative restriction (on trade)

R&D: Research and development

RTA: Reciprocal Trade Agreement (as provided for in the Trade Agreements Act of the United States)

SDR: Special Drawing Right

SEA: Single European Act (of the EC; the basis for "1992")

SIMEX: Singapore International Monetary Exchange

SWIFT: Society for Worldwide Interbank Financial Telecommunication

TAA: Trade Adjustment Assistance

TRIMS: Trade-related investment measures

TRIPS: Trade-related intellectual property rights

UIP: Uncovered interest parity

UN: United Nations

UNCTAD: United Nations Conference on Trade and Development

USSR: Union of Soviet Socialist Republics (a large communist country, now no more, that used to occupy much of Europe and Asia)

VER: Voluntary export restraint

WTO: World Trade Organization (a new institution provided for as a result of the Uruguay Round negotiations)

INDEX